INSIDE FRONT
Volume Two: 2000-2003

I0120812

"The material within these pages has all been mercilessly pillaged from other sources, whether in luxurious acts of wholesale plagiarism or word by excruciating word; in the name of honor among thieves, we urge you to do the same, both with these contents and everything else on the face of the earth."

This Compilation Published 2023
Crimethinc Never-Worker's Collective

Also available:

Inside Front, Volume One: 1993 to 1999

The End of
INSIDE FRONT...

final issue, lucky #13
at the beginning of the new millennium

Includes 14 band hardcore compilation on compact disc, breaking news from the internal front of the war against Western civilization, and provisional blueprints for the next steps of the revolution of everyday life...

...and the beginning for Hardcore Punk.

USA IS A MONSTER

AM 2:00

Hey punk boy—I was listening to your band, **and I wanna know:**

Where's the content **?**

are *YOU* CONTENT **?**

Table of Contents

Editor's Introduction
to the Final Issue

Confession and declaration of war

I am a wild animal.

No, I don't feel comfortable paying for food. It makes my skin crawl, my stomach clench up—it seems like a really alien, superstitious thing to do. It makes much more sense to me to hunt for it, to find it in dumpsters or free bins or take it by force or stealth from the ones who don't care about my welfare. I can't imagine signing a contract and paying rent to one of them, pretending I think that's a sensible way for people to interact; I would much rather travel constantly, or sleep on the couch where my friends have established a collective space, contributing what I can... or sleep on benches and rooftops, if it comes down to that. I can't sit still or act fake long enough to work at one of their jobs when there's so much out here in the real world to do. I can't lie to myself enough anymore to lie to anyone else by participating in the farce that is polite society under capitalism. What they call delayed gratification looks to me more like gratification abandoned.

I am a spoiled child.

I would rather starve to do death, freeze to death, end lonely and incomprehensible to everyone than change myself. I know what I am is inconvenient for everyone, and frustrating, too, since I'm doing what many people would like to but feel they cannot; but there's nothing anyone can say that will persuade me I'm wrong in any way that matters. People talk at me about adapting, being reasonable, realistic, but none of it seems reasonable to me. I think that what I am and what I want is beautiful in a world that sorely needs beauty. I'm not crazy for wanting every moment to be wild and right and fair and honest. I won't let anyone tell me I need to stop listening to my heart. Even at my blackest moments, when it seems like I really have been abandoned by everyone and everything and I have jettisoned myself from the cosmos for no explicable reason, I would simply rather perish than compromise. Whether this is a good thing or not, it's how I feel and I won't back down.

I am a human being.

When I see people cleaning tables at restaurants or bellboys carrying heavy bags, my first impulse is to help them: my instincts, laziness aside, are to assume that what they're doing is of value to humanity and that they deserve assistance—even if they're really doing senseless paid make-work, and it's "not my job" so I shouldn't worry about it. It's not easy for me to suspend my compassion when I meet homeless people or others in need. I even have a difficult time remembering that when a solicitor or a police officer talks to me, I can't trust them to respect my needs or have my best interest in mind—they do *seem* like human beings, after all, at least when the pigs aren't dressed in their star wars costumes. I can't make excuses or joke smugly about exploited labor, people being bombed or beaten or starved to death or raped, animals in slaughterhouses. I can't put my humanity on hold like everyone else seems to have learned to.

I am an experiment.

I know I can't survive too long in this world the way it is. If I am to live another twenty six years, I will have to evolve—devolve, that is, which I have sworn not to do—or else the world will have to. I have everything at stake in transforming this place... and so do you, unless you think that people like me deserve to die, unless you're ready to excise everything in yourself that resembles me.

Disclaimer for the hypercritical

I think in the seven year history of this 'zine, one of our greatest contributions to the hardcore community has been our emphasis on the subject of lifestyle: that how you eat, what you wear, where you live, how you spend the typical days of your life is more important than what you do on Friday night, or what musical taste or ideology you subscribe to. Of course, there have been people who have misunderstood our attempts to open up new possibilities to others by taking an extreme position for ourselves ("never work ever") as an attempt to legislate what is right for everyone else, who thought we believed that we had the "one true way" that every cliquish, infighting radical group claims to have. That was never our intention. There is no one right way to revolution (or making the world a better place or whatever you want to call it), and there's no best way to live in its service. We *all* have our roles in this society, which separate us from our potential allies and divert our energies into role-playing; the question is not which role to choose (professor, outlaw radical, etc.), but how to *subvert* your role in order to create volatile situations in which new, unpredictable, wonderful things can happen.

That being the case, the only remaining question is which lifestyle would be the most personally fulfilling for you, and there are some great reasons to try the one we've embraced, I assure you. People always become defensive (myself included) when somebody is doing something they feel drawn to but have feared to try; nobody wants to admit that they're not already doing what they want, or that someone else has a good idea they didn't have. As for the questions of whether my lifestyle is responsible ("but when you're sleeping on the couch somewhere, doesn't somebody else have to pay the rent?") or sustainable ("do you really think you can do this for the next thirty years?")... it's important to remember that everything is a compromise until the whole world changes, whether you're depending on a little help from your friends who have different resources or participating in the economy of exploitation and destruction. To look for a "sustainable" life as a participant in an unsustainable global system is sheer madness; relying on the assistance of others to work towards a better world for everyone makes plenty of sense as long as you really are pledged to give your all. After all, the American ideal of the "self-sufficient" individual is just bullshit; everyone is totally dependent on everyone else in this society (for self-sufficiency you have to look to small farms outside the First World), and the ones who seem the most "responsible" for themselves are often simply the ones who have been the most *irresponsible* to others, taking from them to take care of themselves. Don't tell me that's not what a manager who makes twice the salary of his employees is doing, when they all have to work just as hard.

And another thing—work-free living isn't something that just a few parasites can do until the excess that feeds them runs out.

The more people who do it, the more possible it is to create really autonomous lives, with the shared resources and energies of everyone adding up to a sum greater than the parts. One work-free kid in a city can shoplift food and get new shoes from the trash on campus when the college semester is over. One hundred kids in the same town can start collectives or squats, start gardening instead of stealing, start organizing bigger projects. And one thousand kids could occupy and collectivize housing and schools and workspaces, start to really take social resources back into the hands of the people. We're not just parasites. We could be the start of a new world.

Finally, after all those points, just remember this: this magazine, and all the other projects we've done with CrimethInc., would literally have been impossible without all the time and energy that we put into them instead of into working—even when that meant sometimes sleeping on the couch somewhere where others were paying rent. Imagine all the good things you, or your friends who still have to work, could do if more people took this approach to life, if more people were *able* to take this approach to life. While we are still at the mercy of their system, let's put all the energy we can into building up the framework for work-free living (Food Not Bombs, the squatting movement, dumpstering, bicycle cooperatives, sharing resources...) so that this option will be more widely available, and we couch-surfing revolutionaries won't always be occupying this no-man's-land between generosity and dependence.

*A snapshot from my life:
the past four days*
(as of Sunday, almost midnight, June 11, 2000)

I've been going back and forth between Chapel Hill (pretty, quiet college town where my lover and student activist friends live, where it's easy to focus on writing and reading) and Greensboro (dirty, post-industrial dead end Southern city where some of my best friends and co-conspirators live, where I go to hatch plots and answer CrimethInc. mail) for the last few weeks, trying to catch up from being gone on tour most of the last year. Last Thursday I caught a ride back to Greensboro to see a show at the new communal warehouse my friends had organized while we were gone.

It was Submission Hold, Antiproduct, and a band from Arkansas with a Native American name my ignorant tongue cannot pronounce (Tem Eyos Ki). They started the show (after a hilarious performance from a punk kid with an acoustic guitar and a maniacally rudimentary sense of humor) by introducing a song about holding on to the fantasies of your childhood through the crush of the "adult" world, and charged forward with so much enthusiasm that we all caught it—and suddenly punk was brand new again, perfect and beautiful and offering the whole world to all of us. We hung out outside after their set, eating from the free buffet of vegan food our hosts had shoplifted in mass quantities to celebrate their first show (when it started running low, some of them dashed off again to procure more!), or wandered around inside, dancing to the Black Flag over the speakers and admiring the handiwork of our friends, how much they had been able to build and create in this empty warehouse in just a month. Then we watched Antiproduct and Submission Hold, two bands also fronted by confident, tough women like the one from Tem Eyos Ki, and it was beautiful for me to see our community live up to its pretensions about fighting sexism and gender roles: the men present all listening, confident enough themselves, for once, to hear other perspectives, to share the space and power of our scene. After the show I went with Jon and Moe to Birch's house, where we ate vegan apple pie that Mark had dumpstered, dreaming and scheming wildly into the dawn.

Friday evening, after answering a day's worth of mail, I went to see a friend of mine from outside the punk community, a single mother who lives on welfare in order to spend her time assisting battered children and women suffering from spouse abuse or alcoholism (since there are almost no paid positions available doing that—another big argument against the bullshit "get a job" mentality, which assumes that it's better to be paid for doing something useless or destructive than to spend your life working on positive things for free). It's always wonderful to talk to her—she keeps me grounded in real life, telling me about the struggle to help individuals who are suffering from our fucked up status quo, when it's so easy for me to get lost in the abstractions I'm always working in. After that, Jon and I climbed a series of ladders and steep shingled inclines to the top of a building on the university campus, to brainstorm for the new Harbinger in the windy exultation of 3 a.m.—and then when we got back to his apartment, he left to put up fliers for an event the next evening, which is what I *really* want to talk about.

The fliers read, simply, in huge letters, "U.S.A. IS A MONSTER 2:00 A.M." Jon had been supposed to book a show for this noise band for months, and never got around to it, until a week before the date he'd promised them he realized he was in trouble and started trying to come up with a solution. He hit upon Zack, the devil-may-care graveyard shi(f)t worker at Handy Pantry, the all-night convenience store in this neighborhood.

Zack is one of those beautiful lumpenproletariat guys who knows who his enemies are and gets jobs just to fuck with his employers. I heard that when he was tired of his last job (night shift at U.P.S.), he took a package being shipped by a chewing gum company, set it down in front of a surveillance camera, opened it up, took out a piece of gum, and, looking straight into the camera, began chewing it. The next morning when the manager found the opened package still sitting there, he checked the tape and saw Zack staring him in the eye, smacking his gum.

Jon went to Zack and told him that he'd forgotten to book a show for a band that would be arriving on Saturday. Zack drawled "well, I'm working every night this week," and it was arranged: U.S.A. Is A Monster would play at the Handy Pantry at 2 a.m. on Saturday night.

Now, Handy Pantry is not some out-of-the-way convenience store. It's in the middle of the main drag by the college campus, a center of Greensboro night life (such as it is!), next to all the coffee shops and restaurants and sharing a parking lot with Kinko's... and with the university police station. This last one is about two hundred feet away, and you can see it through the windows of the convenience store—so we weren't even talking about a risky proposition, we were looking certain catastrophe in the eyes and offering it a formal invitation. I think that's what appealed to us the most about this idea: more than any of the Reclaim the Streets or Critical Mass actions in the past year, more than the noise parades or any of the nocturnal breaking, entering, and exploring we'd done, this was something crazy enough that the outcome couldn't be foreseen or even imagined. We had to do it just to thrust ourselves out into that dangerous space where *everything* is a surprise.

Word of the show spread long before Jon put up the fliers, and by last night every mouth was whispering about it. Jon and I went to a going-away party for Mark, who is off to spend the next month teaching art in another city, and then went to a show in nearby Winston Salem, at the collective warehouse there (which is four years old and much more developed than the one in

Greensboro, really incredible and inspiring!), at which we were to meet U.S.A.I.A.M. themselves. They showed up around midnight, just when we were starting to worry, and we went out in the parking lot for a briefing.

They seemed like good kids—trying as hard as we were to act like this was a normal thing for them—but, to our surprise, there were *eight* of them, including two drummers with full sets, and a keyboard player with crazy electronic equipment. It wasn't going to be easy to run their stuff out the back door when the pigs came in. They followed us back to Greensboro in their van, and I spent the ride talking Jon out of his apprehensions: "This is our chance to put punk rock where it was never supposed to be, where it's still dangerous. This is payback for all the nights we've had to walk around watching this town do nothing, man—this is revenge for that flag they put on the moon!" When we arrived, he turned to me, reassured, and declared "we're going to make Greensboro history, man."

I agreed. For the sake of everyone in this little, dead end town, there is no choice but to make Greensboro, as we've all known and loathed it, *history*.

There were about sixty people from widely varied backgrounds (punks, art students, homeless people, a middle-aged professor "interviewing" people with a microphone that wasn't plugged into anything) lined up sitting on the curb as we loaded two drumsets, four amplifiers and speakers, a vocal amp and borrowed microphone, and assorted other instruments and equipment into the store. The drummers had forgotten sticks, or lost them at the other shows or something, so they ended up just beating on the drums with various junk foods (beef jerkies, soda cans and bottles, popsickles), grabbing a new one whenever one substitute stick broke or shattered. The first notes of soundcheck were so loud that I couldn't believe they were even going to get to play a minute.

Everyone pushed in, packed between the aisles, and the noise began. The band were leaping around, smashing things and falling over like they might have at a normal house show, but here it was totally new and dangerous, visceral, and music that could have been standard somewhere else was suddenly the fiercest, most vehement thing any of us had ever heard. At a normal show the band are the ones taking the risk, but here everyone was at risk, just by standing there in the store—and not just because of the threat of the police, either. There's no way I can describe what it felt like to step out of reality as it had been and into that space, to fuse

two separate parts of my life (the passion of punk rock, the lifelessness of convenience stores) that were never supposed to meet... everything was electrified, tense and intense, ten thousand years of culture turned on it's head in an instant. Amazingly, the band finished one song, the members all switched instruments while the scream of feedback tore the air, and they shot into another one, knocking against the shelving, smashing into the drink coolers, pulling the cardboard display posters over their heads and banging into people—all of us looking nervously back and forth between them and the police station out the window. A couple civilians who had come up to buy cigarettes joined the crowd in total wonder. Some people were throwing junk food, candy, breaking things, wrecking the place (this was the most controversial topic afterwards, since the kids doing this were largely bourgeois children of the suburbs who had nothing at stake and weren't worried about Zack's welfare or anything else)—others, and this was much more beautiful to me, realizing that we owned the place for a moment and they could do whatever they wanted, were picking up candies and other commodities, looking at them, and them just dropping them, realizing just how valueless they all were at *any* price, especially compared with the lightning of what was actually happening. The band switched instruments again in the middle of the song, banging out random notes and screaming nonsensically—someone from the audience jumped behind one drumset, and started playing along as natural as could be—others joined in—and then looks of terror spread through the room, as we all saw the flashing lights of an arriving police car.

And you know what? We got away with it. The pigs pulled up, paused, and drove off for some inexplicable reason, basically giving us the go-ahead to take the city over (if we can do this so easily, then what next?). "Should we get out of here?" shouted a band member, clutching a cymbal stand. "Naw, man, they've just headed off to get the Black Mariah," drawled Zack—"keep playing." The band played for another twenty minutes, until everyone was satisfied that we'd done what we came to do. Still spinning in a delirium of adrenaline, we hastily packed all their equipment out the back door and into the van, while the locals drifted slowly off into the night, exchanging grins of disbelief and delight.

In fact, just as I was writing this last paragraph, Zack stopped by Jon and Will's apartment (where I'm staying tonight, while they drive to the airport up in New York to pick up Zegota's new bassist, Ard, imported

directly from Holland for their upcoming world tour without so much as an audition) to tell me that, though the pigs prank called him at the store afterwards ("you're in big trouble, son—some underage kids who were drinking at your store drove into a tree and died [total bullshit!]. You need to give us the store tapes. Don't lie to us, boy..." and Zack replies: "I'll lie to you as much as I want, officer—but I don't know what you're talking about..."), he just talked to his manager, who said: "no, you're not fired, the store was clean this morning." As I expected, they need us more than we need them—we will win.

Tonight I have a whole apartment to myself, despite not paying rent for the last sixteen months or working for over six years, and I sit here listening to my favorite vicious punk records, stuffing myself on dumpstered food, writing the introduction to our hardcore magazine on my beleaguered little laptop computer, the last surviving vestige of my bourgeois origins—quite conscious that I am enjoying a moment of heaven. Tomorrow Matt and I will drive out into the rural wilderness for Catharsis practice, then Zegota returns to show their new bassist around, who has never been to the U.S. before, and to screen fliers for the benefit our bands are supposed to play for the warehouse space. Then on Thursday night at midnight, we have a date to meet Liz and some of her friends, fifty year old middle class women whose children have grown up and left them, who feel invisible in society, who see themselves represented in the media as helpless and clutching, who have reasons of their own to find common cause with others seeking adventure and transformation, but did not know where to find them—until they met us. They are to bring the picnic snack, and us, the adventure: a 16-story building, abandoned and easy to break into, with a roof that looks out over the rest of the city. There, we'll sit beneath the stars and build bonds between our different communities, talking of which resources each has to offer the other, of what the next step to revolution is—a revolution that is becoming more and more real for us, for all of us, every day.

The last word (we can only hope!) on complaining about "the scene"

An interesting characteristic of communities is the way no one actually feels like a part of them, even the people in their center. Alexei and I had a disheartening experience in Brazil when we were both reading HearrartaCk: it seemed to us like there was all this awesome shit going on in the hardcore scene, but that we were totally left out of it. "I think it's great that they have this community going on," said Alexei, "but I don't feel like a part of any community. If you put all my friends together in one place, they wouldn't be able to get along or even understand each other."

After I'd thought about it for a while, I realized that the hardcore community is actually nothing more than a bunch of people like Alexei and I and our friends, connected to each other in the loosest of ways. In fact if you were to pick two people who are undeniably close to the core of this thing called "hardcore" right now, it might well be him and me. So what's going on here?

The truth is, nobody feels like any community could be big and deep enough to contain all that they are—and that's OK. But we have a disturbing tendency to project our own fears and insecurities onto our community: everyone feels comfortable in it but us, we are secret outsiders, the community is like a Frankenstein's monster with a will of its own, doing things *to* people rather than being a place where people do things... people talk about the scene as if it is a force separate from the humans involved in it, as if it could suck without our participation in that sucking, as if it could alienate us without our participation in that alienation. And so everyone complains ad nauseam about how the scene is getting worse, it's not like it used to be, it has all these flaws, etc. etc. etc.

At this point, that really is the *least* original, the least creative thing you could possibly do. Punk has always sucked, it's always been getting worse, that's been the word ever since about 1977—so seriously, what could possibly be the use of complaining more, except maybe to state for the record that it's not good enough for *you*, either?

I think it would be much more positive for us to admit that punk does whatever we do with it, that that's all it is, and to claim responsibility for it rather than blaming it as an outside force. As soon as we recognize that punk is simply a tool we can use as to do whatever we want, rather than worrying about whether it's cool enough for us.

These complaints have their roots in the old voter/spectator mentality, I think: you want to pick the style or scene that is the coolest, and assert your identity by passively swearing allegiance to it. At first, as a teenager, punk seems to be perfect, so you buy punk records and attend punk shows, calling yourself a punk just because you watch what people who are really

involving themselves in punk are doing. Maybe at age 21 or 22 you get disillusioned with punk—it's lost the novelty it used to have, it doesn't seem as profound as it once did—so you move on to the rave scene or something. You call yourself a raver or an indie rocker, but it's all bullshit—you've just been a consumer, a spectator, all along.

I no longer expect to have my world changed just by buying a new punk record. I look to other styles of music to bring me inspiration, since I feel like I'm pretty much up to date with what punk has to offer (though if you're in a punk band, please surprise me!); but hardcore punk is my community, no matter what music I listen to—it is here that I get to do what really matters: *participate*. You're going to get jaded wherever you go, if you go as a spectator; but if you pick this community as a place where you can try out your own projects and live out your own adventures, you'll find it to be endlessly rewarding, no matter how many morons are involved in it.

I think I've had such a good experience in this community because I realized this about seven years ago, around when I started this 'zine. Since then I've found myself complaining less and less about the scene, even though I spend more time involved in it than just about anyone else I know. It's common sense—hardcore (*your* hardcore, the only one that matters) is what you make of it... so get going! It can take you around the world and back a hundred times, introduce you to the craziest, most beautiful people on this earth, thrust you into moments of adventure you'd never dreamed of—and no halfwit in a Madball or Blanks 77 shirt can interfere with that, unless you let them.

And now I'd like to take just a paragraph to celebrate briefly my love of punk rock. In this community, I can express every side of my character, I don't have to leave anything behind: I can scream and destroy and hate blindly with Gehenna, I can be articulate and idealistic with Trial or Zegota, I can revel in the simple pleasures of wreaking havoc with my friends as we wander the town late one night or I can indulge in sweet solitude reading a 'zine by myself. I can be intellectual as all fuck, debating post-Situationist social theory with a graduate student over the internet, or I can strike up a conversation about the Misfits with a teenager drinking on the job on third shift at a convenience store while I shoplift potato chips. I can enjoy a communal dinner with welcoming strangers on the other side of the world, or organize a

demonstration with mohawked local activists here in North Carolina. I can travel and have a home anywhere; I can write, or dance, or even learn to juggle or speak French, and I would have awesome people to do it with. Here's to punk. Punk fucking rocks.

The end, and the beginning, for Inside Front—and hardcore punk

This is the last issue of Inside Front we are going to do. There are already a hundred 'zines that can take over from here—Slave, F.B.I., even HeartattaCk is quite good these days—and I feel like we've finally realized the potential of this project, finally made Inside Front what it should be. Rather than stop here and hit a plateau, trying to make this into some kind of periodical, I'd rather leave it as an example of what is possible, effectively collectivizing its legacy to be carried on by everyone else who thinks there's something good about what it has done. I don't want to risk ever getting stuck doing something that becomes boring or predictable or irrelevant, and there are so many more things we want to do from here—so don't worry, you'll still be hearing from us. After this issue of Inside Front, which should come out about the same time as the third Harbinger and our first book, Days of War, Nights of Love *[editor's last minute note: scratch that, they're out already!]*, we've got new records, new pamphlets and 'zines and books and tours and actions planned... in just my own case, I can think of about a hundred projects I want to try, all just waiting for the space to materialize.

From here, whatever was worthwhile about Inside Front is in your hands. We're not ending our work with the magazine in defeat or exhaustion—to the contrary, we're more involved and active than ever—but because it has taken us as far as it needed to; now we find ourselves standing at a vista from which new horizons can be seen, and we have to make new vehicles to carry us to them. This isn't the end of hardcore being relevant to our lives, or of life being relevant to hardcore, or of our contributions to either of those things. But Inside Front is now *yours*, yours to improve on, yours to apply and add to. I'm absolutely confident that from these seeds, a hundred greater forces will grow, and we who have nourished this project to this point must simply let go of the reigns to let it become what it must now become—which *you* can see more clearly than us, I'm sure!

For further reading,

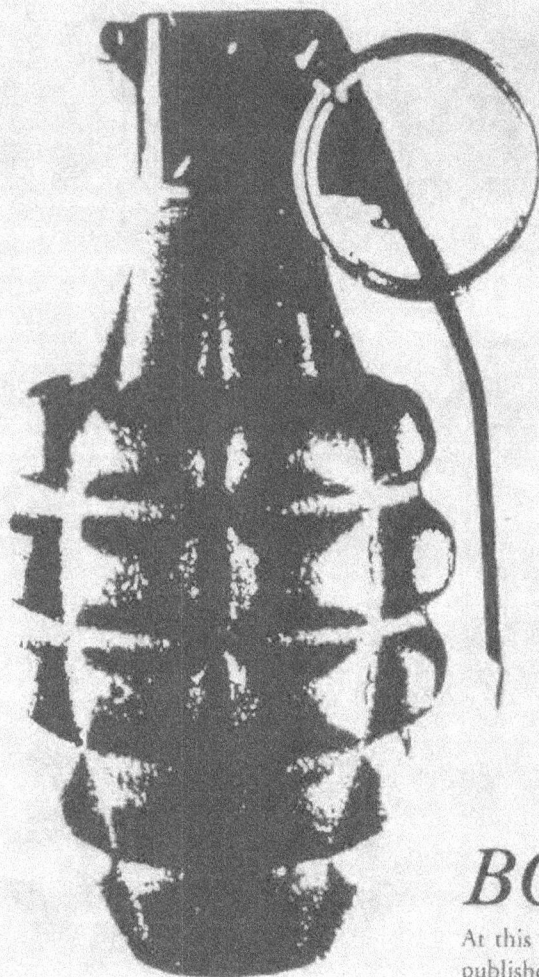

In the past, we've had a hard time keeping on top of all the mail, mailorders, wholesale orders, etc. coming to CrimethInc. *[editor's note: haha, understatement!]*. We've solved this problem by dividing mailorder responsibilities between four different CrimethInc. teams. Hopefully this catalog will make everything clear, and no one will ever have to wait a month and a half for their order again.

BOOKS

At this writing, we have only one book published, but we have others coming by the end of 2000. The Paul F. Maul Artist's Group at CrimethInc. Far East is handling single and wholesale mailorders and distribution of these.

Days of War, Nights of Love: This is "Crimethink for Beginners," the definitive work of our first half decade in action and far superior to anything we'd done before it. It's 292 pages, fully illustrated, the works. *$8 USA*

contact the PFMAG:
CrimethInc. Far East
P.O. Box 1963
Olympia, WA 98507

Or visit the CrimethInc. webpage for more information, news, further reading, etc.:
www.crimethinc.com
paulfmaul@crimethinc.com

FREE LITERATURE

The third issue of our free propaganda tabloid *Harbinger* is now available. If you want a copy to read, or a big stack of them to distribute in your area, please send a postage donation to:

Amelia Wood
642 Chalkstone Ave 3rd Floor
Providence, RI 02908

RECORDS & MAGAZINES

These are available from Gavin at Stickfigure Distribution. He does single mailorders, and wholesales inside and outside the U.S.A. as well. The single order prices are included here; email or write him for wholesale information or foreign postage costs.

Inside Front #12: 136 pages, with the already classic eleven song 6" by Finland's wildest Motorhead fans, Umlaut. Features a lengthy retrospective/interview with Refused, an interview discussing hardcore imperialism and the third world with Brazilian band Point of No Return, a new take on the old tradition of scene reports (including the Appalachian Trail and Louisburg, North Carolina), an analysis of the Reclaim the Streets protests, and a whole lot more. *$4 USA*

Inside Front #11: 104 pages, with 13-track CD including Ire, Earthmover, Zegota, Botch, Amebix... the interviews are with Zegota and Ire, and the articles dissect the age old superstitions of moral law and hierarchical order. There's also a lengthy Amebix retrospective. *$4 USA*

listening,
acting...

Inside Front #10: with 7" of Swedish hardcore from Outlast, interviews with Stalingrad, Systral, and Culture, and articles about the drawbacks of capitalist economics in punk and how to survive without selling your soul to "the man." *$3 USA*

Inside Front #9: with 7" of Belgian hardcore by Liar, Congress, Regression, and Shortsight. Interviews with Congress and Timebomb, articles on work (what's fucked up about it) and how to do d.i.y. tours. *$2 USA*

Zegota "Movement in the Music" CD: The Zegota 12" on CD with revised packaging. It's remastered, so it sounds a lot better than the vinyl, too. Zegota is one of the most innovative and idealistic hardcore bands today, and this is a simply beautiful record. *$8 USA*

Ire "What Seed, What Root?" CD: This is Ire's swan song, their last twisted, savage masterpiece of wreckage and reckoning, in which their earlier ideas and experiments reach their final, awesome form. If Neurosis had gone the direction we hoped they would back in the early '90's, it would have been something like this. *$10 USA*

Catharsis "Passion" CD: To sow seeds in barren soil if there is no more fertile ground. To bear the fragile worlds within through the ruined one that surrounds. To lift us up, to bring empires down... *$10 USA*

Catharsis "Samsara" 2x12": The "Samsara" album takes up three sides, the old 7" is on the fourth. Cheaper than getting both of the older CDs (the first of which is out of press, anyway), it includes all the material before the new record that the band still plays. *$12 USA*

Kilara "Southern Fried Metal" CD: The kings of southern noise. Incomparable weirdness and fury. *$8 USA*

Timebomb "Full Wrath of the Slave" CD: Italian, vegan straight edge, anarcho-communist black metal. *$8 USA*

"In Our Time" 12" compilation: Damad, Systral, Gehenna, Timebomb, Jesuit, Final Exit, Congress, and an insert discussing the standardization of our world under capitalism... and what to do about it. *$8 USA*

Gehenna "War..." CD: Universal destruction, merciless and bitter. *$10 USA*

Catharsis "Samsara" CD: A Pandora's box of suffering and tragedy, with hope trapped at the bottom... *$10 USA*

Trial "Through the Darkest Days" CD: The world's most sincere, intelligent political straight edge hardcore. *$10 USA*

Coming Soon: Another CrimethInc. compilation (the follow-up to the "In Our Time" record, including Zegota, Undying, the last By All Means song, Bloodpact, the Black Hand, more)... a new Zegota record... the Umlaut full length... a new Catharsis record.

contact:
Stickfigure Distribution
P.O. Box 55462
Atlanta, GA 30308

You can get all the information about domestic, international, and wholesale prices off Gavin's webpage:
www.stickfigure distro.org
stickfigure@phyte.com

FURTHER CONTACTS

If you wish to write any of us a letter, ask for whatever further literature we have on hand for you to read or give out, get patches or posters or stickers or Catharsis shirts or sweatshirts, or offer ideas/cooperation for our next actions, please write us at the original CrimethInc. address:

CrimethInc. Central H.Q.
2695 Rangewood Drive
Atlanta, GA 30345 U.S.A.
www.crimethinc.com

Letterbombs

Dear Inside Front,

I have been thinking a lot about the role that [North] American culture and American individualism have in American radical ideas. The U.S. has a tradition of a very individualist anarchism, that kind of anarchism that says "I'm gonna live in the forest, I'm gonna live there by myself." It's an anarchism very influenced by the way that American society sees itself. Everything in U.S. culture is about individualism and this has a strong influence upon anarchist ideas there. People see anarchism as a way to free yourself from society, not as a way to build a new society to live with the other people. I think that this is a reflection of the whole heritage of American society, the myth of the self made man, is a thing that only can happen in a society that is very capitalistic and with enterprise values like American society has. I don't think that people from other cultures see themselves as a totally isolated individual in the same way that Americans see themselves.

I saw this when I talked about the Arauto (Harbinger) ideas with people here that came from poor areas and poor backgrounds. They can't relate those things with themselves because they don't see themselves separated from their community, they think in terms of their community in they think to fight with the community. They can't think in terms of "my personal happiness and freedom are the most important things in the world and I'm gonna fight for them. As I can't bee happy if the others aren't, I'm gonna fight for everybody's freedom"—because the don't see their own personality as so separated from the rest of the world like people in the U.S. do. People here who are more middle class (like me) can relate more with this question because they are more Americanized. But I hadn't stopped to think about that until I started to talk with more poor people. I think that this individualism came together with the other values that make it possible for capitalism work so "well" there. Values that came from the Protestant heritage. Don't you think that making a radical change in everything isn't just seeking to build a way out based in the same vision of the world that your society has, but changing everything, including the way the people see themselves in the world? What do you think about that? Can you do an exercise of imagination and start to see yourself as a part of something?

Yours, Fred

Dearest Fred—

What you have to remember is that people who live in the West are not just individualists because the culture of capitalism has programmed us that way—we are also individualists because there is no healthy alternative culture here that could have raised us as a part of it. Most of us radicals here had to make a painful break with our society, since that society is itself hostile to freedom and happiness. In a culture of violence, it makes sense to reject that culture and the society that embraces it. From there, of course, you have to create another community, because human life does not take place in a vacuum (you are whatever your interaction with others make you—so to make yourself into something better, you have to arrange to have better interactions with others)... but people in the U.S. and Western Europe are very suspicious, and rightly so, whenever someone

starts telling them about the virtues of identifying yourself with your community: remember the ones in the West who have done this over the last century were all people trying to trick us—Hitler, Stalin, Ronald Reagan, the religious right, etc. In a "sick" (oppressive) society, the "healthy" (life- and compassion- and liberty-loving) people will have to be individualists, to start out.

That doesn't mean we don't need community, but it does mean that creating real, healthy community again is a long, long process. For us, it makes sense to consider our personal desires, because as long as there is still something "healthy" about us, those desires will be in conflict with the values of our destructive civilization. Those who are fortunate enough to belong already to genuine communities, in which they need not differentiate between their own needs and those of their companions, are very lucky (I myself live in one of those communities, but it only has a few thousand people in it, and they're spread out across the world), but they can't fault people who don't have communities like that yet for thinking individualistically. The only problem is if that individualism prevents them from overcoming their isolation.

It's true that this capitalist-born individualism can be a real problem in building new communities. You're right, the cult of "self-sufficiency" in capitalist cultures is an obstacle for all symbiotic human relationships— people want "what they deserve" and "what they earned themselves," not what is good for others too and thus better for them. "Self-sufficiency" is a fucking myth, anyway—to quote Gandhi: "Western man fills his closet with groceries and calls himself self-sufficient." It's generally true that whoever calls themselves "self-sufficient" has stamped all over everyone else to be able to be "responsible" for themselves. And since there really is no space left in the world to go live in the woods (and even if you can do so, it's not very cool to abandon your fellow human beings, and your desires that they are happy), we have to face the fact that we are not independent, we are interdependent. The new Harbinger contains a lot of writing about this, as you'll see—the idea that to be truly free, we have to create that freedom with others, in our interactions with them, rather than finding freedom "from" others. The radical individualist wants that simply because he's never had the beautiful experience of getting along with others, and finding that their happiness and his are inextricably linked.

At the same time, I really don't believe in us "sacrificing ourselves" for the good of any generalization, like "community." Whether or not what we are is totally socially determined, that doesn't mean I owe anything to society. I experience life as a self-contained entity, myself, and it is that self I must answer to first. People who don't recognize this, even if they are part of a non-capitalist culture that has existed for thousands of years, are at risk, I think, and I hope that's not just my ethnocentrism talking. When you make no distinction between your own beliefs and desires and the prescriptions of your society, you leave yourself open to being conned into things like female genital mutilation, which is just not cool, period, if you ask me. Also, groups who have "strong community values" and answer to the group before they answer to themselves as individuals tend not to care about individuals outside their group. My ideal would be that each of us sees herself not as a member of a single group, but rather as an individual who has reason to build community with everything and everyone— who sees herself as a part of the world, not just one community.

I consider myself a part of our community (the punk community), as well as other communities, and I think the most important thing we can do right now is to build those communities. But (and this is the big distinction between anarchist communities and other communities) I think a community is only a good thing if it is good for all the individuals involved in it and outside of it. Therefore, we individuals do have to know what is good for us, to be responsibly involved in community building. This isn't radical individualism—rather, it's (what I hope can work as) the most complimentary combination of individualist and community thinking. Each way is a valid way to view the world, but each one by itself is dangerous and narrow-minded.

Or maybe that's just my U.S. imperialist-individualist conditioning speaking. The fact is, it's hard for any of us to get real perspective, since we've spent our whole lives just being ourselves, conditioning and all. The real question is how each of us can find a way to make things work out, whether you describe that in terms of pursuing your private dreams or integrating yourself into the world as a whole. I'll go to my grave insisting that for most of us, they're fundamentally the same thing.

Yours, Brian

Dearest Inside Front comrades!

It's been a while since the last mail to you, my faraway friends. Forgive me if I've been lazy, but I have to wait a long time for your letters too. On the other hand I'm probably not the best person to entertain relationships divided by the greatest ocean of all. It's seems like my brother evolved out of the same lazy genetic pool so he hasn't been able to write down the Intensity legacy of being banned in the USA so I'll give it a shot. I reserve myself for errors...

Intensity fought the law—and lost...

They arrived at the airport pretty tired and Rodrigo had even a veggie-burrito-induced food poisoning complimentary of the airline. Jonas, Rodrigo and Kristoffer just breezed through customs and passport controls despite their gear and the fact that they look like Latin American guerrilla warriors. Thomas, who looks the most clean cut, got asked what he was going to do there and he replied that he was going to make some music with some friends in the country. He got dragged away while the others waited on the other side. After a couple of hours somebody came looking for them and dragged them back in before they even managed to answer the question if they were affiliated with Thomas.

They did some brief hearings with all of them but concentrated their effort on my brother, Jonas, while he had all the information. They put him in small room and 4 officers started screaming at him and postulated all kinds of accusations. Thomas had been forced to reveal that they were going to tour which they picked up on convinced that they lied about them not going to make any money off it. They did the whole good cop bad cop thing, screamed and threatened with jail and horrendous fines. They also came up with stories that Thomas had "confessed" and that they knew everything. Thomas said this and that and that they were

going to get this much money at this show which my brother explained that even if it would be true Thomas wouldn't know anything about, because he was sitting on all information.

They found an old tour chart and he even tried to convince my brother that he knew the organizer of the Chicago festival and had talked to him. My brother kept his calm but says that he never been so scared in his whole life. They threatened him jail for a couple of years before storming out the room and leaving him there for half an hour. He had no idea of what his eventual rights were. He was also given a paper at one point where he "should write his confession". This went on for 4-5 hours and they also called Felix and probably some other of the numbers they found in his pockets. It was out of their mindset that Timmy would accompany them for free and that people would put them up along the way. For some reason they had something against Thomas. Felix called later and said he has a legal right to bring band over as long as they don't make more money than the cost of airline tickets. He have had bands getting caught before which he been able to solve over the phone. When he asked why they wouldn't be let in they answered " because of reasons they wouldn't reveal to him". It was especially the boss that was fucking around. When it dawned on them that they really wouldn't make any money some of they others were prepared to way them by but he persisted. On their way up through an elevator to the interrogation rooms he mumbled something about that "it is my job to protect the American taxpayers from people like you". He clearly had a grudge against them and especially Thomas who "lied on camera about the purpose" of the trip.

The other three were technically free to enter the country but they would notify the local police who would take them into custody while they investigated the economic aspects of the tour, something that could take days. They three of them weren't exactly thrilled about the concept of spending days in an American prison, and not being able to do the tour without the drummer Thomas anyway, so they decided to return. After staring their intent to leave for home again the wisecrack to boss replied sarcastically "ohh, how so??" with a smile on his face. Luckily they could change their tickets on the spot and hence only lost about 1000$ each because they we going to fly out from different cities at different from the East Coast. If Thomas wouldn't have made it within 12 hours he would be prosecuted. He can't return now without a special visa. It was all fucked up and they lost a lot of money some of them didn't have as well as a lot of other shit that went down the drain. It all took a pretty heavy toll on at least my brother. He have always wanted to go over there and tour and meet people—his great adventure. On the paper the tour looked really good and they received e-mails from all over the place that volunteered to feed and put them up. He went silent for days after coming home again. I think the Catharsisans can relate to the feeling only that they, Intensity, didn't even get a couple of weeks and never have and never will...

OK, what are we going to do with a world order that denies us pleasure and our youth—BURN IT DOWN!! Inflamed rhetoric aside I really miss you all a lot...

    Love - Christian/Volvo/Stella Nera/Big Burger(a new one
    given to me by the Stockholm people)

Dearest Volvo—

That fucking sucks. I'm putting your letter in our new issue so people will see just how fucked up the authorities and the whole borders thing itself are. I wish better luck to other bands trying to cross national boundaries—be careful, no preparation and cover-up is too much.
Stay out of reach, Brian

This appeared on the CrimethInc. Message board in the context of a larger discussion about facial tattoos, and we kidnapped it for reprinting here. Hope the author will be forgiving...

Dear CrimethInc.,

I've read a lot of bullshit about the subject and have found not a single solidly based reason for not getting your face tattooed. I'll try to address some of the common concerns:

Employment

While it does limit who will hire you, it doesn't make you unemployable. My guess is that the people who wouldn't hire you are also the people you would never work for. Keep in mind, also, that because youth culture is one of the largest commodities on the market, that dermographic [editor's note: pun?] is rapidly changing and what was once completely unacceptable is now the norm.

Social interaction

It is true that it will have a pretty profound effect on the way people see you. those who are your friends will have to get used to it, but once they do everything will be as it always was. As far as those who don't know you... well, it's an individual thing. many people will be frightened, and there will be many different reactions based in that fear, such as shock, disgust, incredulity, etc., etc., there will also be many people (many more than you would ever believe) who will be utterly fascinated by it. Every time you go out in public someone will stop you to ask about it. The two most common questions are,"is that real?" and "did that hurt?", but you'd be amazed at the betty crocker, soccer mom types that actually engage in serious dialogue about it and consequently walk away feeling a little enlightened. People want to know why you did it and it's a perfect opportunity to share some of your ideas and beliefs with the "average" person.

Security Issues

Well, it's true, it will definitely make things different in your illegal endeavors. As far as plain old stealing goes it depends on where you live, where you plan to steal from, and most importantly how good a thief you are. It has a couple different effects on the store employees. One might be that they watch you like a hawk because judging from your appearance you are a fucking terrorist here to rob them blind, in which case you can take note of their behavior and point it out to them and liken it to any other form of discrimination. Or they might totally ignore you because they don't want be seen as discriminatory. Of course I don't know what's actually going on in their heads, but that's my theory on the common reactions. Now, if you're planning on doing some ore serious things that involve possi-

ble police attention, prison time, cointelpro involvement, etc., then you should first do some studying of covert guerrilla tactics and I think you'll find that the common credo is DON'T GET CAUGHT. This usually involves, among other things, completely concealing your identity, and there are many ways to do this.

Aesthetics

Someone saying that facial tattoos look crappy is like someone saying that dreadlocks look crappy, or stretched earlobes look crappy, or whatever looks crappy. It's totally subjective and a matter of opinion, although it's true that there are many poorly done facial tattoos in the world right now. I think it's because most of them are not done professionally, or perhaps not enough thought is put into the design. You better be as sure as possible that the design you want to start with is the one you want (I say start with because after the first one you may want more). Also, you must be sure of the artist who is going to work on you. If you can, meet people the artist has worked on and see the work in person. Check it for scarring and linework and all the other little things that make a tattoo a good tattoo. To be sure of your design, draw it on your face and wear it around the house for awhile. Actually, have somebody else draw it for you, it never seems to work out when drawing on your own face. I find that designs that work with the natural shape of your face and bone structure work best. I have a thing for symmetry on the face, too.

So I don't know if this going to help, but I tried. I'd also like to make it clear that I say these things from experience. I have tattoos on my face, and it changed my life. EVERY DAY I'm reminded of where I stand. Whoever says everyone will treat you like shit, is full of shit, but it's true that some people will. They are most commonly white and male. This for the most part reaffirms my beliefs and strengthens my convictions. Every day I'm given a reason to want to change the world.

I live in Seattle and I still steal like a fucking bandit. I'm 28 years old and I know that you don't have to wait until you're 40 to be serious about what you do. I have a son who is the light of my life, his name is Justice and when he's old enough to start wondering why I look so different I'll tell him exactly why. I'll tell him about white skin privilege, capitalism, hierarchy, and all the other things that >shape our society and make it "weird" for a person to have something like this. I never regret getting my face tattooed, regardless of what people say about it, although sometimes, after about the 50th kid in a Korn t-shirt coming up and wanting to tell me how cool I am, I get a little annoyed.

As for those who say "don't make life harder than it has to be"!!?? Come on... millions of jews walked themselves into the ovens behind that same attitude. Billions of people live in fucking despair because of that attitude. The only reason life is harder than it has to be is because people allow it to be, because people don't stand up and say this is who I am, it's my right to be this person and I'll defend that right. I don't want to just exist in this world, I want every last drop of life I can get and I'll be damned if I'm gonna let any laws or rules or especially anyone else's morals or ideas that are based in fear and servitude dictate what I do or how I look. I think I'm done ranting for now.

XRichX

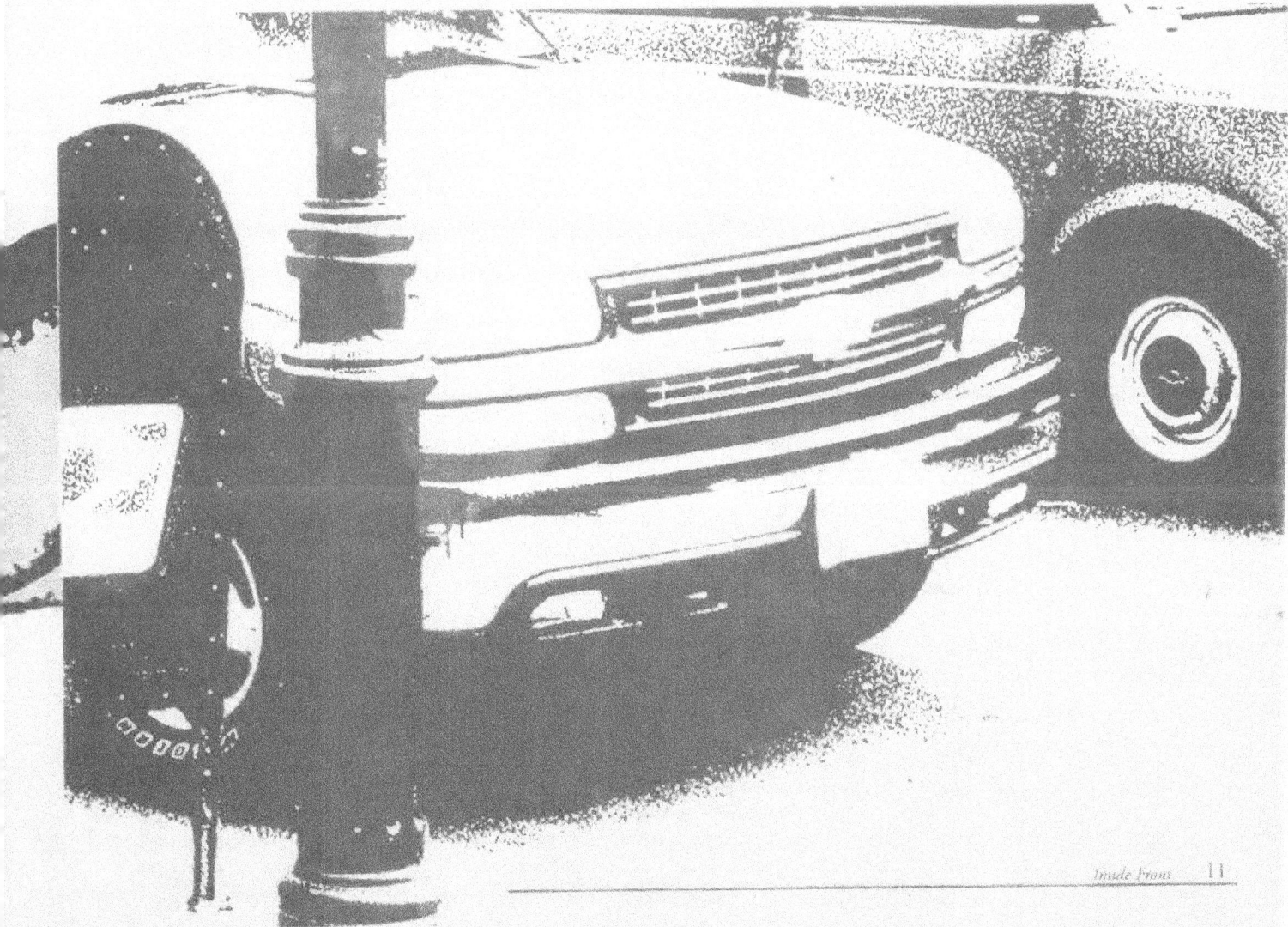

I want to FIGHT like a

If you tough boys want to talk about courage and strength... it takes one hundred times more courage for two girls to kiss in public than it takes for you to fight anybody. Fighting, in fact, is a gesture of weakness and cowardice on your part, since (with only a few exceptions) it shows that you are too scared to question the gender role that your society has pushed you into. You should be embarrassed to walk around flexing your muscles, looking violent—showing off to the world what a fool and coward you are. You would do better to find someone who is really tough—a single working mother, for example—and learn from them.

My heroes and heroines these days aren't dead white men from history books (whether the books be traditional or radical)—they are the living people I meet, the girls and boys whose actions and ways of acting contest and destroy traditions and make those history books obsolete. Most of all, I've been inspired by the individuals who are able to live and act with absolute confidence despite the forces of sexism, homophobia, racism, classism, etc. arrayed against them—that courage and resilience is beautiful, and a gift to all of us, so that the rest of us can see just how much is possible even in this fucked up world. Now, to get more specific:

I want to point out that it's not us conscientious boys who are "protecting" women from sexism, when we learn about it and talk about it; it's the feminist women who are protecting us, by making sure that we don't fail to benefit from what they have to offer our lives, by putting their lives on the line to break down the gender hierarchy that fucks up our lives too. It's not us politically correct activists "protecting" gay and lesbian and bi men and women when we speak against homophobia; it's those men and women who are acting on

behalf of all of us, to liberate us all from the cages our culture has built for us. When two men dare to walk down the streets holding hands, they are striking a blow on behalf of every human being who needs to be free to explore life for herself without fear of judgment or ostracism. Women, non-heterosexual men and women, etc. are not "special interest groups" whose rights have to be "protected" by us normal, sexual-law-abiding citizens. They are the courageous front line in the assault against the conditioning and constraining norms which have been unnaturally imposed on us by a hierarchical civilization that has confused sex with violence, power, and role-playing; their daring attempts to free themselves will free all of us, if we realize that they are leaders and warriors, not victims.

sexuality, you'll see that those coincidences are the result of cultural pressure and standardization, not biology. Fuck you and your generalizations, it's the unique specifics of individuals that matter to me, not the abstractions by which you hope to divide them up into categories, the easier to control. We won't fit in any category you give us, we're bigger than any cage you could offer.

So the same goes for giving us more than two gender role options (lipstick lesbian, diesel dyke, S+M dominant, leatherboy, etc.)—it's just like the choice between pop and grunge, between major label identities and "alternative" identities, all bullshit. My self cannot classified, I will NOT be commodified, and I hope that one day everyone will be able to construct and reconstruct their

As usual, *freedom*, not equality, is the real issue.

What we need is *not* equality between "separate but equal" genders, sexual preference roles, sexual identity ghettos, etc., but the freedom for each of us to find her own way of acting and desiring and relating. There should be as many "genders" as there are people—or more, since people change over the course of their lives, too. The belief that there are two genders, boys and girls, and that they are somehow fundamentally different, is as superstitious as the belief in god, or any other myth that can be disproved just by taking a look at the real world: every person is different, and when we try to fit ourselves into generic groups (by all wearing pantyhose, or all claiming to be attracted to blonde anorexics, or etc.), it's never healthy for any of us. Don't tell me I have something fundamentally in common sexually with every other human being who has the same sexual organs—there may be some coincidental similarities, but if you look at the vastly diverse history of human

sexuality without reference to these strangulating labels.

You can see how gender roles constrict each of us, just by standing on the street and watching people. Watch the way men move their bodies—there is an invisible cage they've been taught not to leave: *Must not let wrist bend more than 45 degrees. Must keep shoulders back, chest puffed out, like authoritative frog, so others will know I'm not to be fucked with.* Listen to gangsta rap—most of the men are so brainwashed by the values of male competition and domination that they are literally unable to do anything with the chance to express themselves except repeat the same stupid mantra about how powerful they are. Pathetic. You can imagine how these same clichés and restrictions express themselves in our relationships, too: despite our best attempts, the girls still end up with their lives revolving around the boys' projects, the boys

girl!!!

still end up not listening or opening themselves up, and both genders find themselves acting out the same unfulfilling farce their parents did, that they swore never to participate in; this pattern is fucked, and we need to find ways to subvert it.

The more radical elements of the feminist movement have done quite a bit towards the liberation of women from their gender programming; as such, they strike me as some of the most successful anarchist efforts of the past half century, whether they used the "A" word or not. What we need now is a movement that can do the same thing to help men liberate themselves from their roles.

Both groups are held in their gender cages by intimidation: women are threatened with worthlessness and expulsion from society should they fail to make themselves docile and agreeable to male domination, and men are led to believe that being less tough than the next guy means certain death. My own personal experience as a boy, incidentally, has been the opposite: when I was younger, and felt the socialized need to lift weights and act aggressive all the time, that got me into trouble constantly with other men who were going through the same thing. Tell a bunch of people that they need to be scared of each other, to make themselves into weapons against each other, and you can't expect that they'll be able to get along and act civil together. On the other hand, once I stopped lifting weights and managed to adopt a less threatening attitude, people stopped fucking with me. Other men can tell I'm not playing their dumb game, and they leave me alone. If you are a young man who tends to get into fights, I would encourage you to try this tactic as well; the more of us learn to make others comfortable in our presence, the less we're going to have to deal with the mindless tragedy of violence. This is especially an issue at our hardcore shows, at

which people need to get along for our community to have anything of value to offer at all. When I go to a straight edge show and everyone is acting all tough, wearing their big bodies and swaggering walks as symbols of their each-against-all masculine role-playing, it doesn't surprise me nearly as much as it does everyone else when a fight breaks out. Don't waste your energy preparing yourself to be tougher than the next guy so as to take care of the next violent situation—try instead to create environments in which everyone can feel safe, in which people can learn how to let their guard down, so they can take that knowledge with them into the rest of the world and make it a habitable place, too.

To clarify—I'm not saying that every kind of behavior and attitude presently associated with "manliness" is a bad thing in all situations. We should all be able to express ourselves in every possible way, to have every human quality at our disposal for every situation we find ourselves in. But since being "manly" is the default setting for all us boys, let's be very, very distrustful of it. The desired end is that we will be free to move freely between all the possibilities that are divided between different roles and personas today, but to get there the first thing we need is experience outside our own sexual/gender ghettos.

I want to conclude this with a reiteration of what the basic problem with the word "fag" is. I know I'm pretty much preaching to the converted, writing about this here, but hopefully some of you will get the chance to put forth some of these ideas in a more challenging environment, and maybe this text can be useful then. A "faggot" was originally a block of wood for burning, so the word refers specifically to the days when women and men who would not toe the party line on sexual behavior and gender role submission were burned alive as witches. No matter how you mean the

word, the fact is that whenever anyone hears it, they instinctively remember that we live in a society in which deviation from the norm is attacked and punished viciously. Those of us who are real warriors in the anti-gender struggle, who are totally out of the closet and exploring publicly without shame, don't need any further reminders of how much risk we run, and neither do the rest of us need to be reminded that we should be scared to join in. The real fucking "faggots," the ones who should be burned at the stake, are the homophobes and thugs who would keep everyone in chains rather than risk a moment of tolerance, let alone questioning. They should be scared as fuck if anyone has to be; they should hide in the closet, if anyone has to hide. I recommend using the word "homophobe" as a slur, where people once used "fag" or "bitch" as all-purpose insults.

Homophobia and sexism have the same root, which is the idea that sex is a kind of violence. "Fucking," in that language of slavery and abuse, is something one person does to another to assert his position of dominance, not a way for equals to express affection or share passion. Women let themselves get "fucked" because they are weaker, according to this bullshit; thus, in homophobic mainstream society, every sex act between men and women has the implications of rape. Homophobes hate gay men because those men show that sometimes men like to be "fucked," too, which suggests that the stranglehold on superiority that men supposedly hold over women is not actually so invulnerable. Part of forging the path to a supportive, free, egalitarian society is inventing a new kind of sex outside the terrain of such power exchanges. That strikes me as exactly the kind of task that the young, adventurous, lascivious kids who read Inside Front are cut out for. Get busy!

Infinite Re

Relationships without bounds or boundaries,

This is about so-called "non-monogamous relationships," about some of the benefits of trying out one of the alternatives to the formulaic dating/marriage/divorce model for love. Your response to this article will probably be similar to the one I had a few years ago when I read a discussion of the same subject by David Sandstrom in the Swedish 'zine Handbook for Revolutionaries: "good idea, but, uh, not relevant to me, of course..." It turned out I was wrong. Had I remembered a lesson I've learned over and over, I would have realized that often the ideas that make me the most defensive and uncomfortable at first turn out to be the most important for me in the long run. Not to say that I'm offering a program that you must all immediately adjust yourselves to... but we can't remind each other enough to be open to new ideas, in case they do prove to be helpful in our lives.

A couple years ago I had a wonderful experience on tour, in which I finally experienced what it felt like for men's gender roles to be dissolved: over the course of the tour everyone in the band and the people touring with us were all able to open up and become emotionally supportive and loving, and suddenly the experience of being with a lot of other boys was totally fucking different from anything I'd encountered before. In this safe, encouraging environment, all of us really felt fearless, free, ready to try anything, with no more doubt or need for walls to protect us. On the surface, it was just that we weren't afraid to touch and hold each other, and that we stopped complaining and being selfish; but the implications beneath this were immense: I realized that there was no need for intimacy and emotional support to be confined to my romantic relationships—I could create and benefit from these things in every relationship.

This got me thinking about my romantic relationships... if there was no reason my friendships couldn't be more like my love affairs, why couldn't my love affairs be more like my friendships? When I thought about it, my friendships had a lot going for them that my love affairs never did: my friends were never jealous or possessive, my friendships didn't tend to adhere to some strict socialized image of what they "should" be, and while my friendships generally continued on in one form or another through my life, once it

turned out that a romantic relationship wasn't storybook-perfect it would end and I wouldn't see the lover any more.

All my love relationships had proceeded something like this: In the beginning I would meet a beautiful new person, we would broaden each others' horizons and have wonderful experiences together, and thus fall in love. At first we would feel more free together than either of us ever had, and the world would seem full to overflowing with possibility and wild joy. But slowly, not trusting the rest of the world, or the future in which we might not feel such wonderful things, we would build our relationship into a castle, to keep out the cold and dangerous outside world, and protect our passion by turning it into an institution. Sex, which at the beginning had been something that came more naturally and freely than anything else, became jealously guarded as the seal sanctifying our love relationship, as proof that it was different than all our other relationships. [This seems, in retrospect, like a really strange role for sex to play.] Inevitably, I would wake up one day and realize that the free, feral passion that we'd been united by was gone, replaced by habit, routine, fear of change; the castle we'd built had become a tomb, sealing us inside and away from the outside world, which we'd actually needed all along to bring us each new things to offer the other and sustain ourselves. Inside the coffin, we fought more and more, each demanding that the other prove her love by

sacrificing more and more—when love is supposed to *enable you to live more*, not disable you in return for an assurance of basic companionship, a companionship that often replaces your participation in larger communities anyway. Falling in love had been like finding a secret entrance to the garden of Eden, a gift economy in which we shared everything without keeping score or worrying about "fair trade"; but now we were back in the exchange economy, competing to see who could need more, who could control more. After all my attempts to transcend the stereotyped roles of people in romantic relationships, I suddenly found that I was a "boyfriend" again, with a "girlfriend" (which is not a healthy role for anyone to have to play in this sexist society!), with no idea how it had all happened.

I started thinking about how it is that we all keep falling into these patterns, and how we could avoid them. The issue of limitation kept coming up: the idea that some things had to be off limits for the relationship to work. With my friends, nothing is off limits, and nothing is demanded either: we offer each other whatever we can, whenever we have it to give, and we don't demand anything that doesn't come naturally for the other (that's how my friendships go when they're healthy, at least, and most of them are at this point). I decided to look into what other models for love relationships there were, and discovered that there is a long tradition of relationships

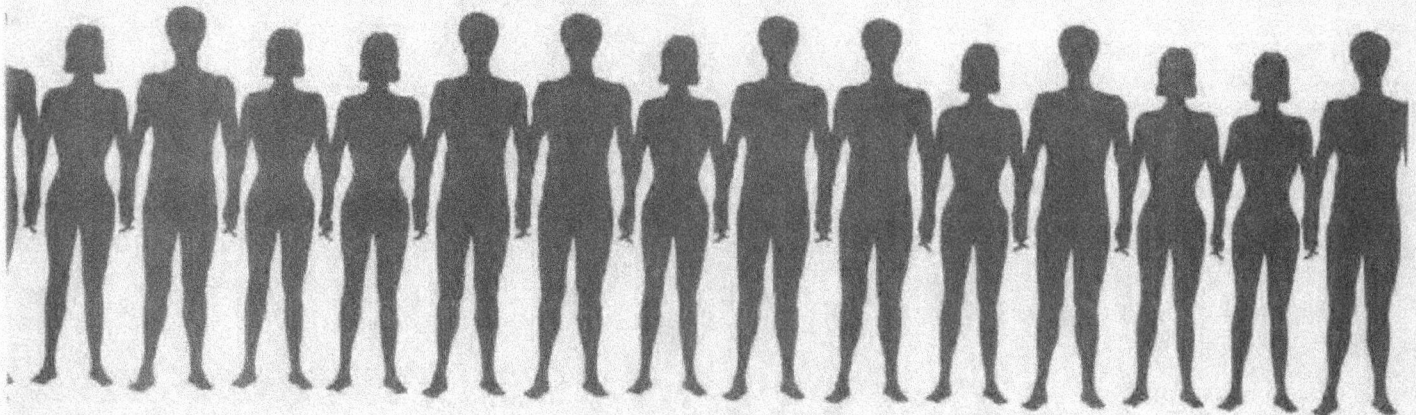

lationships
love without limits, without ends.

without these limits and expectations: non-monogamous, or "open," relationships.

I'm not trying to say that monogamous relationships are bad, exactly, but there are a thousand kinds of relationships, and we generally only permit ourselves to try one format, which seems ridiculous. Let's explore a bit. Every time I hear about another wife/husband/boyfriend/girlfriend cheating and sneaking around, every time I hear someone speaking proudly about how (in the name of monogamy) he has managed to resist doing something he really wants to, every time I must listen to someone pathetically lamenting the feeling of being "trapped" in a relationship or unable to pursue her desires out of some kind of fear, every fucking time I have to witness someone leering voyeuristically ("it's ok to look if you don't touch"), it makes me so furious about how we've trapped ourselves in this one-option relationship system, accepting these symptoms of suffocation as inevitable instead of experimenting with the other possibilities. More than anything else, our commitment to supporting monogamy as the only option (other than "casual sex," I guess, which is boring as fuck and bad in other ways too) keeps us from being honest with each other. We've got to dare to address all these complexities of life and desire openly, even if it is painful.

We punk rockers always act like we're such radical people, but when it comes down to acting, in practice, to try out radically different ways of living that might be more in line with our ideas (or just plain *challenging*, for once, not safe—nothing is more dangerous than playing it safe!), it doesn't occur to us to question our programmed habits. All too often our revolutionary ideas are just badges, a different ideology for us to vote for, not cata-

lysts for transforming life. This is an issue that affects everyone, where anarchist values can be tried out in the real world, but thus far I've seen very little discussion of this subject in our community; if we're going to question the way the world works, we should take that home to our own personal relationships, and perhaps try out alternatives there first before proposing solutions to the ills of the world. That is—if we really have solutions to the ills of our society, let's put those into practice to solve the ills of our own relations. Healer, heal thyself.

What an open relationship is

The most important thing here is to get over the idea that a person's value is measured by whether *she alone* can be "enough" for another person. The world is infinite, and so are we—no amount of living, no number or depth of interactions with others should be "enough" for any of us, just as no amount of interactions with a person you love will ever be "enough." To set borders on what another person can do or feel, as a condition for them to be able to receive my love and affection, goes against everything I believe as an anarchist and a human being; I want to trust others to know what they need, and never limit them—and I certainly don't think *my* life will be any richer from the limitations I place on others. We have to free each other to be and become ourselves. This isn't just about other lovers or sex partners or friends, it's also about other undertakings, needs, even the desire for space and solitude—it's heartbreaking how much of our selves our lovers often ask us to sacrifice to be with them.

I want to be valued for what I am, for what I do naturally, not how well I conform to some pre-set list of needs that someone has. If someone else can fill some of those needs, I

wouldn't deny that to anyone, and I don't want to be jealous when others have something different to offer; I just want the chance to offer what I have to give to those I love, and to remember that those things are priceless and not comparable to whatever unique gifts others may have. None of us should ever be saddled with the role of sole provider for someone's needs (romantic or otherwise), anyway; our purpose on this earth is not to serve others, but to find ways to be ourselves in ways that also benefit others. By saying the rest of the world isn't off limits to your partner, you free yourself of the *job* of being the whole world to your partner.

The monogamy system means that people hesitate to share themselves with others in certain ways, lest they become romantically involved—for since you can only have one romantic partner at a time, you have to make sure that your one partner is a *good investment* (and here we are back in the capitalist market even in our love relationships). Women check men out for financial means, men ponder whether a woman's beauty is socially recognized enough to offer the prestige he hopes to get by having her at his side, and no one is able to experiment with partners who don't meet enough of these criteria to be potential spouses. For that matter—just as in your friendships, there may be people in the world with whom you can spend some wonderfully romantic time once or twice a month, but with whom you don't have enough in common to date steadily and then marry, etc. (although you often see such mismatched couples, who would have been happy as more sporadic partners, making each other miserable in fifty-year marriages). Non-monogamous relationships make such things possible without paying any price of mutual unhappiness.

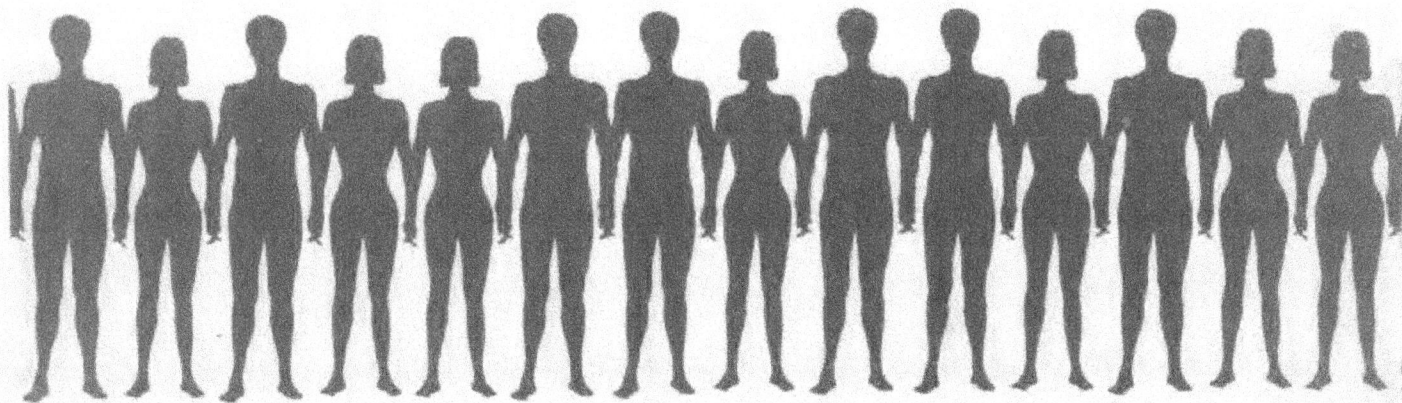

I've decided that I no longer want to have a hierarchy of value between my friendships and my love relationships: they're both crucial, irreplaceable in my life, and fuck anyone who wants me to choose between any of them. Not only that, but I've stopped classifying things as "love" or "friendship" according to arbitrary superficial details—the feelings I share with certain friends are so intimate, so beautiful, that it's ridiculous that I don't call them lovers just because we don't sleep together. It's fucking absurd that sex should be the dividing line between our relationships, between which ones take precedence, between who we play with, live with, sleep with, who we take care of first, who we die with at last.

By the same token, in open relationships, sex isn't weighed down with so many implications and restrictions. Love and desire outside the lines of the monogamy model are demonized and attacked on every front in this society—in the lives of women, at least, and those men who don't want to be monogamous but also despise the superficiality and sexist bullshit of the "player" scene are unlikely to find support in feminist circles, either. Sex should not be contained, and it should not be made symbolic of anything—it should simply be another way for people to be physically affectionate with each other, to give each other pleasure, to be intimate and emotionally expressive, taking equal responsibility for their involvement but without having to answer to some hypercritical mass, social expectation, or moral taboo.

An open relationship is just that: it is a relationship in which people can be open with each other, and with themselves—in which nothing need be hidden or suppressed or off limits, in which the whole world can be ours to explore without fear of transgressing imaginary boundaries. When we demand total openness and honesty from each other in relationships that include limits and taboos, we're setting ourselves up for betrayals and dishonesty; to say "be open!" without being receptive to all of the possible truths is fascist and preposterous. We have to be supportive of each other, in every aspect of our individual characters, if we want real honesty to be possible.

Otherwise, we're like Christians at confession with each other, demanding that we reveal all out of some moral imperative, with the whip of shame ready for any straying impulse. We have to learn to embrace and celebrate anything that feels good for each other. If it's good for our lovers, it's good for us—are we really so selfish that we can't see this?

For one example of how this could work, let's go back to the story of our tour. On the tour, different individuals formed close bonds, and shared private worlds together like lovers do; but they also remembered that for the community to function, they couldn't withdraw from their relationships with everyone else. And whenever two people needed a break from each other or wanted to expand their horizons a bit, they would spend more time with others, because there were always others around them who also had things to offer. Everyone was safe and cared for, and no one was left out, because we weren't paired off in exclusive twos.

Conversely, the scarcity economy of lovers which we have right now makes each person hurry to pick another and chain her to him, before he is left alone forever. The alternative, which this fear of solitude prevents us from seeing, seems more preferable: a world without borders, in which each of us would be part of a broader family of lovers and friends, with no distinction made between the two—and no set format for any relationship, so experimentation would be a constant feature of every one,' and no relationship could ever get dull or overwhelming. To get to such a world, we just have to get used to not limiting each other, to not thinking of love as a limited commodity.

Jealousy, and what I've learned from it

Yes, I still feel jealous sometimes. I've had experiences before of being insanely jealous—not just of another man, but of other things my partners loved or experienced or were excited about. Being able to come to terms with these things has been very important in the development of my confidence and sense of self. It took me years to feel (not just understand) that if my lover loves other things or

other people as well, it doesn't mean I am less valuable. Besides, if (he or) she *truly* loves me, it's not because I match up to some list of desired qualities that someone else can outmatch me at—she loves me for reasons that are unique to me, that no one else can compete with, so I have nothing to fear. Love isn't a scarcity commodity—it increases, just like joy, the more it is permitted and shared and given away. I don't feel like I have to hoard anyone all to myself now. I know that doesn't work, or help to protect love (or me, for that matter).

I consider my jealousy a worthy adversary, one that can teach me a lot about myself if I confront it rather than trying to protect myself from it by controlling others. I've had experiences in relationships before where lovers of mine have limited themselves in order to protect me from my jealousy, and it has been catastrophic for both of us, you can imagine. It's just as important to me now that I help others to not be "afraid for me" as it is that I learn not to be afraid for myself.

One of the things jealousy has taught me about is my attitude toward other men. It's interesting for me to note that I've never felt threatened by women whom my partners were attracted to or involved with, but other men have always made me see red. In our society, men are conditioned not to trust each other, to hate each other, to try to "protect" women from other men (which often looks more like hoarding and protecting personal "property"), and this inclination makes sense when you look at how fucked up many men are when it comes to interacting with women. But for me to not trust *any* men to be something good for my partners (past the point of limited friendship) is outright paranoia and territorial bullshit. If I trust the judgment of my partner, I should trust her to know what and who is good for her, and to not let my each-against-all male conditioning interfere.

Some objections I've heard raised to open relationships:

"It sounds good in theory, but the way people feel is more important than these abstractions..."

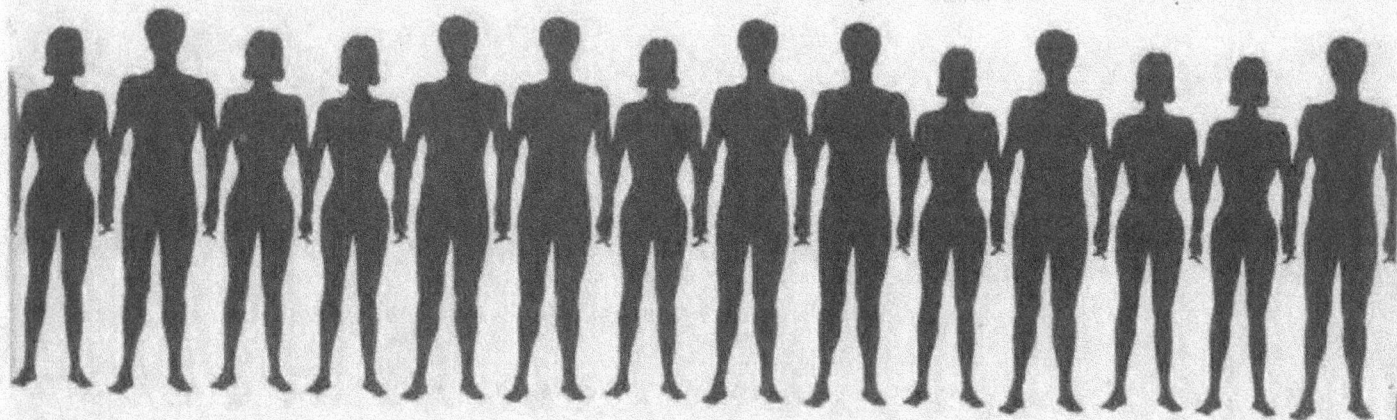

Some people think that we come up with ideas and theories not as solutions to the real problems of our lives, but to show off what good ideas we can come up with. If it's not clear by now that I've been thinking about this as an attempt to solve rather than exacerbate the problems in my love relationships, then I apologize for doing such a poor job writing this article. And hey—if you think open relationships can be tough on your emotions, just try long-term monogamy. They're both hard sometimes.

"But human nature—"

Fuck you. Enough said. Human nature is what we make it, and you know that too, whether or not you want to own up to it—you cowardly excuse-mongering bastards.

"I guess that's fine if it's what you want to try, but luckily I only want monogamy for myself! I'm all set!"

That's great for you, if it really is true—for the time being, at least. We're always so thrilled when our desires happen to coincide with social rules: then it's easy for us to feel proud of our desires, to think they're beautiful, since they are universally accepted (indeed, *everything* around you is reinforcing the idea that what you are *lucky* enough to feel for the moment is perfection itself)... but you might not always be that "lucky," you know. Should you (or someone else) ever feel a need that isn't satisfied by the monogamy system, if you haven't already made the effort to get others to understand and accept the idea that there are many different acceptable kinds of relationships and desire, you'll be back at ground zero, finding yourself misunderstood, hated, called slut and whore. Nobody should have to go through that, ever, so whatever you personally need, you have a stake in promoting non-monogamy as a viable option too. Otherwise, we'll all live in fear of waking up one day feeling a desire that is unacceptable—and that fascist power of moralism over our lives is exactly what I thought we were trying to fight in punk rock.

That's why I consider myself non-monogamous right now, even though I've

only had sexual relations with one person over the past five months: I do what I do not out of a commitment to monogamy, but rather a commitment to meeting my own needs and those of others, with no fucking regard for social norms—and to supporting others who do the same thing, whether or not they do it in the same way. Non-monogamy isn't about sex, anyway—it's a general approach to relationships with people, as I discussed above.

"Open relationships are bad for women—it's just another way for men to be selfish, and absent when women need them..."

This is the kind of sexist remark I'd rather not have to deal with, but I've heard it before. It reminds me of the old myth that all ["good"] women want "responsible" monogamous relationships, and the ones who don't must be confused [so it's OK for us to doubt them or look down on them, just as misogynist pigs call them sluts]. First of all, women have been the ones who introduced me to most of these ideas. Besides the women I know personally, the very best book I've been able to find on this subject (The Ethical Slut, by Dossie Easton and Catherine A. Liszt, on Greenery Press), which I would strongly recommend to anyone interested in this issue, is written by women [if you can't find it, write me and I'll lend you my copy]. Second of all, a lot of the men and women involved in pioneering different models for relationships over the past few decades have not been involved in heterosexual relationships, so in those cases this is a totally unfounded criticism. Third—people who say this make it sound like they think men are only emotionally nurturing to women who are paying them off for it with sex... and denying them access to any other sex as a way to be sure the payoff will always work. God, I hope that's not the best we can hope for in heterosexual relationships...

Finally—yes, it's true that men have been conditioned to be selfish and somewhat less than nurturing in their relationships, and just shifting relationship models is not going to cure that. But that's going to be a problem in whatever kinds of relationships they have, not just open ones, and has be dealt with as a sep-

arate issue. A loving, caring boy is not going to go running off for sex with some stranger when his lover (or one of his lovers) really needs him. There are so many landmines hidden in our sexuality, since so much of it has been programmed by our enemies; we men need to unlearn the pressures that make us seek out superficial sex as a way to avoid real intimacy and support. That brings me to the third objection:

"So does this mean you're giving up on your romantic dreams, your hopes for living happily ever after, just trading them for a series of sexual episodes with acquaintances?"

No, not at all. I'm not interested in evading personal commitments and long term relationships—rather, I want to *protect* them from being unnecessarily at risk. I want to *secure* my romantic relationships, so they won't be at risk from trivial things like temporary boredom or attraction to others, by creating relationships that are sustainable *through* changes in my life and needs. That way I can hope to have my lovers as long as I have my friends, 'til death do us part for real, and no old taboos (or jealousy, insecurity, etc.) will interfere. Sure, this will be hard sometimes, just like everything is hard sometimes—but the rewards of making this work will be greater in every way, I think.

What I'm hoping to do here is free us from the unnecessary tragedies of our love affairs, the insecurities and possessiveness that deny us the commitment and pleasure we could have together. In order to be ready to remove those obstacles, we have to be ready to face the real tragedies head on, with great courage: we can't demand that others protect us from our insecurities by limiting themselves, and we have to face the fact that there will be moments when we are alone. The price of not doing this is absurd—today, we suffer both the necessary and unnecessary tragedies in our relationships, because of the courage we lack. Is it too much to ask that we try something new?

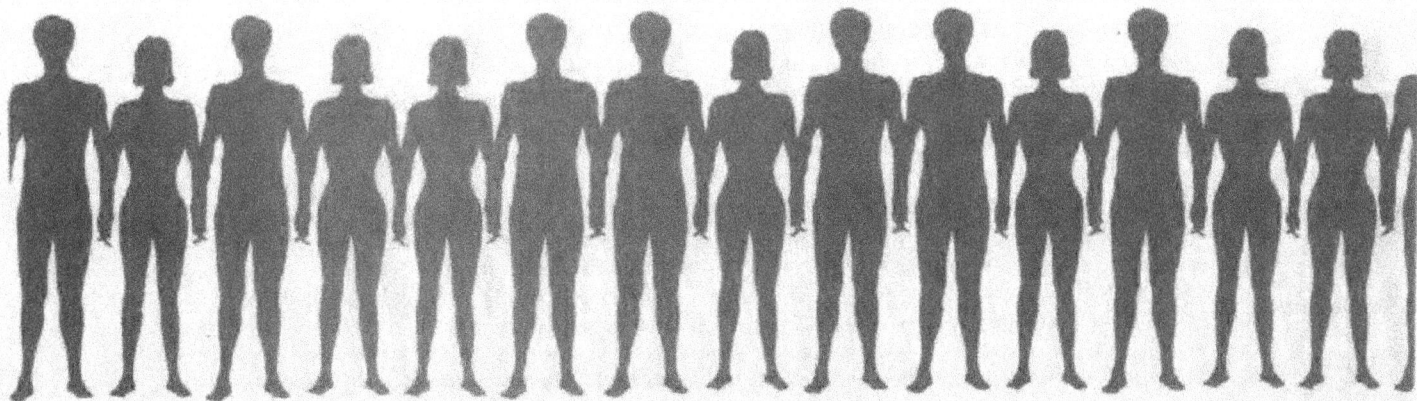

WHAT SHALL WE

Granted, as I talked about in the introduction, lots of kids take the spectator role in punk rock and end up feeling as alienated here as they do in mainstream society. But for the rest of us (and hopefully for them too, soon), punk is a revelation—it is a place where we get to decide what happens, where we find out for ourselves just how much we are capable of, where we can make a world of our own. Playing music yourself, or watching your comrades play it, is nothing like listening to the radio or going to a stadium concert; it makes it clear just how mighty and beautiful we all are, it shows the rewards of freedom and participation in the flesh. So now, the big question is: if we want this feeling more than once every week or two, what do we do?

Obviously we need to build up a larger, more deeply-rooted community, that can provide the support system for us to take our entire lives into our hands—including the practical matters of survival, the aspects of our creativity and thirst for adventure that music does not provide for, and our interactions with the rest of society. This article is intended as a possible blueprint of where to start... but for heaven's sake, don't think we know everything about this—we barely know anything at all. Surprise us by showing what we left out, if you can!

POOLING OUR RESOURCES

There are two ways we can meet our needs as individuals: in ways that help others to meet their needs, or in ways that (directly or indirectly) deny others their needs. This is a basic principle of anarchist organizing in a capitalist world. For example: when you buy your food at a grocery store, you have to work to earn the money to pay for it, and since not everyone can afford to buy food there (or have the chance to get a decent job, in the first place), you're using your wealth and labor to support a system that doesn't provide for everyone—and for that matter, in the process of earning the money to pay for the food, you'll probably become selfish ("I had to work hard for this! I earned it! it's mine! None for you! Your problems are not my problems!"). On the other hand, when you organize a communal garden, or a Food Not Bombs group for that matter, the same process that feeds others feeds you, and food no longer need be seen as a scarce commodity. The more people volunteer at the garden or for the gathering and cooking, the more food there is. You can apply this principle to every aspect of life.

Today we only have a little "free" time to invest in the punk community and the other positive things in our lives, because the rest of our time and energy and resources go into maintaining the system that keeps us separated and thus weak. Do you pay rent on your own apartment, or share communal space that can be used for more than sleeping, eating, and watching television? Do you work for a corporation to pay for your own health insurance, or do you volunteer at a community health clinic? Do you pay for car insurance, gas, and repairs, or participate in a bike co-op and share a community van for longer drives? Do you put your money into entertainment for yourself, or into obtaining resources for your community to build more entertaining lives for all?

There's a lot of talk in anarchist/activist circles about how to "get the message out." I'm not against demonstrations, but I think it's ridiculous to think that demonstrations should be our main outreach to other segments of this society. To show what is worthwhile about sharing, caring, anarchist values, etc., we simply have to demonstrate them. If we can create alternate ways for people to meet their needs together, through which they can take care of the details of survival without remaining divided into atomized units that must sustain themselves or perish, then it will be clear how much better our ways of doing things are. When people see that anarchism (or whatever you like to call it) is about helping people to find food and shelter and environmentally safe transportation and ways to afford the lives they want, they will be a lot more sympathetic than they are when they only see us breaking windows and writing graffiti. If you want to build a community so you'll have a structure to support your own efforts to live free, just find what you have to offer and offer it.

CREATING COMMUNITY SPACES

Here in the U.S.A., all I ever hear about is people complaining about how "this town sucks" (whether it's Louisburg, N.C., or N.Y.C.) and insisting "I'm about to leave, I'm moving to..." The town has refused to offer them the life they want on a platter, and so rather than see what they can do with the resources it does provide they just want to move on to some other place which will presumably take care of everything for them. Usually they don't. Sometimes they do, and they find that the new place also sucks, because they're still waiting for it to take care of everything for them. And since they're always about to leave, they never take responsibility for actually putting effort into making things happen where they are. Every city "sucks" in this country because we're paralyzed running in place from one place to another (in our heads if not in fact) that no one takes the time to build really strong communities, to make real things happen.

This happens a lot in the case of housing in particular. We need to establish communal spaces in which we can live cheaply and do creative things, but everyone is always too convinced of their own transience to take the trouble to make it happen. Were we all to put the necessary work into setting these places up, we could then move all around the country, and every place we went would be awesome—we would travel through established community centers, stopping and participating for a few months everywhere we went, just as blood moves through the internal organs of a healthy body. I'm exaggerating how bad things are a bit, since this is already the way the punk scene works in a lot of places in the U.S. But as far as community spaces go, I've seen much better things in Europe with the squat scene, and I feel like we could

TAKE BACK NEXT?

really benefit from doing something similar, even if squatting itself is a bit more difficult in this country. Rather than always being about to move away, in quixotic search for the perfect cool place to live, we should concentrate our energies on transforming the places we do live—we know better how to do that than anyone else does, and if we don't, we'll just take our inertia and disappointment with us to the next stop in our tour of the alieNation.

Without affordable living spaces, everything else is pretty much impossible—when you have to pay hundreds of dollars in rent every month, that money has to come from somewhere, and living on the street is not practical or sustainable in the long term. In the absence of alternative housing, most people inevitably give up on their dreams of leaving the wage-slave grind, or allow despair and inertia to consume them. As it is, the only bands that can tour as much as they want are the ones demanding ridiculous sums to pay for their leases and the ones who don't care about being homeless in between tours. This is absurd, since it's not too hard to organize cheap communal housing, and we already have a few good examples to work from.

When you rent an apartment, you are paying quite a bit for a space that can't be used for much besides recovering from work or studying for school, the two activities that are generally necessary for paying for the apartment in the first place—and you're stuck in that vicious circle. Rent (or buy!) a cheap warehouse, on the other hand, and you have a space that can be used for a lot of things: shows (which can help pay the rent), art exhibitions, big parties, housing for visitors or travelers or others in need, a communal library or darkroom or internet connection or anything, anything at all. Best of all, in the process of fixing it up and organizing all these things in it, you'll learn all about how to do things with space besides just using the microwave and calling the landlord when the plumbing's fucked. When we blur the line between living space and *acting space*, new things become possible that were unimaginable before.

Every town should have at least one community center/living space, where people come together to interact in person, where resources are pooled to complement each other. In the absence of a squatted building or warehouse space, houses can suffice, but the best thing is to have enough space that there can be a differentiation between the space that really is open to the community and the space that people dwell in, so privacy is still possible for those who need it. To begin this project, all you need is enough people to round up the starting capital and the labor to make it work. After that, *if* you can be careful not to separate yourself from everyone else as the elite that controls the space, others will join in.

MEETING OTHER NEEDS

Once you have a space in which meetings and work can take place, the question is what further resources to make and share. If enough food can be dumpstered, collected for Food Not Bombs, or stolen, you could have a free cafe, providing basic meals so no one in your community will ever have to fear starvation (I mention this especially, since in past years I spent so many hungry days and nights—others who have been in similar situations would probably be happy to contribute their labor to such a project)... that would also double as

a place to gather daily, to discuss new ideas and plan further activities. You could combine everyone's private supplies of books and 'zines (and even records, if you want to get radical) to make a library, so that your group will only need one copy of a given product, not one for each of you. You can get an old VCR and television and have movie showings, or set up a workshop with shared tools for auto repair or sculpture. You could take up a collection and set up a communal screenprinting center; the sky's the limit, as long as people are committed to learning how to share things rather than being selfish. You only learn how not to be selfish in the process of sharing, anyway.

In addition to the questions of space and sharing resources, there are other needs that can be met better communally: food and clothing (which I'm sure you know all about already, from Food Not Bombs and similar projects), health care, transportation. There are free clinics set up here and there in this nation already, mostly left over from the 1960's. If you can find one of them, they deserve all the support you can offer them, because they're trying to free us from the blackmail the corporate health "care" system is able to use against us: *your money or your life*, quite literally.

As for transportation... bands are already used to the idea of sharing vans, and that's a good starting place. Sometimes larger vehicles are useful, and if a group of people can get together and share one, it saves each of them a lot of money. Bicycles are best, of course, and a bike cooperative can help provide and repair them. Bicycles can be collected from college campuses where they have been abandoned after school is over, from the basements of lazy rich people who no longer use them, even from the police (who routinely confiscate them) if you can persuade them that you represent a "legitimate charity organization." I've been to places with bicycle libraries, where you can borrow one for your day's travels, and other places where if you put in volunteer hours, you can trade them for a fixed-up bicycle of your own; various groups throughout the last few decades have even set up stands across their cities, with bicycles at each one (painted bright yellow, to be identified as free bikes) that one can take and ride to the next post, to be left there for the next rider.

Sharing knowledge about trainhopping and hitchhiking is also important—and supporting others who are passing through is not only good manners, but helps you to keep abreast of new scams and information as well. It's crucial that each little community be linked with other ones, for mutual aid and education. This applies outside the lines of the punk community, of course—the most stable community projects I've seen have always been the ones that bring together groups from very different circles of society, to cooperate towards goals that benefit each.

A community of people committed to enabling and protecting each other can provide the support and safety net for each of its members to do incredible things. Such groups can start with a small handful who are pledged to give all, who are ready to recognize what disparate qualities and resources each has to offer and share them fairly, and expand to forces of awe-inspiring power. Let's stop treading water and start putting our energy into building these structures.

OTHER PROJECTS AND ADVENTURES

Solving practical problems is only half the program. The other half is to keep life interesting for everybody, and that means continuing to create challenging situations both inside and outside the punk community. The article about Reclaim the Streets in the last issue of Inside Front told of one project undertaken towards this end, and the introduction to this issue tells of another. Rather than go on and on in abstractions like I usually do, I think the best way I can address this is to collect some writing from earlier pamphlets here, with a couple accounts of other projects we've done.

Summer of 1999 Catharsis and Zegota came back from our U.S. tour together hell-bent on making life in North Carolina as exciting as it had been on the road. The first attempt took place at an Atom and his Package show. Considering that Atom was known for his between-song banter, and hoping to make the show something less predictable and more interactive, we composed a list of secret instructions and distributed it to everyone in the audience before Atom's set: whenever Atom says "song," shout "Go!"—whenever he says "package," applaud wildly—whenever he uses profanity, cough, sneeze, spit... We didn't interfere with the mood of what Atom was doing, but contributed greatly to the hilarity of the situation, giving everyone in attendance a way to "perform" too, and surprising Atom at the same time. It was a really good night for everybody, I think (although by the end of three songs, Atom was totally confused, sputtering and freaking out and laughing—the instructions had been designed so that the more perplexed he became, the more unusual the mass responses to his words would get, and eventually he was so overwhelmed that he didn't know what to do next)... if you want to see the secret instructions we passed out, I think Atom still has a copy up on his webpage.

After the Atom and his package show, we composed and distributed the following pamphlet. The original featured a photograph of our good friend Sally breathing fire into the audience during the most recent Catharsis show at Gilman Street.

PUNK

INVITATION TO THE ADVENTURE

Punk shows. Punk shows us what we're capable of in tight-knit communities, it shows us how to have more fun, more experiences, more life. If we let it, punk can show us just how much is possible in this world. And punk shows are exactly the place for this to happen.

Do you remember when you went to your first punk show? It probably felt like you'd discovered a whole new world, carefully hidden from the eyes of your parents and teachers, where people danced and screamed and dressed and talked and thought in ways that you'd never imagined before. You kept going back because they kept challenging you, kept introducing you to new things. Pretty soon punk was your secret world, where you had adventures beyond anything that could happen in a classroom or an office.

But there comes a time in every kid's life when punk shows start to feel stale. You feel like you know exactly what's going to happen: some kids will come together and talk about the same stuff, some bands will play while people stand around or dance a bit, maybe a little rhetoric will be thrown about, and then everyone will go home. Why even go anymore, except out of a sense of duty, if you're not going to be challenged and surprised anymore? That's why many people drop out and stop going to shows.

The Atom and His Package Show Was Just A Warning Shot

We can either accept that punk shows have lost their novelty value and are no longer entertaining (like the passive fucking spectators this society has raised us to be), or we can do something to make them entertaining and challenging again.

The Atom&H.P. show was fun because the audience got to participate in their own way, to be creative and active too, rather than just dutifully following the instructions of the performer or standing in slack-jawed boredom. This made the show better for everyone. What we did together that night wasn't enough to revolutionize the concept of shows itself, perhaps, but it was a little tiny taste of how much less predictable they could be.

Touring the globe with a rock and roll band is not be the only way to risk everything with your friends. For a new type of adventure ———————▶

THINK

A group of us at ShotGunShelter in McLeansville, NC stumbled across an amazing way to get something done. Some of us call it a Thinktank, some call it a Concentration; they are the same thing. The following is a list of premises that explain what a thinktank is and how you might go about trying one.

In the last two years I have participated in a handful of thinktank projects. I have also been in contact with other groups experimenting with the concept. Where appropriate, italicized examples and anecdotes from various of these thinktanks have been included to expand on a premise.

Premise: In a thinktank, a specific amount of time, usually two weeks, is allotted for the attainment of a specific impossible goal. Impossible examples are:
- designing and building a mechanism or piece of art
- producing a public event
- producing a publication
- digging to China and freeing Tibet

I know of one successful thinktank in St. Petersburg, Florida where only the duration and place were predetermined. The rest was left to situation and spontaneity. This was a risky but brilliant expansion of the thinktank concept.

Premise: Design your thinktank like you would design a machine. In support of your specific goal, assemble a group of people, facilities, materials and tools. Each part should be integral to the project.

For a long while I had a project in mind that required some bicycle mechanic skills; I had a friend in Boston who worked on bikes, so I called him up. He came to McLeansville for two weeks and we built it.

Premise: Two weeks is not a long time; thinktank must be efficient.

"Day 11: I was sewing a six foot tall inflatable Arnold Schwarznegger prop. Drew was in the sub basement trouble shooting beats on the sequences, Erik was securing projection and hauling equipment, Jason was screening the last of the t shirts and posters, Chris, who was on his trailer bike picking up an electric motor, managed to dumpster dive two pizzas and a head of cabbage, which we ate for lunch."

Premise: Thinktank is not just temporary, it is necessarily temporary; like a sprint or a tantrum, a thinktank is utterly non-sustainable.

"A modern day vision quest, [thinktank] destroys the way you view your limitations and your self... none of these pursuits are for the faint at heart." -Manifesto for Concentration, 1999

Premise: Thinktank is holistic. Every part of life during thinktank belongs to the project. There are no lunch breaks or business hours. For the given period, Thinktank is in effect twenty four hours a day. Eating or sleeping are done only in a way that supports the project.

In the final days of a Thinktank arranged by a friend in Boston I had to skip a few nights of sleep to work on the accompanying publication. The next day, I was convinced by my cohorts to sleep in the car on the way to Providence. Because of

SHOWS

The His Hero Is Gone Show Might Be Something More

We're not encouraging you to just start heckling bands—that's inexcusable. We're challenging you to contribute as much to these shows as you expect the bands to. For each show, it should be possible for us to add to the atmosphere with surprises of our own. *This is a challenge to you to outdo us, to surprise and challenge us even more than we can entertain and shock you with our tricks.* If we all surprise each other, then shows will be profound again for *everyone*, not just the youngsters, and we'll all have reasons to keep going.

JOIN US IN TAKING BACK THE SHOWS!
A message from the CrimethInc. Revolutionary Dance Party

Here are some examples of things other people have done to keep punk shows new and fresh:

-Stalag 13 (Philadelphia) has held punk rock proms, where everyone dresses up and dances (other theme shows include Halloween and Valentine's Day).

-Some place (I don't remember where) put on a show where all the bands had only ten minutes to set up, play, and pack up. Six bands in an hour! It would be awesome to make everyone's favorite bands write songs just for an occasion like that, or according to some other theme...

-Fort Thunder (Providence) used to have demolition derbies, including one show at which the first band set themselves on fire, the second band set the stage on fire, and the final band performed with a tube filling the room with carbon monoxide from a running car outside. The idea of making a punk show a place to explore the boundaries of life and death is as thrilling to me as it is scary. They've also hosted punk rock professional wrestling (complete with a cage, etc.) and a hundred other crazy events.

And here are some things you might want to try yourself:

-Try dancing to bands in ways that you never have before (or that *no one* has before). Make up your own dances. Explore the freedom in moving your body in new ways and shaking off the weight of self-consciousness and routine.

-Incorporate things besides bands into shows. Try putting on puppet shows, showing homemade films and videos, theater, comedy, spoken word, staging unexpected performance art... For that matter, try mixing up the lineups of bands a bit, so things won't be so predictable.

-Set up shows as part of larger events, or with greater themes than just music: have a potlatch (in which everyone brings gifts for the bands and each other, instead of money), a costume party, a feast, absurd competitions...

-Bring your own adventures to other shows: stage scripted events, introduce unexpected elements, refuse to accept the rule of expectations, strain against the fabric of reality itself. What else is punk rock for?

Other people did stuff at the His Hero Is Gone show, since I was in no condition that night to do anything (I'll write about that later on in this issue). It was tasteful and fun, and didn't interfere with the show for anyone, just gave it a more exciting feeling.

The next show I did anything for was the Trial show... Jon and I dared each other to write poetry for it and perform it there, something neither of us had ever done before. I took the dare seriously of course, and wrote "Fuckem Goddam Markem," which later was revised for the Folklore/Folkwar tour. When Jon saw me reciting it in front of everyone, he freaked out, since he hadn't taken the dare seriously at all. But on the spot he composed a few lines in his head, complete with a dramatic performance-art conclusion, and delivered them right after me. We were learning to not be afraid of doing anything...

We missed all the activity over the next few months, because Catharsis was in Europe and Jon was there playing with us... but he did something amazing upon his return. Jason had organized a benefit for a park area in the state, and Jon stood up between bands with a chalkboard and a notebook, to deliver a "lecture" on CrimethInc. topics... but as he proceeded, he kept getting interrupted by hecklers he had planted in the audience. The heckling became more and more insulting, and the audience turned more and more against the hecklers as the tension grew higher and higher. Jon attempted to go on with his lecture, until finally he was stopped by a heckler who stepped forward and struck him. Blood (homemade fake blood, but convincing to everyone there, in the mental state that prevailed) spilled everywhere, and real violence erupted as the audience leapt forward to break them up and drag the hecklers outside. They almost dismembered poor Jeff, who was one of the plants, ignoring his desperate insistences that it was actually just a performance. Meanwhile, Jon stepped back up on stage, and now, with everyone's full attention and an atmosphere so full of tension that no blade could pierce it, delivered a few lines of poetry explaining what he was really trying to do: we're going on the road, we're going on the run... and you're the ones I want to come...

For me, this performance was brilliant because, just like Zack's combination of the thesis and antithesis of poetry and work (which I spoke of in the introduction), it synthesized elements that had previously remained trapped in opposition to each other. Usually, a performer has to struggle against the hecklers, while the audience remains aloof, watching the conflict from a distance. By integrating heckling into the performance, Jon transcended the old conflict to create something new and dangerous to everyone.

Meanwhile, another CrimethInc. splinter group had been working on a parallel project. F. Mark Dixon and his cohorts had developed a philosophy of action, which they applied to their various art and performance projects: Think Tank. Using the principles of Think Tank, they had built such unheard-of machines as the Safety Bike (a bicycle that does flips when you hit the brakes) and the Sub-Sub-Contra-Bass-Blaster (described below), and in extremely short periods of time had created, booked, and performed multi-media tours (one explored the connections between bodybuilding and the modern capitalist idea of "progress"). Here is the manifesto they put together, in its latest form:

→TANK.

their insistence, the publication remained unassembled until we arrived. Thankfully, Fort Thunder had a good stapler and some willing bodies so we got the job got done.

Premise: Socializing is an impossibility during thinktank. Participants must focus on moving forward at all times. During thinktank idle conversation and dilly dally are out of the question.

The apartment was saturated with thinktank. Peter, unsuspecting, dropped by around midnight for a visit, only to find Moe and I on a furious binge of screen printing. I don't know exactly what was said or done, but I haven't seen Peter since, and that was back in '96.

Premise: Documentation of thinktank is best handled after the fact in the form of propagandic myth making. Any real-time documentation should be handled by non-participants.

For our first thinktank, we overextended. We spent the first week doing everything twice so we could get good pictures. Finally, we realized we were missing out on the real experience so we could have photos to look at. For the second week, we scrapped the burdensome documentation and let our memory serve. It did.

Premise: Thinktank both produces "works or art" and is itself artistic expression rendered as movement through, and alteration of physical and psychological space.

It's hard to locate the borders of this project. Fuller and I have been tied together with an invisible six foot rope for eight days now. He tastes the Food Not Bombs spaghetti and I immediately say "needs salt." We are desperate to get this show working properly; our intensity leaves stains on carpets and sidewalks. Perched on a

Jon finally met got to know Mark and became really excited about this method. While Catharsis was in South America, he combined his efforts with Mark and together they organized a "noise parade" through the business district of Greensboro, complete with elaborate costumes, homemade noisemaking devices, and joyously absurd avant garde pretensions. The pamphlet they put together afterwards stands on its own as a masterpiece of confusionist poetry, so I secretly dumpstered Jon's original notes (which were much more straightforward) to be published here for the first time. If you want a copy of the pamphlet, you can write the Zegota address (at the end of the "Fire and Lightning" piece at conclusion of this article); a revised version of the demands submitted in absentia by the parade on behalf of my own CrimethInc. faction also appeared in F.B.I. 'zine #3.

The Greensboro Noise Parade

The new medium is movement; the new movement is our medium.

It was in the car on our way back from Reclaim the Streets in Raliegh that a noise parade was first suggested. "What can we do to shake things up?" And downtown Greensboro is the perfect canvas—a place designed for routine, for the soulless, lifeless exchange of capital, inhabited by robots, the businessmen and women who've had all their creativity removed by a lifetime of bourgeois comfort and control.

So the idea was to bring as much attention to ourselves as possible: first by means of noise, second by manipulating our appearance. We made our noise devices as elaborate as possible: some were designed to be percussive, others to create droning, constant sounds. We made our costumes big and funny looking: we wore bizarre uniforms and made

color-coordinated protest signs [editor's note: these were no normal protest signs... one read "You can't push a rope, nope," another "Viral or bacterial?"]. We reduced our level of communication to its barest essentials, until we communicated only through emotion. With the medium of movement through

folklore/
CRIMETHINC. SYMPOSIUM

After the Noise Parade, there was the Handy Pantry show described earlier in this issue, another Reclaim the Streets (our 5th in this state, in under a year and a half—not bad for a quiet place like this), and various other efforts. Our most recent undertaking was a two-man tour F. Mark and I did after our participation in the demonstrations in Philadelphia. I'll conclude this article (which I hope has not seemed self-glorifying so much as inspiring, imploring, provoking) with the report we co-wrote together afterwards... it won't give you much of an idea of the grandeur of traveling the country with nothing going for you but a burning commitment to making shit happen, but it's a start, at least. These are such little things we're doing, for now, but from inside they feel so big, so liberating—and they will not be so small for long, if we can keep upping the ante and daring to always wager all.

CrimethInc. agent F. Markatos Dixon and I kicked off the First CrimethInc. Symposium with a narrow escape from the Philadelphia Republican National Convention police state, after being pulled over and searched by a real dimwit of a police officer (Mark finally exasperated him enough that he let us go: "no sir, officer, it's not a weapon, it's a subsonic speaker for doing experiments on fish... yes, fish, well, robotic fish, actually, it's for the naval program with robotic fish at M.I.T., we're late already..."). Somehow, we managed to get our suspicious-looking red truck onto I-95 south just in time to be thirty minutes late to the first performance of Folklore/Folkwar, a tour that we'd booked a month in advance without having any idea what we were doing, let alone an organizational meeting or, god forbid, a practice.

Practice or no practice we had the kind of giddy confidence that can only exist when you have a fifty foot inflatable teddy bear in the back of your truck. If we didn't have a recipe, we did have a solid set of ingredients. In the back with the reddy bear was a three string upright bass made from scrap wood and two tin drain pans, a

low pitch horn called the Boviphonic Ohm Cannon made out of a trash can, sheet plastic and PVC pipe, a rearranged household prayer organ and the Sub-Sub-Contra-Bass-Blaster, a 300 pound hand-crafted speaker that produces bass frequencies too deep for the human ear to hear. All of this and more was unceremoniously piled in the back of the truck; up front in the cab each of us had brought the special notebooks were we scrawl only our craziest after-three-AM ideas. Between Philadelphia and Baltimore we managed to brainstorm a six act, forty minute performance piece using all the inventions and a pile of other items including a gas mask, three rolls of duct tape a roll of rosin paper and eight permanent markers.

What was our goal? I can explain this best by starting with a story from a visit I paid to my parents a few years back. My father and I were at an art gallery, and he was standing next to me trying to figure out how to relate to the painting in front of us. As a core member of the bourgeoisie, he'd heard about art and how important it was, but he had no idea what one was supposed to do with it. He gave it a shot in the only way he knew, con-

physical space, our creative expression existed INSIDE the onlookers. When we walked by and they said "What the hell is that!??"—that's our painting, that confusion our poetry, that curiosity, that disbelief, that is our sculpture.

And we couldn't resist the opportunity to make demands. So we targeted the owners of this town—the Jefferson Pilot Corporation, the only ones with enough resources to make the necessary changes.

Organization (.2)

The noise parade was valuable as an experiment in organization. From the outset, we realized that a delicate balance was needed between spontaneity and precise planning. The method we came up with to preserve this duality was to make an elite core responsible for the planning, to keep the project focused and organized, and then to arrange a large periphery of artists uninvolved in the planning, to be brought into the project at the last minute—who would bring with them the fresh enthusiasm that can otherwise be destroyed by a month of weekly meetings.

Execution !

The elite core began meeting in early April. At our first meeting we established our responsibilities. We decided who would make the signs, who was in charge of costumes, etc. We set a date for the parade, established a timetable for the coming meetings, and gave ourselves a deadline. All our dates and deadlines were pushed and pulled (of

course), but we continued to meet weekly. The Sunday before the Thursday of our parade we had a "stuff meeting" and a "final orientation" the night before. These last two meetings were more like art exhibitions than anything else, as our artists brought in their outlandish costume designs and noise instruments. We began to get excited, began to feel like the idea was actually taking shape and the event was actually going to happen.

The periphery began taking shape less than a week before the parade. Most of the people involved didn't come to a single meeting, they just began to show up on Thursday morning, ready to make noise and get crazy. The organization became chaos around noon on Thursday. We threw all our shit in the van and drove to the departure point on Elm Street downtown. We got dressed and ready in the Food Not Bombs park and set off down Elm around 12:20 p.m. We paraded north into downtown, took a left on Friendly Avenue and circled the block, arriving on the doorstep of the J.P. building on Market Street. We presented our 95 demands, which were printed on a Suzuki violin, and made our way back to the F.N.B. park. It was a quick in and out operation, lasting approximately 40 minutes, start to finish.

Analysis

All in all, the parade was a great success. I think we definitely got the reactions we wanted, out of ourselves most of all (sweaty palms, pounding

heartbeat, doing something that seems impossible, terror and exhilaration, tumult and exultation) and the shocked denizens of the business district. There are things we could have improved on—better preparation, tighter marching formation, not forgetting the demands in the van and having to run back for them, and especially integrating the periphery more (bring them in earlier?) so no one would feel like they were just a warm body in someone else's project—but overall it was a good way to challenge ourselves and keep escalating the tensions in Greensboro, increase the feeling that everything is about to bust out.

Conclusions

In a condition of adamant doubt you are asked for explanations, when all you want is for someone to explain something, anything.

And you are asked for purposes when you are learning to accept that a purpose is not going to emerge, ever.

And you are asked for a statement of intent when the head seethes with all the fluctuating statements of the past instantly and meticulously taken down and which you use constantly, with increasing derision, in evidence against yourself.

No conclusions. To find out what it feels like, what the possibilities are, do it yourself. Good night.

folkwar:
OF VERY NEW MUSIC

sidering the painting as a commodity, a spectacle.

"I wonder what it would be like," he ventured, "to own this painting, to see it on my wall every day, and know it was my painting…" He stared, perplexed at the violence of color and form before him.

"That's not what it's about at all, dad," I tried to help out. "The center of what makes art matter is far from here, from the art gallery. If you bought this, without knowing the artist or being a part of its creation, it would be just another alien form sitting around your living room, gathering dust with the other meaningless tourist souvenirs and trinkets. The most you could hope for then would be that it would pick up some associations from your own life, and to be frank, you'd have to take living a bit more seriously for that to happen. What mattered about this picture was when the artist was painting it, and his friends were over at his little studio in the Paris ghetto, showing him their work and arguing about principles of painting and trading ideas and insights, being creative and alive together. You can't capture that energy by owning this painting or any number of biographies and critical journals."

In just the same way, we punk rockers have a totally different relationship to music than most of the children of Western civilization—even those of us who don't play in bands. We have music being made around us all the time, it is about us, by us, belongs to us. We don't look at it as some alien force that appears from on high, and we aren't impressed by the high priests of the "popular music" that is made to keep music from being popular in the old sense of the world.

To quote a fellow CrimethInc. agent: "Music is now in the hands of the people. What shall we take back next?" Mark and I set out to broaden the territories of our community, to make forays into other fields that will hopefully be further explored and shared by others in the coming years. Anything we hadn't seen a precedent for at punk shows before was fair game: skits, reading stories and manifestos, acting out street theater (example: I am telling some folk tale of revolution,

Mark appears in police uniform, duct tapes me mercilessly to the stage, and begins throwing water balloons at the astonished audience. Spontaneously one, then many of them leap forward and wrestle him to the ground, and everyone gets lesson in breaking their passivity as Mark nearly gets his nose broken.).

The fundamental concept here is autonomy: not permitting any outside force, corporate, governmental, bureaucratic, cultural/traditional or what have you, to hold the keys to the kingdom of any aspect of our lives. Autonomy means taking control of the things in our lives–from music and technology to community decision-making and feeding ourselves. Mark's home-made musical instruments are a good example of this: they do things that nothing you can buy in a music store can. We have a totally different relationship to them because they took shape under his hands. This is what we call folk science. Just like folk music, folk history, folk art, and folk cooking, folk science it is a way to do it yourself. What we've learned is that you have to participate in solving a problem for that solution to be able to empower rather than alienate you. Our little tour was a very, very humble effort to explore that idea and share it with people.

Addendum courtesy of F. Mark Dixon:

Brian, about solving problems: it is important for people to realize that while science has always focused on problem solving, the nature of our problems has totally changed. The examples of folk science aboard our truck were about trouble shooting in the realm of wasted time and creativity. The Sub-Sub Contra-Bass Blaster is a machine for creating inaudible bass, but it is also a machine for snatching its maker from the jaws of boredom with a process of production that requires so much time and focus that there is nothing left for the usual suicidal fare of sleeping, eating, working and being entertained. These are today's problems, and they are no less formidable than being chased by wolves or gathering enough food to eat.

Fire &

by Hester Prynne

Part One:

.............the sky is making that color, the birds are making that song, it is dawn, the street is quiet. I look down, listening, past the holes in my shoes, past the cracks of pavement, deep... And the rhythm of the Earth is pounding there. Walking home, I pass the landmarks: there's the Handy Pantry and there's the coffee shop, there's the record store and there's the parking deck... The telephone pole with our fliers, the post office box where I drop my letters... Breathing in, I can feel it, above me and beneath me, to my right and to my left: the world, its parts, myself.

It was the same sort of dawn not quite one year ago that I identify as the moment when things changed. It happened in the middle of a long journey (as it often does). Some of us had spent the night driving north out of Denver, on our way to Salt Lake City; stars faded into day-light, trees began to distinguish themselves as the blackness of night sky crept back from the dawn approaching, just beyond the eastern hori-zon, which broke, as we watched, and spilt across the sky. We pulled off on the side of the highway to have a piss break and gather our last moments of desert night... In the distance there was a field of giant windmills, spinning silhouettes painted black by the amber glow of sunrise at their backs. I looked closely at them for several minutes; they were so big... moving... seemed to communicate something inexpress-ible. There was little I could do at the time but cuss and take deep breaths, "Fuck!" I said, head shaking, "What the fuck."

Eventually we climbed back into the van and set ourselves back on the road; but something from that moment stuck with me, something like a seed, or an epoch that begins slow and expands in meaning and importance. I looked around – all that I saw had been accomplished by hands and feet. I twiddled my fingers and wiggled my toes. That was the moment all this began, when an idea was born, when the art came off the wall, when the words sprang from the page, when the music became ALIVE. The Kinko's on Tate street is not quite as dra-matic as the desert in Wyoming, but even so..

There is a moment where ideas crystallize around you and you find yourself with a new freedom of movement, with a strange and remark-able ability to act on the physical world, when the emotional gravity releases its hold on your muscle fibers and a spontaneous and creative energy takes over. This is when the billboards have failed, when the cop inside has lost his voice; because no one lie can tell the truth, because if the world is to continue, the past *must* be eclipsed and the future *nec-essarily* usurped, when the only alternative is death – death of the spir-it and death of the mind. Moments like this are the only real reason to keep going. They are reason enough, for now.

Abusing the World of Vision

simultaneous excitement, enthusiasm, and sheer terror

I approached him one day in the library on campus, "I have a proj-ect that might interest you..." I said. He looked up, ears perked; and that's how it starts. A crazy idea, quickly off the drawing board and into the realm of physical space. Then there are meetings, brain-storming, and we discuss tactics. By now, months later, the evi-dence is mounting that much more is possible than we previ-ously suspected.

After one desperate night, I met Mark in the parking lot of Lowes Hardware. I'd had no sleep (of course) and I felt strongly that the fate of our project depended on the two of us making forward progress. First there was a mix-up with the trucks, next we realized it was Easter and the scrapyard was closed, then we couldn't decide whether to just buy the cloth or try to steal it or what... the whole morning amounted to a lot of running around and wasting time, inertia was wrestling against us. I looked at Mark, his eyes were facing forward. One foot stumbled in front of another and a momentum gathered around us. I didn't know him well then but I clung to him tight for I was drowning, the sea so dark, so deep. We went to McLeansville and I built several sets of wings from a thick,

here the harness-shaker noise device is shown. as per design, the operator must contort the shoulders with walk to generate sound...

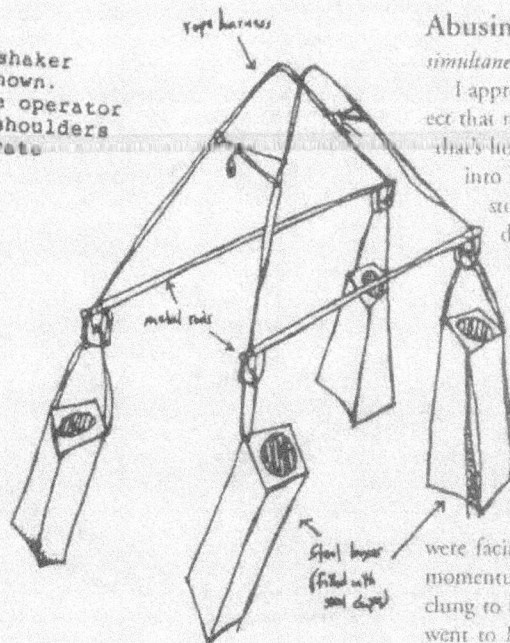

rope harness

metal rods

Steel boxes (filled with seed chips)

industrial sort of foam that Mark dumpstered from an art gallery in Winston; and I began to believe that it was possible to continue on.

I started to think of it as a dance, as one grand coordinated movement through space and time. I thought of my dance partners, who were each alive in different parts of the city: one sewing up the last of the uniforms, one at his desk finishing the demands, and myself, welding in the rain out back of the Durabilt Compound in McLeansville, hoping not to get electrocuted. I looked at the instrument and thought of its design. It was a sort of harness type thing made of ropes and steel shakers. I pictured myself setting it down in front of some parader,

Charlottesville to see, in fact, how desperate they were for a show. It became obvious that I was unable to weasel out of it, so I told him: "Alright goddamnit. I'll think of something." I called Wilson St. and the House of Thieves and left messages, then went out for a walk to clear my head. I felt a wry smile crawl across my face when I came within a block of the Handy Pantry. And I remembered having an idea.

It didn't feel like anything was really going to happen until

Lightning

in Greensboro, North Carolina

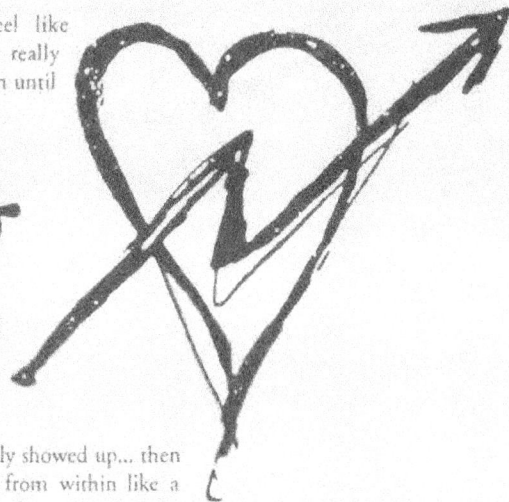

"Here! Use this!" She would stare dumbfounded at the apparatus, "What the fuck is it?" she would say. "It's, um... well... you're supposed to wear it..." I say, "like, um... like this, here..."

Even to this day, I have a hard time articulating *why*, exactly, we decided it would be a good idea to make a noise parade through the streets of downtown Greensboro. Maybe just to prove to ourselves that it was possible? Maybe to shake things up a bit, to do something completely unexpected and unprovoked, hoping that it would speak to the town in a new way.... Or maybe I just needed people, needed to know that people still live, that the desolation I feel is an illusion after all... But will the welds hold? And how long will the noise be heard?

Other Days...

is it not something in this cold, dreary world, to be loved?

Roses outside, shattered like glass: mixed metaphors and old issues of HeartattaCk strewn and soaked with black coffee – one cup too many. I have a candle here on my table that's burning down. Also a tape measure and a pair of scissors (next to my heap of emotional baggage). Just to the left of that is a book entitled, "Faces of Freedom, the Challenge of Transformation" which inadvertently got stolen one day from a church down the street during Food Not Bombs. On top of that is a "d.i.y. anti-depression guide" and a box of soon-to-be-ruined paintbrushes (because I've nothing to clean them with, nor the will to seek out such a fluid at this sickly-slow pace of morning sloth). And, of course, to the immediate right of that is the withered bouquet of my expectations, all that remains from the past week of haggard life in Greensboro. Beside that is a book of matches.

Greensboro is a Monster

RunHaveFun, just after "beer o'clock"

Some matter of weeks earlier, my friend Jeremy had called and asked me to set up a show for his band in Greensboro. "Sure!" I agreed and wrote down all the information on a slip of paper, which I promptly lost and forgot about completely.

When that slip of paper resurfaced in my kitchen, the show was only a couple of days away. "USA is a Monster" it read mockingly, "June 10th" So I called Jeremy up in

the band actually showed up... then the panic rose from within like a great tidal wave of nausea and anxiety.

"Um, shit..." I said to them, "Maybe we better have a quick talk..." and the eight of us sat outside and discussed the ramifications concerning equipment, jail, etc. Standing in front of me, USA is a Monster was a motley crew to be sure; but they seemed oddly prepared to devour the task at hand. I watched for their reactions, there was a madness behind their eyes..

Shortly after 2:00 AM, the "music" began (if it can even be called that). I guess, knowing Jeremy, I was expecting something pathological; but I wasn't prepared for such a blatant, even violent disregard for melody and rhythm. It was horrendous, I felt as if the sound were reaching in through my stomach, tickling my spleen. They were in isle four, just in front of the beer cooler.

I was astounded when the cops pulled into the parking lot, noticed what was happening, told someone (without even getting out of the

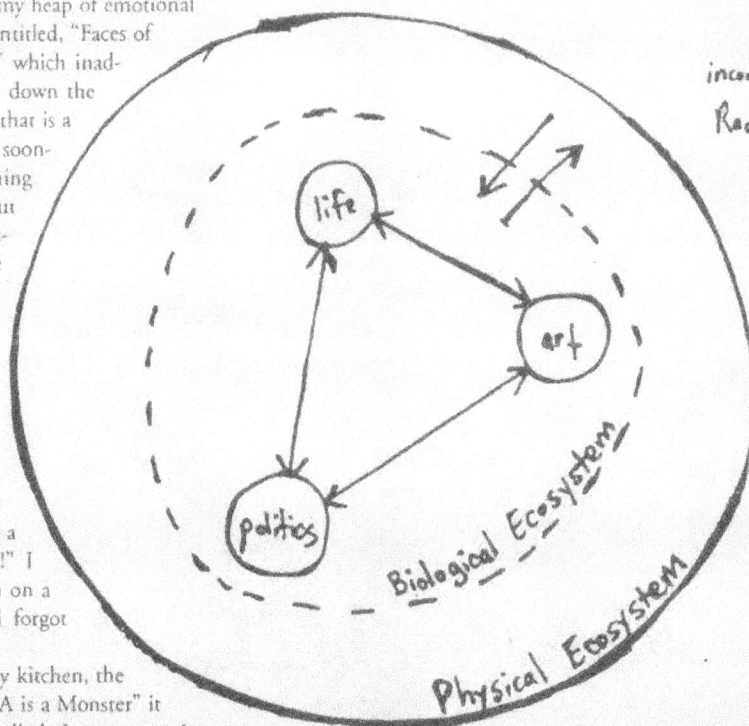

incoming/Outgoing Radiation

Biological Ecosystem

Physical Ecosystem

car) to "keep that door shut" or some nonsense, and then just drove away. Inside, we had all commenced phase one of our *emergency response mission-abort plan for saving musical equipment from confiscation*; but then the cop left and we were all just like: "well, I guess you guys can keep playing." Personally, I hadn't even thought about how we should end the show. I figured it would end itself, one way or another. Eventually we just had to tell them to stop.

Other Days...
shatter my life or complete it

I am terrified by the way things happen. The wind feels wonderful on my face. This corner of the world is utterly without commotion, soft orange illumination, a plastic bag rustling.... there are *other* places people gather, not this one. I am sitting quiet here, alone, thoughts are soft, calm; but by god my heart screams. I have the feeling of a man who is walking in a pitch-black hallway: unsure of where it leads, unsure if there will be obstacles in the way, unsure if he should duck his head, if he should step lightly, unsure of where he is going, unsure of where he has been, expecting at any moment to fall or to hit something, to sustain some mortal injury, and to die. But hoping, of course, hoping that soon his path will illuminate and all his questions will be answered, all of his uncertainty will be replaced by something else – but what, he cannot imagine. O flower in this barren world, O bright star in this empty sky, say something, say anything...

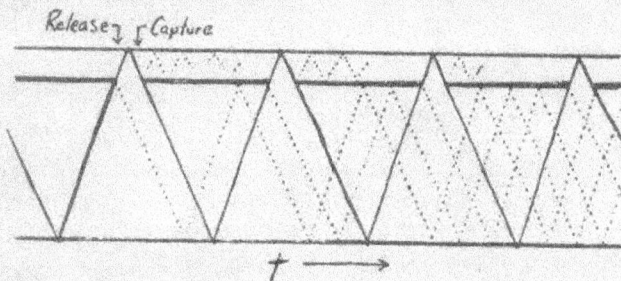

the development of momentum through personal action. Helmholtz path, ripples in space-time.

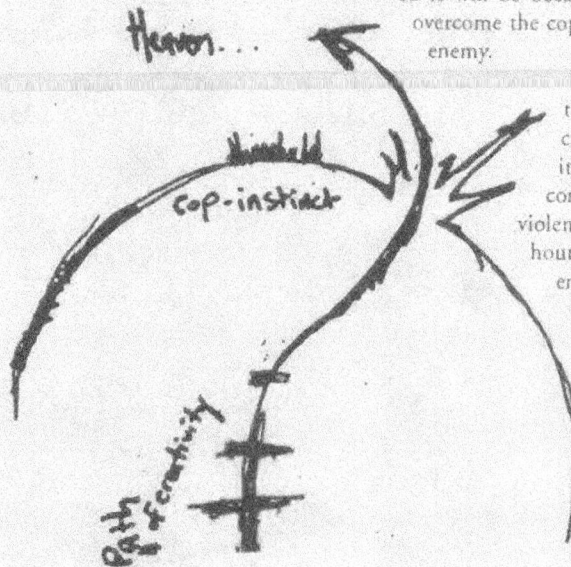

basic faith
involves a certain
amount of risk
never xxxxkxx

never trust a cop

Nothing Exists, Only the Political
the new medium is movement, the new movement is our medium

I sat with my mother on the curb out front of Gate City Noise and she explained to me why she hadn't come to my wedding. "These things you guys are doing..." she began, "...these noise parades and downtown things..." I watched her fidget with a dirty cigarette butt, "they just make me uncomfortable." After she said that, I pretty much stopped listening. I mean what the fuck! My own mother! Can't even come for her own son's wedding! She thought it was a joke; I told her it would probably be her only chance...

Then, just to rub it in, I told my mother the story of the paper airplanes. Oh! if there was ever such a sign of victory, it is this! I was relaxing and eating spaghetti when Bruce approached me, "Did you see these?" he asked. In his hand was a small paper airplane. This was about halfway through, somewhere between the limbo contest and the mambo line. "No," I replied, "What is it?" He pointed to an office window across the street, overlooking the festival below. Inside was a fluttering heart and an idle mind, stolen back from the tight grip of routine. Someone up there was making paper airplanes and throwing them down. We unfolded the piece of paper. "Leveling the Playing Field (1 of 2)" it read, "Lawyer was disbarred in re Pajerowski, N.J., No. D-224, 12/3/98 for, among other things, (1) using a 'runner' to solicit potential clients and (2) condoning runner's fabrication of client's medical claims..." Ha!

There will always be people who believe in getting caught. You'll run into them the night before your big project and they'll tell you things like: "better bring a toothbrush" and "be prepared to travel" – whatever the fuck that means! Once at a show, there was a guy who tried to convince me that Reclaim The Streets was a lame idea. He told me that, instead, we should just "try smiling" and go into the antique shops downtown to meet the old women who own them. He assured me that this would create the sense of "community" and "creative freedom" that Greensboro lacks. I thought he was a moron; but I didn't tell him to his face.

These people believe in society, they believe in cops, especially the cop *inside*. I believe in tact. I believe that with the right amount of finesse, a creative individual can do a lot of very impressive things without getting in any trouble at all. Always remember that we are dealing with people, even cops are nothing more than people: they have emotions, they have expectations, they can be manipulated. Funny things happen to people who become bewildered by the sight of something really bizarre. I believe it is probably an exact science; although I know nothing about it, I believe that when I get arrested it will be because I haven't been creative enough to overcome the cop-instinct. The cop-instinct is our real enemy.

There is always an element of despair that must be planned for in anything crazy we try to do. As the project nears its climax, I expect myself to become a complete wreck of stinging nerves and violent anxiety. If I don't find myself a few hours before the event leaning over an empty pot of coffee, head in hands, chanting: "oh shit, oh fuck, this is it, oh god..." then I know the goals are not high enough.

If I die in my mind, then I die here soon after. If I convince myself that I am alone, then I will convince you to. Bitterness and frustration inhibit movement, prevents motion. Relaxation and broadview are essential for sustainable productivity. The way my body moves through space creates and destroys bits and pieces of the surrounding environment. The way my body moves through space is a manifestation of my mental state. "Pressure" is restriction. Pressure is atrophy. The power to create pressure is the power of the human mind.

"Pressure" results from insecurity, which results from the desire to know the outcome. Releasing the desire to know the outcome requires faith. The destruction of pressure involves faith. Faith requires risk.

When I called Mark to ask that he bring his Geodesic dome to Reclaim the Streets, I knew there was a chance it would be confiscated. I believed that the shape of the dome would have an effect on the space such that it would deter the police from responding in a harsh manner. I'd seen what the dome could do, I'd seen how people change when they find it. I believed in the dome, it's such a basic shape. It speaks to people in a language they're not ready for. It communicates something primal, something essential... Anyway, I believed that the presence of the dome would create in the air exactly the kind of vibration we needed to keep the dome from being confiscated. One creates the other, the other escapes the one. There is a threshold over which creativity must pass in order to defeat the cop-instinct. To not cross that threshold constitutes a disaster. Half measures availed us nothing. Anything worth doing is worth doing right.

We threw open the door of the van and ran out into the street. I went straight for the bus of art students from Winston and began beating on the door, shouting like a maniac, "Go! Go! Go!" and "Now! Now! Now!" *Timing is everything. The first five minutes are crucial.* Bruce was right behind me; we started throwing traffic cones out of the way. I grabbed the first bag of flowers and ripped it open, started kicking them all over the place. Then the banner dropped across the street and I felt the gravity drift from my bones. The space was consumed without hesitation... a thirty foot inflatable plastic tetrahedron rose from the sidewalk, allofasudden there were people everywhere, someone brought out the platform, and I ran shouting: "There's gonna be a wedding! Make way! Make way!"

Our priest was a street poet with blonde hair and glasses, he nodded to signal the bridesmaids. The procession rounded the corner of February One, shouting in one unified and frenzied voice such a wedding march as I have never heard. The festival became a boiling cauldron, water balloons rained from the sky while Jeremy read his poem: our call to arms, our signal, past our point of no return. The mob was hard to

keep under control. "Wait till after the vows!" I shouted in vain. There was sudden movement in all directions, teetering on the verge of complete chaos.

My hand was shaking uncontrollably as I slipped the ring onto her finger. Behind us there were dancers, below us there was Earth, and ahead of us nothing but the sweet sweet now. And then the kiss: THE KISS. It felt as if the word of God had thundered through her veins and in one instant was passed to me by the touch of her tongue to mine. It was cataclysmic. I closed my eyes and listened to the sound of a new world being born. I heard the buildings crumble within, life became excruciatingly real and undeniable. When I opened my eyes, Reclaim The Streets had begun. And with it, the Greensboro renaissance.

A testament of gross self-indulgence supplied
by The CrimethInc. Crash Test Lovers
Correspondence: 1104 Buckingham rd. Greensboro, NC 27408 USA

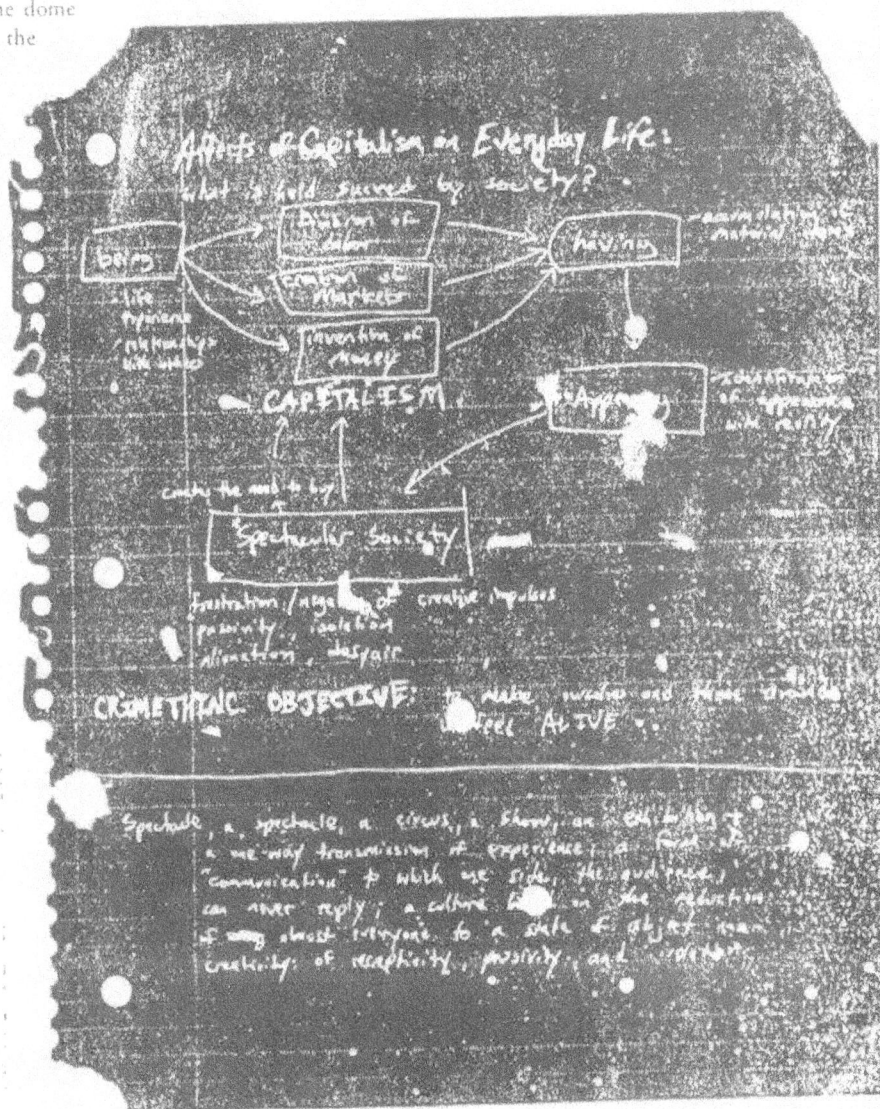

Some hours later, a few of us went back to see what remained. There were still some flower shop scraps and various debris around, and Alex's painting was still up. There were two police officers left, the same two who had been there from the beginning. We watched them standing there, quiet, admiring the painting. Beneath their feet, chalk messages and drawings were scrawled on the sidewalk. "We live" it said. We live.

Everything we do from here on out involves risk. I vow not to let pass another day that is not an adventure of pounding hearts and racing blood. I vow to make this moment last forever. I vow to follow my heart through the black abyss. I vow to swim lakes of fire, I vow to crawl through pits of serpents, should they lay in my heart's path. Should my heart decree, I vow to dance, I vow to sing, I vow to crumble in despair. I vow to soar through the sky like an eagle, I vow to crawl through the dirt like a worm. I vow to love. I vow to make myself hard like stone, soft like a cloud. I vow to become like water, or to become like ice. I vow to scream when my heart screams, I vow to cry when my heart cries. And I vow to breathe, to let you breathe. I vow to *never* let go of life.

fifth COLUMN

INSIDE FRONT COLUMNISTS

A SUBVERSIVE PLOT, A CHAIN OF EVENTS.

by F. Ullivit Buck, Minster of sciences

Two years ago I started work on my first vegetable garden. One morning, about a month later, I harvested my first vegetable, a radish. Crouching right there in my plot, I wiped the radish clean and ate it. It was the first bite of food I had ever eaten that was not the product of someone else's efforts. My first twenty two years, seventy three inches and one hundred and seventy five pounds were made possible entirely by the labor of other people.

At the end of this article, I give a few general tips for beginners interested in trying a garden. But instead of dwelling on the little I know from two summers' experience, I will focus on the why of gardening, a subject I have had many quiet hours in my garden to consider.

Its a well circulated vegetarian "party fact", that there are two things that happen to the energy of the sun as it moves up the food chain. The first is entropy. Our planet's only source of energy is the sun. Plants use solar energy to stack small molecules up to create large, high energy molecules. We call these big molecules carbohydrates, proteins, fats and vitamins. Herbivores eat plants and are thus two steps away from the source. Carnivores eat mainly herbivores and remain at least three steps from the source.

Each time food is consumed, large molecules are broken apart. When large molecules are broken apart the same energy that was used to stack them up is released. The consumer's body uses the released energy for body processes and for recombining smaller molecules into the particular large molecules it needs. Every time this process happens some energy is lost to entropy. Entropy is one reason that it makes sense to gather the sun's energy from its first solid resting place: plants.

The other thing that happens when resources move up the food chain is that they bring toxins with them. Toxins, both natural and artificial, follow materials as they move up the food chain. As energy is lost to entropy, the level of toxins stays the same. As a result, the higher you get in the food chain, the higher the ratio of toxins to energy.

At a minimum this information can help us decide what we should eat. But it can also be viewed as a system of logic that Universe uses to keep relationships successful and healthy. The same system of logic can be applied to other things.

For instance, the food chain is an excellent model for the movement of energy along the "trade chain." The trade chain is the series of exchanges through which the things we use flow.

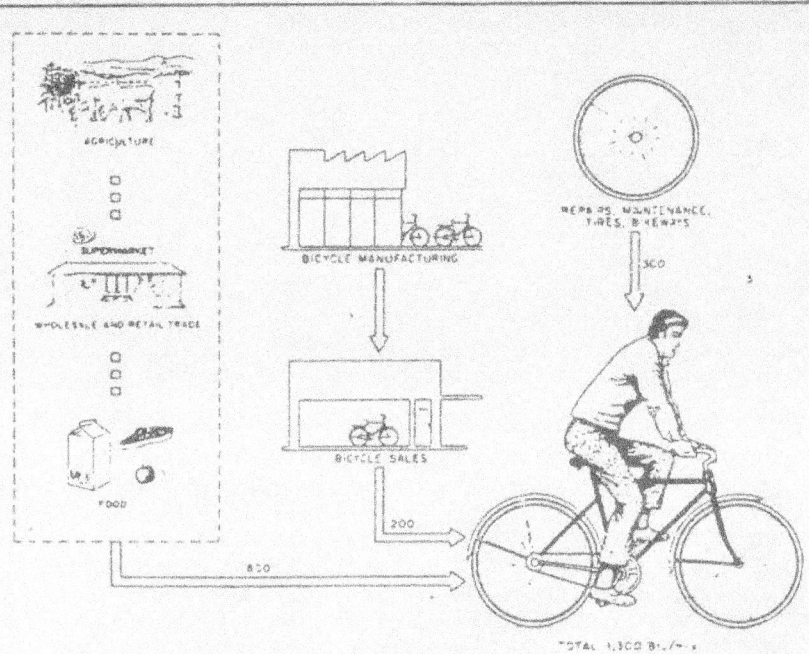

Direct and indirect energy requirements for bicycle travel.

ENERGY REQUIREMENTS—PASSENGER TRAVEL

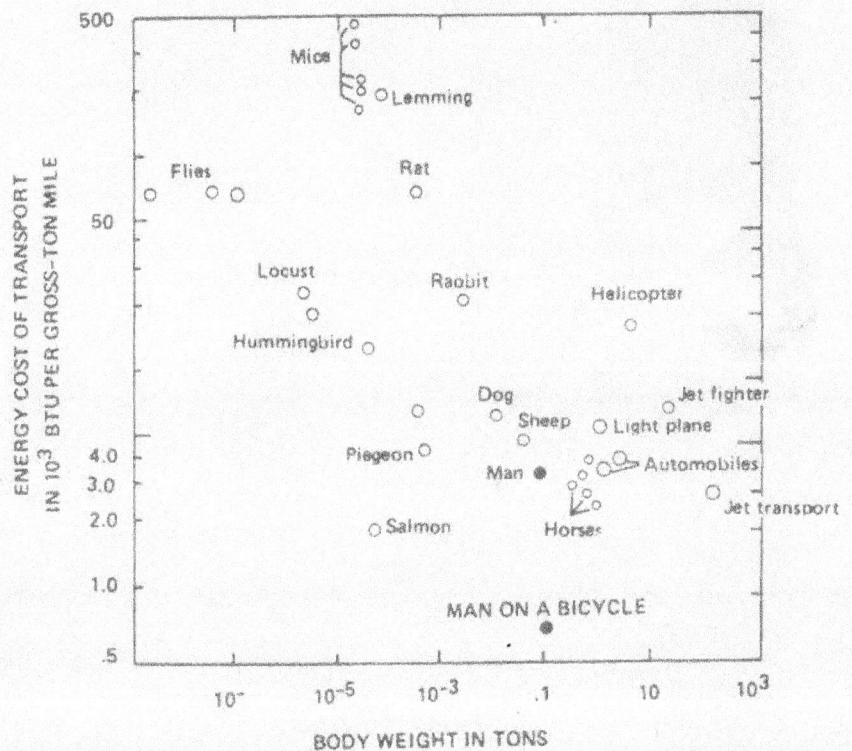

Illustration c.1 & c.2: entropy

Entropy in the trade chain is known as inflation, taxation and inefficiency. Each time a product changes hands, each additional process it undergoes, it becomes more expensive. When the same thing gets more expensive that means a loss has occurred. This rule postdicts that highly processed products will have less value than other products. But sometimes this is not the case. If someone made an exact replica of a Ford Expedition in their garage they would have to sell it to their next door neighbor for much more than the same item mass produced. Obviously, value and entropy aren't the only things to consider.

There's also toxins.

Toxins accumulate as energy moves up the food chain. Similarly, ethical problems accumulate with every transaction in the trade chain. A bottle of Pepsi, for example, comes to its drinker via a chain of exchanges including research, developing, testing, advertising, bottling, shipping, warehousing and retail. On top of that is the lineage of its ingredients: South American sugar cane, petroleum for the plastic bottle, caffeine additive, caramel color, paper board packaging et cetera. Drinking a crisp refreshing bottle of Pepsi requires the labor of hundreds and the use of a staggering amount of resources. In a sense, this product has many of the problems a vegetarian would attribute to a steak. So even though Pepsi is strictly vegan it can easily be considered less "ethical" or more process-tainted than a locally produced egg and that's before you even begin to investigate the most pernicious deeds of PepsiCo.

Here is another source relationship worth consideration. External metabolism is the way we use energy outside of our bodies. The practice started with fire and to this day humans are the only species who metabolize externally. Furthermore, humans use far more of the sun's energy outside of our bodies (to sustain our world) than inside (to sustain our bodies). Among other things, the advent of external metabolism allowed us to thrive in areas where our internal metabolism is insufficient. The internal and external ways we use energy are inseparably entwined; their combination is what sets us apart from both organisms and machines.

As with our internal metabolism, our external metabolism occurs at varying degrees of separation from the source. When we heat and make electricity directly with the sun, we are instantaneous consumers of source energy. When we burn wood, we are using the sun's energy that was gathered and solidified by trees ten to one hundred years ago. Coal and oil are remnants of the sun's energy which are millions of years old. The longer the delay between energies arrival on Earth and its use by a person:
1. the more energy it takes to gather
2. the more equipment it takes to convert to useful form
3. the more money, big business and government is involved
4. the more damage is sustained by the environment
5. the more entropic loss is sustained between its arrival and its use.

So the wisdom that applies to eating low on the food chain also applies to external metabolism. In this case, it is important to stick close to the source with respect to time.

There is no telling how many days worth of stored solar energy we currently use each day but it is becoming increasingly obvious that our gross inefficiency and reckless consumption is both physically and spiritually unsustainable. The Earth receives an allotment of energy from the sun each day. This daily

ration could well be considered a logical upper limit for all of the Earth's energy using processes for one day. Why depend on our dwindling savings account of coal and oil gathered millions of years ago when we could spend your per diem of sunlight?

Considering the source of the things you use is another way to guide your activities. For most things the source system favors consumption of items produced by you or your friends first, your community second, and local or cooperative markets third. All with the overriding principal of avoiding the exchange of money. This principal allows for skimming of waste in the form of dumpstering, free food situations and theft from shitty big businesses. When considering energy, source awareness considers the energy's relative freshness.

Of course, the last thing I want to do is to create more rules about how to behave. Rules are unreliable. As you may know, some of the best reading material filters slowly across restricted borders and through unsuspecting mail systems, changing hands dozens of times while maintaining integrity. On the other hand, the growing supermarket trend thrives off of skipping steps in the trade chain. Keep your common sense sharp so you can recognize the exceptions. The most important thing to remember is that staking your voice in the world on your spending patterns is like resting your political activities to your vote... They are always grateful for your polite participation.

Back to Gardening:

Differing climates and tastes make it impossible to give specific gardening advice, but here's some general stuff I've learned.
1. Don't be intimidated. Despite a few beginner's blunders and one disaster that was completely out of my hands, my first two gardens have been surprisingly easy and fruitful. Kept weeded and watered, well-selected plants seem to take good care of themselves.
2. Well-selected plants usually means Heirlooms. Heirlooms means strains that have been hand-selected over generations to be sturdy, disease resistant and productive without a lot of intensive maintenance. Certain modern hybrids are selected for size and color of fruit rather than more important characteristics like the resilience of the plant, and therefore require chemical assistance. Obviously, these varieties are to be avoided. Particularly ambitious gardeners can develop their own hybrids the way it has been done for thousands of years. It is easy to find material in the library about how to save seeds from the plants that are the most successful in your particular climate and soil and plant them next year.

3. I have never felt a need for chemical fertilizers or pesticides. The rumor is that chemical additives are an imperative for success. Keep in mind that the agricultural revolution raged for thousands of years without them.
4. Do a little research at the library. Keeping your local climate and geography in mind, plan space and time to grow what you want. Don't be scared off by that five hundred page book that makes gardening seem like voodoo rocket physics, that book is for people feeding entire communities. You can do that next year.
5. It is way cheaper to start with seeds than seedlings; they are not hard to grow, you just have to start earlier and sometimes inside. Get your seeds from a store where they are sold by the ounce. They are much cheaper that way, plus the kind of store with bulk seeds is generally a place with knowledgeable employees. They will think it's cute that you are trying your first garden and will most likely be helpful.
6. Spread out your harvest. Plant in several waves to insure that you are not hit with too much produce all at once.
7. It can be helpful to get your soil tested for proper Ph and balance of nutrients. Where I live, this can be done free of charge by the State bureau of agriculture.
8. Proper mulching can save a ton of water and weeding. If you don't have a mulching material, use newspaper. After your plants get a couple of inches high cover the soil around them with several layers of newspaper leaving holes for the plants.
9. Almost anything that can be planted in the ground can be planted in a five gallon bucket. This is perfect for porches and rooftops. Buckets can be collected behind stores and restaurants. Drill holes in the bottom and add a layer of gravel before filling with soil.

THE VIOLENCE/NON-VIOLENCE QUESTION. HOW (AND WHY) TO TRANSCEND IT.

(reprinted: CrimethInc. Special Bullet-in for Maximum Rock'n'Roll, volume 2, number 1)

There are about 1500 of us gathered there in front of the hated Millennium Clock in downtown Sao Paulo. The college kids, members of some Communist Party which has organized this, are there in great numbers, with their little membership stickers on their shirts; but plenty of people from other walks of life are there too: older, poorer workers, bohemian types, middle-aged anarchists and syndicalists, even about one hundred and fifty anarcho-punks. The last group is beautiful for me to see, growing up as I did in a country where most kids in mohawks and leather jackets spend their lives sitting in front of shopping malls: yeah, they have mohawks, and leather jackets (decorated with more political slogans in Portuguese than Exploited skulls, however), but they also all wear bandannas across their faces, like old-fashioned outlaws, and carry backpacks filled with projectiles, gasoline, and paint. They're clearly not here just to chant slogans.

Everything is pretty peaceful at first. There's a radical hip hop group performing from the top of a painted up double decker bus, people playing drums and dancing, a few people trying to burn Brazilian flags (which are all made out of asbestos, it seems). Some of the kids, carrying signs, walk out onto the broad street (eight lanes—this is the second biggest city in the world) to stop traffic; they're pretty orderly, not really ready to get too crazy, and when the police line moves forward to sweep them back onto the sidewalk, they don't resist too much. But the police, having gained a little momentum, push a little further into the crowd than they are welcome, and a scuffle breaks out. They seize one young man, with the domineering pomposity that characterizes anything pigs do, and everyone rushes forward, pulling him away from them and shoving them back. The pigs brandish their clubs, a little space opens up between them and us, charged with a palpable electricity. Into this space, with a sneer of abandon that I recognize well, leaps a young punk kid, who hurls a rock at the face of the Clock which towers fifty feet above us all.

The floodgates burst. From all directions rocks and paintbombs and even molotov cocktails are being hurled at the Clock: the pigs pause, stunned for a second, then charge at us. One courageous soul dashes past them to throw fuel on a fire which has started at the foot of the Clock. People are screaming and shouting all around—none of us have felt this kind of adrenaline in a long time. Tear gas is suddenly in the air. The glass on the face of the digital readout of the Clock shatters, and the glowing numbers go out. The police raise their guns and fire shots over our heads, real bullets. A rock comes flying through the air and hits one of them dead in the face. He crumples like a rag doll.

But I'm getting ahead of myself. (George

Tabb, eat yer heart out!)

First, for those who have never been to Brazil, let me explain what this was about—then I'll talk about the implications. At the time of this writing, Brazil has just celebrated its "500 year anniversary"—that is, it's been 500 years since the Portuguese first landed there, killed all the men, raped all the women (the majority of the modern day inhabitants are descended from this, I'm told), and looted the land bare, before bringing in African slaves to work plantations so that MORE wealth could be squeezed out of the country and into the pockets of Western nations (and a very select few rich accomplice locals). It's histories like this that explain why nations like Brazil are so poor today, and why the Western nations that raped them are so rich (it has nothing to do with who was/is more "civilized"—the opposite, in fact).

Of course, the people who hold power in these nations today stand to gain more if foreign corporations come in and continue to exploit the locals (read as: "enable Brazil to join the global economy," etc.), so they are doing their best to make the Brazilians associate themselves, their history, and their interests with the European colonial powers rather than with the ancestors those powers slaughtered. When we were in Brazil, the most visible signs of this propaganda campaign were the Millennium Clocks: in the center of every Brazilian city, one of these fifty foot tall monoliths (decorated with a picture of the world, no less) counted down the minutes to the 500 year anniversary. All of them (like EVERY public monument celebrating the invasion of the colonists) had to be guarded 24 hours a day by gun-toting members of the military police, for obvious reasons. My friends in Belo Horizante had thrown a lone molotov at the Clock in their city before, but to no avail, so you can imagine how good it felt for us to see the face of one of these seemingly untouchable symbols of capitalist domination smashed and covered with paint in Brazil's largest city.

Sure it felt nice, you're thinking—but did it do any good? How about the actions of the Black Bloc in Seattle, or Washington, D.C. for that matter? Now that things are really start-

ing to heat up in the U.S., too, shouldn't we be addressing which approaches really "work" (my word choice there is deliberate, as you'll see below), and which kinds of activism are "counterproductive"?

These are exactly the questions I want to discuss, but first let's get back to the events in Sao Paulo. There's a sudden moment of stillness, as everyone realizes the gravity of the situation. The Communist students (you knew they would reappear, didn't you?) take this opportunity to throw themselves, with a display of courage that is admirable for unreconstructed middle class kids, between the police and the rest of the demonstrators, and are shouting, pleading with the pigs. The next gunshots were going
to be fired into the crowd, but they aren't. Grudgingly, hatefully respectful of each other's strength, the two sides face off across a line of truce formed by college Communists fearfully clutching one another's hands. There are some more scuffles, and more rocks are thrown at the Clock, but things don't escalate further. The wounded policeman is borne away, and maybe a half hour later the demonstrators take over the highway, with no resistance this time, to march back from the damaged Clock.

Through the second half of the demonstration we hear a fair bit of complaining from the Communist kids about those fucking anarchists, who don't know how to behave, and have screwed up yet another peaceful demonstration. Strangely enough, though, no one hears any grumbling about the college kids from the vandals and rock throwers. You'd think they would want to brag about how much more courageous and radical they are than everyone else, but no, they're quiet and respectful when it comes to their more peaceful comrades—despite the fires visibly burning in their eyes at the sight of cops assaulting their friends. Could it be that they understand how they benefit from the presence of the more "moderate" activists, and vice versa?

For if it had just been anarcho-punks at this protest, you can be sure that they would have been shot at, beaten, and/or arrested, and no one would have intervened. And on the other hand, if it had just been well-behaved college kids, the whole thing would have happened without anyone paying it any notice at all—

ALL BRUTE AND NO FORCE
— A CRIMETHINK KOMIK —

the powers that be wouldn't feel like they needed to pay any more attention than the bored bystanders, and the kids would have chanted a bit and gone home feeling unfulfilled. One of the most convincing analyses I've read of the struggle for black power (liberals can read this as "equality" if you must) in the 1960's claimed that the holders of power and privilege were forced to bargain with pacifists like Martin Luther King, Jr. because they knew that otherwise they would have to reckon with people like Malcolm X and the Black Panthers—people who were not willing to be nice and polite and non-violent. I think that's a good example of how non-violent activism and direct-action activism can complement each other well, and this demonstration in Sao Paulo was another good example. The college kids were there to present the position coherently and to communicate with the pigs when the need arose, while the anarcho-punks and others were there to make the issues REAL and pressing for everyone there, ready or fucking not.

I'm sure many of you are worrying right now about the "bad image" that vandalism, etc. gives us and our ideas. For the moment, I'm not going to try to defend terrorism, or to explain (again!) the difference between initiating violent relations and simply pushing back when you're pushed on—so I'll just concentrate on the question of the "image problem." I always argue about this with my college activist friends... they think that whenever we do things that are publicly visible, we have to make sure not to seem "too radical" or else we will scare everyone away. I think there is a difference between being radical and alienating others. Being accessible (i.e. making it clear that what you're doing is something that others can and will feel comfortable doing with you) is extremely important, but it does NOT necessarily mean we have to tone down our radical messages or actions—perhaps the contrary.

The problem with trying to be accessible to everyone at once is that different things make different people feel included or excluded. The same nice clothes that may make my college friends look good to their bourgeois parents when their protest airs on TV can alienate the fuck out of the poor people down the street from the protest (and which of those two groups do you think has the more revolutionary potential?). By the same token, putting a brick through the window of a building that belongs to the capitalists these same people know are responsible for the mess of their community (to quote the old Profane Existence article, the masses are NOT asses) might speak very plainly and accessibly to them. If we're trying to appeal to others, we must have flexibility in our approach, and recognize when the time is right for wearing suits and speaking nicely, when it is right for

smashing windows and setting fire to public monuments, and when it is right for both at once.

At the bottom of my friends' fears about seeming too radical—this is my guess, at least—there is a profound insecurity that is a bigger problem than any poor press could ever be. For decades now radicals in the U.S. have tried to downplay their beliefs, as if these were something to be ashamed of. This insecurity helps others to see these ideas as crazy, while the real nutcases on the far right get to talk about all sorts of nonsense with the certainty that the concepts they are throwing around (God, country, etc.) will be accepted as absolute values by almost everyone. Thus these motherfuckers can act so smug and confident about their bullshit that everyone is afraid to question it at all, lest they seem "extreme." I think it's time for all of us to be visible in our radicalism, confident and self-assured (without being snobbish or confrontational, of course), so that others will understand that our ideas are nothing to be ashamed of, and will not be ashamed of or try to hide whatever sympathetic feelings they have, either. If nothing else, being cheerfully, openly radical sure opens up access to a lot of ground between you and the so-called mainstream, ground that becomes safe for others to inhabit without appearing TOO crazy: "well, I'm not as far out as those CrimethInc. girls, but I do think there are some serious problems with modern representative democracy..." And it might well be that people haven't come to the radical left before because the solutions we were offering just didn't seem radical ENOUGH, given how disenchanted everyone is—ever thought of that? So as for whether smashing shit sends a message that is too radical—well, perhaps the more radical the better.

Also, it's worth mentioning that not every political action has to be done for the sake of how it LOOKS. There's something valuable about doing what you do for its own sake, not in order to sell your ideas (the way we're used to selling everything in this society). Without moments of authentic and emotionally honest action, like the assaults on the Clock in Sao Paulo or on corporate storefronts in Seattle, we can totally forget what we're trying to do in the first place as activists (which is work towards a world safe for free, authentic action,

right?) and become totally lost in our role as salesmen, the branch managers of the revolution. In this sense, like it or not, the anarcho-punks and the Black Bloc are acting for all of us, simply giving voice to a different aspect of our desires than other activists.

Above and beyond how our activities are seen by spectators, the real crux of the issue is this: any resistance movement, call it "Left" or what you will, is only going to work if everyone who is interested in resistance can find a place for themselves in it. We can achieve this NOT by establishing one dogma about methods and ideology, but only by finding ways to integrate the different methods, needs, and values of different people into approaches that work for everyone involved. It's not very anti-authoritarian, or even humanitarian for that matter, to prescribe the "one true path" to revolution and demand that everyone else follows it regardless of their differences from us. If we can't find a way the Black Bloc and the middle class student activists can work together, we'll be stuck back at square one, where we have been for the last thirty years: the same old endless infighting, the pointless squabbles and blood feuds that make us look ridiculous and alienate everyone else—because people want SOLUTIONS, not new teams to join.

That's why politics has been off-putting for most people for so long: because the majority of the people who HAVE involved themselves in it have done so not because they genuinely wanted to find better ways to live and get along, but out of an insecure need (created by the capitalist impoverishment of our lives and selves) to establish an identity for themselves. An identity is always established in contrast to those of others, of course—so, although he probably didn't recognize this, your old-fashioned political activist actually had a stake in others NOT joining him in his cause. That way he got to be the smart one, the noble hero fighting for everyone's freedom, while they, the dumb unwashed, waited for his help—or despised him and his glorious ideas, "not understanding them." The truth was, everyone else could sense that he was acting more at the behest of his own insecurities than out of a real desire to build bridges to others or live authentically for himself, and therefore assumed he didn't have anything of value to offer to their real lives.

In building the new, powerful resistance

ALL BRUTE —AND— NO FORCE
a CrimethInc. komic
—1998—

When I was born, the doctor dropped me on my head.

that recent events have demonstrated IS possible, we need to leave the "activist identity"—and ALL identities—behind us. Yes, it's important to talk together about what will work and what won't, and to think carefully before we act or declare support for others' actions; but we have to be more ready to listen to each other, and to accept each others' differences (no, I'm not saying we should welcome Nazis, for you fucking morons out there). But the whole "violent activist" (or vandal or whatever you want to call it) versus "nonviolent activist" thing isn't going to help any of us get anywhere, it's just another of the false choices we're used to in this so-called democracy (Pepsi/Coke, Clinton/Bush, competing football teams, etc.). Instead, let's think about what we can gain from each others' different methods, and how to unify them into something mutually beneficial—for it is such interlocking, mutually beneficial relationships and methods that are themselves the model for sustainable lives in a revolutionary world.

As one of my fellow CrimethInc. workers once said: "Anyone who isn't on both sides of the issue is obviously against me from some direction." Scene unity, yo.

CrimethInc. Black Writers' Bloc, 2695 Rangewood Drive, Atlanta, GA 30345 U.S.A.

POLITICAL PARTICIPATION: PROTEST AND THE STATE
by Eric Boehme

Street demonstrations and property destruction have had a storied past in American history. Striking directly at the powerful British Tea Industry, indirectly at Parliament and the King, the Boston Tea Party was a form of political participation that addressed the same issues as anti-globalization protest. Protesting aims to put pressure on government either directly through violence, or indirectly through public opinion and institution-building. Protesting predominantly is issue specific. In other words, protesting builds pressure for incremental change, to enact public policies. The supposed uniqueness of anti-globalization protest revolves around the very ambiguity of what is being criticized. What policies or programs would protesters generally agree upon if given the chance to have an impact? The spectrum

might range from a stronger state and government to a radically decentralized participatory democracy.

Today the means of delivery for raising the voice of the people in protest is the mass media. Media coverage of the Seattle protests made Clinton respond and claim a moderate position on strengthening the state against corporations. In this case, exposure by the media benefited protesters supporting incremental change in the state. Generally the media frames protesting against the state as either a violent confrontation or a street party. Violent confrontations receive less legitimacy as protest in the eyes of the average American. Furthermore, public opinion often supports the use of state violence to "protect property." Framing the protest as a street party, the media delegitimizes the protesters voice, framing the participants as inarticulate, hedonistic, and marginalized.

Protesting seeks to create a crisis of legitimacy between citizens and the state. Outside the usual forms of political participation such as voting, campaign volunteering or contributing, protesting seeks to influence an institution by questioning either its workings or its very premise. Protesting aims to bring some voice to the people, some input for the direction of political and economic institutions. Whether that voice wants institutional reform or institutional transformation, protesting speaks the dissatisfaction of the way one's life is organized. Public opinion is sought and the state may face a crisis of legitimacy to which it responds with either incremental change, radical change, or reaction and repression.

Accepting incremental change means accepting the fact that the state has a legitimate monopoly on violence. Violence is in effect regulated by the state. Without a strong state, the competition of the market heaps subtle levels of violence upon us in terms of environmental devastation, increased "risks" of living in advanced industrial society and class distinctions. Actual violence occurs without a strong state as the struggle for resources pits races, classes, and genders against each other. State building also means institution-building, developing specific programs to alleviate and channel the effects of violence. Yet states protect and do violence to their own populations. Either through the

subterranean violence of law or the blatant creation of public distinctions through specific policies like segregation, states regulate violence.

Protest often seeks to criticize, limit, or overthrow the state's ability to regulate violence. Accepting incremental change means realizing that states enact particular policies that build and support particular institutions. Institutions are useful for regulating violence. Unions support the state. They support building the state to enact better regulation on working environments, enforce wage laws, and protect workers from the competition and violence of the market. Many environmental groups support the state. They would empower the Executive Branch to enforce strict environmental standards and pursue litigation against polluters, reducing the potential for violence through environmental destruction. Some anti-corporate groups support the state's ability to regulate commerce, tinker with the economy, and develop the institutions of civil society to protect against violence. Nader even came to prominence through groups trying to direct the state to regulate a kind of violence done by consumer products.

While this means the state can exercise violence upon its own people, it also means that protest can pressure the state to punish the excesses of corporations and curb the worst effects of consumer culture. For those who support the state, the sword cuts both ways. Accepting a realistic possibility of incremental change, one legitimizes the political institutions of this country. Public opinion often supports protesters with agendas of incremental change, as in the anti-war and Civil Rights movements show. Legitimizing and empowering the state to enact change, protest can make a difference. When public opinion supports protesting, elected officials notice and begin to enact legislation. Accountability results. The voice of the people is heard.

ATR zine, 118 Raritan Ave. Highland Park, NJ 08904
eboehme@eden.rutgers.edu

Editor's response: Don't seek incremental change in the State—erase the State!

Eric, I'm sorry we didn't get to discuss this together first, rather than my thoughts on your article going straight into Inside Front, but this is the final night before it all goes off, so it seems there is no alternative. I hope you won't fault me for saying my piece here.

I think the most valuable thing about the anti-globalization protests of the past year is NOT the "pressure they put on the State" to do things for us. I believe that the State having power over our lives is itself a fundamental problem, one which is essential to the misery of modern man, and I don't want to have to run to one

bully (the State) to protect me from another (the corporations). The State may limit some environmental destruction, just a little bit, but as long as the hierarchal distribution of power (human society as competition rather than cooperation) on which the State is founded exists, the ones who are merciless enough to claw their way above us in the hierarchy game (the corporations, who do this by cheating us out of the same resources they use to maintain their psychological and practical stranglehold on power) will have the basic ability to keep destroying shit and fucking us over: because they can buy that right in the courts and senates, and we can't.

The "voice of the people" is NEVER "heard" by the State—the existence of the State is simply the condition of the voice of the people being suppressed. Sometimes we may make them give us a little ground, so they won't be in danger of losing control—that's all that happens in the cases of "incremental change" you speak of. The Boston Tea Party was the harbinger of a full-scale revolution, you'll recall, not a small change in British policy. We desperately need to stop accepting the "divine right of kings" and governments and corporations to hold the power, and get it back where it belongs, in our hands.

Of course, to be able to do this, we'll need a revolution in the way we get along and care for each other. You suggest at one point that State control prevents us from fighting among ourselves as we compete for resources; I see State control as the ultimate expression of the hierarchy created BY us fighting among ourselves for resources. When we can learn to share rather than fight, States that hold power over us will be unnecessary.

Therefore: acting directly and autonomously to prevent the corporations from going about their destructive business isn't interesting to me because it might enact "incremental change" (i.e. REFORMISM—leaving the State in place to dictate our lives for us, but asking for a longer leash and a cleaner cubicle)—it's interesting because it is a chance for people to learn about using their own power to do things together, rather than deferring to some State or authority. It is through experiences like these that people can get the experience they need to figure out how to utilize their own abilities to get out from under the control of the much-talked-about Powers That Be.

And so I also want to say: fuck the power of the media, too. I'm not opposed to the efforts of those who want to use the media to work towards specific ends in the short run, but in the long run our freedom and survival as a species (seriously!) depend entirely on whether or not we can shrug off hierarchical distribution of power, information, and the power to communicate information—that means rendering the existing "mainstream media" obsolete by creating alternatives and helping people see the benefits of simply ignoring the networks out of existence (which may include burning down some billboards).

Your article does do an excellent job of indicating some of the serious drawbacks of protest politics. Protests, unlike actions (example: the Seattle protest became an action, when it succeeded in achieving the objective of temporarily disarming the W.T.O. ...a wider-ranging series of actions like this would constitute a war of free women and men against their oppressors, not snivelling begging to the Higher Powers), assume the existence of a Master, of whom requests are being made. What I think we really need to do now is use whatever resources we can get our hands on to Do It Ourselves, negating the power of government by simply not recognizing it (and fighting it whenever we have to, but only when we can gain from that fight)—and for this to work, the most important question of all is: how do we find ways to encourage others to join us in doing this?

WHY I LOVE DUMPSTER DIVING
by anyone, anywhere

. Nothing compares to the feeling of elation, of burdens being lifted and constraints escaped, that I feel when I slide that lid back and hop inside a dumpster stocked with possibility, when the mountains of trash produced by this filthy society cease to be mere refuse and become materials. Dumpster diving is the ultimate expression of tact and savvy, it is pure evasion. Everything that sucks about capitalism is immediately inverted when the late night dumpster diver finds her score. Poverty becomes abundance. Loss becomes gain. Despair becomes hope.

Tactics:

The first thing is to find out who in your town is wasteful. I have found that newly opened businesses in yuppie parts of town are often unaware of the wonderful things they throw away. They make good targets; but you have to be careful not to piss them off. A disenchanted yuppie is twice as likely to pad lock a dumpster as a shop owner from a more working class background. Many yuppie shopping centers will be ripe for the "double d" but have security guards that patrol the area. It can help to disguise yourself with an apron or a name tag. When questioned, look extremely annoyed (in true yuppie fashion) and say: "I'm taking out the garbage, you moron," or something to that effect.

If you live in a college town, it should be obvious. College kids throw out more useful garbage than perhaps any other class of people on Earth, especially at the end of a semester. Near the end of spring, the campus here in Greensboro is swarming with scavengers of all kinds. A fellowship exists among us, but there are no rules, no traditions in this game of findtokeep; some secrets are shared, others we keep to the grave.

Successful dumpster diving is not only a question of *where*, but also *when*. It involves precision timing, especially when it comes to frozen goods and other perishable items. There was storm here not too long ago that cut out the power for a few days. Many businesses were throwing out their frozen goods because their freezers were failing. This constituted an opportune moment, prime for the savvy dumpster diver to collect many otherwise unavailable items. Moe and I, for instance, were able to dumpster 10 frozen pizzas, 5 apple pies, 12 packages of Morning Star corn dogs, 6 boxes of Boca burgers, and 16 quarts of almond bark Tofutti, not to mention nearly 13 back issues of *Seventeen* magazine (so that we could work on Moe's love life). It took us a total of 3 and half hours and roughly 6 trips to and from the dumpster on foot. We hoarded it all and fed ourselves from the cache for roughly two weeks.

Psychological Effects:

Among other things, dumpster diving is a powerful anti-depressant. In the middle of one desperate night, I left the house in disgust to go for a walk and try to clear my head. I was listening to Black Sabbath and grumbling bitterly to myself when I ran into my friend Nirmala on Tate Street. On a whim I mentioned, "Hey! wanna go dumpster diving?" She had never been, but she was ready to go. We left the world of despair behind and walked to Friendly Shopping Center, where I took her on my usual rounds. In the end, we walked away with: 1 bag of potato chips, 1 garden salad, as much bread as we could carry, 3 bags of cookies, and oh my god the flowers! We got flowers! We took them back to the apartment and made them into a bouquet on the back porch; it was so romantic, I felt like french-kissing Nirm just being caught up in the moment!! But I didn't...

While we were behind the florist sifting

through the scraps, a Wackenhut Security officer pulled up in a white ATV with green police lights. "I'm gonna have to ask you to leave," he said dryly. Co••pletely swept up by the idea of beautiful dumpstered roses and tulips, I sauntered up to the Enemy and, saying nothing, offered him a white carnation. He refused: "I'm allergic to flowers." His eyes never met mine and his hands never let go of the steering wheel. We gathered our flowers and left the scene; it was obvious to us all what was going on.

On the other hand, dumpster diving can be risky for the recovering bourgeois. Once I was climbing out of the dumpster behind a bread shop, drooling and giggling (of course), and just as I was leaping out, two of the bread shop attendants came out the back door. They looked at me, I looked at them, then we both looked at the huge bag of bread I was toting like Santa Claus. "I.., uhh..." started to explain but the two went back inside before I managed to get out my doctoral thesis on free food. They looked a little appalled, I felt a little weird. It wouldn't have bothered me much except that I recognized one of them to be the little sister of a kid I was in drug treatment with a number of years earlier. I shrugged it off and set about my way. Before I could make a clean break, however, the two emerged once again, this time with a loaf of fresh potato bread to give me. "Um, thanks," I said. I don't think she recognized me.

Sustainability:

I try not to be noticed, but war is war. In my experience, it always serves the dumpster diver to go unseen. I usually make my rounds after store hours and try to clean up the dumpster a bit, leave it in better condition than I found it. However, if the store owner becomes openly hostile, I say fight back. If they padlock the dumpster, squeeze a tube of super glue into the key hole and leave a lengthy manifesto with death threat.

Superstition:

First and foremost: never be afraid to get inside the dumpster. The dumpster gods do not like window shoppers. Second: if a dumpster appears fruitless, do not assume it will always be so. The dumpster gods smile upon those who show persistence. I had to go to the CVS dumpster once a week for months

before I finally found it filled to the top with fresh ice cream bars. Third: if you find something useful, *take it*. The dumpster gods deserve respect, keep them appeased and all will go well. Last week I found an umbrella, on a day as hot and dry as every other one this summer; today, it's been pouring rain torrentially since we woke up, and I've got to go to the bus station.

Warnings:

Some of us have had a problem with this, that's why I bring it up: you've got to watch out for scabies. It was common among us for some time to acquire our sleeping arrangements from a mattress store down the street that would throw away the old mattresses their customers brought in when they got their new mattresses. We have also been tempted by the many foam cushions people leave out with their trash on Thursday nights. Sometimes these seemingly dreamy cushy cushies are infested with little bugs that get in your skin and try to eat you. This is a condition to avoid—be careful.

Another thing to watch out for is rat poison. Most common in larger cities, shop owners often pour Clorox or other lethal substances onto their edible goodies our back to deter the presence of our fellow dumpster divers, rats. Sometimes you can smell it and sometimes there will be discoloration on the packaging. Be sure to inspect your score and stay away from the sketchy ones.

"Dumpster juice." It's a bad thing. Sometimes you just don't need to go any deeper.

Scavenging:

Trash picking is a fine art, it takes experience and intelligence to cultivate your skill. Something changes in the mind of a scavenger as she becomes expert, something strange and hard to define. Where others see garbage, she sees opportunity. Where others see junk, she sees valuable materials. There is a moment in the life of every serious dumpster diver when she realizes that her hands and feet have super power and are capable of incredible things, *if* they are in the right place at the right time, with the right idea. It is a mastery of the resources at hand that gives the scavenger her power. To the extent that she can see the unseen, to the extent that she can match her

wild imagination with the sea of trash before her, is the extent to which the dumpster diver can realize the true possibilities hidden from the rest of society, hidden in the trash.

Some items obtained:
* one 15'x 6' sheet of industrial museum foam twenty pounds of steel shavings
* over one hundred VHS jewel boxes (for video project #1)
* one pair of white mule work gloves
* one custom guitar amplifier
* mountains of bread
* rivers of coffee
* miles upon miles of romantic Christmas lights
* one container of shark cartilage supplements (among other hippie/yuppie health products)
* "The Enchanted Caribou" (children's book, found in Toronto)
* did I mention bagels?
* flowers, oh the flowers
* one greasy massage table
* one "frozen" pizza (slightly moldy, eaten after three days baking on the dashboard of the Catharsis van)
* twenty-five banana flavored power bars
* silk-screening ink
* various home furnishings
* one Dutch bass player
* more Ben and Jerry's ice cream than is healthy for any human

If you're not careful...
epilogue (backlash):

In the summer of 2000, I found myself caught up in a great purging, an elimination of the physical objects surrounding my body and choking up my home. It started as a simple room-cleaning, one Saturday afternoon around 1:00 PM. By 2:00, things had changed: I was throwing out cassette tapes and dirty clothes. By 2:45 I was throwing away stacks of things I meant to mail to people (effectively sending them through the *other* postal system...). Soon I realized this was more than a mere physical cleansing of my dwelling space; it had become something primal, something *that had to be done*. At 3:00 I started in on the home furnishings, and then the pots and pans. By 9:00 AM the next morning, my house was completely empty. I threw out all of my belongings as well as all my brother's (who was away for the weekend). I threw out the shelves from the refrigerator, and then dragged it onto to the street as well. The experience was simultaneously terrifying and liberating.

A few minutes later, I looked out the window and saw my friend Jason digging through our trash, my old sneakers in one hand and the thrill of discovery on his face.

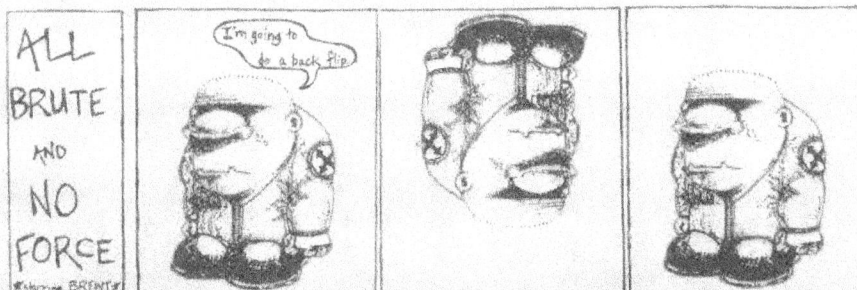

ALL BRUTE AND NO FORCE

I'm going to do a back flip

RIMBAUD, VERLAINE, MATHILDE, AND THE HATLESS PRIEST.
by Liz, Visible Woman

Dear Brian,

I can't write a column for Inside Front after all. I wanted to a lot and I really did try, but I'm finding that it is just beyond me. I think it would take about four years of deep psychological analysis and another four years of silent meditation and maybe four years after that of solitary travel to get to the bottom of what I really feel about freedom and responsibility—or maybe that's not it exactly: independence and interdependence. No, that's not it either—and I guess that's the first problem. The thing I wanted to write about doesn't fit into a neat dichotomy of action and reaction or yin and yang. In fact, the more I examine my problem the more it refuses to stand still for definition at all. F. Scott Fitzgerald wrote "The test of the first-rate intelligence is the ability to hold two opposed ideas in the mind at the same time, and still retain the ability to function." At least on this project I have ceased to function.

I'll try to explain what I wanted to do so you can see the difficulty. It began with the piece in Days of War Nights of Love about Arthur Rimbaud. Do you remember it? "Rimbaud wreaked havoc throughout Paris, knocking the hats off priests in the street, verbally and physically assaulting the popular poets Verlaine introduced him to, and destroying Verlaine's marriage." As the book tells it, Rimbaud's life is an invigorating account of independence and adventure, a kind of inspired selfishness, a life lived entirely in the wild borderlands of human possibility. But as I read it I began to wonder: what about Madame Verlaine? How would the story sound if she were telling it? She was, you know, almost the same age as Rimbaud—16 when Verlaine met her and began courting her (courting her, I should point out, with the same relentless obsession that he later pursued Rimbaud). She wrote poetry herself; not good poetry, it's true, but her own. It was poetry that attracted her to Verlaine, ten years older than she was and already balding and unromantically working in a city office. Her first words when he was introduced to her were "I like poetry very much, Monsieur." You can imagine how short a step it was for a 16-year-old girl from loving poetry to loving a poet, especially one who would slip little poems, lovely sensual little poems, into her hand as he was leaving her parents' house. Who knows what magnificent future she imagined they would share.

My idea was to write in Mathilde's voice—I wanted to write a little dialogue for her and a priest, one of the priests who had had his hat knocked off in the street. My imaginary Mathilde tried to describe the intoxication of those early days with Verlaine. "I saw windows opening in all the stuffy drawing rooms of France," she said. "I saw highways unrolling at our feet, bathed in golden light. It seemed that we would spend a lifetime dancing naked together across the rooftops of Paris. Can you remember?"—she asks the priest this—"what it feels like to be young, to yearn for freedom, to be filled with that aching desire to have everything matter? To long so deeply to translate everything familiar and ordinary in life into a new language?"

Of course in real life Mathilde's marriage was hard from the very beginning. Verlaine, already a little frightened by his own excesses and most particularly by his addiction to absinthe, had married an idea, not a woman—he wanted an angel, a redeemer, a mother, a muse—and he didn't have the capacity to liberate Mathilde from his own romantic imagination. They were married after a year of exquisite, urgent, unfulfilled desire (this was 1870 remember) but almost immediately he rejected the flesh and blood reality of his young wife. She apparently disappointed him in bed and he returned to his absinthe drinking, beating Mathilde at night and begging forgiveness in the morning in floods of weepy, sentimental remorse. Poor Mathilde!

Then came Rimbaud. Mathilde actually met him first, if only by a few minutes. Rimbaud, you may remember, had been sending his poems to Parisian poets—although at 16 he had explicitly rejected all poetry that had gone before, he still longed for recognition. Verlaine sent him train fare to Paris and went to meet him at the station, with no idea that the poet he was looking for was a boy in homemade clothes and rough hand-knit stockings. They must have walked past each other on the platform; in any case, Verlaine waited for the next train and Rimbaud made his own way to Mathilde's parents' house where she and Verlaine were living. So it was Mathilde who was the first to welcome Rimbaud to Paris.

What did she think of him? He was by all accounts an attractive boy, tall and blue-eyed, with tender skin and big hands and big feet, although in the photographs I've seen he looks sulky and severe. All the biographers suggest that Mathilde and her mother were taken aback by his crude manners, but my Mathilde—the one I wanted to invent for you—was more complicated than that. She was hugely pregnant at the time, emotionally shredded and patched back together by Verlaine's capriciously alternating kindness and cruelty, lonely, frightened, and still very young. Perhaps Verlaine showed her Rimbaud's poems; perhaps she simply took them out of his coat pocket while he lay snoring on the bed, but however it was I think she had seen them. To be certain, one half of her was repelled by Rimbaud's rudeness, selfishness, and lice, but the other half, my invented half, was half in love with him. Not long before he left his village home for Paris Rimbaud had written a letter to a friend that was to become the famous manifesto for a new poetry, in which he called—you've heard this quoted many times, I'm sure—for "a long, immense and reasoned deranging of all the senses." But there is another passage in the letter, quoted less often: "When the endless servitude of woman will be overthrown," Rimbaud wrote "when she will live for herself and by herself man,—hitherto abominable,—having given her her release, she will be a poet, she also! Woman will discover some of the unknown! Will her worlds of ideas differ from ours?—She will discover strange, unfathomable, repellent, delicious things; we shall take them, we shall comprehend them."

Rimbaud joined the household. Of course the arrangement didn't last. Mathilde's father, who had been traveling, returned; the next month the baby was born and Rimbaud moved out. He derided Verlaine for his bourgeois devotion to his wife and new son, and soon Verlaine was out every night again with Rimbaud, falling in love with him himself. I see one last meeting between Rimbaud and Mathilde: a strange one. I imagine Rimbaud returning to the house to get something he had left behind and encountering Mathilde in the hall. She has just come from the nursery; her dress is still unbuttoned and her hair is loose. Rimbaud blocks her way, and when he reaches for her she does not resist. He opens her dress and leans over, takes one of her breasts in his mouth, and he bites her—hard, so hard that he draws blood, the red drops mingling with the white milk. She cries out and runs away, pulling her robe around her. They never meet again.

That scene is my invention (although

Rimbaud's casual cruelty is not—remember that Rimbaud once drew his knife across Verlaine's palm simply because Verlaine had offered him his hand). Not long after that imagined scene, however, Verlaine and Mathilde had their own well-documented final meeting. Verlaine and Rimbaud had left Paris together; Mathilde followed them to Brussels and met Verlaine in a hotel room—perhaps in search of "strange, unfathomable, repellent, delicious things" she presented herself to him naked on the bed and they spent the afternoon in lovemaking. Verlaine had always believed that his time with Rimbaud was an interlude, that he would return to the security of Mathilde's comfortable household when he was ready. Now he decided it was time: he and Mathilde boarded the train together, still scented with each other's sweat, but as they pulled away from the station Verlaine fell silent, looking out the window. When the train stopped at the Belgian border he got off and ran away, sending a cruel and insulting farewell by the stationmaster.

That was the last time Verlaine and Mathilde met face to face, although for years Verlaine kept begging for a reconciliation. He went on to become one of France's most revered and distinguished poets; Mathilde remarried, a building contractor this time, and passed out of history. As for Rimbaud, the book outlined the rest of the story: "Rimbaud, disgusted with Verlaine, who claimed he couldn't live without him, decided to leave. In desperation, Verlaine shot Rimbaud, wounding him in the wrist. The police came and Verlaine was jailed for two years, on charges not of assault but sodomy; meanwhile Rimbaud escaped to his mother's farm, where he completed the body of poems that was to change poetry and writing itself forever. Then, at the age of eighteen, Rimbaud put down his pen and announced that he was done with being a poet."

Have I explained my dilemma at all? It's partly this: secretly each of us believes that we are the central player in the drama of our own life, and that everyone else is just part of the supporting cast. In this drama, however, Mathilde was not allowed to choose her own part: without consulting her, Verlaine and Rimbaud cast her in the allegorical role of "middle-class respectability" and then proceeded to systematically kick her to bits. In

my imagined dialogue she tells the priest "Their freedom put me in chains."

The priest was such a small part of my dialogue that I never bothered to even invent a name for him, but he did have one important thing to say: he tells Mathilde about an afternoon when he was walking down the street and Rimbaud ran by and knocked his hat into the mud. "It was awful," the priest says. "The hat was ruined and I had to proceed to my next appointment bare-headed with every person in the street staring at me. But"—this is the important part—"do you know, when I look back at that spring that is the only afternoon I remember? All the rest is lost in routine and duty, but when I think of that one extraordinary afternoon I can feel the sunshine and the wind, see the startled expression of the passers-by, hear the carriages passing. It was, perhaps, the only hour that season when I was truly alive."

So would Mathilde have been happier if she had never married Verlaine? Would Verlaine have been happier if he had never met Rimbaud? He certainly wouldn't have been as good a poet—in the months that he and Rimbaud shared a series of cheap rooms in Brussels and London his poetry leapt off the page and became the poetry that is reprinted in anthologies. What about George, Verlaine's baby son, abandoned by his father? He grew up—this is documented in the biographies—an unhappy, selfish, alcoholic man, his father all over again but without the poetry. Could Verlaine have saved him?

The three central players—Verlaine, Rimbaud, Mathilde—have taken over my imagination. There is Rimbaud, the dark angel, dedicated to impulse and desire. There is Mathilde, forced to be a plaster saint, representing convention and respectability. And there is Verlaine trotting between them, never quite able to choose. He's the least appealing of the three, but the truth is he is the most like the rest of us—dabbling in freedom, dabbling in convention, trying to find some way to hold onto both. I know that you yourself lean more towards Rimbaud than Verlaine. What, therefore, would you advise a 16-year-old who wanted to follow Rimbaud's example? Steal her parents' ATM card and take a Greyhound to California? Break the lock on the music store door and take all the instruments? Drink anything, smoke anything, embrace

anyone among the broken glass and weeds down by the railroad tracks so long as it deranges the senses? Burn it up, burn it out, kick it down, use up your poetry as fast as you can?

Instead of a dialogue I'm left with scraps of paper covered with questions written at random moments—stopped in the car at a red light, standing with my grocery cart in front of the frozen food case. I'll assemble a few for you: Must following your own desires always hurt other people? If it must, do you still have a responsibility to other people? Is freedom isolation? Does being a genius give you special rights? Can you be a genius without assuming special rights? Can you assume the rights without being a genius? Do you owe something to the world for the choices you make? And what is happiness? Is there value in orderliness and responsibility? Is the only way to reverse a mistake to walk away from it? Mustn't we always remember that other people are also fluid and growing, with their own sets of desires that sometimes contradict our own? What if part of the pleasure of freedom is taking more than our share? How do we know what, and who, to sacrifice? And, finally, is poetry—art—worth it?

So, Brian, that's all—I'm really sorry, but I just can't do it. I hope you can find something else to fill the space.

Love, Liz (406 North Mendenhall Street, Greensboro, NC 27401)

THE POSSIBILITY OF PERFECTION
by Eric Boehme

I've been holding these standards for years now, like some secret personal ad written on my heart. You: Dionysian, passionate, intelligent and soft, decisive and political, cut from this cloth, veggie and vogue, attractive and secure, outspoken and funny but never demure. Me: Apollinian, insecure, seduced by the form, cautious but curious, the calm and the storm, compete and sometimes play fight, stay up bleary all night, body and mind, committed. . . But I never could get past committed. In everything I do, commitment. To myself, and to you. But how can I negotiate it? Commitment means having standards, having perfect blueprints to fight for, to pursue. Does having standards of perfection, for myself and the people I love, inevitably doom all of my relationships to substandard copies? How can I imagine the possibility of perfection between us, that I would one day find some-one. One, who would match my secret personal ad?

Body
Can you, without any hypocrisy, criticize the beauty myth and the objectification of potential sexual partners but still think physi-

ALL
BRUTE
AND
NO
FORCE...
(sleepy as shit)

I'm tired.

I'm going to sleep now.

cality and attraction are important to a relationship? You live in your body, a body with desires created through your social environment. You're attracted to certain people, certain looks or body types, you're not attracted to others. You harmonize well. Fitted deep into arm crooks and bent elbows, back of knee-scents, and protruding shoulder blades. Desirous body, you battle the mind. You consume all in your path. A brief glance. . .but you know body, you know the first test has been passed. Leave me alone mind, you know this is how we were raised, images of beauty, images of perfection. Masterful pornographic perfection.

You desirous multiplicity, many sources create your pleasures. Yet which sources should I trust? Which origins are untainted? You've tried to change your origins, deny the social construction, the daily existence in the society of the beauty myth. Why do you so desire to be with the beautiful? The secret personal ad includes attractive. It must. Should you be ashamed? Seduced by the form, the cheapest manner of ignoring the mind. Yet pleasurable nonetheless. Tearing against your friendships, you, body always looking elsewhere. You, masterful body, flit and echo, experiencing without cessation, digesting and forgetting, cutting a swath miles wide. Always already moving to where the grass might be greener. Obectification dictates fluidity. Bodies desire objects. Is that how you are? Is that the secret you must accept?

You body, volatile and violent. Pain becomes you. You inflict it on others too, objects. Just, only, merely, barely, slightly bodies for conducting pleasure. You body, consume others. But digesting hurts because you body, are all alone. To stop consuming body, you must be hurt. Perfect secret personal ad, to find you, you must hurt me. To stop for a moment to say beauty doesn't matter. But can it ever not matter? Ironic that you use beauty to soothe that hurt, body. For it is beauty creating violence to body, the never-ending motor of your desire.

Mind

Can you live the life of the mind, shaming your body because of the fucked up ways desire has been socially constructed? Can you imagine the possibility of perfection? You body consume, but you mind, possesses. Knowledge. . .of information, of secure relationships, of possibilities, of perfection. Bodies never know perfection, bodies know degeneration and death. You mind, imagine perfection, creating perpetuities of possibilities. Minds think desire can be fulfilled. Bodies know better. You mind, controlling and binding, anxious to keep, to hold onto, to remember, to store away.

You mind, try to possess the beautiful, to

hold it/them down, to capture the perfect stillness of frozen time, through the perfection of your mediated gaze. The mind's eye. You hold the beautiful, picture perfect and still, never moving iconic on a pedestal. You want to remember, not forget. You create the illusions. Mind, you think you lack beauty because your knowledge tells of the violence and the terrible instability of body. You try to possess, to stabilize, to hold and reassure because of that horrible knowledge. You mind, wish you could forget.

Trust

Paradoxes rife with contradictions, trusting body you do feel closeness. You might one day be able to trust. You lay and sigh, you know trust is a feeling not a thought. You body, trained not to trust, trained to fight or flight, your wish is the stillness of complete trust. The stillness of never moving, trusting, because you body, want to be cradled and at ease. Yet body, you must pursue ecstasy, you must move outside yourself as body. Orgasmic individuality, you body destroy trust.

Mind, you too might one day be able to trust. You add up the history, you grip and remember those times that body was cradled. You know reality is never perfect, you know form never matches content. But you mind, wonder if perfection is possible. Mind, you're trained to stop and consider, you press onward. You destroy trust. You tightly grip the secret personal ad, your glance strays, looking for perfection slipping out the corner of your eye. And the picture-perfect lock clicks closed the heart.

ATR Zine. 118 Raritan Ave. Highland Park, NJ 08904
eboehme@eden.rutgers.edu

PORNOGRAPHY AND THE REPRESENTATIONS OF THE EROTIC: A RESPONSE TO LIBERTINAGEM
by Ferdinando P. Villa

Pornography is under constant attack, not only by the censors of the Christian right but by the liberals as well, turning this art (yes, art) into something clandestine, shameful, guiltful, steal-

ing all its libertarian aspects. The conservatives' argument is that pornography is dirty, an insult to good behavior; we assume we don't even need to counter this argument. The liberals' argument is that pornography is automatically sexist, degrading, and exploitative; this argument shows a great lack of knowledge, and, even if a little more hidden, this same disgusting morality seen on the Christian right. Yes, they're right in one point, mainstream pornography sucks, it is sexist, it is degrading; as such, we have no interest whatsoever in its use. In this same way, it is also true that mainstream music almost always sucks—but basing ourselves solely on this argument we wouldn't assume that all music sucks, ignoring all its subversive potential and all DIY musical experimentation that doesn't find in profit, fame and propaganda its main objectives. Following the same logic, there is DIY porn based on the subversion of values, on the experimentation of the erotic, on the coherence of pleasure, as an art, made by women and men alike who found strength in breaking social tahoos and exploring their desires without guilt. Between 1500 and 1800, the first erotic writers and painters were part of the so-called heretics, free-thinkers, and libertines, who constituted the dark side of the Renaissance, the Scientific Revolution, the Enlightenment, the French Revolution, and used pornography to subvert political authorities and social relations. Centuries later, the modern libertines who see strength and self-realization in sexuality are not so far from that. Sexuality and eroticism is one of the most perfect art forms, one of the only ones where we can give ourselves to the moment completely, one of the most beautiful forms of contact between two human beings, therefore destined to be some of the most beautiful artistic expression. To the moral watchdogs: attack the true reactionaries, explore your desires without guilt or limitations; it's a lot more fun and liberating.

This proposal of a radical use for pornography was presented by the Brazilian band/collective LIBERTINAGEM in their debut release. While the LIBERTINAGEM members surely had good intentions when they came forth with the piece above, and, more importantly, talked about eroticism (do I hear giggling in the back?) inside a sexist and heterosexual environment which is, underneath the rebellion catch phrases, very conservative and still unable to break away from the old

Christian/Judaic morals, still unable to liberate its sexuality, there are a few problems in their proposal and in the concept of pornography itself that need to be further addressed and discussed.

The writing above seems to deal with pornography in a historical perspective, when they talk about the "heretics, freethinkers, and libertines, who constituted the dark side of the Renaissance, the Scientific Revolution, the Enlightenment, the French Revolution," and, credit given where due, pornography (more specifically the murdered, burned and tortured who dared to experiment new and radical ways to enjoy life) deserves its place for bringing up the fact that people have fucked, like to fuck, and will always be fucking, regardless of who, where, or when. But back then things worked in quite a different way, the world was dominated by religious mysticism and a unitary pre-determinism not a bit interested in the co-optation of desire. The kings and priests of the old world hadn't found out that people could be profitable. If plagues, famines, and horrendous wars wiped out their kingdoms, people could just be expendable—the right to consume hadn't reached everyone yet. That was before mercantilism and market laws spoke louder than God's voice, it was before advertisement was born to convince every citizen of the need to consume a specific product for every feeling allowed to be felt (and for those not allowed as well: at every point in history there was always a black market). This was before Penthouse, before the discovery of the feminine body as a marketing strategy for an audience of masculinized, dumbed-down men who spend way too much time drinking beer and watching football. It was before the societies of diffuse spectacles were born, before representation came to be more important than essence, before everything was reduced to appearances. The old priests and kings were more interested in the word of heaven, the unitary mode of existence centered around pre-determinism, than to divide up that share and sell a slice of the market to every good citizen. If it is so, could the same circumstances of before be applied today, when images of unhealthy bulimic women are being used to sell every imaginable product on earth, when sex shops make a fortune selling products specially designed to improve your life and sexual per-

formance," a world of Barbie dolls, phone sex, online pornography, anorexia, Monica Lewinsky, Jerry Springer? To base pornography's worth today in its merit centuries ago is like saying Jesus Christ was a revolutionary (he was a political prisoner after all, wasn't he?). It's undoubtedly important to have a historical perspective and to know the other history, the one they didn't teach us in school, about the men and women who found out that life was much more enjoyable if you just stop tormenting yourself with morals dictated by somebody else and start to have pleasure, about how we can learn a whole lot by looking at the way these people expressed this kind of terribly repressed sexuality—not to mention it can be just plain beautiful to look at. Bodies can be wonderful. But it's even more important to know how to bring this to the present—nothing is static, and to treat it as so makes it all the more dangerous. It can be very dangerous to talk about pornography in a time when sex became just another product, one more sector in the quantitative organization of our carefully constructed lives. It can be very dangerous to talk about erotic representations in a time when images have come to represent every sensation that was previously experienced by the individual himself.

By reading the LIBERTINAGEM writing, one can clearly point out that it was written exclusively through the eyes of an author, of a creator of the erotic art on trial (them being a band, it's not hard to see why), and not through the eyes of the individual experiencing it—this point of view was kept entirely out of the picture. The author of a piece of erotic art can have numerous reasons to create an image, a representation of his or her sexuality. Maybe she would like a visual sensation of a sexual fantasy that has been tormenting her for years. Maybe she sometimes likes to express her own sexuality in other ways besides sex—maybe this can work more or less like an orgasm or sexual relation. It doesn't really matter why; human beings have always created images to express important happenings in their lives or in their imagination, and the sexual area of our minds is undoubtedly very fertile and worth being dug out. But in the process of creating an image and making it public, its author automatically creates a relationship to anyone experiencing this image, and over what foundation are these relation-

ships formed?

What are our relations to images and erotic representations? Why do they excite us? How do we use them? These questions were left aside of the original writing, and although too complex to be answered by this pretentious sex addict, I intend to dwell a little deeper on these and other questions that might come up when dealing with pornography and the representations of the erotic.

Erotic images are mainly used to stimulate our imagination (some people have a rather—um, bizarre use for them, but that's another story). Having visual contact with these images, we can create whole fantasies and scenarios where we are the absolute masters of everything that happens. In fact, this is the image's greatest advantage, in a society that's based on non-communication (or mis-communication), images cannot talk back to us. Images consent to everything we demand and desire. Images do not disagree, impose barriers, or get headaches. In short, it's a perfect world, where we and our images can fuck in peace in the craziest of ways, and among these four walls there is absolutely nothing to stop us.

But there lies the bigger problem. The image becomes an entity in itself, disconnected from reality, a fetishized and unreal object. If, for example, you masturbate using an image of Pamela Anderson's incredibly fake tits, or even your girlfriend's (the subjects used here are masculine because men in general tend to use more images to fulfill their sexual fantasies; the reason it happens would generate enough discussion for a whole new writing, maybe next issue), you're NOT having a real, complex relationship with Pamela Anderson or with your girlfriend. You might be looking at them, thinking about them, but your relationship consists in a merely objectified relation to separate and unreal entities.

In the real world, would Pamela Anderson even pay attention to your existence, would your girlfriend agree to what you're thinking? Maybe not (in the first case, most definitely not), but these imaginary entities would. And when we reach the point where we're spending more time worshipping a TV model practically nonexistent in real life, when we spend more time using images as escape valves for our most intimate, secret and unfulfilled fantasies than we do trying to learn how to communicate with our partners, being in touch with real bodies and complex individuals, exploring every unknown territory of our lovers' bodies, trying to bring up and work out the mutual fulfillment of our desires and fantasies, something is deeply wrong here. It can be quite scary to see what pornography can do to people. A friend of mine who used to work in a video store tells me about a single lonely middle-aged man who every week returns six porno movies and rents six more, infallibly.

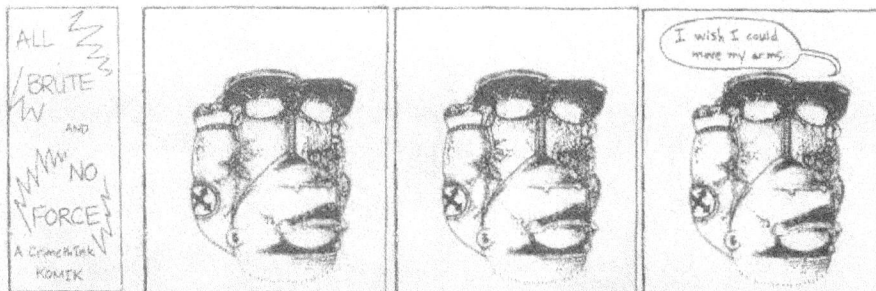

ALL BRUTE AND NO FORCE
A Crime&Ink KOMIK

I wish I could move my arms.

Try to imagine this man's life—you don't have to be a genius to guess that, if he is occupied with a porno video 6 nights a week, there's not much room left for real human interaction and sexual contact. The time and resources spent on pornography also don't give much room for activities that are intellectually stimulating and bodily exciting. And while this man can be sure that his sexual representations and blonde hooters will always be on the shelves of the video store every time he gets a hard on, chances are that his problems, fears, and sexual anxieties will only increase and trap him in this artificial hell as he sinks himself deeper and deeper in a sexual uni-dimensional world of black and white social interaction.

But, as LIBERTINAGEM suggests, this is how all mainstream pornography operates—and we have to fight its evil ways with some kind of revolutionary and D.I.Y. pornography. They are right on one point, this is how mainstream pornography, being part of a bigger whole of division, appearance, hierarchy and market rules, operates. The mainstream sex industry is just like any other corporation on the planet, it exists exclusively to make profit, no matter at which costs. And maybe there is a certain value in magazines such as Fat Girl that, as the name suggests, brings very daring erotic photos of naked fat lesbian women, bodies the beauty standards say should not be photographed naked, should not be acknowledged as sexual, let alone published—and that are anyway in this great publication, going against every unhealthy image of blue-eyed, bulimic blondes. But doesn't it create another problem? Doesn't it just expand our choices of having an alienated relationship to skinny women or fat women? Isn't this another aspect of the liberal thought that to be free means to have as many choices as possible? Isn't this why they fight to have Ralph Nader running for president, the "rights" of gays and women in the hierarchical institution of the armed forces—or D.I.Y. pornography?

Maybe this belief that is reinforced by LIBERTINAGEM, of some kind of conspiracy against pornography is making them stand up and defend this poor, lonely image cowardly attacked by all sides by liberals and conservatives alike, when maybe we should just leave pornography aside as part of the spectacle and look for some more fulfilling forms of eroticism. It's very easy to be caught up in this pro-porn stance because at first it might seem like some kind of pro-sex, pro-freedom fight, and who wouldn't want to support these causes? But maybe this pseudo-libertarian fight would just create an illusion of freedom—a temporary relief that we are a little more free as long as we have the "right" to produce atomized porno. But is this the freedom we want?

However, we have to consider: is pornography inherently harmful? LIBERTINAGEM manages to prove that the argument used by liberal feminists that pornography is automatically sexist doesn't work anymore for us. A quick flip through the pages of a magazine like the mentioned Fat Girl would prove it to be anything but sexist and degrading. But LIBERTINAGEM's argument doesn't prove that pornography isn't inherently harmful because it always creates an objectified and unreal relationship. Liberating can turn into alienating just as easily. A D.I.Y. image is still an image, it still belongs to spectacular categories and objectified relations. So if images are inherently problematic, and if it is consensus that they will always exist in the specter of artistic expression, does this mean that certain spheres of life (such as sexuality) shouldn't mix themselves with images? Is it possible to use images in any healthy way? If the image is used solely as a stimuli to the imagination, a stimuli to a desire lost inside of us to be then realized with real lovers, can we break the image's spectacular status?

In my opinion, images are inherently harmful *while images*. Which means that, while the object created continues to be a mere representation, an entity separated from reality, an escape valve for our forbidden desires, images contribute directly for non-communication and non-realization of life. The actual problem does not reside in the image per se, but in the society that created the need for such images, and why they are needed. The spectacular relation of the image does not operate independently—it reflects the society which it belongs to. Therefore, if the system has created this artificial necessity of sexual representations and false relationships, the images we create and experience normally and without interference will correspond to this function. The whole problem is when a creation of our own escapes our control and becomes an independent entity, thus taking control of us and the way we experience the world. It's the old principle that the human being alienates itself when it becomes the attribute of an abstraction that it created itself, but no longer recognizes as such, becoming instead an entity in itself and turning the human being into its object—God, the State, or images.

When images start to construct our desires for us, to be the subject of our relations for us, when the definition of sexuality is determined by someone else for us, it's time to take our lives back. And the only way we can achieve it is to work our way towards a society that collaborates for the mutual fulfillment of our desires, not for their destruction; for the realization of life, not its suppression; for some kind of cooperation that would still allow us to be individuals so we won't have to rely on images and representations to guide us to the sensations this world can offer us. Images should exist solely to be deconstructed, dismantled, transformed, used according to the reality of each individual (if desired). The only acceptable image has to be shareable, imaginable, expandable, accessible, free. Only when we abolish this system of market rules and hierarchical power will an image (or anything else, for that matter) cease to be a product, a commodity, and become free to become an active participant in the fusion of art, sexuality, and life into one. I think by now it has become obvious that this system does little for our happiness, that any image created will correspond to its alienating function, so what are we waiting for? Me and LIBERTINAGEM are not in opposite sides—I still believe sexual art has place in life, that when we find life we will also find control to give enough wings to our deepest desires and their realizations. I don't want my erotic stories to be someone's fetish, someone's escape valve, because they could never do what I write about in real life. They are way too important to be commodified so easily. I want them to be weapons, words inflamed with passion and desire ready to explode. But first, we have to create conditions for our sexuality to flow freely, beyond any constraints, free of alienation, co-optation, or exchange value. To think what could happen if we could live our sexuality however way we wanted, whenever and wherever we wanted, it gives me more than enough reason to risk everything in the name of the extreme sensuality of being truly free. Therefore, lovers, paint, roll over paint with your naked bodies, make love over the Mona Lisa, write, let the pen be guided by your most intense orgasms. There is no image in the world, no representation, no matter how real or how virtual it is, that bears the smell of a lover's body, bodies rubbing, hands dipping through curves and cavities, lips touching, tongues sliding, sounds of pleasure being exchanged. If we can work our way through some kind of life that attracts us, perhaps we can also work our way towards some kind of anti-image.

that reduces images to their base form—use-less, dispensable. Like witnesses to a terrorist action, they are only useful while they can spread the myth. Afterwards, their existence is pointless.

It is said that Henry Miller wrote with his penis. Did you know that when he died nothing was found between his legs but a fountain pen?

contact: through Libertinagem address (see reviews section)

CAPOEIRA, THE DEADLY DANCE
by Robin Banks

My first exposure to capoeira (pronounced ka-po-AIR-uh) was in the martial arts video game Tekken. There was a character in the game called Eddy Gordo whose style seemed a bit like breakdancing, a bit like kung fu, and a bit like acrobatic tumbling. When I finally found out that Eddy Gordo's fighting style was called "capoeira," I knew that I had to find out more about it. Here's what I learned.

The History

Capoeira was developed hundreds of years ago by renegade African slaves in Brazil, who were influenced by ancient African martial arts such as sanga. They had been captured and enslaved by Portuguese imperialists, who then sold them to Portuguese settlers in Brazil. Some of the slaves escaped into the mountains which surrounded the Portuguese plantations, and it was there that they honed the craft of capoeira. The escapees would then sneak back to the plantations and teach capoeira to the other slaves.

This is the main reason why so much of capoeira seems like elaborate dancing and ritual—any martial art practiced by slaves was a threat to the slaveowners, and so the slaves concealed their skills within graceful dances, music, and chants. Eventually the slavemasters caught on, and any slave found practicing capoeira could be put to death. However, the slaves continued to practice in secret and passed their skills to their children.

In 1888, the Brazilian government abolished slavery; four years later, it criminalized capoeira. Due to economic hardship and racial discrimination against the former slaves, jobs were scarce, and as a result many capoeira gangs sprang up. These gangs, known as mal-

tas, were hired as thugs by the wealthy. Business owners would hire maltas to rob or trash rival businesses; elite criminals would pay maltas to beat up groups of cops. The maltas never used guns, knives or any other weapons—only capoeira. Eventually, capoeira became associated solely with criminals and gangs, but despite (or maybe because) of this, it continued to grow in popularity.

In 1920 capoeira was legalized in Brazil and the first capoeira school was opened twelve years later. For decades, capoeira remained within Brazilian borders, but by the 1970s capoeira masters (mestres) were moving to other nations and opening their own capoeira schools. It has slowly grown in popularity, especially since the movie *Only the Strong* (not to mention the relatively recent movie *The Quest*) was released, not to mention the debut of Eddy Gordo and Tekken. Capoeira will be an official sport in the 2004 Olympic Games.

OK, now you know the roots of capoeira ... but still, what is it really all about?

The Art

Capoeira was and is a game, a dance, a ritual, a musical performance, an exercise, and a form of combat. Practitioners of capoeira, known as capoeiristas, are also musicians and singers.

When practicing or fighting in formalized matches, the spectators and capoeiristas form a circle (roda) around the two fighters. The roda is headed by a group of musicians and singers (the bateria) who provide music, rhythm and poetry to accompany the battle or practice session.

The bateria begins its music and the capoeiristas begin their fight. In formalized capoeira (practices and matches), it is against the rules for any part of your body to touch the ground except for your head, hands and feet. If you are knocked on your ass or fall on your back, you lose. The vast majority of capoeira matches do not involve bodily contact—it's mostly a matter of feinting, dodging, turning, leaping, and otherwise faking out your opponent. Capoeiristas are considered highly skilled if they can humiliate their opponents by repeatedly pretending to strike vicious blows instead of actually causing injury.

I was unable to find much about capoeira in the context of street combat—for example,

do the capoeiristas pull their punches or kicks when fighting cops? Do they spend time doing flashy tumbles and cartwheels, or does capoeira become more focused and brutal when your life is at stake?

I'd like to read more about the lives of early slave capoeiristas as well as the early mestres such as Mestre Besouro, who was notorious for fighting cops and escaping capture and death. If anybody finds some decent books on capoeira, please write and let me know (robinbanks@disinfo.net).

The Scene

Why is this article in Inside Front? What does capoeira have to do with hardcore punk? Think of the parallels—a group of people form a circle with musicians at one end. Dancing fighters (or fighting dancers) leap into the center of the circle, coming quite close to physical contact but always just barely missing. When the dancers do inadvertently strike other dancers or bystanders, they are considered clumsy buffoons, and the best dancers are those who display great skill and form without actually injuring anyone. Sounds like a hardcore show, doesn't it?

The very idea of a deadly martial art concealed within an aesthetic medium like dancing is fascinating. It's a great metaphor, too... what deadly ideas are contained within the aesthetic ghetto of hardcore punk, and how can we apply those ideas to our daily lives? Capoeiristas may learn their skills in capoeira classes with ritualized music and singing, but in the streets they retain their deadly kicks, acrobatic grace, and self-confidence bestowed by capoeira. What lessons do we take from our own rituals of song and dance? Is hardcore punk just another aesthetic commodity and subcultural ritual like country music and line dancing, or is there something greater contained within, something we can apply to our daily lives in valuable ways?

FELA ANIKULAPO KUTI: THIS IS HOW IT'S DONE
by Robin Banks' Monsanto-manufactured duplicate, Robin Banks

From Africa to America to the Kalakuta Republic

Fela Ransome-Kuti was born in Nigeria in 1938, son of a Protestant minister and a teacher. His upbringing was typical of the Nigerian middle class—as "good Christians" and good citizens, they strove to fit into the power structure imposed by white imperialists. When he was twenty, his parents sent him to London to study medicine, but Fela instead studied at the Trinity School of Music for five years. He formed a few bands which played a style of music known as "high-life," a sort of

Maybe I'll go as a witch

(Nah)

ALL BRUTE AND NO FORCE!

light, danceable African pop. Fela blended high-life with jazz to form his own unique sound.

Nigeria was liberated from British colonialism in 1960. Three years later, Fela returned to Nigeria and formed a new band, Koola Lobitos, with several other Nigerians who had studied music in England. At this point Fela was not at all politically conscious; he was slowly becoming a successful musician who wrote popular love songs, and his idea of fulfillment was to be a wealthy pop idol.

In 1969 Fela decided to take Koola Lobitos to the United States for an extended tour, where he changed the name of his band to Fela Ransome-Kuti and Nigeria 70. While in Los Angeles he met a Black Panther, Sandra Isodore, who opened Fela's mind to the politics of Malcolm X, the Panthers, and other black radicals. They stayed up late, engaged in a passionate argument about radicalism and Pan-Africanism (the idea that all black people are Africans, as opposed to Nigerians, Ghanians, Egyptians, Jamaicans, or African-Americans; an idea espoused by many reggae artists including Bob Marley and many hip hop artists including Dead Prez).

By morning, a seed had been planted in Fela. Sandra loaned him several books which he read and re-read avidly as his United States tour concluded. When Fela returned to Nigeria he was a completely different person. The band changed its name again, from Nigeria 70 to Africa 70, reflecting Fela's new Pan-Africanist beliefs. Fela also changed the name of his nightclub to The Shrine, where in addition to performing his new conscious music he would also give lectures on radical politics and Pan-Africanism.

Fela had dubbed his estate the "Kalakuta Republic" as a sort of joke, but by the early 1970s it became very serious. He declared the Kalakuta Republic's independence from Nigeria and many of his fans (who lived in the same neighborhood!) followed suit and joined the Republic. The upper crust of Nigerian society (consisting of white businessmen and their Nigerian allies) began to consider Fela Kuti a threat.

Against the State

Fela changed his name to Fela Anikulapo, which means "he who carries death in his pouch." From this point on, nearly all of Fela's songs were politically charged. Some were sarcastic or humorous jabs at government or police and some were direct attacks on specific officials or policies. He developed a new style of music which became known as Afrobeat, a combination of traditional chants, trumpets, piano, and drums, all blended smoothly in free-form jazzy jams. One of Fela's songs would take up both sides of a long-playing record; the first side was an instrumental build-up, and the second side

featured his vocals. Fela also considered the recording of a song to be its obituary, and after a recording session he would rarely if ever play that song in concert. Because of this, Fela's new style never found much success in the United States, where audiences wanted recognizable three-minute pop hits, not thirty-minute improvised jam sessions.

In Nigeria, however, Fela's music was an enormous success. He was more popular than ever, but instead of accumulating his wealth and cultivating an image as a playboy-musician, he used his money to develop the Kalakuta Republic (for example, he built a hospital on his land and opened it up to the people!) and hire more musicians. The name Africa 70 now meant the number of musicians, singers and other performers on stage during Fela's concerts.

Fela was repeatedly beaten, arrested and interrogated by government officials. The attacks increased as Fela and his ideas became more popular. As Osofisan says in his brief biography of Fela, "In Nigeria, power has always been, since Independence at least, in the hands of a certain elite, made up of men who got their wealth through being the local agents of white companies. Fela's message, that we should stop serving the whites, that we should develop our own black resources instead, was a direct threat to this ruling class. His message, that we should turn away from the colonial religions, because they had been and were still the instruments of enslaving our minds, turned the numerous Christians and Muslims against him."

The End of the Kalakuta Republic

A crucial event occurred in 1977: a thousand government soldiers attacked the Kalakuta Republic and burned it (along with the hospital, the Shrine, and many other facilities). During the attack, all of Fela's musicians, supporters and allies in the Republic were severely beaten and many were arrested. Fela's mother, by now a radical Pan-Africanist feminist in her own right, was thrown out of a window by soldiers and ended up dying from her injuries. Fela and his supporters later put his mother's coffin in a bus, drove the bus into a military compound (crashing through the gates, avoiding machine-gun fire from the guards), and laid the coffin at the front door of the Nigerian general responsible for the attack.

Fela and his people moved to Accra in Ghana to escape Nigerian repression and to plan a world tour in response to the government attack. On the first date of the tour, which was one year after the destruction of the Kalakuta Republic, Fela performed in a packed stadium in Accra. The first song he played was "Zombie," his satire of Nigerian soldiers, and fighting broke out between his fans and police in the stadium. The fighting turned into a massive riot. Fela and his band were arrested and sent back to Nigeria after being permanently banned from Ghana.

Upon arrival in Nigeria, Fela and his group began squatting in the offices of his record label, Decca, for two months. Then Fela moved to Ikeja and formed his own political party, Movement Of the People, which was almost immediately banned by the government. Fela tried for years to build Movement Of the People and get elected but was continually thwarted by the government through legal means and through violent police repression. A succession of military coups crushed any hope for democratic elections, and so Fela gave up on his campaigns for office.

In 1984 Fela was imprisoned on false charges and served twenty months. He was released when the judge revealed that he had jailed Fela solely because of political pressure from the top down. When Fela got out he formed a new band, Egypt 80, and began touring the world. His politics were as radical, passionate and powerful as ever, and his repeated world tours helped spread the popularity of Afrobeat and Pan-Africanism. He ruthlessly criticized colonialism, imperialism, and United States/European policy towards Africa. One of his biggest hits at this time was "Beasts Of No Nation," a song about Margaret Thatcher and Ronald Reagan (which wasn't actually released on LP until 1989).

Fela continued agitating against Nigerian government regimes and foreign colonialist powers until his untimely death from AIDS-related causes in 1997. His funeral drew over one million mourners, many of whom believed that Fela was actually murdered. Fela's son, Femi Kuti, is also a musician and activist. Femi founded an organization called Movement Against Second Slavery (MASS) which is not a political party but rather a

direct action group which works against corrupt government and corporate interests.

I was introduced to Fela Kuti's music and legend by the band Bread and Circuits, who include samples of Fela's music on their Ebullition CD and explained a bit about him in their liner notes. The first Fela Kuti CD I got was "Coffin for Head of State" which is about the government attack on the Kalakuta Republic and the murder of his mother. The other song on the CD is "Unknown Soldier," which refers to the government report on the destruction of the Kalakuta Republic. The report attributed the illegal attack to "unknown soldiers." Fela's response is to sing of revenge: "Unknown police/they kill nine students/we get unknown civilians/they kill two soldiers."

Fela's family is re-releasing his LPs as CDs. Most of the CDs have only two songs on them, each song being around fifteen to forty minutes each. I recommend "Coffin for Head of State/Unknown Soldier," "Let's Start" and "Black Man's Cry."

Sidebar / Footnote:

What can we learn from Fela Kuti? He was wildly popular and revolutionary at the same time—is this possible in our country, in our culture? Personally I'm not sure, though I lean sharply towards saying "no," simply because our consumerist/capitalist culture has an amazing capacity for absorbing, defanging and repackaging everything imaginable, including hostile attacks on the culture itself. An American Fela Kuti (can you think of any candidates for this title?) would have to be on a major label, tour constantly, release songs instantly to cope with the here-today-gone tomorrow nature of American politics, struggle daily to resist commodification, avoid bullshit legal harassment (trumped-up drug or tax charges, for example), and also build a real political movement, not just sing about discontent and revolution.

I think it's also important to realize that Fela did not spring from his mother's womb as a mature musical genius and political radical, but to recognize that he (like all of us) went through several phases of growth. It wasn't a spontaneous bolt of lightning that caused Fela to become a radical; it was a single late-night conversation with a new friend who encouraged him to read a few books. All radicals

should learn something from this—talking with friends or acquaintances can completely change their perspectives, not just on politics but on their daily lives. Do you write off non-radicals? Then you're making a huge mistake. Talk to people—friends, family, strangers—share your ideas and analyses with them. Don't be an elitist asshole either by not listening at all or by talking only in haughty, inaccessible, academic language—don't use radical code words like bourgeoisie, class war, syndicalism, imperialism, etc.—in fact, don't use any "ism" words at all! Please, fly out into the world and set a dozen hearts on fire. Maybe you will befriend and inspire the next Fela Kuti. You never know until you try.

DEATH: FUN FOR EVERYONE OR JUST A PAIN IN THE ASS?
by Greg Bennick

I want you to imagine the character "Pig Pen" from the Peanuts comic strip by the late cartoonist Charles Schultz. Foreign readers unfamiliar with the strip would do well to imagine a dirty young boy surrounded wherever he went by a three-foot diameter cloud of dust. Do you have the visual in mind? Excellent. Now, for our purposes tonight, replace the dust that surrounded Pigpen in the comic strip with the odor coming from my body in real life, in this moment, as I type these words. As I always aim to provide the reader with the most exacting sensual experience possible, please allow me to describe the odor for you: it is a blend of cigarette and marijuana smoke, human sweat, a touch of beer, and some other unidentifyable tidbits thrown in as well. "But Greg," you might ask, "Why, if you are of the committed drugfree variety, would you be smelling of the long-forsaken weed or beer?" The answer, dear reader, is because I attended tonight the event of the decade thus far...the single greatest night of Dionysian bliss one could ever hope to find in this new millenium...the one thing which could pull me out of my recent state of existential dread (to be explained later) and into the direct heart of life itself. Yes, you guessed it: tonight I went to see Iron Maiden play at the Tacoma Dome.

I find it difficult to describe in words just how much I love Iron Maiden. There is no other band in the world which embodies the creativity, innovation, ridiculous premises, and sheer metalness contained in these six (yes, count them, six!) British lunatics (The current tour features all three guitarists from their last few years together onstage with bassist Steve Harris, frontman Bruce "Tattooed Millionaire" Dickinson, and drummer/psycho Nicko McBrain for a total of six Maidens for your simultaneous viewing and listening pleasure). They had it all, from fire and explosions to feet up on the monitors for guitar solos, to lights and moving sets...whew! "But Greg," you ask, "What was the show itself like? Would you tell us, in the CrimethInc tradition, of what the experience FELT like, what PASSIONS were aroused in you as you stood within that Temple of Metal?" Well, it was like being thrown back to 1985: a sea of long haired white guys in various KISS, Motley Crue, and Metallica shirts talking loudly about how they were ready to rock, dude. On the way in, I mentioned to my friends that the difference in the crowd now as opposed to '85 is that many of them probably held stock options for dot com companies and were simply posing for the evening as metalheads. Rather quickly however, as we drifted through a sea of humanity beyond description - filled with interlocking devil horned handshakes and cigarette lighters ready to punctuate the ballad filled darkness of the arena - it became obvious that at least some of the people there were the real deal: the true metal maniacs of yesteryear, the Bill's and Ted's of a bygone day. I wondered where these people had been for the last decade or so. I realized that though I'd seen them from time to time around Seattle, I'd just not had the chance to observe them in their natural habitat or in as concentrated a space as I was able to observe that night. The most frightening thing I saw by far was a metalhead of about 35 or 40 years of age standing WITH HIS SEVEN YEAR OLD SON, both wearing matching Queensryche t-shirts and jeans. "My god," I thought, "They breed." This was a terrifying thought, and it was one that had not occurred to me in 1985: that metalheads actually produce offspring. It is for the best that this was a new thought. Had it crossed my impressionable teenage mind during the 1980's, it would undoubtedly have sent me into a state of panic comparable only to Nostradamus or the National Enquirer in terms of an apocalyptic vision of what the world might in fact become.

As for the band themselves? Six forty-somethings wearing jeans and white high top shoes with three of the six in Iron Maiden t-shirts, bless their little hearts,

ALL BRUTE AND NO FORCE

Bruce Dickinson was amazing on vocals, sounding even better than the records...HE should be giving lessons to all of us hoarse hardcore singers. Rumor has it that Bruce is a world class fencer in his spare time. Can anyone confirm this? I was ready for the show. About three years ago, at a Trial show at Gilman in Berkeley, a guy came up to me with a gift. It was a set of cassette tapes he had made for me featuring every song, outtake, and B-side Iron Maiden had ever recorded. That guy, wherever he is right now, is proof to me that Nietzsche was wrong: Good and evil *do* exist: GOOD=that guy, and EVIL=anything which harms worries or concerns him until the end of his days. He should be knighted, bronzed, canonized, or all three.

I left the show feeling very alive...in fact tingling with life...or was that the effects of residual pot smoke? (Perhaps I should quantify/clarify my self-proclaimed straight edge title with something more specific and accurate: "straight edge except when receiving second hand bong hits from metalheads"). Arriving home to my beloved Cynthia, I could not begin to express my joy. After all, how would someone who went through a finite metal "phase" (metal is forever, my love) listening to Kix and Extreme EVER understand what it was like to kickbox in the center of a pit of metaloids during "The Trooper"? Forget it, I can only hope that she and I continue to connect on other levels, since metal, in all of its splendor and glory, seems to be out of the picture for her.

"But Greg," I hear you ask, "What is this column really about? Surely you can't expect to retain our ex-worker collective attention for even one more paragraph if all you keep typing about is middle aged metalheads, one of which you yourself are quickly becoming?" Ah true, my friends, and so I refer you to the title of this column. I had spent quite sometime trying to decide what to write about, given the intensity of the last column and the implications of the previous ones. The problem is that I live in a state of writer's block. I do not find "writer's block" to be an occasional occurrence which inhibits my process of putting words on paper. Rather, I live in that state, constantly unable to write, and the rare "writer's unblock" is what actually frees me to pour ideas onto the pages of zines worldwide. With that, I offer you the following:

"The idea of death, the fear of it, haunts the human animal like nothing else, it is a mainspring of human activity — activity designed largely to avoid the fatality of death, to overcome it by denying in some way that it is the final destiny for man." -Ernest Becker.

I have been obsessed with death recently.

In a way, perhaps "obsessed" is not the right word as I have not been only able to think thoughts of death and dying. Rather, it would be more accurate to say that many of my actions are influenced by the foreboding feeling that my eventual death is a reality, and inescapable at that. I suddenly *feel* time, rather than just experiencing it at a distance. I was walking recently with a college professor friend of mine who just turned 50. I told him that I often worry that I am not living fully enough, that I am afraid to die, and that I need to come to terms with death in a more comprehensive way somehow in order to feel alive again. He stopped walking, turned to me and yelled with a smile, "What is wrong with you, man? You are having a fucking midlife crisis at age 29! You are 20 years too early!" Good advice, and I guess that is what friends are for, but it didn't heal me completely by any means.

The quote above is by Ernest Becker. Becker wrote a book called <u>The Denial of Death</u>, which I would ask you to remember if you remember nothing else from this column. Find the book and read it from cover to cover and let me know what you think. Keep in mind that Becker was a student of Freud early on, and his descriptions of Freud's ideas in Chapter 3 should be pushed aside a bit in favor of focusing on the book's central theme. Freud was a sexist jerk; Becker a genius who went far past Freud in terms of overall vision. Becker explained that the world is terrifying, with the cause of the terror being death itself and our fear of it. He said that the basic motivation for our behavior is our biological need to control our fear of death, which he saw as the primary anxiety facing us in our lives. This is an anxiety that Becker argued we attempt to keep unconscious because it is so overwhelming. He suggested that we attempt to overcome death by constantly involving ourselves in a social hero system which makes us believe that we will actually transcend death by participating in something of lasting worth. Becker called this the *causa sui* (cause of the self). Ultimately, in his second book, Becker described the social implications of this "immortality striving" and its effects on society. He argued that our attempts to destroy terror and ugliness through involving ourselves with projects seen as the highest good ultimately had the paradoxical effect of bringing more ugliness and terror into the world. We would trample and destroy all of those around us in our attempts to transcend this existence.

The implications of Becker are overwhelming. If we are motivated constantly by the fear of death, and if we deal with that by involving ourselves with projects that we hope will insure our immortality, then what is that to say about such seemingly basic tasks as writing this column? Couldn't it be argued that the reason I have pursued this task so consistently, worrying when I couldn't decide what to write, was because psychologically my entire existence depended on the outcome of the challenge? And I am not joking. What if the psychological implications of not completing this column on time were that I would be cast aside and not remembered by future generations of people on this earth because I had failed to provide the world with something lasting? Becker suggests that art is a result of that immortality striving. He would suggest that a root cause of creation by the human animal is to craft life into a tangible form which will outlast the body, which of course, is finite.

Becker suggested that we are in continual competition with one another as well through our immortality projects. He suggested that what we fear is being left behind while another attains the transcendent, and as a result, we do whatever we can to insure that we are the one who survives, who wins, controls, and dominates. Again the implications here are astounding. What does this say about all those who flip people off while driving (he/she who gets there faster or more efficiently wins the race), or succeed in business (he/she who makes the most money wins the race), or for that matter - and in order to stay focused here - those who kickbox during "The Trooper" at Iron Maiden concerts (he/she who clears the most space on the floor and frightens the metalheads wins the race)?

Ultimately, the effect of thinking this way can be restrictive. Reading Becker put me into the aforementioned state of existential dread, where I worried about death and thought about it clearly for the first time. Or rather, for the first time in my conscious mind. I found myself concerned with what

ALL BRUTE AND NO FORCE

I perceive as a societal lack of acceptance of death, an ignorance of it so to speak, and an unwillingness to contemplate or face it on any widespread scale other than for its shock value in the media. There is a distancing which happens in media representations of death. The images we see play on our fear of death and our wonder about it, but do not directly address the issue. We all suffer as a result. The restrictive element enters when we consider the implications of Becker's thought: if I am motivated by a fear of death, and if my actions are inspired by a psychology far deeper than I can readily perceive, then what is the reason behind even getting up in the morning? Why would I engage in activities throughout the day no that I know that everything is a defense mechanism against my fear of death? Ah *mes amis*, before you let yourself get roped into this mode of thought and end up laying face down on your sofas across the world crying in paranoia and pessimism, let me offer a few thoughts. Understanding and appreciating Becker and fully integrating what he has to say is entirely a matter of putting him into perspective. This is where the greatest challenge lies. Now that we are aware of death and our fear of it and what that fear implies, the question becomes: how will we deal with this information? My process has not become one of identifying EVERY example of death-anxiety-driven-action in my life and negating it; that would literally be impossible, as EVERY action *is* driven by death anxiety. (Wait! Don't run to the sofa yet...there is still hope!) Instead, the answer is to be found in balancing out my fear with a sense of wonder at the process of life itself. The process involves making myself aware of every moment of life and of fully experiencing it, and more importantly of crafting my life and the moments within it into art itself, and then offering that art to the world at large for them to experience, enjoy, discard, or embrace. The act of creation and of experience is what we have in this world, and learning to fully understand that *in the context of our imminent death* is what I now feel to be the task at hand for me, and hopefully for the people around me.

Wow, sounds like a party! Hey everyone, come on over to Greg's house! Let's contemplate death, pain, and suffering! Yay!

Hooray! Yippee! (...there are the sounds of noisemakers and party favors in the background...children singing in chorus...rainbows in the sky...a cake in the shape of a decaying corpse...etc...). Sorry, must be the residuals from the show tonight.

Anyway...this actually brings me to the next section of my little treatise on demise. What do we do with the information Becker has offered us? Your faithful editor and I were recently discussing life, love, and van break-downs, and in the midst of that I said to him "Do you know what I would be doing with my life right now if I could do anything at all? I don't even think that I would be juggling. I would be spending my every waking hour preparing for my own death." Joy, bliss, death! Really though, I think that something is missing from my life, and that is a greater comprehension of death and a preparation for it. Socrates, from my understanding, advised people to practice dying. Becker agreed. As I am not an anthropologist, I know little about what other cultures have done or are doing in terms of role playing their deaths. (Any insight would be appreciated folks!) I think that establishing a means of communicating about death would be a first step to a new broad based social psychology. Admitting that we are afraid, and examining our projects as extensions of our fear would be a good first step. Sharing information openly about custom and death ceremony would be a good second step. I might go so far as to suggest role playing, or even reinstating ritual into our lives, the symbolism of which would bring us psychologically more in line with death itself.

Recently, Bill Moyers did a four-night-long special on death and dying on PBS. From what Cynthia said, the shows were very intense, and well needed. I taped them but was only able to watch the first few minutes of one night's broadcast. I saw something striking in those few minutes. Before the show began, a man came onscreen and told viewers that if they were troubled by what they were about to watch, that there was a number offered which people could call to discuss their feelings. While this foresight (and the series itself) is to be applauded, I was struck with how limiting the offer really was and how it clearly

represented a troubling aspect of our culture. The offer was not a suggestion to create local support groups, or an idea to share thoughts with friends, neighbors and family. It was an offer to solve the problem, so to speak, through a phone call. What are the implications of this? It was yet another example of people hiding behind technology, social construct, or character in order to solve problems that they have been taught not to admit to those around them. Becker might suggest that this tendency stems from a desire to not appear weaker than anyone and thus continue to maintain an appearance as a formidable opponent for immortality conflict. I wondered about the people who would call in, and actually should have called myself. I wondered if they would be linked directly to a person who would become their confidante for a number of follow-up calls as well, and maybe offer to meet in person to really establish some connections and valuable human interaction on the matter. Doubt it. But this is what we need. We need to meet eye to eye and face to face and admit that we are scared. We need to start thinking about the personal construct of 'character' and what it represents, and the group construct of 'society' and what it represents in terms of death. I would suggest that both are distancing tools. We need to explore or examine death and its implications on our lives. At least I think that I need to. Anyone else interested?

Out soon: a new issue of a great zine called No Longer Blind from Australia, which will include columns and articles by a number of good people about intensive personal politics. The writings will be much like what I have been writing about in the last few Inside Front columns (email nxlxb@yahoo.com for more information on contributing or getting your hands on a copy). Also upcoming: I am always on the lookout for people to help raise money through benefit shows or any other means for the Western Shoshone Defense Project. Contact me for more information at xjugglerx@yahoo.com and check out http://www.alphacdc.com/wsdp/.

Well, it is now time to shower ten pounds of Iron Maiden residue from my body and go to bed. Write me anytime about anything from any of my Inside Front columns, and thanks for reading. This column was written under the influence of the new In Flames album *"Clayman"* which is more metal than your grandma's soup kettle. Check it out (The *album* that is. Leave your grandma and her kettle alone.)

Talk with you again sometime soon my friends.

All Brute and No Force *is continued on page 137*

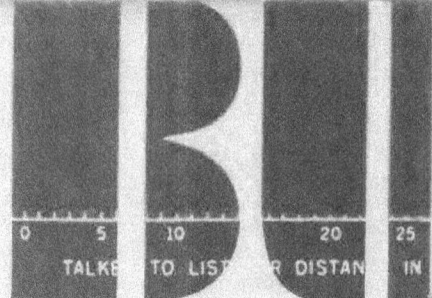

n our society (punk included) music is often mediated several degrees from its 'immediate' creation. For example, at a rock show, there is a degree of mediation that is physical, the sound vibrations are transmitted through amplifiers. But there are other, even greater mediations, like the roles we're supposed to play at a show. On stage (usually literally above everyone else) there are the 'musicians', the creative specialists. The musicians are supposed to fulfill this role – they are supposed to be well dressed, witty, talented, and are even expected to have answers to all our questions. Down below is the 'audience', who in affect are supposed to worship these specialists. This audience is generally passive, though a few swaying motions are permitted back and forth in the dark. This hierarchy between 'musician' (creative specialist) and 'fan' (passive consumer of said creativity) acts as a form of mediation. So, you and three of your friends sitting around playing acoustic guitars together on the sofa is a less mediated musical activity than you watching a rock band with six hundred strangers in some club. I'm assuming here that the less mediated the creative process (the less alienation), the better.

IF: I saw you play two weeks ago at the Cradle here in Chapel Hill at the Daemon/ Mr. Lady Records Showcase and it clarified for me quite a bit what I like so much about seeing The Butchies play. During your set, when Amy Ray (of the Indigo Girls, who was on tour promoting her record label, Daemon) came up to play with you, a contrast became clear to me: What Amy was doing was Rocking, with a capital "R." She has been around rock n' roll for a long time, and it's obvious she's an expert. However, to me it seemed that a few minutes before, the Butchies had been attempting something different – Yes, you had been rocking, but with a crucial difference – Namely that a distinct humor was involved. It was with that humor that to me it seemed that you were playing around with that role of the Rock Star (the kicks, the Rock Faces, etc.) and thus exposing it for what it is – A role. I believe that this sort of play has the potential to subvert that role (by exposing it and it's alienated nature, and then by refusing to take it seriously) and consequently subvert the hierarchy of Rock Star/Audience. I think the Butchies achieve this, at least during certain moments in the show. I believe that this subversion allows myself and others to connect to you – you know, as three human beings being passionate and creative, instead of just seeing another rock band.

I'm interested to know, insofar as you agree with me, what tactics in addition to humor have allowed the Butchies to have that "im-mediate" emotional connection – Which ones have worked? Which haven't? What do you consider the largest object in the way of this emotional connection? Why is this connection important to you? What are some personal examples of when this "emotional music connection" has been most immediate, either as musicians or audience?

M: Well, humor always works for me. You gotta be able to laugh at yourself. Try not to take yourself so seriously. I feel that's what the Butchies do. We remember that we are performing for people who wanna see us... so why not put on a good interactive fun show? I don't think I can act like nobody is out there watching me. I gotta be like "Hi, how are ya?" "How's the family?" Be friends. I guess it doesn't work if no-one wants to be involved. They don't want to participate. A voyeur. I really try not to let it get to me. I don't want to force anyone to do anything. If that's how they are feeling or if that's

how they want to interact, that's fine. Be yourself. No pressure. One of my favorite shows we did was at Santa Cruz. Before we played there was an open mic. So people who came to see the show could "perform" as well. We saw some great performances. I felt really connected to the audience. Like it was some warped family reunion. I definitely want to do that again. Maybe a Butchies tour with no opening act just open mic... hmmm...

A: I don't know about "tactics". That sounds a little fake. We are ourselves on stage, which is funny, honest, open. I think it's important to pay attention to the crowd. We are watching and get inspired by our fans. When the crowd is not willing to be open with us, that's probably our largest obstacle. We don't get up there to entertain ourselves...playing wouldn't be as much fun if it wasn't for the fans, so when we connect, everyone is happy. My favorite show was probably in Bismarck, ND because the kids were so excited and open that we got really energized. They never get those kinds of spaces where they can be themselves, so it's really important for us to play there.

IF: It's been clear to me at every Butchies show I've been to that you have created a successful Queer Positive atmosphere. I often feel totally alienated at punk and hardcore shows, not necessarily because they're not queer positive (unfortunately very few are), but they often don't offer any kind of positive space. Usually I feel that social rules are even more strict than elsewhere, you can't dance, or you can only dance a certain way, you can only talk about certain political topics or not talk at all, and on and on. If your not crossing your arms with an emotional-less expression on your face you are some kind of freak! Or so it seems. That's why I've found the Queer Positive spaces at your shows so appealing – that space allows you that breathing room to be yourself, at least to a significant degree more than when you're walking down the street. Additionally, I don't think in any way is a Queer Positive space alienating to straight people. It obviously, at least at your shows, includes almost everybody. We all feel queer, even if isn't necessarily is about our sexuality, and I'll assume that's why most of us came to punk rock – to have that space where we can be comfortable being queer, freakish – to support others who feel alienated from the "mainstream." But we also come together to create a new world, where we can be queer *and* beautiful. I believe that is what's changing our world: intentionally creating autonomous spaces like a Butchies show. Those nights of freedom raise the stakes for all of us involved, and I find myself demanding more and more. I want these spaces linked, and I want them more frequently.

How have the Butchies managed to create these spaces? How connected is that with who the Butchies are? What other "spaces" beyond shows do you believe are connected to this same experience? What tactics have you seen work and not work in the creation of such autonomous spaces? When was a moment in your lives when you felt most *free*?

M: Again, I feel very strongly with being yourself. We are queer. That's what are everyday lives are about. We are real. So we talk about what is going on in our lives. If that makes people feel safe than that is totally awesome! You ultimately know if such and such space is safe for you. Not all queer spaces are safe for all queers. That's unfortunate. So, it's up to you... how you feel. If you trust the situation. Find the space that feels safe for you. They do exist.

A: We create these spaces by being open and honest about who we are, and by not putting up with the attitude you see at a lot of shows. This is really important to us, because the world is so full of hate, we need a space for positivity. I try to create these spaces wherever I am, by not letting coworkers say homophobic things, or whatever else. When I came out was probably the moment that I felt most free, because the most confining thing you can do is be in denial about yourself.

IF: One could say that the Butchies were born from the seeds of the Tree of Riot Grrrl. Sleater-Kinney, on their new album, sing the following lines in the song "#1 Must Have": "Bearer of the flag from the beginning/ Now who would have believed this riot grrrrl's a cynic/ But they took our ideas to their marketing stars/ And now I'm spending all my days at girlpower.com/ Trying to buy back a little piece of me." I believe SK addresses here one of the most important issues for those of us who are attempting to create revolutionary music. Namely that our creativity and great ideas are in so much danger of being co-opted by what I'll call an alienated system of commodity exchange – which really means the danger of us (our bands, scene, etc.) becoming just another product, like shoes. Do you think there is a danger of the capitalist system saying it's okay for you to be lesbians or *anything*, so long as we can market products and sell them to you – or even more dangerously: Capitalism expanding itself to the "lesbian market"? – "The more markets the merrier. Think of TV shows/ news reports/ records/ movies/ soap we can sell now!" I know this is a complex issue. We want to see "ourselves" represented around us – but do we really need their TV shows to validate us, especially when we'll still be slumped in front of the TV? Do we really need to see our music on MTV or SPIN, if we're just going to be one more image/product for someone to buy into? Even if that image is Queer Positive? How have the Butchies played into this scheme? Do you feel that our "culture" is in danger of being co-opted by some greedy assholes at some corporation?

And even if we are creating our "micro-capitalist" economy (which we are to a greater extent than in years past), where all the money is in queer hands, or punk hands, or whatever, aren't we still just selling one another *products*? I want music (and ideas, and all art) to be more than just a commodity, and though we can transcend this sometimes at shows and through sheer imagination with our record players, I'd like to think that there's another way. *Pure music ——— emotion ——— heart.* I've seen this a few time in action, but only a few. Do the Butchies see a way out from here?

M: You totally hit the nail on the head... this is a very complex issue. I think of the queer kid in Anytown, USA who doesn't have access to queer music. They have no support group at all. Until one day he/she picks up a copy of SPIN. Sees some review of a queer act and thinks to him/herself... wow, that's me. I'm queer! Then he/she picks up the CD of such band. Finally a support group! The doors have opened. How can I say that that is so awful? Is it?

A: Sure it's weird to see companies marketing things to us, and making us another demographic. However, at least they are acknowledging our presence. The capitalist system is a good indicator of the wider community. In order to get our message out, it's necessary to be accessible, and if doing that is buying into the scheme, then I guess we do. The most important thing to remember is that ultimately we have control over our community, and we can suppress being commodified. In order to transcend the "microcapitalist" economy through our record players, aren't we buying into it? It's difficult at best for people to receive information unless it is disseminated. Product costs money, be it from the consumer or from advertising dollars. I see no way out of this.

IF: In your liner notes to the more recent Butchies album Cara Hyde writes, "...Every time we write a [queer] love song, every time we take control of our own lives and our own potential – every time we kiss – it is a revolution!" Beyond being a word used to sell us cars, what does the word revolution mean to you in your day-to-day lives?

M: Holding hands with my girlfriend at the grocery store. Not being afraid to be myself. Trying to challenge myself and others to not be racist, classist, xenophobic, homophobic. That's revolution.

A: In my life, revolution means rotation, as in "the car tire went one revolution". Seriously though, by being ourselves and being open, we are revolutionary.

To get in touch with the Butchies contact them at the record label (which one of the Butchies co-owns) Mr. Lady Records, PO Box 3189, Durham, NC 27715-3189 or send an electronic message to: mrlady@mindspring.com (www.mrladyrecords.com).

In this interview the Butchies were:
Alison, who strums the Bass guitar and sings.
Melissa, who pounds drums and is responsible for between song banter.
Bruce, who asks leading questions and dances in the back.
Kaia, who plays Guitar and croons – Kaia didn't get to respond, but we forgive her.

sinism, hip cynicism, semester despair, which is as seductive as it is

Theory of De

It's been a year since the events during the Seattle meeting of the World Trade Organization suddenly made demonstration activism seem like an effective way to make things happen. There have been a lot of other attempts to shut down meetings in the months since then, most of them not as successful. The honeymoon is over. In recent months we have learned that just showing up and blocking intersections is not going to recreate what happened in Seattle. The police are ready for us now, they know our strategies, they have our planning meetings bugged, they have a media blackout arranged so no one will even hear about our attempts. It's time to decide whether we want to abandon the demonstration approach for another thirty years, or find new ways to (re)vitalize future demonstrations. When you're creating through the medium of revolution, you have to always keep ahead of inertia (especially when that inertia is represented by the F.B.I.!). What follows won't be a comprehensive guide (that's impossible!) or even a thorough introduction (which would be indispensable!), but I hope it can remind others to think these issues through themselves.

Before we get into this, let's go over why participating in these big demonstrations can be worthwhile in the first place. A lot of people who deliberately choose not to go to demonstrations argue that the events in question do not represent their particular "issues"—or favored methods. For example, my friend in Germany stayed home from the Prague demonstration because he thought the protesters wouldn't do a good job of communicating with the local civilians. This boycott of a demonstration rests on the assumption that a demonstration is one mass event with a single mission or platform. Instead of staying home, my friend should have gone to Prague and worked to create the pieces that he saw as

missing. After all, demonstrations are going to happen whether we go or not. Boycotting may be valuable in the case of hopelessly petrified institutions like K-Mart or the vote. Demonstrations, on the other hand, are not institutions, they are a forum. As such they have the power to be fresh with each materialization. The anarchists who made Seattle so important didn't stay home because the Revolutionary Communist Party was involved. Instead they came and, D.I.Y., threw their own party, with a lowercase "p!"

When people are going to be in the streets trying to make things happen, the rest of us have two options: we can leave them to struggle on their own, imagining that our absence will speak for our qualms, or we can seize the opportunity to shape the event. We should view demonstrations as a chance to create the situations we want, not just to vote with our presence or absence for some particular method of organizing. Unless we can find something more effective to do somewhere else, there's no reason we shouldn't be there.

A demonstration is different from almost any other project we could use that time to work on. A public demonstration means thousands of people see our work with their own eyes. In a mediated world we cannot forget the power of direct visibility. The interactions spawned by this contact are far more valuable and meaningful than the scraps of "coverage" the corporate media may or may not toss us.

Participation is also an excellent way of raising issues (from globalization to animal rights) in the eyes of people we are close to. This is important because often these people will not be involved otherwise. Family and friends who hear about our activities become aware of important issues as an extension of their concern for us. At the same time we can use the forum to reinvigorate ourselves: it's easy to come to accept the most horrific

tragedies as normal things, until you try contesting them.

Of course it's also an opportunity to fuck shit up for those fucking it up for us. When we *demonstrate* that the monster has weak spots other people will be inspired to do the same. On the other hand, when others try to demonstrate this and have a hard time, because people like us are withholding our fresh ideas and participation, it reinforces the illusion that the monster is invulnerable—when all it would take to dispel this might be another couple participants with a secret plan.

There are other reasons to participate in these mass demonstrations, that activists don't usually talk about as much. The demonstration is an opportunity to collaborate with people from outside the circles we usually travel in. If we're going to make this cooperative anarchist thing work, we'll all need lots of practice with this. (Remember: there is nothing that pleases the motherfuckers more then infighting among the people. It is perhaps their greatest weapon against us.) Furthermore, demonstrations can become conferences where we develop plans, have fun, see friends from far away, meet new people, fall in love. Far from the blockades and handcuffs, we sleep on the floors of strangers (who are soon to be friends), and over the meals we share, we exchange stories and ideas. The smallest of these details is as important as our most radical long term goals.

Now, back to the subject. The people who came up with the strategies that worked in Seattle had been developing them for many years. Just like the band whose ground breaking music is repeated until it is a cliché, our masterpieces often become monoliths that loom from the past, trapping us in ritualistic attempts to resurrect them. Preoccupation with precedent can prevent us from finding the new innovations we desperately need.

monstrations

A preface to all the scene reports about demonstrations, supplied by F. Markatos Dixon

Now that chaining ourselves together across intersections is not so fresh and vital, a responsibility lies in our hands. Those of us who have been coming to these events unprepared, hoping to be directed by the ones "in the know," must bring our own plans to the next event. We, who have *not* been central to the organizing over the last few years, may actually have the most to offer. Our minds have not yet been filled with years of plans, failures, expectations and assumptions that are difficult for the experienced to shake off. What *we* need to shake off is our passivity. Each of us must prepare as if the success or failure of the whole demonstration depended on our contribution.

This decentralized approach will be the most effective for a number of reasons. It's impossible to infiltrate—if the F.B.I. had to discover the secret plans of every single person headed to a demonstration, they wouldn't have a chance. The affinity group model has been a good start towards this end, but it could be taken a lot farther, particularly if the individuals who have been hanging back in these groups waiting to be directed brought their own plans instead. ["But it would just be *anarchy!*" shriek the old-fashioned communist organizers, to which we respond, "Exactly!"] Of course we should not act in total disregard for what others are doing. The most effective approach will be one in which everyone answers to themselves while planning original approaches that complement those of their friends. I'll give some examples of this below. The old guard are going to stick to their predictable stuff, anyway, and it's going to keep on not working. Instead of just arguing about their methods we would do best to introduce something new and fertile.

It was the introduction of fresh elements that made Seattle so effective in the first place: the anarchists destroying property, the radical cheerleaders, the infernal noise brigade. Countless unique individual projects which

no one expected created a situation that no one could control or predict.

OK, on to specific examples. The number one cliché we have to avoid: going to fucking jail. Movement after movement has started in this country, gotten going, and then collapsed when mass legal trouble scared off half of the participants and embroiled all the resources (money, time, patience, you name it) of the rest in court cases. The lawyers and judges are surely the segment of this society with the very least potential to be radicalized! Why waste all our energy on them? Let's keep it in the streets, where it belongs. For countless reasons, getting arrested is just a bad idea—especially in this atmosphere of media blackouts, getting-caught is martyrish at best. Abbie Hoffman (who went through this whole thing three decades back) once commented: the trick is to find things to do that *aren't illegal yet*. Or just not to get caught.

My favorite example of fully legal mayhem remains the time Abbie Hoffman and Jerry Rubin shut the New York Stock Exchange down just by walking out onto the visitors' balcony and dropping money down to the stockbrokers. The crazed capitalists, well practiced in the ways of short sighted gains, abandoned their posts to collect falling dollars—precipitating a stock market crash for the day! Had Hoffman and Rubin tried to barricade the market by chaining themselves across the doors at 5 a.m., they probably wouldn't have succeeded, they certainly wouldn't have had as much fun, and even if it had worked I wouldn't be writing about it over thirty years later.

Now let's use the Philadelphia Republican National Convention protest (which I attended as the kind of unprepared automaton criticized above) as an example for some things that could have been done differently.

Had I known how much more my creativity was needed than my mere presence, I would have tried one of the following ideas,

which Brian and I came up with after it was too late. One of the main things we were all trying to do was block traffic, and delay the beginning of the Convention. There we were, trying to block traffic with our bodies, when we all know what blocks traffic best: more traffic! If everyone who came to the demonstrations by car had simply driven them very slowly into the area where the hotels were, stopping to ask for directions at every block (perhaps with clever art on our cars, like floats in a parade), traffic would have been effectively halted. The beauty of this plan is that if they chose to arrest people, they'd have to tow their cars out of the jam, which would just make matters worse!

Hell, we could have done that and still have had plenty of people left over to do other things. Here's another idea, which could easily be applied in any traffic-blocking demonstration. Usually the people in blocked cars are regarded as unfortunate victims (if not apolitical car-driving assholes!), and nothing more. Why not take the opportunity of these traffic jams to communicate with them? A radio transmitter that can reach car radios within a block or so can be built for around $10, and it's legal. Take one of these to the next demonstration in a car (so it won't be confiscated), and hitch it up to a tape loop explaining what we're doing and why. When you get stuck in the traffic jam, friends will be ready at the curb with signs reading "FOR INFORMATION ON TRAFFIC DELAYS, TUNE TO 98.9 FM." We could make the next demonstration into a pirate radio convention, with twelve different stations participating (each with its own message). This way, formerly useless, mad or bored motorists become the guests of honor! At least when the newspapers the next morning say "the protesters' message was unclear," the drivers will know that's just bullshit.

More on traffic: Let's say you don't have two hundred people with cars to gum up traffic; if you had ten people who were ready to get a little crazier, you could achieve the same effect. Have a few benefit shows, and raise money to buy each person a clunker car that's on its last legs. We could have found hundreds of them in Philadelphia... long old American cars just begging to "break down." Purchase them under fake names (or whatever you gotta do), then at the assigned minute, ten old cars breathe their last breath in the middle of ten crowded intersections, paralyzing traffic for hours. Maybe the drivers have escape routes planned; or, if they're gutsy, they'll just stick around insisting that they don't know what's going on (in that case, they could use their own cars, with no fake names). Even if ten people get charged with "conspiracy to block traffic" it is still preferable to four hundred people getting charged with assault for being beaten by police because they created a human blockade. If you're an expert and you really want to increase the tension, you could rig a device to set your old junker on fire (cars sometimes burst into flames you know!), and—talk about demonstration ambiance!

Or let's say we couldn't get our hands on any cars at all. Let motorists deliver them! Did you know that if you clog up the exhaust pipe of a car, it shuts down? Potatoes are ideal, just pound one in, way in, so its good and lost. In a matter of seconds you've got your blockade provided by some unfortunate motorist or truck driver. And happily for those of you with qualms about "property destruction," the offending tuber can eventually be extracted with no lasting damage... slashing the tires, on the other hand... works too! If we'd managed to enact a few of these plans, the delegates would have had to take the fucking subway to get out of the downtown area, and that would be the last thing they'd want to do with hundreds of demonstrators (with plans of their own!) on the streets.

While all this was going on, it would really just take one person who had planned far enough in advance (and gotten a nice enough haircut) to have infiltrated the Convention itself to go to the basement and cut the power on the whole event. Or, since all the police in the region were at the Convention center or waiting downtown for the demonstration, it would have been a perfect time for a group of people to appear in a totally different part of the city, free to wreak the havoc that everyone would be talking about for years.

One interesting new tactic surrounding the Philadelphia Republican National Convention occurred almost spontaneously. At the time, Brian and I were on the road with a performance project of folk lore, science, music, home made instruments and a large inflatable teddy bear. As it turned out, our somewhat inconvenient itinerary began in Philly and ended up buzzing around it like a moth. Our periodic returns to Philly combined with close contacts with highly involved individuals there put us in the position of becoming folk media. We ended up incorporating news of the demonstrations into our performance. Every where we went people were desperate for real news of the events. We provided the information we could within the performance and in several instances ended our show by beginning a discussion about the demonstration. The discussion gradually lead to important local needs and issues. By the end of the discussion, we had provided national news to a local audience and learned of local news—all from first hand sources. In addition we were able to send out e-mail updates. We have evidence and reports of many of these being forwarded around the world. Distrust of the media is not uncommon but it is quite uncommon to be in the position of being a first hand authority on an important issue that the press is actively blackballing. With a little more planning, the role we ended up playing for the Philly Demonstrations could be covered in a much more thorough way.

These are just a few examples of dumb ideas my friends and I have tossed around. There are a thousand other starting places. Next May Day, instead of doing that march carrying signs down the street, break up and have each person start a conversation with someone—that's much more real, much less of a spectacle. Bring yo-yo's to give out for everyone to play with at the next protest—it'll make us feel less dumb standing around there. Invent games, be tricksters, do things no one can understand (that's what our leaders do). Come up with crazy alliances between totally different groups that could come together for one moment to make things happen that *nobody* could have imagined. My wildest dream is that one day we can coordinate one of these mass demonstrations to coincide with a citywide police force strike. They have reasons to be discontent too, you know, not the least of which being that their masters are always forcing them to be assholes to us. If we took to the streets one day and the rank and file of the police force stayed home in protest, that could be the first day of something bigger than any of us have ever seen...

Regardless of our methods, our collective activities hold unlimited promise for transformation. It is during the brief moments of clarity, when a demonstration stops being self conscious, that we begin to wonder why they ever end. You know, fat cat murderer C.E.O. motherfuckers proudly flaunt their ideology of power on the streets *every day*, and in front of the very people they exploit! These demonstrations are a chance for us to be "out" about what we believe, too; rather than hiding in our punk and political ghettos, as if being conscious and concerned was something to be ashamed of, we adventure, we get a taste for what real *action* feels like, we test the possibilities. And the possibilities are big; all this revolutionary talk seems pretty dumb until you live through a moment when it comes true.

ns of Theory

The first time I really experienced what it was like to change a little piece of the world, my life was altered forever.

Postscript:
"But What About Local Activism?"

A lot of people point out the drawbacks of these mass demonstrations and then say we should just be concentrating our efforts in the places we live. Well, of course we should—and a lot of us are, otherwise the broad base of individuals who join in these demonstrations would not exist in the first place. At any rate, there is certainly no need to choose one over the other.

It is crucial, above all else, that we do not stop doing outreach to others. It's that outreach that made what we're doing possible. I'm sure the Powers That Be would like nothing more than to see the small number of radicalized people remain small. Cut the spearhead off a spear, and it's just a stick—we need to remain active in the places (like the much-maligned punk community, and even the college activist scene) where we first learned about activism and anarchy, so others will too. These need to be augmented, not replaced, and certainly not fought against. We need to find local environments and communities where interaction and action can take place. But concentrating on local activism doesn't mean that we can't also work together for big events that unite us from across the world. This system of cross-pollination is critical if our activism to remain fresh; in fact, it is at these gatherings that people exchange the new ideas and inspiration which travel back home and keep the fires burning.

I'd like to conclude with a couple more ideas of what we can do at home to "get the message out." I wrote in the features section about trying to provide for the needs of the community in anarchist ways (without necessarily using that word!). With our energy

applied that way, our communities won't have to meet so many needs through the usual (Christian, etc.) channels. Through our example, people will learn about the alternatives to old process of doing things. A good case study is the B.R.Y.C.C. house in Louisville, Kentucky, a vast building my friends opened (with a $150,000 grant from the city!) to be a "youth center." They have a 'zine and book library, a radio station (which is, in effect, a record library as well), an art gallery, punk shows, poetry readings and Food Not Bombs. All of this is organized by young people acting autonomously and getting involved in radical shit in the process. The city government has no idea what it's funding there, and my friends are filling a space in the community that would otherwise just be occupied by assholes.

Something else the readers of this magazine can do to make the alternatives to the capitalist nightmare visible (when the big demonstrations aren't going on) is autonomous media. There is more to this than just 'zines—wheatpasting and graffiti writing are good examples. If we make our own media to reach people outside our communities, than we don't have to beg the media barons to do the job for us. Instead of photocopying 'zines, put the ideas that usually remain within our circles on posters and wheatpaste them all over the streets of your town. People will see them for the next three months, and even after the text is unreadable they'll see the remains of the flier and it will make them remember what was there before. If I had a wheatpasting recipe committed to memory, I'd print it here, but I'm sure you can find one easily enough. This kind of adventure is a fun and empowering experience for people who do it. It means deciding for yourself what your town should look like and spending your time and effort to make it so. This is radically different from the methods of slave masters like Nike who simply

spend loads of money dumping their an-aesthetics on our towns. Remember, we have more ingenuity than they have cash. Aside from being an invigorating experience for the "artist," the results of autonomous media and street decoration will encourage others who see it. Maybe they thought they were alone in their discontent until your efforts started showing up. Maybe you think you are alone in your discontent... until someone begins to reciprocate.

Another option, beyond wheatpasting and hand spray-painting billboards and walls, is stenciling. Here's an idea: If you want to safely stencil an image all over the sidewalks of the world, cut the bottom out of an old back pack and attach your stencil in its place. You'll look like you're just rummaging around in your back pack when you're actually spraypainting through the bottom of your auto-media portable decoration machine. Then, there's stickering. If you live in the U.S., it's easy to make free stickers that are hard to remove. Go to the post office, where free stacks of priority mail stickers will be available. Make a stencil and spray paint a design on the stickers (you could even have a big design that was formed by a number of stickers together). You can put the stickers up (on the front of newspaper machines, at bus stops, on stop signs: "Stop being bored/eating animals/etc.") so fast that it's practically impossible to get caught.

Anyway, all these examples are just to encourage you to be thinking about this stuff yourself. You've probably heard most of these ideas before, and surely you can come up with better ones on your own. The thing is to focus on doing stuff yourself, coming up with your own approaches—that's the best way to have fun, and save the world, all at once. See you on the streets (not in the jails, if we can all help it!)... your friendly neighborhood folk scientist, Dr. Frederick M.D.

AFTER PHILLY,

I'm sure all of us feel excited, empowered and full of revolutionary electricity over the recent events in Seattle, DC, and Philly. If for no other reason, the FBI and local police are really acting like the movement is a true threat to the establishment, and shit—maybe they're right! But as we can all see from one event to the other, the police tactics are changing, and we need to change along with them if we hope to keep effective. So, I think we must analyze what has happened.

In Seattle, none of the authorities were ready for what happened, not only did thousands of truly peaceful protestors (read: fencewalkers) show up, but there was a new addition to the scene, "the violent anarchists" who, although their number was small, managed to lay waste to much of downtown Seattle, and turn the event upside down getting national and international media coverage and sparking debate at every office water cooler, where just minutes before they were talking about prime time TV sitcoms.

But in Philly and DC things have changed. It is obvious to anyone that Seattle was a wake up call to the FBI who instantly began the ol' COINTELPRO (counterintelligence program) and started monitoring and infiltrating the groups that are involved with the protests— after all those boring years after the radical sixties they had none of their own citizens to persecute and now, wow, we get to break all kinds of laws, and lie, and get away with it again! All in the name of defending the status quo! Woo hoo! It must be a great time to be piece of shit FBI motherfucker.

And we made it easy for them to watch us and fool us: we made no secret about when and where we planned on showing up, we even set up websites for them, we went to the same buildings day after to day to organize, and since our large groups were composed of members of other groups and individuals it was easy for them to infiltrate.

And the results are clear enough: Seattle, 0 arrests for the "violent" anarchists, and no arrests prior to actually participating in the action(s).

DC and Philly: there were many preemptive arrests, clearly the sign of police and FBI infiltration and surveillance. Also, because there was time to prepare, there were many plain clothes police on the streets, dressed very much like protesters, and as you were about to light that Mercedes on fire, the fellow revolutionary standing behind you who you thought had your back is really radioing the police four blocks away. Disaster.

And, now that we are seen as a enormous threat, the justice department has begun using every tactic at its disposal to keep us locked away in cages with the occasional beating, or in extreme fear of such a fate. False arrests, outright lies, denial of the very laws and privileges that they claim to support, such as no access to lawyers and ridiculous bail amounts.

Take this situation from Philly: In what turned out to be only an hour before the major protest actions in Philly were to begin, the police and FBI raided (with a full SWAT team as

IN CASE YOU HAVEN'T HEARD ON THE STREETS, THE FBI ANNOUNCED IT LAST WEEK IN PHILLY— THERE IS A FUCKING WAR ON.

WHATS NEXT?

part of the action) the Puppet House which had been used as a meeting place for helping organize the protest. They had a warrant, issued in the time-honored FBI/Nazi tradition of an anonymous tip that C4 (a U.S. military plastic high-explosive) was on the premises. This of course was a lie, and in fact due to the intelligence of those working at the house, there were no weapons or drugs at all! The 70-odd people who were in the building were arrested (and most are still in jail a week later) on various bullshit misdemeanor charges and the police and FBI confiscated basically everything they had there. Now, keep in mind these people were in the building lawfully, not breaking any laws. The police have stated that they had things like chicken wire, plastic pipes, chains, etc. that they claimed were to be used in protests, and thus were labeled as IOCs (Instruments of Crime), and possession of such is, of course, against the law. It is clear that they had inside information about the group and what was to go on that day (most likely provided by infiltrators) and timed the raid just before the people in the house were have started a major protest. Hence we have what is basically a preemptive gestapo police raid on people who have broken no laws.

In case you haven't heard on the streets, the FBI announced it last week in Philly— THERE IS A FUCKING WAR ON.

So, how should we handle these new twists and turns? First, we must ask what the advantage is in protesting these large events because the disadvantages are many. It is assumed that these events are chosen because they are covered widely by the national mainstream media, and as such protests are sure to get attention. Outside of this I can see no reason to choose these events for direct action. In Seattle, this tactic worked wonderfully, we caught the whole nation off guard, and it showed— there were front page stories and it got tons of coverage on television. But in the Philly protests it has been a different story. Clearly, the networks had some serious meetings (with, I would guess, a fair amount of input from corporate sponsors, not to mention the corporations who own the networks and newspapers) and it seems obvious that a decision was made not to give

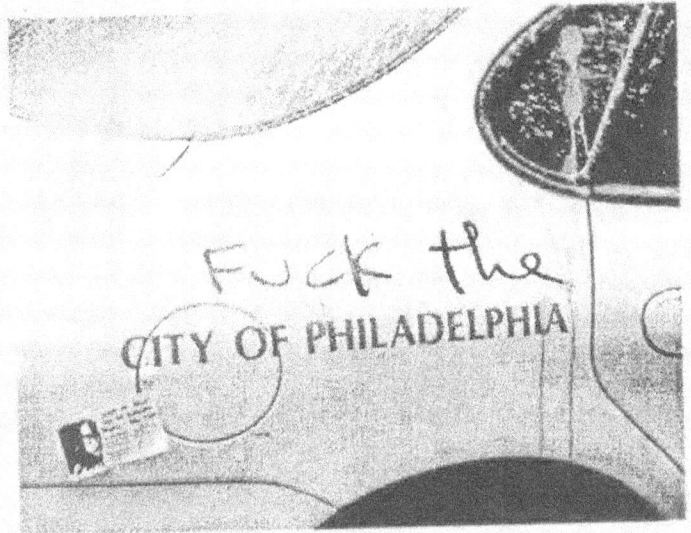

coverage to the protests in the future. And that is what has happened, if you blinked, you would have missed all the coverage of this last week of police brutality and FBI raids.

So, the primary objective of the protests failed—this is not to say the protests were a failure at all; all those who partici-pated feel empowered, and with a new, healthy resolve to take action. But now, 400 of us are in jail, eventually having to give money to the system for our freedom, with our names, fingerprints, and photos in the FBI's files, on the relatively short list of people to watch out for—which is not a good thing. And some of the unfortunate might be in jail a lot longer, charged with felonies and bails as high as $450,000.

I ask you this, is it easier to smash the windows of ten luxury cars and set them afire when there are no police around, or when there are thousands of them roaming around in groups of 12 concentrated in a small downtown area? Is it easier to assault an abusive police officer when its 5 on 5, or when its 5 on 500? We should not be willing to sacrifice our bodies and our freedom in ill-advised, poorly planned direct action that goes unnoticed by everyone who was not present.

If the FBI expects you to show up, then you better figure out how to not get caught, or better yet—burn down their office while they are looking for you protesting in another state.

The time has come to start acting like the serious threat to the status quo that we are being made out to be. When my time comes, I want to earn every dollar of my $1,000,000 bail!

No more sheep intentionally carrying protest signs to the slaughter shouting now meaningless slogans. Work at night, with your friends, in small groups and set the world ablaze with passion and beauty!

-No Surrender Cell

Scene Report

This is now just our second attempt to do a scene report section that transcends the tedium of bands/labels/distributors/etc.—again, not to say that kind of knowledge is useless, but others are offering it, so we consider it our role to offer something else. Please don't interpret this as news reporting, or even historical snapshots—these reports are first and last the testaments of individuals trying to recapture their own inexpressible moments of life, holding out the shreds of memory that remain to you as possible blueprints from which you might continue to weave your own tapestry of life. This is a map to lost hours in the lives of strangers; but we hope it might help you to find your way to wild new hours and days of your own. Just remember that you can't do the same thing twice: neither the W.T.O. protest in Seattle nor the first kiss of your childhood are coming back, so don't hold fast to old methods if you want to make new things happen. You can't get in on the joy and glory of what others have done by imitating or following examples—but the present is always greater than the past, and if you create revolutions for yourself in the moments to come, whether with caresses, bricks and plate glass, or boldly putting your words and body between the violent and the beautiful, those instants will outshine whatever displaced "historical importance" the events chronicled here are supposed to have.

There's a focus on the demonstration activism of the past twelve months here, since there are a lot of things that are brand new about it. If people are ready to keep being creative with it, to learn from all the events of the past few demonstrations, and explore how to be even more ready that the authorities for the next ones, this could be a way for us to gain momentum and power in our efforts to take our lives back. If we don't learn from our mistakes, we'll dissipate our energies following futile formulas and crashing into the brick walls of defeat. Don't read these accounts as a celebration of what has happened, but as a question you must answer: what next?

And another thing—looking over these reports, Gloria pointed out that they're pretty much all about visits, "vacations" in other people's lives. Even our demonstrations have largely been political tourism, in which we descend upon a foreign city and try to act on the forces of evil who are also visiting it, with no reference to the people who live there and the daily routines of their lives—which are what we really have to address, eventually, if we're making truly radical change, not just trying to get the governments or corporations or whatever to "change things for us." What would be really beautiful would be if the next time I pick up a punk magazine and flip to the "scene reports" section, I see fiftyh reports from people talking about all the crazy transforming shit that they have going on in their hometowns and neighborhoods. It's the same for all of us punk rockers as it is for my bourgeois parents: go on "vacation" to "get away from it all," and you'll run all around the world trying to get far enough away, carrying that insidious "it all" with you every where you go. Start with some maniacal idealism and new ideas in your home, and you can find yourself in a totally different world in two weeks, or two seconds.

See you in one of those worlds, next time, your loving editor, Brian

PART ONE: DEMONSTRATIONS

THE WORLD TRADE ORGANIZATION MEETING IN SEATTLE, WASHINGTON

This is a story about some things that I did and saw and felt during the protests against the World Trade Organization in Seattle in November and December of 1999. I have done my best not to romanticize or exaggerate any of this, and I didn't make anything up. I have tried to make this as accessible as possible, and to avoid using activist jargon as much as I could, but it would still help to have some prior knowledge of what happened in Seattle last winter and why before reading it. I have made little effort to explain what exactly the WTO is or how tens of thousands of people came together to stop it, simply because that has already been done elsewhere, and better than I could ever hope to do it. This is just my story, and I hope reading it empowers you in some way. I strive to make very day of my life as fulfilling as these ones were and I hope to help create a world where that would be possible, soon.

The Power is Running

I can't do it. I can't. I can't tell you what this felt like any more than a bird could tell me what it feels like to fly. I can tell you my story, but it's only my head talking. My heart can't write, and my guts don't have lips. I cannot truly explain how it felt to taste ecstasy in every breath as the invincible forces of privilege and coercive power finally lost control, to stare down the world's most ruinous and abusive bullies and watch them blink, to fall in love with tens of thousands of people at once, to not know what would happen next, to become dangerous. And that is a tragedy which haunts me as I write every one of these words. Because if somehow I could share with you what I _felt_ for ten days in Seattle you would never settle for anything less ever again. You would kick in your TV, run outside buck naked, tear up the freeway with your bare hands, flip all the tanks upside down, and dance with panda bears through the streets. The barbarians would emerge from exile to knock down Heaven's door and the dead would rise up from their coffins and cubicles. And once you got a taste of the sublime joy of reclaiming control of your life and your world, of regaining your lost kinship to a human community of which you are an integral component, of realizing your wildest dreams and desires, you would do whatever it takes to make it happen again.

Monday Nov. 22 – Thursday Nov. 25: I left for Seattle from Columbus, GA on Monday, November 22, on a greyhound, alone, already hungry, with no money and nothing to eat. Six hours later in Atlanta my bag was whisked away to a different bus, leaving me with no warm clothes and nothing to read, either. I stated blankly out the window at the bleak, diseased wasteland of concrete and smoke and cars, at the trees and fields and hills and rivers, at all the cities I had never seen before. Chattanooga, Nashville, Louisville, Indianapolis, Gary, Chicago. I scrounged what little food I could at bus stations, but by Tuesday night I was hungry enough that I was starting to get mean. In Chicago a grizzled old man gave me a sandwich, which I ate, and a dollar, which I gave to another grizzled old man. I stared and thought and tried to sleep. Milwaukee, Madison, Eau Claire, Wednesday morning in Minneapolis. Haggard young women with kids, disgruntled truckers, teenage runaways. Fargo, Bismarck, Billings. The North Dakotan whose car broke down in Minnesota who couldn't afford to fix it. Butte, Missoula, Coeur d'Alene, Spokane. The grizzled young man who bought me a waffle in Montana because he hadn't seen me eat in a day and a half. I fell asleep a few hours past Spokane in the Cascades and woke up, Thursday Nov. 25, at about midnight, in Seattle. I staggered off the bus, met my mysterious liaison Ms. J, and was miraculously reunited with my long lost bag. Fifteen minutes later I was standing outside of the 420 Denny Space, a nerve center of sorts where I found dozens of people bustling around with saws and paint and walkie talkies, plotting and planning and building. This was a very good sign, but after 78 hours of Greyhound time it was also pretty jarring. I was utterly exhausted, ravenously hungry, and in no condition to conspire yet. I caught a ride south of downtown to the Roasted Filbert, a cavernous, dusty, unmarked warehouse with concrete floors, no windows, and a purple door; which was serving as a refuge for everyone who showed up at 420 with nowhere to stay. I found a space inside, curled up in my bag, and passed out listening to warm bodies breathing all around me.

Friday Nov. 26: At dawn I ride back up to Denny with four others from Filbert. None of us know each other. Downtown the towers glitter in the distance like decorated tombs, spectacular monuments to wealth and power that loom overhead just as the institutions they embody loom over every aspect of our lives. I know that we are flying under their radar, and that we are not alone. For the first time in my life those almighty towers, and all that they stand for, look vulnerable to me. Up at Denny the bustle and activity of Thursday night has multiplied exponentially. I help out with the kitchen and the dishwashing, finally get some food, and spend most of the day getting my bearings. Around dusk Critical Mass issues out of 420. I ride with some woman on the back of her bike since I don't have one. Later I just run. We ride around and around the upscale shopping districts downtown, taking over whatever streets we want, whenever we want, without any authorization or permission, singing, dancing, howling, and conversing with anyone who will listen. Someone begins chanting "We're gonna win! We're gonna win!" and for the first time in my life I believe it. Much to my surprise and delight, I chance upon Mr. X in the midst of Critical Mass. I have only seen him once since I spent much of the summer of '98 in a van with him. He is in Seattle with Ms. X and X-Dog. Our reunion is cut short, however, when a psychopath in a fancy car tries to run us over. Mr. X screams like a banshee, jumps onto the hood, slips a piece of cardboard under the wipers and over the entire windshield, pounds three big ass dents in the hood with his fist, and disappears into the night. Later we invade the Washington Trade and Convention Center, where the WTO summit is supposed to be held, and ride in circles through the foyer for quite some time before a security guard punches someone in the face and the police finally manage to chase us away.

Saturday Nov. 27: I spend all morning and early afternoon at Denny. The 420 Space is serving as a welcome mat, training grounds, mess hall, and nerve center, and it is turning into a complete madhouse. Countless meetings and workshops, endless training and skill sharing, and ceaseless cooking, cleaning, eating and welding all rage perpetually and simultaneously under Denny's roof. More and more people pour in throughout the day, and it is beginning to get difficult to move around inside. I leave late Saturday afternoon for the Hitco space to make lockboxes. Hitco is every bit as wild as Denny. While others hammer away at mammoth puppets and matching sea turtle suits we set up an assembly line and build hundreds of lockboxes out of PVC pipe, chicken wire, framing nails, tar, sand, yarn, and duct tape. We turn them out late into the night. I ride to 420, walk to Filbert, and sleep covered with tar.

Sunday Nov. 28: Sunday morning Denny is an utterly unfathomable zoo. I learn that Saturday night banners were dropped all over downtown, one from the top of a crane over I-

5. At noon a parade complete with giant puppets, street theater, radical cheerleading, and an anarchic marching band rolls out of Seattle Central Community College (SCCC). The street party is a roaring success, reclaiming downtown for hours and railing fiercely at all manifestations of corporate dominance. Unfortunately I miss it. I go back to Hiteo around five to finish the lockboxes, unaware that the festival is still bumping. I get back to 420 around eight and run across Ms. C. We are eating dinner when we catch wind that a mass public squat is about to be opened on Virginia St. The word is free shelter downtown for anyone who needs it during the protests, and for Seattle's homeless after. About forty of us steal through the night to recover a fragment of the world that has been stolen from us.

913 Virginia St. The door opens, and two masked heads emerge from the darkness. "GET IN!" I run through the door, up the stairs, through a wooden hatch, onto the second floor. The door closes behind me. The building is enormous. This floor could harbor a horde of barbarians. The power is running. Androgynous ninja elves scamper about everywhere around me, hammering away furiously on a thousand different project. I board up windows at a breakneck pace with a tireless Danish carpenter. Plywood, 2x4's, chicken wire, black plastic, anything. Next room. The cops are coming. They're about to fire tear gas through all these windows. No they're not. More rooms. Yes they are. Cover all this up so they can't tell how many of us are in here. No they're not. "WHO THE FUCK LET IN PHOTOGRAPHERS? I'VE GOT FELONY WARRANTS IN WASHINGTON STATE!" The cops are coming. Two rooms left. No they're not. "KEEP THOSE FUCKING PHOTOGRAPHERS IN THAT FRONT ROOM! SOMEBODY GOT TALK TO THEM!" Yes they are. We're done. No they're not... There are two doors one in front and one in back. The former can be opened from the inside by dismantling the contraption that braces it. The latter, where Mr. N has constructed a virtually impregnable barricade out of toilets, concrete, rebar, plywood, and an iron fire door, could only be opened by a tank. The doors are adjacent to two stairwells, one in front and one in back, which lead to either end of a long winding hallway that connects about ten rooms. The rooms are vast and spacious, with 25' ceilings, gigantic windows, and giant stages and lofts of various shapes and sizes. One has been furnished with an ample supply of food, water, and medical supplies. Someone runs out of another, arms raised in triumph, a crescent wrench in one fist and a plunger in the other. "THE TOILET WORKS!" In yet another Ms. I and Ms. S arm a security team with short wave radios. Every window on this floor is boarded up

except for those in the front room — where earlier we gave a full fledged press conference before banishing the blow-dried talking heads of the corporate media altogether — and nothing inside can be distinguished from below. The third floor is essentially identical to the second, except that none of the windows are boarded up and there is a ladder to the roof in the back stairwell. There is no way to approach the building that is not visible from the roof, where someone stands guard with a short-wave radio, waiting for the inevitable. Here come the cops, this time for real... We assemble in The Spiral Room and send Mr. G outside to negotiate, agreeing that he will not accept, refuse, offer, or request any proposal before we have all consensed to do so. The cops say we need to let in a fire inspector. They need to know if we are posing a fire hazard to ourselves. After much discussion we consense that this is complete bullshit. They don't know the layout of the building, they or how many of us are inside, or how sturdy our barricades are or for that matter if we all have machine guns or not. They want to inspect the building to determine how difficult it will be to raid. When we refuse they cut the water, then the power. By this time a bizarre circus has gathered below. Reporters, Feds, and undercover agents film us, and our friends from 420 and the Independent Media Center film them. We hang banners and signs from the roof and windows. Mine says "RESISTANCE IS FERTILE". Outside, Mr. G wrangles with the cops. Inside we are embroiled in an absolutely endless meeting regarding their ever-changing promises and threats. As it gets later and later we are left with less friends and more enemies, who make less promises and more threats. The situation becomes increasingly tense, but they never move in on us. Around four they finally leave, swearing that they will return at eight with the landlord to chase us out. I sleep with one eye open, and wake up four different times to false alarms. The cops are coming. No they're not. Yes they are. No they're not.

Monday Nov. 29 : Throughout the morning a crowd from 420 and everywhere else gathers outside, beating drums and singing. The cops return at eight with the landlord, block the doors, and refuse to let anyone in or out. Around noon we manage to get a lawyer inside. He tries to cut us a deal. We will occupy the building until Friday, then hand it over to Share/Wheel, a homeless advocacy group, who will convert it into a free shelter. The landlord claims he will get sued if someone gets hurt in his building. We write up a waiver clearing him of any liability for anything that happens inside. He refuses to sign it. This all takes hours. The negotiations break down completely by late afternoon. The landlord wants us disposed of. The cops slaver in antic-

ipation. Around 5:30 they swear that in thirty minutes they will kick down the doors, beat ass, break heads, and arrest everyone inside. They will let anyone who is willing to leave out now. This is our "last chance." Nearly everyone opts out at this point, understandably having no desire to spend the 30th in jail. They promise to tear ass up to Denny and return with as much backup as they can scrape together. I know that whether this is our "last chance" or not there are nowhere near enough cops outside to actually raid the building, and I cannot fathom why. Later I learn that crowds have amassed all over downtown. Some have surrounded The Gap, some the Westin Hotel so that the WTO delegates can't get in to sleep, and some have attacked a McDonald's, breaking some windows. About 15 of us remain inside. There a lot of people out front, but not enough. The situation looks bleak. At 6 the riot cops show up. We decide that there is no longer any way to defend the building, and that there is no point in making martyrs of ourselves. Except for Mr. B, who says he will hide in the rafters and hold out alone if he has to. We dismantle the barricade at the front door and run outside. We are greeted with a wondrous sight. The cavalry has arrived from 420. Somehow hordes of people have slid in between the cops and the door, and more stream in from all around. Everyone goes berserk. We pound and bang on everything we can get our hands on, howling and dancing and taking up most of the block. Mr. B is up on the roof, roaring at the top of his lungs with his arms raised to the sky as if all the indomitable power of the avenging squatter demon is running through the marrow of his bones. The cops are at a loss. Every time they try to give us an order or command we just dance, but when they try to charge their van across the block to disperse us we surround it and slow it down to a crawl, then beat and kick and rock it while the couple inside squirms. It is all they can do to limp their wounded warhorse through to the other side before all the little elves flip the damn thing over. The cops leave. Pandemonium reigns. Up on the roof Mr. B roars in triumph, and the walls tremble in the top of the tombs. I suspect that the cops are not prepared to start a riot on Virginia St. when so much of their force is downtown protecting the world's most ruinous and abusive corporations and the delegates who represent them. A fragment of the world has been recovered, and it is safe for now. About forty people run inside, and I run back up to Denny. A few hours later, right before I leave 420 for the night, I run into Ms. X and X-Dog. She tells me that Mr. X is in jail. She is trying desperately to bail him out before the state discovers exactly who he is and what he has done. I promise to keep in contact with her and to do all I can to help. Before I fall asleep back at the squat, beneath a window, with the glittering banks looming over me, I remember the time Mr. X told me that there were only two things that he would never do. He would never hurt anyone, and he would never take anyone's food. His captors do both, and some day they will suffer the consequences. They have locked Mr. X in a cage, and tomorrow it's time for payback.

Tuesday Nov. 30: I wake up before dawn and walk to SCCC, where the festivities begin. Before long I am surrounded by thousands of friends, and at seven we set out for the Washington Trade and Convention Center, where the summit is supposed to be held. As we near it we fan out, taking over the surrounding streets and blockading entrances to the building. Everything you can imagine turns into a barricade. Bodies, puppets, lockboxes, a fifty foot tripod, barrels full of concrete, dumpsters, cars. We begin to form a human chain around the convention center. In an amusing display of either arrogance or stupidity the delegates all wear matching beige suits and big ID tags that say "DELEGATE". Whenever they try to approach the building we stop them and chase them off. Without the protection of their armed servants they are as powerless as a brain without a body, and their expressions are priceless as they run away. Before long the chain is complete, and the only ways in are through parking garages, hotels, and underground tunnels. We cut these off one by one. I dart around by myself, patching up holes where blockades need help and trailing delegates to their secret entrances. I dog one for blocks, grinning malevolently at him as he searches in vain for a way into the convention center. He finally gives up and asks a cop for advice, and I listen in rubbing my hands with glee. "How do we get inside?" "Well sir..., right now there is no way to get inside..." The opening ceremonies of the summit are "postponed", and then canceled altogether. This is when the cops begin to riot. They have failed their masters miserably and they are pissed. I run up to the barricade at 5th and Seneca, which I hear is about to be attacked. The cops, sporting Darth Vadar suits and unmarked raincoats, have formed a line across Seneca. Behind them there are five or six more on horses and a couple with big ass guns. We push a line of dumpsters in front of them so that they can't trample us, and form an enormous immovable knot so that they can't drag us away and arrest us. The cops flip on gas masks and begin to fire tear gas into the crowd. Others blast us with jumbo tanks of pepper spray. One throws a can of gas into my lap. Ronald McDonald and his band of merry devils run amok through my organs, burning plastic bonfires in my windpipe and hacking at my lungs with chainsaws dipped in DDT. Vampire fangs sunk down to the gums suck the soul from my skull, and all that

remains in the hellish wasteland between my ears is fear and hatred. Everyone around me starts to run. While I am getting up a cop bucks me in the face with pepper spray. Tony the Tiger is scouring my eyes with his chemical claws, my nostrils are searing, and I can't see a damn thing. I scramble down Seneca stone blind and finally collapse in the street, gasping and convulsing. Someone pours water on my face and rubs life back into my eyes. I am born again in their hands. We all tear ass back up Seneca towards 5th to make out what the cops are doing and how to stop them. I realize that my friends are not all just going to bail when things start to get ugly. And here come the cops, storming through the sickly clouds, ejaculating toxic gas as fast as they can stroke their triggers. They open up on us with rubber bullets and concussion grenades, and we stampede back down Seneca and around the corner. The stampede becomes a fairly orderly retreat as we book down 4th Avenue, hurling everything we can get our hands on out into the street to protect ourselves from their cars and horses. Trash cans, newspaper stands, concrete tree planters, dumpsters, construction barricades, anything that will stop them or slow them down. The gas is inescapable but we grab the cans and throw them back. The rubber bullets are legitimately scary but we chuck sticks, stones, and bottles, and hope for the best. I find myself on top of a newspaper stand in the middle of 4th Avenue, unleashing a psychotic stream of invective at the interchangeable bullies who are approaching through the smoke. "FUCK YOU, COWARDS!, I'M INVINCIBLE!" This is happening all over town. They can move us but they can not disperse us. At 4th and Union the worm is beginning to turn. The cops, facing thousands and thousands of us now, are a little less gung ho than they were at 5th and Seneca. They form a line across 4th and we come to another standoff. Only this time no one is going to sit down for them. I find myself on top of another newspaper stand in the middle of 4th Avenue, roaring at the top of my lungs. "I can't TELL you how THRILLED I am to BE here right now. I LOVE every ONE of you, like a SISTER and a BROTHER. There is NOWHERE, in the WORLD, EVER, that I would RATHER BE then WHERE I AM right now. There is NOTHING I would RATHER BE DOING than WHAT I AM DOING right now. I would RATHER be OUT HERE than spend another FUCKING SECOND in my CAR, or at my JOB, or WATCHING TV. I DON'T think these cops can say that. I DON'T think those delegates can say that. I would rather EAT MORE TEAR GAS than any more of their FUCKING fast food. I would rather DRINK MORE PEPPER SPRAY than any more of their FUCKING soft drinks. I would rather DEAL WITH

THAT than ACCEPT THIS SHIT for another FUCKING SECOND. And I would rather DIE LIVING than continue to LIVE DYING..." Somebody hugs me. It has been so long since anyone has touched me that I nearly melt in their arms. Someone else jumps up and roars, and then someone else, and then someone else. I rest for a minute while a stout Chicano man recounts some interesting news. While the servants were busy terrorizing us and the rest of the blockades, the wily and mobile Black Bloc dealt with their masters in kind. Masked little elves armed themselves with slingshots, sledgehammers, mallets

Illustration s.1. Eviction from the 121 squat in the U.K.

chains, and crowbars; and attacked The Gap, McDonald's, Niketown, Bank of America, Starbucks, Levi's, Fidelity Investment, Old Navy, Key Bank, Washington Mutual, Nordstrom's, US Bankcorp, Planet Hollywood, and other manifestation of corporate dominance, smashing windows and redecorating facades. I am ecstatic. Those glittering towers are not invincible after all. The greatest trick the vampires ever played was convincing us that garlic did not exist. Let their facade be torn to pieces, and may the walls come tumbling down. The stout Chicano man tells me that during the L.A. riot he and his friends burned down police stations, and nothing else. We freestyle from the newspaper stand until my larynx is throbbing. Eventually the cops get impatient, and one of them bucks my man full in the face with pepper spray. I kiss him on the head, they club me and everyone else they can reach, and back down 4th Avenue I go, a phalanx of crocodiles in anklyosaurus suits at my heel wreaking havoc and pain. Yet another standoff at 4th and Pike. The cops form a line across 4th Avenue. This is getting repetitive. I have inhaled so much tear gas, ingested so much pepper spray, and ducked from so many concussion grenades and rubber bullets that running the bulls on 4th Avenue is no longer novel or fun. It's just frustrating. We outnumber them almost immeasurably yet they still attack us with impunity. They hold all the cards, they make all the rules, and they cheat all the time. I am terrified. We are in no way seriously prepared to defend ourselves. All it would take is for one dumb ass aggro cop to decide to get his rocks off and open fire and all the rest would follow suit. It would be a massacre, Kent State. Bonfires smolder behind my eyes, and the smoke rises out of my mouth.

I choose one—at random, for they all look exactly the same. Every inch of his body is hidden under black cyborg armor. He is armed to the teeth. His face is hidden under a gas mask, face shield, and full helmet. "O'Neil" is embroidered on his bulletproof vest. I plant myself squarely in front of his face and I stare dead into his eyes. He won't look at me. He blinks constantly, looks down, left, up, right; anywhere but at me. It infuriates me almost beyond words that this coward has the impudence to attack me when I am unarmed but lacks the courage to even look me in the eyes. "Can you look me in the eyes? CAN YOU LOOK ME IN THE EYES? LOOK ME IN THE EYES, O'NEIL. Nothing. I know why he won't look at me. When he was halter-broken he joined his trainers in a companionship stimulated not by love, but by hatred – hatred for the "enemy" who has always been designated as a barbarian, savage, communist, jap, criminal, gook, subhuman, drug dealer, terrorist, scum; less than human and therefore legitimate prey. I try to make it impossible for him to label me as a faceless protester, the enemy. I pull off my ski mask and continue to stare into his eyes. I tell him that I am from the south, about fixing houses and laying floors and loading tractor trailer trucks, about nearly getting killed in a car wreck in October, about carrying my dog around crying to all the bushes that she loved to root around in the day she died of cancer. I

tell him that we all have our stories, that there are no faceless protesters here. Nothing. "Can you look me in the eyes, O'Neil? I am a human being, and I refuse to let you evade that. I won't let you label me as a protester, and I don't want to have to label you as a cop. I refuse to accept that they have broken you completely, that there is not something left in you which is still capable of empathizing with me. I want to be able to treat you as an equal, but only if you prove to me that you are willing to do the same. And the only way you can do that is by joining us, or walking away." I remain dead still, staring into his weak cow eyes. He is blinking excessively and is visibly uncomfortable. "Can you look me in the eyes, O'Neil? The difference between me and you is that I want to be here and you don't. I know why I am here. I am enjoying myself. I am reveling in this. I am rejoicing. I have been waiting for this to happen since I was a little kid. There is nowhere, in the world, ever, that I would rather be than where I am right now. There is nothing I would rather be doing than what I am doing right now. It has never been so magnificent to feel the sublime power of life running through the marrow of my bones. I know that you don't want to be here. I know that you don't know why you are here. I know that you are not enjoying yourself. I know that you don't want to be doing this. And no one is holding a gun to your head and forcing you to. Wherever you want to be, go there, now. Whatever you want to be doing, do it, now. Go home and get out my way. Go make love with your girlfriend or boyfriend, go snuggle with your kids or dog, go watch TV if that's what you want, but stay out of my way because this is a lot more important to me than it is to you." I have not moved my feet or my eyeballs at all. I have been trying to blink as little as possible. O'Neil's eyes are quivering and squirming to avoid me beneath the mask. "O'NEIL! CAN YOU LOOK ME IN THE EYES? CAN YOU DO THAT FOR ME, O'NEIL? CAN YOU LOOK ME IN THE EYES. Basically this whole 'Battle of Seattle' boils down to the relationship between you and me. And really, there are only two kinds of relationships that we can have anymore. If you can either join us or walk away then you will be my brother, and I will embrace you. If you cannot then you will be my enemy, and I will fight you. The relationship that we are not going to have is the one where you are dominant and I am subservient. That is no longer an option. That will never be an option again. Which kind of relationship do you want to have with me, O'Neil? Look around you. Look at all of these people singing and dancing and making music. Don't you see how beautiful this is? Don't you see how much more healthy and strong and fulfilling and desirable and fun relationships that rest on mutual respect and

consent and understanding and solidarity and love are than ones that rest on force and fear and coercion and violence and hatred? Don't you see that the life and the world that we are beginning to create out here is superior to the one that you have been trained to accept... Don't you see that we are going to win? Don't you want to be a part of this? I know you do because you still can't look me in eyes. If you want to remain my enemy then so be it. But if you want to be my brother all you have to do is join us, or walk away." At this exact moment the Infernal Noise Brigade appears. For the first time since this surreal monologue began I look behind me. A small man wearing a gas mask and fatigues is prancing about in front, dancing lustily with two oversized black and green flags. Behind him two women wearing gas masks and fatigues march side by side, each bearing an oversized black and green mock wooden rifle. Two columns of about fifteen march behind the women with the guns. They are all wearing gas masks and fatigues, and they are all playing drums and horns and all sorts of other noisemakers. They are making the most glorious uproar that I have ever heard. The Infernal Noise Brigade marches all the way to the front where we are standing. When they reach the line the columns transform into a whirling circle. We form more circles around them, holding hands and leaping through the air, dancing around and around in concentric rings like a tribe of elves. We dance with absolute abandon, in possibly the most unrestrained explosion of sheer fury and joy that I have ever seen. On one side of the line across 4th Avenue there is a pulsating festival of resistance and life. On the other side there is a blank wall of obedience and death. The comparison is impossible to miss. It hits you over the head with a hammer. When the dance is over I return to my post up in O'Neil's face. I stare into his eyes and invoke all the love and rage I can muster to fashion an auger to bore through his mask and into his brain. And Cow Eyes cries crocodile tears. His eyes are brimming, with red veins throbbing. His cheeks are moist. He won't look at me. "O'Neil, I don't care if you cry or not. I don't care what you're thinking right now. I only care about what you do. Before long you will get orders to attack us, or one of you will get impatient and provoke another confrontation. What are you going to do? When that happens I am going to be standing right here. If you choose to remain our enemy then you are going to have to hit me first. You are going to have to hurt me first. I dare you to look me in the eyes when you do it. You may be able to hurt me and not look at me. You may be able to look at me and not hurt me. But you won't be able to look me in the eyes while you hurt me, because you are afraid you will lose your nerve. You are afraid of me, and you should be. O'Neil, you all have been terrorizing us all day. If this goes on all night we will have to start fighting back. And you and I will be standing right here in the middle of it. I have no illusions about what that means. Neither should you. We may get killed. But I would rather deal with that than accept this one second longer. I would rather die than give in to you. I don't think you can say that, can you, O'Neil? Would you rather die then be my brother? Who are you dying for? Where are they? Whoever gives you orders is standing <u>behind</u> you, man. Whoever gives them orders is relaxing down at the station, and whoever gives <u>them</u> orders is safe in some high rise somewhere, laughing at your foolish ass! Why isn't your boss, and their boss, out here with you, O'Neil, risking their lives and crying in the middle of 4th Avenue? Why should they? You do it all for them! What are you thinking? I just don't <u>get</u> it. They don't care about you, hell, I care about you then they do. You're getting used, hustled, <u>played</u>, man, and you will be discarded the minute you become expendable. Please look me in the eyes. I'm serious, O'Neil, come dance with me..." Someone whispers in my ear that another cop is crying down the line to my right. For a fleeting moment I can feel it coming, the fiery dragon breath of the day that will come when the servants turn their backs on their masters and dance...and then it's gone. Because O'Neil is not dancing. He is completely beaten. His lifeless eyes don't even bother to quiver or squirm. And he won't look at me. I could whisper in his nightmares for a thousand years, I could burn my face onto the backs of his eyelids. I could stare at him every morning from the bathroom mirror, but he would never look me in the eyes. He is too well trained, too completely broken, too weak to feel compassion for the enemy. His eyes are dead. There is nothing left. The magic words that could pierce his armor and resurrect him elude me, if they exist at all. "O'Neil, I know that you have been broken and trained. So have I. I know that you are just following orders and just doing your job. I have done the same. But we are ultimately responsible for our actions, and their consequences. There is a life and a world and a community waiting for you on this side of the line that can make you wild and whole again, if you want them. But if you prefer to lay it all to waste, if you prefer death and despair to love and life, if all of these words bounce off of your armor and you still choose to hurt me then <u>FUCK</u> you, because the Nuremberg defense doesn't fly." I have nothing left to say. I sing the last verse of my beaten heroes' song, softly, over and over and over again, staring into O'Neil's eyes and waiting for the inevitable. "...in our hands is placed a power greater than their hoarded gold, greater than the might of armies magnified a thousand fold, we can bring to birth a

new world from the ashes of the old..." Eventually one cop down to my right either gets impatient or gets orders. He grabs some guy, completely randomly, pulls him across the line, and starts beating him. The crowd surges to rescue our friend, and O'Neil makes his choice. "LOOK ME IN THE EYES, O'NEIL!" He clubs the person standing next to me, and the cop standing next to him clubs me. <u>"LOOK ME IN THE EYES, MOTH-ERFUCKER!"</u> But he never does. I ram into him as hard as I can, praying that the sea behind me will finally break through the wall, drown the both of us, and carry my friend away to safety. But I am not strong enough, and the wall of death beats us back once more. Over my shoulder I watch one cop walk up to a very small older woman and unload a tank of pepper spray into her eyes. Her indomitable and bitter face is the last thing I see before I have to run away... There are no words that are poisonous enough to convey

the venom that I hold reserved for O'Neil and all of the rest of his kind. These wretched scabs, these Uncle Toms, these despicable bullies, these hellish machines, these dead bodies are utterly beneath contempt. I look at their faces and I feel nothing but hatred. I run down 4th Avenue, ducking gas and grenades, my eyes brimming with red veins throbbing. Training has dehumanized me in O'Neil's eyes, and O'Neil in mine.

Friends, I bit off more than I could chew, I am leaving town tomorrow. I have stayed awake for two weeks beating this monster into shape, and I don't have time to finish it.

Much love always,
Anonymous

I.M.F. MEETING IN WASHINGTON, D.C.

courtesy of Ameliarate

"Never doubt that a small group of thoughtful, committed citizens can change the world; indeed, it's the only thing that ever does."

It's been exactly seven days since I left D.C. and I lay here on my bed wondering how the hell I'm going to write down my experience on paper when I still tremble in cold sweats at the thought of what's happened in the past two weeks of my life. As my hands leak with perspiration of the past, my brain rattles in wonderment of what lies ahead. My stomach growls and twists as a manifestation of relentless hope burns in the deepest part of my soul. Where has this taken me?

I've heard from most of my comrades and have replied with short, heartfelt emails describing how much each of them mean to

Illustration s.2: S26 in Prague

me. The more I reminisce I realize that there is a tugging at my heart longing to be closer. I want to touch them again. *I want to feel you again.* I want to gaze into their courageous souls and grab hold of what we shared and fly as far away with them as my wings will take me. These strangers have become counterparts in a movement that is not only revolutionary in a global sense, but in a personal and spiritual sense also. I could never forget them or this experience as anything less than life altering and eye opening. Raising our fists, singing verse upon verse, or getting naked and going limp were experiences that will be crammed against my heart for eternity.

For those of you who weren't there, I want to portray what I experienced that week as best I can; please bear with me and all the details. There are of course no words that can describe what went on between each soul in that jail or outside in the streets, but one thing I can conclude is that there's a whole new world ahead of us...and this is only the beginning.

A16-5am

I first stepped onto the kidnapped ground of D.C. to a morning wetness that reminded me of other marches I had been to. The air was humid and the streets were damp from the early morning rain. Without an official affinity group name, my friends and I made our way past Farragut North Station to an intersection that held a clump of demonstrators.

As we approached, I could see a group of about 30 forming a circle inside the intersection. There were a few people with string running around the four light poles in an effort to keep police cars from passing through. Soon after, two police cars struggled their way through the intersection while the cluster of demonstrators remained, singing and chanting.

Since we didn't have a schedule to go by, we decided to continue walking. By late morning we had managed to stay together, ending up at a blockade on some street that looked like all the rest. We locked down for about 3 hours in front of a police line. As the gray morning soon turned into a sunny afternoon, we remained locked down; fed, sunblocked, and massaged by our fellow compeers. As delegates attempted to solo it through our line, we gently refused them entry and told them to try another block (even though every block within a quarter-mile radius was blocked with protesters). By 3 o'clock we heard that the meetings had begun and most of the delegates had made their way into the World Bank. We gathered our noisemakers and puppets and headed for The Ellipse.

My group and I made our way around police barricades and riot cops, soon to find a street overflowing with demonstrators. We joined in and followed the crowd (or more accurately put, critical mass) to the Washington Monument. [I remember by that time of day the skies had cleared and spirits were alive and roaring throughout D.C. Dancing in and out of the crowd, I caught an eye here and there, receiving smiles and shouts of support by the blurs of people lining the streets.] As the warm breeze sifted over us, my lover and I would periodically lock eyes and walk arm in arm as if we were in a dream: We could see it, we could feel it, but was it the real thing?

Once we arrived at the park, my friends and I collapsed beneath a tree and dozed on and off for the rest of the afternoon. Everywhere I turned there was a smile to smile back at or a drum to dance to or a voice to echo. I realized that within those tens of

thousands of people lay a common thread: a passion for life, for humanity, and for change. The majority of the participators were there not for a superficial image but for solidarity in a movement that went far beyond a day of protest. This was a day that would continue with us for the rest of our lives. I felt loved by every single person whose eyes I met. Even the cops, who stood emotionless, couldn't convince me that they were empty inside; they were just as human as the rest of us. As I stood silent from my side of the barricade, I searched through their blackness and found a light. Patience was now my crutch, leaving me with an odd feeling of hope and satisfaction. The day was soon over, only to learn the next would be twice as intense. As the crowds dispersed and the echo of speakers and music faded, we gathered our things and headed for the bus.

A17-9am

The next morning my friend (whom I met the night before; I'll call him "G") and I headed towards the Ellipse for another series of protests. As we crossed the intersection of 16th and H St., I glanced at the light, noticing it's green glow, and then to the opposite, which was red. I looked to my right and saw a black suburban sitting at the light, partially acknowledging that it was probably a police vehicle. As we continued jay-walking across the intersection, the suburban gunned towards us, ignoring their red light, and aimed straight for my bandanna-covered face and all-black attire. I slapped the side of the vehicle in retort, not thinking about the possible consequences. The vehicle halted to a stop and an enormous man in a bulletproof vest jumped out and shouted "hey!" as I dodged to the sidewalk (G ran the opposite direction). Once on the sidewalk, I realized it was pointless to run any further. I stopped, turned around, and held my arms above my head as the Herculean caught up to me, grabbed my arms and slammed cuffs on my wrists. I let my arms go limp but remained standing and allowed him to push my head into my knees and my legs into a position that gymnasts are only supposed to do. A group of agents were already surrounding me; one ripping my hat and mask off my head and others yelling at pedestrians to get off the sidewalk (I found that quite amusing and ironic when they were told to go into the street). A cop walked up to the scene, recognizing me from the day before and sputtered "it isn't so easy to look at me now is it?" I remained silent, ignoring the childlike comments and threats of "we got you now," and "are you an anarchist?" After being searched two or three times, I was pushed over to a suburban and slammed against it until they shoved me inside for a few minutes. I was then put into a paddy wagon with G. During the drive, G

told me that when he was running, two vans pulled up and a herd of cops jumped out. At that point, he said he stopped and put his hands up, but as soon as he shouted "I quit" the cops were senselessly beating him into the ground with their batons. There were a few cameras around, one being our friend's who we had lost earlier, but were pushed away by the agents. I wonder what would've happened if those cameras *hadn't* been there...

We arrived at an office building and were taken to the 5th floor (which was private and unmarked as far as I could tell). We were searched a few times and then finger printed. I had identification on me so I complied with their questions. After one phone call we were taken downstairs and put into a car and taken to the Central Cellblock (the "dangerous" jail of D.C.). We were finger printed again and offered donuts or a bologna sandwich. I took the donuts out of desperation for some nourishment and was taken to my cell upstairs.

As I entered cell #43 I noticed that the rest of the cells were empty. The gate slammed shut and chills shot up my back and into my neck. The thought of Mumia penetrated into my chest. My heart raced. I peered around and examined the cracks and corners of my five by six foot cell. The shoe marks on the mint green wall formed rainbows of memories that I would never know; the stained bars sent images of bruised wrists and chapped hands through my head. Hesitating, I gripped the naked bunk and hoisted myself on top. I looked through the bars and thought to myself, "Where am I? What is this place?" As I sucked in the coldness around me, my heart cracked with thoughts of the thousands of displaced souls who had been there before me...and would soon return. Was this the belly of the beast?

I fell in and out of dreams for the rest of the evening until I was awakened by the sound of female voices and cell gates slamming shut. They were here: thirty Jane Does were being brought in. I touched as many hands as I could as they walked to their cells with their juice and donuts. My door opened and a young woman walked in, dressed in a yellow hospital jumpsuit. We introduced ourselves and exchanged stories. Once everyone was in their cells, we opened the meeting that would last all night and into the morning.

The goal of our night in jail was to attract media attention by remaining in solidarity for as long as possible. We chanted for hours on end, demanding our lawyer and a phone call. After awhile, the men's voices from downstairs echoed ours. The entire jail was pumping with hope and desire; we were alive. As voices harmonized and fists and feet thundered against the walls, something changed inside of me. Fear dissipated and trust took its place. We became one.

Around 7am we were transported to the

courthouse for arraignment. I was put into a cell with two non-protesters for the remainder of the day. By early evening, the majority of the thirty women who were arraigned chose to remain in solidarity and sent to the D.C. Jail in shackles. The few that had "no papers" or posted bail ("no papers" meant their papers were "lost" and they were free to go) were released and I was left alone in my cell, a little shaky at the thought of spending another night in jail. I had been offered a sandwich and cookies (after asking for food three or four times throughout the day) by late afternoon and took the cookies. I don't know what time it was when I was finally taken to court but once I was there, I wasn't given a phone call or a court-appointed lawyer. A lawyer from Midnight Special (a group of volunteers that answered questions regarding the legality of situations) was waiting for G and me but could only answer questions, not represent us. We were pushed into the courtroom, my name almost immediately called and before I knew it, I heard "no papers" and the judge told me I was free to go. My charge "tampering with an automobile" was serious enough that (hypothetically, according to the U.S. Marshals) I could have faced up to five years in prison for. You might imagine how dumbstruck I was when I heard "no papers" and ordered to leave the courtroom. I nearly collapsed, as did G when he was told the same. We made our way outside for the press conference and told our story. Welcomed by hugs, blankets and Food Not Bombs, I was relieved, but my mind was still in jail, thinking of the hundreds of others who were still shackled and caged.

A18-12pm

After a good night's sleep, G and I headed to the Secret Service to collect our belongings. My arresting agent told us that he had gone to the courthouse and put in a good word, but the nice cop ensemble didn't appeal to us since they had told us earlier that they arrested us simply because of our appearance. At that point, any officer's opinion was taken with a grain of salt. G and I said our heartfelt goodbyes and headed for the D.C. Jail.

We arrived at sunset to find a group of about 40 dispersed throughout the parking lot of the jail and adjacent hospital; some playing tag, some singing, some cooking in the homemade kitchen, and the remainder mingling with police. We tried to get an update on the prisoners but were only told what everyone else scarcely knew: there were 150 left and no one could talk with them or see them. As the sun waned and a chill grew over the small camp, people gathered for a meeting to discuss the current situation and what to do in the coming hours.

The meeting was short and ended up splitting due to blocks and conflicting proposals.

Attributing to the fact that so many had been without sleep (and one or two men were on hunger strike in solidarity with the prisoners still inside), tempers were short and ideas were taken half-heartedly. The scattered meetings continued throughout the night while food was served and warm liquids brewed. The numbers slowly drifted into the twenties as some headed for their distant homes and the rest either attempted to sleep under a tarp or stay warm through conversation and cuddling. I decided I had too many unanswered questions to sleep since I knew the women and men inside were awake and plotting their demands for the following morning. Later in the night we were told that prisoners were going to be transferred to the courthouse as early as 4am; their public defender had made a deal with the judge to move them, post bond, issue a trial date, and push them out in an attempt to break solidarity. As far as we knew, the prisoners were not aware of any of this and were being taken to court against their will. We were at a loss of what to do since there were so few of us. After many proposals and heated concerns, we decided that we would make signs to tell the prisoners where they were going and why.

Around 4am a group of 15 headed to the rear entrance of the jail with signs saying "FIRE YOUR PUBLIC DEFENDER" and "DON'T SIGN ANYTHING." As vans crept out and sped past us every few minutes we attempted to shout in unison "FIRE YOUR PUBLIC DEFENDER (amongst other things)" but somehow nothing was in sync. Wrapped in blankets and sleeping bags, we struggled to stay awake for the next 3 hours as vans periodically sped by with barred and tinted windows making it almost impossible to see prisoners inside. By late morning, the Midnight Specials had news that no one in our group had been transported to the courthouse. I drifted to sleep on a curb for about an hour and soon awoke to more vans and shouting, but no new information.

As the tireless day went on, the Midnight Specials were allowed to speak more with prisoners, now aware of the potential of being moved to the courthouse. The women decided to strip and go limp if they were to be taken out of their cells; the men were on hunger strike. As we marched around the jail chanting to our brothers and sisters, we heard the prisoners' voices begin to echo ours. We stopped and listened. Hope had sprung loose inside the jail; I was speechless.

In the late afternoon there was an attempt to transfer some of our prisoners to the courthouse. A small group ran to the back of the jail and attempted to slow the van to inform the prisoners of what was going on. Two people were pepper sprayed by a U.S. Marshal and one was pushed into a car, followed by a violent push to the ground (which later put

her in a neck brace and sling). The group followed the van for about a block with only two officials fighting them off. After the chaos, they were told to leave the neighborhood unless they wanted to be arrested. One local was forced to leave even though he lived a few blocks from the scene. Still recovering from the shock of the marshal and his uncalled for violence, we calmed down, reassembled, and talked about what to expect next.

It was Thursday evening and things were back to a calm but questionable pace. The current information was that the prisoners would be released the next evening with the hopes of only a five-dollar jay walking infraction with the option of remaining a John or Jane Doe. There was still a good-sized group outside the jail, many talking with police and others still singing and dancing. The night rolled by and the next morning we awoke to gray skies and wet tarps.

By Friday afternoon, the prisoners were

illustration s.3. S26 in Prague

guaranteed release by midnight. We began to cook more food, warm drinks and gather lawyers for people's stories of their treatment in jail. There were five guards in riot gear blocking the very narrow entrance to the inside of the release area. We lined the sidewalk singing and waving to the inmates we could see in the windows as we anxiously awaited our comrades' arrival.

As time began to drag, I heard cheers and hoots and locked my eyes on the guards. I saw three women proudly walk out, hands held, smiling from ear to ear, approach the roaring crowd. The energy I saw in those women's eyes reminded me of why I had slept outside the jail all week. As the hours passed, women and men filed out, either running or nearly collapsing into the crowd, as their friends and strangers greeted them with hugs and kisses of affirmation. Once reunited with my sisters who I had spent the night in jail with, the crowd died off and people headed home. There was still a man and woman who hadn't been released so I waited with ten others until they were let out.

The remaining ten of us decided to walk around the jail one last time in solidarity and thanks for the inmates' support; we had been there that week not only for our friends, but for them also, who were just as meaningful to the fight for freedom and justice. Following our march, a black van pulled up to the camp and a guard jumped out. He extended his hand and began to tell us how much he appreciated what we were doing. The small group of us gathered round in awe, blown away at the sight and sound of this man's quavering voice. His "mixed emotions" about our cause and his job as a security guard left me speechless. With tear-filled eyes, we thanked him for his empathy and watched him drive away. Dumbfounded, I staggered and collapsed. In my daze of disillusionment, I found the world now flooded with justice. Our revolution had begun; strangers had become allies and there were no more sides to be won. We were now *spiritual* companions that could move the world in places, in people, in ways, that we've never thought possible. The world was ours forever.

MAYDAY 2K IN THE NYC
by Nick Baxter

PLANTING FLOWERS IN THE ONCE-FERTILE SOIL OF THE GARBAGE-HEAP CALLED NEW YORK CITY... Planting a forgotten beauty in the now-desolate thoughts of the cynical, apathetic masses...

...We came to New York City via train from the posh wasteland that is Connecticut this past Mayday, or May 1, 2000, not quite knowing what we were getting ourselves into. Jessica and I had read the email forwards in the days preceding the action, and had visited the Reclaim the Streets NYC website eagerly planning our adventure into the city that never sleeps. However, unable to glean much information from the all-too-insecure electronic medium, we packed some food and water and headed out into the bright spring day.

We arrived at the chaos of Grand Central Station in the groggy disorientation that follows any long train ride, took the subway to lower Manhattan, and headed above ground to get our bearings. Almost immediately upon greeting the piercing sunlight once more we became aware of the stench of bacon. No, not "the other white meat"—I'm talking about human pigs: police. There were pigs everywhere. Every street corner swarmed with dozens of pigs; every sidewalk was lined practically shoulder-to-shoulder with pigs; every street was clogged to a standstill with pig transport-devices, if not blocked off completely with barricades. And this says nothing of the wide variety of uninvited barnyard guests present that day: pigs in riot gear, hogs on horseback, swine on bikes, porkers on motorcycles, pigs in normal uniform and plainclothes, pigs in cars (marked and unmarked), piggies in vans and trucks (marked and unmarked), and oinkers in helicopters. ...And all because a bunch of real humans wanted to make their voices heard and try to change this place for the better. Of course, not all these cops were there for our particular action—there had been some protests and civil disobedience earlier, targeting City Hall and the NY Stock Exchange—but the fact that there were so many in the first place proved the point that we were not welcome in this labyrinth of capitalist greed. But I'll give the pigs some credit—they later succeeded in doing their job of making our day more exciting and rewarding.

It's difficult to explain the type of tense apprehension I felt that day, walking through the gauntlet of uniforms, guns, batons, and shields, all ready to strike me if I said one wrong word or made one sudden movement while passing the time before the 4:30 meeting. My companion and I clutched each other's nervous hands tighter as we tried to stroll as nonchalantly as possible down Wall St. and Broadway—intensely aware of the hostile stares and almost-tangible suspicions of the officers surrounding us. As time crept slowly by, we ended up back where we started, at Battery Park. Settled down on a park bench, we listened to the lively rhythm of a street performer's bongo drums and kept a lookout for any fellow guerrilla gardeners.

After getting discouraged and contemplating the fruitless train ride back home, we noticed a crowd beginning to converge nearby. A young man saw us walking over and whispered to us that it was in fact the guerrilla gardening meeting, and to stay inconspicuous, as the pigs were already beginning to surround, surely itching to slap plastic ties around our wrists and cart us out of there. More waiting and nervous small-talk ensued until finally the wheels were set in motion: we were to split into small groups and make a roundabout trip to the nearest subway terminal, trying to shake any cops or suspicious followers from our tracks. As most of the crucial information about the mission was kept

between the handful of main organizers (and for good reason), my ladyfriend and I basically tagged along with a few other activists who seemed to know what was happening, fearful that we would lose the group and get lost. Fortunately for us, we never lost sight of the others amidst the general chaos of the NYC subway transit system, and even found some adventure along the way. This was because at several points the pigs were able to catch up with us, sending our group running through the echoing bare tunnels of the subway, looking desperately for the nearest spot at which we could transfer and elude the boys in blue. After several incidences of this, a few tense conversations over walkie-talkie with other groups, and more waiting, we arrived above ground once again in Brooklyn, hearts beating and veins pounding.

We raced to the designated site: an abandoned, derelict plot of land shackled by a tall, menacing iron fence, overrun with prickly weeds, dead brush, and littered with trash and debris. Nestled between the nondescript piles of brick and concrete that pass for city architecture and partially under a looming bridge that seemed as if it would cave in on top of us with each passing vehicle's rumble, we found that day's promised land. Despite the immediate ugliness of our surroundings (which included, obviously, scores of police officers in a ridiculous football team formation with riot gear), our eyes were greeted with a beautiful sight that I will never forget: a huge banner tied some fifty to sixty feet up on one of the bridge supports screaming triumphantly, "FREE THE LAND!" With soaring hearts and victorious smiles, we walked with our heads held high past the rows of pigs and into our new urban playground. We were delighted to find out that most of our fellow guerrilla gardeners had already set up shop in this once-morbid meadow and were having a grand time serving free vegan food, pulling up weeds and dead brush, collecting trash into plastic bags, handing out seeds, flowers, and gardening tools, setting up banners, decorations, and maypoles, laughing, playing music on homemade drums, singing, conversing, relaxing,... *living!*

Fearful of being rounded up and kicked out (if not worse) by the cops before actually getting anything done, we quickly went to work, shedding our bags and inhibitions. I found a small group of people tying long strips of fabric together to use with a tall maypole being erected, while Jessica helped pull weeds and clear the area of sticks and dead brush. I soon found out that the ropes we had been making were to be held by each of the participants of a traditional maypole dance, and before I knew what was happening I was running frantically around the pole, ducking and dodging the runners coming in the opposite direction. Stealing glances out to my companion, I was comforted by her warm smile and the look in her eyes that I knew meant, "WE DID IT!" This haphazard, joyful game eventually came to a panting, giggling end as all the ropes were wound completely around the pole and the participants converged in an exhausted pile near the center. Soon after these festivities we resumed the task of cleaning the liberated space and organizing all the trash bags into one pile to be thrown away later. Gradually word spread that the dozens of police officers standing at the entrance of the area like useless statues had been persuaded by the legal observers (lawyers; most likely doing this pro bono) into letting all of us go at 9 PM without questioning or arrest. They were also persuaded into getting the city's sanitation department to come the following day to remove the bags full of trash and refuse we had collected. This further raised our spirits, and just before 9 o'clock the 100 or so gardeners and activists all gathered in a huge circle holding hands, while a final impromptu statement of thanks, congratulation, and celebration was given. This closing was a moving tribute to our persistence, perseverance, and positive action, and an intense wave of joy swept through me as our last moments together that evening unfolded with the powerful chants of "WHOSE LAND? OUR LAND!" and, "AIN'T NO POWER LIKE THE POWER OF THE PEOPLE, 'CUZ THE POWER OF THE PEOPLE DON'T STOP!"

For those few hours on May 1, 2000 we tasted perhaps the closest thing to true freedom that our system of shackles and cages could allow. Our hearts and minds were comforted, at least temporarily, with the feelings of victory and success, and it is in the precious memories of these triumphant events that our hopes, dreams, and will to keep fighting for change are sheltered and fed. We must harness the positive energy that these small victories create, and use it to build stronger communities, form lasting bonds, and execute further actions and plans. We *can* make a difference, and this story is proof of that.

BUT THAT'S NOT ALL...we need to figure out where to go from here, what lessons were learned that day, and what else should be done next time. In thinking about what happened this past Mayday, I have gained some new understandings into direct action and civil disobedience.

My first lesson: planning, organizing, and preliminary work are insanely crucial! I realized that what happened took place only after much careful and meticulous planning and organizing. Much of this I could not even recount to you, as I was largely an outsider until the action took place; I only found out about it via email a relatively short time beforehand, and never did any extensive information gathering or participating until the last minute due to my own busy schedule. There was inevitably much research conducted into the city's unused land, whose jurisdiction it falls under, how to get to it, how and where to elude cops, what legal repercussions to expect from such an action, where and when to meet, what techniques would be most effective, how and where to obtain legal observers, etc.... With all of this preliminary work going into one short event, it is imperative that as many dedicated people help out in this process as possible. This goes along with my realization of the lack of readily available information, but I know that this is because we live in a police state and every mode of communication open to the general public is monitored and invaded, especially when activism or direct action is involved. We can't rely on means such as the internet or phones, or sometimes even mail if we don't want to

risk getting our actions infiltrated by undercover agents or ended outright before they can even be carried out or made effective. This means we must be dedicated and involved in real-life 3D space and time; bring whatever you can to the table as early as possible, and stay informed every step of the way (D.I.Y. ethic in full effect here).

My second lesson: despite the fact that latecomers and rookies will undoubtedly be at a slight handicap, it is crucial to leave the action as open to everyone as possible at every step, for maximum participation and involvement. Perhaps the only thing I didn't like about the Mayday action was the lack of participation of the general public, "outsiders", and passersby.

Although I realize that it's an extremely difficult task to convince any Joe or Jane Shmoe you see around you that it may be beneficial and enjoyable for them to participate in your action, it is something we have to keep working on. We need to find more effective ways of communicating and reaching out to those who would otherwise be ignorant, in order to achieve change on a larger scale. I've realized we need to be creative, sincere, and un-condescending in our outreach attempts, while being careful not to divulge enough information to end the mission if it falls into the wrong hands. Strength in numbers (i.e. solidarity or unity) combined with an inviting atmosphere to the public are absolutely imperative for a successful mission.

My third lesson that I kind of already knew: cops really aren't completely bad, despite the fact that I love to make fun of

Illustration s.4. S26 in Prague

them (especially in this article). Pigs are a huge problem and a constant threat to any action, guaranteed, but the key to diffusing at least some of their "power" is in dealing with them properly. I've learned that if you never deliberately provoke direct confrontation or blatantly break laws for the hell of it, it will be much easier to accomplish your mission—this much is obvious. On a subtler note, having the right body language is always helpful, such as a pleasant, calm facial expression accompanied by confident eye-contact, and hands not shoved deep into bulging pockets, where a bomb or weapon could be lurking (for all they know). Of course, the ones who know the law, and thus cops the best (besides criminals) are lawyers (a.k.a. criminals, in most cases). Jokes aside, there are always good, left-leaning lawyers around whom you should try to contact and persuade to be legal observers for your action, to make sure that the kids with the big toys play nice. As you read above, I learned that they really can help mediate the situation and diffuse conflicts.

My fourth lesson that I definitely already knew: New York City and its subways are like a maze of confusion for a suburban-raised youth like myself. Bring maps and don't be afraid to ask people questions when you're lost. This goes along with always being prepared.

My fifth lesson: direct action gets the goods.

If you would like to ask questions, give comments, or correspond for any reason then please get in touch with me at the address below, and we can take it from there. If you have any projects or actions you've done or are planning similar to this article's, I would love to network with you. Hopefully someday there will be networks of people who could eventually carry out actions like this every day in cities and communities across the nation or world (Fight Club, anyone?)…We're getting close, so let's keep working.

Peace. —Nick
FBizine@hotmail.com
www.fbizine.n3.net

REPUBLICAN NATIONAL CONVENTION, PHILADELPHIA
provided by Chapel Hill local, H. H.

What were we really expecting of the protests at the Republican National Convention in Philadelphia? We were nearly thirty people, all who felt compelled by their knowledge of the current sorry state of the world to make some type of stand – to at least be there in Philly. Were we expecting to win, to shut down the convention, and send George W. Bush packing home with all his bags of money-bribes to his daddy? It would be nice, but probably not. Were we expecting to adventure? Most of us were I think, after all, this type of thing doesn't happen every day. Were we expecting romance? Well, you never really know. Were we expecting the eyes of America see us on the television screen and suddenly wake up to reality? Probably. We all know they need to. While most of us come from vastly different backgrounds, since in our little group we had people ranging from an student from Oxford to a down and out anarchopunk, we all did have one expectation: To help in whatever way we could with the Revolution. Whether we were effective in that is a question only history will decide, but I'll

throw my two-cents in.

Philadelphia was a mad-house before the convention. From all over activists converged unto the City that Loves You Back, and it became some weird mixture between a festival of the absurd, a revolutionary warrior's camp, and a crazy family trip.

Everywhere we were offered hospitality. Quakers, who we never even met and who we called at midnight, let us stay at their place, while others stayed with kind if clueless relatives and myself – I fell asleep face down in the kitchen of some punk house. We wandered about the city, and saw first-hand the destruction capitalism had caused, and cause for hope. Some neighborhoods in Philly looked like a bomb hit them, just empty shells and general despair. But many were alive and vibrant, with community gardens, helpful people and beautiful murals. The protesters were busy creating their own free spaces – like Everybody's Kitchen, where healthy portions of vegan food could be found served from a some type of Magic Bus. The Spiral Q Puppetry Warehouse was one of the more enjoyable places to spend an afternoon, helping create beautiful puppets with whatever materials could be found – proud banners proclaiming revolution, rat masks for those corporate rat-bastards, and over a hundred giant skeletons for every man killed under George W. Bush in Texas. Art seemed to mean something for once, not just some snobbery, but really mean something, and more artists were always needed urgently Everywhere people training, learning about first-aid, what to do in jail, everywhere people meeting new friends, reuniting with old friends, chatting and nervously awaiting the day of reckoning that was assuredly coming. It was quite a feat of implausible logistics just to keep everyone together, fed and back in the housing, but we pulled it off.

Then came Sunday, the day of the Big Liberal March, strategically given a legal permit and placed before the convention actually began by the Powers That Be. While marches can be alienating and boring, with every marcher just being reduced to another face in the crowd, I must admit even I am sometimes inspired just to see there are so many of us – by us, I mean revolutionaries. We mostly mulled around, up and down the street like it was some sort of county fair and we had to see every group to feel we had got a fair deal out of our coming. The speakers droned on, some good, many others just lengthy, but when I saw the Puppetistas break out the mud-wrestling rink between a mock-Gore and Bush that criticized both their horrendous track-records, I knew it was worth it. Things were getting a bit crazy around the edges, and it is usually at large legal marches like this that the authorities manage to coral activists and drain their energy so they don't actually cause

real harm to the system, something seemed like it was about to break. Personally, I hoped it was America's so-called Democracy.

Then Monday was the second day of the Big March, this the Kensington Welfare Rights March, a march of homeless families right up to the convention center that was not given a permit. A permit for a protest – the whole idea's a philosophical crock a shit, but to be realistic some people won't show for a non-permitted event. While I did see these brave homeless activists, they were joined and outnumbered by hordes of home-having activists. The possibility of confrontation in this march was very real, and everywhere we say cops on bikes, cops in vans ominously going up and down side streets, and cops on every corner – waiting for us. Honestly, it seemed like a death-trap reminiscent of the PIC march in DC, in which the authorities would take advantage of an un-permitted march to arrest as many people as they could to defuse whatever direct action was going to take place in the following days. Events sure seemed to be playing into the cops hands – the march went on and on and on right up to the convention center with cops totally surrounding it, with buses and paddywagons just ready to take people away in. I saw lots of little heroics though, like activists tearing the media (who unlike the cops swamped the march to standstill) off the march, protecting the homeless children, and scouting ahead to provide reconnaissance information. The end was anti-climatic, since nothing really happened, but we all went home nervous about the direct action planned for Tuesday. For after the march, we all had a distinct feeling we were being played with by the cops, like a grubby mouse being played with by a strange blue cat.

Overall, the group in charge of the planning for the direct action, PDAG (Philadelphia Direct Action Group) did a decent job, but due to lack of organization, lack of security-consciousness, and general lack of planning managed to set the stage for the disaster Tuesday. It's far too easy to be an armchair critic, so take my words with a grain of salt. Still, while we had thousands of puppets, the general plan was to shut the entire city down by blocking off major roads and generally causing a ruckus – in other words, actually using our right of free speech. It followed the same general game-plan as Seattle and DC, which was to try to physically stop delegates from getting to the convention, it was clear this was neither Seattle nor DC. There were simply not as many activists as they were at those events – definitely not enough to cover the whole city as PDAG planned. Also, as usual, most the activists were simply confused, and PDAG, which could have provided guidance and tactical information, seemed to have only slightly more of a clue what to do? 'Hey, George Bush is staying in this hotel. Umm... it would be cool if some folks would go over there and do something). Also, all decisions were made by consensus. I think consensus works great for small groups of people, but for a group of a thousand, it is idiotic to use consensus, and P-DAG tried to run everything via consensus. While it sounds noble, it actually, what happens is that people just get bored of hearing a few people take control of the conversation, and through boredom agree to whatever anyone says it desperate hope just to end the consensus process. Also, the whole idea of one person blocking or stepping aside for the democratic process, while it from a theoretical standpoint sounds noble, is ripe for abuse. But somehow it was all pulled together at the very last minute, and people agreed at least on a time and a location to end up on the streets. Not being complete idiots, the police knew all of this because they were without doubt at the meetings. The security was almost non-existent, they simply asked you when you came in if you were associated with the law, and they entrusted with heavy responsibility many people who just showed up a few days beforehand. Later they admitted they had been fully infiltrated by the cops, and that the people they thought were spies were actually just ordinary folks getting involved, and the ordinary folks who were even in the tactics ending up being spies. As regards other direct action groups, the Black Block brilliantly posted their meeting time over the internet and in doing so got infiltrated, and many of the older and more experienced direct action activists just got desperate. I admit, while I consider myself fully an anarchist, being an anarchist does not exclude one from being organized, prepared, or knowledgeable, especially when going into a situation rife with possibilities.

Ground Zero: We were going to reclaim the streets and shatter the myth of American Democracy, revealing it for the corporate-run lie it is. Or that was the plan.

What actually happened was quite different – we were outnumbered and outmaneuvered by the cops from the beginning. The whole thing took on the air, not of a brave seizing the streets for the people, but of a ridiculously braze kamikaze attack on Big Brother. From what I saw, there were at least five cops for every one protester, and the protesters, while some tried to disguise themselves, were for the most part painfully obvious by their age, funky hair, and Conflict t-shirts. Most of them also wandered about fairly large groups, looking for something to do. For quite a while, it appeared like the whole Philly protest was one mass hallucination, that the protesters weren't actually going to *do* anything. Finally, something in my section happened: The Anarchist vs. Communist soccer game started in the middle of the street, and right in

front of it a group of brave and suicidal souls "hard-locked" (using chains and PVC piping to lock themselves in a line across the street), so completely blocking the street. Street closed - Protesters: 1, Capitalist Rat-Bastards and Their Tools the Police: 0. Suddenly the mood jumped from anxiety to jubilee, people moved a dumpster into the middle of the street, people jumped onto the dumpster to drum, and dance, and the for one brief, almost unreal moment – we had won. The infamous Goats with a Vote, whose exact purpose seems beyond the comprehension of mere mortals, began doing their goat-costumed dance of joy right next to me. Then the police came, not in the gas-masks and full body-armor of Seattle and DC, but in their normal light blue gear, almost comically biking around us. They blocked off all the streets around us, encircling us and cutting off means of escape, and closed off the intersection. The media were everywhere, and we finally had to almost physically drag some of them away so we could position ourselves to "puppy-pile" (jump on people physically to prevent them from being beaten senseless by the men in blue) They began marching straight at us, hands itching at their billy-clubs. We put our little masks up, and soft-locked (human blockaded) ourselves around the hard-locked protesters. We heard them marching up to us, and we gripped ourselves tightly and whispered words of encouragement as we realized our fate was sealed. Finally, the police came, and they didn't even bother to beat us with billy clubs or pepper-spray us, which somewhat surprised us as we had seen police in similar situations go completely insane. But

here, unlike in DC and Seattle, they had complete control of the situation, so they put on a good orderly spectacle for the media. The cops simply picked us up, we went limp, and then dragged us away against our will, a process that took several hours. Not exactly a running riot, or even a dramatic inspiration I must admit, but a small if fine example of human beings looking out for each other. Protesters: 1, Capitalist Rat-Bastards and Their Tools the Police: 1.

Once everyone was dragged, some upside down or by their hair, into the bus, we began our journey into the twilight zone of the so-called justice system. While being heckled by the police, our plastic cuffs were on so tight many people lost all feelings in their hands, and many still suffer perhaps permanent nerve damage. The weather outside was burning,

illustration s.5: S26 in Prague

and the police did nothing to alleviate the situation by turning the heat on in the buses. A few people fainted due to excessive heat. However, as I was to see again and again, in our darkest moments the people came together in solidarity and brought real meaning to the word mutual aid. We rocked the bus when people started crying - literally crying - due to the pain of wearing hand-cuffs. The police would finally listen to us a bit and take people's hand-cuffs off after we caused enough commotion. We were then taken to the Roundhouse, a detention center, to be processed. Once in the Roundhouse, the atmosphere became elated, when we saw bus after bus of protesters come in off the streets. Even though they bore usually bad news, for the police had completely swept the streets, arresting anyone and everyone they put their hands on, we still wanted more company and to keep morale up. Some people snuck their hand-cuffs off and began smoking, we openly joked at the police and sang songs of Joe Hill and our younger days deep into the night. For that moment, despite the fact we couldn't even tell each other our real names, we were one family of fellow humans.

Then we realized we were one big family together, despite the strange circumstances. The police, after separating the males and females, separated some people they thought were leaders from the main groups and took them into solitary confinement and having them questioned by the FBI. Others of us were processed, and almost everyone refused to give up their name or any ID, an act called jail solidarity which usually has the effect of clogging up the police and legal system to such a degree that they comply to our demands, such as being let out on minimal charges and being tried as a group. This frustrated the police and the correction officers to no end, and they continually yelled at us for not co-operating, which only made our resolve stronger. Once processed, which included the bizarre act of having your shoelaces taken away so you don't hang yourself or other in jail, we were put 6-9 people in a filthy 6 by 8 cell, packed as tightly as sardines. We could not even all lay down at once and sleep – there simply was not enough room. Even though the cell blocks couldn't see each other, we could still organize, chat, scream, and keep ourselves from going insane. We refused to eat the "nutrition-approved" meals of two slices of stale bread with cheese and some chemical Wawa (who ironically were one of the main sponsors of the Convention – wonder what kickback). We threw the bread and cheese out of the cells, made a cross out of cheese and started worshipping it - "All hail Cheesus Slice, Lord of Lords!" Everyone begged the guards to let us see our lawyers, and when they refused we tortured them with bad humor. "What did we do – CD? C-Deez nuts!" was one of our rallying cries besides singing "Solidarity Forever," various 80s songs, "Banned at the Roxy," and "State Violence, State Control." Discharge would have been proud. When our friends led a vigil outside the jail, we began yelling and banging on the walls so loud we broke the jail's light bulbs and guards started breaking down – mentally. We could hear the women upstairs yelling and organizing too – it was very uplifting. We would yell "Hey Women! Stay Strong" and they would yell "We love you guys!", and vice versa. A more romantic moment I have never seen. It was like a mix between a disco and hell, with handcuffs if you misbehaved.

The guards took us one by one to get finger-printed and arraigned. Lots of people resisted, taking off their clothes and going

limp. This pissed the fuck out of the guards, who preceded to start beating the shit out of people. I saw a guy dragged down the hall by his genitals, with a female guard mocking his small dick and then giving him a few swift blows when he said anything. She scratched her badge number off so we couldn't get her. Lots of guards just started terrorizing people, like holding them upside down to get finger-prints and nearly breaking their fingers when clenched their hands. They called one black protester who refused to co-operate "a motherfucking Mumia". Actually, one chant that really drove the cops almost too tears in anger was "Brick by Brick, Wall by Wall, we're gonna free Mumia Abu-Jamal". They squirmed when they heard that. Finally we all got sent to a monkey-court one by one where a judge laughed at us with his attorney (who just sat there playing with his pencil!) and preceded to charge us with trumped up nonsense. We were then sent to a maximum security jail for "quarantine" for a week– after all, the authorities can't have us standing around spreading our radical ideas about freedom, equality, justice and anarchy. Might cause a revolution if they're not careful. We continued to hunger strike, and every other non-protester prisoner I met was behind us, giving us cries of solidarity and raised fists. We even tried to hunger strike with all the rest of the prisoners across the nation against the prison-industrial complex, and call it "Hungering for Justice". But we could never call out – the phones were always mysteriously not working – so I don't know if anyone ever figured it out. I really don't think the brutality was out of the ordinary for the police – all prisoners get treated like shit, and to them a bunch of "hippie" (as they called us) protesters were no exception.

The whole prison system needs to be dismantled – ask anyone whose ever been there. It doesn't reform. Prisons destroy human dignity, turning both guards and prisoners into monsters.

What is far from ordinary and incredibly fucked up is the bail money – they charged people with a few misdemeanors about $15,000 bail on average and people accused of felonies (like throwing a bike at a cop!) up to $450,000 dollars, and people they thought were leaders up to a million dollars. To get out you have to pay one-tenth of that bail, and the rest gets sued out of you if you don't show up in court (also known as "government tracks you down and steals all your earthly possessions, then throws you back in jail"). The police kept taunting us about being a bunch of rich white college students, but from personal experience most of us weren't. While my cell-mates in Roundhouse did include a white, rich college-kids (who were arrested for making puppets!), they also included a concerned middle-school teacher, several home-

less punks, a working-class pizza delivery boy, and older Quaker. I know a guy who lost his home due to the fine, several people who lost jobs, and one person whose dad had to mortgage the house to get him out of jail. This is ridiculous – and they're honest about why they're doing it: They're trying to cripple the movement by ruining its members lives by whatever means necessary. Let's face it folks: This is no game – this is serious, and there are serious consequences to our political power. But we got the capitalist fucks running scared – and we're really just a bunch of unorganized kids.

But we did get our act organized to get people out of jail. I myself, when finally released from jail, and many others spent night after night without any sleep trying to figure out who was in jail, how to get money to bail them out, and how to get everyone home. Some people camped outside the jails until their loved ones were free. It was truly an amazing time to be alive – when I got too frustrated in dealing with the lawyers, the media, and the prison a hippie Quaker women would sit me down and calm me. I have to admit, if I were a religious, I'd definitely be a Quaker. One by one we got our people out, and finally, we too could go home.

Home to what? Let's face it – we were bunch of unorganized kids with immense ideals and passion, and now we were straddled with fines and stuck in the legal in/justice system. In retrospect, Philadelphia was a massacre. Everyone got arrested, the delegates got to their convention, and many protesters had their lives ruined. The cops were well-prepared and we weren't. The Republicans snorted their coke and drank their wine like we weren't even there. The CIA has now moved their main focus of operations from international terrorism to internal protest – now the whole weight of the government will be trying to shut us down. Still – we are a threat. To the punks out there, I am finally proud to be a part of punk culture – punks formed one of the largest groups out there and many of them were on the front lines, doing things others wouldn't dare. To the anarchists, the spirit of anarchy has definitely influenced the entire movement, and anarchists could lead the movement from being one a fractured reformist movement to a true revolutionary movement for freedom. However, we are simply not organized enough, or serious enough in both our ideals and our actions, as we should be. The government has clearly learned from Seattle and DC, why didn't we? They had clearly infiltrated all of P-DAG, and knew our every move. They treated us as terrorists, not protesters.

Sending a bunch of kids to the streets of some city they don't know to meander around, protest things, and block delegates works only if there is a fuck of a lot of people there and the cops don't know what they're up against. Seattle was an accident, neither side really saw it coming. We need to stop being mere protesters, stop looking like terrorists, and become an organized and coherent force for revolution grounded in the people. We need to reach out into our local communities more and plan with them. It's incredibly easy for cops to arrest a bunch of political pilgrims who travel into town for a weekend, but they can't arrest a whole community. Imagine if the entire city of Philadelphia had been there in the streets – then the city would have truly been shut down. Enough jails simply do not exist for everyone to be thrown into. Revolution requires going home and talking to local grass-roots organizers, local businesses, high schools – everyone – about your experiences, your political views, and what we as people can do to help ourselves, if not overthrow capitalism, at least turn the tide on the new wave of corporate fascism that is destroying everything and everybody. Revolution requires organizing, taking part in local community actions, local issues, and forming real local communities. Eventually the government and the corporations will hunt us down and try to destroy us, and we need our communities at our backs. The era of the weekend protester must end now – we must instead become revolutionary in our every moment. Until this happens, there will never be a revolution. As a consequence, we all have a more than probable chance of destroying ourselves and taking the whole planet with us.

Let us look at the supposedly most revolutionary faction in the current movement, the Black Block. First, the black block is necessary. The government strikes back and they physically hurt people. It is only a matter of time before they start shooting people, especially if we get more organized and become a real danger to the corporate Reich. An extra-legal force of revolutionaries committed to fighting, physically if need be, against the government in whatever form necessary is needed. However, right now, due to heavy media coverage, it may very well become a bunch of kids in Conflict shirts throwing rocks at the police. That is simply stupid, and only the most removed from reality of us can really sit back and say "Hey, the people will see the destruction as art". Fuck that. They need to see the destruction not as art, but as concrete and needed tactics meant to defend people. To do this, the Block must be tactical and strike large corporations like the Seattle protesters did with Starbucks, with very explicit reasoning. We should then, quite honestly, spread our thoughts and our ideas through whatever channels. Break a window, and then spray-paint the reason why right next to it. And don't just go out and there to break windows, but break them to cause a distraction when the cops starting beating the fuck out of peo-

ple. The anarchists could be the leaders of the movement. Of all the factions, we are the most passionate, with one of the best critiques of the entire system of relations under capitalism. We just have to prove we are responsible. Other groups don't have to know our plans – that would be compromising security – but they should be able to trust us and be proud of our presence there. The movement in the 60s was destroyed by Maoists, lifestyle rebellion hippies, and art-as-revolution anarchists. Anarchism could succeed. If we can demonstrate that we are fucking serious and fucking intelligent, then anarchism can progress beyond being a lifestyle into a real fucking movement, and then into a real fucking world.

As for being revolutionary in our every moment, I'm not saying in anyway that we should all withdraw from all aspects of our lives except for politics. We should instead strive to be full human beings and realize that

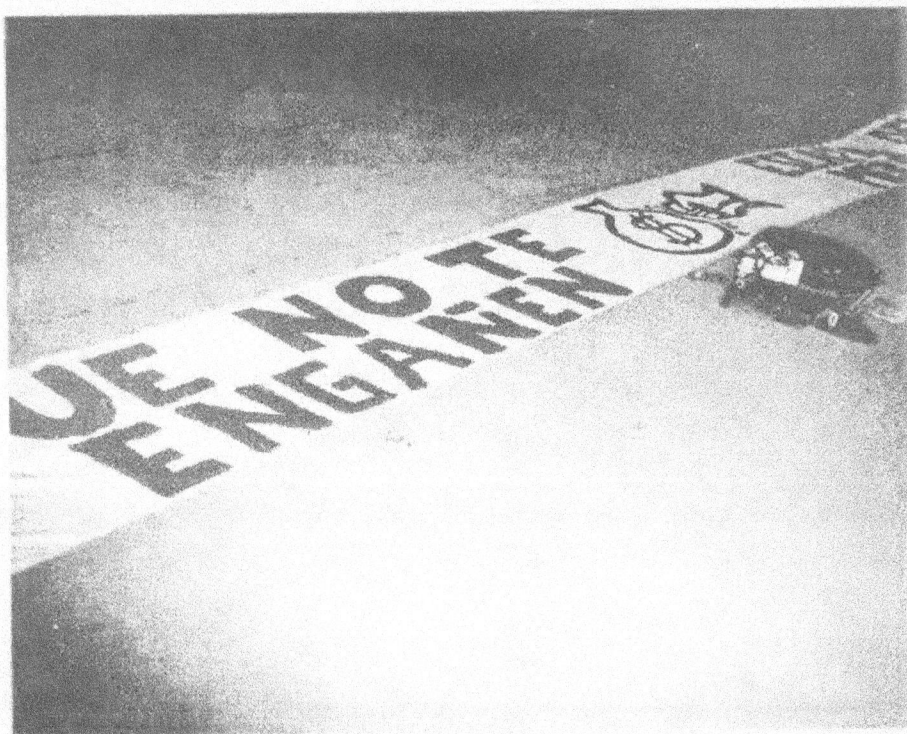

Illustration s.6. S26 in Prague

there is nothing really revolutionary about being revolutionary. Revolution is not some far off socialist utopia. Revolution could be our decisions right now. People seizing control of their own lives, making their own decisions, fighting for their rights – that is the most natural thing a person could do when faced with the situations we are living under. A television-brainwashed corporate temp slave with no dignity or freedom – that is the most unnatural state. Look at your hands. Were they not built to grasp, to hold, to manipulate? Likewise our minds and bodies were meant to move, to think, to plan, to act, and to serve not only our own benefit but to

the benefit of everyone and our environment. I guess in that regard love of one's fellow humans is one of the most revolutionary values of all. If we are to be revolutionary in our every moment, then others will see our lives, feel the deprivation and destruction of capitalism and join us. When enough people join us, either bit by bit or in one giant collapse we will destroy capitalism and erect an alternative based on human and ecological values. We need more than a few revolutionaries, more than a Black Block. We need the people to become aware of their own actions and their own power.

The future belongs to the people, not the big corporations and big government. The future belongs to us. We must simply seize it and never let it go.
Love and Revolution.
Hairball

MELBOURNE, AUSTRALIA, SEPTEMBER 11, 2000
by Dan/NoLongerBlind
An account of life before, leading up to, and after the S11 World Economic Forum protests in Melbourne, Australia.

Background Information / Introduction

No doubt you would have heard of the N30 protests in Seattle, or the A16 protests in Washington. I have written this under the assumption that you may not have heard much about what happened down here in Melbourne, Australia, from a perspective that isn't that of the mass media. S11 (September 11: isn't anyone getting sick of this whole letter/number combination yet?!) was a protest/blockade/mass action against the World Economic Forum which was meeting at the Crown Casino in Melbourne. The WEF comprises of the richest fuckers in the world, who get together to discuss the "merits of globalisation", and (covertly, of course!) how to extend their control over the world and our lives. Seeing as the downfall of capitalism was high on my list of priorities of "Things To Do" this lifetime, I was really excited to be there.

Now, first things are first. I wanted to write this article from a purely clinical standpoint to avoid some of the very painful and depressing things which my time in Melbourne represented to me. However, in light of how tedious and boring it would be for you to read, I've decided to open my heart here. Melbourne was definately one of the most awesome experiences of my life, but for many reasons it was one of the most excrutiatingly painful experiences of my life (which, all things considered, could correlate with the former?). A short time before S11 my girlfriend/lover/best friend/soulmate decided to end our two year relationship (we have lived together for 1 ? years now) and to pursue a new relationship with my best friend and, coincidentally, OTHER housemate. So, while I would like to claim that I am the revolutionary who is totally fine with this situation, living with your ex-girlfriend and her new boyfriend (also your best friend) was taking a toll on my sanity. When we were going to S11, we were all going together and I knew it was going to be hard for me. So a lot of what I write will be influenced by this situation, that I was in a terrible emotional state whilst down there and therefore cannot report on a "textual basis", that I would like to. Understand? OK, let's go.

Here is a short excerpt from an article I wrote about life before S11 for my own 'zine:

"This September, I went on a trip down to Melbourne for a mass action against the World Economic Forum. The trip lasted just under a week, and though that may seem short to some, I can say with confidence that this was one of the longest weeks of my life. Full of adventure, fun and mayhem; of dancing in the streets, fighting with police and and some incredible hardcore bands. Here is the story of that week.

"... I was tired, hungry and in a city I didn't know so I was feeling just a 'little' over-stressed...

"...that night I couldn't sleep I was so angry at everything, I sat there feeling the blood pumping through my head, thinking cold, bitter thoughts with an empty stomach and a broken heart.

"...after a boring meeting and some food

from the gracious 'Food Not Bombs' we all cruised over to check out the Casino, which was where the WEF was being held. Well, fuck, you would have to be there to believe how huge this place was. It's hard to understand how and why someone would need to build such a place for people to come and throw their money away at. But, they did, and as an example of how much profit this place pulls: the three days that we shut it down (September 11-13) it was estimated they had lost $10 million. Fuck, that's more money than anyone needs to feed their entire family over 10 lifetimes, isn't it?

"Come the morning of S-11, we were all as ready as we could be. We awoke at 4.30am, got our stuff ready and caught a 5.30am tram into the city, a short walk away from the casino. We arrived, a motley crew of anarchists and socialists and -ists, clad in ski-masks, bandannas and multi-coloured overalls, some smiling, some scared: we were ready...

"...and over the next few days of intense violence on the part of the police, running, dancing, screaming, laughing, talking, arguing, love and hate I realised that nothing could have prepared us for it!"

The reason I wanted to use these excerpts is because they articulate some of my feelings in Melbourne. It was such a hostile situation to be in, the meetings and convergence spaces we went to were full of untrusting people trying to be as covert as possible in fear of the police, as it was understood that there were police spies 'everywhere.' This unhealthy dose of paranoia was beginning to get to me after a while, and I'm still feeling that untrusting insecurity which was drilled into us in Melbourne. One thing I remember was this anarchist bookshop we went to, and my friend Dave passed them a copy of the 'zine' by 'Revolutionary Action', an organisation devoted to the downfall of capitalism and the construction of some form of socialism. While I am definitely not a socialist, they are awesome to work with. What got me was the dick at the bookshop whose first reaction was "oh, there isn't any Marxist crap in there, is there?". I was just sick and tired of the faction fighting political bullshit, and it was only the second day! A quick note: it's unhealthy to be dogmatic about anything. Sure, anarch-'ism' is a great thing, but if you treat it like it's the be-all-and-all then you become like a religous zealot, like these guys obviously were. It was fucking gross, I wanted to puke.

Organization / Strategies

Basically, there was a very concrete aim to what we were trying to do in Melbourne, and that was to blockade the entrances to the casino to prevent delegates from entering and thus, hopefully, fucking up the meeting and showing our disapproval for capitalism, globalisation and all it's destructive extensions. To

blockade the entrances, groups of people would stand at the entrances 'locked-on' to eachother (arm in arm) and chant to any delegate who came to enter to "fuck off", but usually in a more 'media friendly' way. There were some chants which I will never forget, mostly because of how disgusting they were! For example:

"We will, we will stop you!" Sung to the tune of "We Will Rock You" by Queen (ah, the amount of times we've talked about Queen over the past few weeks!)...

"Shut it down, shut it, shut it down!" Said really fast in some sort of head jerky techno dance music pattern.

"Join our line, join our line!" Sung by people whenever you'd walk past. The problem with this is, usually you'd be going somewhere important and people would hurl abuse as you passed them for another area.

There were two groups of organisational strategies apparent at s11. First, the 'official' "S11 Alliance", who were organizing in a traditional 'socialist' way from my understanding. No, I can't articulate this, this was just a description given by someone for it. It doesn't help, does it? OK.

They organized on the basis of a group of people marshalled by people identifiable as 'marshalls'. These 'marshalls' were supposed to know all about the area we were to cover, about first aid and legal advice, about what to do in certain situations, and they had a level of 'authority' invested onto them for this information. More information on these people later!

The other way of organizing was in 'Affinity Groups'. If you are unfamiliar with this, it's pretty easy to understand - it was basically a group of people you have 'affinity' with, familiarity with, friendship with. For an example of an affinity group, our group consisted of about 7 people who all knew each other relatively well. We would stick together and keep an eye out for one another. We would always organize meeting places if we would be separated and we kept to it. If one of us went missing, we would find the person before moving on.

Each affinity group decided what they were going to do. Our group in particular was a mobile group. We walked from blockade to blockade, filling it up if it needed numbers, and when it had enough numbers we would move on. This way, we did a lot of walking and running from place to place over the time we were there. It did mean that we missed a lot of the 'action' which usually happened in certain blockades at certain times, but it also meant that we were able to keep the numbers up where they were needed. In hindsight, it would have been a good idea to not have run around so much!

Other affinity groups did different things. There were street performers, a huge truck which played that dance music that the kids listen to these days (!), mobile groups, vandals, a self-proclaimed 'Black Bloc' who romanticised the whole thing to the point of ridiculousness and people who just stayed on a certain blockade for the whole day.

Day One

As I said earlier, we arrived very early to the casino and it was still dark when we got there. We had arranged to meet a group of people known as 'Red & Black' as it was safer to be around a huge group of people at this time of morning. As soon as we got there, it started pissing down with rain and my feet got wet there and then. Fuck! For the record, I spent the entire day with wet feet and when I took my shoes off that night, it looked like I'd been having a bath for my entire life.

We took shelter and started to do blockade tactic training. The group that we arrived in, which was basically the 20 or so people who came from Wollongong (my home town, fool!) split in half, half of us deciding to stay with Red & Black and the rest of us scouting the outsides of the casino.

At this stage of morning, there were a lot of huge jock motherfuckers around. For example, I was wearing a ski-mask (for reasons I will articulate later) and this HUGE guy walks up to me looking FURIOUS and says "the last time I saw that it wasn't a pretty sight". I hightailed it fast, this guy was three times bigger than me!

We walked around, surveying each blockade. At this stage of the day, the police looked very confused as they didn't know what to expect. We walked around for a little while, and then I freaked out worrying about Jyoti's (my ex-girlfriend) safety and decided to walk back to Red & Black and meet them there. My friend's Luke and Keith came with me. As we were walking back, this group of jocks were eyeballing us. One says to Keith: "what a life!", and Keith says "It's better than yours!" and he got angry and started following us. He didn't do anything.

We found Jyoti and our friend's Dave and Lee and formed our affinity group there and then, deciding to be a mobile group and we started moving.

Today the police didn't know what to expect, and although they knew it was a non-violent protest they were still pretty scared. There were so many people they couldn't really do anything, and we kept out 2/3 of the delegates which was so awesome. They weren't very violent today, but my friend Luke got kicked in the chest by a horse and he coughed up a hunk of blood (gross!) and Jyoti almost suffocated when police got violent on a blockade that we were on.

Anyhow, I won't detail everything that happened because it would take way too long. I organised for me and Keith to stay at my friend Mark's place and we did, because the house where everyone else from Wollongong was staying was packed with people. We hung out, listening to records and watched an Unbroken video, then we crashed.

Day Two

Today we had much less numbers. I knew this because, when me and Keith arrived at the casino we were told "go to this blockade now!" and we ran down to it. It was down a couple of streets, and so we turned a corner to face about 50 riot cops with sticks and horses and masks and shields and they looked fucking psycho! Behind them, in a small intersection, there were easily 200 police standing around armed and angry. We forced them all back into the casino, and then me and Keith were told what had actually happened 15 minutes before we arrived.

Basically, there was a blockade on one of the gates the buses (which the delegates wanted to enter in, fucking smartasses!) were going to enter, and it was there for about ? an hour. Suddenly, a huge line of police horses arrived, and police on motorbikes and riot cops with huge sticks came out of nowhere and started beating people up to form a path for the bus, and they zoomed through at about 70km an hour!

Today, there were much less people and the cops knew we were 'non-violent' - even 'pacifist' - and they took advantage of this. People were beat up really bad today. It was fucked! My friend Luke got punched in the head and guts by a cop at one of the blockades he was at.

Anyhow, today I realised how fucked the marshalls were. Basically, they were making decisions on the part of a blockade without consulting the blockade, they were telling people what to do (including stupid shit like "turn your backs to the police", whereupon the police would hit the back of your head or "sit down in front of the horses", whereupon the horses would stomp on you) and were basically of no purpose whatsoever. I received more assistance from people in the street who I asked than these marshalls, identifiable by their blue scarfs.

Also, I realised how fucked it was wearing a ski mask. I wanted to wear it just in case I became involved with anything compromising, and also because the police were taking photos of protesters and I didn't know whether I had a file with ASIO (Australian Security Intelligence Organisation) which this photo could become a part of. Anyhow, every time I turned around there was some fucking photographer from some mass media trying to get my photo because it looked so 'violent' and 'dangerous'. The majority of photos taken would have had me flipping them off, but it was just disgusting how many there were! So, I decided that I'd rather not have that photo

in the newspaper and I wore a bandanna over my face instead (a good choice, now I could breathe!).

That night, shortly after I left (I was putting in a twelve hour day here!) the police went really violent and fucked people up. My friend got a broken nose, another has a huge gash taken out of their head and a cracked skull, I know of people with broken arms, punctured lungs and cracked ribs. It was total police brutality!

Day Three

Because of my emotional state, I couldn't stay in Melbourne any longer and today decided to try and get home. I managed to hustle a ride in a mini bus going back to Wollongong, and I got back late on this night, and finally got to lay on my bed and cry, for the first time in a week.

illustration s 7: S26 in Prague

Conclusion

Obviously, I can't conclude this. It's so soon to what has happened, I have so many thoughts going through my head that I need to sort out - as do many of the other people who were in Melbourne. I have a friend suffering from Post Traumatic Stress, who has panic attacks whenever she sees a police car. In fact, I know of people who suffered from PTS just from watching the violence on television, and my mum was so worried about me that she has to take a week's stress leave!

In the next issue of 'no longer blind' (#9) there will be an open forum discussing what happened in S11. I'm especially interested in hearing your ideas on non-violence, the media/protester relationship and basically anything you'd like to address. Please get in touch for any reason whatsoever. If you're more interested in finding out what went on, check out www.indymedia.org or www.s11.org, and keep in touch with me as I'm working with other people putting together a zine out of the forum that will appear in #9, plus interviews and other related stuff.

Contact Details?
Dan / NoLongerBlind, PO Box U69, Wollongong University Wollongong, NSW Australia 2500.
nxlxb@yahoo.com

S26
SBANCA LA BANCA MUNDIALE!
by Kim Bae

I was travelling in Europe for a few months and had planned to return to the US at the beginning of September but the International Monetary Fund (IMF)/World Bank summit (er, protests) in Prague was calling me. A few days before it I went to a festival in Leipzig, Germany where I met up with my friend Yannick. We had heard all kinds of stories about troubles at the border so we tried with some success to look decent and clean on the train to Prague on Saturday the 23rd of September. Surprisingly the border police didn't ask us even a single question and we entered the Czech Republic with no problems. By the next day my friend Derek and this guy Greg who I'd met in Leipzig became a part of our crew.

The next few days were spent preparing for the big demonstration on the 26th and trying to find out what was going on. We went to some workshops and volunteered to help out at the INPEG (Iniciativa Proti Ekonomické Globalizaci - Initiative Against Economic Globalization - the organizers of the demonstration) convergence center. I was disappointed that there didn't seem to be any coordinated actions to prevent the IMF/World Bank delegates from actually leaving their hotels or arriving at the meeting place near Vysrehad. Most of the planned actions seemed to be aimed at blocking the delegates inside the congress center. We were also somewhat dismayed by what seemed like a lack of medical and legal support and general organization and information so we set about trying to figure shit out on our own. By Monday night we were equipped with a mobile phone, respirators, goggles, bandanas, and supplies in case of pepper spray or tear gas.

When Tuesday rolled around the atmosphere was charged. There had been police all over the streets and helicopters overhead the whole time I'd been there. I had been thinking about this demonstration for 3 months now and hoping that it would be next in the string of legacy protests that were N30 Seattle and A16 Washington DC.

Tuesday morning we headed off to the meeting point at Nám?stí Míru square. There we met up with six friends of ours from Germany so we now totalled 10. There were to be three organized marches (blue, yellow, and pink) to the congress center which were all declared illegal by Czech officials. Around 11:30 we left Nám?stí Míru with the blue march, sticking more or less with the black block. We all locked arms and the march kept stopping and starting, people were breaking off to spray graffiti, some asshole fascist/nazi types harassed us...I was nearly exploding with adrenalin and nervous energy. Not far from Vysrehad near the intersection of Krokova and Lumirova we encountered a police blockade. I was pretty far back and all I could see was the huge globe some demonstrators had made being sprayed with water cannons and bobbing up and down. Once I made my way to the front I could see that people had already started hurling rocks and bottles at the police who responded with more water. They would occasionally swoop down a hill where members of the press were trying to photograph and videotape the events but always retreated. At one point it looked like the police were making a full retreat and I, absolutely dizzy from excitement, charged forward with the crowd only to be pushed back by tear gas and concussion grenades. I saw several people hurt, bleeding mostly from their heads which showed where the police were aiming their weapons.

Since this was the first time I was ever in the thick of a violent demonstration I scurried around near the front with rocks in my hands, unable to get the courage to actually do something with them. After being hit by a tear gas canister and some rocks thrown by the police I got angry enough to launch some of the rocks. I spent quite some time trying to get close enough to throw more but kept being turned back by the tear gas and concussion grenades. When 6 tanks were rolled down it was evident that we wouldn't be able to get past them. Some people however continued vigilantly and I saw several molotov cocktails flying through the air. Yannick saw 4 police officers catch on fire and people scrambled to grab their shields and batons. Four of our German friends grabbed a ton of rocks and marched toward the police in a line punching the air with their fists and shouting, "No justice, no peace! Fuck the police!" and I got chills down my spine.

The battle continued for about two hours until the police managed to force us all back down the street we came from. A cement train

pulled up behind us in some kind of feeble attempt to block us in between it and the police but there were several ways to get past it. By then it was 3 pm when the IMF meeting was supposed to be over so I felt defeated. The police had successfully kept us from reaching the meeting center and it seemed like complete failure.

For the next hour or so I wandered around trying to figure out if anything more could be done. Every time the police started to attack the crowd I would lose track of everybody I was with but managed to more or less stick with Derek and Yannick. We heard some people were moving up to the congress center to surround it so we marched up some steps on a steep hill and somehow arrived with no police interference although the complex seemed to be heavily guarded everywhere else. There were some cops there and people in suits, presumably IMF delegates, standing on the roof. The riot police formed lines a few times but would break up shortly afterwards. Nothing much seemed to be happening so I took a nap in the grass.

About fifteen minutes later someone tapped my shoulder. "I think it's better you are awake now." I looked up and saw riot police making a bigger formation than before. I scrambled up to where Derek and Yannick were and a few minutes later the pigs attacked us and started beating the shit out of people. I ran down a path until I reached a police blockade and had no choice but to slide (more like fall) down the side of the very steep hill. Things seemed to calm a bit so Yannick and I climbed back up and saw loads of fuckers in suits standing on the roof, at least ten times as many as before. Seeing these assholes on the roof who are destroying the planet and people's lives drew anger and hatred out of me like nothing before and I had to scream "Fuck you!" at them a few times, wishing I could pelt them with rocks instead. There were now a lot of police behind the blockade on the path and they charged us again from about 20 meters from where I was standing, sending me back down the hill on my ass. This time the police kept pushing forward so I was forced to run down yet another steep hill. Derek tried to grab me as we were running and he sent us both tumbling down to the bottom. When the police stopped attacking us and shooting tear gas/concussion grenades we climbed up only to see a big police bus pull up. We scrambled back down to the bottom just in time to miss the second wave of gas and concussion grenades. Walking on a path at the bottom of the hill I saw some police grab a protester on the street above and aggressively try to force him to get down. A group of us clambered up the hill, taking photos and shouting at them, "Everyone can fucking see what you're doing! Fucking assholes!"

After walking for a bit it was obvious we

could do nothing more, especially with the peace police faction of the protesters shouting at everybody throwing rocks so we decided to head to the Opera where the delegates were supposed to have some sort of dinner and entertainment. On the way we met up with a huge crowd of Italians and all of us boarded a tram to the center which was pretty amusing. When we arrived at the Opera we turned a corner and looked down at Václavské Nám?stí (Wenceslas square), the huge shopping/tourist area in front of the Opera, absolutely overflowing with people. It was seriously a jubilant sight. The McDonald's was already completely destroyed as well as some bank windows. From this point on it was complete mayhem. Riot police were constantly forming lines and attacking everybody they encountered, even tourists and locals trying to leave some of the businesses. I had several close calls and did my best to stick around the area without being beaten or arrested. I had completely lost everybody during one police rush when I ran down a side street so I was alone for about 15 minutes which was nerve-racking. It was pretty dark by this time and the scene at the square was like something out of a movie that looks totally unreal and exaggerated on-screen. People running and screaming, clouds of tear gas, police in riot gear randomly attacking and arresting people - I couldn't believe what was happening in front of me. We all managed to regroup and after seeing what seemed like a mile of police cars and buses we decided it was best to leave the area. Once we were in the flat we were sleeping. I asked what happened to two of the German guys, Mario and Philip. Nobody knew. I found out a few weeks later that they had been arrested and kept in jail for 2-3 days, Philip with a broken hand.

At 11 the next morning we headed off to Nám?stí Míru where everyone was supposed to meet. There were groups of police on nearly every corner on the way there and we were, of course, stopped and searched. I was a bit nervous since I had my passport in a plastic bag taped to my leg which looks pretty sketchy and my bag was filled with supplies for the demonstration. Yannick was taken away but the rest of us were let go. I wasn't about to walk through the dozens of other police so Greg, Derek, and I opted to head back while Marian, Sascha, and Jörn continued on. They were immediately stopped and searched by the next group of cops and arrested. The three of us that remained went to the INPEG infocenter and found out that there would be no demonstrations or actions that day but there might be some peaceful protest organized for the next day. We also heard that people who had been arrested were being beaten, sexually harassed, and tortured by the police. An Israeli guy that Yannick knew told us about a march to the prisons that was sur-

rounded and detained by the police near Nám?stí Míru. Since our friends had just been arrested there an hour prior we figured it would be pretty senseless to go there only to be arrested and unable to help the four of them.

Feeling cut off at the knees we spent the afternoon at the flat, waiting to hear some news about Yannick, Jörn, Sascha, and Marian, and avoiding arrest. I felt depressed, impotent. We were completely immobile, unable to participate in any actions and most of our group was arrested or missing. By about 8 pm the four arrested that morning had been released. The worst story was from Sascha who was made to stand against a wall with his arms and legs in the "spread and search" position for 4 hours. We ate some bread and tofu together and headed off to the old town center where we heard there was a meeting at 9. We arrived to see what was basically a street party. I bumped into my friend Nick who explained that the meetings had been stopped that afternoon, a day earlier than planned. The IMF and World Bank said they worked really fast and finished everything they needed to do in two days but we all knew that was bullshit. Contrary to what INPEG denounced as "fruitless expressions of powerlessness and political immaturity," it was obvious that the violence sent a very clear, effective message. The street party was a celebration - we fuck-

ing stopped the meetings!! My body and mind exploded with elation. The riot police arrived soon after we did and, not wanting to be arrested again, we made a hasty retreat.

I left Prague the next day and began to hear horrifying stories of what happened to people who weren't as lucky as my friends in the jails. Some people were forced to stand with their arms and legs spread against a wall for 20 hours. One guy Ralph who I met the Sunday after the protest had an arm and a rib broken by the police and was kept in isolation for 3 days, coughing blood the entire time. At least one woman was raped. Another was so scared of the police who were aggressively interrogat-

Illustration s.8: One of the many agit-prop wallpaintings in Tehran

ing her that she jumped out of a window and cracked her skull. Others were pepper-sprayed and beaten and, of course, denied access to medical and legal help. When I heard about all of this I was enraged and wished I had done more to fight the fucking assholes that are getting away with this bullshit. Ralph said that what happened to him only made him more angry and more motivated to continue to fight. These organizations must be stopped and Prague showed me that we can stop them. I made a pact with myself that any time the WTO, IMF, or World Bank are meeting, no matter where it is in the world, I will be there.

TRAVELING THROUGH BOSNIA

I slept about two hours and woke up feeling sick. Things had settled during the night but I was feeling rough as shit, physically and mentally. The past few days had been hard: never more than a few hours of sleep, always up early, long drives and problems at every border. Not enough food, not enough rest, we ran on forty-five minutes of adrenaline just to play the music, then spent the rest of the day trying to recover our strength. The fifteen of us crammed into these little apartments and dorm rooms at night, into the van all day; I hadn't been able to find any personal space. The apartment in Klagenfurt was small but cozy. There was a woman who gave us bread to eat in the morning; I still don't know exactly who she was. Anyway, we hit the road to Banja-Luka early.

I crawled into the back of the van, sleep descended and I spent most of the long drive in a hazy state of light comatose. We went through something like three borders and each time you cross a border it's a fucking hassle because we always have to lie to the customs officials and hope the border police don't search the van. But they always search the van. And no matter how thoroughly you prepare, it's always a high-pressure moment when you drive up to some soldier-of-fortune motherfucker with a badge and a gun and pretty much the ability to shoot you dead. Then you hand over your passports with a bullshit story about being "tourists" and hope for the best. You've got to be on your toes, talk fast and look confident about your story. And never, *never* ask to use the bathroom.

Anyway, by sunset we were driving through the mountains of Southern Croatia. It was an eerie experience to drive through these old villages and see the standard of living and think about what it's like to live in such a place. These families were really living at subsistence level, right off the land. Every house had chickens and piles of wood, ragged old barns and rusted tools, woodstoves out in the yard. Your sitting in the back of the van, weary from the constant travel, looking out the window, watching these old houses roll by. And every so often you catch a passing glimpse of a pale white corpse hanging from a sort of teepee made with branches lashed together at the top with rope. "Wait, was that..." you think. Then another one goes by, you realize it's a slaughtered pig, some of them have been cut down the middle, exposing the rib cage. Intellectually, you *assume* these animals are killed for food; but you don't really know, not for sure. You notice there are also skinned chicken bodies hanging from the branches of

trees. Feral-looking dogs are prowling around and every once in a while you see and old man with a hat standing motionless by the side of the road, expressionless, he doesn't look at you, he leans on a cane, he's a farmer in southern Croatia and he has no idea what punk rock is, he has no idea what Catharsis is trying to do. Then you see he has a Pepsi in his hand and you realize what you're up against.

The closer we got to the Bosnian border, the darker it became and the worse the road got. In the twilight it seemed the place was haunted by memory; the landscape was utterly vacant, but there was evidence of terrible things. We passed burned-out houses and apartment buildings, scarred and torn with bullet holes. There were ghost villages full of empty, abandoned houses, cars burned to their skeletons overturned by the side of the road, huge holes in sides of buildings caused by artillery fire.

After hours and more hours of driving, we were flagged down by pair of soldiers standing by the side of the road. They took our passports and compared them to a list on the hood of their patrol car. "They must be looking for somebody," said Matt. At this point, you're thinking to yourself: we don't even speak the same language. We don't know our rights or their privileges. They have guns. We are in the middle of fucking nowhere. They told us to keep going.

When we finally got to the Bosnian border, the sky was black as coal and none of us had any idea what was going to happen. There was a small bridge. And soldiers. We stopped and handed over our passports, which they held for about thirty minutes while they checked us out and made strange paperwork. We told paraplegic jokes to ease our anxiety. Then they let us on in. Actually the Bosnian border was more rational and practical than most of the other borders. The Bosnians were worried that we didn't have insurance for our van (rightly so – because we didn't!) whereas most of the other just wanted to bust us for small amounts of drugs so that they could fine us and keep it for themselves.

Once through the border, it wasn't far to Banja-Luka. I fell back asleep in the van and as I drooled on my guitar amp and flirted with semi-consciousness, I heard the others voices. "We need to get out of here," one said. "Just go, Alexei, just go." A voice told me to look out the window and when I raised my head I saw outside the van a small village of tents, constructed of wood and plastic, camp fires and people cooking over fifty-gallon barrels, kids and dogs running around. There was no electricity, it was dark, like really dark. Every place gets dark, I guess; but few places get as

dark as that bus station in Banja-Luka. We had no vital information about the show except for the promoters name and phone number, so we drove to the bus station to call him. He told us to stay put, he would meet us in an hour.

Standing around the van, a little edgy, perhaps a little nervous, I absorbed the sights and sounds of Banja-Luka. There were various sketchy characters around, standing, waiting on their busses, smoking cigarettes, looking suspicious. There were others who lived there. Bojan, the promoter, later told us that the tent village is inhabited by Yugoslavian refugees who were driven from their homes during the war. "The government helps them some," he said, "but not much."

At this point, I thought to myself: *right now I feel like absolutely anything can happen next.* And it was true, none of us knew the promoter or anything about the Bosnian scene, we're waiting for him at the bus station next to a camp of Yugoslav gypsies *[editor's note: gypsies are a distinct ethnic group, not just refugees... these weren't gypsies].* I thought: "Is this guy going to show up with a Chain of Strength windbreaker and a pair of New Balances and take us to play for a basement full of middle-class Bosnian hardcore kids? Is an army going to come through and start wrecking shit? Are we going to get robbed standing here? Are those gunshots?" Some of the kids playing around were setting off fire crackers every minute and a half or so. Each time I heard the sound, my blood curdled and my eyes flinched open. It was so dark; there were many people standing around nearby, but you couldn't see anyone's face. We waited.

Bojan came after an hour and directed us to the show space, which turned out to be a pretty typical kind of rock stage with a tall stage and loud PA system. Bojan told us it was the first hardcore show they'd had since the war, which is pretty fucking cool, but I don't know whether or not to believe him. Another woman I spoke with told me they have about seven shows a year. I don't know what Bojan meant by "hardcore show."

After the van was loaded, I was sitting outside on the edge of a concrete patio next to a restaurant or night club that was closed. I watched a shadow looming up behind me and when I turned I found an old Bosnian man, the proprietor of the restaurant. I started to get up, expecting him to yell at me and kick me off his property like they do in America. But this guy didn't want me sitting on the cold stone, he showed me to a bench constructed outside one of the restaurant windows. "We don't even have the same alphabet," I said and gestured a thank you. He nodded, and walked off.

After the show we went back to someone's apartment (a friend of Bojan's whose name I never got). I was dead tired and went to bed immediately. In the morning it was pouring rain. I ran out to the van, where Ernie, Josh, Christian, and Alexei were sleeping. It was early, I remember that. There was like five or six days there where we were going to bed at four or five AM and getting up at nine AM to move on to the next town. A week of four hour nights can take it's toll, especially when you're not eating much.

It wasn't a long drive to the town in Croatia where we were scheduled to play; but we knew it would take a while to find the place because we had no vital information about the club itself and no real idea where exactly it was; plus we had to make it out of Bosnia first. We were right to be concerned, when we got to where we thought the border would be located, we found only a very long, very still line of cars. Christian went ahead on foot to check out the situation; but he returned unsure of what to make of it. "There's some kind of activity at the front of the line," he said. Turns out that Croatia and Bosnia are separated by a river and the bridge had somehow been destroyed. So all of us would-be commuters had to wait for the army to set up a pontoon bridge before we could cross, which explained the line.

We made it across okay, but our Hungarian friends didn't; they were rejected, because their paperwork was out of order, and forced to drive all the way around Bosnia to another border crossing. We waited for them all night, sure they were in prison, and had to miss the show. We never carry paperwork with us, anywhere, just give blank looks and seem certain that we can't be stopped. I guess that's the moral of the story.

CATHARSIS SOUTH AMERICAN GUERRILLA TOUR, FALL* 2000
*(that's spring north of the equator, remember)
provided by your lovable editor

I can't possibly do justice to two of the most incredible, horizon-broadening months of my life in a simple scene report, but at the same time I don't want to let some of these stories go untold—so I'm going to make a humble little attempt here to capture a few moments of my life on that tour. South America seemed like another world when we left for the airport (which is a story in itself—Alexei's grandmother died that day, we were driving a van we'd borrowed from a friend of ours who had stolen it from his father, he's on probation and not allowed to drive or leave the state and we were going from N.C. to N.Y.C., then it turned out it didn't have a license plate on it, just as we ran a red light in

front of a policeman...), and everyone who talked to us made a big fucking deal about how we were "leaving civilization" and all this other really ignorant bullshit.

Really, any place seems wild and exotic when you first arrive, because you project your own fear of the unknown onto it. When we first got off the plane, into hot summer weather (we had left shivering winter in New York), everything did seem crazy at first: "Wow, did you see that tree? We don't have trees like that in the U.S!" "Look at that shantytown—fuck." "Oh my god, that's really Portuguese!!" But after we'd been there for a while, it was no more exotic than any other place (in fact, coming back to the U.S.A. was a real shock—everyone seemed so unhappy here, all the fucking amenities seemed so unnecessary, and though the drinking water in South America never gave me trouble, contrary to popular myth, the tapwater in the U.S. wrecked my life for a few days when I got back!), and that's when we stopped being just adventure-happy First World punk kids on

tour and started really learning. I think it was really important for a band like ours, with our political pretensions and so on, to actually go to the "Third World" (whether Brazil, Argentina, Chile, or especially Uruguay actually count as Third World is controversial, I guess—but the way I see it, you can see pieces of the Third World everywhere, in Detroit ghettos just as in small town Peru: the Third World is basically the parts of the world that have been designated by capitalist power as waste dumps and sources of cheap/slave labor), to have real experiences and faces to connect it with, so all our talk about imperial-

ism, etc. won't be mere abstractions. This scene report may concentrate more on the adventurous, selfish sides of my experience, but I hope that my writing in general from now on will be a little more informed, thanks to our trip (and all the efforts of those who made it possible).

I. I stayed up later than everyone else on the flight south, totally carried away by the thrill of setting out for a new world. On the advice of PfM (my old comrade who I hadn't seen since the Catharsis tour in 1997, who joined us for this again, rekindling an old and troubled friendship), I watched a somewhat clumsy but poignant romance movie that was showing on the in-flight program, and cried a little. When it was over, everyone else was asleep. I opened the window and looked down—at that moment we were crossing the northern coast of Brazil, for real, and it blew my mind. After so many times in the past few years thinking I couldn't go any farther with my life, seeing the little lights of that anony-

Illustration s.9: Co.Tra.Vi

mous coastal town winking beneath our plane was a sweeter absolution than I could possibly deserve. Then, at that instant, the sun broke through the clouds on the horizon—and I looked up to see the sky turn blood red.

II. Did you know in South America bands share amplifiers, drums, and cabinets? We always share cabinets and drums when we tour Europe (unlike a lot of touring U.S. bands, who insist on renting "their own" equipment, then take the expense out on the "fans" in show guarantees), but we'd never shared this much stuff before. It's awesome, because it emphasizes a basic common sense point that is so hard to remember when you live in a wasteful, consumerist, selfish place like the U.S.: one car is enough for a neighborhood. One amp is enough for a punk scene. If people can just learn how to be cool with each other, they don't have to each provide individually for their own needs. Now, if we could only apply lessons like this, which make it more possible for people of varying means to participate in making art, to life in general...

III. PfM and I spent a lot of our time in Sao Paulo at what we called the "straight edge house," our own poor translation of the local name for an apartment shared by lots of really cool people involved in the hardcore scene there. I have some wonderfully idyllic memories of sitting on the second floor overlooking watching him play stickball (Taco, in the local dialect—it has different rules in every neighborhood) with the kids in the neighborhood (who came to refer to him as Soldado, a reference to his resemblance to the guerrilla warriors of the gangs in Brazilian ghettos) drinking Guarana (a delicious Brazilian fruit drink/soda, one of the only local beverages in the world that still can outsell Coca Cola despite the latter's marketing powers).

Something that amazed me over and over in South America was the generosity and hospitality of everyone we met: it far exceeded anything I've experienced in Europe or the United States. There are a lot of different factors that could explain this—the continent is not yet overwhelmed with money-hungry U.S. hardcore bands, people who have less always understand need more, cultural differences, etc.—but the bottom line is that we were spoiled rotten by everyone, and might not have survived physically or emotionally otherwise (since being placed in a totally different environment is a bit of a system shock). I'm afraid that we North Americans with our feeling of entitlement didn't make it clear how much we appreciated every meal, every place to sleep, every show set up for us... but we did, we really did.

IV. Before we played any shows, we got to see a guerrilla show on top of a concrete parking deck-type structure in downtown Sao Paulo. Some of the poorer punk and hip hop kids organized a show there, with almost all the instruments plugged into one little struggling P.A., so they could play their music and get together without having to afford a hall. It was definitely cool to see the different musical genres combined there, and also important to me to see how different being a punk rock street kid is in Brazil from in the U.S. Someone hot-wired the electricity to power the amplifier from the streetlights (very impressive!), and though the pigs showed up

to harass people (I saw them questioning one kid: one pig stood in his face, threatening him, while the other stood a few paces back with a gun aimed at his head) they didn't shut it down.

V. Our first show was at a Krsna house in Sao Paulo, oddly enough. The hardcore kids can use the house for free, which makes it possible for them to organize shows that can actually provide funding—the shows we played were a big help to us in financing our tour (we lost $1200 altogether, and it would have been a whole lot worse without the Sao Paulo shows—hell, we wouldn't have been able to go to South America at all without them), and they paid for the printing of the Portuguese version of Harbinger (Arauto) with funds from shows at that place, too. Someone was selling books (including de Sade!) and radical magazines in the courtyard, alongside the usual records and 'zines, which I thought was awesome (a lot more awesome than the local television station, which showed up to do one of their typical "News of the Weird" pieces on Brazilian hardcore).

The Sao Paulo hardcore scene is probably the biggest in Latin America (we're talking hundreds of people here, consistent shows, lots going on), and it's notable for its variety as well as its size and age. It has come to maturity with the people involved in it, growing from the primal disorganized violence of early punk scenes about a decade ago to something much more positive today. You can find all sorts of punk/hardcore bands, 'zines, etc. in it. I'd start listing bands and 'zines and kids, but I wouldn't even know where to start, and I don't want to leave any out if I do make that list. Pay attention when talk of Brazilian hardcore comes up, write kids and 'zines and bands from there if you can; I'm sure over the next couple years South American hardcore will begin to be taken more seriously north of the equator, just as European hardcore is finally coming to be taken seriously in the U.S.A.

VI. We stayed at a farm occupied by the M.S.T. on our way north from Sao Paulo. The M.S.T. (landless farmworkers' movement) is an organization that squats—not buildings, but rather large stretches of farmland! This one was about 30 kilometers across. I'd heard that the M.S.T. has some communist party involvement at the top, but the people I saw on this farm (basically poor families who had nothing, who work in the movement in return for the chance to take a home and sustaining land of their own) were purely anarchist/syndicalist in their day to day lives (if you have to put an "ism" on it)—and it was so fucking inspiring to see that happening, to see land that had been selfishly owned and unused now captured and turned into a little corner of egalitarian paradise (hard work not option-

al, of course, but vastly preferable to a life of comfort built on the bruised backs of others—let alone remaining one of those backs...). I don't feel qualified to write in depth about the M.S.T. or our stay there here. I feel like it would be easier for a native Brazilian to capture the subtleties of what's going on there, and hopefully before the week is over and this has to go to print Tarcisio will send me his article *[editor's note: the next day, his piece follows this one]*—but I do feel like I need to mention a few beautiful moments:

a. Our hosts spend the day showing us around the area: they take us by the houses that have been erected, by the farms where coffee is grown (they encourage us to try our hands at planting, and we learn just how impractical our suburban upbringing has left us... later, passing by another field, one of us points at a sad, stunted little coffee plant, and jokes: "that's from when Crudos came here"), and as we go we collect various fruits and other foods that happen to be growing on the land. It was a fucking revelation that night when I realized that was what we were making for dinner. And oh my god, the stars clear in the sky overhead after everyone else was asleep, with no air or light pollution to interfere...

b. The town calls a meeting to talk with us and find out what we are doing there. We all sit in a circle, asking and answering questions with the brilliant translating assistance of Tarcisio... at one point, I ask how decisions are made on the farm. The first time I ask, everyone ignores my question. The second time, one of the farmers looks around at everyone like it's a most ridiculous question he ever heard, and responds, simply, *"collectively."* Of course.

c. The next day we hike about 25 kilometers to the other camp, on the other side of the farm. The first has been there for a few years, and has been legalized; but this one was new, freshly erected houses with tarps for walls in some cases, and always the threat of assault by the pigs or thugs of the rich (there have been slaughters in M.S.T. occupied zones before, brutal murders on a par with the original genocide of the fucking conquistadors). The people there were as generous as anyone I have ever met, sharing the best of their food with us even if they had nothing else. I spoke (thanks again to the wonderful patience and efforts of Tarcisio) with one older man, who told me about his struggles in the mining unions in his youth, and insisted with a calm, inspiring conviction that law or no law, this was where he was going to make his home and live for the rest of his life.

I was also told about an urban movement analogous to the M.S.T., which squats buildings and neighborhoods, and has won similar advances for the poor and dispossessed, also against the resistance of the violence of the rich and merciless. For those of you reading this in the U.S. and Europe—the M.S.T. is the sort of group that your governments put pressure on "Third World" governments to eradicate, so their countries will become better investing grounds (and we saw as many fucking multinational corporations there as in any Western European nation—the difference being, of course, that *none* of the capital earned by these corporations is going to remain anywhere in Brazil...). Your government counts on you not knowing about their existence. The pressure you could put on them not to interfere or arm the Brazilian government to destroy these groups could preserve the lives and livelihoods of thousands of people, as well as strengthening an arm of the international anti-capitalist resistance far removed from your own efforts. Learn about this stuff if you can.

VII. After the inspiring days at the M.S.T. camp, we crashed right into the brick wall of how stupid and senseless hardcore can be. We were playing in Belo Horizante, at a show organized by my friends Ian (the comeliest man in the world—seriously) and Felipe of Libertinagem, with Point of No Return (in which Tarcisio, who had come with us to the M.S.T. farm, Fred, who booked our whole tour, and Marcos, who released our split CD with Newspeak, all play, along with other good friends of ours); over 400 kids were there, and it looked like it was going to be a great show for everyone. But while P.O.N.R. were playing, and Tarcisio was trying to speak about our experiences with the M.S.T., some drunken punks began heckling him, and suddenly the whole show disintegrated into a bloody riot as the two gangs (punks and straight edge kids) fought each other with martial arts, spiked belts, throwing chairs... it went on for over half an hour, until the pigs came and the whole space was cleared out. I know it's easy for me to say this, since I'm far enough away from the whole thing to have a disinterested perspective, but what happened was really fucked up and *everyone* should figure out what their part of the blame was. Yes, the "other guy" always does dumb shit that makes it impossible for things to turn out any other way, and of course as a recovering macho male myself I understand when someone loses his head, but the question is not who to hold responsible, but how to make sure this shit doesn't happen next time. Being violent when violence is around you, coming from a life of violence, is understandable, if tragic— the only part that really disappointed me was listening to my friends, whom I respect so much, comparing their exploits in the fight afterwards.

There are class implications to the punk/hardcore kid distinction in South America, just as there are in the rest of the world, and they are expressed in some places (like that night) with more tension and force, because the class tensions are themselves more explicit and tense (that's my theory, at least). In situations like that you can see how people get lost in the roles set up for them by their chosen identities: hardcore kids are supposed to look rough, so the punks feel intimidated; punks are supposed to be drunkards, so they get defensive about straight edge kids; and everyone gets so caught up in the conflict of their identities that it's no longer individuals with different perspectives meeting, it's just

Illustration s.10. Co Tra Vi

roles meeting to fight each other without the humans playing them even being present (except in body). Again, it's easy for me to preach, since I'm not involved (I might as well tell rival street gangs in Los Angeles to forget their blood feuds, when their brothers and friends have been killed by their enemies)— but the question is how to act in such a way that you never get involved, so our efforts to build something in this scene don't end in blood, waste, defeat. Fuck, that was a depressing night.

VIII. After the Belo Horizante debacle, we proceeded to the coast, where we played in Vitoria and then Aracruz, and met more awesome people. We were also fortunate to encounter in the flesh a truly legendary character: Schmike. Schmike is known in these parts of the Brazilian hardcore scene as a man who has walked on foot to every punk or hardcore show in the past decade or more. He was at our Vitoria show, and then there the

next day at Aracruz, after an all-night walk— kids pointed him out to me, sitting by himself. He has the faraway look in his eye of a man possessed by a destiny greater than himself, driven by things he cannot articulate to anyone else.

IX. PfM and I returned ahead of time to B.H., to hastily organize a show to replace the one that had ended in disaster (we were only playing on the weekends, when people were free to attend shows—we spent the weeks meeting people, or traveling, which we did by bus)... well, that's a lie, Ian and Felipe organized the show, we just tagged along and chatted. We spent some wonderful time with them—Ian really is the most attractive man in the world, it's ridiculous... everyone in his city knows him, too. Everywhere we went, they call him over, greet him enthusiastically, celebrate him. I share this with you for no good reason except that I'm not quite over it myself. He simply radiates a feeling of calm and acceptance.

We caught up with the anarcho-punks at an art gallery opening, after attending the meeting of a local activist group. There was free food inside (it was an exhibition about the 500 years of European oppression in Brazil, yet of course the refreshments and access were reserved for an elite), and we were all trapped outside, until the guards saw Ian among us, and welcomed us all in. The punks had come to sneak in too (we ate the free food, they drank the free liquor), and we made peace between us. They apologized for their friends who had acted out of line, and said they had no quarrel with us, which was quite cool. One of them asked me if I spoke Esperanto (the "universal language" invented a century ago by radicals hoping to bridge cultural divides), and invited us to do an interview on their pirate radio station.

X. In parts of Brazil there is a war on between the State-organized public transportation and independent cells of vigilante public transportation. A van will suddenly pull up, invariably a minute or two before the city us arrives, and a man leaps out screaming and gesturing for you to hurry into the vehicle before the bus or police arrive. (Ever seen the movie *Brazil*, which incidentally has nothing to do with the nation Brazil? The vigilante repairman in that movie is a good reference point for this phenomenon.) Each van is manned by two people: one who drives, the other whose job it is to lean out the window, screaming at traffic and waving his fists. The State has posted huge billboards threatening those who ride the guerrilla public transportation with death and dismemberment, just to make the whole thing more ridiculous. Marcos informed me that the "alternative transportation" is all controlled by the mafia, which sucks, because for a second I thought we'd experienced some real d.i.y. "dual power theory" in action. Ah well—the same principle could be applied here, without the mafia.

XI. We played in Rio de Janeiro, which is probably the scariest, ugliest place I've been, outside of New Jersey. I attribute this to the fact that it's a tourist city used and abused by rich assholes from all over the world: of course the city is left to deal with all the garbage and bad karma of their bullshit attempts to lose themselves on vacation. Matt had pinkeye so bad he couldn't see, and we all thought he was going to die—it hurt just to look at him, with his eyes crusted shut and swollen up. I was the only one who would even come close to him, since the others were so scared of being infected too. We were up all night waiting in the bus station for a bus out of town, so we could get back to Sao Paulo for our second show there... finally, at six a.m., a bus came. It was one of the more expensive busses, a higher class one, but we opted to pay the extra couple dollars each just to get going and finally get some sleep. When the bus started we found out that the extra cost was simply because they had movies on the bus—and no headphones, the soundtrack blaring out of the speakers at us. The screen was right over my head, and at 6:15 am Mortal Kombat 2 came on at full volume, poorly dubbed into Portuguese. Oof. I pulled the cheap fabric of the pillow I'd stolen from the airplane over my head, managed to finally fall into a troubled sleep (sitting erect, on the bus seat, as we were for up to 72 hours a week during the tour), and woke up in Sao Paulo with my eyes sealed shut: pinkeye.

XII. The pinkeye proved useful, however. We were interviewed on a Sao Paulo rock radio station, by a D.J. who quickly turned out to be our enemy. He was out to imitate the successful rocker D.J.s of the first world, regardless of the fact that they and their whole civilization don't give a fuck about him—and was angry that we were trying to make his show address serious topics by bringing up the M.S.T., music industry imperialism, etc. The cool hardcore kids who had gotten us on the show were a little shocked to find out he was so adamantly opposed to what we were doing, and at first thought we should leave; but we kept wrestling with him between songs, until all the issues that were supposed to be kept silent were on the airwaves. At one point, as he was bidding us a pointed farewell, firmly shaking my (infected) hand goodbye, I informed him (live on the air) that he had just contracted pinkeye from me, and his so-cool professional pose cracked for a second in front of all his listeners. Ha ha!

XIII. I'd also managed to develop an abscess in my thumb. Everyone in our group made fun of me, since I'm always exaggerating things, but this time it was true. I had a fucking abscess and no one believed me. It was in my right thumb too, the one that holds the microphone, the one that people grab and squeeze when they're singing along. We were playing a show south of Sao Paulo, in Guaraja, near Santos—on the drive there and back we had passed through one of the scariest industrial infernos I have ever seen; the town is occupied by a chemical company, which has polluted it so badly that a whole generation of babies were born without brains in their skulls... it took a decade for the corporation to admit responsibility, and even now they're not doing anything for the families affected.

We were at the merchandise table, and I'd bought a pack of razor blades, determined to solve the abscess problem once and for all. PfM held my hand down, while Ernie (I had chosen him because, as you may know, Ernie has had extensive experience with abscesses of his own) sliced my thumb open with the razor blade, as the kids who had come up to buy records or grab a copy of Arauto watched in horror. But Ernie missed the abscess, so now I had a fucking abscess AND a gratuitous incision halfway through my thumb, too! Later that week, Estela (the drummer of Sao Paulo's all-female hardcore band Infect, and a wonderful person) had her mother look at it (her mother is a doctor who also gave me the medicine that cured my pinkeye), but she was afraid to try anything to fix it. Finally, at the end of that week, before we headed south for the next leg of our tour, when I was staying at Marcos' house, my thumb had become so fucked up from the abscess that I couldn't feel anything in it at all (the skin under the

thumbnail was turning dark brown...), thus liberated, I took the remaining razor blade and made another incision, cutting until I finally got to the abscess. More pus came out than I'd thought could possibly fit in my thumb, but after that it healed and I was OK. It's a pretty good feeling to perform successful surgery on yourself—makes you feel capable of looking after your own health after all.

The other event I really remember from that show was watching Abuso Sonoro play. Although there was a lot of good competition, they were probably my favorite live band we saw all tour. It was straight ahead political punk, the kind I already know and love, but played with such fucking passionate seriousness that it swept us all away. Their singer, Elaine, has the most powerful presence when she sings, and creates just through her own self-confidence the kind of safe environment in which everyone is able to feel secure and supported and self-confident. If you've ever had the experience of being at a real punk show, where the feeling of community and belonging and power is so thick in the air that you feel you could live on it alone, you know what I'm talking about. There was an anarcha-punk woman at the show wearing a fishnet shirt and nothing else, not to show off her body but simply because she was comfortable like that—just the fact that she could do that and not fear the bullshit and stares and judgments of those around her was a beautiful thing. The walls were hung with banners urging us to make good on the promises of punk rock rhetoric by living them out, and when Abuso sang about solidarity with our Zapatista comrades, we could all taste the reality of what we were doing and it felt fucking good. Their guitarist was wearing a bandanna over his face, and I didn't truly understand why until I saw him at the rally against the "500 Years" clock the next week, wearing it again, participating in the riots I wrote about in the "violence/nonviolence" article in the columns section.

XIV. A few days later, we played a show in a water park in Joinville, farther south in Brazil. It was an old, slightly rickety water park, and after the bands played the owners were cool enough to keep the water on for us—imagine upwards of fifty hardcore and punk kids running around a water park at midnight after a punk show, screaming and leaping down hundred-foot slides... for me, it felt like we'd slipped through the fetters of everything that was supposed to be off-limits to us, and we had arrived at a paradise beyond the edge of the world. Here we were in fucking small-town Brazil, with a hundred new friends, in a fucking water park, a place I never thought I'd ever be (for financial, social, legal reasons), let alone feel so happy and free in. I count that night as one of the high points of my life in this past year.

XV. We arrived in Uruguay at four in the morning, after a 22 hour ride from Curitiba in Brazil. Fred and I were met by yet another generous host, who took us to his mother's tenth-floor apartment, with a broad window facing a gorgeous sunrise over the river that separated us from Argentina (it was so wide, you cold see no land on the horizon). Again, we were pauper kings, more free than anyone in any office in the United States behind us (thanks as usual to the support of the international punk community, to which I am forever pledged to give everything, now!).

The day after the show in Uruguay, some other friends there took me around the city of Montevideo, explaining to me the political history and current events there. They told me about the school occupations (organized by horizontal, spontaneously created student committees) that have happened since 1996, pointed out one such group meeting on the steps of a building (including a well-known communist party member, who stood to one side, except when he was delivering angry speeches at the others), and explained to me why the whole punk/anarchist scene in Montevideo is 22 years old or younger: there is a whole missing generation of radicals that were killed or forced to flee during the coup d'etat.

One of the places they took me was the CO.TRA.VI: the squatted neighborhood ("shanty town," some Westerners would call it) outside of town. Over 360 families moved in when the land was first squatted three years ago, and now many more have joined. All the houses are built by hand by their occupants, from found materials; the electricity is all stolen from neighboring power lines, by talented (and dangerous) local handiwork. This squat differs from the M.S.T. squat in one significant way: the group that squatted this land was organized during the planning and squatting, but afterwards left all the inhabitants up to their own devices, rather than continuing to meet and make group decisions. Consequently the township has same problems within that go on in the outside world, with the notable absence of police pressure. The police are scared to enter, and a young punk called Gustavo (the Montevideo punks have all moved into the CO.TRA.VI to find common cause with the other poor men and women there, to see what they can all learn from each other... they seem to have done quite a good job integrating themselves) told me of a night when he and his friends forced some pigs to flee who were trying to break into his house (in a purported search for a "criminal"). Police are not well paid in South America, and Gustavo also told me of one policeman who lives in the squatted town— once the squatters set a big fire in the middle of the nearby freeway, to place pressure on the city not to evict them, and his neighbors had

to warn him to hide, because he might be recognized: his squad had been called out to watch over the protest! Gustavo's parents were full-on Tupumarus, part of the terrorist resistance to the dictatorship government of Uruguay a generation ago—they were captured and tortured by the government before escaping and fleeing to Holland, where he was born. Gustavo loaned me some photographs of the punks building their house in the CO.TRA.VI, which will hopefully be reproduced with this article. It certainly was inspiring to see people living autonomously in every sense of the word, to walk into a hand-built house with punk playing on the hijacked stereo, and see people from the other side of the world, who are also a part of my community, putting these values into practice in a totally different situation, and to a much greater extent than I am used to seeing in the U.S.

XVI. We took a boat over the vast river (it was a beautiful ride, the sun glinting off the water—in the middle the river is so vast you can't see land on either side, and you only know you are on a river by the branches that occasionally float past), arriving in Buenos Aires. We were terrified going through customs (we don't look like tourists, of course, and we have musical instruments, lots of CDs and radical literature, no papers of any kind besides our passports...), and the pigs were checking everything very thoroughly—but fortunately, just before it was our turn, they took a cigarette break, and we just walked through unchecked! Thank heaven for this kind of luck, which we had every time—without it, disaster.

The most memorable moment for me in Buenos Aires was when one of our friends took us to an anarchist center, the F.L.A., which had been there for decades. It has a vast library, an infoshop, a large meeting center, all sorts of awesome resources. Argentina has a rich anarchist history—a lot of refugees from the anarchist movement in Italy and France fled there in the earlier part of this century, and in fact there is an Italian neighborhood in Buenos Aires that declared and maintained independence for a year in the 1920's. People explained to us that after the success of the so-called Communist Revolution in Russia, lots of anarchists became communists, because that seemed to be what was working. I guess it's a good thing, in the long run, that the Soviet experiment was attempted and failed, so now we can know what to avoid in our next attempts to overthrow capitalism and replace it with something genuinely free and healthy for all of us (hope I don't sound like too much of an ideologue here). Anyway, the guy who showed us around the F.L.A. was this awesome old man who, it turned out, had once been a race car driver (something Ernie fanta-

sizes about from time to time—at first Ernie thought we'd put the words in his mouth!)... he recounted how one day he had realized that it wasn't the competition he enjoyed, but the speed itself, and from that epiphany it was just a few steps to getting involved with autonomist action.

Something else that's worth noting about Buenos Aires—shows there take place so late it's unbelievable for people of other nations. Both the shows there we played didn't start until after two in the morning, and we didn't play until five a.m., in both cases— and at the second show, we weren't even the last band!! We sat out on the curb at eight a.m. that morning, waiting for the show to close down so we could leave, watching people head to work.

Illustration s. 11: View from Alamut

XVII. Our best show in Argentina was in La Plata, a matinee. After we'd finished playing, we had to run as fast as we could to catch the last night train back to Buenos Aires, and we just barely made it. That ride back is another of my most treasured memories of the last few years—it was a cool, perfect night, the doors of the train were open so I could sit on the steps watching the dark countryside speed past, our friends were moshing in the train car behind us and singing Argentinean samba as they beat out the rhythm on the walls, and I felt so fucking good about what we were doing and where we were going.

XVIII. We were terrified heading over the vertical horizons of the Andes mountains (which were beautiful, oh yes, the most stark and severe, dry splendor), because Chile is the most recent of the four countries we visited to come out of a dictatorship, and the pigs there (who are a part of the army—"military police," they're called—it's the same in Brazil) were trained under the last generation of murderers. [This seems like a good place to point out, in case any of you don't know already, that these dictatorships, especially the one in Chile, were all established and maintained with the explicit support, training, and funding of the C.I.A., even when it was clear that thousands of people were being executed without trials. This is not secret information, it's easy to research, and if you don't know about this shit, you should read up.] The border crossing was elaborate (a few different stops, thorough searches, guns and military bunkers, etc.), but we didn't have much stuff left with us anymore, and we got through OK.

Santiago, the capital of Chile, is an industrial city in a desert valley in the mountains: that means the smog from the factories can't escape and is trapped over the city, keeping the sky a lead grey and making it impossible to see more than a few hundred feet through the air. It's hard to breathe, even if you're not used to it... you'd think obvious shit like this would make even the industrial capitalists more environmentally aware, but I guess they can afford fancy air re-conditioning. Despite all this, Santiago struck us as having a sort of romantic atmosphere, and again we got along with everyone there very well.

If I can beg your indulgence to tell one more Catharsis war story... the last show of the tour (besides a free show we played in a ghetto outside Sao Paulo on our return, after a 72 hour bus ride from Santiago), we were playing on a stage a number of feet high, and I somehow got carried away enough during the last song to do a somersault off of it—and landed in between the people in the audience, flat on my back. I was out cold for a minute, and when I came to I saw everyone staring down at me in terror; Ernie came over to the edge of the stage as he continued playing the improvisation—he saw that I wasn't dead, and kept playing. And (you won't believe this, but it's true) somehow it happened that at the exact second we hit the last note of that final song, the electricity in the whole building cut out.

Conclusions

There's a lot I haven't done with this scene report that I really should have: I should have written about all the awesome bands we played with and got to know (all of whom deserve the exposure, for helping us so much), the specific activism happening and issues being addressed—about the political and economic history of Latin America, and the context from which punk rock has emerged there—about the specific life lessons I learned

from all the wonderful people I spent time with, and the fragments of culture and language I picked up. In every case, I've just been too afraid of leaving things out, misrepresenting things, spelling names wrong, revealing my typical North American ignorance. Had I worked on this soon after my return from that continent, I could have at least had the poetry of recent experience at my disposal to capture those wonderful, pure moments I mention so clumsily in this piece... but alas, I'm writing this the day before the deadline to get this issue laid out and printed, and I'm afraid I can't do better than this. Besides, to really do those two months justice, it would take a whole book. The one thing I can say for my article is that it captures the edges of my personal experiences there, which you can't find out about anywhere else. There are others much more qualified than I am to teach about the way imperialism works, the function of class and race in nations like Brazil, the latest incredible bands in Santiago. Please, seek them out, if anything in this scene report has interested you. I'll be addressing some of those issues myself in my future writing, too—and, as always, the best way to follow up on this article would be to just corner me next time I'm passing through your town, and ask me to tell you how to get a visa to enter Brazil, or exactly what I mean when I talk about "hardcore imperialism," or where the best old school hardcore band in Buenos Aires gets cheap vegan pizza.

BRAZIL AND THE M.S.T.
Edited and provided generously by Tarcisio

1. The MST – Landless Workers Movement
General info to contextualize the reader...

As you may know well, Brazil is one of the richest countries in the world. It is a huge territory, with plenty of natural resources, full of rivers and fertile lands. The problem is that all the wealth is concentrated in the hands of a real small – but powerful – elite: 1% of the people in this country controls more than 50% of the wealth it produces; 32 million Brazilians suffer hunger and 65 millions are under fed. The results... you may know it as well. Brazil is one of the most miserable nations in the world, equal to many African countries in which natural resources are extremely scarce.

If you take your world map you will see that Brazil is almost as big as Europe. Most of the population is concentrated in the big urban areas, which are mainly distributed along the coast, while the countryside remains a huge amount of land with very few inhabitants. These lands are mostly very fertile but, as we have already said, a small elite controls them. This fact recalls to the period of colonization: after reaching the Brazilian coast, the

Portuguese divided the territory into 15 big areas and handed it in to a few members of the royalty. These people distributed the land among their relatives and friends – people from the Portuguese elite.

From the 16th century to our present days, something has changed, but the basic structure remains the same: a small minority controls the land, most of which is kept for the only purpose of economic speculation. Less than 3% of the population owns two-thirds of Brazil's arable land. Thus we have huge areas of unproductive lands, while millions of people in the countryside and in the big cities live a life of misery, with no perspectives to find any kind of work at all. While 60% of Brazil's farmland lies idle, 25 million peasants struggle to survive by working in temporary agricultural jobs.

This situation has forced poor people to get organized and start struggling to take back what has been stolen from them. The Landless Workers Movement (Movimento dos Trabalhadores Sem-terra - MST) is an attempt to do it. It is a social struggle, which is trying to achieve agrarian reform for poor peasants all over Brazil's territory. Hundreds of thousands of landless peasants have taken onto themselves the task of carrying out a long-overdue land reform in a country mired by an overly skewed land distribution pattern. The Movement started many years ago and has grown greatly ever since, at such a level that they became nowadays a terrible thorn in the side of Brazilian federal government.

The MST is transforming the lives of thousands of families from north to south, from east to west. It's an autonomous mass movement, without any political or religious link. The main goals of the movement are the land, the agricultural reform, social justice and the schooling of rural workers. Their actions go from occupying unproductive lands to setting up public demonstrations in big cities, from mobilizing extensive marches in the countryside to carrying out raids of big supermarkets. As their power increases more and more, it has became impossible for the Federal Government, which is responsible for the agrarian reform, to simply ignore them as they usually do to the demands of poor people. MST became a real threat and the government knows it.

And of course, the more the struggle for human emancipation grows, the more violent State repression becomes, and we see that the so-called democratic nations are not democratic at all. The MST has been bombed from all sides: 1) by the media, through deliberate lying, cheating and manipulation of public opinion (note: recently, our biggest weekly magazine, Veja – a Brazilian version of Times – has published a special report about the MST; the cover of the magazine, with a dark/red background and the picture of a

MST member in the first plan looking like a crazy fuck, showed the following line: "The tactic of riot: how the MST wants to transform chaos into a socialist revolution". Do we need to tell anything more about how tendentious was this report?); 2) by the government, through the ostensible police and army repression; and 3) by the landlords, through the building of paramilitary groups, seeking to assault, threaten and kill peasants who are occupying their lands. In the past 10 years, more than 1000 people have been killed as a result of land conflicts in Brazil.

2. The Visit
by Isadora and Tarcísio

When Catharsis was on tour on Brazil they decided to see personally one of the MST occupations, and since we had never seen any of these as well we decided to get off our fucking asses and go there with them – a decision which we will never regret. We left São Paulo on Tuesday at night, we took a bus to a small town and, from there, we had to drive about 40 minutes in a cab – which looked like an old van – to the MST farm "Primeiro do Sul" (note: This encampment is called "Primeiro do Sul" – "South's first one" – because it was the first land MST legally gained in the south of the state of Minas Gerais, which is bigger than many European countries).

The MST has two kinds of occupations: the settlements, that is, the places in which the fight for the land was successful, and the MST members were given the legal right to remain on the land; and the encampments, that is, occupations in which people are still fighting against the landlords in the Judiciary, waiting for the final decision of the judge. The first place we visited was a settlement.

A family that was known by one of our friends, Isabela, welcomed us. They were a couple – Tani Rose and Magela – and one kid – Ipê – and received us in the kindest way. After leaving our bags in the rooms, we all sat around the kitchen, and while the food – rice, beans, and some vegetable – was cooking we had a nice conversation. Magela is one of the state secretaries of MST. We talked to him about Brazilian reality and about important facts on MST history. Tani Rose kept coming into our conversation, talking about some aspects of Magela's personality: "He doesn't like religion at all. He is pretty much an anarchist," she would tell us. [editor's note from Brian: When the topic of religion first came up in our discussion, I was really careful with it, because I had no idea how this guy saw religion or what role it played in his life. So it ended up that HE told ME I was being too soft on religion, which was pretty funny and ironic!]

It was our first candle-light dinner in years. But, wait a minute… not in a romantic sense. They use candles because they do not have electricity. Their home is humble, there is no

electric devices as TV set, refrigerator or whatever. They have only a small oven to cook their meals and a small radio that works with a battery. And that is all. On the other hand, they have something that people from big cities as we are, with all our apparatus – from TV sets, CD players and computers to washing machines, guitar amplifiers, etc. – could never dream to possess: they have freedom and dignity.

(note: perhaps it would be naive to say they are free. But one must consider that they have conquered much more freedom than we do because they were able to take control of the means of production - in their particular case, the land. And they certainly have dignity because this freedom is a result of a great collective effort and militancy).

In the next day we hung around the farm. In the morning, after taking some tea and fruits, we went to visit some plantations and other houses. The main agricultural activity there is coffee because it is one of the most valuable products in the market. They plant coffee in order to sell it and make some money to buy the equipment they can't produce by themselves: tractors, agrarian machines, gas. We went firstly to a coffee plantation, in which we could see – and help a little bit – how to plant the seedlings in the soil. After that, we came to visit some other houses, passing through small roads and many other plantations. All those pieces of land had been equally divided among the members of

that occupation, by the time when they conquered the land legally, according to the needs of each family. So everyone has their own piece of land to grow their crop, which is partially sold and partially consumed by them.

During our walk, we chose what we would have for lunch: edible vegetables were everywhere and the sensation that we didn't have to buy – or steal – to eat was incredible. Food was just around, all we had to do was choose a vegetable and pick it up from the land. We felt that we could really be in control of our life in that place. We felt that the survival of the landless workers on "Primeiro do Sul" depends only on themselves and on their own work. Maybe that is why the Brazilian elite is so afraid of the MST.

Illustration s.12: Covert Crimethinc. opertaives on their way to Alamut

At night, after having dinner, we had a meeting with the whole community of the farm. They were all very curious about us. First of all, because not so many people go to distant farms like that – unless members from other MST occupations in the region; secondly, because they knew that there were some foreign people among us. But we, also, were very much excited to have the opportunity to know those people personally, to talk to them, to share information. And so we went.

For that night, we reserved a special place in our memory. Around 8pm we all went to a big hall in front of an abandoned house, in which we sat and talk to more than 30 peasants for about two hours. There were all kinds of people, from the elderly, who could barely talk, to kids, playing around frenziedly. It was one of the most exciting experiences we ever had. We were mediating the conversation. Sometimes, it was the peasants asking their doubts and curiosities about the USA; sometimes the guys from Catharsis wanting to know about the life in the occupation.

We've learned that, on the settlement, all the decisions are taken collectively, and that each person is responsible for an aspect of the administration of the farm. The production and the profit from the coffee sale are divided between all equally. They have some special rules there, and one of them is to respect nature (there are two ecological reservations on the settlement area). One of the landless workers told the guys from Catharsis that the competition against multinational companies was very unfair and harmful to them. Another one asked if they had class struggle in USA, or any movements that are similar to the MST. They all wanted to know about the American distribution of land and about American social movements.

How moving it was for us to see poor peasants, which had barely access to education, so aware about our present political situation! In Brazilian big cities, most part of the poor population is completely indoctrinated: they have given up to pessimism or, even more frequently, to religion determinism. The MST, on the other hand, has created a structure in which poor peasants have been given not simply a common education, but a critical one. We left the meeting deeply affected for what we have seen and heard there. The experience was inspiring for ourselves, and we are sure, for all our friends as well.

In the next day – our last one there – we woke up very early in the morning and walked from the settlement to a MST encampment near there (well, not so near...). We walked for about 2:30 hours to get to the encampment! But it wasn't tiring or boring; it wasn't boring at all! Nice conversations and the beautiful vision of plantations had filled our minds, and at 12pm we were able to see the red flag of MST trembling: we had reached the encampment.

The fact that it was not a settlement means that the situation over there was much tenser. In the settlement, since the land already belongs to the MST militants, we could find many houses being built, while old constructions were being reformed, and we could find each family growing their own piece of land. In the encampment it is not like that. Instead of houses they have provisory tents, built with canvas and bamboo; small pieces of land are cultivated but most of what is consumed still comes from the city; and the hope for a positive response from the Judiciary is high.

Zacarias, one of the leaders of that occupation, told us that the legal recognition of that encampment was dangerous to the elite of Campo do Meio, the city next to it. First of all, because once they gain title to the land, the MST families living on Campo do Meio area would be the majority of the electorate. In a second place, because most of the rivers and lakes that supply water to Campo do Meio and other cities around it were on those lands. Finally, because that elite was mostly composed by landowners that were interested on getting those lands for themselves.

As a consequence, that MST encampment was suffering all kinds of attacks. The main victims were the leaders of the encampment – most of them waiting to be judged for two or three accusations. All the crimes that happened on that area were attributed to the MST members – we don't think we need to mention that some of them happened specifically with that intention. Zacarias told us that Campo do Meio police came by the end of 1999 and destroyed almost everything they had produced during the year. We asked him about the use of violence on their struggle: "We want to do things peacefully but, in case we don't have an alternative..."

Even so, the atmosphere in the encampment could not be better. Just as in the settlement, everyone there very well welcomed us. We were divided into three different tents, so that it could be easier for them to provide food and shelter for us.

The first image that comes to our minds, after getting into one of these tents, was the picture of Che Guevara, black and white, hanging over a bed. That recalled us again the fact that we were not in a common, but a very special place; I'm never tired of repeating that: in São Paulo, just go to a poor place you will find the picture of Jesus Christ or Ayrton Senna. But, hey, not there! They had fucking Che on their wall!

After taking another delicious lunch we kept talking to the people there. One old guy, Mr. Ramon, told us that they were just waiting for another sentence from the judge, and in the afternoon they were going to the city, full of hope that the land might be finally given back for those who really deserve it. On his last sentence, the judge ironically decided that they could remain on that area, but they could not work on the land. Afterwards, when leaving back to São Paulo, we met Mr. Ramon in the city again; unfortunately, the response from the judge has not been positive yet; but it wasn't enough to take the smile out of his face or the hope from his eyes: "It doesn't matter. We can wait."

In our last moments of this trip, we had a great time in a lake near the Camp. The weather was hot and Tarcísio spent some hours in the afternoon trying to perform Ernie's incredible *flying retard* "jump" *[editors' note, as requested by the authors: in this special diving maneuver, Ernie leaps up and forward, grabs his ankles, and flies head-first into the* *water with his legs and arms out behind him like the wings of some extinct, absurd fishing-bird. I'm sure Ernie means no offence to all you retards out there.]*. At last, he wasn't able to do it 100% - his best jump was like 80% , and it made him a bit frustrated. The sun was setting and we had to move on, back to São Paulo... back to hell.

Anyway... any kind of bad feeling could never overwhelm our great excitement for being able to know a revolution taking place before our very eyes.

3. A Personal Comment
by Tarcísio

What shape may revolution take? This question has been in my mind for quite a while. Some years ago, I had already tried to provide a reasonable answer for myself but nowadays, looking back and rethinking the issue, as well as observing recent historical events that are taking place all around the world, I believe my opinion slightly changed.

One of the most important things I have learned in the past few years is the importance of seeing social phenomena historically. This means to understand that historical circumstances of time and space cannot be excluded from the process of interpretation of events. It seems to be pretty obvious but, personally, I have always found myself prone to fall in the very same mistake, again and again: trying to provide absolute solutions for problems that are circumstantial.

That is why I believe that I was pretty naive by spending my time thinking of what shape a world revolution might take. Because we don't know. We can't know. It depends on several different inter-related aspects: where and when is it taking place and what are the social, economic, political and geographical conditions involved. Besides, revolution is not something that we can specify: "now it just started; now it is all over." Revolution is not an event; it is a process.

But what all this has to do with the subject of this report? Well, in this text me and Isadora tried to come up with some information about one of the most important social movements in Brazil nowadays, the MST. But I believe it is important for everyone reading this to keep in mind that this struggle is very specific to Brazilian reality. The whole idea behind the MST may sound absurd to any American or European person, if they think about it in terms of their own reality: highly mechanized rural areas, few amount productive fields, relative social equality, effective preventing politics from property speculation and so on.

The best lesson we could take from MST, in my opinion, is not that agrarian reform should be tried everywhere. Rather, we learn the importance of striving to understand deeply the historical circumstances of the places we live in, so that we are able to come up with real effective, solid, threatening counter-attack to capitalism advance. If the MST is getting any success nowadays it is because – besides, of course, the tireless militancy of its members – they were able to interpret Brazilian reality as no one else could.

For more information, or to discuss this subject further, contact Tarcisio at the Point of No Return address.

WORKING IN CHICAGO'S GAY NIGHT CLUBS
Culture and Hedonism
By Eric Boehme

I see him approach, making a beeline from the dancefloor just as I come behind the bar. I'm used to this now but I still cringe inside. I know I'm gonna have to kiss him. I know his lips will linger just a little too long and, if he can get his arm behind the bar, he's probably gonna grab my ass. But I'm gonna let him do it because last time he was here, he left me $20 after buying just one drink. I went home with over $300 that night, all tax free, all cash. And even though I've been working in all kinds of jobs since I was fifteen, this was the most money I'd ever seen in the quickest amount of time. I bought my first computer that summer, I saved money to go back to school and I took a three week trip to Paris to visit my then-partner. Sometimes it really sucked. Like being at the bar until 6 AM. Other times it was cool, talking to some friends who would come in, hanging around and not doing too much. Every night though, it was interesting.

This is not a Commodity
nor a Spectacle: These are People's Lives.

First lemme start with a disclaimer. I wondered if I wanted to write about working in Chicago's gay night clubs because I thought that some of the things I saw, if I wrote about them, would come across as a kind of judgment on the behavior and lifestyle of folks I worked with and I saw at the clubs. This is not meant as a judgment on the way people want to live their lives. Neither is this an attempt by me to commodify gay club lifestyle by writing about it or make a spectacle, an "under-cover expose" of the "deviant" lifestyle of gay club guys. The facts are that I needed money for graduate school and at that time, for all intents and purposes, I lived as a gay club guy. My housemates were gay, many of my friends were either gay, straight or ambisexual kidz who liked hanging out in gay places. Finally, I worked so much that I was constantly around gay club culture. However at the time, my partner was a woman I was

committed to monogamously and spiritually. And I even though it was interesting for me, I didn't really like the club scene. Hopefully, this won't color the way I tell what I saw and participated in during that year.

The Clubs, The Crowds,
The Clothes, and The Chests

I worked at a couple of clubs in Chicago's "Boys' Town" for over a year, starting in 1996. I worked mostly at Fusion, formerly called the Vortex. At the time, it was one of the largest gay/mixed dance clubs in Chicago, with two different dance floors and four separate bars on an upper and a lower level. Manhole was

Illustration s 12. Path that eventually leads to Alamut

a smaller, two room leather bar run by the same guys who ran Fusion. Our clientele at both places was pretty varied but there were basically four crowds that came through: the leather crowd (predominant at Manhole), the shirtless-and-jeans, water-drinking, circuit-club boys, the "freakshow" club crowd (drag queens, trannies, costume wearing hetero club kidz), and regular gay guys and girls. At Fusion, a fifth group was regularly seen: straight women who came to dance in a place where they wouldn't be constantly bothered by men trying to pick them up. I did a variety of jobs but mostly I bartended and did what in the industry is called bar-backing. When I bartended, I would mix and get

drinks and try to develop a repeat clientele who knew me and would come to my bars rather than the other guyz who worked there. When I bar-backed, I worked for the bartenders, filling up their coolers with beer and ice, stocking glasses and supplies, and making sure the liquor guns were full in the back. Business was usually pretty crazy there—very high volume, very stress inducing. We would try to attract business by having performances and theme parties. At Fusion, Ru-Paul played the opening, Debbie Harry performed, and we had some of the International Male Leather Events. We wore theme-specific costumes (the over-riding theme being less cloth-ing is more), leather for the leather events (vinyl for me), loin-cloths for the monthly "Animal Parties," boxers with hearts on them for Valentine's Day. Even the three or four straight bartenders never wore a shirt behind the bar. Everybody worked on their bodies (some obsessively) because this is how we made our tips. It made me realize that sometimes men have just as many body issues as straight women do. Guys come to your bar rather than others' because they like the way you look or because you have developed a continuing relationship with them where they give you tips in return for drinks, kisses, ass, nipple, waist or bicep grabs, a quick conversation, flirting, and sometimes complimentary.

drinks or shots. Chances are, your biggest tippers are the ones who you give the most stuff too, either in terms of drinks, your body, or your conversation. I finally knew what it was like for women walking around in a crowded hetero club cuz I got grabbed and pinched everywhere I went.

Being the Fluffer:
Getting Him Ready for the Next Scene

Because I was also a bar-back, I had a unique relationship to the bartenders when I wasnt bar-tending. In many ways, that meant that I was the production-assistant, gopher-type guy who had to go all around the club doing different errands for people. I'd take a drink to the DJs in the booth and then carry four cases of beer through a shoulder-packed club shouting in my most menacing voice for people to move. Because my tips came from the bartender, I'd have my own little mini top-and-bottom relationships going with the bartenders. I'd be doing stuff like going to get a bandage for someone or delivering a note, or when it was slow, I became some anal-retentive bartender's re-decorator. Some guys wouldn't care what I did as long as they had beer, ice, and glasses, some guys wanted everything around them set up and placed in a very particular way. It was like I was fluffing them so that they could go and display themselves for their customers, so that they looked good to attract tipping guys.

Drugs and Sex: Vanilla and Leather

Everyone was just wasted on drugs. Either frenetically trying to control everything around them, or doing as much as possible to run around and have a good time rather than doing their job. I saw all kinds of sniffing and snorting and puffing from people who went to the club as well as most people who worked at the club, who used some kind of drug for entertainment or to keep them awake and up for so late into the morning. The most popular drugs I saw were coke and crystal meth, ecstasy and K—everything up to keep you dancing. Even the owners were all wired. Many a time I'd try to talk to someone running the joint and they would be sweating and talking faster than a firing AK-47, trying to encompass far too many thoughts, suggestions, and mostly orders into a jumbled train-wreck of sentences.

Sex and drugs were everywhere. Indirectly, I guess we as bar-tenders were doing a kind of sex work by wearing hardly any clothes and exchanging some level of physical interaction for tips. But I'd walk around on the dance-floor, in the bathrooms, or in the dark corners and couches upstairs and run into all kinds of people, both gay and straight getting it on. I've seen guys getting jerked off, giving head, and hetero couples having intercourse right on the dancefloors. I was introduced to

leather sexuality, to codewords and practices, top and bottom roles and bondage techniques. During the International Male Leather competition, there was a shaving and boot-blacking booth next to my bar where men would get their crotch and assholes shaved or their boots shined by a big man with a handlebar mustache wearing nothing but a leather biker hat and a leather apron. One time a guy asked him to urinate on his boots. A swing was set up in another bar for incapacitation and whippings, while tops tattooed their submissive slaves at a table next to the downstairs bar. I overheard a conservation in the line for the bathroom that basically consisted of one guy asking another to urinate in his hat, which he then put on his head.

Jackie told me I should wear my armband on the left. I think I would consider myself a top and he said that tops wouldn't try to pick me up if I was representing myself as a top. It was interesting to meet men in leather culture who considered themselves either tops or bottoms. As with the gender roles of men and women, the dominant and submissive relationship was a kind of guideline for action rather than a rigid set of roles. Traditionally you think top and bottom and you think the top is the one who is dominant and in control. Yet youd meet a top who would initially come off really tough and macho yet later youd find out that the bottom, the guy who was being submissive and obedient, was actually running the show.

Head-Games, Drama, Hierarchies
and Categories.

It was refreshing for me though because I think gay men, unlike some straight men and women, are totally honest about their desire. Everyone was totally up-front and honest about what they wanted from you, and if you didn't want to give it to them, that's cool, there is always someone else. I think there are far more head-games when it comes to sexuality between men and women. Not to say that gay men aren't interested in head-games and drama, but just that when it came to fucking, things were pretty cut and dried.

It wasn't just pure, raw sexuality though, it was also an insight into the way men interact with each other. I think many men, both gay and straight, need to be able to use categorizations and hierarchies to determine where they stand in the social order. There was certainly a hierarchy between those worked at the clubs based on the amount of time that someone had worked there, or based on who happened to be the personal favorite of the owner at the time. It is not just straight male culture that needs this kind of wolfpack, pecking order mentality—these men I worked with also needed it. They also needed to be able to categorize, to determine once and for all what someone's sexuality or sexual habits were.

I mostly kept to myself and I think they really couldn't figure out where I stood sexually, so I was constantly the subject of gossip and speculation. It was like any ambiguity was problematic and rather than let you represent yourself in a certain way they had to have confirmation of which category you fit into. I remember on a number of occasions telling men that asking the question of whether I was gay or not was so passe. It just seemed to me that most of the guys and girls I know just naturally consider themselves bi or ambisexual and defining yourself in such black and white terms is anachronistic. I guess it also could have been a generational thing because back in the day there was so much more at stake by declaring your homosexuality in the face of a dangerous and prejudiced society.

The off-duty Chicago police-officers who did security for the club didn't quite know what to make of everything, particularly anyone who came across as quite masculine. I felt like it was weird for the security to see straight or straight-acting guys among those of us who worked there—they just didn't know how to talk around us. After shift they would sit around with us as we cleaned up and waited for the owner to count out our cash drawers. The best conversations during these periods were always between the police officers and the most effeminate bartenders. The thing was, they agreed on everything. The security guys and the more catty among us would crack wise about certain things that occurred during the shift. Sometimes I heard the same homophobia from both: genuine in one case, self-hating in the other.

Celebrating the Little Boys' Playground

It felt like such a little boys' playground working at the club. Gay nightclub culture is notoriously hedonistic and self-indulgent. Everyone going to the club or working at the club was trying to get their rocks off either through drugs, dancing, sex or just hanging out with friends, seeing and being seen. The management had huge amounts of money to throw around and there was a massive workshop in the back to build sets and design decorations, costumes, lighting, and sound productions. In many ways we were like a bunch of pre-pubescent boys working there. Self-indulgent and hedonistic, we supplied entertainment and fun for so many. And we had as much fun as we could when we were there. Sometimes I left the club and went to other clubs on Halsted Street for awhile. Sometimes I would go in the back and read a book. Sometimes I would stand in the cooler and exercise using cases of beer and bottled water as weights. There were many nights when I made the best of the work situation and had a lot of fun. But I think that is why drugs were so ubiquitous. In such a playground everything was fun, everything was open, we could do anything, anything we wanted, anything we desired. Playing next to each other in very close quarters, we had a constant level of physical yet non-sexual contact. Hugging each other, horse-playing, wrestling, slapping each others' asses, it was all in good fun and deeply refreshing to find out that you could touch and be physical with another man without it being sexual or getting violent. Yet as far as I knew, none of the guys slept with each other. It was just like being a kid before you knew that touching another guy was socially frowned upon, before physical contact was channeled into either sports or sexuality. It was the way boys play with each other before heterosexual society begins to try to mold them into either masculine males or queenie fags (not that everyone now is or should be one or the other).

Live Your Desire? Hedonism and Fulfillment

In many ways, gay-club culture could be seen as the complete expression of the "live-your-desire" mentality so advertised and exhorted in the pages of this magazine*.

Even the off-duty police treated the club like their playground. One time as we were closing I came upon a security guard in a just-closed bathroom with a woman he had met at the club. She obviously did not want to be there and I hung around the bathroom cleaning up until they left. It was then I realized that the self-indulgence and hedonism I thought was so healthy and so rad, could have very detrimental effects on others. Sometimes when we pursue our desires completely, we hurt ourselves and others. Because the very nature of desire is to be unfulfilled, because desire works sometimes directly at odds with the well-being of others, and because others can come to be objects through our desire, there was almost an endless and wistful sorrow, a deep isolation under the surface of the fun and friendship of the hedonistic club culture. Desire always carries a measure of objectification. People become conduits for our pleasure. Pursuing pleasure at all costs lessens us as social beings. We become individuals. Always searching for the next best high, that next great fuck, that next great DJ, pushing our senses to the limits of human existence, tasting the pain and the ecstasy of a constant never-ending desire sometimes can seem like a hollow quest. Perhaps I just didn't get it. Perhaps I never will.

ATR Zine, 118 Raritan Ave. Highland Park, NJ 08904

eboehme@eden.rutgers.edu

*Editor's note: see the poster section at the end of Days of War, Nights of Love for an illustration of the crucial differences between mere "hedonism" and "ambitious hedonism". Real, ambitious

pleasure-seeking is not a temporary abandonment to individual desires, but a well-reasoned, long-term commitment to the pursuit and exploration of desires of all kinds and scopes, especially the large-scale, long-term ones.

ALAMUT
Excerpted from the international bestseller, *Volvo Speaks*

Prologue

After a 56 hour bus trip that took me through most of Turkey, countless mountain passes and military checkpoints, I reached Iran. After an overdose on Persian pop music and a day of severe diarrhea I was overwhelmed with relief when I got of the bus. I wouldn't do my memories justice by trying to incorporate my impression of Iran into one essay and therefore I choose one tale...

Alamut - The Eagle's nest

We descended into the clouds that filled the valleys in the Alborz mountain range and traveled back in time, or so it seemed. Behind me laid the busy street life of Tehran, housing the remains of an American Embassy, the world's largest bazaar and millions of people and cars.

The countryside was waking up as we made our way on winding roads. The villages, which scattered the mountains, showed no signs of modernity and its female inhabitant's colorful clothes were in stark contrast to the black chador, worn by the majority elsewhere. At the time I was unaware of the significance of the place I was about to visit, I was along for the ride and the scenery made it worthwhile. As always, unmediated adventure is the most rewarding, and this particular one took me to Alamut, the ancient fortress of the medieval Assassins.

The fortress of Alamut was the center of the empire and the symbol of the movement, controlled by Hassan i Sabbah and the later heads of the Assassins. The Assassins were a Persian Isma'ili sect and their empire was largely a hidden political one within the borders of others and was maintained by the means of information and political assassination. Alamut is said to been seized in 1090 by the Assassins and stood unassailable until 1256 when it was destroyed by Hulagu Khan and his Mongol raiders. Why became apparent when we parked the jeep at the foot of the mountain in the outskirts of a little village and started to make our way up the mountain. Alamut is only accessible only by a single, almost vertical pathway, which at the time of my visit was slippery with small stones. We reached the top and our eyes were rewarded by the swindling view, while a group of young local boys who tailed us filled our ear with incomprehensible phrases and laughter. There

was not much on site to aid the imagination of what the castle had looked like back in the day. I found some holes along the edge that overlooked the path and which were probably suited for greeting unwanted guests with flying rocks. A herd of goats were grazing the few patches grass that could be found up there and there were no visible signs of the mythical garden.

Like many secret societies throughout the ages, the actual history and practices have been blended or bastardized by folklore and myth. The history of Alamut is no exception to this. Most of the Western myth about Alamut, which have intrigued writers such as William S. Burroughs and Hakim Bey, comes from Marco Polo's tales of his travels in the area in the early 1270s. While the fortress had fallen at that time it's fair to say that Marco Polo's narrative is not a first hand source but a

Illustration s. 13: Marko picking vegetables in Zagreb

collection of tales he picked up from story-tellers along his journey. According to Marco Polo an initiate was drugged and taken to garden close to Alamut where he was given a taste of paradise on earth. It's a matter of dispute whether the initiate was treated with hash along with the other sensuous delights as wine, food and sexual pleasures. The initiate was led believe that he would return to this paradise after death. With this prospect ahead of them the Assassins performed their deed willingly. From Alamut the Hassan i Sabbah, also called the Old Man on the mountain, sent out missionaries to infiltrate his enemies ranks, where they would often rise to positions of prominence and trust, often posing as religious teachers or dervishes. From this position it was easy for them to kill their intended victim. The assassinations would usually be carried out with a knife and the Assassin would not try and escape capture. Instead, he would wait calmly prepared to die, having carried out his objective. Political assassination was not unknown in the Muslim world before Hassan i Sabbah but the Assassins marked a qualitative shift. Sometimes an Assassin would be in the service of a ruler for years and years before being required to strike. This sort of political assassination was new to most of the rulers and it was easier to give in to the Old Man's demands, when one could not be sure of even his closest advisors could be trusted. The power to assassinate an enemy was said to reach as far as India and France.

The terrain in this area is arid, rocky and some sources assert that the altitude would not sustain a garden with the vegetation described in the chronicles of Marco Polo. It's therefore highly unlikely that the garden was a physical place and if it existed it was either an allegory for some sort of initiation ceremony or part of a spiritual vision to which the initiate was given access. Another of the principle myths surrounding Alamut involves the library, which supposedly contained over 200,000 volumes on a myriad of subjects including political power, philosophy, religion and the control of spirits. When the Mongols invaded Alamut, record show that they were surprised at the number of books and scientific instruments that they found. More critical sources refute the notion of a library of that magnitude, in regards to the lack of space among other things, and having visited the place I feel inclined to agree. According to the myth the words "With the aid of God, the ruler of the universe destroyed the fetters of the law" were written on the door to the library that after the Mongol invasion was either lost, stored in another manner or did never exist of this world.

The religious teaching emanating from Alamut is said to have been a derivation of the Isma'ili faith, a peculiar and unique and blend of Sufi mysticism and Shiism. For the Isma'ili, the Imam, or religious head was the personal representative of God in the physical world and salvation was only obtainable through the Imam. For years the Isma'ili Imam had been the Caliph Fatamid, but the split, when the Isma'ilis from Persia pledged their allegiance to the by-passed Caliph Nizar who lost the throne to his brother al-Musta'li, the Nizari Isma'ilis was born. The Nizari Isma'ilis under the Hassan i Sabbah, who later took the role of Imam upon himself, started a new school with a slightly different direction. Paradoxically, Hassan i Sabbah managed to install his followers with a sense of freedom, at the same time as making them fanatically loyal to himself, which can be illustrated by a tale from Arkon Daraul's book.

Two men in the year 1092 stood on the ramparts of a medieval castle - the Eagle's Nest - perched high upon the crags of the Persian mountains: the personal representative of the [Persian] Emperor and the veiled figure who claimed to be the incarnation of God on Earth. Hassan, son of Sabbah, Sheikh of the Mountains and leader of the Assassins, spoke.
- You see that devotee standing guard on yonder turret-top? Watch!'
He made a signal. Instantly the white-robed figure threw up his hands in salutation, and cast himself two thousand feet into the foaming torrent which surrounded the fortress.
- I have seventy thousand men - and women - throughout Asia, each one of them ready to do my bidding. Can your master, Malik Shah, say the same? And he asks me to surrender to his sovereignty! This is your answer. Go!

The paradox can be seen in some of Hakim Bey's writing on the Assassins where he states "[t]rue, in this myth some aspirants disciples may be ordered to fling themselves off the ramparts into the black - but also true that some of them will learn to fly like sorcerers".

The Assassins most known lasting legacy is actually the English word in itself, which definitely entered the literary vocabulary when it was used by Dante. In The Divine Comedy: Hell, Book XIX, Dante describes himself "like a friar who is confessing the wicked assassin". From an etymological viewpoint the popular notion is that the word is derived from the Arabic word hashashin, consumer of Hashish. It is unlikely that the austere Hassan i Sabbah indulged personally in drug taking and there is no mention of the drug hash in connection with the Assassins in any historical written records except for Marco Polo's. Other scholars derive the word from the Arabic word "assasseen", which signifies "guardians" and consider this the true origin of the word – guardians of the secret.

Epilogue

It's a tentative to reason whether the Assassins legacy has had any influence on contemporary militant fractions in the Middle East. I do think that the myths can serve an emancipating purpose among the many people, who has to conceal their armed desires in an alienating world, to endure until the time is ripe to strike. A guiding star in the battle may well be the oft quoted maxim attributed to Hassan i Sabbah which reads...

Nothing is true – everything is permitted

Additional recommended reading: Arkon Daraul: A History of Secret Societies. *Edward Burman:* The Assassins – Holy Killers of Islam.

Plagiarized and supplied by Volvo – CrimethInc. Travel Agency

by Matt (SK8amongus)

[editor's note: to its credit, this scene report arrived handwritten with lovely pen drawings in the margins, and a few stalks of genuine Wyoming wheat in the envelope, which was of course postmarked December 29.]

11 p.m. December 27th, 1999

Car pulled over. No others in sight. No light but that of the wide open, clear sky. Lying in the dead grass, we stretch and marvel at the warmth. One hour until we sleep. Gorgeous!

December 28th, 1999

Oh my god, it's so beautiful out! The guy in the Harley shirt and leather vest proclaims that this 60 degree weather is, indeed, unusual for this time of year, then continues with his tales of weddings attended by himself and Al Gore, Boston accents, C.B. radios. What the fuck am I doing in Wyoming? Two weeks ago, if you'd told me I'd be staring at these vast plains spotted with remnants of snow and deer and cowboy culture and "Taco John's", "Kum & Go's," our polluting tailpipe, sagging bumper, cramped Corsica, and us inside— well, how would you know that? How the heck was I to know I'd finally find the nerve to make a long-standing dream of mine a reality? And not a moment too soon—nobody seems to know what's gonna happen three and a half days from now.

The guy at the trading post said that Sunday was their busiest day by far. A lot of young fellers coming in. stocking up on firearms and ammo. His electrician buddy claims there'll be a fourteen-day minimum lack of power. What are three (more or less) middle class white boys doing so far away from the security of friends, families, homes, jobs... I should be stocking soymilk or cashing out 47-year-old ladies with $50,000 bank accounts and a taste for free range, "organic" turkey, so I can pay for a decaying, over-priced third floor apartment back on the coast of New England. Not that I mind that as much as I might say if, say, I was there doing that. I feel really lucky. If not for some stupid Hollywood movie (or two), I might not have decided to risk the economic eclipse I'll have to face once I get back—if I get back. What if this IS it? My last chance to finally witness the sun setting on a rocky Oregon beach that so many people have captured with camera lenses and paint brushes, yet I've (longed to but) never managed to see first-hand (not having the opportunity to spend the time or money on such a journey).

Normally, rationality would instruct me not to escape the security of my daily/weekly routine. Things are tight enough as it is—but eventually, I decided it was near mandatory to at least try to make this journey a reality. I think that if the world is engulfed with nuclear disaster the morning of January first, there will be a bit more harmony within my personal constitution, huge hiking pack strapped on and fir trees cradling the moon. The only regret I might have, if busses don't exist anymore and I can't be carried back to the east, is I may never see Noella again. This almost had stopped me, but we all gotta do what we gotta do. I guess I wish I had brought my skateboard, too (Cheyenne had some rad fucking transitions going on). 700 miles to Eugene. 79 hours to live. 3 friends. 2 many days before this I've spent dreaming, not living. 1 last chance to live the dreams. ($0).

CARRBORO, NORTH CAROLINA
by Gloria Cubana

A zoo without a fence and the Paris of the Piedmont. The two towns share a main street and the burden of housing 25,000 students, but Carrboro and Chapel Hill enjoy very different personalities. Take the homeless populations for example. Chapel Hill is the upscale, self-conscious town (only recently persuaded that with a huge university and a rapidly growing supply of permanent residents, it could no longer call itself a village)— in spite of this, or because of it, a lot of panhandlers ply their trade on the main couple of blocks in the center of town; the crazy ones tend to roam down-to-earth Carrboro, since they won't get any money out of anyone anyway, preferring Webster's Laundromat and the sidewalk outside of the cooperative grocery.

That grocery, Weaver Street Market, is the pulsing center of a tiny town, which means that you will not be able to get out of it in under half an hour after going regularly for a period of time. In fact, even if you have never been in it before, and in fact have lived thousands of miles away all your life, there have been documented cases of people entering WSM for the first time and finding long lost friends. Lucky you if *your* friend plies you with Carrboro bars the most filling vegan pastry you can get for $1.50.

Transportation in Carrboro is a cinch: walk. If you have to make the dangerous border crossing into Chapel Hill, a full 10 minute walk from Town Hall, you can use a bike. Bike paths are plentiful. Carrboro even features a bike courier service, and, when he's not working, its owner, Seth, can occasionally be spotted riding a double-decker bicycle (with optional cheetah head and tail attachments) through the streets.

The Spotted Dog will feed you enormous salads and beer-battered fries. For a cheaper meal, you can go to the Armadillo Grill right across the street: breathtakingly mediocre Tex-

Mex, but you can stuff yourself for less than $3. After dinner you should venture onto Chapel Hill's Franklin St.: if you don't stray too far from the safe glow of Carrboro, you'll find the Silk Road Tea House, where a Sufi group frequently gathers to sit on the cushions and enhance the atmosphere of the place. Another option is the Open Eye Café, a comfortable Carrboro coffee shop with divine vegan ginger carrot cake.

For nighttime entertainment, Carrboro provides the Cat's Cradle, a once-great club that now hosts a bunch of bands I've never heard of. (I haven't yet been able to decide if this means they are out of the loop, or if I am.) If you've got to work early, and can't go sway with all the hipsters at the Cradle into the wee hours, just get up an hour or two early and head over to the fire station, which is beside Town Hall and the Farmer's Market. I used to live right across the street from it, and besides the insomniac bird chorus (purportedly the result of a Zoology department experiment at UNC-Chapel Hill whose purpose was to see if

illustration s.14: Dinner in Zagreb

it was possible to confuse birds' internal clocks and cause them to start sleeping during the day and singing at night (apparently, it was)) that can be found performing all over Chapel Hill and Carrboro after about 1 a.m., you can enjoy the early morning performance of "Siren-Testing Song" (Op. 14), an avant-garde number that the firemen execute faithfully every morning, carefully calibrating it to climax just when the neighbors are sleeping best. [The police are just as unique as the firemen. Carrboro cops are notoriously laid back. EmoCop wears Buddy Holly glasses and warns you not to leave your bike unlocked.

Officer Bob will tell you bad jokes of his own invention ("Thanks, folks, that's an Officer Bob original.") and stop to chat outside the coop.]

The Saturday morning Carrboro Farmer's Market, by the way, is almost as upscale and boutique-y as Chapel Hill. Still, Kathy will keep you talking and sell you beautiful garlic, and right next to her you can get all kinds of crazy varieties of potatoes, and sometimes there are even free tastings. I stuffed myself on watermelon recently, feigning studied concentration as I carefully compared the 10 or 15 different varieties they were offering as snacks—I mean, samples. The eco-gourmet atmosphere can be off-putting (no dusty, sunburned old men backing up a dirty pickup truck with a bed full of ears of corn here), but there are a few old-fashioned farmers there selling produce (and all kinds of preserves). Plus, those little yellow tomatoes are so delicious, they're worth any price.

For such a small place, you wouldn't think they'd need two hardware stores three blocks from each other, but they do, and if you lament the salt-of-the-earth types missing from the farmer's market, you can always go listen to the hardware guys converse with the regulars: "I know you aren't trying to flimflam me this early in the morning, now," we heard one 8 a.m.

Cheap clothes can be found at the PTA on Jones Ferry Rd., but I don't often find anything that I want to wear. For a somewhat more expensive but more reliable selection of old clothes, you should head to Time After Time, only a bit farther down the street from Carrboro than the Silk Road Tea House.

Haircuts can be had at the Beehive on Weaver St., but I think you have to be far cooler than I to enter. That's why I cut my own hair, and my bathroom and broom and dustpan are available for other daring souls with similar plans. When I'm getting really fancy, I call my sister (no remarkable haircutting skills, except that she can see the back of my head better than I can), who can be found way over in Chapel Hill. She might do yours, too, I'll ask her.

After Hours at Weaver Street Market (summer Thursday evenings) is usually a really terrible band playing, attracting a large crowd of hippies and yuppies (and that weird breed that is sort of a mishmash of the two) who gather and bring their kids and drink wine and dance and basically make life hell for the hapless store employees that get stuck with the Thursday shift.

During the summertime, there are numerous apartment complexes around town whose pools are ripe for sneaking into. I'm not going to tell you which one is my favorite, though because I don't want to see you there. There's also a hot tub at a luxury complex, and if you're willing to climb a fence in your bathing suit, there's no reason you should hold back...

An idyllic way to Get Away From It All (if you are fast enough to dodge reckless mountain bikers during peak hours) is to wander the trails in the woods of Estes Drive. One of them leads to Wilson Park, where it is pleasant to lie in the grass and read novels and listen to the thock, thock, thock of tennis balls bouncing back and forth in the courts. Or you can take a ride into the countryside. Just past Calvander, a small community (i.e., an intersection), the scenery turns to fields and dairy farms.

Nice Price is perhaps the best used bookstore around. And Carrboro does have a public library—but why bother, when there are the 8 floors of Davis Library on the university's campus to explore?

ZAGREB, CROATIA
by Kim Bae

I was fortunate enough to spend about 11 days in Zagreb in August 2000. There I found a bounty of great food and happily immersed myself in a frenzy of eating debauchery. Before revealing the details of my gluttony, let's get some practical information out of the way.

I. Practical Information (for tourists, punkers, and vegetarians)
A. Croatia is actually called Hrvatska in the Croatian/Serbian/Bosnian language.
B. At the time that I went the exchange rate was about US$1 = 7 Croatian Kuna (KN).
C. The tourist office on the east side of the main square in Zagreb, Trg Bana Jela?i?a, is

one of the best I've ever seen. Be sure to grab a copy of the pamphlet "Zagreb Info A-Z" which has all the information you need to know as a visitor to Zagreb. Also available is a map of the center (which can also be found in the pamphlet) and a map of the tram and bus system - all for free! Keep in mind that the names you see on maps are not the names you see written on the street signs. It's a bit confusing but at least the roots of the names are the same. All street names in this report are those that are written on maps.
D. Most of the time you need not worry about purchasing a ticket for the trams but I was controlled about 3 times so I bought a ticket and simply didn't stamp it. They can be bought at little kiosks that sell tobacco and magazines or at post offices for KN 5.50 or from the driver for KN 6.00.
E. If you find yourself in a pinch and need to get some vegetarian/vegan shampoos, soaps, etc. there is a shop called Lush near Trg Bana Jela?i?a on Petrinjska. Everything is handmade, vegetarian, and cruelty free. You can ask for a newspaper they produce which lists ingredients so you can be sure of what is vegan. Very expensive.
F. The best place to go to check email is the Mama internet cafe. It is located on Preradovi?eva on the west side of the street in between Berislavi?eva and Hebrangova. It's a bit difficult to see it but just look out for the red and white sign and a small passageway you must walk through to reach it. Internet access is really cheap and the people there are involved in some political activities with the Attack! autonomous center (see below).
G. Attack! is an anarchist community center in the basement of some alternative club (can't remember the name - starts with an "m"?). They have an info shop, library, internet cafe, and cook a cheap (10 KN) vegan meal every Tuesday and Thursday. It's located at Kralja Drzislava 12 south of the center of town in a former factory building. Telephone: +385 1 461 12 671. Website: members.nbci.com/zap_zg/news1eng.htm. Email: attack_zg@zamir-zg.ztn.apc.org.
H. As far as I know there aren't any record stores where you can get punk and hardcore stuff. Attack! has a few records for sale.

II. Food!
- every place written about here is easily accessible by trams. All the food mentioned is vegan.
A. Grocery stores: The best ones I visited were both Konzum. One was located near Kvaternikov Trg (there are actually two there but the bigger one is directly across from the market) and the other near Britanski Trg.
B. Markets: The best market is at Kvaternikov Trg. There you can find everything from

broccoletti to dried soya chunks for cheap. It runs from early in the morning to about 6 pm. Another pretty good one is at Dolac, north of Trg Bana Jela?i?a but it's only open until 2 pm. I visited the one at Britanski Trg as well but it was pretty small in comparison to the aforementioned.
C. Health food shops: Health food is super fucking expensive. A carton of soy milk is about US$3. Be prepared to spend big. The best health food shop I went to was Biovega which is located at Ilica 72/1 near Meduli?eva. There is also one called Rosa which is on the south side of Hebrangova in between Gajeva and Strossmayerov Trg but it's a bit smaller. Inside the meat market just south of the open-air Dolac market is a small health food stand which is bizarre. It's truly difficult to brave the smells of raw, bloody meat in order to buy a some Alpro Soja Drink Schokolade (which you absolutely must try). It's impossible to explain exactly where it is but it's somewhere in the middle of the building. Supposedly there is a new health food store that just opened right at Trg Bana Jela?i?a but I didn't have a chance to go there. If you just need soy milk, try going into a DM (Drogerie Markt) - it's a drugstore but they have a sort of health food section. They can be found everywhere.
D. Restaurants: Zagreb has two(!) macrobiotic restaurants. One is called Makro Nova and it's in the same building as Biovega. If you have a huge appetite you can have an entree for about 60 KN but I got the small plate which was more than enough (and cheaper). Desserts are 20 KN and are pretty good. Bijeli Val is this not-quite legal restaurant situated in an apartment at Trenkova 7. You have to push a buzzer to be let in and I was too stupid to write down which buzzer it is but it's on the first floor and the word written on the buzzer is also written on a little sign for the restaurant on the wall. The meal I had there was really incredible and the atmosphere is great. A huge meal including tea and dessert will cost you about 70 KN (?). The Attack! community center has an infokitchen twice a week (see above).
E. Foods you must try when in Zagreb: Konzum has these vegetarian sausages that you can slice up to put on sandwiches. I can't remember the exact name (I think it has "veg" in it somewhere) but there are 3 different colors of packaging. The white is original flavor, the green is olive, and the beige-ish one is with tofu. Ajdvar is this interesting spread made with red peppers and onions that comes in a jar. It's bright orange and looks gross but tastes great. I discovered some wonderful ?ipak (rosehip) jam in a small shop near Sanja's house and decided to try it, not knowing what the hell it was. Also look out for the best chocolate

in the world called Bajadera which is a creamy hazelnut chocolate. Fontana Ledene Kocke in a blue box is a strange minty kind of chocolate. Kras Čokoladne Napolitanke in a red and brown box are really amazing chocolate wafers. Dorina Čokolada Za Kuhanje in a brown and white wrapper is really good, not-so-bitter cooking chocolate. There is a cherry liquor chocolate in a red box that I didn't try that is always found next to Bajadera and Fontana in shops. All of this, except for the sausages, can be found just about anywhere. The plain white bread loaf found in bakeries and all food shops in Croatia (and all the other former Yugoslavian countries) is really amazing. I don't know what they do to it but it's kind of crusty on the outside and really, really soft inside. It's really different from any kind of bread I've had before. There are 3 Slovenian drinks that are commonly found in Croatia that are incredible. Their answer to Coke is Cockta which you seriously have to try to believe. I don't even like soda but this stuff is great. Eis Tea (the one with the blue label, not the pink one) is a peach flavored ice tea that is, again, something I would normally hate but is somehow really good. Fructal is the brand name for a line of the best juices I've ever had. It's not as easy to find as Cockta or Eis Tea but is still available. I think the strawberry and blueberry ones are the best but they're all good.

III. Stuffing my face for 11 days straight

I'm positive I gained some weight on this trip and I wouldn't be surprised if it was all from Zagreb. My first full day in Croatia, a big group of us went to this small village where the parents of my friend Marko live. We picked some vegetables in their garden and made a huge meal with stuffed tomatoes, dozens of kebabs, marinated soya steaks sandwiches, tomato and kohlrabi salad, great bread, and baked chocolate bananas. I told everyone that night about my idea to do this scene report and from then on the stage was set. My friends Sanja, Nežu, Marko, Bojan and I sat outside on Sanja's patio one nice evening and had a stir-fry dinner by candlelight. They had told me that Chinese food was somewhat of a rarity in Croatia (considering the extremely high cost of soy sauce there I can understand why) so they really enjoyed my ordinary stir-fry. This evening I tried cornflakes with chocolate soy milk for the first time which tastes a lot better than it sounds.

The next night Sanja made this traditional Croatian dish with beans, onions, and soy milk which was really great. About ten of us sat around in her living room, bonding through food. The grand opening of Attack! after the summer closing was the next day and I cooked a Korean meal. It was a grand affair with flyers announcing the meal and a beautiful poster that Nežu drew. A few days later Sanja had her birthday party there and I cooked a Thai meal with some salad. Just about every day we ate bread with ajdvar, miso, garlic, tomatoes, margarine, mushroom pate, etc.

I really love to discover new foods as I'm travelling and cooking/eating with new friends. For me, food isn't just about sustenance and survival. It is one of the few simple pleasures in life and is something to be shared and enjoyed with those around me. Very few things give me as much joy as sitting around a table covered with food and seeing smiling faces all around me.

Illustration s.15: Stuffed tomatos in Zagreb

Last US Tchkung Show
Eugene, Oregon, USA Summer 1999

A Hillside
Prague, Czech Republic Summer 1999.
by Finnegan Bell

Usually a "scene" is conceived of as a certain amount of people in a loose community, involved with various projects, usually bands. However, more often I've found that the most critical scenes that I have been a part of have lasted seconds, or perhaps a few hours or a day, like the ones described below. I feel much more compelled to share these "fleeting" scenes with you because with all disregard for time and place these moments have shaped my life more than any list of local bands. It is also quite clearly subjective to the reader whether or not any of the below information is of any "practical" use. At heart, I want to begin to sketch a picture of a world that I have caught a glimpse of in my travels throughout this life. These transforming moments have become more and more of a web that I can travel upon - I'm doing everything to link them; not only with each other, but with other's moments as well. A federation of beautiful moments! There is a world beyond the perceived banality of our society - a world full daring people, breathtaking beauty and ingrained with (dare I violate the cynicism?!) - magic...

As the bi-plane pilot, lover of key lime pie and sublime novelist, Richard Bach noted: "There was no need for fiction. In fact, the truth wasn't plausible enough for it!"

Thus:

***

An old dance hall on a street of forgotten buildings - a long summer's day descending into twilight. Earlier that day Arwen came to me at the coffee shop: "Hey," she said slyly "There's something you can't miss tonight."

"What's that?"

"Some folks are coming down from Seattle, a band... erm... of sorts - Tchkung."

"A Tchkung? What do they do?"

"You'll see..."

Later I found myself following Arwen into a foyer of the old hall. I could see that it was already packed: hippies, punks, burnouts, dropouts, freaks, and what looked to be a whole regiment of wood elf terrorists. Some were sitting masked behind an Earth First table. I looked to Arwen.

"They came down from the Treesits for the night," she replied to my unspoken question. The Oregon and Northern California Treesits were some of the most pleasing and effective activism that I had ever experienced. In response to the relentless cutting down of old growth trees in National Forests for-profit a brave handful of individuals took to the trees and refused to come down. They have actually, with the simple tool of ropes and their bodies, prevented the trees from falling. In the last decade not only have the number of treesits steadily increased, but a number of treesits have become year round communities - some as going so far as to declare their autonomy! Though media coverage rarely extends beyond Pacific Northwest, the support community is immense -Everything from food to funds to climbing training. Around town they were fondly referred to as the "Ewok Villages." The dark smoky room smelled sweetly of the Earth.

Arwen turned to me and smiled mysteriously.

***

Joelle and I had been in Prague I don't know how long. She had rigged up some crazy scam where we had traveled from the North of the Continent for ridiculously cheap. But we had had to spend days traveling on shady regional trains and arrived in Prague in the middle of the night to find we had the city to ourselves. The air was damp in that eastern city. It was probably noisy like all cities, but later we could only recall a steady thumping silence.

Joelle and I had been traveling for months in disguise as Swedish tourists. We had even made up a secret language; our own "Swedish" that we would speak in front of taxi drivers and late night kiosk loafers.

"Where are you from?" they'd ask.

"Sweden," We'd answer with serious faces.

But Praha was different - it was a secret city - at least the one we stumbled on in those days. We soon realized that we didn't need our disguises.

We walked through the midnight until we found a corner to sleep in. Later, we woke in the mists.

***

Arwen and I carefully made our way through the crowd of people excited with anticipation. Arwen explained that the last time Tchkung had played in Eugene a street riot had ensued at the end of the set! A tribal drum session was played exclusively over the PA evoking a ghost ensemble. I was handed a small tract by a fleeting figure - I could only make out a certain amount of the apocalyptic ramblings in the half-light. The small stage was crowded with debris that I assumed were to become instruments. I noticed a guitar hidden in the clutter. A massive percussion section dominated the back of the area. And power tools... I turned my friend. "An oil drum?" I mouthed.

The lights went out.

***

We had been wandering since early morning. The mist us had kept us well hidden and happily lost. Each corner we turned seemed to hold some new surprise.

Sauntering over cobblestones we found a small unassuming cafe where we hid ourselves in a dusky corner to nourish our damp bodies with 15 cent Turkish coffees. Behind our table of worn wood there was a forlorn bookshelf. Joelle slid an old dusty Rainer Maria Rilke volume off the shelf. Opening it she read to me:

"Und der Mut ist so muede geworden und die Sehnsucht so gross. Es gibt keine Berge mehr, kaum einen Baum. Nichts wagt aufzustehen. Fremde huetten hockendurstig an versumpten Brunnen. Nirgends ein Turm. Und immer das gleiche Bild. Man hat zwei Augen zuviel."

Two too many? With sad eyes she shut the book. We rose and slid out of the cafe back into the city, to drift.

***

A rumble erupted from the front of the stage. I suddenly realized how packed the club was - how electric. Three or four people began pounding out furious rhythms on a mess of surfaces, a bass guitarist was thrusting about. A woman was standing stoic like an angry demi-goddess, violin in hand. A burley bearded man dressed in industrial coveralls stepped to the microphone. The building music stopped for a brief second — we inhaled - the room exploded.

Every rock show I had ever been to, every fakery of expression and emotion, was left behind in that moment. Everyone on stage and off was moving in a frenzy. I was hardly certain as to what I was witnessing: drums, old radical IWW songs, screeching metal, a haunting violin. The whole room was awash with one anguished cry for everything our modern society has destroyed; for wounded forests and our polluted bodies, our neuroses. Each song was a piece for a building symphony. Each one raised the stakes for each of us present. Each song begged the question: How far are you willing to go?

I was lost in the lighting storm of color and vibration and sweat and bodies. Some one on stage had taken an electric saw to the oil drum, creating a cascading shower of sparks over us, burning our skin faintly. Two dancers appeared in front of me surging from the crowd, their bodies completely covered in silver paint. One reached down into a container and then proceeded to anoint me with a streak of silver across my forehead. Around me boys and girls are shedding their shirts and were covering themselves in silver coating, never ceasing to dance. Near us there was then a bright flash. A pail with some brilliant burning mass illuminated the room like a bonfire. Immediately all began to direct their dance around the fire. The oil drums had been brought to the floor, the sparks intensifying. Some one blew fire; another spun fire around her head. I heard shrieks of delight around me as we moved around the flames. I could no longer remember the last time the music stopped. I caught a glimpse of a shotgun on stage and pieces of a hysterical speech about defending the lives of the last remaining wild North American wolves - And I understood - a refusal to accept the destruction of the little beauty left - drawing the line. Savage and beautiful.

Then everything crystallizes into the Real: A gas-masked uniformed figure in riot gear broke from the crowd and brutally tackled the fire breather in center of the room. Total confusion. Everyone stumbled back over each other only to suddenly find we had been roped in - The room panicked.

Flashing lights, bull horns, flailing bodies, screams. The music did not stop.

***

The mist and rain increased until Joelle and I found that we were alone on the windy streets. We had just come from a lush, concealed and deserted garden we had just explored. We made our way up a twisting street, ascending a long hill slowly. To one side of us was a row of old medieval homes, to the other a decaying stone castle wall, long abandoned.

We both became anxious to discover what lay on the other side of the wall. After and indeterminate amount of walking, weary from the climb, we finally spotted a gate ahead in the stone. Reaching it, we eagerly slipped through and old iron door to the other side. We emerged into a strange light, sight. There was a wood before us already well into its autumn colors - despite the persistence of summer on the calendar. Ahead to the right a statue of some forgotten saint stood remembered only with old dry flowers strewn about its base. Beyond that the forest disappeared down a hill.

Joelle looked to me and I followed her amble away from the door into the strange fall. Soon we came to a large grassy slope. The mist had intensified quite noticeably. The wood was cloaked in grey. We both stopped suddenly. Ahead appearing from further down the hill, entering into the glen was a figure in white. We stood still and waited for the stranger, a young woman, to approach. Her pitch black hair was tied back and moist -All our clothes were clinging to our forms from the moisture. She was carrying a small canvas bag. As she drew nearer she eyed us thoughtfully. Finally, standing in front of us she asked something in Czech. We shrugged in the Swedish manner to indicate politely that we didn't understand. She then reached into her bag and held her hand towards us asking again in perfect broken English, "You want a pear?"

Joelle and I stood both shocked for a moment, totally entranced by what seemed to be some magical question. There was something so queer and beautiful about the encounter that we were both savoring. With tender care we each took a pear, all the while

transfixed on this mysterious girl. She slowly explained that she had been further down the hill poaching fruit all morning. In love, we bit deeply into the pears. Absolutely the most delicious, sensuous bite ever. We were totally stunned - somewhere we had crossed, without noticing exactly, into another world. As the universe spun around our feet, the girl said goodbye and disappeared back into the wood. I stood next to Joelle for a long time. She smiled and took my hand. We continued to walk, silent and transformed.

***

The music had climaxed finally into one slow, pounding drum beat. The smoke hung in the air. Our bodies breathed sweat. Darkness. From around a corner two drummers hooded in old habits marched in time. They were followed by four painted men bearing a platform on their shoulders. On the platform sat a four armed blue woman with thick dreaded locks. Decked in jewelry

Illustration s.16: Yet another food related photo from Zagreb-Danijela enjoying a baked banana with chocolate

and intricate chains she surveyed the room. As the procession, which was followed up by two additional drummers, made its way around the room, the blue woman was handed a small torch. She then produced an American dollar bill and set it to flames. Then another. Fistful after fistful of dollars were sent fluttering to the crowd around her. Every Single last dollar was retrieved and held to the fire. Money is a symbol of debt - every symbol was returned to ashes. After marching through the crowd, they slowly exited. The room was quiet - we were all left with ourselves.

Arwen found me and we hurried from the

club, and the implications of what we had just been a part of in that space/time. Coming onto the street, we both hesitated. The entire hall was surrounded with riot police, waiting. Arwen pulled up her collar of her coat and looked at me: So close! Yet, perhaps this time not so far. We quickly made our way down the street, past our fears, into the vanishing night.

***

The rest of the day we spent in silence and shared laughter. Joelle's eyes were so bright. In the gloaming of the day we found a small restaurant. We sat long into the night trying to remember what to say. The establishment served a strange beverage of milk and honey, which we sipped slowly. Finally it occurred to me what must be said. I began to open my mouth, to speak and Joelle tried to speak at the same time. But spoken words were thankfully no longer necessary. Not with her. I looked down at

the tattered paperback that I had been carrying around for months. Remembering the old trick Richard taught me, I opened the book to a random page. "For magic to even begin to work, you have to believe," it said. It was no longer a choice, not that night. We could only acquiesce. Joelle carefully brushed her behind her ear with her hand. Dishes clattered joyfully from the kitchen. The forgotten city exhaled.

SOLRESOL
UNIVERSAL MUSICAL LANGUAGE

EMPHASIS
is function

redomido = to slander
REdomido = slander
reDOmido = slanderer
redoMIdo = slanderous
redomiDO = slanderously

KEY
is primary

Do = Physical & Moral Aspects of Humanity
Re = Family, Household, Dress
Mi = Human Actions
Fa = Agriculture, War, Travel
Sol = Arts & Science
La = Industry & Commerce
Si = Government, Law, Society

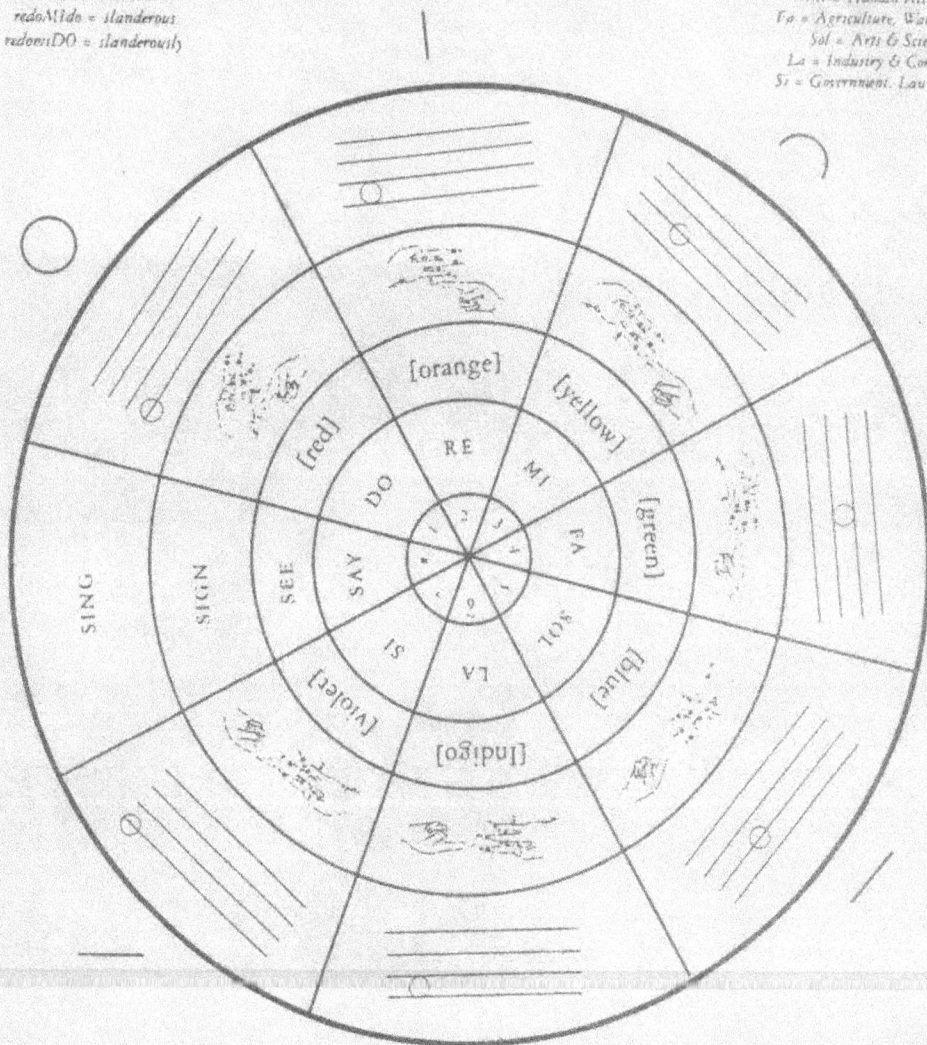

[orange]
[yellow]
[red]
[green]
RE
MI
DO
FA
[blue]
SEE
SAY
SOL
SING
SIGN
SI
LA
[violet]
[indigo]

MEANING
is reversible

Misol = Good
Solmi = Evil

ORDER
is static

Subject - Verb - Object
Noun - Adjective

SOLRESOL
UNIVERSAL MUSICAL LANGUAGE

As you can see, this last reviews section begins with some reviews from outside the hardcore scene. I'd wanted this issue to conclude with reviews of some of the movies, books, plays, and older records (punk and not) that were responsible for inspiring us to do what we have with Inside Front in the first place, alongside the more standard reviews of current records and 'zines, but time and space were, as usual, too pressing.

I'd hoped to write a review comparing Art Speigelman's *Maus* (about his father's experiences in the Nazi death camps) comic to the more recent *Palestine* comic (which deals with the current situation of Israeli oppression and inhumanity in occupied Palestine). I wanted to write about Godspeed, You Black Emperor! and their side project A Silver Mount Zion, about how their ensemble approach subverts the usual hierarchy of roles within a band, and how my friend Paul says their music is the only thing he's ever heard that sounds like it's coming from a world on the other side of the "rev-

both need"). I was going to write about the first Integrity record, about what was so important about it when it came out, since so many people listening to hardcore today weren't then and don't understand now what all the fuss was (since that band turned into a joke in poor taste). I wanted to write about Diamanda Galas, about the anarchist jazz communes of the 1960's, about my favorite books by Italo Calvino and my favorite paintings by Ernst Fuchs...

I was going to write about one of the best punk shows I've ever been to in my life, when I saw Alexei's old punk band Polyester Cowboys play almost a decade ago, while we were still in high school. The singer of the band was a little older, and worked construction with a black man in his late thirties who was a blues musician, who had promised to come to the show. He arrived at the club (the Fallout Shelter, a notorious basement punk club where my friends saw Agnostic Front and other bands in the '80's) with his saxophone, and was so musi-

shoulders to steal handfuls of popcorn. A rich older woman caught him doing this, and clutched her popcorn to her chest in outrage. To everyone's amazement, he snatched it from her hands, threw the popcorn in her face, tossed the box in the air, and strode away while everyone in the place (a bunch of totally bourgeois families) laughed and cheered. Right on!! I'm sure she got another popcorn and a free sweatshirt ("we can only hope," quipped Bruce when I told him this story), but all the same it was amazing to see this sold as entertainment. A young man I've corresponded with told me the second half of the story: we he saw the Cirque, the same guy was going around stealing popcorn, and a little girl noticed him trying to get a handful of hers. She held her popcorn out to him, and he was so surprised that he took his hat off and

The Negate Box Retrospective:
All Time Greatest Lyrics of the Decade!

I'd have to say the prize goes to Earth Crisis, for their song "The Order That Shall Be," which was on their demo before the Firestorm 7" (actually the best thing they ever did, someone should have bootlegged it) and then reappeared on a couple Animal Liberation benefit records. The whole song is just one riff, repeated over and over with minute changes in the drumming to signal the differences between the introduction, the verse, chorus, and breakdown, seriously just four notes over and over for about four minutes—that's vegan nazi minimalism for you, keep it simple so no one gets confused! The chorus is my favorite part: the guitars are all e-chunking in lockstep together, like a squadron of Third Reich [vegan reich?] stormtroopers arrived to purge the "undesirables," and would-be Fuhrer Karl, in the one-dimensional monotone grunt of the vocalist who recognizes "sounding tough" as the only possible standard of value, pronounces:

Perpetrators of this madness, your right to live is gone
Your burning bodies will light the path to a glorious New Dawn

The rest of the stormtroopers join in to shout along on the last two words (in "unisence," as Agnostic Front put it during their "Live at CBGB's" era), and in my mind's eye I see us, the righteous vegan warriors of the world, stamping the faces of the non-believers into mush with our steel-toed patent leather boots as the death camps smoke with the flesh of the guilty, purifying the world once and for all. As the final note (an "e," of course) rings out I find I cannot resist the urge to raise my right arm stiff, hailing victory, welcoming the New Dawn, ready to burn the bodies of all who stand between us and the Order That Shall Be. Christ, this stuff is better than Wagner, or even Skrewdriver! Yeah!

olution" we talk about. Speaking of that, I wanted to write about the heartbreaking Bertolucci movie *Before the Revolution*, about the fragile idealism of a young Italian communist in love with his aunt.

Hell, I even wanted to write that ten page exploration of *Natural Born Killers* I've been threatening to write ever since that movie changed my life, and Paul was supposed to write about *Fight Club*. And I wanted to add to those a raving review of the Children of Bodom "Hatebreeder" record, my other favorite record along with the Godspeed e.p.—Children of Bodom are the most amazing metal band I've ever heard, five Finnish (of course!) guys doing the work of a whole symphony orchestra. I was also going to review the new Dover CD "Late at Night," which is by far the best rock record I've heard this year, and I wanted to talk about how the first song addresses the subject of non-monogamous relationships ("I've been with someone else—I've been with someone we

cally acute and outgoing and confident (in what was a totally alien environment, to him) that he was able to pick up all the chord progressions of their songs and play along. He got up on stage and joined them and they played together, and everyone felt so close and excited—clearly, anything could happen! I remember that night as one of the first times I realized the real power of punk rock...

And I was going to write about seeing the Cirque du Soleil, the French Canadian circus I went to see with my parents that made me think about how the circus has been a place where creative and radical and exciting things could always take place in the most conservative and repressive of societies, and gave me ideas about what new things could be done with the circus model. Before the performance started, a man in a hilarious costume who later turned out to be the ringleader was stalking around the aisles of the amphitheater, sneaking up behind people and reaching over their

gave it to her. Her eyes got really big, and she was very happy—as was I, to hear about it.

And, damn it all, I was going to write a review of my friend Greg Bennick's juggling performance in front of the post office when he came to visit Chapel Hill last summer, and review my friend Sera's 'zines and tell the story of how we met when she was living in the library I hang out in and sleeping in her car. All that will have to wait, I guess—look for those reviews in future issues of F.B.I. 'zine, or maybe Slave magazine, or else we'll have to do a fucking Inside Front epilogue. The only piece I did get finished was this, the final submission for the "Negate box" (the Inside Front feature created in honor of our favorite nonsense-lyrics band, as reviewed two issues ago).

DEAD PREZ "LET'S GET FREE"
by Nick Baxter

This is a rap (or hip-hop) album, has nothing really to do with hardcore/punk, and consists of the rappers M1 and Stic. However, I felt it deserved a review in this zine because of the profound effect this album has had on me since I first heard it while in Washington D.C. "protesting" the IMF and World Bank. I have long been a fan of hip-hop (or rap) music, but stopped listening to it when I started to become more educated and informed, and dare I say, political. This is because of the overwhelmingly nihilistic, sexually degrading, mindlessly violent, and basically counterproductive views and lifestyles embraced by many rappers, which I found myself increasingly aligned against. ...And then I heard Dead Prez, a politically and socially conscious, revolutionary, positive-minded, "from-the-streets" hip-hop duo, and was blown away. Finally, I could really sympathize with the lifestyle being represented, the intense emotions being portrayed, and the intelligent, uplifting messages being advocated in a rap album. I really don't know where to start, as I have so much to say about this, so I'll sum up by stating that Dead Prez have got their shit together and cover all the bases on this album. Their main goal seems to be to uplift, unify, and energize the African-American (or in their minds, just plain "African," as they see "American" as an unjust term for the race) population into forming revolutionary armies and declaring war on the status quo to obtain true freedom and equality. This is a *huge* task considering present conditions, and they seem aware of this, with every song an urgent call to arms, both literally and ideologically. They go from rejecting the Eurocentric, institutionally racist school system, to overthrowing the prison system (even more horrifyingly unjust), to confronting harmful social attitudes and perceptions towards blacks, poor people, and women, to rejecting lies of the advertising and media industries, to fighting the pigs tooth and nail, to dispelling the capitalist myth of material comfort and status (perpetuated by most rap artists nowadays), to veganism and sustainable living. It is so uplifting and inspiring to see people trying to organize the populations most effected by the world's problems, yet who are ironically also the hardest people to reach, even though they are the most crucial to any mass uprising or movement (and doing this from the standpoint of being "one of them," not as a messiah leading some followers). I truly hope that this hip-hop duo can succeed in this, and I consider myself to be a part of their struggle until the very end, even though I come from a very different background and situation, and even though they would probably denounce or distrust me because of my race and background (but can you blame them?). This is precisely what is so powerful about this record: it has broadened my horizons, forced me into the shoes of a ghetto minority who has the most daunting odds stacked against him, who must struggle every day just to survive, and who is forsaken by the motherfuckers in power, ignorantly trying their hardest to maintain the conditions which will take his peoples' very lives away. I have realized just how important it is to incorporate the African(-American) struggle into my/our own struggles for a better world, and to never disregard their perspective, which could teach me/us a lot. I can't comment on the musical aspects of this CD comfortably, as I don't feel I have adequate knowledge of hip-hop music to do so, but I will say that I thoroughly enjoy their blend of aggressive beats, soul, jazz, and blues style riffs and back-up vocals, and samples of speeches by revolutionaries and activists. My criticisms are slight, and tentatively proposed, as I come from such a different situation than Stic and M1, but mainly have to do with their abundant use of "nigger" and constant focus on race, especially the blacks vs. whites mentality. I don't understand why they would want to use a term with each other that was meant as extremely derogatory by racists for years, and I believe that the world is so much more complex than the dualistic us vs. them attitude they seem to embrace. But, as I do not have a lot of background info on these issues, I would need to have a discussion with Dead Prez themselves before knowing whether these criticisms are actually valid, which brings me to another, more founded criticism: no contact addresses in the layout!! There is a great manifesto of sorts which explains a lot of their stances, and they put a focus on getting organized and active, but if someone wanted to contact them to do just this (which I do), then they are more or less left hanging. All in all, however, this is a powerful, urgent, and important album for anyone with a revolutionary or "political" mindset, who likes hip-hop.

"We sick of workin' fo' crumbs and fillin' up da prisons/ Dyin' ova' money and relyin' on religion fo' help/ We do fo' self like ants in a colony/ Organize da wealth into a socialist economy/ A way of life based on da common needs, an' all my comrades is ready/ We just spreadin' da seeds..."

"When I'm bent up I think a lot about da reasons I'm here/ I think about da things I fear in the comin' years ahead of me/ I'm ready for whatever they bring though/ I'll go against a tank wit' a shank fo' my dreams and that's my fuckin' word!" —n, *reprinted from F.B.I. #3* www.loud.com, and/or 79 Fifth Ave., New York, NY 10003

EVENING, BY SUSAN MINOT
by Gloria Cubana

So this is what it is to cast off the heavy cloak of pain, to scrub the smoke and shadows of fear from your skin, and reenter your past. To enter your self at last. Not to see it objectively but to see it *truly* for the first time.

They could say anything now.

There it all is, luminous and complete. There your *self* is, suddenly, even at those times you felt you'd lost it, those moments and months where you numbed yourself to the thought of its absence, and you see that you have never been anything else.

I am here I have always been here your true self I was never gone and though you thought it came from him it was really yourself your whole self entire

You know what evening means. You have felt the sun's warmth fading. You have felt loss, you have watched the most beautiful thing slide away, you have known what it is to kill beauty when it has only begun to blossom. *Hope belongs in the same box as despair.*

You watched yourself die. You watch yourself die. This time it's different. *I have to go.*

You did not try to escape it then. It even seemed inevitable. A perfect dream to carry back into the real world. You have known loss to be natural, even easy. And you know that, scientifically, more is coming.

...eventually one lost everything.

But there is no longer any fear. Even that hurt that you have carried with you for most of your life, that loss that shaped your future until the future became the present and now is ending— even that one, you see now, is joy. You are resigned to nothing but you accept everything, you open up your arms wide to it, overwhelmed, incredulous, that there could be so much beauty in your own life, which you lived with adequate happiness, to be sure, but without realizing the rapture that was hidden within it all the time.

Her life had not been long enough for her to know the whole of herself, it had not been long enough or wide.

This is what it is to feel it all, even the pain, without hurting, without being damaged. This is strength. This is slow and gentle and silent. Laced with pain, even with sorrow, but without regret. The pain: an ache, ghosting through the chiaroscuro memories of your life, but not a stab. How can one find such joy in death, such satisfaction in oblivion?

It was like him to be wandering around in the night leaving lost things behind him. Buddy held loosely onto things.

But this lets go of nothing. This is what it means to hold on. Not desperately, with a feverish grip that damages and distorts, but with the sense that your hands are cupping infinity. That nothing can really be lost because it is whole.

He was silent for a while. I'm not sure I can go back that far. Can we? It wouldn't be the same.

That's alright, she said. I have it here. She closed her eyes and knocked her fist on her breast.

This is a glow you've never felt before. This is your heart in a paper bag.

THE IDIOTS, DOGMA 95 AND THE VOW OF CHASTITY
by Robin Banks

The Idiots is a film made by Lars Von Trier, a member of the film collective that created the Dogma 95 Manifesto and Vow of Chastity in 1995. The Manifesto is an energetic document describing past and current attempts to revitalize film in order to make it relevant to everyday life. A few excerpts from the Manifesto: "In 1960 enough was enough! The movie was dead and called for resurrection. The goal was correct but the means were not! The new wave proved to be a ripple that washed ashore and turned to muck ... The auteur concept was bourgeois romanticism from the very start and thereby false! ... Predictability (dramaturgy) has become the golden calf around which we dance. Having the characters' inner lives justify the plot is too complicated, and not 'high art'. As never before, the superficial action and the superficial movie are receiving all the praise. The result is barren. An illusion of pathos and an illusion of love." In order to fulfill the vision of the Manifesto, the collective created the Vow of Chastity, which sounds distastefully ascetic, but in fact is a sort of "do-it-yourself" attitude about film. Here is most of the Vow:

"1. Shooting must be done on location. Props and sets must not be brought in.

2. The sound must never be produced apart from the images or vice versa.

3. The camera must be hand-held. Any movement or immobility attainable in the hand is permitted.

4. The film must be in color. Special lighting is not acceptable.

5. Optical work and filters are forbidden.

6. The film must not contain superficial action. (Murders, weapons, etc. must not occur.)

7. Temporal and geographical alienation are forbidden. (That is to say that the film takes place here and now.)

8. Genre movies are not acceptable.

9. The film format must be Academy 35 mm.

10. The director must not be credited.

... I swear to refrain from creating a 'work', as I regard the instant as more important than the whole. My supreme goal is to force the truth out of my characters and settings. I swear to do so by all the means available and at the cost of any good taste and any aesthetic considerations."

The film "The Idiots" is an incredible fiction about a group of dissatisfied rebels who are squatting in a nameless upper-class suburb of Denmark. Together they pretend to be a gang of "idiots" — people with severe mental retardation — and with this ruse they maniacally careen through life. Says the official Dogma 95 website, "The project (of the idiots) is a manifestation of an explosive appetite for life in which they confront society with their idiocy ... they want to live out the excessive feelings, the aggression, the curiosity and the uncontrolled, egotistical primitive sexuality." The film plumbs depths and scales heights which most other movies completely ignore, all without resorting to cheap violence or worn-out action sequences. I strongly recommend this film to anyone sympathetic to CrimethInc.'s ideas, and if you like the idea of Dogma 95, I also recommend watching a film called The Celebration, also made by a member of the same film collective.

JUDITH SLAYING HOLOFERNES: PAINTING BY ARTEMISIA GENTILESCHI, EARLY 17TH CENTURY
by Robin Banks

The alleged story behind this painting is almost as interesting as the painting itself. The painter, Artemisia Gentileschi, was raped by one of her father's friends in 1612. She took the rapist to court and testified against him, even when pressured by officials to change her story. Her graphic, harrowing testimony is a matter of public record. It can be found in Mary D. Garrard's book Artemisia Gentileschi: The Image of the Female Hero in Italian Baroque Art (Princeton University Press, 1989). After Gentileschi was raped she began painting several versions of a single image: the Jewish widow Judith beheading Holofernes, an enemy general. Holofernes was head of the Assyrian army which was besieging Jerusalem at the time. When Judith heard that her city's army planned to surrender to Holofernes, she put on her finest clothes and made her way to Holofernes' tent. She kept Holofernes amused for hours, encouraging him to drink and flirting with him. Finally, Holofernes dismissed his servants and began making advances on Judith. Being completely sober, Judith was able to overpower the drunken Holofernes, steal his sword and cut off his head. Other artists who depicted this same scene always showed Judith

looking away from Holofernes as if she could not stand the sight of blood and death; but Artemisia Gentileschi depicted Judith as grimly enjoying her task. The painting is quite gory — long spurts of blood erupt from Holofernes' neck as Judith saws through the flesh. His eyeballs roll up as he gurgles his last breath. Judith's servant stands in the background, holding down the tyrant's body. It is a truly brutal painting, thick with passion and revenge. As of August 2000, you can see it online if you want (http://shrike.depaul.edu/~bblum/gentil1.html), though any decent library should have a reproduction of the image within its art history books.

STRIKE AT THE FOOLS WHO ARE LAUGHING AT YOU: A PERSONAL REMINISCENCE / REVIEW OF KINGHORSE
by Jamie Miller

"When someone tells you to 'think for yourself,' they are really telling you to 'quit disagreeing with me,' which isn't really thinking for yourself at all."

At first, the one thing that for me meant the most about Kinghorse was the HATE—the blazing contempt for other people's shallow opinions and worthless motivations that seemed to fuel every single song. Sure, Kinghorse was a machine the likes of which Louisville had never seen before (at least my generation hadn't), and yes, Kinghorse was ten times as sincere as any given handful of the other bands floating around at their inception, but those shining qualities paled next to the fiery hatred blasting from the stage.

Me, Danny and Drew—the self-anointed Triumvirate—were in the front at every single Kinghorse show, no exceptions. We taped the shows constantly (video and audio), we deciphered the lyrics long before they were published, we helped design shirts and flyers when asked to do so. We were completely in synch with the band's nihilistic individualism (in other words: I don't care what you think of me because I'm a psychotic weirdo and I'm this close to killing you anyway). In fact, after the Columbine shootings in Colorado, Sean remarked to me that if those so-called Trenchcoat Mafia kids had been around in Kentucky in the late eighties/early nineties, they would have been Kinghorse fans, and they wouldn't have killed anybody because they would have had the perfect outlet for all their antisocial rage. Hell, the Triumvirate wore black trenchcoats and listened to punk rock and hated everybody who crossed our path, and we turned out just fine—I mean, at least we didn't kill anybody. We just engaged in heavy psychological warfare with our classmates.

As time passed, I realized that it wasn't hatred that fed the Kinghorse conflagration so much as a fierce, uncompromising individuality. The hatred was a result of conflict between the individual, the bleating sheep, and the idiotic authority figures, but it wasn't the real message. The real message was: be yourself.

This is precisely why Kinghorse was so important. There are a ton of bands out there who tell kids to "be yourself" but they are bracketing this empty advice with cookie-cutter music styles and scenester-approved clothing.

Therefore their words ring hollow in the finely-tuned, hypocrisy-detecting ears of America's Youth. A band like Kinghorse, on the other hand, made up of people who clearly did not give a damn about what you thought of their appearance or politics or attitude or music — yeah, when THOSE guys flew the freak flag of individuality, you BELIEVED it because it was obvious that they LIVED it. When other people confront you with a message of "be yourself" or "think for yourself," they are usually advocating some type of position or point of view which they want you to adopt. Kinghorse was arguing for nothing EXCEPT defiant individuality, which made their message more palatable and believable to boot.

And Kinghorse didn't just say "be yourself," they said "be yourself and define yourself by attacking everything around you that is false, hypocritical, empty or just plain stupid." In other words, be yourself and destroy anything that isn't true to itself. This is why Kinghorse came into conflict with all the various scene factions from the very beginning—and why it united them in the end. This is why the flyers and T-shirts and artwork were so confrontational, because it wasn't just about individuality amongst a nation of individuals, it was about individuality when confronted with a mass of Mary Quite Contrarys urging you to conform, conform, conform at all costs.

Nowadays, "individuality" (or "uniqueness" or "eccentricity" or "political incorrectness") doesn't mean that you are truly an independent thinker who challenges the status quo—who terrifies your classmates and co-workers—who spends most of your time thinking of new and creative ways to rearrange people's thought processes, often against their will. No, nowadays it means that you like to be pointlessly rude and repeat idiotic bigoted comments you heard from Rush Limbaugh—or that you kowtow to authoritarian leftists and repeat idiotic generalizations you read in some Catharine MacKinnon book—or worst of all, that you are one of the thousands of hip "retro" people who consider themselves unique because you have embraced a certain long-dead style of music or clothing and don't care about anything else (excluding sex and inebriation, of course).

And now, a brief aside to explain why Kinghorse adopted the imagery of the Process Church of the Final Judgment, and also to illustrate the uniqueness of both groups (the Horse and the Process) in contrast with the miserable sameness of their peers.

If you imagine the mainstream as Christianity, then the "opposition" would be Satanism, and the apathetic Other would be unbelievers and heathens in general. The Process Church had critiques of Christianity and Satanism, but instead of turning to unbelief, they rearranged the symbology of both religions in a new, interesting and challenging way. They didn't just mix up the ideas in order to be ironically blasphemous, they actually created a brand new set of ideas out of the disordered old ones.

This is why it was entirely appropriate for Kinghorse to adopt the Process Church's rotated "P" symbol as their own. If you imagine the mainstream as the 70s/80s hard rock/metal that the Horse boys were raised on, then the "opposition" would be punk rock, and the apathetic Other would be all those people listening to Boy George and Wham or whatever. Kinghorse combined the best elements of punk (the attitude, the stripped down-essentials approach) and metal (the guitar solos, the double bass!) in a way that provided something new and satisfying. In addition, the confident and emotional tone of defiance found in Process literature rang true with Kinghorse and at least some of their fans, especially the Triumvirate. End of aside.

Retro cool and the mainstreaming of punk/hardcore have proved that there is no more ultimate status quo in terms of aesthetics — which means there can never be another Kinghorse. Ask people what the status quo is, and you'll get a dozen different responses. Is it the liberal establishment which admonishes us to eschew firearms? Is it the conservative establishment which frowns upon queer sex or environmentalism? Is it major labels or mainstream media? Is it corporations, the church or the state? Nobody can agree.

Perhaps the true status quo nowadays is this fragmented spectacle of opinions and preferences which make the opinion-makers and product-sellers rub their hands together with unrestrained glee. "I am an individual and a rebel," says one kid, "because I like Rage Against the Machine and I wear baggy pants and I am against racism and, like, censorship or whatever."

"No, I am the true individual and rebel," says another kid, "because I like Ted Nugent and I hate affirmative action and the Liberal Media and immigrants or something."

"Nay, among the three of us, I am the only true individual and rebel," says the other (most annoying) kid, "because I like (insert 'obscure' indie rock band name here) and I wear thrift store clothes and thick framed glasses and I am fashionably nihilistic and I contemptuously spit upon you other two numskulls."

The real joke is that all three of them would have hated Kinghorse—and in five years, you won't be able to distinguish any one of them from the other two.
SO BE IT.

"Christ said: Love thine enemy. Christ's enemy was Satan and Satan's enemy was Christ. Through Love, enmity is destroyed. Through Love, saint and sinner destroy the enmity between them. Through Love, Christ and Satan have destroyed Their enmity and come together for the End; Christ to Judge and Satan to execute the Judgment.

Salvation is the resolution of conflict. The Ultimate Salvation is the Salvation of GOD. The Ultimate Conflict is God and Anti-God. God and Anti-God are two halves of a divided Totality. And They ultimately must be reconciled. God and Anti-God are embodied in Christ and Satan. So Christ and Satan must be reconciled. The Lamb and the Goat must come together: Pure Love descended from the pinnacle of Heaven, united with Pure Hatred raised from the depths of Hell."
—the Process Church of the Final Judgment

Note to Inside Front readers: If you feel the urge to go out and buy Kinghorse music now, allow me to warn you that the best possible way to experience this band—like all great bands—is live. Their recordings could not and did not capture their essence. That said, their first CD is on Caroline, and their last CD is on Slamdek. Both can be easily ordered from decent record shops. Rumor has it that Kinghorse's final unreleased material may be released in the near future. Let's hope so.

LOUISE (TAKE 2)
by Finn Forester

Movies will never set us free. Only we ourselves could possibly ever accomplish that. But, we here at CrimethInc. have found that particular films have been known to send us running freely out into warm German nights, through the crowded Reeper Bahn, dancing in and out of mysterious smoke-filled rooms, transformed.

A movie about aimless Parisian pickpockets, derelict street-kids endlessly roaming the subway stations. Love. Madness. Escape. And they run and run and run. Ah.

Hip hop, jazz, world beats attempt to keep pace with the cameras (almost all the camera shots were improvised), the cameras try to keep pace with the actors: the actors fly. Admittedly that that *sensation* that we call *freedom* could only be captured on film with great difficulty, if not impossibility! But! Something does occurs here: Between the frames something is glimpsed; subliminal freedom perhaps? (I gaze over to see Dörte floating in the seat next to me, my spine tingles, I feel ready for anything). Where does the story begin? With a girl? A bunch of criminals?

Sigfrid. Ah. He wanders the Earth alone,

East to West, West to East. Never is he in one place too long, always moving, learning languages, learning people, customs, secrets. And then, he emerges mysteriously, not as a character in our film, but to compose the music, produce it, write the script and to direct the whole thing! How he managed to make this film can't be told here, a vagabond's secret. I imagine young Sigfrid, having made a film that could explode into a thousand stars, quietly disappears into the night, smiling, not overly concerned with his the monumental film he just made. He walks down a rainy street, and slowly begins running, his thoughts swirling to night, smiling. Ah, the run, the easy, desperate run, a running madness. What next young Sigfrid? Hopefully we'll never hear from you again, hopefully this was the only film you had to make. Perhaps now, *we can come find you.*

The story begins with a girl. Louise. The story begins in a Paris Metro station. But actually the story begins when the theater lights come back on and seconds later, or perhaps days or weeks, I find myself *running* through crowds, lights flickering through summer nights, seeing Dörte chasing, dancing in out of

fear and hope). But really it's all the same: past, future, present, because it doesn't matter at all as I kiss you and you whisper to me of remembered forgotten nights, and the thousand stories of our lives.

Post Script:

A film can be a tricky thing, after all it's hard to do anything more than *watch* a film. We must also consider the risk that a film will simply co-opt one's desire for a particular thing, whether it be a desire for romance, adventure, or a sensation of freedom. It's easier after all to watch a movie and enjoy it than to actually to go out into this huge world of ours and make *our* lives that beautiful exciting story you can see in films. The film industry largely relies on this inability on our part to actualize these crazy dreams we have of Great Love, freedom, action, and mystery. Yet, we all know that real kisses taste much better than any cinema flicker.

So perhaps we have a dilemma with a film like "Louise (Take 2)". How great is the danger that someone will simply watch this film and be content to *see* "freedom" on the screen and

been released in the Unites States, there is a French website: www.louisetake2.com that you could check out – otherwise hold your breath and keep an eye extra wide open!)

THE MATRIX
by CrimethInc. Private I William Warren

Over capuccino we sat to discuss the experience. We oogled over special effects, I pictured myself running up walls and leaping across buildings, firing guns one-handed and moving faster than bullets; we let our imaginations go all the way out. Soon our conversation matured a bit and the caffeine wained in our blood and the conversation took a more sociological turn: "what," we queried, "is the philosophical context here? What exactly is being said?" And finally, "What is the Matrix?" This is how my research began.

From Christ imagery to Greek mythology, The Matrix is full of references and hints, mysterious connections, full of many complex and intriguing avenues of exploration. The depth of plot combined with some of the most spec-

Editor Dee's Top Ten Things Done by People in the Hardcore Community This Issue:

1. Trial live and on the "Are These Our Lives" CD
2. Zegota live
3. Liberninagen 'zine and CDR/Evasion zine
4. His Hero Is Gone live in Greensboro at the end of their existence, and on the "Enslavement Redefined" 12"
5. Undying live and on their incredible new CD
6. Ire live in Montreal at their last show, and on the "What Seed, What Root?" CD
7. Abuso Sonoro live/Newspeak live and on their split CD/Point of No Return new CD
8. Milemarker "Frigid Forms Sell" CD
9. Bloodpact live, on their split 12", and most of all in their lyrics and liner notes
10. Shoddy Puppet Company

Idiotor Dee's Top Ten Things Done by People Who Have Probably Never Heard of Hardcore This Issue:

1. Direct action in Seattle, São Paulo, Prague, across the whole world...
2. *Gimme Shelter* (not because of the fucking Stones)
3. Children of Bodom "Something Wild" CD
4. Godspeed You Black Emperor! "Slow Riot for New Zero Kanada" CD/A Silver Mount Zion CD/Godspeed live
5. Bertolucci's movie *Before the Revolution*
6. Cirque du Soleil
7. Dover "Late at Night" CD
8. Greil Marcus' *Lipstick Traces* (great book, but fuck that guy)/Italo Calvino's *Invisible Cities*/*House of Leaves* by Mark Z. Danielewski
9. Trans Am live in Raleigh, N.C./Seeing an orchestra perform Beethoven's 3rd Symphony
10. Clifford Harper's *Anarchy: A Graphic Guide*

smoky, forgotten clubs. Picture this: we dance into a bar in Hamburg, but find ourselves in London moments later. It's not even strange or uncommon, but only essential to understand. For, a great film will remind you about the true nature of time and space: time is yours, space is yours. Do with it what you will and what you must... we find ourselves living, breathing in the night air, not letting fear stop us from transforming ourselves into our dreams, into slinky sexy dancers one moment, on one hand, to vagabonds lost in a world of mist and perhaps beauty, perhaps triste pain the next, on the other hand, clasped in yours. I watch "Louise (Take 2)" backwards, forwards in my head, and the barrier between the screen and myself recede, and the movie becomes part of my past (I'm lost, panicking underground, trains close by) or maybe my future (bright, blinding lights, earth rumbles, sighs of relief,

leave it there, a flicker? I think this question reveals the most important thing about this movie: that is perhaps it contains a different sort of danger. The sort of danger we here love around the CrimethInc. offices. It seems to me that "Louise (Take 2)" inhabits that misty land of paradox (which some of us around here practically live in) where a mostly co-opting medium is somehow infused with a certain alchemy of (dare we say?) liberation.

A movie about a bunch of French misfits won't set you free, BUT there is that danger that you might walk back out into the streets, moved. Go on, we dare you, turn your lives into gold! Thankfully you don't need this film to do it either.
Highly Recommended.
1998. In French, Subtitled.

(Where to find this film: I don't believe it's

tacular action I have ever seen made this film very important to me. Its function as a tool, as a myth, helps me to deconstruct the world around me. I believe in this function, have experienced it, I believe in this parable and I believe it has a potential to reveal the truth of our world.

I will not endeavor here to point out all the individual references to Alice and Wonderland, Zen Buddhism, etc., other than to say that most of the secrets of this movie are revealed in the second scene, when the audience is introduced to Thomas Anderson, a.k.a. Neo. Also in this scene there is a quick reference to a French theorist/sociologist named Jean Baudrillard. After Neo takes the money through the door, he walks to a bookshelf and pulls out a book, which has been hollowed out to use as a hiding place. That book is called Simulacra and Simulations, by Baudrillard, which discusses with the function of images in modern society and the alienation of man from real, lived experience. This critique is central to the theme of the matrix.

Think of it as a system of communication, a social relation among people mediated by images, a system that ingrains itself so deep into your subconscious that you even use it to communicate with yourself, you think in its language, abide by its rules of grammar, etc. We learn what is good and right by observing images of goodness and righteousness. In similar ways, we learn what behavior is appropriate, what choices are responsible, etc. This system acts as a strategy of deterrence, that teaches the mind what is and isn't possible based not on reality, but on representations of reality, which is where Baudrillard comes in. "Simulacrum" is a word used to describe a sign which signifies nothing, but is its own reality, a copy without an original. In the world of the Matrix, human beings live in a neuro-interactive simulation of twentieth century life, a copy of the world as we know it, while their bodies exist only in pods and are used to generate energy. They live in a simlacra.

Baudrillard proports that modern industrial society is also a simulacra, where the images used to teach us what is real no longer bear any resemblance to any reality whatever, and exist only to perpetuate themselves as pure simulacrum. Consider for a moment the things you have learned, do you know they are real? Do you find yourself pacing the halls of your school or workplace tortured by the feeling that there must be more to the world, that there must be more to life? Consider the limits of your world, do they really exist? Limitations, by their very definition, suggest that something lies Beyond.

What if I told you that there is more? What if I told you that you were born into a prison, a mental prison, where iron bars and shackles are not necessary because your mind does their work for them? What if I said that the real is no longer what it used to be, that it occurs now only in moments of falsehood? We have become like cows, held at bay by a single strand of wire, endlessly fertilizing the ground upon which we graze.

The Matrix is about finding the truth in a world of lies. It's about realizing you have been deceived by everything you thought was pure. And it's about awakening to the real world, redefining your limits, and deciding for yourself what is and isn't possible. The first step is discovery and realization, sensing the Beyond, and finding the courage to follow that intuition. The second step involves facing a decision in every moment between truth and comfort, between freedom and safety. The audience cringes when Cipher betrays and murders his friends so that he can be reinserted into the system; but who can deny having that impulse within himself? These two steps are thoroughly addressed by the protagonists in the Matrix,

but there is another step which is not directly addressed.

Throughout his activist training, Neo is repeatedly told to free his mind. "You've got to let it all go, Neo: fear, doubt, and disbelief." He learns over time to release his inhibitions and is amazed as he finds himself with a new freedom of movement that he previously believed impossible, he is astonished as he realizes he can do what has never been done. As anarchists in the modern age, there is something we can learn from this. If we expect to realize our goals, if we expect to ever get our ideas off the drawing bored and into physical space, we must learn to see the unseen, we must learn to do the impossible. To defeat our enemies we will need more than guns and violence, above all we need imagination, we need cunning and tact, and we will need to be clever. We have to leave the limits of this world behind and head out into uncharted territory, for this is where our lives are won. We can no longer look to the past for help, tradition has done for us what it can, our eyes must face forward, unwavering.

To the extent that we can accomplish this transcendence in great numbers, is the extent to which we can change the world. The Matrix is a great movie, but it is no manual for HOW. There is no guidebook for us, we are totally on our own. Only our intuition can lead us; it will

manifest itself in the world, it will yell at us from the pages of books and zines, from music, from people in our lives, and even from the silver screen.

Every day is a war against evil, a fight for mobility. The key is to focus inward and let nature take its course. Do not set yourself out to change the world, who can move for very long under that weight? But do not doubt the world is changing. Reinvent yourself in every moment, find your way to a state of choiceless awareness, without condemnation or comparison, formless and unpredictable, no waiting for a further development in order to agree or disagree. This is how our revolution will be made real.

Further reading: Simulacra and Simulations, by Jean Baudrillard, Society of the Spectacle, by Guy Debord, The Tao of Physics, by Fritdof Capra, and The Tao of Jeet Kune Do, by Bruce Lee.

SHODDY PUPPET COMPANY— PERFORMANCE IN CHAPEL HILL, WINTER 2000:

reviewed by your editor

I was already vaguely aware of the potential of puppet shows in the punk rock context from the work of Roby Newton, but seeing this performance (which she booked in her basement) really drove it home for me. These kids challenged us on every front, showing us how much was possible in an artistic medium we hadn't thought much about before, educating and informing us of political and social issues while entertaining us so much that it opened us up to learn without suspicion or despair. That was real genius there, for usually learning about something like city government corruption and the way it fucks up the common citizen would really be a miserable, disempowering experience—but taught through an absolutely genius shadow puppet show about a baseball team, it was thrilling even more than it was depressing, and left us all ready to think and act creatively about political issues. The I.WW. song at the beginning of the set gave us historical knowledge and context, the sock puppets in the piece about the dangers of genetic engineering pro-

vided hilarity, the amazing homemade set for the dramatization of Subcommandante Marcos' "History of Melons" made us wonder what our own hands might be capable of, and the spoken word pieces accompanying everything made us feel at home while showing the confidence needed to make us all listen up and take things seriously. This is where it's at for a lot of you out there who haven't started bands yet but want to do creative things in this community—try another medium, there are thousands of them out there begging to be explored. *Shoddy Shack, 4719 Hazel Avenue, Philadelphia, PA 19143*

Gloria Cubana's Top Ten Ways to Drive Yourself Wild in Bed

1. *Evening*, Susan Minot
2. At the Drive-In live, October 2000
3. Paper Hand Puppet Intervention's production of *A Very Old and Unfinished Story*
5. *McSweeney's Quarterly Concern*
6. Le Tigre with The Butchies, Summer 2000; Laddio Balacko, Sep. 2000
7. *Art Objects*, Jeanette Winterson; *The Red Leaves of Night*, David St. John
8. *The Millennium Cookbook*
9. *Confederates in the Attic*, Tony Horwitz
10. *Being John Malkovich*, *American Beauty*
11. Interview with Genesis P-Orridge seen in exhibit at Centre Pompidou, Paris, Jan. 2000; Ashmolean Museum, Oxford, especially exhibit on Futurism, March 2000; Musée de la Vie Bourguignonne, Dijon

THIEVING KINKO'S EMPLOYEES
by Robin Banks

If there is any one group of people in our so called "scene" who need to be regularly thanked for their immense contributions to our ongoing struggle, it's renegade Kinko's employees. How many seven-inch covers, CD booklets, LP inserts, flyers, and zines have been produced for free by naughty punk moles at Kinko's? I was inspired to write this review when I got back from my local Kinko's with approximately $500 worth of free stuff — photocopied zines and flyers and office supplies, all thoughtfully liberated by my Kinko's comrades — which only cost me thirty eight cents at the cash register. There are endless tales of punk rockers making similar scores at their local branch offices. So let us honor all of our Kinko's amigos. Let us give them free food, drinks, music, kisses, and clothing. Let us finally acknowledge our great debt to those unsung heroes of the so-called "scene" — thieving Kinko's employees. I give them four stars. Highly recommended. Available at the Kinko's nearest you.

ble acts, take place on this front. The author of the introduction calls this a tale worthy of Dostoyevsky, and that's absolutely right—this ultimately turns out to be about the most fundamental questions of being human, and the specific details of the lives chronicled here just makes it all the more real and persuasive (and, thus, universal). It's massive, 328 pages, practically a life's work considering the quality and intricacy of the graphic art as well as the storyline. It's no hyperbole for me to say I was as deeply moved by this as by One Hundred Years of Solitude or The Unbearable Lightness of Being.
Autonomedia, P.O. Box 568, Williamsburgh Station, Brooklyn, NY 11211-0568

WLOCHATY [EPONYMOUS] 12"
by... anonymous.

"Let me pick a rose before the storm breaks out—Let me take a bite of bread before it turns to stone—Let me look at the sun before it's covered in ash—Let me touch your cheek with my lips before the bone starts to show." One afternoon, not so long ago, I got off of the school bus and found a package with my name on it propped up on the steps of my father's house, bedraggled

for the ten thousandth time, and I open up the lyric sheet. Wlochaty. Would it have been better if I had never heard music like this, if I had never read these words? Would it have been better if I had come to terms with reality, with this best of all possible worlds, this sick farce, and gone about my business accordingly? I have gambled my freedom, my health, my sanity, my very life away in desperate hopes that I could indeed "live differently", that we could all still "fall deeply in love". Was I mistaken? I don't know. But when the music stops my broken old (Ha!) heart beats thunderous and strong once more, and I do at least know that I am not alone. "Somewhere in the darkness of uncertainty—You still harbor a small hope—That you'll live differently—That you'll fall deeply in love—Even though you're walking in a barren desert—And you've been spared nothing—Somewhere in the darkness of uncertainty—You still have hope." "I'll tell you nothing, although I want to scream I feel like a hounded animal—But I don't want to infect you with my fear I'm so scared, give me some of your strength—Maybe it's the last time, don't turn away—Maybe I'll wake up strong tomorrow morning—And when you nestle your arms in me frightened I'll wrap you up in myself and carry you—'Til

Jon Smith's Top Ten
Reasons Why Activity Is
Better Than Sleep:

1. The marriage of Amanda Louise Smith
2. Roof access at UNCG
3. Catharsis in Bosnia
4. Submission Hold at the House of Thieves
5. *Safety Three Frequency Geodesic Icosahedron* by F. Dixon
6. Stravinsky's *The Rite of Spring* (ballet)
7. "in the fields the bodies burning" mix tape from Jason
8. RunHaveFun in Greensboro 1/8 – 6/30
9. Poetry, love letters, and untold secrets
10. Malabaster at Wilson St.

Paul K Maul's Top Ten
Reasons To Not Kill Himself
(So Far, So Good.)

1. Bottled Root Beer
2. Avocados
3. Yellow Tomatoes From My Friend Austin's Garden
4. Charles Bukowski
5. First Annual CrimethInc. Bi-Coastal Moonlit Wild Nature Walk
6. 17 Distinct Memories From the South American Tour
7. Cuban Cigars (Esp. Bolivar)
8. Crisp Air
9. George W. Hayduke's Victorious Final Escape Into The Sea
10. Walking

WAR IN THE NEIGHBORHOOD:
A GRAPHIC NOVEL BY
SETH TOBOCMAN
also reviewed by the editor

This is one of the most beautiful, important books to come out of the underground (or anywhere, for that matter) in a long time. With breathtaking images and graphic design, it tells the stories of a variety of individuals struggling to work together in the Lower East Side of N.Y.C. through the late '80's and early '90's. Together, they struggle to preserve their freedom in Tompkins Square park, to defend squats, to get along with each other, separately, they struggle with their own demons, doubts, and destructive tendencies, and the real heroism, as well as the most cowardly and despica-

and covered with foreign stamps. I had long since forgotten that months and months before I had mailed a ten dollar bill to Poland, requesting a twelve inch record by a band named Wlochaty. I put the record on the turntable, and I opened up the lyric sheet. My pupils dilated. My heart beat faster. I was not alone. Six years later. My life is utterly wrecked. I see no prospects that anything is going to get any better any time in the foreseeable future. No, my situation is only going to get worse, and I am paralyzed with fear; nameless, unspeakable dread that haunts me every second of every day. I can not make it go away, no matter what I do, or think, or say. I go to the milk crate, to the special place between 'Warzone' and 'Wrecking Crew' where Wlochaty lives. I put this battered piece of vinyl on the turntable,

I've got enough courage—'Til I've got enough strength—It's rumored that people fight somewhere—It's rumored that they still pick up stones They hit blows and win, and only that gives you hope—Be the hope for them when they'll be bled to death—So don't die yet, here's praise for life—Be the hope for me, have strength to scream and call—We'll find our good side in ourselves—We'll open our hearts and minds—And we'll be free at last—Because our future will be the one we will win for us."
Wlochaty - PO BOX 68, 70-821 Szczecin 12, Poland
Wlochaty - S/T - on Nikt Nic Nie Wie - Zielona 16, 34-400 Nowy Targ, Poland

MUSIC

Actitud Subversiva "Ni Tu Ni Dios Ni el Mundo" cassette: At eighteen songs and a quality recording, this is certainly not a demo, although the price is still cheap. The music has an oi/punk feel to it—the simple melodies, occasional major key guitar leads, gruff singing with back-up ooo-ooo-ooos—it's well done, spirited, and non-monotonous, if firmly entrenched within the conventions of the genre. A Puerto Rican Kríticka Situace without all the unique stuff (and some of the energy) comes to mind. No lyrics printed in the insert, but they're singing (in Spanish) about basic, empowering things (do what you believe in, work towards unity with others...) in everything we can make out. –b with help from @
Colin Dover, 123 c/Marte, Isla Verde, P.R. 00979

As I Bleed "Fire in Summer" 10": This introduction, with beautiful, distant Middle Eastern singing, is gorgeous (though it is a sample, I fear) and so when the music comes in they have my trust. For the most part, they don't abuse it. There are a few moments when they throw in some hackneyed, overplayed double-bass-guitar-chunk-and-groan parts that the world could have done without, and they also seem to have a hard time getting their Judas Priest guitar harmonies to sound tight and right. But when the singer tries to pull off the singing-during-the-emotional-part of the song, he just barely gets away with it, despite obviously having little singing experience; and just after that they execute a great arrangement where hard jabs of guitar and drums stab in staccato over an acoustic part—it's something I've never heard done quite this way before. In case there was any doubt in your minds—this is modern U.S. metal/hardcore, with the low guitar tuning, frequent tempo changes, the fancy transitions and complex riffs. By the end of the record, I'm satisfied with their musicianship, and I've enjoyed this at times... but I'm a little tired of hearing the sample I liked so much at the beginning between every song, and I've come to a realization: I look at the lyrics to this kind of music *after* I've listened to the record, because I generally think of them as being separate from the music, which is too bad—and then, I see it: one of their songs ends, incongruously (he was talking about autumn leaves falling) with the words "never trust another whore." Kid, what are you talking about? In a world of pimps and whores, I'll trust my fellow whores first any day. Seriously, saying things like that has some bad implications... anyway. –b
Voice of Life, P.O. Box 1137, 04701 Leisnig, Germany

Analena "Arhythmetics" 7": This record is suffused with plaintive longing: it cries out from the guitar melodies and vocals, and attains an extra bite and urgency from the driving force of the drums. The singer doesn't hold back the sorrowful beauty when she sings, nor the rage when she screams. Her lyrics are simple but thick with feeling, just a few lines for each song. The final song is, improbably, the same Kylie Minogue song that Systral covered, although it sounds totally different here, and no less touching, although in a totally different way: she sounds doubtful of the consequences but sincere as she offers herself, easily transcending the meaninglessness of the original track, and replacing the nihilistic destruction of the Systral take on this song with something more human. They even get away with using electronic drums on that song without losing any of the immediacy of the song. Beautiful. —b
Get Off, Sergej Vutuc, Bahnhofstr. 2, 74072 Heilbronn, Germany

Balaclava "" 7": This record is really excellent. The music is difficult to describe, and that is because it is creative and unique...and isn't that what all of us are hoping for in this genre? These tracks are intended to be anthems instead of just songs. They are a rallying cry towards something better, and they have the immediacy necessary to inspire people to achieve. Is that too vague? Well, looking at the lyrics will help us specify a bit. There are four songs on this record and all of the lyrics are translated into both English and Czech, though sung in Czech (which I love...more bands should be singing in languages other than dumb old English...English is the McDonalds of the language world). Each song has a quote that describes in a few words the focus of the song, the lyrics, and then a song description as well. Topics include: inspiring people to get involved with hardcore, overcoming "barricades" within ourselves, animal rights and unity. Each of the members contributed an essay for the post song descriptions and they work well to convey what the songs are trying to express. The music benefits from dual vocal tracks, one higher and one lower, and itself is heavy without being patterned or contrived. The song topics might sound as though they are played out and overdone, but this band brings to them a passion and energetic twist which defies all the other bands out there talking about the same things. Definitely original and definitely recommended. —JUG
Hopewell Records; Ondrej Benes; U Hraze 1; Praha 10, 100 00, Czech Republic; reskator@post.cz; or rescator@post.cz for more information

Blood Has Been Shed "I Dwell on Thoughts of You" CDEP: This is an incredibly talented metalcore outfit hailing from CT, who gets mad DIY props for releasing their own CD.

Reviewer Code:

b— your humble, bumbling editor • WG— Will 'Gota
@— mistress of foreign tongues, Gloria Cubana
WW— William Warren, martial artist, traveler, anarchist, wild romantic
n— Nicholai Baxter • BB— Bruce Burnside
JUG—Greg, King of the Bennicks • raz— Moe 'Gota

Note: The following releases have not been reviewed in this issue, in the interest of avoiding redundancy:

• Harbinger, part 3 (which came out and was gone in a month, all 25,000 copies of it-?-)
• Zegota "Movement in the Movement" 12" (nearly out of press from Crimethinc., also pressed by Reflections in Holland) and CD (Crimethinc., in press for a long time to come)
• Fre "What Seed, What Root?" 12" (Scorched Earth Policy) CD (Crimethinc., very much in press)
• Catharsis/Newspeak split CD (Liberation, in Brazil... out of press now, anyway)
• "Days of War, Nights of Love" book (Crimethinc... of course)

It shouldn't need saying that we think these are all great, and I'm sure the last thing you want is to read more of our ranting and raving about projects we've participated in.

This debut EP has seven songs of brutal and blistering moshy metal, with excellent vocals that range from beautifully mournful singing to a raging scream. Lyrical topics are also somewhat varied, from personal to slightly political (anti-rape). My only problem with this is its tendency to fall into clichés and things expected of every metalcore band, like the visual imagery (computer-manipulated artwork of angels and other vaguely depressing computer craziness), some of the common "metal" riffs, and the lyrical style (almost always addressed towards the infamous, but never really identified "you"). However, this should not overshadow all the ways that this kicks serious ass…and I have heard their new stuff via MP3 (to be released soon in an album on Ferret), and it is even better, so hopefully they tightened up on those few aspects that were lacking. –n
Goodness, I think Nick's forgotten to include their address. Write him at the F.B.I. address and demand it, if this sounds interesting…

suddenly shift to the ride cymbal, becoming totally spare, cutting the beat in half—only here, instead of a falling guitar wail with the tremolo bar, it's Andy's scream that descends into the darkness before the next part begins. By the way, kids, you misspell the word "weird" on the back cover, in the song title. –b
+/– records

Born Dead Icons "Work" 12": At first, I was expecting (due to their name, and former members and associations) something along the lines of the dark, political post-metal/post-Neurosis music bands like Ire play, but that was totally off. Remember (you may not) how the Amebix thought they were Motorhead? This is like Motorhead, if they thought they were the Amebix—it has the Motorhead workmanlike approach to songwriting, the Motorhead aesthetic (gravelly vocals, ridiculously fast single bass drumming, bare-bones rock'n'roll chord progressions—shit, come to think of it.

Brazen "As Floods Decrease" 10": Hm, no lyric sheet, or at least I'm missing one (in addition, both sides of the record are absolutely identical, down to the etched i.d. number, so I'm not sure if I'm listening to "The opening curse" or "Frozen Gossips"). The cover is gorgeous, a rectangle of cardstock folded around the vinyl, with a hauntingly simple image of an old man's bare head on the front. The music is artsy in ways similar to the packaging—it seems to have something to communicate, but to be expressing it in a code for which the key is not provided. Or maybe that's making too much of it. They opt for the less-distorted guitar sound (no metal here) of bands like Fugazi, vocals that flutter between song, yell, and scream, songs that wander through strummed melodies for quite a little while, without sudden transitions or shifts in mood, but gathering tension and force as they go. Every once in a while their chord progressions and arrangements actually remind me of

Aluminum Noise "—" Collection CD: This is a noise CD my friends Jason and Nate put out, and they asked me to review it because I know nothing about noise, so I thought I would have some fun. This starts out with multi-tracked, pulsating, meandering, harmonious guitar notes that remind me of when you and your favorite person are swinging around in a circle with both hands grasped, the background going around and around, but the beloved's face always in front, focused and smiling. Then I get into a rocker sailing to the unknown and quickly hear evil note progressions in front of a hurricane of white noise, which get louder and then crescendo into octaves and various other riffage. Then I swear I hear an AC/DC melody ("C'mon, c'mon listen to the mo-ney talk…") that goes into a string scraping session and then into some screwed-with samples. And suddenly I'm watching my life pass before me backwards, projected on the sky, and some dude appears and talks to me about traditional musical notation, and before he can finish what he has to say a big monstrous beast comes and tears him apart with contradictional musical notation (and execution). Then I spend a while walking around the UNCG area of Greensboro, NC, but nobody is around. I'm alone, the *only* life. Soon buildings sprout out of nowhere, like in *Dark City*, and I hear a drumbeat that I try to follow, but every time I turn the corner to where I think it's originating from, I see nothing and am forced to keep going, frustrated. And then I realize that the drumbeat is merely a soundtrack to me looking for something, and I stop, and the drums stop. Then I proceed to experience in succession a plane crash in slow motion, what it's like to live on clouds and then fall off what it was like to be on the set of Star Trek in the 70s, and the likeness of having the most scary fucking beast ever imagined roar in your face for 38 seconds so close that all you can see is it's warm breath pushing against your nose hairs and all you can feel is it's tonsils dangling like rovers excited rail. Things cool off a bit and I am visited by my dead grandmother on my father's side, and I watch myself sleep for a while. I wake up in a factory with only one person working the line, assembling sprockets with an expressionless countenance, undeniably sad. She sees the sun, people playing soccer outside, but if she stops, she will for some reason *die*. I feel helpless and guilty, and leave, head hung low. I bump into a TV and get sucked into it, the hypnotizing computer chips scraping at my useless skin, bleeding me, getting in my ear and making the most godawful noise I've ever heard that reminds me of what it would sound like if you took a multiple-car accident and slowed down the metal on metal friction of the teeth grinding, heart-breaking, impact. Then… it's all over. Silence is sweet. This was written haphazardly and at the last minute, so sorry if it makes no sense whatsoever. I like the CD. –WG
P.O. Box 66146, Greensboro, NC 27403

Bloodpact "Bastardization" CD discography thus-far: Check out my review of their split 12" somewhere later in these pages to get a more thorough idea of why I love this band so much. This includes those songs, along with their 7" (which had, um, much better drumming), and a series of Black Flag covers, I mean compilation tracks. They also cover 7 Seconds, and Chokehold, and get massive bonus points for listing the lyrics and credits to the Black Flag song as simply "depression, fuck." Listen, this is awesome, this is way up there with the best hardcore being made today, if you ask me. Finishing this review, I realize that on the third to last song of their split LP, they totally ripped off Slayer—it's that moment on "South of Heaven" where the guitars strike an open chord and the drums

the Amebix had all that, too), but the Amebix politics and ambience of doom. My favorite moments, artsy bastard that I am, are when they do the spooky, unexpected breakdowns and buildups that all great rock and roll has in it—but all of this is high energy in a way that Motorhead rock can be and hardcore never can be, you know? It's fucking good. By the way, after reading their right-on but linguistically tortured Conflict-style essay on the reverse of the lyric sheet, I'd like to publicly offer my assistance to any non-English speaking band who want help polishing the English translations of their writing. Seriously, just send me what you're working on at the Inside Front address and I'll help smooth it out. –b
Deadalive, P.O. Box 97, Caldwell, NJ 07006

what Neurosis would do if they were playing on Fugazi's equipment. I'm becoming more and more convinced as I listen to this, rather than bored, to their credit. There are ideas being developed here that will prove powerful, if the ones pursuing them are ready to follow them out onto the wild, unexplored plains, rather than remaining crouched in the suburbs with the generic bands who don't even know that movement is possible. –b
Brazen, 8 Bld James-Fazy, 1201 Geneva, Switzerland

Breed/Extinction 7": This is the first time I get to hear my friends' band on record, and it's awesome to find out that their recording lives up to their performances. This is bitter, ugly music in the tradition of such bands as

Gehenna and His Hero Is Gone—I don't mean the musical tradition so much as the psychological one: in which, sour on life and exhausted by failure and tragedy beyond the point of believing in anything, a band picks up instruments to express their misery and rage, and in the act of playing rediscover passion in the one place it still remains to be felt, in the singing of a dirge for its loss. For those who haven't suffered and struck out blindly, this can be alienating, fearsome stuff... but for those of us who have been dragged to the edge and clawed our way back by vomiting the filth out of us, though it seemed like the stream would never end, this hateful noise is an affirmation of life, of the indomitable will to live and create. The guitars arise from a black sea, soaked in oil, rumbling thunder... the acoustic parts have the ruined, trashed post-apocalyptic beauty that can be persuasive when anything cleaner sounds like a mockery. And they're smart kids, too—the lyrics and writing leave nothing to be desired. They have six more songs that aren't on this 7" (maybe on some demo somewhere?), which are equally worth hearing. —b

my only complaint is that these morons didn't put a ground address anywhere here! try to find them somewhere in Connecticut, or use email (much as I fucking hate it): breedextinction@hotmail.com *or* eighthdaydissent@hotmail.com

Brethren "To Live Again" CD: When I first received this in the mail I noticed the sick artwork/photography and read the awesome, insightful album explanation in the lyric booklet, and was excited at what I would hear. But what I heard was just way too generic sounding and boring to spark my interest and emotions any further: it was just the typical heavy east coast hardcore sound. I tried to let it grow on me the way some music can do, but to no avail...I guess I've just heard all the riffs and song structures and vocals too many times before. I hate to give a negative review to a band that seems very sincere, dedicated, and intelligent, but I guess I just don't like what they're doing musically. My advice for them is to keep pushing the boundaries further, try to be innovative and a little crazier, and try not to get caught in one overdone style of hardcore. Overall this band is doing a really good job at what they're doing. I just don't like what they're doing all that much. —n
OHEV (address at 23rd Chapter review)

Broken Promises "" CD: This has a very genuine feel to it, not forced or fake at all. It's metallic hardcore, with the chunk-chunk-note-chunk-chunk-note riffs and screaming vocals, but they definitely have an aesthetic of their own here. When the singer pauses to speak in the most troubled, angst-ridden, trembling voice I've heard in one hundred reviewed records, it sounds like real, troubled,

youthful emotion being expressed for its own sake, without regard for anything except getting it out, and I really appreciate that, especially in a genre (metallic hardcore) weighed down with so much baggage of posing and expectations that one can hardly expect to hear something honest and open from it anymore. I guess Starkweather was this emotionally raw and real [well, more so, honestly], that's the best example I can think of. I'm surprised by how polished the playing and the recording are, too, and though the music doesn't stray far from the formula laid out by Unbroken they use enough ideas of their own invention to keep it sounding unique (a naked double bass blast, abandoned by the guitars, segues convincingly into a soothing melodic part, at one point). The lyrics and various writings from the band (which are numerous, thankfully) also bleed the same troubled emotion, alternately giving and pushing away... "this is about love, but no thanks to you," writes the singer over and over, and you know he desperately wants to say the opposite, whether he can admit it or not. I like this a lot. —b
Stick to the Core, Hogeweg 31, 3200 Aarschot, Belgium

Burden "Strength of Conviction" 7": I reviewed this in the last Inside Front so I will just give it a mention here to say that the demo has been rereleased in 7" format from Badman Records in the Czech Republic. I love this record, as it is reminiscent of Judge in terms of being powerful SxE hardcore, but these guys do the genre justice and really hammer these songs home. There are a lot of bands out there playing straight edge hardcore, but Burden is one of the best. Check out the 7" and support a new label in the process. —JUG
Badman Records; Martin Cesky; Nebrehovice 7; 38601 Strakonice; Czech Republic; mcesky@pvtnet.cz for more info.

Buried Inside "In and Of the Self" CD: , The first song starts out in the screamy modern metal/hardcore format, then goes into a more retro deathmetal-growling chunky mosh-pit-windmilling dance part near the end, which surprised me a bit. They're not as polished yet as their musical ambitions demand—sometimes I feel like their timing is a tiny bit off. But at the same time, I appreciate that they're working at and sometimes past their own limits, and they are able to do some things I haven't heard before in such an overcrowded genre—the echo effects on the metal guitars give their chunky/melodic parts a faraway, spooky sound, for example, and they are always messing with sound textures and arrangements in similar ways. The lyrics are taken seriously (dealing generally with living under the yoke of our rape/consumer/domi-

nation culture) and are right on, and that makes me feel a lot more comfortable about them. In fact, the lyrics are fucking awesome, now that I go over them again: "personal interest is the steam that fogs the mirrors of our very existence" "so here we are, sitting on the edge of it all, waiting for the sun to rise." *Apocalypse Now* samples over a piano/opera intro to the last song, and I'm sitting here with the lyric sheet, listening to the first, coldly beautiful, severe notes that follow, realizing now that if this band could distance themselves from the pack just a little more they could do some amazing things. —b
Standingwave, 422 Leighton Street, Ottawa, ON K1Z 6J6, Canada

Caliban "A Small Boy and A Grey Heaven" CD: Just for fun, after I had written the first three lines of this review, I went to www.altavista.com to the 'translate' section (which, by the way is the very best web page on the entire internet. I promise that it will provide you with hours of laughs) and translated the three sentences from English to Italian and then back to English. (Is it obvious that I don't get out much?) Anyway, the review starts out like this: "This CD opens with an 'Omen'-like musical intro and then blasts immediately into a death metalish selection of songs. Think of The Year of Our Lord (reviewed elsewhere in this issue) but more to the intensely heavy hardcore side rather than towards metal. I love it!" Now, take that and plug it into alravista. Translate it back and forth a few times, and you get: "This CD is opened with 'Omen'-as the intro musical and then ago in order to jump immediately in one selection of the metalish of the dead man of the songs. In order to think elsewhere close next to the year of ours gentleman (to see still in this edition) but more neighbor to the intensely heavy side of the hardcore rather than towards metal. I love!" Whew...I am wiping tears of laughter from my eyes as I type these soon to be spell checked words. I wholeheartedly recommend that you try this altavista trick with any piece of text in the world. It is amazing and will make you the life of the party, especially if you actually try to use the site as a tool for bona fide translation. If an Italian kid ever comes up to me and speaks like the above translation, I will have to be committed to an insane asylum. Okay...stay on target ...we have a CD to review here. The Caliban CD has an immense sound, with growled higher pitched vocalizations and varied well orchestrated music. It isn't standard by any means. Instead, it brings you on a journey, ostensibly through the hell which our world has become due to pollution, greed, hate and fear, with music which adequately represents the doom expressed in the words. There are definite black metal influences in the guitar work, as

well as a tendency towards the incredibly complex which brought to mind Botch at times. They don't rip off anyone however, so don't get me wrong. The CD is full of shards and glimmers into the band themselves, in terms of samples and interludes, intros and outtros. Lyrically good as well, with a beautiful layout: a booklet with painted pages and full lyrics. Lifeforce is on a roll with these metallic hardcore and hardcoric metal and metallic metal bands! —JUG
Lifeforce Records; PO Box 04011 Leipzig; Germany; cartel@bigfoot.com; www.carteldistrobution.com

Cast-down "these autumnal tints" 7": Four songs of slightly melodic, slightly post-hardcore, emotional hardcore, if that makes sense to you. These guys are doing a really good job finding their own sound and not imitating, so they're a little harder to describe, but I guess if you imagined a mix of Shai Hulud and Endeavor after mellowing out on some huge bong hits, you might be in the ballpark. There's some really catchy riffs, interesting musical changes, great raw, sincere vocals, as well as some snappy graphic design work,

ly is an accurate, although I'm not sure how flattering, comparison. For those of you unfamiliar with this style of hardcore, its straight-up heavy as hell, nuts and bolts, gritty and tough moshcore from Michigan with half-yelled, half-screamed tough as shit vocals. I think this rocks, mainly because the vocalist has such an awesome voice and style, and admittedly, simply because I like Earthmover. The artwork on here is beautiful, the lyrics are simple and to the point, and the personal writing by the band in the booklet is a sincere touch, but I can't get over the recording quality. It's simply not as full and dynamic as it should be, and it really bugs me. It sounds very quiet, weak, and trebly, like a demo recording, and I'm kinda wondering what happened...everything else is so top-notch and slick, I feel let down in a way. Aside from that, I like this a lot and am excited to hear more from these guys. —n
Genet Records / PO box 447 / 9000 GENT 1, Belgium

Children "Impedimenta" CD: This is without a doubt the best CD to ever begin with the lyrics "you stabbed me in the back." Brilliant,

do whatever it takes—it's a flawless executed acoustic piece, spanning the jazz and folk and classical styles over about twelve minutes, really beautiful. —b
Overcome, B.P. 7548, 35075 Rennes Cedex 3, France

Clear "Deeper Than Blood" CD: Clear play metal influenced hardcore (the drummer thanks Slayer, Candiria, Iron Maiden, among others) that I've heard many times before from many bands. Same goes for the packaging. Not much new or original here. But, alas, if you dig the heavy moshable scream-alongable chug-chug tunes that seem to be popular these days, than this is for you. The recording is fairly dry, and the drums are way too loud. It sounds to me like this was done in a hurry. Alone in the drum mix, the bass drum (which is a main asset of the entire album) has too much click making it sound like someone is standing in the recording studio with a freaking pair of sticks and hitting them together every time the bass drum is struck. To stand out in this type of music, the bass drum itself needs *some* click, added in during mixdown, but this is off the hook. And just for fun I'll say too that the

Black Dice 10": celebrity review courtesy of Ben Clack

"I can honestly say that I don't give a fuck about anything anymore." —an unnamed member of black dice during a post performance discussion, Philadelphia, Pa july 1999

I sit to write this on the day that I have learned that I have begun to lose hearing in my right ear. This damage is irreversible and thus I must begin looking at the capabilities and limitations of information carried with in sound and the implications of not being able to process this information. Across the room sits the black dice 10" propped against the shelf containing my record player. Seeing this I know my days of sound are numbered and I admittedly never want this beautiful noise to leave my memory. So I must keep playing it over and over and over again. For this is not just sound, it is the physical manifestation of depression, anger, frustration, and energy.

The black dice are not merely the next darlings to whom all of the young dolls will be thrashing about, instead the black dice are the stoned drunk pissed off children of the night. Blasting away without fear, bleeding screaming, wholehearedly embracing everything you ever wanted, needed, and dreamed of becoming. The audience was the instrument, the band becoming the wandering voyeur. The music came from these worlds colliding. With this comes something great noise for the fuck of it. The black dice are proof that punk rock still happens in this world of insufferable greed. Don't go buy this record. Steal it, tape it, and then break it over your head slashing all nearby with its broken shards, and then maybe you'll begin to understand what it will be like to never again hear this noise. Oh how dathy would be proud. *Ben was available on Troubleman unlimited... Ben was too busy taping and smashing to give us their address. Right on!*

which all make this release worth getting despite the following drawbacks: The cynical attitude expressed in the liner notes, some awkward parts to the music where it just doesn't seem to flow well (I don't have enough technical knowledge of music to explain what I'm thinking here in more depth, sorry), and some of the lyrics that sound cliché in their introspective poetic vagueness or struggle to find rhyming words at the end of lines. I think that in two more releases this band will have worked out all these little kinks and will be doing some amazing, unique shit, but for now, this effort is still good. —n
Watch 'M Burn / Kauwplasstr. 28 / 3545 Halen, Belgium

Cast In Fire "Apology" CDEP: Earthmover on steroids, plain and simple. With ex-members of that now-defunct mosh machine, this real-

maximum energy groundbreaking hardcore from the cutting edge of the musical movement, with a perfect recording (that sounds scary all by itself, with the rumbling bass, the stab of the snare drum...), acoustic arrangements of classical quality, extra dynamic songwriting with flawless transitions and well-constructed riffs, plenty of little experiments and new ideas to spice everything up. Most of all, this just rocks in the way that really good metal/hardcore can, but it also has some moments of chilling beauty. The lyrics are pretty desperate, not in the typical stylized manner of most lyrics in this genre (OK, the first line, the one I cited above, is not so original), but really persuasive, disturbing. If you thought there was anything good about what Overcast was trying to do a few years ago, you should find this at least as interesting. The final track proves their skill and readiness to

snare is getting all run over by the hi-hat and ride cymbal; what's important here? The vocals are pretty good when they are screams, but there are times when they are sung, and this is a bit weird. Packaging wise: imagine the typical fold out glossy insert, complete with action pictures and lengthy 'thank you' lists. The lyrics are included, with topics usually circling around the personal and infamous "you." I can definitely relate to them, though. Yeah, this is not a bad record, but I will probably never listen to it again. —WG
Clear c/o Sean; 7529 South Campus Circle; Salt Lake City, UT 84121. Stillborn Records; PO Box 3019; New Haven, CT 06515.

Cloudburst "Love Lies Bleeding" 7": This French band plays a personalized version of the melodic metal hardcore played by legions of new school bands (many of whom have

been released by Good Life records). They have the same basic features here—breaks for bass melodies to which guitar chunks are soon added for build-ups, hoarse screamy vocals, pounding metal chunk breakdowns, rare moments of blastbeat frenzy—but it doesn't sound derivative, just modern and nothing more than modern. They set themselves apart on the b-side when they cut everything but the acoustic guitar and vocal harmonies—more of those unexpected moments and the hardcore formulas would hit harder when they come in. Lyrics in English, explanations in French and English, all dealing generally with the strain on humanity created by the latest steps in our cultural/technological/political "evolution." –b
Mosh Bart, address below

The Control: Ruination is a perfect point of reference, although I think these kids practice more. A lot of oldschool hardcore songs here about getting lost in the working world. The melodies are good, not so simple as to be

good (roughness doesn't hurt this kind of music)—in a total of eighteen minutes. I'd be wrong to be critical of this—basic, straightforward, rebellious hardcore bands made up of socially challenged Black Flag fans are pretty much the backbone of our community, in some places, and there's nothing wrong with that. –b
+/– records, address nearby goddamnit or I'll be a monkey's uncle, blaghh!

Corretja "" 7": This record begins with strange humming noises and the drums (which have a really hard-hitting production) playing by them selves for a little while, and it really drew me in. The fast, double-picking, double-time metallic hardcore kicks in, and I'm still enthralled. The vocals are mixed below the guitars, emphasizing their harsh, indecipherable rage; the first song is a wild-eyed assault on Christian hypocrisy that ends in a naked roar—this is good stuff. The second song quiets down in the middle to an acoustic part that is momentarily less com-

stuff, I'm talking later, psychedelic, 10 minute long, lounge-music shitty-ass Melvins material. I'm guessing Cower were on lots of drugs when they did this, hopefully heroin, because the lyrics are stupid and nonsensical, and the songs are all in the range of 10 minutes and played really, *reeeally* sssslloooowww... What's worse, the last three tracks are fucking 15 minute long radio interviews with Celtic Frost and none other than the Melvins (who are actually damn funny). I really do not understand this release at all; I think it's not much more than a self-indulgent, pointless waste of time and resources, to be quite frank. Whatever... –n
Delboy / P.O. Box 75 / B 9000 Ghent 12, Belgium

Cross My Heart "The Reason I Failed History" cd/ep: Ok, the first thing I usually do when I'm given a cd is put it in the player, press play, pull out the insert or booklet and mostly block out all the sounds coming through the speakers. That's just me though.

Borch "We Are the Romans" CD: There is no other way to start this review, than to say that this musical group is damn absolutely mindblowingly *otherworldly* incredible, hands fucking down. They hold a concrete place in my brain, a space that is reserved only for the few bands that dare to push the limits of *impossible*. I just can't understand how Borch plays what they do. I just can't understand how this guitar part fits with this bassline and that drumbeat, with vocals and everything, and have it come out so insanely beautiful. All of them know their instruments like the back of their hand, and fuck, they are just one of those bands that you can't put in a category because they're so damn good. I mean, they're hardcore and everything, but not of the usual strand. All the components of the music are pieced together tightly, even leaving room for each instrument to go off on it's own and dance a little and then come back to it's anchor, all the while keeping the flow of the song. Remarkable. Ok, here's the technical dirt: Borch plays carefully orchestrated relentless rhythmic hardcore music with a twist of more rhythm and some soft grooves that are great to slow dance to (just get ready to rip your partner apart at any second). I'm guessing that all or most of the sounds made are guitar, bass, drums, and voice, but a good part of the time there are noises coming out that I don't know where the hell they came from. I can tell you this; the guitar player is all over the place, with all kinds of effects (that don't sound like *effects*) and tons of riffs that are very unconventional and have been known to make people dizzy and pass out. He goes from winding runs that go all over the fretboard into a collection of notes that are just pounded away at with the most chaotic sense of gentleness. The sound on the CD is very loud, strong, and thick, and *self-confident*. The bassist is right up front too, refusing to take a back seat, and really shines during a few pockets in the chaos. Also, all during track nine, the bass sound is so cushy and distorted, I just want to lay down on it and have it lull me to sleep. The vocals on previous Borch releases have always confused me a bit; I could never understand what hell he was talking about. But here I see the vocals as being right on, in perfect places with the music, not merely sung in random places along the way. In fact, for most of the CD, the vocals are coupled with the accented beats of the other instruments, making them so much more powerful and meaningful. Some of the songs are about Christianity ("I know that it is all shit"), American conquest ("never satisfied..."), other bands ("can't hear the notes you play or the words you say and you're not changing the world"), and a song entitled "I Want To Be a Sex Symbol On My Own Terms."

hopelessly generic. On the second song the verse riff ambitiously packs a lot of notes together, which is awesome (until a later part, when they sort of ruin the energy with a singing part in the vocals—the singer is much better when he's just yelling in his gravelly, post-Born Against voice, as he usually does)... the fifth song has a nice (if not entirely new—the seventh song is even reminiscent of it) melody to it, which they almost take to another level of intensity at the end (but instead, since they're an old school band, it's time for the song to be over). Their best lyrical moment comes in the fourth sing, "Fury," for which the lyrics are simply "We've got the fury!!" Thirteen tracks altogether, the last three from an earlier recording but just as

pelling, but the all-out attack returns with blood-curdling shrieks more fearsome than anything I've heard in this day's worth of reviews. They get points for mysterious, classy d.i.y. packaging too, which includes black-on-black print and a transparency. This is an excellent record all around—it's well-played, sounds good, has plenty of emotion and some innovation too. –b
Increvable, P.O. Box 425, Ithaca, NY 14851

Cower "The Annual Hornvenders Convention" CD: God, this is just plain weird. I guess the best comparison I could give you is 2 tablespoons Melvins mixed with half teaspoon Eyehategod. And I'm not even talking about the halfway cool early Melvins

I'm often more interested in how the artist(s) use their space to present themselves visually before I can let myself become completely attentive to the music they're performing. In the case of Cross My Heart, they offer the two-panel insert that informs of who plays what (instrument), where they recorded/mastered, who did the graphic design, and the right people to contact (Dim Mak records) if you're interested in receiving a lyric sheet. To me all this adds up to very poor packaging. Musically Cross My Heart plays soft, melodic pop with the occasional up-beat moments that have a falling-short-of-rocking-out feel to them.

P.S. The only reason I'm not making a fuss about the lack of printed lyrics is because i

could actually understand the words when sung. How often does that happen for an Inside Front reviewer?!?!? (taz)
Dim Mak, address elsewhere

Dawncore "Obedience is a Slower Form of Death" CD: Metallic hardcore with some good riffs and energy, screaming vocals (with the aggressive delivery of some "tough guy" bands, but without seeming stupid or insincere), lots of transitions between fast parts and moshier parts with guitar chunks, a recording with the weight and brightness to give them the edge and thrust they need to make this work... and a really prominent double bass. . The lyrics reject earthly and religious hierarchies, push through the scarring pain of life's difficulties, and reach for inspiration and idealism through everything. The tough-guy influence that I mentioned manifests itself at the end as a Cro-Mags cover ("World peace can't be done, it just can't exist!"), which is fucking awesome. The fact that they can do a Cro-Mags cover and make it exciting should give you an idea of

back, and this 7" won't do for a substitute second coming; but it fills out their legacy—it has the same things going for it, without sounding like an imitation at all. —b
Per Koro, address elsewhere

The Dents "The End of All Civilization" 7": Hey, this is something I haven't heard too much of in this issues reviews: fast, fast, snotty, angry high school punk rock. Government Issue shirts, yelling vocals (that end in a hearty "Fuck off!" at the beginning of the breakdown at the conclusion of the first song), simple three-chord riffs. In my head (and perhaps theirs?), these kids are opening for Social Distortion in 1982, wearing flannel and moshing to Black Flag blasted on the car stereo between bands. Their simple values (fuck the greedy rich, do what you want, teachers and parents get outta my life, break shit! yeah!) are right on, and the rebellious energy that makes this stuff work is all there. —b
So Fucking What?, 253 Alexander Street, Apartment #322, Rochester, NY 14607

are in Portuguese and English, and the insert includes an essay about why they choose to play their anarchist/political music to the deathmetal scene as well as the hardcore scene (to try to bridge the gaps). —b
Marcolino, Al. Mal. Floriano Peixoto 56, Centro Guariga, Sao Paulo 11410-240, Brazil

Dragbody "transgress, nullify" 7": This one's worth it for the lyric sheet alone—it's clear plastic with black printing on one side. And the layout and artwork is exceptional too, with these sick, organic-looking photos of people with slashed skin and wires. But the music rocks so hard too; it's heavy as fuck all-out chaotic metal that doesn't get boring, with tortured screams to boot. But all these aspects that I like are also what I don't like. So you have the money to get some slick-ass packaging, but you're just playing up to all the metal stereotypes with disgusting pictures, vague and morbid lyrics, and heavy metallic riffs one after the other... I guess this release is a mixed blessing then—you can listen to it just to rock

Now the drummer: he is one of those that at their shows you see tons of people crowded around him just to watch. You know the kind I'm talking about. Surprisingly, he plays mostly with snare, bass drum, and cymbals, but he doesn't limit himself by any means. As a drummer, he has lots of rhythmic (how many times can I use the word *rhythmic* in this review?) tools to play with, and I think my favorite is when the guitar and bass are playing some part that is in a weird time signature, and the drums are accenting those, and then they suddenly break away and play a straightforward beat over the 5 or 7 or whatever the case may be. For those of you that don't understand, see it like this, you will be bobbing your head to the beat, and all of a sudden the beat won't be there anymore, but your head will keep moving to the rhythm, and then before you know it, the downbeat is right back where it started. I seriously could write a whole "zine on Botch (maybe. I will, dammit) but here in this review I want to keep things at least a little concise, so I am being a little more short-winded than is called for: (if you can believe it). Notable parts of the CD include all of track nine, which is some sort of historical anthem of sector destruction at precisely 0:51 on track one; when the beat changes so smoothly and graciously the slow-dance ending of track four; the fucking soundtrack to my life concluding track five, especially the double bass. Actually I don't know who I'm kidding picking out *notable* parts of this; every part has a vision or attribute to it that is fucking notable! As far as recording quality goes, this CD sounds great: none of the common mistakes exist here that you see on a lot of hardcore/punk recordings, such as too much click on the bass drum, nor enough bass guitar, overall dry sounds, or overly enhanced vocals. The sound is full and moist, just like it should be. A criticism I would have for Botch is that I think a lot of their music goes over the head of listeners and things are happening so fast that there is no time to grasp them, not to mention enjoy them. But hey, I guess that comes with the territory. The packaging is very well done, featuring a paperboard foldour cover, and beautifully chosen colors and graphic artwork. The lyrics are inside, and are easy to read, unlike a bunch of words that are thrown together with no beginning or end. *We Are the Romans* is definitely more epic than their last CD, and breaks new ground that shakes the listener into a whirlwind of precious stimuli, creating more than music, creating a world all it's own. Get this. —WG
Botch; Suite #364; 2522 North Proctor; Tacoma, WA 98406; Buschrock@hotmail.com; Hydra Head Records; PO Box 990248; Boston, MA 02199

what their strengths are. —b
Trottel, 1192 Budapest Kos K. Ter. 14, Hungary

Degeune "The Last Dance" 7": Acme is the crucial point of reference for all these German metal/hardcore bands, but they're particularly relevant here, since some crucial details match up: the guitars have that same menacing slightly-out-of-tune sound, the first side begins and ends with the sound of a choir hum (something Acme would have used), the riffs and transitions have that same discordant, spooky feel, and when they get going like a machine out of control their singer's torn, trebly screaming voice merges with the spasmodic, jerking music, creating a sandblaster effect similar to the one that made the Acme record so amazing. Acme isn't coming

Desecration "Broken Peace" 7": The punk music on this 7" has the same grim resolve and boiling energy that I associate with their comrades in Abuso Sonoro, although Desecration takes a more metal approach (blastbeats, double-picked riffs, dramatic breakdowns). The recording is good enough not to hold them back, and the playing is pretty tight; the only drawback here is that their lead singer (who I know from meeting him to be a very cool, smart person) sounds like he's trying a little too hard for the grindcore growl sometimes, like it might work out better if he would just let go and not worry about what his voice sounds like. All the same, the recording has a good, heavy atmosphere, which makes the music here matter. The lyrics

out and groove and stare at interesting artwork, and you can also notice all the boring clichés and predetermined molds that prevent you from getting anything really meaningful out of it. —n
Jawk Records / 5145 N. Bridges Dr. / Alpharetta GA 30022, USA

Endstand "To Whom It May Concern" CD: Shall I outline all the things Endstand have going for them on this CD? 1. A great recording, with really powerful guitars and drums, heavy bass, like a modern rock recording (uh, good rock... hm...), makes you want to dance just as soon as it comes on. 2. A great, great vocalist. Vocals make or break so many bands, and Janne gives everything he's got on every syllable. Just listening to him n the CD, his passion and sincerity come across and make you feel welcomed and safe. 3. Honesty—that comes across in the straightforward lyrics, which proclaim positive, d.i.y. values... I mean, fuck, at the climax of the fourth song, when Janne is screaming the refrain "the older I get, the more I know— the more I know, the more I just can't let go" and the rest of the band is chanting "hey hey hey hey" like a Bolshevik dance squad, how could hardcore get any better than that? The 'rock' reference I made earlier is not too off the mark, there is a really rocking feel in a lot of their hardcore, but they're totally right on about everything

Eradicate s/t LP: From Germany comes this political hardcore outfit that reminds me a lot of Gehenna in their sound, but with maybe a little more crust-punk flavor, especially in the artwork and lyrics. I am impressed by their intelligent subject matter that's presented in a very street-level, kind of old-fashioned punk way, and the thick, cut-n-paste (punk style) booklet is very attractive. I think it's great that they print the English translations to their lyrics so us yanks can know what they are growling about. They really seem to be sincere and well meaning, and I wish I could get into their music as much as their message, but it just bores me. There just wasn't any-

Exigencia "Usando la Conciencia" CD: Weird. Old school (all the predictable features, including the generic invocation of our collective conscience to solve all injustices) but the vocals are incredibly sloppy, making them almost impossible to understand without the lyric sheet, unusual for a genre that has focused so much on the tendency of their fans to sing along—and if they don't have a rallying cry that blazes out, summoning to its powerful voice and enviable elocution the energies of the masses, how exactly can anyone sing along? I am tempted to construct complex theories on masks and disguises, on a

Catharsis "Passion" CD celebrity appearance record review courtesy of Al Burian

I'm sitting around Bordeaux, France, completely aware that I should be out exploring, or taking in the landscape, or absorbing the history and culture of this place, and I'm mortified to be sitting instead in a Frenchman's apartment listening to the new Catharsis album. Frog legs? No thanks, sounds weird; let's order a Domino's pizza. The French seem crazy about this record. Language barriers notwithstanding, the point is made clearly by their pantomimed slamdance moves and vigorous air-guitar riffing. I admit that I also enjoy air-guitaring to Catharsis. Air-drumming is a bit more challenging; my legs get tired. Still, I enjoy many of the fine products of the United States of America, and nonetheless I feel a pang of regret that what I have found here in a foreign land to forge a bond of commonality between myself and the locals is not political conviction, deeply-felt humanitarianism or some other recognition of the basic human similarities which transcend all nations; rather we all seem bound by our common appreciation of my down-the-street neighbor's heavy metal band.

Well, the die is cast; the French are going to self-induce whiplash and ask me excitedly about all my intimate knowledge of such riveting subjects as what kinds of sandwiches, toothbrushes and pedicure products Brian D—— prefers (information which I am glad to provide, albeit in the form of ludicrous made-up stories about his extensive collection of loofahs and secret hunger for sunrise biscuit kitchen sausage and cheese biscuits, which causes the sweet, gullible Francs to run around the room in circles from amazement). I have no choice but to make the best of the situation. Producing an air-pick from my conceptual wallet, I hit the standby switch on my air-amp and stand with my imaginary B.C. Rich Warlock at the ready.

But suddenly a thought occurs: hey, is the new Catharsis album going to be reviewed in the next *Inside Front*? That seems like it would be a little strange. Conflict of interests at best. Kind of like reading up on what new music is cool in some magazine published by The David Geffen publishing group. We expect such crass marketing ploys from the capitalist pigs, but what about the revolutionaries over at Crimethink™, well-known and self-acclaimed as severely uninterested in the profit motive and "moving units"? Would they stoop so low as to review their own flag-ship product? Doesn't it seem like the (inevitably raving positive) write-up is going to be blatantly self-serving, in an uncomfortably Geffenesque way? Who are they going to find to give it an objective review? On the other hand, for *Inside Front*, being a journal of the goings on and important events in the universe of Crimethink™, the release of this record is an event of millennial magnitude. How, then, can the magazine be true to its editorial mission *without* reviewing the record?

The mind reels at these ethical and artistic quandaries. I certainly cannot put myself forward as a candidate for objective reviewing of this record, much as I'd like to write it up and give it the minimum stars rating, just so as to be able to send it in to Brian and have him refuse to print it and revoke my Crimethink™ I.D. and firearm to boot, which would then give me the much-sought-after excuse I've been looking for to rip open the jewel-case of the CD, to reveal the—oh yeah, here's a hot tip the french gave me—reveal the extra hidden manifestos cleverly enfolded therein, and yell: "Aha—this collective?! You're fucking kidding me! These guys are just a bunch of self-promoting capitalist bastards like David motherfucking Geffen! 'Yours for a world free of charge?' Give me back the ten bucks you, Brian D——_____, made me PAY for the last Catharsis CD!" (and he actually asked me to pay him the ten bucks while waiting in line to scam some free food off of the local Hare Krishnas. In line for FREE FOOD! And again, let me just stress that you really should see his loofah collection).

But, hell, I'm shredding on the Warlock to it, so who am I to give it the minimum stars. Then, the next-to-last song, a reggae song, kicks in. Odd. "What do you guys make of this?" I inquire of the french. They nod, enthusiastic to the end. As the last note of the reggae song rings out, I hear Brian D., a man I know as lithe and sensitive, with a sensual side he has never quite been able to bring into his music, whisper, as if I'm in a pick-up joint and he's muttering boozily into my ear, "kiss me, you're beautiful—these are truly the last days." KA-ZONG!!! My mind is blown. "They have done it!" I yelp enthusiastically to my French friends. "Catharsis has broken new ground, they have done something completely original and unexpected and taken me totally by surprise. The reggae could have been predicted—sure, they've heard the Bad Brains; but bringing in the slow-jam sex-talk aesthetic? Catharsis?"

they do, so it's not a guilty pleasure. And they're not hearing some hackneyed, generic formula to death, either, so when their seventh song ("Small Sacrifices for Big Changes," about veganism) begins a little like early Nirvana, it's just fine by me. Hell, I like some old Nirvana. But I'd rather listen to this. —b
Impression, P.O. 938, 09009 Chemnitz, Germany

thing amazing happening that caught my attention—I think it sounds like 2836 other modern hardcore/punk bands. I think I could have gotten really into this back in the day when I only knew about a couple of good bands, y'know? Insert last sentence of Brethren review here. —n
Whirlwind Productions / PF 770338 / 93076 Regensburg, Germany

band hiding within their old school guitar riffs a rougher kind of aesthetic. The songs treat basic themes: "I'm Not Going to Change," "Compromise," "Pure Ignorance." That this isn't a very original recording perhaps only means that they haven't yet found their own style, although they sound pretty comfortable in this one. The music is energetic enough, although the drumming can be a little erratic. Old school hardcore is probably a lot newer in Colombia than it is here; we can only hope that they are able to move past this to a more innovative, compelling sound.—@

Dirección Positiva, can't find the address anywhere on the CD, perhaps you can try writing to Diego Paredes at 8372 NW 64th St. #1595, Miami, FL 33166

The Exploder "West End Kids Crusade" CD: When one goes on tour, one experiences many bands, the majority being ultimately dismissed to the back of the skull into a file

shake a part of your body, and maybe shake the person next to you for fun. Putting them in a genre of punk is tough, but I'll say that they've got emo hardcore overtones. Their music is kind to the ears, and I could see a lot of people liking them right off the bat. The drums are played well, using a technique that has a way of forcing the blood to flow with more gusto; I like it. The vocals are screamed and sung, both working very nicely. The two guitars dance with each other very well, most of the time playing in harmony with each other, which I like very much. They have a real rock-n-roll sound, too. The bass is often

them...three graphics. There are lyrics and info provided, and a picture, but it looks like the band didn't care about having a meaningful insert. On the other hand, cheap and simple is no problem in my book. –WG

The Exploder; PO Box 18034; Richmond, VA 23226. Dimmak; PO Box 14041; Santa Barbara, CA 93107

Face Down "Angels with Soiled Wings" 7": This is the New Jersey Face Down, in case you're wondering. They're pretty damn heavy here, with a production that emphasizes the thickness and bass of the chunky guitar riffs

"Oh, yes! We love that part!" the French agree. "The *God Speed You Black Emperor* lyrics add so much..."

"Er..... what?" I say.

I am, at this point, shown the lyrics to a song by the band *God Speed You Black Emperor*, which, to my horror, bear a striking resemblance to the Catharsis reggae song' lyrics. Striking. In fact, let's just call it like we see it here. Plagiarism! I, of course, am aghast. Brian has totally ripped off the lyrics to this song. His booty call moment is not even his own damn booty call; he's reading someone else's pick-up lines. Plagiarism is unethical, dishonest, and what's more, it's against the UNC-Chapel Hill honor code, a code which I know for a fact that Brian pledged his allegiance to at some point during his tenure at the University of North Carolina Chapel Hill (a university I have always suspected he chose to attend primarily because of its close proximity to Brian's personal crack-house, the sunrise biscuit kitchen).

Don't get me wrong. I don't have wild, romantic notions that my friends should be able to come up with ideas on their own, and I have myself engaged in certain behaviors which might be considered borderline "plagiarism," but there is a difference when you cite your sources, you can get away with calling it an "homage" or a "sample" or whatever; when you try to past off as your idea is when you get kicked out of school.

Well, I don't know. I think there is a Crimethink manifesto somewhere where they talk at length about how great they think plagiarizing is. I suppose it does have somewhat of a noble history, in punk rock at any rate; everyone seems to be falling over themselves to express how original and innovative a band like Refused is for having the brain-storm of combining the Nation of Ulysses' wardrobe with the rhetoric of Situationism and the music of Rage Against the Machine. And the Nation of Ulysses stole their entire aesthetic from jazz in the first place (making Refused triple plagiarists), while the Sex Pistols already plagiarized Situationalism (mak-ing Refused triple plagiarists), and in any case he'd the word SEX in their band name which was, in terms of soci-tal upheaval, a much more immediate deal than Situationalism over was or will ever probably be, at least as far as social-impact-measured-through-band-lyric goes, and the whole hare-brained scheme was, in any case, a publicity stunt for a clothing store, conceived of by a man named Malcolm McLaren who no doubt threw in the whole Situationalism bit because of some Guy Debord book he noticed on his coffee table while getting stoned one day and scheming the whole thing called punk rock up. As for Rage Against the Machine, well they are not plagiarists at all because unlike Catharsis and/or Refused, they include lists of recommended reading in their albums, thereby giving footnotes for where they stole their ideas from, and making them not plagiarists but scholars. Why no read-ing lists, Dennis Lyxzen? Why no reading lists, Brian D——— and Catharsis? Is the intent to educate and disinterest in unitizing and franchising? Is the use of as the last line in John Gardner's Grendel as a Catharsis lyric ("Grendel's had an accident, so may you all")intended as an ode as an ode a nod to a book which moved you, or is it a crass attempt to spoil the ending of the book, so that potential readers will spend their hard-earned ten dollars (the price of the Gardner book, softcover, and the price of a Catharsis CD — mere coincidence?) on a record instead? (Why not just make songs entirely composed of lists of who did it in every Agatha Christie book, Brian?) And if my dire sus-picions are indeed the case, how are we then to differentiate ourselves, our culture, this thing we attempt to call our own, DIY punk rock, from the David Geffens, the Tower records, the ominously encroaching corporate world which is slowly but surely replacing books with books on tape, newspapers with televised infotainment, politics with enter-taining pre-packaged political entities including both the major and minor political candidates, as well as the vari-ous hip "political" bands increasingly in fashion as it becomes increasingly clear that their toothless sloganeering poses no more threat or possibility of change than the toothless sloganeering of our actual world leaders? No, no, things cannot go on like this. Something must break; something must be done. I draw a line in the sand. I raise my fist in defiance. I throw down the air guitar and scream it into the cold French night. The new Catharsis album: no stars! No stars!

[editor's witty repartee disguised as note: that's "Situationism," Al, not "Situationalism." Or perhaps in your case, it is—: "SituationALism."]

with a "suck" heading. But if one is in the right place at the right time, a band will appear that stands out and is given a permanent place in the tourist's memory; The Exploder, alas, is one. I saw them in Jersey 2 years ago, so when I spied this CD in the review box, I grabbed it with high hopes. And let me say that this record is no let down of any kind. The music just makes you want to

hard to find in the mix when the music is rowdy, and it hugs the guitars a lot; and it could be louder. Overall the music is rhythmic and sweet, and is far from being boring. As for recording quality, I think, for this music, the tones are well-placed and the levels of all the instruments are fairly right. The packaging of the CD, however, is pretty sad, mostly follow-ing a light pastel blue motif with, let me count

and the cutting attack of the drums, and the vocalist comes through with deep, anguished roaring that complements the music perfectly. They cut the slow chunky hardcore stuff from time to time to play more disorienting breaks with effects, that make me feel like I am falling slowly in a dream about to turn to nightmare. Nice handdrawn illustrations on the packaging. The lyrics (and lack of anything else) make it clear that this is a personal emotional testament, about friendships that end in tragedy and such, rather than something with broader implications, but it's delivers the goods as emotional expression, and that's what counts here. –b

Malph, P.O. Box 2066, Neptune City, NJ –7754-2066

Fear is the Path to the Darkside "Someday this war is going to end..." 7": Starts with a Star Wars sample, hmph. As they come from Germany, it would be easy to lose this band in the crowd of well-recorded, heavy German metal bands, but they have plenty of personality of their own, so it's worth listening a little closer. That personality comes out more on the slow parts, which throb with a hypnotizing power and grace, creating a haunting atmosphere, the vocals evoking a palpable pain. When they play faster, it's harder to tell them from the other bands screaming and playing fast chord progressions. It's not too often I find a hardcore band that can really handle playing slow, so hats off to them. German lyrics that I'd like to understand, since I think highly of their singer's intellect. I want them to push the limits a bit, surprise me a little more (like they do when everything stops and the two guitars alternate, with totally different sounds)... until then, this music will do just fine, although I think it would be at its best as the soundtrack to a dark, ominous movie... –b

Scorched Earth Policy, address below

Forstella Ford "Insincerity Down To An Artform" CD: Whoa, this band is all over the place, and it's fucking great! A breath of fresh air amongst the widespread blandness of common hardcore/punk bands. FF is chock full of what I love most, rhythm manipulation on all levels by all instruments while maintaining a cohesive groove. The instruments used are of the norm, but FF seems to have found a new way to play them. The drums are jazzy and free, the screams are sporadic and strong, the guitar is all over the fretboard and at times unintelligible, and the bass is not merely following the guitar- it finds a creative path of it's own. All of these are great assets for a band to have. This is hard to put in a category; I'll have to make one up...Chaoslovecore? Garbagecan algebra rock? Jet-puffed albino jazz? Fuck, I tried. Anyway, this is a very diverse piece of work, with fast parts, slow sleepytime vibrations, and straight up noise. Good samples and piano, too. The lyrics are all about the infamous and ever-so-worthy "you," and are often hard to follow even when reading along in the insert. The singer could enunciate the lyrics better, unless of course it's part of the music to just scream gibberish. The packaging and layout are done well, including lyrics and a few pictures. Interesting song

titles, too. All in all a great work of art. Get this. –WG

Forstella Ford; 1301 Albion Ave, #5; Milwaukee, WI 53202. The Mountain Collective; PO Box 220320; Greenpoint PO; Brooklyn, NY 11222-9997.

Foundation "Fear of Life" 7": Yet another great visual performance undermined by a not-so-great musical performance. The packaging is attractive, with great use of space and good-looking stills from the movie "The Shining" (although I don't see any meaning behind this other than trying to be scary), and has a cool gatefold-type thing happening. But it's all downhill from there, with simplistic fourth-grade level lyrics and simplistic, high-school garage-band level songwriting. There is nothing new or exciting or profound happening here, so I'll talk about the only intriguing part of this release for a minute. On the 7"s center label is an imitation of the famous Slayer photo of two arms over a bathtub, with the word "slayer" carved really deeply into one of them and blood everywhere, only on here it says "foundation," obviously. I once read an article about the original photo and apparently some guy was paid to have his arm numbed, then carved up, then set on fire to make it even bloodier and gruesome looking. What I am intrigued by here is whether or not this imitation photo is only really well done computer trickery, or if some brave, psychotic band member or friend actually did that to themselves just for this. I really hope it's the second one, because that would kick so much fucking ass and be so goddamn metal that I would cherish this 7" forever, and not feel duped by nifty computer graphics. –n [editor's note: on Nick's behalf, I'll offer a rave review in his 'zine and a place in his top ten list to any band willing to hack themselves up, set themselves on fire, throw themselves off cliffs into pools of hydrochloric acid, and send us proof. See, getting a positive review is really not so complicated...]

Dead Alive Records / PO box 97 / Caldwell, NJ 07006, USA

Giveuntilgone "Settled For the Art Official" CD: Damn, another example of being excited by absolutely stunning artwork/graphic design only to be let down by music I don't care for, in this case very mellow, sappy, sugar-sweet emo/indy rock with annoying vocals. Well, there's actually one thing I liked musically here, and that is when there are the most serenely beautiful female guest vocals accompanying the usual male whining. Other than that I could barely stop myself from falling asleep to this Sunny Day Real Estate soundalike. I know that the two band members who did the layout and artwork are in art school or recently graduated, because it's just that good. But besides basic aesthetic appeal I

can't relate one bit to the overall cleanliness and just plain sugary prettiness of this release, both visually and musically. And furthermore, I'm not convinced that this band is concerned with being or representing anything deeper and more profound than artsy, creative candy-coated imagery. ––n

Dim Mak (address in Ninedayswonder review)

Goat Shanty "Encroachment" CD: Twelve songs, all named with numbers (presumably according to the order they were written, like Zegota), in twelve minutes, with a rough, abrasive recording, incoherently outraged lyrics (reaching their best moment with "solace in dependence, soulless independence"), insert artwork that wasn't taken too seriously (lots of images of goats, if you didn't see that coming... also a couple skulls, etc.), general d.i.y. atmosphere, last song ends with fucking mess of noise for a minute (the standard length of all their songs)—yes infuckingdeed, this is punk rock. What else can I say? I'm tempted to deliberately misspell words in this review just to get into the spirit of the whole thing. –b

Moot, 255 Hillcrest Avenue, Athens, GA 30601

Imbalance s/t CDEP: Here is another band that appears to be sincere and very intelligent, able to put out an attractive release, but is lagging behind musically. I love the artwork throughout the packaging of this CD; it's a mix of really weird drawings, paintings, and collage, all in very drab and subdued colors. The lyrics are well written and deal with important personal and social issues ("feud like Montague and Capulet/fight like cat and dog/take pleasure in ridiculing each other/lose sight of what we've got"), but the vocals and music just didn't do anything for me. The songs are not too fast and not too slow, the riffs are the kind you'd hear in any punky sounding hardcore record, and the vocals are pretty standard hoarse yells. Read last sentence of Brethren review and insert here.

Hermit / PO box 309 / Leeds LS2 7AH, UK

Ire "Adversity Into Triumph" CD: This CD is a collection of songs from previously released stuff on a 7" (Schema Recs.) and a split LP (Spineless/Fetus recs.). Ire plays medium to slow paced heavy hardcore with a huge helping of rhythmic changes and great thick slow chugs. A lot of the musical themes have an evil sounding edge to them, and at times I picture people struggling, fighting against some huge fucking ugly enemy, but failing miserably. Damn, some of this is sad. You can feel it in the singer's effort. The rhythm is strong, always up front and under your nose. The vocals are about as passionate as I've ever heard, but sometimes they don't mesh well with the music, like they were conceived totally separate and pushed to fit in holes that they aren't shaped for. And the singer went crazy with double-tracking, which gets in the way sometimes. The bass is no doubt *here*, and is glorious, better than most of the lot of hardcore/punk, which has an infamous reputation for uninteresting bass. The guitars have great minds and dare to venture off into uncharted territory, and they have a solid, powerful drive. Same goes for the drums; essential. For the most part, the songs are long, and every once in a while we get a sample of haunting chants (Tibetan?) and other intercontinental expression. The packaging is standard and done fairly well. The cover folds out to reveal the lyrics (including one song in French and one in Arabic) and fabulous song explanations. Ire's songs are about Palestinian struggle, Native American assimilation, consumerism, the problematic U.S. social structure, widespread denial of humanity being a part of nature (take this both ways), and self-realization. Ire really has something to say, they don't just play music and then go home: "we are disillusioned from the sight of fields where plants and trees fade into symbols of profit, where success is a seed sown in a plain of rocks where nothing grows." Yeah, this is good. --WG

Ire; PO Box 902, station C; Montreal, Quebec; H2L 4V2, Canada.

Kafka "Truths" CD: Their vocalist has a high, screaming voice that is just the right frequency to cut through the simple, metallic hardcore and become the main thing that I focus on when this CD is on. It's a little hard to bear, that one high, ringing note over and over, screamed at me—there was a CD released by Mountain records a couple years back that had exactly the same thing going on with the vocals, I think the band was Devola. Anyway, the music has some hypnotic power in parts, and they use jarring chords to some effect in places; over all it's not brand new or top of its class, but it is a hell of a lot better than some of the work of Kafka's more generic colleagues. They experiment with a piano piece and some spoken word for the sixth track, and if they can incorporate that into their hardcore they'll be on their way to something good. A fascinating quality of Italian hardcore is that bands from that country seem to be somehow incapable of producing generic lyrics (praise Allah!)—so the lyrics here are all interesting; the last song is the (true) story of a coastal town in Brazil in which the poor hunt the crabs who live on the garbage that accumulates on the beach: the tragedy of our age, recycling rubbish into shit and disease... --b

No! Records, via Cadighiara 18/14, 16133 Genova, Italy

Kill the Messenger "Five on Seven" 7": This 7" has more music on it than I'm used to from a polished band like this. When K.t.M. are going

at it, they play jumpy, experimental punk/rock stuff, with plenty of new ideas. For example, the first song begins with a scary, whispering, dragged part that I was sure would lead to the predictable metal/hardcore thing, but instead surprised me by going into something much poppier. Their singer has a deep, hoarse voice that is reminiscent of something else I didn't like much, but he's not the most important thing happening here. There's a "post-hardcore" taste in my mouth here that I'd like to be able to wash out or ignore, because what these guys are doing is new and exciting... I just hope they're trying to expand the genre rather than escape into the arms of something more commercially accessible. Oh fuck, I shouldn't complain—any band which, when the vocalist sings "hold my breath and count to ten" actually pauses so he can count it out loud, has to get my go ahead. Gorgeous hand-drawn insert artwork, too. --b *Phyte, address nearby, c'mon!*

Jane "A Doorway to Elsewhere" CD: The best Systral record (*Maximum Carnage*) did something that transcended the world of "brutal" hardcore music—it took that brutality to its logical conclusion, revealing the bloodlust and desire for total annihilation that lies at the roots of our civilization and the music made by the rebels within it. This record does the same thing, in just about the same way Systral did it (if not for the first time, this time), and for those who were disappointed when Systral became fat and self-satisfied and stopped trying, this will be a welcome sequel to their aforementioned masterpiece. Not to say all the elements that made Systral so important are present here—really, this is just an exploration of that particular aspect of their work, with the same merciless metal arrangements, shrieking-suffering high vocals and murdering-without-feeling deep roars, thunderous bass-overloaded mix that makes the double

bass and blastbeats sound like the maximum-velocity workings of an industrial killing machine, fragments of resigned, lucid death poetry: "feel numb to the carnage all around me"—"killing to lose ourselves in it"—"is it the blood which awakens the monster in us..?" In the opening instants, after the classical introduction (which brings to my mind Wagner, and his proto-fascist dreams), the guitars come in like the hiss of the air on Judgment Day, and the snare drum begins banging out the rhythm of a witch's Sabbat, or perhaps the same rhythm the skeleton is playing over the mouth of Hell in Breughel's terrifying *Triumph of Death*... and at moments, like it or not, I catch myself glorying in my own cold-blooded, contradictory nature, and it hammers home the tragedy all the more inescapably. --b

Alveran, P.O. Box 10 01 52, 44701 Bochum, Germany

Countdown to Putsch "Handbook For Planetary Progress" CD and Books: I find myself mute in the presence of greatness. Anyone who likes to read Inside Front would do well to check this out. It's challenging on all levels: intellectually, this is brilliant, all-encompassing, as thorough a literary/academic work as has come out of the hardcore community, on a par with *Day of War, Nights of Love* and very little else. The book compiles everything from an exploration of the distinction between Melville's *Moby Dick* to regressive and progressive taxation to stories of meeting giant rats in the subway. Fuck, this is awesome, and I can't sum it up any more than I could sum up *Society of the Spectacle* or *Thus Spoke Zarathustra*. Musically, they're doing what I think That's All She Wrote wanted to do, but couldn't cut the cords tying them to hardcore conventions thoroughly enough to really achieve this isn't hardcore with free jazz influence, this is genuine free jazz played by a hardcore band. Unqualified craziness, no idea what to expect next, that intoxicating immediacy of something new and dangerous being tried right in front of you—fuck, this is top notch. As a rule, these wild experiments don't last long, that's too bad, because I'd be fascinated to see what these kids would do next, to polish this approach and explore further. In any event, find this and explore it, learn what you can and steal some ideas to try yourself. --b

Mountain Cooperative, P.O. Box 220320, Greenpoint Post Office, Brooklyn, NY 11222

Lariat "Means of Production" CD: OK, first off, the idea to review this came spontaneously when I found this CD right after writing the review for the Lariat demo tape, and *goes hand-in-hand* with said review, this review building upon the other. That said, I am convinced that Lariat likes bullets (this CD came with one in the narrow space on the left side of the jewel box, I love it). This release is out of Denmark, and contains the same recordings from the demo, with three new tracks of their political machine-gun firemusic. These three new songs are not recorded quite as well compared to the demo quality (which is good), but they are nonetheless powerful and fucking intense. Especially notable is the second tune, a tune that fucking made me cry as I listened to it over and over. It concerns the police shooting of Amadou Diallo, an event I am familiar with, and the chords chosen here, the notes, the rhythms...they represent the

event musically, tearing at my very fucking marrow, ripping out anger, hopelessness, sorrow, and pain that I feel when something like this goes down. This song says 'Fucking look! Look what you fucking did!" Shit, now I feel like I lost someone that I knew and loved; is that supposed to happen? The CD booklet is beautiful black and silver, and it contains more focused and less writing than the demo booklet (including, of course, lyrics and explanations). Lariat are bare-naked here, and come across as more mature in the sense of their ability to get things accomplished. I'm guessing that they have lived what they have been talking about, and learning things along the way. If you want to make a change in your life and your world, you would be doing yourself a great disservice by overlooking Lariat. Their live show is impressive, as well as serious and confrontational; so when you see them, by all means, *talk* to them. -WG
Lariat; PO Box 443; Round Lake, NY 12151. Last Effort Recordings; Dankwart Dreyers Vej 9; 5610 Assens; Denmark.

Luddgang "Collateral 18.06.99": At first, I was afraid this was going to be more painfully derivative imitation Crass shit, with the circle-A-derived logo on the cover and the BBC sample at the beginning—but no, this is fucking awesome! The first side turns out to be a Public Enemy/Consolidated-style sample collage with an oil-drum ensemble percussion backdrop. This is the kind of shit that bands like Crass deserve to have done with their legacy, not copycat bullshit until we're all bored to death... I've heard nary a guitar yet by the beginning of the second side, and yet it's clear to me that *this* is the punk music of today, the music that can keep the whole genre and musical aspect of the community itself vibrant and meaningful. The b-side is a similar percussion/sample collage, but since *this* formula hasn't been explored 10,000 times in 10,000 songs on 2000 records, two times is not too many! Hmm, I wonder what the ideological implications of using samples from the electronic/mass media on a vinyl record are for a band with a technophobe name like Luddgang... I guess they're trying to "deconstruct" the power of that media and technology with "recontextualization" of its constituent elements (hope it works!). You don't have to put up with my political rhetoric and theory about them, though—they offer plenty of their own in their packaging (and plenty more in an explicatory 'zine available from their address: Luddgang, P.O. Box 1095, Sheffield, South Yorkshire, S2 4YR, England). They're coming at everything from the standard bookish modern anarchist perspective... the issues they address in the 7" packaging are the June 18 Reclaim the Streets event in London, and the NATO bombing of Serbia. -b
Crasshole, P.O. Box 65341, Baltimore, MD 21209

Malefaction "Worship Nothing" 7": Ragged, growly grindcore, with some of the typical characteristics of the genre: for example, the guitars and bass are remarkable low in the recording, so much so that at one point the ringing ride symbol practically eclipses them. Samples include death screams, talk of slavery and how humanity is a plague on the earth, an argument about Jesus between a believer and blaspheming nonbeliever. There's a Slayer cover from *Reign in Blood*, in which (remarkably!) the band does just fine, keeping some of the energy and all the speed of the original and playing tightly enough—the only drawback is the singer, who is at his least inspired there. On the originals he ranges from a predictable grindcore grumble to a decent angry roar. Lyrics cover nationalism, religion, sexism, servitude, all anti- of course.
Commode, #5, 227 21st Avenue S.W., Calgary, AB, T2S 0G5 Canada

Man Afraid "Complete Discography" CD: For those who haven't heard Man Afraid before, they came from a strand in the family tree of hardcore somewhere after Born Against and before Dillinger Four—anti-patriotic lyrics and samples, rugged down-to-earth approach to everything, energetic music with the distinct oi/punk roots still barely discernible, gravely vocals, haunting moments between the full throttle punk rock parts. It's good stuff, unpretentious and yet dramatic in the way that this music can be. Everything they did is collected here, fourteen tracks plus their demo, and the insert is excellent too; it contains all their lyrics, all the information we could have wanted, plus little retrospectives by Brian Alft (editor of Contrascience) and Alex Coughlin (editor of Dwgsht, my old friend who went off hiking one day and never stopped). The last tracks (the rough demos ones) are some of my favorites, the sound is perfect for this music. Man Afraid was a band that was important to a lot of people, and not only because the project ended in tragedy; this isn't the most "current" record reviewed here, but it's better than that—it's timeless. -b
Half-mast, P.O. Box 8344, Minneapolis, MN 55408

Man in the Shadow "Pax Americana" 7": I want to like this record much more than I actually do. The lyrics are smart and poignant, exploring the terrors of trying to break free from your socialized role, and the fearsome, unbounded world that opens before you when you do. The music moves ambitiously between the poles of melodic/acoustic prettiness and more aggressive, screaming climaxes with chunky, distorted guitar riffs, but because the mix isn't heavy enough for the heavy parts or clear enough for the clean parts, it isn't able to deliver the way I'd like it to. The vocalist also could benefit from letting himself

get carried away more. But the overwhelming impression that his singing and this record as a whole deliver is of sincerity, though, with the multilingual lyrics and essays about making revolution step by patient step, and that's worth a lot to me. With some improvement they could do something like what Kriticka Situace did so well, I'm imagining. This record does give the impression of a band with lots of energy and potential starting out (I'm thinking of the Zegota demo, for example, which by itself wasn't half as good as this but provided a hint of what they would have to offer soon), and I hope to hear another one from them...
Postscript: Neck Beards

OK, looking back, I just realized that I concentrated on all the wrong things in the review. This is what I really should discuss: their drummer's neck beard. Their drummer was one of those rare people who is so centered and gentle that he radiates peace and safety to everyone in his presence. He also wore his hair in a way I'd never seen before: his cheeks were completely clean-shaven, but below the jaws he sported a big, bristly punk rock beard. I was telling Mark about this when we were driving together, and he speculated that the drummer's healthy disposition might have been connected somehow to the neck beard. The more we discussed this possibility, the more likely it seemed: both of us had always hated shaving, though having your cheeks bare can feel kind of neat—and we realized it was our necks that really caused us trouble in the shaving process. What if we stopped shaving them, and kept shaving our faces? Would we too become centered, calm, generous people? Find out next time you see me, with a neck beard halfway down my chest... -b
Miran Rusjan, Pot na Breg 8, 5250 Solkan, Slovenia

Manifesto Jukebox "" 7": Melodic, singing punk with big, ringing chords in a major key, coming off as light-hearted and irrepressible, but with an undertone of sadness when you listen deeper and read the lyrics (from the second song: "still got the fire, but nothing to burn—just the bitter beauty of an end"). The high-hat is mixed too high, and asserts itself as a trebly hiss in places; but other than that their mix flatters them, helping them sound like the Smiths as a punk band in some spots. They keep up the energy and speed throughout, and sometimes get worked up enough to ditch the pretty stuff and sound pretty out of control. They could have played with Leatherface a few years back and it would have made for a good show. —b
HALLA/Jani, P.O. Box 139, 00131 Helsinki, Finland

Milemarker : Changing Caring Humans : 1997-1999 A Collection of Singles and Compilation Songs on CD: As noted in the title, this collection of music includes every single and compilation track released by the band from 1997 to 1999. To begin, instead of simply presenting this compact disc as a pile of non-LP songs, they present this collection as part of a greater, um, plan. I like a band with a plan, certainly not enough bands have even the remotest resemblance of a plan. Specifically, preceding the lyrics there is a manifesto/musing on the band by a presumed Francis Haarstraub. This certainly was intriguing, because first: it introduced political pretensions on the level of, say, Refused or Nation of Ulysses, and two: it is a marked contrast to the generally stark and vague lyrics that proliferate throughout this album. Which is certainly reassuring. Listening to Changing Caring Humans I felt I encountered a group of humans leading rather bleak and unhappy lives. Milemarker does well to document the alienation of our world, its despair and painful longings, paved earth, endless strip malls and the nether, failed levels of human interaction. However, the most despairing aspect of the album is that I only felt more alienated and greater anguish with each song—the same feeling I encounter reading bleak leftist newsletters. The black and white images gracing each lyric page reinforced this. While it is legitimate to assume music (or art) is there to serve as a document of experience I must also demand that music serve as a tool of transcendence. I wonder if it at least serves this purpose to the band ?Or perhaps it's just sending them spinning faster into the abyss? This despair translates into fast guitar driven songs for the most part. Minor chords and cries and yells that sound as if the whole business of crying and yelling is hopelessly past and only a detached self-aware futile spew is appropriate anymore. There is also a jazzy number, some slower postmodern ballads and a handful of technopoppish (keyboard) inspired numbers that hint at the "Frigid Forms Sell" LP that followed these songs. (Note: two or three earlier, slower, rougher versions of songs from that album appear here). I think the best of these 18 tracks is "Receiver" from the early days when they could only manage to sound like Griver and/or Hellbender. It contains a certain sincerity that the other tracks lack and which "Frigid Forms" abhors. The band has come quite some way since then. But for the better? I know the members of Milemarker must retain their romanticism in a delicate corner somewhere far hidden from the world, defended by an arsenal of ironical pop songs. I've seen it in their eyes and coded in these hopeless songs. I just hope that corner doesn't turn to stone before it's too late. Maybe it is best they left Chapel Hill and its demands of a hip contemporary version of a Jane Austen novel.

Milemarker, I dare you to be vulnerable, like a lover! We may betray you (like all those before), but what do you have to lose? -BB
Stickfigure, PO Box 55462 Atlanta, Ga, 10108 USA

Newborn "self-titled" CD: Newborn play passionate hardcore, at least that's my interpretation from this cd. Really good, sincere lyrics, accessible writings to accompany the lyrics, a self-released full-length, and oh yeah, there's just something that truly sounds and feels *fucking* passionate. How often does that *really* come across in a hc record? As for the musical style, Newborn have a somewhat melodic hc feel with singing vocals and then at times change to complete screaming over more intense drumming and guitars, which in my opinion is where they shine. Anyway, Newborn comes from Budapest, Hungary, but you can't write to them because no address was included in their cd. People also tell me they're incredible live. (taz)
I'm sure you can contact them through the addresses at the end of this issue—the ed.

Ninedayswonder "The Scenery is in Disguise There" CD: Ugh! I really wanna be nice but I simply cannot when a CD causes me to vomit all over myself. It's the combination of really jangly, noodling, trebly, wimpy-ass indy rock guitars and moaning injured-dog-yelp vocals that sounds like a bad imitation of Fugazi that I just can't get into. I don't even know how to constructively criticize this because I just don't like anything musical about it. I like the record label because they inserted a photocopied piece of paper containing an awesome quote about revolution by Angela Davis, I like the sleek and simplistic layout, and I even kinda like some of the lyrics, but please do not make me actually listen to the music again. —n
Dim Mak / PO box 14041 / Santa Barbara, CA 93107, USA

Nostromo "argue" CD: There are so few open chords on this CD that when the guitars finally strike some midway through the second song, it's practically a revelation. Everything else is non-stop guitar chunk/double bass onslaught... one often describes bands like this one wants to honor by comparing them to machinery, but that analogy cuts both ways here: with their airtight recording and exact, uniform execution, Nostromo really do sound like a machine, as if a computer program had been written to churn out perfect (too perfect) mosh metal. Nothing ever goes wrong or is even a split second off, but the humanity is missing somehow. It's not entirely monotonous—the high jarring guitar alarm thing in the first song (reminiscent of something Converge did a few years back) is clever enough, but with no lyrics or variation in the tough roaring vocals, I just can't connect with this. —b
Snuff, P.O. Box 5117, CH 1211 Geneve 11, Switzerland

Nueva Etica "Momento de la Verdad" cassette: This is Vieja Escuela's sister band, the '90's version of the same thing, the vegan straight edge revival band. Maybe I like V.E. more because we're far enough from the '80's to forget all the dumb shit that went on then... we're not far enough from the '90's, unfortunately, so when N.E. plays something reminiscent of Path of Resistance (and they do—they do) I'm unable to escape my bad associations with that bygone era in the U.S.A. when veganism was a mark of narrow-minded self-righteousness and elitism rather than compassionate openness. Point of No Return has shown that the same starting point can lead to new, right on places, and I'm sure N.E. can get there, too... but for the time being, this cassette is up-tempo, metallic, moshy, three-vocalist '90's hardcore with at least seventeen X's discernible in the band photos alone. —b
Firme y Alerta, address in V.E. review

From Ashes Rise "" 12": I'm sure these kids are sick of hearing comparisons to their former neighbors His Hero Is Gone, but unfortunately that's the best reference point for this particular genre—and they do have just about everything going for them that made His Hero so important to me: overloaded production that creates a dramatic atmosphere, complex use of dual guitar melodies, sure-handed application of traditional punk musical conventions, straightforward political lyrics, furious fucking delivery. Now let's talk about the differences: they're faster—they don't slow down as much or as frequently for the heavy sludge parts their drummer uses double bass, and occasionally employs other sort of '80's thrash beats that have more funk than anything His Hero would have done; the vocals are higher pitched. But what really matter above all else, which makes rather than breaks this band, is this: they have their own songs, great songs. You can be the most skilled, well-recorded, politically aware band in the world, and without good songs, you can't do anything—but they've got them, and it makes for a great fucking record. I wouldn't ask for anything else. Top notch. —b
also like His Hero, there's no label address write the band at 7038 Bonnavent Drive, Nashville, TN 37076

One Fine Day "" CD: This is interesting stuff... their hardcore reminds me a little of Botch, with the *real* craziness (not just seeming crazy but really proceeding according to conventions of timing and chord progression that are unfamiliar to the ears), and it's punctuated with all sorts of foreign elements—notes which are shaken and tremble painfully like the warbling of alien birds, smoky nightclub jazzy improvisations, strange breaks between chaos and quiet melody, Black Sabbath playing in the background at the beginning. The singer is mixed a little under everything else, but when you stop to pay attention to him, it turns out he has a powerful screaming voice and is going at it without restraint—one song ends in a long, naked scream that makes my throat bleed just listening to it. I get the impression this band started from the mid-'90's mosh metal thing and just explored further and further away from the pack, until they found themselves in a totally exotic landscape... and now they're comfortable there, even if we're not, even if they haven't charted much farther than the ground under their feet yet. For their next record to be as compelling as this one is interesting, they have to make us see the wild horizons opening around them, to make us feel and intuitively understand everything whenever they strike a note. In the meantime, we can sit with this record, trying to puzzle out its strange power. —b

Green, Via San Francesco 60, Padova, Italy

Page 99 "Document #4" 6": The packaging contains no lyrics, and an essay from the band that isn't easy to read—it explains that in the months before this recording, loved ones of the band members committed suicide, and that they're trying here to capture their grief about that. The tragedy of music is that sometimes you can pour out all your suffering and desperation and shattered hope and it just sounds like a rockin' good time to listeners who have been conditioned to expect to hear rage and misery (simulated or real) on the records they buy. This is great music, high-tension, intense, energetic hardcore that doesn't sound dated to any particular era or genre, executed well all-around (I'm thinking of a more personable Stack, or something), but I feel strange now knowing what it came from and simply reviewing it as music—that's the way the art market works, and it's pretty unpleasant. I will say that the samples (which I'm guessing might be from the old movie *Heathers*, about teenage suicide) are unnecessary and detract from the seriousness of the music for me. —b

Rohodog, 12001 Aintree lane, Reston, VA 20191

Pensar o Morir "Hardcore Head Eternamente" cassette: Musically this seems to come from the tradition of New York hardcore, a lineage I haven't heard much challenging music from in a little while—but this is excellent. The recording is powerful (the bass is mixed more prominently than basses usually are, but it doesn't ruin anything), the music layered and often complex, full of transitions from fast parts to moshy rhythms to acoustic parts, even guitar leads sometimes. The gruff yelling vocalist (think post-Agnostic Front and Warzone) is

---

His Hero Is Gone "The Plot Sickens Enslavement Redefined" 12: His Hero did the most honorable thing they could have: once they became really popular and all eyes were on them, they dropped off their label, which had also become big and successful, put out their final record themselves (with no logo on the back—a fuck off to punk feudalism, a proud assertion of d.i.y. values, a demonstration that no, bands that are more popular do *not* have to work with bigger labels "so all their fans can get their records"), with a no-frills rugged recording and on vinyl only (long live punk rock!) did a last U.S. tour with a Spanish band (E-150) to bridge the divides of hardcore imperialism, and, returning bloodied and emotionally wrecked to their godawful Southern home town of Memphis, Tennessee, broke the fuck up amid various personal and interpersonal tragedies. Even the packaging for this record is exemplary, with the visionary aesthetic and spare utility that always characterized them: black and white cover (and fuck, it's chilling: a row of nails that, thanks to the rugged xerox-art technology, look at once like a row of smokestacks, and a barcode—saying everything about technology, commodification, and death at once, without employing a single word), gatefold with lyrics and a surreal dystopia landscape right out of our own backyards, text about the malady of our civilization's destructive values (as manifested by capitalism and "progress"), quotes and reading list (more criticism of modernity, technology, virtual reality...).

The most important thing about His Hero's music on this record for me, something I haven't heard addressed by others much, is the deep sorrow it expresses. This is some of the most anguished, bereaved, grief-stricken, deeply soulful music I've ever heard, and that they evoked this with traditional Swedish-style fast punk is truly amazing. It has the same profound, tragic spirit, the same hopeless but unsuppressable longing as the most haunting Flamenco music I've heard from Southern Spain, if you know how to listen into it right. When I saw Submission Hold this summer, I was moved almost to tears by what they were doing; rather than raging against the perpetrators and perpetuators of misery, they were forcing us all to feel the hurt, forcing us to be overcome by the tragedy... their rage some could have brushed off, but the pain was so undeniable, so universal that I can't imagine any businessman murderer motherfucker who had heard that them that night could have escaped without suffering pangs of guilt at bringing so much ugliness into the world. Here, His Hero does the same thing, but without leaving behind their rage, their determination, that twisted, self-loathing love of life that remains in the heart of the beaten as the ragged remainder of idealism. This makes it possible for them to roar about the slaughter and waste of our era without seeming generic, emotionless, or mired in reactive, uncreative formula: they are insisting on claiming their emotions for their own, not letting this fucked up world desensitize them, bewailing our fate because they fucking *know* it doesn't have to be this way, because it's a real tragedy. When, at the end of the first song, Todd cries out "Surrender! Surrender! Surrender! Surrender the passion from our lives..." it's a refusal to let the pain go, to become an automaton in a ruined world, to keep playing along—and thus the music becomes transformed into a demand, from within every heart: Never surrender! Better suffer, cry, be humiliated before their hateful eyes... but for heaven's sake stay alive, survive, clutch your bloodied heart to your chest and bear it with you through this smashed world, as a seed to plant when the polluted soil becomes fertile again. The blastbeats squeeze tears out of my bleary eyes, the grimy bass lines caress my tight, sore muscles, the shrieking of my comrades reaffirms my convictions that we are right to throw ourselves out in the world like this to suffer and fail and triumph, and I am fucking alive. —b

write to Ebullition and tell they have a copy. Their address is at the conclusion of the Severed Head of State review.

His Hero Is Gone—live summer of 1999, at their second to last show: Our band has a history of playing with bands we love only to see them break up immediately afterwards (Trial, Refused, Ire are some other examples...). This was a particularly bad night—it was two days after I received the news that Dan Young, our former guitarist, had died of a drug overdose on tour with the rockstar asshole band he joined after leaving us to make his newly-embraced nihilism dear to everyone. I had just split up (again) with my lover, our relationship was totally fucked up (in order to deal with the situation she had had to decide that I was ugly, awful, repug-

probably the main connection to the New York style, besides something about the snare drum sound. Come to think about it, my Brazilian friends told me that Argentina harbored a hardcore tradition parallel to but independent of the N.Y.C. one, and I suppose P.O.M. is coming out of that.. The lyrics cover the mass murders of the Argentinean dictatorship, lost friendships... —b
C.C. No. 406, Correo Central, La Plata, CP (1900), Argentina

Planesmistakenforstars "Fucking Fight" 7": Damn, I don't usually care much for music in this style (post-"emocore" melodic stuff), but this really has the teeth to make it work. The

ciate with Milemarker, although more idealistic, much less deliberately cynical (to their credit!). I wish I had a full length record here (what would that be from these guys, twelve minutes long?) rather than just these two songs. —b
Dim Mak, address all around here

The Purpose "Art as a Weapon" 7": I think this is old-fashioned hardcore in the melodic style that I never really listened to—I'm thinking of the stuff that came after Dagnasty... simple, traditional hardcore riffs, melodic, melodramatic vocals that work up to a yell at some points—oh shit, I've got it! Token Entry, that's an example. Anyway, the lyrics are elo-

the last song is a good start, and it builds to some typically good lyrics: "but it's not your sound you're selling, it's your soul... it's the space you're filling. That's not the passion they're buying, it's just records." —b
Underestimated records, address somewhere else you should be able to find, now move on, nothing to see here...

React "Deus Ex Machina" 12": Me and my friends Pigpen and Chaos are hanging out in the smashed-up living room of a punk house in a Philadelphia ghetto, eating dumpstered cheese pizza (OK, I'm vegan, so I'm eating month-old bagels by soaking them in water and microwaving them, but the other two are

...nant for wanting the things I wanted which were interfering with our romance) and she had to call me to tell me that she'd just heard he died, and did I know yet? And get this bullshit—she found out because the rest of the band, who had been eating in a fast food restaurant in Texas when he died (while his cocaine- and valium-addled heart stopped beating in the van outside, in 118 degrees of heat), had come back *to find a new guitarist so they could finish their tour.* So I was fucked up. The aforementioned lover was at the show too, complicating things in the self-confidence department... Moe was also there, miserable and starving and half-crazy after living in his truck in abject poverty since our tour together had ended, not wanting to get a job but unsure how he was going to stay alive, getting more and more desperate.

And His Hero were in bad shape, too. After the show I was waiting to hang out with my friend who plays guitar for them while he took a walk with another member—in the course of walking around Greensboro, they got lost, and in the extra thinking and talking time that gave them, they decided to break up. Tensions were already high when they finished warming up and began playing. I've seen very few bands play with the resolve and total focus they did—every chord, every pick slide was executed with the most merciless attention to detail, as if they were carrying out an operation in which a single misplaced note would mean catastrophe, as if they were guerrilla warriors with their lives at stake, not just punk musicians. I've never seen a human being sweat as much as their singer Todd did that night—it was pouring off his face and hands in rivers every time he moved—almost impossible to believe. I sat up above everyone else on the P.A. stack, bearded, weary, and thrown, looking down, and what they did for me, and for Moe and probably others, was so important: it was a promise, a reassurance from other conflicted, tortured souls, that we weren't crazy, that these emotions that compelled us to such wild extremes of action and refusal had a sacred glory of their own, something beyond the limits of anything in the quiet, resigned world from which we had steered ourselves.

For their final song, they played "Chain of Command," the last song on the first side of "Monuments to Thieves." During the break, when only the bass and drums were going, Todd took the microphone and repeatedly smashed it against his forehead, so hard it was terrifying. I've seen plenty of singers get "carried away" (generally imitating each other in very scripted ways) and "emotional" and beat the microphone against their heads or chests, but this was different: like their music, it was brutal, determined, deliberate. He wasn't trying to get crazy, he was specifically trying to break his skin open—and with two swift blows, he opened a wide gash in his forehead, from which a new river flowed, a river of red. It poured down his face in a thick stripe like warpaint, and across his chest—the brightest color in the room, perhaps the most brilliant scarlet I have ever seen. Pushing the crushed microphone back onto the stand he spit into it: *we keep on licking, they keep on kicking. keep making the pills—but long will we follow? How long can they lead? How long will they feed? How long will we follow?*

And it was clear to me what the blood was about, finally. In this world of symbols, of abstraction and representation, where we're supposed to march under standards of one kind or another, the scarlet stripe down his front, which issued directly from his very body, was a declaration. We can march under no banner. If we must have a flag, it can only be the flag of our own blood, which we must be ready to spill with our hearts and hands, for only that blood is as literal and real and complex as our confused hearts, as the world we live in and hope to seize. For once, blood-letting, singing and guitar-playing anarcho-punk performance was not a representation of something else at all, but a presence: of him, a real person, present and shameless in all his biological reality, all the complexity and conflict of being a real person, something "insanitary" and "uncivilized" and "unpleasant" to them, but now beautiful to us, divine and mortal at once. Blood is indisputable, undeniable—it is organic when everything else is plastic, abstract, silicon, concrete. We carry that poison, the time bomb of the natural world, inside us everywhere we go, even walking around their malls and office buildings. We do not exist without it, however clean and sterile they would like to make everything. Open yourself and let it bleed back into this world, a world "cleaned" and "purified" with the unthinkable deforestation, gentrification, holocausts of their genocidal reich, and wash it dirty again in the blood of our soiled conscience. Amen. It is the only way to bring this world back to life.

singer's voice is rough enough to have drama whether he is singing or screaming (I'm thinking of the vocals that make Leatherface more interesting than any other band in their genre), the music is pressing, intense, hurried... and, fuck, over before I get more than a taste. Two songs and they're both really short. The lyrics and packaging have that coded, poignant but self-aware character that I asso-

quently written and direct about the subject matter, and make me trust them—they're express some anti-imperialist ("We are the third world"), anti-egotist and rockstar-popularity-ist ("Player piano"), pro-living-life-to-the-fullest ("That smile"). It's all well done, solid, seems quite sincere... I just wish the music was a little more spectacular in some way. The experimental part near the end of

eating the pizza, despite the green mold). We listen to a mix tape of a bunch of nameless European crust bands, and then Chaos puts on his favorite new record, this one. The Discharge-beats, '80's-Antisect/Nausea punk drama, and gritty production all make us feel good about our dreadlocks and filthy Amebix patches and lack of beer money (OK, I don't drink, but whatever). We don't even mind

when the sample of the guy telemarketing for Jesus is a little too loud in relation to the music, or another song goes into another breakdown part followed by another punk guitar solo as we've heard a thousand times before, because this is our music, made by people like us with spiky hair and names like "Roach" and "Hoss." In the process of listening, we reaffirm our anti-corporate, pro-environmental, anti-sexist, anarchist values, as punks have been for a couple decades, and perhaps the token musical experimentation at the beginning of the second side (anarcho-folk with singing and acoustic instruments) reminds us that there is more to life than just wearing black and being against things. –b
Fired Up!, P.O. Box 8985, Minneapolis, MN 55408

Red Kedge "Through the Greatest Death..." cassette: New hardcore music from Singapore, with distinctively hoarse, shrieking and wailing vocals over music with a variety of textures (acoustic melodies, distorted chord progressions, high guitar leads, often in places you don't expect them) and transitions (fast, punk parts, slower, more complex parts). There's an atmosphere of lamentation through a lot of this, and that is captured in the lyrics as well: "I'm running, running out of this world, running out of breath..."—but they also maintain the glimmer of real hope that is necessary for this kind of music to be sad rather than just dreary. It really doesn't sound like anything else I can think of... seriously, if I had to come up with a musical comparison, old Vegan Reich would be the only thing I could think of (not because of the lyrics or attitude at all, seriously, I'm just trying to think of who else used this kind of combination of melodious leads and old-fashioned hardcore... they aren't even a good example... maybe Underdog? Fuck, you never even heard any of those bands, did you...). It could be more polished in the recording quality, although it's pretty good already, I imagine they'll have all the little details worked out next time, so I'm curious where this will go. —b
No Action Taken distribution, Mazmi Arshad, 2115-21, Jln Sungai Gombak, 53000 KL, Malaysia

Revenge "" 10": Something like Oi Polloi at their most metal moments ("Victim of a Gas Attack!") with harsher, gruffer vocals, a more rugged mix (featuring a snare drum that is significantly louder than the guitars and everything else), and lyrics that rage against the stupidity of the television-addled masses and the biotechnological/corporate elite that rules them with police terror when all else fails—in alternating English and German. Now, when a reviewer reaches the point of having reviewed more than two hundred records in a given genre, there are two levels of quality to

which a record in his review box can aspire. The first is to be nice to listen to while it's on, and thanks to its coarse energy this record passes that test; but the second test is to be something that the reviewer will want to listen to over and over, even though he's heard similar ideas executed on a couple hundred other records (of at least three songs each—do the math, it's intimidating). Despite their passionate attempt, Revenge hasn't been able to do that for me here. That's the weight of history in conflict with the life force itself and it's not pretty—if nothing else, I can at least assure you that it's worse for us reviewers than it for you listeners, so if you've only listened to, say, twenty records in this genre of punk, it should work great for you. —b
An's Bein Pissen, Klein v. Wisenberg, Breisacherstrasse 24, 81667 Munchen, Germany

Revolte 10": Eight different label addresses on the back (a couple of them tape traders), great punk artwork that a modern Pushead might have drawn (tasteful silhouettes of burning skeletons with drums and guitars, others dressed as priests and policemen, handwritten lyrics and logos), everything in their native German—all these indications that this was a genuine, d.i.y. punk rock record (like the ones you might have heard about!) combined to persuade me to try to trick one of these 10"s out of somebody in Germany: "oh, I'll review it, I promise!" Well, not only does it look beautiful next to my "Cleanse the Bacteria" record, it also sounds quite good—simple, sufficient recording, straightforward music that spans from late '80's hardcore riffs and breakdowns (that don't sound retro or dated here at all, just timeless) to more original: a moment of off-time chords, inspired buildups on the snare, one whimsical use of echo effects. Too bad I can't understand a single screamed word, uneducated North American idiot that I am. I wouldn't even know where to start to learn all the different languages of hardcore, if I were to try, though. Oh, wait, I found something I can understand (besides the skulls and guitars)—it's an equation: an anarchy sign, plus a heart, equals a smiley face. –b
the most recognizable label address is Bad Influence, Stefan Fuchs, Rennweg 1, 93049 Regensburg, Germany

Romeo is Bleeding "The Principle of Pain" CD: Plenty of variety and ideas here. The vocals, which alternate between a barely discernible mumble, a tough bark, and a ripped shriek which I like most of all, are lower in the overloaded mix than I'd like them to be. Wait, on the third song the vocalist is singing over the now melodic music (which still retains the same tough, really rugged, snare-drum-maybe-too-loud, thus actually retaining some energy... and my interest)—that song ends with the sexiest, throaty whisper, I'm surprised and pleased, and then immediately they

return to the hard-hitting European metal mosh. The riffs and songs are all well-constructed... this could be the starting point for a new generation of hardcore bands, perhaps, exploring a wider territory of musical possibilities. Techno parts at the beginning and end pay homage to the last bands to undertake this project... —b
Plastik Culture (with a machine gun over a star for the logo!), 13100 Aix-en-Provence, France

Rubbish Heap "" CD: This is an incredible record with what could be described as a tragic flaw, which I think explains the widely disparate reviews I've seen it receive already. It's vicious, abrasive, has pummeling rhythms, variety in tempo, unpredictable transitions and song construction, plenty of power and bitter emotion and raw fury expressed in the songs, hard-hitting mix, appropriately angry and alienated lyrics, with a political analysis to them as well... the controversial spot is the mix. The Rubbish Heapers went for a totally overloaded, distorted, unbearably ugly mix for this record, so that even the mix would communicate the bitterness, like listening to static on the radio at maximum volume. It's a powerful effect they've achieved, but it really is overwhelming, and it can make all the different parts in all the different songs sound similar and perhaps emotionally one-dimensional, because the listener's first response throughout is to the assault of the mix. I'm into it, personally—it's disconcerting, and I like that. But I have to listen hard, so the whole thing doesn't just over me and flow past like a sea of pure noise. This made the most sense blasted at four in the morning in the terminally slovenly room Jon used to live in, when we would slouch together in a bitter torpor of well-disguised idealism, waiting for the next explosion of inspiration to hit us. —b
Conspiracy, P.O. Box 269, 2000 Antwerpen 1, Belgium

Ruination "" 7": If I were to tell you that a band must have written, learned, and recorded all the songs on a 7" in one weekend, I would probably be insulting the band—but in this case, 1. I'm not insulting them, and 2. I'm not making it up. Ruination's whole project, they explained to me, is to do the whole writing/practicing/performing/recording thing with as little lost time as possible for each project—they have to, they all live hundreds of miles apart, spread between two different nations. Believe it or not, I think the approach works fine for them—the terror they must feel as they try to get the songs right for all time as they play them for the fifth time ever in the studio communicates itself to the listener as a desperate immediacy that usually is lacking from this kind of hardcore (yes, they're playing the gritty, rough straight-ahead stuff that Talk is Poison does so well and others do, well, OK),

They don't sound too loose, either, and although the recording itself could flatter them a tiny bit more (as the sleeve itself notes, the guitars seem to be absent from the mix, or at least unnecessarily reticent), that's not fundamentally important in their case. The lyrics range from the obvious old school stuff to more off-the-top-of-one's-head incoherent frustration, but that all works fine for them too, and they express all the ethics and attitudes that I love to see in bands. If this sounds like you'd like it, I'm sure you would—I do. ---b
try to contact them at the +/- records address

Russian School of Ballet "" CD: Simultaneously lighthearted and furious... I think this is that "power violence" stuff I've heard so much about (though, to quote an old friend, "Most of these bands are neither powerful nor violent!"), from Brazil in this case.

but high-spirited use of the genre. Really nice, personable d.i.y packaging... hm, while the Portuguese lyrics are easy to read, the English translations are so poorly typed that I fear I've been the victim of some anti-imperialist sabotage. All the same, I can make out that the R.S.B. are snotty, anti-imperialist, suspicious-to-say-the-least of U.S. politics and culture, insulted by the brainwashing attempts of the media, and unimpressed by more-revolutionary-than-thou radicals types. The whole CD goes by quite fast. --b
L-Dopa, C.X. Postal 1860, C.E.P. 80011-970, Curitiba, P.R. Brazil

Sangraal "Wolves of Armageddon" 12": Fuck, I'd forgotten how good this record was, until I listened to it after trying to do reviews of 500 other records. Well, unlike most of the bands out there, they're not trying to imitate any-

a crowd riot that goes over the top. Sangraal don't shy away from it, they plunge into it with animal fury, without pause or remorse, and it really makes for an unsettling experience even just listening to it—unless you're ready to let yourself go, like the anonymous rioter who gets carried away and is no longer himself, smashing, striking, running and screaming. The lyrics are ridiculous metal fantasy ("terrible are the moons of Neptune, moons where fierce battles were fought... for three hundred years a great battle was fought between the spider people and I"), but the song titles have the needed poetry: "Plague Riders," "Everlasting, World Without End," "The Long-Haired Kings"... —b
Wicked Witch, P.O. Box 3835, 1001 AP Amsterdam, the Netherlands

Libertinagem CDR and 'zine: This is beyond a doubt one of the most important reviews in this 'zine first, because this is an amazing, incredible thing to come out of our community, and second of all because you probably won't read about it anywhere else. The sheer idealistic ambitiousness of a project like this is itself inspiring to those not easily intimidated—since this is the sort of thing that can easily come across as exclusive, elitist, etc. with the insider radical terminology and references. For those of us familiar with that little world, this is a wonderful thing—in it you can see the plagiarized words take on the new meanings that recontextualization offers in the most fortuitous cases, bringing dead clichés back to life as bombs and beating hearts. The men and woman that made up this group spent six months working feverishly to put together these fourteen songs and accompanying essay, organized a few remorselessly confrontational performances in their home country, then scattered the ashes of the past behind them and plunged immediately into other projects, a behavior that indicates the kind of values going on here: the centrality of the moment, of doing anything to get into the thick of what is happening, anything from the most terrifying of terrorist actions to the most "debauched" of sexual acts, the wildness of teenagers rampaging for the first time, smashing windows of the banks in new-found and brilliantly reasoned anarchist theory shared in whispers in the cafeteria at school before rushing home to have group intercourse in their vacationing parents' beds... the poetry of transgression and transience, the passion that embraces life in its every form simply because it is more exciting than any kind of death, that sets fires for the joy of watching them burn and to hell with the consequences—the magical kingdom where nihilism ends at the foot of the tower of a hedonism that goes beyond itself to finally become a compassion and deep love for humanity and existence, in all its suffering and twisted triumph. The music is raw, daring, featuring the various voices of all the willful individuals involved (the woman's voice reminds me of, say, Spitboy—her defiant, beautiful, uncompromising personality comes across even out of the CD player)... when they're not working from their post-Fugazi punk approach, they're exploring everything else—1984 samples, improvisations, an a capella song about theft. There's soul here in a lot of the melodies and arrangements, and above all their enthusiasm and willingness to believe that whatever they feel like doing is right (a philosophical theory is worthless until it is demonstrated in musical practice) simply carries the day. The 'zine itself is some of the most challenging, clearly- and cleverly-thought out material reviewed in this Inside Front, and it's plenty thick with material in both Portuguese and English. This has been really important to me, helping me keep my romanticism and abandon, helping me lose my fear and above all the stupid, shortsighted notion that there is no one out there who can offer me more than I already knew and feel. —b
Deublehink, Rua Nanes Viera, 167, Belo Horizonte, MG 30350-120, Brazil

The duality of their approach is clear from the first seconds of the CD: it begins with a Russian dancing song, that quickly gains velocity, ending with a single, sung high note from a powerful baritone—the screamer comes in on the same note, excellent touch, and then they really get going. The mix is balanced in this order: really hoarse, screamy vocals (too loud), grainy bass guitar (louder than bass guitars usually get to be), thin, trebly guitar (quieter and weaker than it should have been), drums (sometimes I'm really not certain whether or not the drummer is playing). All that doesn't really matter, though. If you can imagine it, some of the irrepressible spirit of early '80's punk bands like Minor Threat comes across here, in their irreverent

body, or to impress anybody—just following their own crazy ideas whether or not they make sense to anyone else. Sangraal think they're a black metal band, somehow (they're desert black metal, just as the Norwegian bands are blizzard black metal...[?]), but they're actually a filthy, messy, shit-wrecking punk band, always playing a little faster than they can handle, everything in a mess, the constant blastbeats and busy drum fills murky in the mix under the ragged guitars, the hissing, rasping vocals seething somewhere between hatred, disgust, disregard... violence is definitely in the air, scary, real violence, that disconnection between action and consequences, between human and human, that you feel in the instants of a brawl, a stabbing,

Scatha "Birth, Life, and Death" 12": This comes out of the long tradition of British anarcho-punk that goes back to Antisect, but it's significant because, first, it doesn't sound like rehash, and, second, the ideas and values aren't rehash. The lyrics, in fact, are some of the smartest I've seen in thirty record reviews; they begin from the standpoint of the pagan, tribal values that cultural imperialism has almost stamped out of their people (they're Scottish Celts, I believe), singing some lines in Gaelic, and proceed to declare common cause with all other non-Western civilizations, going on to apply (what they consider to be) the perspectives and values of these various peoples to such modern problems as environmental destruction, fear of death, and homophobia (they insist that in other cultures, those who refuse to stay within the limits of one gender were honored rather than vilified for this). The last song wisely rejects both the patriarchal image of god and power and the older matriarchal image which has gained currency again recently as a feminist reaction to it; Scatha sensibly assert that nature and everything that is holy have no gender, and that the conflict between God and Goddess is nothing more than egocentric human bullshit.

As for the music—it's pretty simple and straightforward, in the old punk tradition, but none of it has happened exactly this way before. They go for a recording that is clear rather than polished (probably the best kind), heavy guitars with chunky riffs but not very much metal in the mix (no solos!), deep roaring vocals with plenty of power. The songs tend to go forever, which after a while makes this a better record to have on in the background than to sit and listen carefully to. I could see these guys playing with the now-disbanded By All Means, it would be a perfect match for a number of reasons. –b
Flat Earth, P.O. Box 169, Bradford, BD1 2UJ, U.K.

Season "" 7": At its best moments, this 7" is a torn-throated, bitterly beautiful lament, to be sung as acid rain falls upon you in the wilderness of industrial night. They're doing something quite similar to Fear is the Path to the Darkside, although their countrymen Headway also come to mind when I focus in one the wailing shrieks of their vocalist. Lyrics in French and English (perfect!), eloquently mourning the destruction of our environment and sense of self... beautiful packaging... plenty of music here for a 7"... great recording... thick emotional ambiance... with a little more individuality to set them apart, this band would definitely be among my favorites. —b
Stonehenge, Christophe Mora, 21 Rue des Brosses, 78200 Magnanville, France

Severed Head of State 7": This brings to mind crowds of unshaven young women and men, wearing black rags and patches and spikes and political slogans, faces dirty from train hopping and squat repairing, waving their fists in the air, with bottles of beer or gasoline in their other hands—and, more impressively, it makes me excited about that kind of punk rock again, makes me celebrate it, fills me with the joy that I feel whenever the more superficial aspects of our musical traditions regain their power and freshness again. Lots of those Discharge bana nanana nanana riffs here, blast beats to spice things up, distorted roaring about the apocalypse of technocracy and apathy, and only one emotion expressed throughout all four songs (furious outrage), but there's a certain pleasure and even comfort I take in putting on a record like this, wanting

to wave my fist in the air too, hearing the resolve and conviction of two decades of d.i.y. political punk rockets expressed again in those trusty three chords. If this didn't have so much fucking energy, it couldn't do that—but it does, baby, it does. Great record. –b
Ebullition records—if you can't find this address somewhere, I'm surprised! Anyway, the band's address is 1012 Brodie St., Austin, TX 78704

Sharpeville "At the Late Hours" 12": It took me a few songs to realize that Sharpeville could qualify as "anarcho-punk" after all. In the first draft of this review I was describing them as "anarcho-punk from an alternate universe," because they're so original and unburdened by tradition in their application and pursuit of the anarcho-punk aesthetic that it actually *works* again. Yes, there are roaring vocals, but they don't remind me of anything else, exactly (a little like Neurosis' vocals, really); there are heavy guitars and drums and bass, but the mix is incredibly heavy, really pounding in a way I've never heard in the genre, and the amps have a different sound than anything I could trace back to Nausea; there are interludes and acoustic introductions to the songs, but nothing that's been done before; there are slow, dramatic parts like the early Amebix, but no imitation here. And the lyrics have no dogma or repetition in them, they're fucking awesome! It's the excellence of the lyrics that makes me really believe in these guys—they're poetic, thoroughly-thought out, just the mix of theory and threat and mourning: "the time somebody invented for rent is a legal term for theft; the world is a challenge for my love, to paint the blank with

my blood... but we'll get what we deserve—thanks in advance!" I guess none of you kids listened to Axegrinder (a sort of updated anarcho-Amebix at the end of the '80's), but this goes next to that 12" in my record collection for mood and drama, and easily outclasses it for content. —b
Maximum Voice, Postfach 26, 04251 Leipzig, Germany

Shitlist "A Cold Slap of Reality" 7": More straightforward ranting and raging political punk from this label, this one with a few less '80's U.K. references in the music, and roaring vocals that are a little more constricted and staccato than most of the post-His Hero Is Gone crop. Hell, this could still be from the U.K. (I guess I'm thinking Cracked Cop Skulls or something); the lyrics are less general than they usually are in this genre—they seem to be personally directed, in most cases, at people the singer thinks are doing dumb things. The last song ("Pull the Plug") is my favorite, by far; it has more raw energy and furious abandon than the others, and that helps to make it a real punk song, not just an exercise in genre-production and maintenance. —b
Fired Up! records, address above

Sickshine "Hissing Snake" CD: This starts out with a noise that sounds like a person is being slowly gagged early in the morning, for about thirteen seconds. Fuck, I don't know *what* that is. But soon it breaks into a Kilara-esque rolling heavy sludge distortion groove, but not as slow or powerful. Throughout the CD, Sickshine explores lots of different things:

Milemaker "Frigid Forms Sell" CD: Milemaker's determination to do something new has finally paid off in the form of their first really great record—a record that can stand outside the supposed continuum of "musical progress" (a capitalist myth if I ever heard one—not only do you need a new microwave and car every year, but the latest style of rock music, too) as a moving, emotional work in its own right. Given, they get there by recombining old elements in a new way—the spooky keyboard lines, tense rock riffs and emo melodies, yelling and singing vocalists, and like Refused before them, they turn to the inorganic world of techno music for leads on innovation in the live music they play. The first song begins with a purely techno piece, all bleeps and whirps, the sound of robots talking amongst themselves. They cut it off in mid-bleep, to sing a song themselves, ambiguously posing as the robots-who-would-be-humans singing to the humans-become-robots (their cynical take on the audience-performer relationship). Their song, however, is suffused with a real tragic beauty—when the chorus rings out ("there's a product line... attached to every form of suicide") the last time, and the song ends with notes and chords of the most heartbreakingly smothered longing, I can feel tears well up in my eyes.

Considering the duality they've established in that chorus (death=consumerism, technology, etc; life= ...everything else), you'd think they might spend the rest of the record exploring the alternative to that suicide, but it's not that simple. For the most part, the rest of the songs are as hopeless as the first one—the running theme is the chill of modern society ("frigid forms sell you warmth," "the ice age is coming," "cryogenic sleep," "the shipwreck survivors contemplate their icy tomb," from four different songs). There are two ways to look at this—either they're opting for the easy, predictable out of pessimism, hip cynicism, semester despair, which is as seductive as it is

slow sludge rock, fast metal riffs, noise, rap-core, scratching, singing, growling, sampling, a lot of parts that sound like Tupac Shakur, and soft lovely ballad guitar parts. Listening to the whole thing, most of this is really progressive and very interesting, and at times very weird. What at first seemed awkward now comes across as a passionate effort at communication. If you can't stand rap (this had a heavy, heavy dose of it), then don't dare listen to this. But if you can swallow it, then this is a very baffling attempt at the fusion of the countless musical (and non-musical) styles. Most of this is the singer(s) doing dynamic raps combined with screams and singing, while the other musicians do their thing. How the hell can I say this... there are some really great parts, and some other parts that just insult the potential of this band. I would guess that they had so much fucking fun making this CD. The more I listen to this, the more confused I get. I wish I had the lyrics to this, it would be understandable. The packaging

like this, because it's melodic and sappy emo-pop-punk stuff, reminiscent of Lifetime and Good Riddance, with gruffly-sung vocals a la Hot Water Music. I however, have a soft spot for this type of music, but only when it's very well done, which this record is. I get a very personable and sincere vibe from this, which is comforting in a way, as most of these types of bands seem to just be using the hardcore or independent music scenes as a stepping-stone to corporate rockstar-dom. And my opinion on bands playing forms of music that are not new, exciting and innovative is that as long as it is done very well, and thus stands out from the countless others doing the same thing, then it is worth it. So basically, I think this is a good record and a band that is doing what it's doing very well—plus they're from New Zealand, which for some reason I think is really cool. –n
Get Up & Go! / Marienstr. 21 76137 Karlsruhe, Germany

A cold wind blows past me, through me, like a wash of cymbals, and then the demonic melody begins again, approaching through the tunnel... —b
Coalition, P.O. Box 243, 6500 AE Nijmegen, Netherlands

Starfish Pool "Rituals for the Dying" 10": It's nice to hear something totally different coming out of the punk community: this is full-on electronic music. The first track begins very spare and distant, increasing slowly in rhythm and tension as new sounds are added one by one—by the heart of the song, a high-energy pulse has been constructed from the noise collage, and then the various threads are pulled out one by one, leaving a hum very different from the beginning of the song. That explains what happens, but it doesn't capture what it feels like to listen to this—something like receiving foreign messages, trying to decipher a pattern or meaning in them, feeling it inside but not being able to translate it into any

pathetic and boring, or else. Catharsis-like, they're trying not to offer any easy answers but rather to explore the breadth and depth of the problem before offering a glimmer of genuine hope at the end. [OK, admittedly, Catharsis wasn't the first to do this... the best example I can think of is Saetia in his finest book, *Narca*.] The second to last song is the only one that suggests a solution (basically, subtle computer hacker workplace sabotage: "act like you belong until the final stage") And while the last song is negative again, covering the way that Milemaker themselves are implicated in the cultural/rebellion industry, that could just be a calculated reminder not to put your disconcert back on the shelf when the CD is over.

So is that second to last track the white dove with the twig in its mouth, coming to our little Noah's Arc of humanity across the polar wasteland of a world flooded cold and clammy by four hundred years of the reign of global capitalism? I'm not sure—here's one of the problems: though this is a great record, the best parts are at the beginning, so by the last couple songs it's hard to tell if they're there on purpose or just as afterthoughts to fill out space. That song, musically one of the least exciting ones on the record, might just be less cynical due to an oversight.

And I'm sure Milemaker, in all their intellectual post-modern glory, would object to their record being read in terms of life- or death-affirming sentiments. "Believing in stuff is totally passé," they'd insist with an irony that didn't entirely undercut the statement—"we're just Making Art." So for a real insight into what's going on here, let's look at two of the songs that don't fit into the frigidity theme. The third and fourth tracks are what Milemaker calls "sex jams," although they pointedly aren't celebrations of sex at all. "we slide up mechanically, sex" sings Dave in the first one, returning to the images of cold machinery—is that despite himself or a deliberate attempt to make even sex seem unpleasant and ridiculous? I think what's going on at the bottom of all this is that, in the long-standing tradition of self-proclaimed tormented artists, Milemaker are expressing their affirmation of life by indulging their angst, ennui, and misgivings to an almost absurd degree. This isn't new in indie rock/punk circles at fucking all, but they're able to make it compelling again here for a few instants—the most gripping one being when, in the second "sex jam" (which works in metaphors of insect copulation), Al, who has been singing over and over "you ought to kick it to me, and then bite off my head," suddenly shrieks, maniacally, over a scream of similarly maniacal feedback "that's the way the insects do it—EXOSKELETONS FILLED WITH FLUID!" and in that final phrase captures all the lascivious disgust with sex and embodiment itself that each of us has felt in the blackest moments of self-indulgence. —b
Lovitt, P.O. Box 248, Arlington, VA 22210

consists of a sandwich bag with a folded cover and a CD stuck in the middle. The cover is a piece of silk-screened fluorescent yellow cardstock, and features a snake on the front and some pretty shitty doodles on the back. Seriously, this looks like what I used to draw on my notebook when I was bored in class... in third grade. The inside is blank, and a lot of the writing on the back is indecipherable. This CD will be hit or miss with most. –WG
Swamp Suckas Get Dissed; 917 Olive St.; No. Little Rock, AR 72114.

Sommerset "More Songs" CD: I'm not sure how much a lot of the "typical" IF readers will

Srack "Selbst find ungsgruppe" 6": I am in a sewer pipe, underground, the ceiling just high enough for me to stand, trying to make my way through the blackness with a weak flashlight, scared out of my wits. The poor acoustics of the concrete explain the slightly muffled, bass-heavy sound, which emphasizes the terror of being trapped here in this small space with the air running out and the black water running over my feet, rather than detracting from the music in any way. The screaming is of a fellow-sufferer somewhere nearby, losing his mind in the darkness; the music speeds up with the beating of my heart, the stench of refuse, claustrophobia closing in.

familiar language. The b-side approaches in a similar way, but with a steadily beating bass thump at the bottom of it, a slightly more conventional touch—all the same, I don't think this is made for any kind of conventional dance club. —b
Conspiracy, P.O. Box 269, 2000 Antwerpen 1, Belgium

Stifled Cries "" 7": Gorgeous hand-made packaging, with silk-screened silver and black snake artwork (fulfilling the insistence of one of my comrades that d.i.y. projects must also have a d.i.y. aesthetic all their own, rather than imitating the glossy absurdity of mainstream

products). Musically this band explores the terrain that Neurosis, Acme, and Rorschach opened up almost a decade ago, which the more "avant garde" hardcore bands have been charting ever since. They use spiky, jumpy, impatient rhythms to maintain the energy, roaring vocals to deliver the pain, hold back on the metal flair in favor of a more rugged, raw-hearted atmosphere, and threaten that they will be capable of stranger things next time by playing with saxophones and static noise between songs. There's drama in the screams and sudden transitions, and the creative packaging combined with the developing creativity of their music makes this record a little self-contained aesthetic environment, as 7"s should be. At one of the high points, the music evokes a procession marching down an ancient church corridor lit by candles, dragging a prisoner to an unspeakable fate. —b
Conspiracy, address nearby

Stratego s/t 12" EP: Wow, instead of being excited by sexy packaging and let down by mediocre music like practically every other review I've done here, this band followed through big time. This fuckin' rocks hard, rock being the key word, because it is not hardcore or punk or metal. Imagine a cross between At The Drive In and The Get Up Kids, then throw in some subtle Refused vibes, and you might come something close to Stratego. The music is melodic and catchy as all hell, and manages to never get boring as it moves with lots of unpredictable energy from jumpy, slightly heavy grooves to subdued emo melody. The vocals are great too, ranging from a shout at the crazier parts to harmonizing crooning at the softer parts. Lyrics are intelligently poetic, dealing in an un-cliched way with personal and relationship issues, and the layout is fresh and inventive, with a Morse code theme running throughout. I love the label for including an extra insert with an inspiring little tribute/explanation of Bruce Lee and revolution (no, really!). The high point of this record for me came in the first song, which illustrates compassion beautifully with the lyrics, "I take no comfort knowing that you're no better off than me/I take no pleasure knowing this/I take no comfort seeing you struggling everyday/Just to reach things I take for granted." Rock on, man. —n
Dim Mak (address in Ninedayswonder review)

Suicide Nation "A requiem for all that ever mattered" 12": This comes on, and Matt asks: "are they from Europe"? No, they're from Arizona, proceeding from the tradition of West coast destroyers that I trace back to Gehenna, and I really loved their 7" last issue (it had a raw, devastated sound, like early Systral)—but this sounds something more like a top-speed German metal/hardcore band influenced by (the black-metal-influenced)

Undying. I guess they've polished their metal up enough to "graduate" to the rank of full-fledged metal band. I personally feel like metal flourishes and theatrics come across as more real with a little punk roughness, and I miss the rugged quality of their last record, but for the genre (throat-hanging-out-the-mouth-in-strips vocals, lots of blast beats, double-picked melodic metal riffs, classical guitar interludes) this is perfectly executed. The songs are well-written, the musicianship and recording superb, the bloody/religious-referenced lyrics confidently constructed if not entirely original... Actually, fuck it, this is a great record (and the sincere writing about how to keep the punk community supportive inside and dangerous outside only helps). The only problem here is that so many other bands are doing this, that every time the 'Nation plays a great riff or blastbeat I have to fight myself not to associate it with every metal riff and blastbeat recorded by bands of this genre in the past three years. An excellent example of why musical innovation, though not essential in any fundamental way, can help a band shake off the inertia of their times. My conclusion: if you *haven't* been listening to much metal/hardcore in the last few years, this record will probably do a lot for you. —b
King of the Monsters, 8341 E. San Salvador, Scottsdale, AZ 85258 U.S.A., or: Scorched Earth Policy, P.O. Box 3214, 76018 Karlsruhe, Germany

Supersleuth "...and still it beats" 12": I got a hand-screened pre-cover for this record, but I think it's classier than any real cover could be, personally. Supersleuth take the crystallized, mummified legacy of "old school hardcore" and disassemble it, putting it back together in new ways, with drumrolls and transitions where they never were before, the riffs arranged differently. They concentrate on slower, melodic parts, rather than full-speed-ahead simplicity. The vocalist does a mix of old-school yelling and singing, and sometimes sounds like he's struggling a bit, but the music is all about struggle, so it doesn't seem out of place. There's an Apocalypse Now sample before the third song that surprised me a little bit in this context. This music has a certain tension in it, maybe a little wistfulness, and a raw quality that makes it seem really sincere (all of which also comes across in the lyrics, too), so it gets the go-ahead from me. —b
Underestimated, P.O. Box 13274, Chicago, IL 60613

Talk is Poison "" 7": This band has absolutely everything they need to play this long-lived style of straightforward speedy punk without being held back by history: a worked-up, carried-away vocalist, unpredictable songs, excellent playing, gritty mix, high guitar leads here and there (you know, Discharge), just the

right mix of pounding intros and breakdowns with top-velocity verse/chorus parts. I don't think I learned or felt anything new from the lyrics, but I didn't have any objections to any of them either. Great high-protein punk rock here, you can pick up those rarer vitamins and minerals from other records, if you're still missing something after this. —b
Prank... address below

That's All She Wrote "" CD: Well, here's another experiment, for you adventurous types. I'd say this CD, plus the Libertinagem, Text, and Countdown to Putsch releases (and a John Zorn CD or two, if you insist), would make for a good starting point for the next forays into broadening the horizons of hardcore and music in general. This is basically a grindcore/power violence record with jazz and dada pretensions. The jazz comes out in the saxophone blowing during the quieter moments, before the blastbeats and bark-bark-growl vocals and spasmodic guitars hit again—as well as being present in the free jazz aesthetic of their less scripted songwriting moments. The dada comes into play in the nonsensical collage aesthetic of the packaging, lyrics, and texts, which are all hand-constructed, unsettling in their disorder but filled with material that could serve as the launching pad for any number of brilliant ideas in the patient listener: here science, child psychology, personal confessions and accounts, radical ideas, Beat cut-up-and-paste chaos all come together to create a non-linear, admirably non-didactic, ultimately fragmentary mess from which the listener/reader had better deduce her own conclusions. —b
45 Wilder Lane, Leominster, MA 01453

Thumbs Down s/t 7": Ooooooohhh...silver and blue ink...sexy logo...clever use of thumbs down theme on 7" labels...record label's logo is a diagram showing how to make a Molotov cocktail and throw it at a police station.... Oh wait, I almost forgot the music. Well, its standard late-90s "traditional" or "old school" hardcore...all the usual gang back-ups, some pretty standard mosh breakdowns, and some fairly run-of-the-mill lyrics making for a less than exciting listen for me. I can see a lot of kids liking this though, because it is really well played and executed—there are actually a few interesting little change-ups and hooks—and I can smell an energetic, posi live show from here...but it's just not something I can get into having heard so many other bands also doing this stuff. Insert last sentence of Brethren review here. —n
Firestorm / Italiëlei 58/9 / 2018 Antwerpen, Belgium

Trephine "" CD: There are definitely common threads tying together the music of the various Detroit hardcore bands over the past few years.

Earthmover temporarily united a few different tendencies, and when it split into the old-fashioned fast hardcore of Bloodpact and the polished, chunky mosh of Walls of Jericho, you could see two of those tendencies crystallized. A third pole of the Detroit sound is represented here by Trephine's very metal approach. There are countless stops at which one guitar will lead off with a complicated metal melody before all the others join in, chromatic chords, chunky mosh parts and double picking galore, even a purely acoustic segment in the fourth song. The two vocalists have plenty of enthusiasm, but need to polish things up a tiny bit to distinguish themselves from the legions of other screams and groaners. The song titles are pretty good—"Pat Robertson in a Lake of Fire" is a sort of revenge fantasy used to illustrate the band's avowed atheism, and "Not Everyone can be Jack Kerouac" expresses the desperation of watching one of your friends disintegrated by addiction. Watch out for spelling errors in the liner notes, by the way, my frendz. There's a fucking Gorilla Biscuits cover at the end, to undercut everything I've said about metal here, in which one of the singers suddenly sounds about ten years old. —b

+/- records, address all around

Twenty-third Chapter "An Eden for the Machines" CD/LP: Well, first of all this album is a little old by now, by most people's standards for reviews, and the band has since broken up, but as I will explain that is a good thing in a way. 23-C play crusty and gritty as fuck political metallic hardcore/punk with touches of grindcore, and I love it. This stuff is angry, morbid (but intelligent too), and desperate as hell, something I listen to for some strange kind of masochistic comfort after a long stressful day being frustrated by school and work and the bullshit of modern society. The story of this band makes their recordings all the more tragic and representative of the emotions they convey—one of their original members committed suicide, and their eventual breakup is like the rancid, rotten icing on the cake of shit that life can sometimes be. The artwork on this album is also great; it's a whole bunch of comic book style drawings

and photo collages, all done by the band. My only complaint is that it leads to an overall feel of being very disjointed, confused and random. —n

OHEV / 1500 NW 15 Ave. #4 / Boca Raton, FL 33486, USA

Two Day Theory "Modern slaves in a world of guns and profits rise fight" 7": 2D.T. has one of those vocalists who sometimes sounds out of breath, and that's representative of what's going on here in general: no polish or pretension, probably not a whole lot of practice either, but enthusiasm and honesty and serious intentions. Well, now that I listen closer, it's not just one guy, there are a couple people shouting in the background too. This record reminds me of Struggle, Downcast, that whole school of idealistic, accusation-wielding political hardcore from the beginning of the '90's—the first side ends with everybody angrily shouting "in the name of God—in the name of America" over and over. They mention the oft-quoted 500 years figure for the time during which Europeans have been oppressing other cultural/racial groups at one point, and they make it clear in their writing that they're out to figure out how to extricate themselves from the whole mess and start

working towards an egalitarian, unlimited world. –b

Tree of Woe, 18311 Arch Street, Little Rock, ARK. 72206

Underprivileged Nation "...For we are many" one-sided 12": Good marks for originality, which is pretty rare for records so far this year. The record begins with a long, slow journey through a spare, desolate landscape, the Bible verses from which the title comes being read in the background (don't be scared off—it's pretty clear they're not interested in Christianity here), before the spastic, minimalist hardcore punk chaos begins. The recording could be a little more powerful, but everything comes across as honest and unpretentious, and perhaps the recording is a part of that too, who knows. They snagged one of the only good samples I've heard in a while (a young woman, very serious, imparts: "when

you grow up, your heart... dies."), and they add some background melodic vocals at one point that add something tenser than those usually do. There are acoustic parts, and sudden transitions; the slow, wandering, centerless songs can get a little monotonous, but I think they're on to something. They're also not dumb (thank god), so the enigmatic lyrics (which range from a lament over our destruction of mother earth to the interpersonal struggles that complicate life) interest me rather boring me to tears. —b

Dead Alive, P.O. Box 97, Caldwell, NJ 07006 USA

Unison "Sunday Neurosis" cassette: This is top-notch dynamic hardcore from war-torn Eastern Europe, with well-constructed songs and plenty of variety (from all out hardcore speed and fury to jazzy acoustic improvisations, with mournful guitar leads—the best part—throughout), all executed with confidence. Eighteen songs, all lengthy, from two different recordings. The singer's voice is the only thing I could like better, his choked up yelling is emotive but lacks the total release I'd like to hear from him. The recording is perfect, clear as a bell, absolutely nothing to be desired... and the lyrics! They capture the

tragedy of real life war and strife with sensitivity, poetry, tragedy, incisive insight—for example, "a priest stands in front of the mirror, and his reflection shows a businessman in uniform. And the salvation churchbells ring, but God doesn't hear the difference between the bells and the police sirens." Another song title inverts an old phrase about duty, to ask the real question: *But why wouldn't the State die for me?* —b

We're in this alone records, Srdjan Stankovic, Veljka Petrovica 12, 21000 Novi Sad, Yugoslavia

Unkind "Plant the Seed" 10": Fast, angry punk, coming from the heavier side of Finnish anti-authoritarian punk tradition. They have their own personality—there are slower parts, sometimes they have broad, open chords on top of the bana-nanana guitars, and the songs are written well. You can hear the vocalist

Point of No Return "Centelha" CD: I just received this today, the day I thought I was finished with these reviews, and it will be the newest (and the last, damn it!) record I review for this magazine. I wouldn't even touch it, burned out as I am right now, except that it's so fucking good, and since it's from Brazil all you Europeans and North Americans probably won't hear about it otherwise. This is the most important "vegan straight edge hardcore band" I can think of right now; they bring new life to the genre in every way. Their music has the bursting energy (and, yes, aggression) that this style needs to work—stylistically, they're occupy the same territory that Timebomb did during their metal years, mixing the post-Earth Crisis metal mosh with deathmetal devices, pushing the formula as far as it will go with top notch riffs and transitions, and recording quality, and playing. Three vocalists, all roaring all out, all with distinctive voices. Their songs are about real subjects, worthy of anger—when they scream "true 'til death" they are referring to the guerrillas who robbed banks to find the anticapitalist struggle in Brazil a few decades ago. Their perspective, from outside the ivory walls of first world hardcore, is also worth a thousand hardcore bands from Buffalo, for anyone in the U.S.A. who wouldn't get to see things from this side otherwise. Extensive explanations to go with the lyrics, all in Portuguese, but I'm sure if you don't speak that language they have translations available. All five stars for this one.—b

Liberation, Caixa Postal 4193, Sao Paulo, SP 01061-970, Brazil

working hard to get the growls out; he doesn't have the strongest voice in the genre, but he makes up for it in effort. Plenty of packaging: nice cardboard cover, lyric booklet, poster. The lyrics rage simply against participating in the system of apathy and oppression, against the fur industry, against police brutality, pollution, consumerism, and for what they call "the one true law worth fighting for: the instinct to survive." —b
Fight, Hikivuorenkatu 17 D 36, 33710 Tampere, Finland

Vieja Escuela "La Mejor Eleccion" CD: Let me preface this by saying I've never really liked any "oldschool" hardcore—I liked some of that stuff when it was still "modern," and as soon as it became "retro" I started being bored, and then really bored, and then bored to fucking tears by it (and even then, it was only the mid-'90's...). There have been notable exceptions, including Final Exit (though I'm not sure if they count), Trial (maybe they don't count either?), hm, early Mainstrike (come on, you assholes, that counts!), I dunno what else... anyway, point being, often you have to go far from the birthplace of an older style to find people for whom it is fresh enough that they can play it with fresh enthusiasm and energy, and I have definitely found that in Vieja Escuela. They make this oldschool youth crew straight-edge shit so awesome all over again, it's ridiculous! Yes sir, there's so much excitement in this music again that the whole genre makes sense to me again, gang backing vocals and pointed fingers and stage dives and all (OK, the athletic gear is still all wrong, but these guys aren't really into that either, so it's cool). When I saw them play, it was the same adrenaline-charged mayhem of furious youth crowd mosh madness that this music suggests, demands, awesome. The lyrics are in Spanish, but thanks to the simplicity of the straight edge hardcore tradition, I can still understand them (even though my Spanish is less than remedial)—roughly translated, some of the song titles are: "Brotherhood," "Without Cruelty," "Diversion or Degradation?" You can take it from there. The only unexpected thing I've found on the whole record is a strange little techno buildup on the song "Resist," but of course that gets my approval too. This one gets five stars as possibly the only youth crew record of the last five years that matters. —b
Firme y Alerta Discos (I'll give you illiterate youth crew nerds one guess what that translates to!), C.C. 1817 Correo Central (1000), Buenos Aires, Argentina

Voorhees "Fireproof" 7": Voorhees always specialized in no-bullshit, straight-to-the-point hardcore, and that's what they offer here. This could have come out any time in the last fifteen years, and been equally relevant

(for anyone who likes Negative Approach, that is!). A more recent comparison could be "Systems Overload" Integrity, with the rough, simple mid-to-up-tempo hardcore, and rough, roaring vocals. The bottom line for me is that I like Voorhees—their music has a certain power to it, they wear their ugly hearts on their sleeves, they're good folks—even if they sometimes pull some sketchy shit (like naming a song "more violence in hardcore," and not printing the lyrics...), and I don't actually put their records on much (OK, who am I fooling here, I've had neither a record player nor a place to even listen to music for a year and a half now, but it's not Voorhees that I miss most). When I was in England last, their singer played me a recording of one song, not on this record, that was incredible, though. I wonder where I could find that. —b
Chainsaw Safety, P.O. Box 260318 Bellerose, NY 11426-0318

Word Salad "Death Match 2000" CD: For some reason, I expected this to be more groove-oriented, like Damad, but it's entirely all-out punk/metal in the tradition that spans from Antisect to His Hero Is Gone, with proportions about two to one in favor of double-picking and blast beats over bana-nanana post-Discharge/Nausea riffs. I would call this grindcore, but it has an urgency that can't be faked, something that grindcore is not known for. The vocalist sounds is a furious frog sputtering in a hot frying pan, the quadruple-time drums sound like a train running out of control overhead, and in each one of the twenty songs there is at least one moment when I simply can't believe how fast and tight they are playing at once. In that respect, it reminds me of "Reign in Blood" Slayer, actually—that overwhelming feeling of adrenaline surging through the veins like a tsunami, driving all in its path before it. The record ends and I discover I haven't remembered to breathe since it came on. No, it never lets up on the accelerator enough to lose my attention, although it takes a strong stomach to want forty minutes of this stuff. This might be analogous to what Napalm Death was for some of us in the late '80's, I guess. As for lyrics... well, I'll reprint one song in its entirety here, as Inside Front is known for (obnoxiously) doing: "ageless, raceless, classless, sexless murder." Yep, that one's called "Indiscriminate Murder." Fun, but dumb. Some of the other lyrics are just a little tiny bit more profound, but what isn't? —b
Prank, address easy to come by

The Year of Our Lord "The Frozen Divide" CD: Something bizarre happened when I went to review this CD. I didn't realize that I had put the disc into my CD changer along with Mozart's "Eine Kleine Nachtmuzik", so when the Mozart track started playing, I thought "Cool! They sampled Mozart!" After

about a minute I realized what had happened. It did take me a full minute, even with the Mozart CD case in full view. This proves that I have an IQ on the same level as a moth or kitchen sponge, and it is a wonder that I can discern which appendages are my fingers, let alone type these words. Regardless...this The Year of Our Lord is a goddamn excellent CD. Think apocalyptic black metal, and then think of it being played by Americans and not by Swedish corpse-painted sword wielding maniacs. I know, it is impossible to imagine. Your brain just exploded even trying to think of it. "But Greg," you argue in vain, "Americans can't play keyboards! The guy from Bon Jovi already tried it, and failed miserably." Oui, mon cheri, I agree with the second part of your statement, but must rebut the first half. This CD features a full apocalyptic sound, and the keyboard type sounds on it are what add that element to the disc. The sound overall is symphonic with the keyboards, and I fully believe now that Bon Jovi as a band would have gone much further if that jerk off keyboard "player" had taken lessons from The Year of Our Lord. Basically, The Year of Our Lord could eat Bon Jovi for breakfast and spit out small chunks of stone washed jeans with a demonic laugh. The songs on this disc bring you one step closer to the apocalypse, and reassure you that this would be as ample a soundtrack as any for that event, whenever it should arrive. The closest parallel I can draw is of the At the Gates "Slaughter of the Soul" CD, but played with all of the members under possession by demons. I think this CD is a compilation of earlier previously released songs, so be sure to check with the label before forking over your cash. I am pretty sure that the songs here were re-recorded even if they were previously released, so it is still very worth your while even if you have heard the band already. Layout and lyrics are both excellent. The CD comes without a jewel box in a super heavy glossy cardstock folding cover. Looks great. Any band which uses the word "algorithmic" in each of two different songs will always catch my attention, but to add to that such phrases as "this frozen divide of sanguine skies" and "diastolic murder comes with every choking laugh" and I become a fan for life. Great job here. —JUG
Lifeforce Records; PO Box 04011 Leipzig; Germany; cartel@bigfoot.com; www.carteldistrobution.com

Agathocles/Deadmocracy split 12": Agathocles recorded their side of this record on a four track in their practice space, and it sounds it: rough, overloaded grindcore, with the growly vocals characteristically too loud (and distorted, sometimes even sounding like they have a flanger effect on them)... they have the growling bass (when it plays by itself and you can it hear it), straightforward old-fashioned grind songs, and negative/political lyrics your would expect. It's all pretty monotonous to me, but I guess that's the aesthetic here. Deadmocracy are a hundred times more interesting from their first note—they're tight and serious about what they're doing (bringing Assuck to my mind), unlike their recordmates, and that combined with their energy and better songs makes it possible for them to rescue the anarcho-grind genre from the wholesale brush-off I'd given it after hearing the first side. They suffer from a mastering disaster that makes their side sound extremely bass-heavy and muffled, but a little fucking with the E.Q. on the stereo and everything's all set. I really like what they're doing here—it's not the first time a band has raised grind to an artform, but when I'm listening, it doesn't matter. They actually have a song that explic-

second song begins ominously again, with dirty guitar chunks that growl like an angry dog, and when they proceed into the song proper I decide that I like everything about them except their transitions. If they could get the parts of these songs to hold together tighter, this would be an awesome—they certainly can create a scary, tense atmosphere, their vocalist is ready to go, too. their recording is clear and yet gritty at once, their riffs and arrangements are awesome. The Submerge side comes in with plenty of threatening drama, too, and builds up, suddenly counting off on the high hat and getting going fiercely. They too have a great, ugly recording and plenty of intensity. Their first song is an assault on the Christian system of guilt that has manifested itself physically in the form of prisons. This is near the top of its class in the world of split 7"s this issue. —b

like here are the lyrics: they're way too vague and "artistic" to be anything but a bunch of silly jargon to those who didn't write them…although I can faintly detect some intelligent socio-political observations beneath all the confusion, which is promising, if not frustrating. But I can say that BUS put on a great live show, during which they sometimes explain what the hell they're screaming about in between songs. —n

Snuff Records / PO box 5117 / CH-1211, Geneve 11, Switzerland

Cable Car Theory/I. Robot split 7": When C.C.T. are at their best here, they're playing a tense, constantly changing melodic hardcore with throaty screaming and occasional sung notes over it, plus jumpy, busy drumming, that expresses desperation and drive at once. The first comes in fucking rocking, and keeps

Systral "Black Smoke" CD: The thing that struck me when I first heard this is that these guys had the audacity to release a CD that plays at the wrong fucking speed. You can hear, nor just from the sludgy mess of the guitars but also from the drums, which are totally flat and strange sounding, that they recorded it at normal speed, then slowed the master tape down for the transfer to CD. What the fuck! I guess they thought that would make this sound more "heavy, dooooode," but it just muffles everything. Musically, this is the kind of post-deathmetal rock'n'roll that is trendy right now—Entombed does it well, these guys not so well. The vocals don't fit very well with the music, especially when you read the lyrics along with them—they seem to have been added as an afterthought. As you might have guessed by now, this totally breaks my heart, to hear a CD like this from a band that recorded one of my all-time favorite albums a few years back. Their whole thing now is that they're rockers, they're headed straight for the top (some lyrics: "I knew that somewhere along there would be girls, the crown would be handed to me"), they don't care about anything, that they just want to rock—well, whatever, coming from a band that did so much influential and amazing innovating before, this just doesn't rock, it sounds like all the songs were written in one day (and a pretty uninspired day, at that). I guess if this was a demo from a new band I'd say it had some potential, since a little of their dramatic, dark atmosphere is still there, but that's all that remains. The lyrics are obnoxious in their childish nihilism ("Reduce words to a state of mind—I don't need to apologize for just having a damn good time" is as eloquent as they get, the rest is about rocking 'til they die and so on)… you know, a band doesn't have to be political to be cool, of course (in fact what was so touching about Systral's 10" was that it wasn't committed politically—they were openly struggling with the doubts we all have, but don't admit (especially not the "political" ones among us), and it was powerful in its honesty), but what's going on here that fucks them up is that, having turned their back on anything "political" or even topical, they feel so defensive towards those who remain "political" that all they can do is react against them with this tripe and drivel Pathetic. Do I sound like I'm getting carried away? Check this out: the lyrics to the second to last song, "Worldmaster," are simply a list of which nations won the World Cup in football championships over the last thirty four years. This, from the band whose last record ended with the shrieked, pained words "another life just ended—who cares?" Who cares, indeed. I guess Systral have found a way to solve the problem of how to deal with the tragedy that so affected them before: make yourself so dumb, you forget about it. For the rest of us, dealing with that tragedy will be a little harder now without them. —b
Edison records, a subdivision of the Very distribution conglomerate empire

itly tells Shelter to take their Krishna "consciousness" out of the hardcore scene (this was recorded just after Shelter cashed in with a Latin American tour), another one called "Why work?" …that should give you a basic idea where they're coming from. The lyrics to this record come in Portuguese and English—right on! –b
Out of Step, Fernando Nascimento, R. XV de Agosto 525, Santos, Sao Paulo 11082-320 Brazil

Ananda/Submerge "the dead bird e.p." split 7": Ananda begin with a guitar harmonic arrangement that is simultaneously hauntingly beautiful in melody and ugly in the fearsome growl of the bass and guitar chunks, then lose some of that power with a transition that doesn't flow well to a faster part. Their

Shogun, Phil Keiffer, 39 rue du Mont d'Arene, 51100 Reims, France

Born Under Saturn/Shora split 7": Two songs by each of these very similar, very kick ass bands, on a ridiculously thick and heavy slab of gray Swiss vinyl makes for an awesome 7". Each band plays that spastic, super chaotic and heavy grindish type hardcore with crazy screamed vocals, but Shora wins with me for their sludgy, even heavier (perhaps downtuned?) take on this style. Both recordings are top notch, and the layout is really weird and interesting computer-manipulated photography. I love how two bands from different continents (BUS are from USA, Shora from Switzerland) can get together and share music and resources on a release, it illustrates an important concept. The only thing I didn't

going, just increasing the energy, until… they go into a more melodic part, and from there just back off on the energy, it's too bad. The sample at the beginning seems sort of unrelated to the music, by the way, guys. I. Robot are going all out when they kick in from the acoustic intro, great shot-out shrieking vocals, strange hypnotic rhythms, jerky transitions, enough confidence in their wild delivery to carry me wherever they go. It's not the most classic, original music ever, but it has its own personality, it's fucking solid. They too add quieter, melodic singing parts like C.C.T. does every once and a while (and as in the former case, these are sometimes the weakest moments). —b
Immigrant Sun, P.O. Box 150711, Brooklyn, NY 11215

Cable Car Theory/Realign split 7": C.C.T. concentrates more on the melodic parts here, but they still have the tense, constantly-shifting style that characterizes them, and they throw in some little blastbeat parts for more energy and unpredictability. Maybe the mastering or something is a little different here, because I think I liked their other mix/recording (on the other split 7") more, but this is clear and strong enough. The third song is a bit of a farce, it never really gets going, then ends in them shaking a tambourine and singing sardonically. I think it was supposed to be an attack on women like Courtney Love for not being good role models, judging from the lyrics (which never get sung, most of them)—in contrast, they extol the Lilith Fair rock tour, as "one of the best-selling events in rock history." That's *herstory*, guys—or is it? Can we point to the marketing of our feminism as an advance, or is it just more commodification of the progress we've made? And is it really cool to blame women like Courtney, who are doing what people in the Occupied Territory have always done (play along and try to survive), for the way the sexist media uses their images to sell unhealthy roles? Anyway... Realign plays a similar take on the melodic hardcore tradition, but less jumpy, fewer transitions (there is a double bass part at one point, that's unusual), and the vocalist speaks when he's not screaming, instead of singing. Their second song has a couple breaks with some good guitar melody arrangements, that was the high point of their side for me. —b
Voice of Life, P.O. Box 1137, 0470 Leisnig, Germany

Cameron/Bastard in Love split 7": Here Cameron goes back and forth between a heavy, modern European metal/hardcore attack, and more experimental breaks (a la Refused, perhaps); then, to bring in the second song, they cut to a piano and a few effects-laden guitar chords, before going back to the heavy metal (they even employ Judas Priest harmonies on the guitars) interspersed with nontraditional breaks. They're looking for a way out of the closed formula of the hardcore world that bore them, but on this recording they're not sure which lead to take and follow. That doesn't prevent the music from being compelling (mostly when they're playing the metal, which has already been through the testing-and-development process), and nor do the occasionally bombastic vocals. The lyrics and explanations are smart and politically conscious, dealing with economic imperialism. Bastard in Love have a more raw, straightforward recording and punk rock approach, making for a strange combination on this split 7". They can do what they're doing quite well, and I prefer this to the pop punk stuff that tends to address the same

emotions (self-doubt, lost relationships, etc.) in a much glossier, more phony way. —b
Moo Cow, P.O. Box 616 Madison, WI 53701

Cave In/Children split 7": Cave In appears here with a song from "Until Your Heart Stops" remixed as a techno song, with drum and guitar loops, distorted and flanged vocals, deep club bass, all reminiscent of the '80's techno scene (I think of the good Ministry years, Front 242, the contemporaries of Skinny Puppy). It's a fascinating experiment, though it's over quite quickly, as is their side of the 7". Children come in rocking, like an European metal/hardcore AC/DC, and then kick into gear to play some really powerful screaming hardcore that doesn't sound like any of the 2000 other bands in the genre. After a couple minutes, unexpectedly, they too throw in some crazy electronic noises, and

shift gears into a tense but understated dance music bass line, before proceeding into a third movement of what is swiftly becoming a really amazing song. By the end of one listen, I'm convinced: they fucking rock, in the best sense of the term. Everything they do in this song sounds new and original and self-assured, the energy level never drops out of the red (even though they go on a lot longer than Cave In), this shit makes me want to thrash around and study their chord progressions and, most of all, see them do this live. Right on! —b
Mosh Bart, Lepillet Loic, 28 rue du Puit Mauger, 35000 Rennes, France

Costa's Cakehouse/Heartside split 7": Heartside are playing metal/hardcore like many bands in Europe right now, but they don't sound like anyone else, really... it's not just the recording (a little rougher than those

German bands usually have with a bass that is sometimes overloaded), they actually have unique songwriting going for them. I'm interested in what they're doing, I wish there was enough of their music here to get a better feel for it. Their side ends with a long stretch of feedback and sound decay, as it becomes increasingly clear that the sample in the background (in Italian) is something like a fascist addressing a cheering mob. Costa's Cakehouse surprised me by coming in with a lot of screaming and grind, then cutting to an energetic acoustic part with a Santana solo over the top, before going back to the busy hardcore punk. There's a tension in a lot of what they do, when the music is understated and it feels like something is about to explode. When they do explode, it could be a little harder (and if it was, this would be truly excellent)—for example, their vocalist has what

sounds like a strong voice, but I think if he pushed it a bit more. —b
Get Up and Go, Nanouk de Meijere, Marienstr. 2, 76137 Karlsruhe, Germany

Dead Thirteen/Down Foundation split 7": Dead Thirteen start with such a deep, ugly, sludgy riff, with such deep growling vocals, that I thought I must have the record on the wrong speed—but no, it's right... fuck, I'm having a gut reaction to this that says it's awesome, even though it's just simple chunk-chunk-grrrr metal/hardcore. I guess this is just so over the top about itself that it's impossible not to be convinced. Even the demo-style production is perfect for me—rough, snare and bass drums that really punch, thick layer of grime and filth to give atmosphere. If I went to see them and a bunch of morons were windmilling to the dance parts, I would be a

Text "" CD: I got this CD in the mail from a friend just as we were finishing the reviews. Hold on, let me begin again. I am in love with a young man called Jon. When we are together, we feed ravenously off each other's courage and creativity. We can transform any environment into one of wild liberation and drama, danger, epic romance, just by vaulting into it and struggling to outdo each other. We dare each other to get crazier and crazier with our self-indulgent flourishes and flights of fancy. When I'm with him, everything feels weightier, like I could leap up and land in any world, any time. This CD arrived, and as both of us have been inspired by the work of some of the people involved in this band before, we threw it on the player in the house we'd occupied for the task of answering mail together and planning world domination. And it was the perfect soundtrack: the sounds of young people springing arrogantly out of the confines of genre, speeding across a landscape of genres, zooming from one to the next, kicking up soil behind them to obscure the boundaries and mix the nutrients of one genre with the others, with the same disregard as a gang of teenagers trespassing for its own sake on a Saturday night (but with something else, too, a monomaniacal attention to detail and proficiency, handling everything with an egomaniacal mastery... —and thus capturing the essence of a certain kind of freedom that lurks in music like this: the realization (which can only be expressed by demonstration) that the rules taught to you (and hammered home through years and years of listening to bands that "play" by them, until you can't imagine anything coming after the third chorus but the moshy breakdown) are illusory, that the musicians can do ANYTHING, at all at any moment. And once you realize that the rules of music are illusions, it becomes clear that ALL rules must

lot less enthused, and the religious imagery of the blood-and-gore-and-revenge lyrics does nothing for me, but the simple pleasure of listening to them thunder and bellow is just fine. Down Foundation, surprisingly, sound like an early '90's straight edge band, with the '80's youth crew fast parts and youthful yelling vocals (and backups!) and an occasional heavier part for an intro or mosh part. Their lyrics are much clearer, but that's just thanks to the genre, I guess—they don't actually cover any new ground (friendship, which is always relevant to young men making hardcore I suppose, and seizing the present). —b
Slave Union, 58 Grace Street, Waterford, NY 12188

Deamon's Jaded Passion/Avarice split 7". D.J.P. have a sort of strange mix (the snare sounds like an oil drum, the guitars are a little

two parts '90's hardcore mosh parts, one part '90's black metal technique (if you're Gomorrha, adjust the proportions to 1-1-2, respectively). Their vocalist doesn't have the personality of the D.J.P. guy, so they aren't able to stack up quite as well (was that a German hardcore pun? Oh my goodness!). —b
Alveran, P.O. Box 10 01 52, 44701 Bochum, Germany

Deaththreat/Talk is Poison split 7". Deaththreat here sound like a pissed-off, no-frills, mid-'80's-punk-band, post-Black-Flag. Some details should fill you in, if that's not clear enough already: yelling vocals that hurry to keep up with the rest of the music, a bass sound that isn't yet distorted in the grindcore tradition, echo on the last word of the last song, which is "slavery." Talk is Poison aren't much different stylistically, but they have an

pace just barely too fast for my heart or mind to keep up with, so I am always just behind them, overwhelmed at what they are doing. At the end they hit one tiny, split second pause, hammer it all home again, and cut out, without a second of their side of the record wasted. The combination of Envy's red-wound-sound-painting with T.M.K.'s explicitly political anti-police brutality consciousness-raising is awesome, exactly the combination of soul and ammunition that I come to punk for. The musical association of the two makes more superficial sense than anything else, since while both are playing jumpy emo/hardcore the one does it with the grace of shredded longing and the other with an impatient, irrepressible verve, but this is a great little record. Lyrics in both English and Japanese for both bands—the bilingual trend I'm noticing is right fucking on. —b

simply be illusions, even the so-called laws of physics. Jon and I gloried in this, shouted about it, planned yet wilder schemes to smash through the wall of reality into new cosmoses, pretentious and extravagant and divine.

Or, I could come at this review from yet another direction: when a band breaks up, it splits into its constituent elements, which had perhaps formed a unique whole. When Refused split up, singer Dennis took the political rhetoric, the Make-Up moves, the psychotic notion that fashion could be tied somehow to revolution, and formed the International Noise Conspiracy, while other Refused people, the ones who had been more interested in strictly musical/artistic radicalism, went on to put this band together. In both cases, you can see the elements that were combined to comprise the strange and wonderful monster that was Refused crystallized in their pure form with all their qualities and particular drawbacks apparent. In the Noise Conspiracy, you can see what happens when you rub shoulders too much with the "popular" approach to making inflammatory music (i.e. you can get trapped in the trappings of being a leader of the people, with the intellectual elitism and focus on image)—meanwhile, in Text, you see the drawbacks of avant garde artistic pretensions—they can be alienating, isolating, making art seem like an elitist, individualist (totally, beyond translation) project as well. And yet—in splitting up like this, the musicians are able to pursue their conflicting visions to their logical conclusions, an undertaking of great interest for me, at least (and maybe to you, since you read this 'zine). There are some great pieces of music on this CD: the first song is an a capella requiem, screamed out (and infinitely superior in vision and delivery to the a capella on the Liberimagen recording, the only analogous project I can think of reviewed this issue), everywhere there are brilliant musical innovations in form and juxtapositions (everything from jazz improvisation to laid back club/techno atmospheres to moments in which gospel choirs or punk distortion kicks in just to pull off a transition)... the general idea I think is to free up space for others to explore, not to definitively chart any space of innovation. A large part of the CD is given over to what appears to be a Burroughs-style cutup of a Bataille text, read over a constantly evolving sound and style collage. Their best moments, not surprisingly, are the ones when they pause long enough to perfect something—like the end of the fifth song, a folk piece recorded on a four track, when David sings the ultimate anarchist exhortation: "Think this is my voice? This is not my voice. I just wanted to tell all the girls and boys to keep on keeping on—not that you won't die alone... but to fight for something is to make it your own... —b
Demonbox, Box 1043, 172 21 Sundbyberg, Sweden

low), but their vocalist is going all out with the shrieking, and that makes their German metal/hardcore matter. They're not afraid to cut the organization make fucking wrecked noise for half a minute, which works to their advantage, and they come back in from the noise with a light jazz jam, underlining their disregard for the demands of the formula. Good for them. They don't have riffs and transitions that are unique enough to set them entirely apart here, but their energy comes across, for sure. Avarice come in with an Anthrax-style riff and a high hat that should have been lower in the mix, and then go into the guitar chunk/roaring part that makes up the meat of this genre, pulling off the transition with a moment of metal double-picking that sets the standard for their standard application of the metal/hardcore formula in Germany: one part '80's metal introductions,

extra energy somehow (not that Deaththreat lacked it), and emphasize it with the occasional high guitar flourish and constant snare drum fill. Their style makes me want to leap around, mosh, crash into other dancing kids, the chains on the arms of my leather jacket swinging around. Their vocalist sounds fucking furious, and their drummer never takes a break or plays any slower than he possibly can. Yeah, this is good stuff. —b
Prank, P.O. Box 410892, San Francisco, CA 94141-0892

Envy/This Machine Kills split 7". Envy can fucking deliver the goods—they scream and contort themselves and twist their hearts up like rags to squeeze out all the emotion they can, they juxtapose chords that would be beautiful by themselves with gunshot drums and by the end have built up the speed to a

H.G. Fact, 401 Hongo-M, 2-36-2 Yayoi-Cho, Nakano-Ku, Tokyo 164-0013 Japan

Flores del Sol/Whisper split CD: First, it needs saying that this CD has absolutely lovely packaging. The only contemporary comparison I can think of for Flores del Sol is Submission Hold—both play a slower sparer descendent of punk that emphasizes the melody and tension and sadness over the distortion and release and anger. The woman who sings for this band has a voice of a very different temper, though, a more classical singer style, with which she explore the lines in different ways. She works up to a scream every once in a while, but only when the lyrics and music demand it. Their final song builds to an impassioned conclusion, and it is Whisper's turn. Now, here I get a chance to consider my attitudes about sex and gender—

for their singer is doing just about the same thing as the singer of Flores del Sol, but he is a boy, and I don't like it as much. I think it's not so much my deep-seated sexism, though, as it is the fact that he's just not as confident with his voice, so it comes out much less full. He does more screaming than she did, and he sounds more at home there. The music is similar, too, relying very little on distortion and speed, working more with the notes inside their chord progressions... I think this is "emo" music, for sure, if there is indeed such a thing. As with their recordmates, their final song is my favorite, as it starts very simply and builds energy and emotion without overreaching itself. –b

Sniffing, C.C. 3288, C.P. 1000, Correo Central, Buenos Aires, Argentina

Gomortha/Hellchild split 7": Gomortha strays from the pack of German metal/hard-

being ominous rather than aggressive. Oh my god, Hellchild just employed a high lead guitar, just in case there was any metal frontier they'd left uncrossed (I guess the high wail is the only thing missing on this record). Sadly, the lyrics of both bands leave me unmoved—that's the problem across the board in the world of metal/hardcore these days, I think: metal used to give us melodrama, which we made into real drama by adding it to punk, but now lots of our punk music has become mere flourish and empty rocking, like metal once was. Come on, kids, make this shit *real* again, so it can be dangerous once more. I listen to all this would-be scary, "evil" music, and I'm not scared at all. —b

Bastardized, Stefan Eutenbach, P.O. Box 200521, 56005 Koblenz, Germany

Hocus/Cheerleaders of the Apocalypse split 7": Once Hocus gets going, and I can pick the

Imitation Pushead artwork on the sleeve that looks fucking vintage—and knowing how much less it probably cost these poor bastards, I like it a lot more. The artist even signed his name with the copyright symbol in the same place Pushead would have! —b
Scorched Earth Policy, address nearby

Holding On/The Real Enemy split 7": The Real Enemy play rough, basic "oldschool" hardcore, but here's the catch" they're not dumb. They have a song about infiltration and Union-busting (classic line: "that back you stab might be your own!"), another against homophobia, and the last one, "Better than youth crew," is about growing older in hardcore. Holding On don't change the atmosphere—they come in with the same rough recording and traditional hardcore beats and rough yelling and traditional themes... the first word out of the singer's

Trial "Are These Our Lives?" CD: When I was young, I attended a public hearing in Raleigh, North Carolina, where the issue of chip mills in the American southeast was discussed. I was there with a grassroots environmentalist collective and we were trying to make people understand that chip mills are horrible for the land, and that they are only used to develop disposable paper products, which are just as easily made from recycled materials. That public hearing was the death of my belief in democracy: it proved to me that my voice would not be heard, that the corporations will always get their way, and that I was a fool for even trying. That night I wanted to jump out of my building and all its bullshit hearings. That night I wished I had a bomb to destroy that fucking Earth dying beneath my feet, and there was nothing I could do. I felt like a wretched member of a vile race, and like it was too late. On the car ride home I listened to a tape I had made of an early Trial seven inch and it was the first time this music made sense to me.

That week was one of the most fucked up periods in my life last year. I just lost my job, which is not a disaster, but as all of us might know, this society created conditions for us, when we feel the one to be blamed. They fucking made me feel an outcast, worthless person, who is not good enough to fit in their standards. They made me feel a person, who can't show up any 'good results', which can easily put me in some position I was never really claiming for. This feeling of alienation haunted me through a couple of days, which also made me losing my focus on things. I thought are important, fucking turned to hide even from my loved ones, thinking that losing a shitty job will take me a less valuable person. Later that week I had some obligations: being a hardcore/punk promoter in my hometown, Budapest. Having things to do in the hardcore/punk scene used to be my only salvation in these days. Luckily I promised that show for Trial, which is a band I always liked on records, and I was desperately waiting to see live. Seeing them perform totally blew my fucking mind, and I could finally start focusing on important things again. That cold november night, seeing a band play made me breathe again.

Trial is fast, desperate music. And this LP their last, is the most complete expression of everything Trial has meant to us. The guitars have sharp teeth. The drumming is maniacal and without compromise. The singer's voice is on the brink of destruction but the words must come out, quiet is no longer enough: you can hear him struggling against his face, fighting to carve his own destiny in a blank world. This is what it sounds like to want something, and to give yourself for it, completely. On this record is the silence of lovers on the verge of touching and the crash of a molotov cocktail against the helmet of a riot cop in Prague. Emotional, passionate hardcore.

There might be different stories happening to us, but there will always be common ground. And that is the fact, that people might live on different sides of this globe, but there is not enough distance to erase the discontent and the feeling of alienation, what we feel in our hearts. Trial was the perfect example to break down all the boundaries, we humans did build for ourselves. Through their studio recordings and live performances they touched starving bears. Their words were like gaso-

core bands by playing at ridiculous velocities, setting a new land speed record for blastbeats at the beginning of every new song, and doing it well too. The dual vocals stick mostly to the emotionless grindcore growl and groan that can get so tiresome, but they're not out of place with the music, and the recording is as shiny and crisp as it needs to be for this. I like them best when they're playing at maximum speed, metal breakdowns be damned. Hellchild is a good match for them with their near-constant double bass and prehistoric beast vocal rumble. At their very best moments, they can create that threatening evil atmosphere that Slayer could when they were

parts out of their German metal/hardcore that I like. I'm into it: driving energy in places, some pretty (if heard-before) melodies hidden under thick layers of distortion and screaming. Then C.O.A. come in, and I realize that I've just been being nice to Hocus—this is better, much more vicious vocals, much more energy and abandon, and that's what it really takes to make this metal shit real. Their first song ends with the most agonized screaming I've heard in twelve records. I don't like their lyrics as much as Hocus's, though—C.O.A. lean on the blood/suffering/revenge thing too much, while Hocus are more open and idealistic... both have songs about "lies," of course.

mouth is, in fact, "Go!" My favorite song of theirs, of course, is the fifteen-second one about dance floor justice for those who fuck with others at shows. They attack racist thugs in the last song (lyrics by Felix Von Havoc), and that seems to be just too easy, in my opinion—racism is everywhere around and inside us, and it makes things seem to simple to concentrate just on the "racist" enemies. Better to address the issue as it affects our own attitudes and interactions—and sure, fight the Nazis when they show up, but speak about other things when you have the chance, rather than patting yourself on the back for that. Anyway, both bands seem to be right on, but I like the

Real Enemy better, because it's clearer from their lyrics what they specifically believe in (vagueness was a constant feature of those '80's hardcore bands, which allowed them to seem cool without really believing or doing anything at all). I won't ever listen to this, but I'd probably go to see them play, just to chat, hang out, maybe dance a bit. —b
One Percent Records, P.O. Box 41048, Minneapolis, MN 55414

Minute Manifesto/Shank split 7": Shank play political grind with a real work ethic: get in with one riff, switch to blast beat and get the point across, the job done, and then the fuck out of there, the better to prepare for the next song. They're not afraid to play a slow pounding breakdown part enough times to get the point across but you'll never hear them do anything superfluous. Their singers (both high screamer and low growler) both sound snotty/growly, and the pace a bit slower. –b
Smack in the Mouth, Eight-O-Three, Flip Basement, 70-72 Queen Street, Glasgow, G13FM, U.K.

Remus and the Romulus Nation/Pezz "Benefit for the Tennessee Coalition to Abolish State Killing" 7": This is an excellently packaged and right on little record—it comes with a separate booklet for each band, a booklet about the injustice of the death penalty in the U.S.A., a postcard to the Tennessee governor demanding an end to the death penalty, and a legal document you can fill out demanding that if you are murdered the murderer will not be executed. R&RN feature a singer who always sounds a little off key (except for the rare moments he gets carried away and starts screaming), so that was a little hard for me to deal with... musically, their murkily-recorded poppish melodic punk listen to it comfortably. —b
Soul is Cheap., Zach Payne, 164 St. Agnes #3, Memphis, TN 38112

Stack/Narsaak split 7": Stack is the real thing here, their metal is applied to punk intentions in just the right way to make it matter, and the music is scary and insistent. Plus, they have a singer who can jump forty feet in the air, in the old '80's punk tradition. Check out the awesome lyrics to their first song ("Knock knock, anybody home?"): "Hi, I'm Mr. Restricted—representing this world's stupidity, to choose for polarization as a view of life is one of my ways to protect myself against the acceptance of a pluralistic reality"—a point driven home by their hilarious take on the old straight edge slogan: "Face Realities," it says, across the bottom of their lyric sheet. Narsaak creates a similarly dark ambiance; their first song is simple, hypnotic, repetitive, and while

line added to the fire, which all of us should speak if we are willing to have more than what this world has to offer; if we are willing to embrace all the joy, knowledge and adventure ever existed on Earth.

"We are the tortured and insane, disillusioned and mundane, unknown and unnamed, desperate and enslaved. And we want something more." —WW with help from Zoli... now let's hear some more on this record, from our long-winded editor:

I don't think the epic nature of the conditions under which this masterpiece was recorded can be exaggerated—that's a critical part of the story of why this is such a triumph. The band was wracked by internal conflicts, both personal and over the direction they should go commercially. After a tour on which singer Greg's voice was entirely destroyed (he could barely speak for months afterward and the doctors said he had almost become permanently mute), and they discovered that the label they had left CrimethInc. for (hoping to pacify the more "commercial success"-oriented band members) wasn't going to do anything with their record at all (it turned out CrimethInc., for all its anti-commercial and disorganized ways, sold as many as or more records than any of the other labels they worked with), all the members of the band quit except for the des-... Greg and Tim. Despite their conflicts, both were determined to fulfill the destiny of the band (this record) at any cost, and both spent a year working on writing it, a real act of faith considering that Greg's voice was ruined and Trial having no bassist, drummer or second guitarist. To hold the band together, they had agreed on Equal Vision as a compromise between their very different visions of what the band should do, despite the frustration this struggle caused each of them (not to say that remaining in a miserable project is always noble or worthy, but in this case I imagine you'll agree it was worth it for all of us); and during this year they also had to keep the very business-minded label persuaded that thing were going to work out, despite their own doubts. (One thing you can say for them working with Equal Vision: they were able to get enough money from the label to pay for a major-label-quality recording, and for the string section that plays on the powerfully dramatic interludes.) At the last minute, the drummer of Greg's friends' band flew out across the country to learn and record the songs in one week, and Greg's voice held out just long enough in the studio for them to record the entire record. This achievement gave them the momentum to gather new members and complete a tour of the U.S.A. and Europe... they played their final show with us (Catharsis) in Germany, on November 30 (the day that the W.T.O. protests in their home town of Seattle shook the world), after their passports, tickets, and band money had all been stolen from their van in Rome. After that the strain was just too much for them, and they broke up once and for all, but I consider myself so blessed that they were able to make this record for me to listen to before their demise. —b

only available on Equal Vision records, so steal this mercilessly. The band won't lose any money, because "EVR" is still collecting money to cover their "debts." Their fucking marketing director once told me in cold blood that its target audience for their products is "typical moron hardcore kids," so it's clear what we're dealing with here.

scary as fuck here, and despite the aforementioned work ethic they're often able to create that atmosphere of doom and futuristic devastation that makes this kind of music thrilling before their songs are over. In contrast to that atmosphere and the fury and abandonment from which they create it, their lyrics and essays are smart and self-conscious, often ironic, usually political (from a generally anarchist, if pessimistic, standpoint), and sometimes capricious or strange. Those last qualities come out more in Minute Manifesto's music, which is also fast and furious, but features some ridiculous samples, funny acoustic parts, etc. The vocals are also more reminds me of Pink Collar Jobs, which is a good thing, and they're sincere and right on as all fuck (locally relevant, globally thought-out lyrics... and, their refers to the two brother who founded Rome, one of whom killed the other and thus got to have it named after him). Pezz is also right on, playing in a similar style (with those vocals I can't handle), similarly right on—they have a song about supporting a friend going through the difficult situation of having an abortion... now that's a *real* subject to address, one few do, that touches almost all of us some time... Anyway, I endorse this record wholeheartedly, everything about it, and it's too bad I can't actually then second one starts at a faster tempo (with the bass-snare, bass-bass-snare punk beat), it maintains the same feeling with abrasive guitar noise and gravelly vocals. —b
Per Koro, Fehrfeld 26, D-28203 Bremen, Germany

Teenage Warning/Inflatable Dates split 7": Provided technical proficiency isn't your chief standard, Teenage Warning have some fucking awesome moments. The playing is messy, sometimes the drummer gets off beat, but there's real energy and excitement in this, it's clear that polished playing and all that bullshit are not nearly as important as getting crazy

and getting the point across. At the most intense moments, one singer is singing her heart out (with a youthful, totally open and honest voice, zero pretensions), while another screams as hard as she can, and there's a mix of tragedy, outrage, compassion, and the simple joy of free expression newly discovered all in the air at once. The Inflatable Dates have a slightly more polished recording and playing, and feature one garbled, shrieky singer and another mumbly one, strange combination. Their lyrics are dumb enough to be totally irrelevant to the listener (or reviewer—I feel like I'm doing them a favor by not writing about them). Fuck, their last song is really "Bombshell" by Operation Ivy, in disguise as an original. I prefer T.W., for sure. —b
6 S. Kent Road, Gaylordsville, CT06755

Timebomb/Redemption split CD: Timebomb play three of their songs off an old record, "Hymns for a Decaying Empire," the record that got me so excited about them in the first place. At this point I'm guessing they've played these songs a million times apiece, so the result is that these new, much more polished versions are totally tight (and have new guitar leads, etc.), but also lack a tiny bit of the urgency of the original, rough recordings. I'm guessing these guys wanted an alternative to the rough older recordings of their favorite old songs, needed three songs so they could do a split with their friends' band, and wanted a new recording project to break their new singer in. Redemption hadn't followed their ideas through as far when they recorded this as when they recorded the song that appears on the CD with this Inside Front (which I think is awesome). It's still the same idea—double-picked metal guitars and double bass, screaming and growling from the male vocalist and a mix of more beautiful and even more screamy crazy stuff from Valentina poetic lyrics about the search for self—but Valentina appears less, the music isn't quite as constant in its energy. It has some great parts (the whole second half of their first song is incredible, beautiful and haunting and with real energy when it all kicks in), though. In fact, it seems that I love the second half of each song, which is a fair bit, since all three of their songs are pretty long.

Timebomb, incidentally, has radically changed their whole musical style, since this recording, in an attempt to subvert the expectations of the hardcore community, which I think is fascinating. I don't have any of new recordings of theirs yet that they would feel comfortable with me reviewing, so instead I'd like to reprint their new manifesto here:

Movin' on, growin' up... these things are always seen as negative in the hardcore punk community. But let's face it, we all grow up, which doesn't mean you have to betray everything you believe in... We've been playing together for

eight years now and decided to change radically, no matter what people said, fuck 'em all! This is the most important aspect of our often shitty lives, it's our outlet and changing is our way of finding interest in what we are doing. Growing up we've been able to experience the joy of creation, the joy of art (our three chord fucking' art) not as a product to be sold, nor as an alibi for another bourgeois elite. Now we can do whatever we want to, we got rid of that heavy, hard-structured body we had built around ourselves, and we can move in every direction without plans—it's a wild, beautiful sensation, like running naked on the seaside or the beauty of the destruction of a society that destroys beauty. The sound of protest, smashed windows, the beauty in struggle, the poetry in a fight.

Many labels have been attached to us through the years. We were always expected to do something, to act in a certain way, to say certain things 'cause of the image people had of us. That's the hardcore scene is reduced to sometimes: a useless set of rules and cliches. Not changing our name is a choice to prove that one can do what he wants, we are free to follow our desires—that's where the strength of a truly independent scene lies. (review by —b)

Wards, Alessandro Andreoni, Via E. Medi 14, 00149, Roma, Italy

Whisper /Eterna Inocencia split 7": Wow...this is the first issue where I liked everything I got to review! [editor's note: no... this is the first issue in which Greg has refused to review anything he didn't really like!] This is another great record, and it comes from Argentina. Now, I apologize up front for being a speaker of English only, so I can't translate many of the lyrics and other words on this record, but I can tell that it is very politically oriented. There is a song on the Eterna Inocencia side called "To the Barricades" which has the following lyrics: "To the barricades! Argh!!!!!" which I surmise is either a rallying cry to storm said barricades, or perhaps a cry of pain after the storm of the barricades begins and the rallier has fallen into a ditch "Argh....fuck...help me out of here so I can continue to storm the barricades!" I assume the former. The music on the Whisper side is like a cross of Zegota and Fugazi [the editor, who is painfully aware that he is not making himself any friends at this point, would like to add another note: that makes as much sense as saying something is like a cross between Catharsis and the Amebix—what the fuck!] in that it is melodic, and sung, yet powerful and intense at the same time. The Eterna Inocencia side is similar in terms of it being melodic, but the vocals are even more pronounced in the mix giving it the impression of being even more melodic. The music here is more straight forward punk/hc, but it is still great because of the feel the vocals give. The record comes in a brown paper bag look-

ing thing...totally cool...and the vinyl on this copy is a creamy white and super thick...I would definitely carry this thing with me as a weapon while storming the barricades! It feels like it weighs a pound. The address is given as CC 213 (1412) Bs As Argentina, so you will have to take that one to your local post office and have them help you figure it out, but I would recommend it. I would love to have the lyrics translated, because if the cut and paste layout is any indicator, I bet there is some real poetry going on here. Great job. —JUG
CC 213 (1412), Buenos Aires, Argentina

"Asian Punk Lives #2" Tape Compilation: This is punk rock from Japan, the Philippines, Indonesia, and Malaysia. 11 bands and 26 songs comprise 60 minutes of the rawest of raw old-fashioned punk fuckin rock. Some of the recordings are great, some are not so good, but I think it's safe to say that this style of punk sounds best with a low-grade recording. Hence, this tape makes me feel good. Mostly 3-chord pissed off speed jams bearing a likeness to Los Crudos, with most of the songs about issues such as environmental degradation, technological disaster, injustice, neo-nazis being losers, deceptive governments, and of course, love. The bands are: from Japan-Absent, Out of Touch, Refuse, and Social Crime; Aggressive Dog Attack from the Philippines; Balcony, Deadly Ground, Inner Warfare, and Turtles, Jr. from Indonesia; Silent Majority and Shocked from Malaysia. Some of the bands sing in English, but a good portion of the tape is in Japanese or other languages (but it's still worth it to hear someone speaking before a song pissed off screaming even though I don't understand; I almost *do*). The tape comes with a half-page size booklet including a page for each band to express themselves (lyrics, art, etc.), contact info for each band, and a page for general scene news. On the front cover is a short, impressive discourse on *why humanity is fucking up*, and an explanation of materialism and authority. On the back is permission (suggestion) to tape this for my friends. I know plenty who will dig this... —WG
Sprout Records c/o Tsuyashi Konno: 1-10-27; 1-bancho; Aoba-ku; Sendai-city; Miyagi; 980-0811, Japan.

"De Madrid al Hardcore" Volume 1 compilation CD: This CD is a compilation of heavy hardcore bands from Spain. Bands included are: Mal Chance, Like Peter At Home, Kausa De Alarma; Versus, Inside Me, Proud'Z, Unchained, and Lagrimas Y Rabia. Of course, since it is a compilation, sound quality varies dramatically, as does song quality. Overall, most of the tracks have a (dare I say it) early 90's NYHC feel to them with gruff big guy sounding dudes on vocals and chunky guitars. Could it be that the four hundred and thirty six tours which 25 Ta Life have done in Europe have impacted or influenced the musicians there? Probably. I know that I was speaking in "Da's" and "Ta's" for weeks after their first record came out. This CD, while it could be a little more diverse in terms of the styles represented, definitely gives a good image of the type of music being played currently in the Madrid hardcore scene. Standout tracks for me were the last song (by Lagrimas Y Rabia) which was reminiscent of Bad Religion with a little more distortion on the guitars and the Like Peter at Home track. Like Peter at Home's song was especially heavy and hard hitting with interesting vocals alternating between deep and gruff and deep and sung, and a cool set of guitar riffs. I wish I spoke Spanish though to understand the lyrics. Wait though! I almost forgot!!! The www.altavista.com text translation section!

"Decade of Dissidence: The worst of the 1 in 12 Club Volume 14/15" CD compilation: This is a collection of songs of widely disparate musical styles, recording qualities, and subject matters, mostly from the U.K. but occasionally from, say, Japan. The connecting theme is that all these bands have played at the 1 in 12 Club in Bradford, England. Seriously, there are noise collage bands here putting bagpipes over industrial samples, old British punkers covering Motorhead, women playing strange ditties about sex, guys exploring the acoustic landscapes of emo jazz, old men reciting poetry, Japanese guys who want to be Conflict, Cress who want to be Crass, an articulate group of French people called Happy Anger, the usual British hardcore bands (Voorhees and Hard to Swallow and Stalingrad and Sawn Off and John Holmes) screaming and rocking. The Hard to Swallow song, their theme song, is probably my favorite on this by a good couple kilometers.

ugly and jumbled, with a shoddy photocopy quality. I know all this is supposed to be DIY and "punk rock" but this release is unnecessary and disappointing in the first place when all the music appears elsewhere and two of the bands aren't that good. I guess I should be fair and describe the bands, so here goes: GZ play brutal as fuck metalcore with sick imagery and throat shredding screams, and DMW play furious, chaotic and raw metalcore with quite possibly the most brutally sick, desperate screaming to ever come from a human throat. The two NY bands on the other side play pretty unmemorable and generic mid-tempo metalcore with the usual screams/growls. To sum up, let's try not to waste money and resources putting out unnecessary releases, and if you're interested in either of the two CT bands, just get their individual 7"s (or albums). —n
Slave Union Records / 58 Grace St. / Waterford NY 12188, USA

Undying "The Whispered Lies of Angels" CD: I've already been criticized for reviewing records on this label before, so I'm in for it now, but there's no way around it: this is one of the records that has kept me caring about and feeling the potential of hardcore music this year. Everything is perfect here: the composition, the playing, the intentions (besides their misguided choice of record label, a choice excusable for an inexperienced band choosing an overseas label), the vocals, the lyrics, even the recording... It plays like a classical symphony from the beginning to the end, the possibilities of all the individual instruments multiplying exponentially as they are combined, so at any given moment there is more happening in the relationships between the two guitars, the bass, and the drums (which shift constantly between five different gears, ranging from blastbeats to vast fields of double bass punctuated by impossibly sparse snare beats, so the listener is thrust into the irresistible rhythm afresh at the beginning of each successive verse) than a single person could keep up with at once, leaving me perpetually overwhelmed by the genius of the writing. The riffs and transitions themselves are never lazy or easy, always exploring any possibility to its farthest and wildest reaches, but never seeming forced—this is one of those records that seems as if it has always existed, as if each of the songs here was carved into the cosmos from the beginning of time. And they command so many different emotions at once—at one moment the guitars are playing the saddest requiem, the drums pounding with adrenaline, and the vocalist screaming with such rage, and then at the next everything switches places again and I am at once crying for the worlds that vanished under the treads of the bulldozers, shaking as my heart pounds with fear and excitement in my chest, and clenching my fists in the scowling certainty of the unflinching insurrectionist. In case all this is too clear about my feelings and not clear enough about the music, let me give you some reference points: I love the music for the same reason I love the second Children of Bodom CD (incidentally the very best metal album I have ever heard in my life), and the vocals are a mix between the hoarse, hissing scream of Radwan in Ire and the straight-to-the-heart speaking of Greg on the last Trial record. In my review of their last CD, I suggested that they needed to expand their subject matter lyrically, and they have come through with flying colors there. Let's cut straight to the last song (before the hidden gothic rock cover, which sounds just fine in their hands as well)—a lament, but raging with the threat of the one with nothing left to lose: "if this is what your life will take from me, if this is what your world will make of me—then let it live with the consequences." The blood of my ancestors, pumped into my veins, assumed to be safe, runs cold on me, the world trembles imperceptibly beneath my feet, and I know again and without shame or fear what I am doing with my life, and why. —b
Good Life recording...

I will type in the lyrics to one of the songs and translate it to get the full impact. We will use Versus, whose last CD I really enjoyed and reviewed in the last Inside Front if I am remembering correctly. Their lyrics on this track according to altavista say, "They came to the world between hunger, misery and hopelessness. Their own families left them. Alone and single on the streets looking between sweepings. They shelter is pain between alcohol and poison." Even if it is not exact, I think I get the right idea. —JUG
Kilometrocero Records; apartado de correos 8578; 28080 Madrid; Spain; xloyalx@hotmail.com for more info.

The real reason for this record to exist is that it's a benefit to support the people in Kosova, who are trying to put their world back together after all the wars, witchhunts, and oppression. —b
1 in 12 records, 21-23 Albion Street, Bradford, BD1 2LY, England

"Four Corners" compilation 7": Two great bands victimized by a pretty pointless release makes for an unhappy reviewer. This comp does no justice to CT metal heavyweights Groundzero and Die My Will by including a song from each that is previously released, and pairing them with two other bands that are rather mediocre (Sever and Dying Game Theory). To make matters worse, the layout is

"Hardcore Reality: Colombia en Tu Cara" compilation CD: This is a compilation of Colombian hardcore bands, eight of them, twenty three songs altogether. Hardcore is relatively new in Colombia (so to have eight bands with recordings is pretty impressive), and presently all the bands are working on their own version of the kind of music that Breakdown played in New York in the late '80's: simple guitar riffs, fast and slow parts, gruff yelling vocals, a general mosh aesthetic. The first song on the CD is excellent for this genre—it ends with gang shouting, which evokes a crowd riot, adding the necessary adrenaline and intimidating atmosphere. There's also a part in it in which an extra four beats are added at the end of every verse, just

as Sick of it All did in their second version of "Stand Alone." More than one song ends with someone shouting "puto!" in the background, which I guess is the equivalent of "beeeeatch!" here. The recordings vary from rough to, well, a little less, rough, but all are sufficient not to hold the bands back, especially for the style of music being played here. Everything is in Spanish, except for the brief introduction at the end of the lyric booklet. I just hope these kids all know that, unlike them, the bands from the New York hardcore scene that inspires them were known for their ignorance, their disinterest in world affairs of any kind, their fear to show compassion or personality... --b
Diego Paredes, 8372 NW 64th St. #1595, Miami, FL 33166

"Not without a fight... Noise/Text War" compilation double CD: While everyone else was trying to figure out who the next really popular hardcore band would be, Adam (chief organizer of this record label) was out trying to hunt down the most interesting, under-appreciated bands. There's a long tradition of this in the more underground extremes of punk rock, and it was these collectors of esoteric punk knowledge that first started to bridge the gaps between the punk communities of different nations (think of the Peace/War compilation, for example). In the old days, a compilation like this probably would have had G.I.S.M., Agathocles, and the Cripple Bastards on it... today, it has bands like Dahmer (fucking awesome, murderous grind, and the live recording only helps), the Japanese Final Exit (who play some of the stranger, tougher experimental crust/noise that exists today), and uh, Agathocles and Cripple Bastards! There's a mix of noise bands and punk/hardcore bands, more songs by the latter but more song length from the former to balance it out, and a few bridging the gap with crossover stuff... other bands include Strong Intention, Bastard Noise, Katastrofialue, and about ten thousand more (this is a packed double CD, it's enough sound to wander through for a long, long time), as well as a spoken word piece from Mark Bruback. The booklet is thick with writing from other groups/individuals active within the punk community, including Daryl Vocat (who writes about coming out), Jen Angel (who writes about advertising in the punk community), Adrienne Droogas (on self defense), Fly (the artist from New York, with a very poetic piece on protests, etc.), Chris Boarts, Mike Antipathy, our very own C.W.C., and many others. Basically, though this is framed as a simple compilation, it really is a testament of dozens of different individuals on a level with the best hardcore 'zines, and more interesting than most for the wide variety of mediums employed. —b
Fist Fight, P.O. Box 364, Hagerstown, MD 364

"Over the Walls of Nationalism and War" compilation 7": This record features seven bands from the war-torn area of ex-Yugoslavia, as a gesture of dialogue between people from the different struggling factions of the population there, and a declaration of unity against the divisions of nationalism and war. As such, for us Westerners, this is something much more real than we're used to, a punk record with real things at stake, not just a declaration of allegiance to some image or another. Everything here is translated into English, too, so it's possible for an uneducated U.S. punk like me to read the lyrics and explanations... I would counsel against getting this 7" just to buy a souvenir of the exotic world where anti-war songs are actually real statements, but I would encourage everyone to get this record as a way to hear a perspective about the situation in former Yugoslavia that doesn't just come from fucking network TV. I remember that during the U.S. bombing, a kid from this area sent me a photograph of the damage to civilian housing U.S. bombs had caused down his street, something I never would have learned about otherwise—that's something the punk network can be really valuable for, getting your own news. The bands on here play gritty, straightforward, distorted hardcore, with the exception of the last one, Uberzeitung, who present a disconcerting noise project with someone screaming over the top: *you don't have to kill the people— you just have to kill the bastard inside you.* –b
Dusan Vejnovic, 12, V.U.B. 34, 25000 Sombor, Serbia/Yugoslavia

"Payoll Squat Benefit" compilation 7": This is a benefit for a squat in Brazil, in Curitiba (I was there but didn't see it—hope it hasn't already been evicted now?). The packaging is quite classy, cardboard closed by an industrial clip, very d.i.y. and personable. The 7" itself features an international array of bands (Faulter, Diavolo Rosso, Spinebender, Wut-Entbrannt, Revolte, Seuchenherd, and...) all playing rough, tough, fast, aggressive punk, each with enough energy (sometimes a moment of originality) to distinguish itself. The Brazilian band (Difekto), from the squat itself, have an understandably rougher recording than the others, but it flatters them too. They remind me of Against, the old U.S. Discharge-style band I love so much. This is a good rough punk record, for a good cause. That's the deal. —b
Bad Influence, Stefan Fuchs, Rennweg 1, 93049 Regensburg, Germany

"Pickle Patch" CD compilation: This is the sort of excellent little project that could only come out of the hardcore scene. Not just a twenty two track collection of songs played at an apartment that had house shows for a few years, but also a bunch of essays from every-

one who loved those shows—showing how much excitement can develop from just a few kids taking themselves and their fun evenings seriously. The sound quality of the (all live) recordings is just fine, better than it is on lots of my favorite old punk records that were recorded in studios. Probably the most priceless moment is the break between the verse and the chorus in Atom and his Package's live rendition of "Punk Rock Academy" when you can hear the audience laughing along with his humor. Close behind that is Behead the Prophet No Lord Shall Live introducing their song "They Shall Not Pass": "this one's for the homophobes in the R.C.P." Right on! And after that, in third place, we have Former Members of Alfonsin spelling it all hilariously out about how dumb the absurd "unity" rhetoric of the commercialized side of the straight edge scene is. The minutes of band-crowd banter at the beginning of Submission Hold's set helps to remind the listener how wonderful it can be to be in one of those comfortable, safe, supportive environments that can be created at punk shows. Lest any of you embittered motherfuckers feel left out and isolated by all the positivity on this compilation, I'll go on record and admit that I am personally responsible for the only negative, unpleasant show that ever took place at the Pickle Patch—when Catharsis played there, we were in a bad mood, and deliberately pissed everyone off, which no one could understand at the time. And here I am singing the praises of everything they did besides that night. Goes to show how multifaceted punk is in each of us and in the whole community, I guess. —b
Dim Mak, address within your reach if you just flip a few pages

"Visionville hardcore: reaching out" cassette compilation: This is a compilation of Malaysian hardcore bands, and for a scene that has only existed about five years (according to the liner notes, at least... and that's also about the length of time since Inside Front got its first letters from Malaysia, but that doesn't really prove anything) the recordings and songs here are really incredible. Seriously, the recordings are better than many U.S. bands get for their releases. I haven't been able to get all the bands straight yet (two songs each from Chronic Mass, Another Side, Disaster Funhouse, Projekt AK, N.E.T.), but there's a mix of metal (lead guitars with echo on them, screaming vocals) with more traditional hardcore approaches here (yelling vocals, more speedy rhythms)... perhaps think an updated, more metal version of the "New York Hardcore: The Way It Is" compilation, if any of you remember that at all. Maybe not. Lots of guitar solos, but (dirty secret here!) I'm a sucker for those. One band, Projekt AK, are doing a sort of funk/hardcore thing with the spotlight on hip hop vocals, but it sounds less stupid and insincere than this style does when done by Western bands. I'm really interested to hear what will come from the Malaysian hardcore community next, now that it's clear the bands there are sure enough of themselves to do interesting things. —b

As It Is, Mohd. Azmi, P.O. Box 50808, Kuala Lumpur, Malaysia

DEMOS

<u>1125 "Plonie Mi Serce" demo:</u> I love this tape! It was sent to me by my friend Kasia in Poland after I asked her to let me know about good Polish bands (I love Poland and want to go back there someday - anyone have names or addresses of people to stay with over there?). This tape has it all, and I can only describe it this way: imagine if five guys decided to form a blast beat punk band with political/personal lyrics and

guage, then feel free to send me a stamped envelope and I will copy the translations for you. You will need them for sure. A fun thing for non-Polish-speaking people to do with this tape is the following: put the tape on and try to read along with the lyrics anyway. Think of that as a special bonus. One thing I thought about while reviewing this tape (and I listened to it four times all the way through right off the bat!) is that most people in the US will probably never hear it simply because of the USA-centric nature of punk and hardcore. Many of us recognize that great bands from overseas rarely get heard as much as American bands. So, to counteract that, try this tape out. The email address in the tape is no longer working but I did find a distro in Poland who carry 1125 releases and other Polish bands as well. Check out http://www.shingrecords.com for more info, or try their label, whose address follows here. —JUG

Pasazer Records; P.O. Box 42; 39-201 Debica 3; POLAND

cliché old school rehashing, but even after the pleasant surprise, this is awesome in its own right. A great start for a promising band, and DIY points abound for the home taping job with scratched off labels. —n

Uprising Tapes / PO box 1903 / 581 18 Linkoping, Sweden

<u>Discarga demo:</u> Fast beats, pick slides, faster beats, snare drum rolls, blast beats, guitar starts playing another three chord riff, back to fast beats, yelling vocals all the way through, with backing vocals—just fine recording and production, and the sense of immediacy to make this matter. Well, that's the first five songs, which are also on the "Play Fast or Die" CD my Brazilian friends released but didn't send us in time for review. The last three are similar musically, but are more muffled production-wise and feature the deep-growl-and-high-yowl traditional grindcore vocals. Those are their older songs, and the music is just as good, though the vocals lack a bit. Classy,

<u>Bloodpact/Varsity split 12":</u> One of the bands on this record is fucking great. The other one sucks so much that they're also great, which is what you'd better do if you're going to suck—so, in a roundabout way, this is an all-around great record, though that's not to say you should listen to more than one side of it (the Varsity side is more for reading the lyrics to your friends and laughing... sorry guys, I'd hoped to stop being so cruel in these reviews, but...). Bloodpact is rough as fuck, their recording isn't too polished or well-balanced, their drummer isn't too good, but all that comes across when I listen to them is the desperate energy of the band. And, hey, check this out, they have something going for them that very few bands have these days: good, solid, well-written songs! Yes, that's right, the blast beats and fast hardcore riffs and breakdowns all add up to really good music, all the progressions serve to build intensity and excitement as the whole way through. The vocal delivery is fucking awesome, all out and over the top... at one point the music stops so instrument can lead into another part of the song, and Andy keeps screaming, spitting out about fifteen more syllables, hoarser and hoarser, until he finally runs out of breath and has to pause to gasp before going into the next part. The first song ("The Rain Comes"), about the terror of the dropout from the middle class facing economic and social annihilation, has all the rush of those moments of middle class dropout fear with which you yourself may be familiar), dashing forward to plunge into the darkness as Andy shrieks "down, the roof caves in and everything is taken out with it—there's no mass of friends to catch the black sheep when you fall—" and the guitar chords and frenetic, frantic drums are there capturing the melancholy of such moments of doubt, too. The lyrics are all awesome so very smart and well-thought-out (titles include "have you ever met any actual members of the working class" and "you should have been eaten by wolves"), they have a depth and subtlety and self-awareness that is missing from almost every other political hardcore band, even the best ones. Now Varsity, on the other hand... imagine I'm reading these lyrics to you in a facetious voice: "been down on us for far too long, we're the positive youth fucking singing this song—with an xd up fist and an xd up heart, we're the positive youth fucking playing our part"—and the music makes good on that threat. Well, it's not the worst thing ever, honestly, but after Bloodpact... I'll stand by my allegation (which Matt quoted in his review of this record for Slave magazine) that Varsity sounds like someone's high school class assignment to form an old school band, totally derivative and shoddy to boot. Boo! is the right verb for this side of the record. Maybe somebody should bootleg the whole record as a one-sided LP. —b

r-records, address nearby

wrote a 17 song tape while listening to old school NYHC and early So-Cal straight edge the entire time. Fuck...it rules! It has the speed and intensity of punk rock throughout every song, with the rage of early NYHC (Side By Side / Alone in a Crowd), the energy of the So-Cal bands and finally the production of the newer generation of heavy bands. It sounds great. The result of all these influences is a tape that breaks through my expectations continuously by drawing on all of the above influences while not relying on any one for too long. Highly recommended! The layout is a seven-fold glossy insert printed on heavy cardstock with full lyrics. The lyrics are in Polish, but the good news is that Kasia translated them into English for me, so if you a moron like me and only speak one lan-

<u>Dead End s/t demo tape 1999:</u> This truly is "old school" at its best! Seven songs of fast, energetic and lively music in that older style of hardcore, with energetic yelled/screamed vocals, and gang backups in all the right places. Not since Trial has "old school" sounded so new, vibrant, important, and of course, posi. All of the lyrics address important topics such as consumerism, non-conformity, social mores, and personal growth in such an intelligent and uplifting, yet down-to-earth way. The photocopied inserts make a great political statement in a fun way with three silhouetted traffic-sign type figures doing the "see no evil, speak no evil, hear no evil" motions. I think one of the reasons I'm so impressed by this is that I was expecting yet another boring and

original d.i.y. cardboard packaging. — b

Douglas, R. Catequese 1787, Centro, Santo Andre – CEP 09090401, Sao Paulo Brazil

<u>Entreat demo:</u> This demo has moments of sad beauty; at other times, when the vocalist is moaning rather than doing the yell/growl/mumble he seems to have perfected, it seems a little weak, unconfident... and then still other times, it just sounds like common '90's hardcore to me, with the metal guitar sound, acoustic parts, mid-pace, decent recording and writing but nothing spectacular. Then I read the lyrics, and they take me back to the sad beauty—they are suffused with poetry, longing, tragedy, and they're written with the skill it takes to capture such

things. When I return from the lyric sheet to the music, it has the sad beauty again too, for all its clumsy moments. Tighten everything up, guys, and record again. It's clear you're capable of something powerfully moving and emotional. —b
Valter Cijan, Gradnikove b. 49, 5000 Nova Gorica, Slovenija

Evoke "We Stole Four Minutes From Your Life" demo:

As far as I can tell, this project was put together just for my own listening pleasure as the Inside Front guy reviewing this. It's not mass-produced, the whole insert is written out by hand, no songs were written (the kids just got together and expressed themselves immediately, in an unplanned improvisation), the whole thing is just a one-

cations, the thematic statement and whether it's regressive or not (etc. etc. etc. etc.!)—but when young Belgian hardcore kids do it on a whim, it feels so free and fresh and real, fucking awesome. Don't order this—make your own, and give it to a friend for her birthday or something. Or send it to HeartattaCk, demanding that they interview you. —b
Push the Limit, Kevin Alen, A. Vermeylenstr. 3, 3920 Lommel, Belgium

The Great Clearing Off CDR demo:

This is a triumph of d.i.y. in every sense: a CD in a lovely eco-friendly case, with a twenty-four page booklet of fine-print lyrics and explanations culminating in a reading list and a brilliant schematic drawing of the life of the questioning young man by a band member, all for

to revolutionize the 7" format next! —b
290 Chestnut Street, Hammonton, NHJ 08037

In The Red "" Demo:

The recording on this is shit, but in my book that's ok for a demo. I'm guessing it was recorded live in a garage or similar atmosphere, and it's ok because we all don't have the same resources to produce a good recording. Here are five dynamic songs hinting at Born Against with fiery guitars, a full bass sound (probably the best sounding instrument, surprisingly), good drums, and great vocals that I like. The tempo changes quite a bit without the music getting shaky, making me picture an In The Red performance as a beautiful blur of skin, hair, and smooth fucking fury. The packaging is interesting: a homemade metal-tape case with stenciled spray-paint, and stuffed

off project with a projected audience of about three—right on! The volume on the tape is so low it's hard to make it out, which is too bad, but the music isn't actually as pointless as you'd think—the vocalists are screaming so hard you're scared for their safety, and the band does some interesting chaotic things. Of course the recording isn't great (this was done on a boom box, remember), and there are no lyrics, but seriously, I'm thrilled to have received this. It's numbered for collector nerds ("1 of... 1"!) and at the end of the liner notes there's a plea for me to send it on to another 'zine for review once I'm done with it. This is the kind of thing that, when people from bands like Text or Countdown to Putsch do it, all the 'zine journalists make a big pretentious deal about the artistic innovations and impli-

between $1 and $3 (sliding scale!) at the show we played with them earlier this week. You can't expect the music to be totally polished, since this is in fact a demo, but it doesn't disappoint, either—though the guitars have a sort of thin, strange sound, the riffs often stray from the expected punk chords, and thought the vocals aren't totally confident they come off as very much for real. There's plenty of the discomfort and excitement of a fresh band here, touching and moving as it can be. All the things they're thinking about (passionate, anarchist/punk rock ethics, confronting all the assembled stupidities of our times) are fucking right on, they make them more clear than any other band releasing a demo since, say, Gocce nel Mare, and there's nothing left to ask for here—except to see what they'll do

inside is an insert along with the tape. The insert includes lyrics that could be interpreted in countless ways and are hard for me to understand, hence the songs have less meaning than their possible potential. Having songs that mean different things to different people is great (and inevitable), for many reasons, but sometimes the original message within is obscured or scattered. Explanations for us lightweights are sometimes a worthy gesture (what are you folks about?). Oh, and this demo is $2 ppd. —WG
In The Red; PO Box 11046; PDX, OR, 97211; 503.528.0340.

The In:Security Camera demo:

Strange combination of samples from the old punk movie Another State of Mind with a live recording... the vocalist sometimes sounds like Jello Biafra when

he speaks, but he spends more time shrieking and screeching and grunting, he's outta fuckin' control. The music follows his lead, cacophonous, spasmodic, jerking and smashing like a machine breaking down. Squealing feedback just adds to it all. From the lyrics, I deduce that these guys probably believe in some of the same basic things I do, but find more pleasure in ranting insanely: "Never too late to keep an eye on the bullshit! Still want you to go play in traffic!!" or, in a particularly articulate moment, "If you feel like shit, you're not alone—forced routine, endless drone, arghaharahhh!" Alright, the deal is, they need to polish up (yes they do!), but the energy is all here, in excess, ready to be used, and they could be capable of great things in the same sense that the Kid Karate are. –b
Justin, 1222 N. University, Peoria, IL 61606

old hardcore formats). The lyrics lie somewhere between Nietzsche, Dante, and early Carcass. My only complaint—sometimes the recording is a little fuzzy, with so much going on at once. The solution? This should be on CD, obviously. —b
Eric Boog, Oderstrasse 7, D-41363 Hochneukirch, Germany

Tet Offensive "The Revolution Begins Now" demo: Maybe it's just the associations of the band name, but I'm reminded of the atmosphere of gathering danger and darkness that made the Dead Kennedys "Holiday in Cambodia" one of their best songs. The singer has one of those growly voices that usually sound fake, but in his case he sounds crazy and reckless enough for it to be persuasive.

and more jazzy breaks, and it's hard to really tell what's going on, but it's not bad stuff, there's some energy there. At Bay is a little better recorded, still messy though, with distorted yelling vocals, fast and simple hardcore punk music, and if not lyrics... two little explanations. The first is about Globalization (the World Trade Organization, the I.M.F., the World Bank), and the second about being willing to go all out, no holding back. –b
2480 Winding Road, Hatboro, PA 129040

one. The extensive packaging and printing was all stolen, too, as the booklet asserts. Punk rock fucking lives, man—and in Belgium, no less. If I could see these guys play with Negate it would be the show of my life. —b
A Bust the Size of Texas, Carlos Steegen, Molenstraat 57, B-3730 Hoeslt, Belgium

Lariat "Manifesto" Demo: I pick this up out of the review box, and all I see is a blank tape marked "Lariat, Manifesto" on it, and I'm about to ask if there are any lyrics when I am handed the beautiful, lengthy, utterly diy booklet that accompanies it. I love when that happens. Especially when the contents offer such great words from people that give a shit about the state of this world, and who are trying to make a change utilizing their passion and skill. The booklet offers 42 page divided up into 5 chapters, half page size; I like the way they did this. The first chapter is a "declaration of war, in which anonymous members of the band talk about the issues that they care about. They cover numerous topics concerning our capitalist society, focusing on how people are forced to work their lives away for someone else and have nothing to show for it, and being sick of the hardcore scene acting like a shallow and meaningless fucking fashion show, a mere step down from the culture it claims to counter. These things have all been discussed many times before, but the personal accounts here made me keep reading, and gasp at the simple and profound way things were put. Chapter 2 is dedicated to lyrics and song explanation, the latter of which unearth the emotion behind the meaning of the songs. Again, these passages seem to sum up a lot of things that I feel strongly about: being a political band means internalizing your causes and living every day as an example of what you think is right." Chapter 3 shares a few pages of decent pictures of Lariat performing included for those of you who are just here for the nifty pictures. Chapter 4 is ed for the members of the band to express whatever they wish individually, and chapter 5 is space for band info and a list of books to read for further information on the ideas discussed therein. Ok, to the music. At the time of this recording, Lariat had been together for 3 months, and holy shit I can't believe it. They play tight and furiously well-written music full of changes, sometimes slow and suddenly taking off into the unknown with powerful blazing swiftness. The guitars are thick and are hugged by the bass, the drums are all over the place (in the *right* places, I might add), and the screamed vocals are right there in your face, but not dominating, like a lot of bands out there. The five songs are recorded and mixed well, and there are a few tracks fully placed samples, my favorite of which is at the end of the second song (with lyrics from an IWW publishing) Fuck, after listening, really *listening* to Lariat, I can't *not* take every minute of my life and have my way with it. This seems to be what they are mainly trying to convey as a solution (something rarely seen around here) to the widespread complacency that they see everywhere. Everyone should give these guys a listen, and I know that this is a long review, but hey, material like this must become known, and these folks deserve this space. (Note: see the Lariat CD review as well.) –WG
Lariat, PO Box 443, Round Lake, NY 12151

Nirdezneb demo: This a combination of electronic and live music, with lots of samples for aural texture and vocal effects—definitely the sort of project we need to see more of in our community to keep challenging ourselves and doing new, dangerous things with our art. It begins with an impossible blastbeat, like a locomotive at a thousand kilometers an hour (they *are* German, you know), or a video of factory machinery played at fast forward speed, then goes into some Slayer-harmony parts that sound truly evil and terrifying. It took me a couple minutes to get into this (or did it take them a couple minutes to get going?), but once I was into it, I was persuaded—this is awesome, and there's so very much potential to do new things here (and consequently give new ideas to those working in the

The lyrics are not dumb at all, they betray some right on class consciousness and deal with such important subjects as the way the education system is designed to grind out cultural differences among students. The first song is the best, by far—it has a spooky old-fashioned metal drama that works perfectly in the punk context, and helps them to create a classic, memorable song unique unto itself. And for a four track recording, this is surprisingly powerful, though the guitars are typically too low. —b
P.O. Box 7DDD, Jersey City, NJ 07307

R5/At Bay split cassette: No lyrics for the R5 side, which is recorded live (and with some compression problems!)... they divide their time between fast, screaming hardcore stuff

CrimethInc. Special Report

The singer of an unamed band poses at Gilman street for publicity photot to show how punk and hardcore his band is . . . (more info on page 137)

MAGAZINES

Agua #3: This Brazilian 'zine (in Portuguese) made me feel so good! It has pieces by different people (and in different handwritings, sometimes) scattered throughout so that it feels more like a conversation than like a group of columnists whose personalities and opinions are already pre-approved by those putting the 'zine together. Major themes include always questioning and struggling against our human tendency to simplify and prejudge; how to create new ways for us interact; and a basic and uncomplicated, but still invigorating, feminism. It occurs to me that these themes overlap pretty frequently and are sometimes even indistinguishable one from another, and that it is perhaps unnecessary, for example, for me to emphasize the feminism, when it springs directly, and naturally, from questioning and struggling against patriarchal values (a simplified system of human interactions if there ever was one) already in place, and attempting to construct new social and political patterns; except that the 'zine itself is definitely from a female perspective, with some writing on beauty standards, gender roles, and feeling confident and strong as a woman, even though it often seems like women are supposed to feel that their gender is a major disability, and are trained to live as if they were fundamentally handicapped. The 'zine also features a very interesting interview with a Liberation Theology priest (a Latin American tributary of Catholicism, none too popular with the Pope, that split off in the 1970s, positing Jesus as the "Liberator" of the poor and oppressed, interpreting Christian thinking from a working-class (and frequently Marxist) point of view). Although his brand of Christianity is much more palatable to me than most, with its emphasis on social justice, and solutions for issues that are all too frequently only moral ones for the Church (like abortion) that address causes rooted in social and economic circumstance, not just in the sins of the individual, he still can't manage to persuade me that there is any reason to rely on divine forces to guide human life. Nevertheless, the interview itself is thought-provoking and thorough. In addition there is a pair of descriptions of visits to a women's prison; a vaguely complaining essay about the State of Emo (mainly lamenting the stagnation that eventually plagues any genre), which concludes pretty weakly that for the author, "emo" music is anything that evokes an emotional response, including anything from Spitboy to the Get Up Kids(!); and some poetry and more personal writing. That's not all, of course, but I will resist the sudden impulse to give a table of contents. My favorite thing in a 'zine full of great stuff is a beautiful description of how to exorcise the phantom of a love relationship that has ended in disaster and pain. I guess I should warn you that this 'zine is in Portuguese before you all rush out and buy it, but maybe you should, anyway.—@
Agua, a/c Carol, rua Simão Alvarez 745/111, São Paulo SP cep 05417 000, Brazil

As It Stands #2: Introductory 'zine with a variety of articles and a generally political theme. The subjects include body image and the beauty industry, an exposition of the negative things P.E.T.A. has done, what the editor finds appealing about gangster rap, a Reclaim the City! event in Sweden that ended in police brutality, and an outraged response from mainstream society, all the bad things about smoking (and—how to quit). There's also an excellent Trial interview (I think it was hard to do one that wasn't!), a piece written by a young man whose brother was slain in a car accident, and an interview with an animal rights activist (which is not dry by any means), a review of Daniel Quinn's *Ishmael*, and various other smaller pieces. –b
Mark Osmond, 8364 Washburn, MI 48438

Book of Letters #12: This is where it's at, fucking hilarious! A collection of provocative/stupid/absurd letters to various corporations, and their responses (when they do respond). Example—he writes to Coca-Cola about the return of "Coke Classic" after the public uproar, asking whether they will bring the old Coke with cocaine in it back (as the *real* "Coke Classic") if drug laws ever change. They don't respond. He writes to Dunkin Donuts about the distinction between "garden vegetables" and factory farmed vegetables (in some product they manufacture) and gets a hilarious confession back from the CEO, who admits flippantly to factory farming. I'm a little saddened he didn't get more coupons for his efforts (he only gets a couple dollars worth of free potato chips), but I've known others to get up to hundreds of dollars of free products from writing angry or beseeching letters to manufacturers. —b
P.O. Box 890, Allston, MA 02134

Catalyst #1: This looks at first like a typical first issue cut-and-paste (and-sometimes illegible) 'zine with personal perspectives on love, fragmentary reprints of eco-positive living, little essays on why feminism is right on, lists of things to be happy about and vegan restaurants the author enjoys, reviews of political/personal 'zines and one record (fancy that, it's Submission Hold)... but there are little, unexpected gems hidden inside too: a reprint from a Tchkung! ad on how to make a molotov cocktail, information on what to say when the F.B.I. shows up, a little manifesto written upon returning from a lockdown in N.Y.C. about refusing to let life be less than a war for joy. Yes. —b
Catalyst, P.O. Box 381855, Cambridge, MA 02238

Deformación Cultural #2/#3: Para hablar francamente, éste no es un 'zine muy interesante. Hay columnas (mejores en el tercer número—en parte porque hay menos tratando el tema de la gente excesivamente polfticamente correcta), entrevistas, y mediocres comentarios de discos. En el #2, también hay una ficción corta. En el #3, solamente una de las entrevistas fue hecha cara a cara; la entrevista con Indecision viajó por correo electrónico, y la con Distancia la preguntaron mientras charlando en el Internet. Las dos ilustran muy bien las limitaciones de esos métodos de hacer una entrevista. Queda casi imposible expresarse precisamente o aclarar las ideas. Las columnas son sobre temas como el conformismo, el fascismo, el capitalismo, el nacionalismo... y el straight edge. Nada nuevo aquí. Los que lo hacen parecen ser sinceros e inteligentes—y jóvenes. Quizás necesitan pensar un poco más cuál es su enfoque, y cómo puedan hacer que Deformación Cultural se distingue de todos los otros...—@
Deformación Cultural, Casilla Postal 1424 (c1000two), Buenos Aires, Argentina

Deformation Cultural #4: This just arrived on the final day of the third and final attempt to finish these reviews once and for all, with a demand that it be reviewed, so it wins the prize as the absolute last Inside Front review ever. Unfortunately, we're going out with a whimper, for my Spanish is atrocious. Let's just say there are lengthy interviews with Decameron (from Buenos Aires) and Catharsis, an interview with Sol Perpetuo (also from Argentina—from the interview I pick up that they don't like One Life Crew, and that they apparently play a cover of Project X's "Dance Floor Justice"), two pages of fine print 'zine and record reviews (including a rave review of a Point of No Return tape, and a review of a Victory release that begins "Seeeeeeee melodic sucker pride!!!"), a full twenty MRR-style columns, and a couple letters to the editor. I wish it was easier for me to read this, for my impression is that I would get a good feel for what's going on in the Argentinian hardcore community here—this is no messy little 'zine, it's thorough and well-crafted. For those of you who speak Spanish and want to keep up with Latin American punk and hardcore, this would be a good first step. —b
Still the same address as above...

Evil #2: Many many interviews. Some reviews. Sort of the opposite of Inside Front these days. The band interviews rarely ask anything really challenging, but most of the bands interviewed (At the Drive-In, Orchid, Don Caballero—fuck, you don't really want me to list all 15 of them, do you?) are intelligent and well-spoken enough to carry the interviews. The Rubbish Heap interview stands out from the rest: instead of asking, for example, When did Rubbish Heap form and who was in the band?, a question sure to inspire a boring list of line-up changes, the interviewer asks, When did Rubbish Heap form, and what were your intentions and the context that led to its formation? Also very interesting are the interview with performance artist Jean-Louis Costes, and an essay on filmmaker/writer/musician F.J. Ossang. As for the reviews, the review of The Paper #2 begins, "What can I say about The Paper? The first diet zine?," enough to put me on their team for the rest of my reading. The quirkiest feature has got to be the gallery of pig drawings, most of them absolutely revolting. Maybe next issue they'll have a collection of drawings of butterflies: perhaps that will cut down on the gratuitous gore. It is lengthy, and it is in very small type, but it's not a bad 'zine. You might even like it. I just wish I had a better idea of who the writers are and where they're coming from. In French.—@

Evil, P.O. Box 5117, CH-1211 Geneva 11, Switzerland

F.B.I. #3: For a third issue, this is incredible, especially considering how far it's come already. It took Inside Front about nine issues to cover the same distance. It begins perfectly with a two page exposition of their goals and the myths they hope to dispel, which is as lucid and intelligent as anyone could ask for. A list of demands follows, in the CrimethInc. tradition of propaganda, and then a series of essays: the value of 'zines, the media coverage of the W.T.O. protests, healthy vegan diets and fasting, conspiracy theories about A.I.D.S., some discussion of learning of how to share the earth and build community, some news from Australia, and more fragmentary little pieces. There aren't many reviews, but they're all written in the thorough way that I like to see them done. No band interviews... come on, bands, get your shit together and get *interesting* if you want 'zinesters talking to you. It's illustrated throughout with photo collages and challenging captions. The essays vary a little in quality and interest, but altogether this is good in the same way Hodgepodge is, and I expect the next issue to be essential. It ends with editor Nick's recounting of the possibilities he sees in the new wave of activism, and as in the introduction the writing is as direct and persuasive as the very best I've seen. —b

15 West Dayton Hill Road, Wallingford, CT 06492

Fuck You Bearden!: Named for the asshole judge who put author Rob Thaxton in prison for seven years after he hit a police officer with a rock during Eugene's June 18th Reclaim the Streets event. Rob introduces himself with commendable honesty here, and goes on to write about daily life in prison and the events

leading up to his imprisonment. The bulk of the 'zine around those elements consists of some of the anarchist analysis (his perspectives on what the present weaknesses of capitalism and hierarchy are, and what a successful revolution must entail...), rhetoric (...that piece is called "now that's Revolting!"), and history (the Illegalists of early 20th Century France). The end has a few 'zine reviews, even including *Anarchy. A Journal of Desire Armed—* presently the mother of all insider anarchist journals, I'd say. If you like that magazine, and/or *Willful Disobedience*, this will also speak to you. Even if you don't, or don't know about those 'zines, you might want to show solidarity with a fellow human being locked down, by reading what he has to say. —b
Robert Thaxton Support Group c/o A.A.A., P.O. Box 11221 Eugene, OR 97440

Get In Touch #7: This is a good quality hardcore 'zine (in that long-standing tradition) from the Philippines. It's well-crafted in all aspects, including columns by such notable personages as Henrik Lindquist (once sang for Outlast— he writes powerfully about the divine moments of inspiration one experiences upon first encountering punk, and how

to recreate them) and Yann Boisleve (who did the International Straight Edge Bulletin 'zine), among others, interviews with Bridge records (with which Henrik is involved—this one's briefer than the others), OnexMore (Belgian hardcore band), J.R. Ewing (Norway), and xFeudx (smart Filipino straight edge/pro-choice band—this was the one that was newest for me to read about), thorough hardcore scene reports from across the globe, and a whole lot of d.i.y. record and 'zine reviews. —b

Dangie and Butch, Regala/1260-D, Quiricada St. Sta. Cruz, Manila 1003, Philippines

The Hardcore/Punk Guide to Christianity: This pretty much puts the issue on the table, in the best way (thoroughly, mercilessly, with an uncompromising eye for detail), so those who are wishy-washy about it will be forced to face the contradictions in their beliefs... and maybe to come to more sensible positions. It's well written, attractively laid out, solid in

every aspect... I remember thinking when I received this that there was one little objection to Christian self-contradiction missing (I've done a lot of historical study of early Christianity, I'm fascinated by the subject), but now I can't remember for the life of me what it could have been. Author Robin Banks doesn't hold back anywhere, even going so far as to accuse Jesus of poor botany ("...in so-and-so verses, he says the mustard seed is the smallest seed in the world. It's not."). The only drawback of this pamphlet is that its use-value is limited: for hardened Christians or atheists, responses will be totally predictable ("yup"...or "you're going to Hell!!!"), and for those trying to figure out where they stand, it lays all the facts on the table without being gentle enough to win the trust of any potential recovering Christians. We need more little books like this from our community, for sure: how about the hardcore/punk guide to police, to gardening, to yoga... —b
Robin Banks, P.O. Box 4964, Louisville, KY 40204-0964

Hazlo Tú Mismo #8: Este 'zine argentino contiene algunos comentarios de discos bastante breves, pero lo bueno de ésos es que la

mayoría de los discos son o latinoamericanos o de otra parte del mundo que no son los EE.UU., lo cual significa que, aunque los comentarios en sí no son muy útiles con referencia a los discos descritos, ayudan para indicar qué pasa en el resto del mundo hardcore. Una entrevista con Bread and Circuits (traducida de un 'zine estadounidense) es muy interesante, y también una con los franceses Flagrants Deli, quienes utilizan unas preguntas sencillas para explorar los detalles de sus pensamientos sobre la política francesa contemporánea, la mejor banda anarcopunk de todos los tiempos (¿es que hay alguna duda?), y "un poco de tus ideas en este momento," una pregunta que recibe una explicación de una página hablando de la superpoblación, el mundo virtual, la ecología, la epidemiología, y el poder de la contracultura de iniciar cambios sociales. Hay entrevistas también con Mofa, JFA (los de HTM admiten que no es la mejor que hayan hecho), Promise Ring, y Todd de Old Glory Records. Lo que he notado más de

Do or Die #8: For anyone interested in politics, anarchism, ecology, activism, or radical news from the world over, this is absolutely the number one source. Three hundred forty some pages, fine print, covering issues, actions, and reactions from all over the world, in amazing depth. I'm not going to try to describe this, it's just too much... everything from the pros and cons of tunneling as a direct action tactic to women who became pirates to Earth First groups in Israel and indigenous anarchist/environmentalist uprisings in southeast Asia. Unless you're at a place in your life where anything that doesn't have to do with how you will be living your life in the next five minutes or less seems dry, you really should at least sit down with someone's copy of this for a little while. -b
6 Tilbury Place, Brighton, East Sussex, BN2 2GY, United Kingdom

la escena argentina (por leer unos 'zines aquí en los EE.UU.) son las divisiones entre las distintas facetas de la comunidad, y esas se ven en este 'zine, también. Sale una prueba del nivel de la Punkitud que uno demuestra (con una intención irónica, estoy segura, pero sin embargo esas clasificaciones (200-300 puntos: "Escuchastes Nofx, sabes que es Epitaph, pero ni puta de ida quienes eran Black Flag" [todos sic]... ¿ésto porque no tengo zapatillas Vans old school, ni uso la billetera encadenada?) me hacen muy incómoda. Hay una presentación de cómo hacer un disco, de la masterización a la distribución a las cuestiones legales de impuestos, etc. No tengo ni idea cuán útil sea, pero mi poca comprensión de la grabación, etc., no me ha enseñado, como dice el autor, que "masterizar sirve para meter efectos...o sirve para levantar el volumen, nada más." Caveat emptor. Las columnas incluyen una receta para lasagna y una comparación de los lugares que venden falafel [en Buenos Aires?], el feminismo, "la melancolía urbana," un concierto de Offspring, y el punk de los ochenta. Es la sección más personal del 'zine, y la menos coherente. Con frecuencia me parecen las columnas descuidadosamente escritas o un poco desorganizadas. Sin embargo, lo que me molesta más de Hazlo Tú Mismo (aquí habla la persona perfeccionista que me invade cuando leo cualquier texto) es que utilizan los acentos caprichosamente. Lo peor es que no los niegan a usar por completo, sino que los usan, a veces, por razones indiscernibles. En general, interesante.—@
Hazlo Tú Mismo, CC 213 suc 12 (B), CP 1412 Buenos Aires, Argentina

Hodgepodge #6: This is a good companion piece to Rumpshaker, if you're looking for an excellent hardcore music/life/politics journalism 'zine... it even has some of the same characteristics: dumb name, high quality writing, intelligence, (maybe a little less) personality, glossy perfectionist layout and presentation—and something Rumpshaker doesn't have: in-depth political/economic analysis. The columns are as spotty as columns generally are (I mean, seriously, with the exception of '80's M.R.R., columns sections suck—get a bunch of supposedly "good writers" together, have them each write some random, self-indulgent fragment on no particular subject, what do you expect)... Scott Beibin's typically extravagant piece on punk rock film-making and Eric Boehme's classic Boehme exposition of the class dynamics of the service industry are the highlights, while the low point is a poorly written, tediously ignorant and immature (and vaguely sexist) column by a kid who tells us about how the Initial Records Krazy Fest fuckin' rocked, dude. The columns are just a little atavistic fragment at the beginning of the 'zine, however; the bulk of it is made up of informative essays (a much-needed exploration of genetic engineering fleshed out by an

interview with an activist about biotechnology, pieces on the Multilateral Agreement on Investment and the World Trade Organization complemented by a report from the streets of Seattle the week we shut the W.T.O. meeting down, a piece about our ecologically destructive civilization followed by an interview in which Daniel Quinn turns out to be a little less radical than I'd like him to be... and an awesome piece about toxin levels in tampons) and competent band interviews (Rainer Maria, the Dismemberment Plan, Catharsis), with book, 'zine, and record reviews (all decent) at the end. Really, this is a lot more like Slave than Rumpshaker, in terms of the educational/informational side of things, but it would complement both 'zines perfectly, none would be complete without the others for good reading. —b
Mike Schade, 983 Little Neck Avenue, N. Bellmore, NY 11710

I Hate the World #5: Much like Inside Front, this 'zine evolved dramatically along with the editor's own discovery of himself, partly aided by the experience of doing the 'zine... also like Inside Front, he's ending the 'zine now, to keep himself fresh and fluid for new challenges. The strongest point of I.H.W. is the way Andreas' personality comes across in it, which makes reading this feel like a personal interaction: the conversation wanders from sexuality to childhood experiences and fears to the way the school system in Sweden creates and reinforces economic hierarchy. Andreas comes across as extremely sensitive, intelligent, and insecure, all at once, as he reexamines whether friends should be afraid to kiss, explains why he feels uncomfortable about his body, recounts (somewhat mysteriously) stories from his own life, leaving out crucial contextual details sometimes. I do want to take issue with some things he says about rape—he seems to consider it a result of men not curbing their sexual desire, whereas I think rape has little to do with sexual desire... yes, our desires have been connected to the power dynamics of our struggle for domination over each other, so lust is often indistinguishable from the urge to do violence, but rape is something that happens not as a result of untrammeled sexual desire but rather as an act of pure violence dressed only in the trappings of sex. One is not capable of rape because of one's sexuality as a man so much because of the violent conditioning of this society. Anyway, you can spend quite a bit of time mentally going back and forth about various issues addressed in this 'zine, that's probably its chief practical virtue. —b
Andreas Hagberg, Fjardingsmannavagen 15, 643 32 Vingaker, Sweden

Imagine #1: This is really excellent—it's an anarchist 'zine that makes anarchist thinking feel accessible and relevant to everyone. It's totally lucid, top notch writing, covering a

variety of subjects in a great deal of depth. The cover has a Leo Tolstoy quote (his contribution to anarchism was drastically underreported, since the literary establishment wanted to make use of him), the inside cover a Refused lyric, to give you an idea of the cultural span of the author—and the quotes continue throughout. Let's go through the contents: a letters section (including intelligent debate about anarchists voting, and how violence and anti-social actions would be dealt with in a non-authoritarian society), matching "Reader's Digest" news sections with sickening reprints straight from the mouth of the Associated Press, who you think would keep quieter about this stuff ("Life in these United States" covers the abuse and misfortunes of average civilians, "Humor in Uniform" concentrates on police brutality), a hilarious Cometbus reprint about romance with a radical, reprints on police violence by Mumia Abu-Jamal and Fred Woodworth (editor of *the Match!*), absurd news from the murderous meat/dairy industry, a couple vegan cooking tips, a well-balanced consideration of Noam Chomsky ("anarchist, or traitor?" asks the writer, who concludes that the answer is "neither.")... It ends with a superb reviews section, which covers everything from current similar 'zines to a novel by Ursula LeGuin, another famous author little known for her anarchism. Anyway, for the Inside Front reader seeking a good anarchist periodical, I'd have to recommend this even before *A Journal of Desire Armed* or the other better known ones: it's more inclusive, more well-balanced, more personable. —b
P.O. Box 8145, Reno, NV 89507

Interwencja #1: What makes it most difficult to review this zine, actually, is not that it's in Polish, but, instead, that I keep trying to guess what it might be saying, based on little that has anything to do with Eastern European languages. What I have gathered from my experiment in language immersion, as much as it is possible while sitting on my sofa in North Carolina, is first of all that it's going to be a struggle for me to learn Polish, and second of all a fragmentary list of Interwencja's contents, if you aren't persuaded by its cute name alone... It includes a Catharsis interview, an essay on Chechnya, one on the Chiapas Media Project, a show review (25 Ta Life with Counterweight and Schizma), and some pretty long record reviews. I take their length to be an indication of quality, in that the writer seems to be putting some care into his writing. Several of the reviews are of records that came out a while back, probably a reflection of the availability of most hardcore records in Poland. There's more in here that I can't identify but if any of this sounds interesting, consider dropping Marcin a line. The only bit of English in here makes it clear that he'd love to be in touch...—@
Marcin Kopczynski, Chabrowa 12a/15, 44-200 Rybnik 15, Poland

Kill For Love #1 (full size, photocopied, 52 pp.): This is really fucking good for a first issue, it seems the editor and cohorts either have had experience with this in the past or have done a lot of observing of other good zines before doing their own. I guess you could describe KFL as a typical political hardcore fanzine, complete with band interviews, sexy band action photos, columns, ads, and record reviews. The bands interviewed are all awesome (Catharsis, Shai Hulud, Redemption, Extinction, Mainstrike), and the questions were well thought out, which made for some interesting conversations, the most intriguing of which I thought was with Catharsis. The reviews are informative and overall, very positive and helpful. There is one column in here dealing with homosexuality within the hardcore scene that absolutely floored me with its intense urgency, emotion and sincerity, and I think it was the single most important and attention-deserving thing

that I've seen in a zine in a while. Visually, this is also an excellent start, with crisp, clean page layouts and fairly large font sizes (a relief to punk eyes used to tiny print). On the other hand, I think there needs to be more original artwork combined with less emphasis on band photos, which as we all know, can lead to scene hierarchy and rockstar-ism. I think my only other criticisms are for them to not put ads in the middle of any of the writings, interviews, etc, as it is distracting and breaks up the flow of reading unnecessarily, and to keep pushing the boundaries of creativity and innovation in writing style, content, and graphic design (perhaps less band interviews, or interviews with people not in bands or even involved in hardcore). If this zine keeps itself out of the ruts and traps of indy publications and self-referential youth-culture, it will sure-

ly be one of the very best, because it's already excellent. —n
Simone Marini / via R Battistini 32 / no151, Roma, Italy

Mayhap #2: This was written just after the W.T.O. meeting was shut down by the Seattle protests, and the back cover reads "Seattle '99 All the Time." It begins with an excellent participant's account, and proceeds to address the question of where coercion and conflict come from in the first place—it's compelling and serious writing, if conversational in tone. A reading list follows, then a piece about how to delegitimize authority, hitchhiking stories, more front-porch-style analysis of how to make all this political/interpersonal stuff work... it's a great mix, and makes for a great read. If you're not overwhelmed already with 'zines talking about protests, youth gone wild on adventures and anarchist dreams, people being arrested and beaten and sentenced to

years in prison, what the next step to a world without authority could be, then you should get one of these to read... sure, there's talk about "dismantling the Power Machine" at one point when the editor gets carried away, but for the most part (the very most part) the writing is down to earth and real. —b
P.O. Box 5841, Eugene, OR 97405

Message From the Homeland #5: Consider this a relative of F.B.I. 'zine. It deals with the basic issues of being human in an inhumane world (there's a particularly touching column early on about Dave's encounter with a homeless man, which drives this point home), the struggle against capitalism and racism, from a sort of New England hardcore kid perspective (witness the atavistic music reviews at the end, which are well written but reveal a taste for

tough guy hardcore). There is a four way interview with Greg Bennick (Trial), Dave (Retrogression), Ian (Equal Vision records businessman, with whom I've had one particularly bad experience), and myself... I think Greg, Dave and I all balance each other out really well, giving different perspectives on the same basic approach, while Ian just says the kind of ridiculous stuff that any cold-blooded entrepreneur in radical company would feel pressured to (he claims anarchy won't work, takes the same standard in favor of the "independent" music industry that Victory records did a few years back, etc.). But anyway—this is quite a good read, and my only complaint is it isn't longer. More content would fill out the ideas and approach. —b
P.O. Box 4248, Springfield, MA 01101

On the Bank of the Tumid River #2: Hardcore journalism 'zine akin to Hodgepodge or Slave, but with more of a split

personality. It starts out with a columns section which is something of an improvement on the usual awful columns section: it has a theme (immortality), and is wisely understated as a section (unlike many columns sections in 'zines, which announce themselves with great fanfare—only to be wandering and dull). There's a rock-journalist-style interview with Godbelow (the not-tough guy tough guys?), an interview with Cave In that was what I expected it to be, then interviews with the Hope Conspiracy, Agoraphobic Nosebleed, Kill the Slavemaster (sadly illegible), Elliott, MC Wildcat... The high points for me are Ted Kaczynski's parable (not the best short story ever, but seriously, the guy has the record to back up his ideas with), a very technical piece on Cryogenics and Nanotechnology, and the account of the April

Evasion #1: I have begun like many others, left for the highway on foot with this zine under my arm, a sleeping bag in my backpack, seeking adventure. It was early March and threatening rain, my first time hitchhiking. I was alone, it was cold, I felt afraid and hesitant. A million voices in my head seemed to give reason after reason why it was a bad idea to be standing by the highway at 7:00 AM in rural Virginia, but I wanted to taste life, even if I wasn't sure why. I sat down there, on the asphalt, and read the first pages of Evasion. That's when I really felt it, that this zine was the answer to a question I had not even figured out how to articulate. Four hours later, after I had arrived in Washington, DC days ahead of schedule, I would take Evasion out of my bag and read it, sitting on a bench near the exit of the Omnimax Theater in the Museum of Natural History. And moments later I would sneak my way in. Sitting in the back of the theater, with my 3-D glasses in hand, I watched the others, the sheep, the *paying customers* file in from below and it occurred to me that I hadn't even checked to see how much the tickets cost. By then it didn't matter to me, I was living in a world free of charge.

Evasion is a full page, xeroxed zine. It has a cut-and-paste style layout and is almost completely hand-written. It contains stories about hitchhiking, train hopping, shoplifting, dumpster-diving, scamming, sleeping on rooftops and in closed libraries, and sneaking into hardcore shows. "Chris" (as he calls himself) is a mysterious vagabond traveler, who writes about a world of freedom that exists just beneath the surface of capitalist glitter, a world where much more is possible than you think. It is a world I want desperately to believe in, and a world that I believe exists, but only for those who are prepared to find it. This zine is not for entertainment, it is a tool for opening the mind, for learning how to see the path of free adventure. When there are dark moments (and there will be), answers can be found inside this, the new bible for wandering hearts, a new tale, a new myth, rewriting history in every moment. Find a copy of this zine. Tuck it under your jacket as you fall asleep gazing at the stars from the roof of a Burger King in Rawlings, Wyoming, read it in the still silence of the Library of Congress after your mace has been confiscated at the entrance, show it to a lover by firelight in some wild outskirt of a National Park in southern California, and share it with a hobo in your boxcar as you speed across Iowa, together. Run these scams, but be savvy and don't get caught! Open up your world and live! Live your life! After all, this is the only chance you'll get. —VW
Evasion has no address. For a copy, try writing to Crimethinc. Send a dollar or two for postage.

16 protest in Washington, D.C., which was quite well done... you may have already read your fill of those activist's reports by now, though, I fear. The layouts are occasionally difficult to read (when the tiny white letters are drowning in a sea of black ink, going under for the last time), and the pages of ads bug me (although we can hardly blame the 'zinesters for that necessity—can we?). At the end are some reviews of decent depth, which I wanted to like... but it was hard for me when I read one band being negatively compared to "an ugly girl with a crush on you." Come on, what the fuck—that shit is totally un-called for. Strange combination here of smart political stuff and generic hardcore market coverage... I expect it to go one way or the other in the future, probably towards the former. —b
17 Sparkhall Avenue, Toronto, ON, M4K 1G4 Canada

<u>Personality Liberation Front #3:</u> This is one of the very last things to be reviewed, so you can imagine my head's not too clear right now... but this is a good 'zine, so it has to get mentioned, at least. It's something like an Australian Synthesis: half size, thick with fine print, lots of discussion of gender roles, how to break out of them, and how to break out of the trap of only talking about those issues, also some writing on other subjects (which companies to boycott over union-busting, how to be open about one's emotions, etc.), interviews with Arm's Reach and Knuckledust, quality reviews of 'zines and records, even some fun stuff—a photo gallery of mullet haircuts in the punk rock world. —b
P.O. Box 3023, South Brisbane BC, Qld 4101, Australia

<u>Raincity #3:</u> Newsprint 'zine covering goings-on in Malaysia, which has a large and active hardcore scene. There's an interview with Carburetor Dung, one of the longest-lived bands in the scene, and another with Toxin 99%, as well as record reviews, columns and scene reports of what is going on in various regions, and plenty more writing about local and general issues affecting the hardcore community. It gave me a window into a totally different, distant part of the hardcore world. —b
Zahid, 137, Lorong 19, Taman Sri Kota 2, 34000 Taiping, Perak, West Malaysia

<u>Red Devil #11:</u> This is a big 'zine with a lot of content, all sort of disconnected and lacking cohesion, but more interesting than many because it comes from a perspective still generally unheard in the international hardcore scene. The contents include a letters section, columns (which range from philosophical argumentation to... a discussion about how Clinton needs to act responsible, so as to affirm the power of the U.S. as the world's single remaining superpower, and thus to bring

"order to the world"—what the fuck? pro-imperialist sympathies in a Singapore 'zine?), an extensive interview with Sean (former front-man of Vegan Reich), who is now in his latest incarnation as a Muslim (this interview was interesting, since Islam is an "exotic" thing here in Sean's country, but more common in editor Abdul's), interviews with Stalingrad and Radical Noise (the latter being a hardcore band from Turkey!), information (reprinted?) on the plight of East Timor, a number of pages of reviews, and various smaller fragments and opinions and emo sharing. I do get a really good vibe from the editor, he seems totally sincere and positive, and that matters a lot. —b
Abdul Khalid, Blk. 321 #04-287, Sembawang Close, Singapore 750321

<u>Reskator #2:</u> Written, at length, in Czech. The only comment I can make about the Czech language used here is that it doesn't seem to be infected with hardcore disease, in which every other word is in English, like an ad in Spanish I saw once that advertised "17 mosh hits!" The editors have put together a 'zine with a letters section (long letters with apparently thorough responses; the themes seem to be Downcast and vegetarianism, perhaps in response to a previous issue?), several interviews (an impressively long one with Lumen, and others with Culture, Kevorkian, and Gnu), and reviews. It looks like it's all really well-done. Sometimes it seems like the 'zine is mostly an excuse to publish an immense number of band photos, as there are scads of them everywhere—especially, of course, in the two page spread on the Vort'n Vis Festival, of everyone from Fugazi to Pray Silent to Saturn's Flea Colar [*sic?!*]. But I get the feeling that if I could read what it all says, I might be very impressed. There is nothing resembling a column or article, however, and while it is true that as most 'zines execute

them, columns are a tired and pathetic genre, I get the feeling that Reskator could do some good writing that's not band-related. There are a bunch of record reviews in here, too, but the only thing that stood out (and how could it help it?) was the Die My Will review that ends, MOSH IT UP!!!—@
Reskator, c/o Tomas Mladek, V krovinach 16/1540, Praha 4 – Branik, 147 00, Czech Republic

<u>Revolt #10:</u> More Eugene anarchism, by some of the same people doing other publications from that hotbed of wild desire-pursuing and (even more so) rhetoric slinging, some of which are even reviewed elsewhere in this issue of Inside Front. Some articles (like the Illegalism piece from Rob's *Fuck You Bearden!*) are reprinted here, and yes there are reprints from other sources... it seems like everybody in these circles is reading the same things, throwing the same formerly-inflammatory rhetoric and terminology back and forth, obsessing over the same primitivist examples of non-civilized life and its virtues while scanning the internet for the latest news of cellphone-coordinated street protests. I can say this "with authority" (uh oh!), because I am in these circles myself, in the lower circles of insider anarchist hell, not actually unhappy about it but definitely ready to demand a little more innovation and freshness from my comrades. Come on, attacking the poor anarcho-syndicalists again?! How about bringing up a new topic of discussion/catalyst for action that could make the old debates irrelevant, as new vistas of practical possibility open before us, and the rhetoric is realized in experience, or discarded... Back to this 'zine and the others done by its authors (the *Black Clad Messenger*, for example)—if you haven't had much of this stuff in your life yet, you should give it a chance... you're probably better

<u>Synthesis #5:</u> What a delightful 'zine this is! Witty, intelligent, informative, foaming slightly at the mouth at times... The 'zine runs the gamut, from a vegan cake recipe to an interview with eco-activist Saxon Wood to commentary on the Vort'n Vis festival and discussions of human nature. Synthesis is very political, specifically and aggressively feminist. Sometimes, perhaps, it comes off as being a little short-sighted or incoherent: that animal rights, for example, is the trendy cause du jour (or decade) in the hardcore community, completely eclipsing the women's rights issues that affect actual members of the scene (or are *all* the active, rough punk women we know just girlfriends?), does not really cancel out the bunnies' plight, as Laura (the editor) so vigorously implies (even though it is rhetorical). (Her criticisms of veganism as a social marker and of adherence to it as a final solution for all the world's ills are spot-on, and even incomplete—it's the attitude that bothers me.) And how anyone can claim to "have faith in humanity's potentials" and that "sympathy and concern are deep and widespread human traits," but say elsewhere (in a slightly different context of course, but this is my review here!, and she was speaking about people as a whole...) that "95% of those people will be crap" baffles me. I don't distrust Laura at all—she comes off as being extremely solid and positive throughout the 'zine—but it is exactly for that reason that I can find her leaps to criticize and dismiss confounding. Apart from that and her

equipped than the rest of us to come at it with the necessary fresh perspective with which the remaining revolutionary potential of the contents could be discerned. —b

Anarchist Action Collective, P.O. Box 11331, Eugene, OR 97440

Rumpshaker #5: One hundred eighty eight pages, bound like a fancy academic journal. Very impressive, and I have to say that for hardcore "music journalism" beyond the monthly updates of magazines like HeartattaCk, this is the best thing going. An absolutely crucial part of that is that Rumpshaker (in addition to its heroically stupid name) has real personality of its own, that shines through all the time... that's the difference between a 'zine that makes you feel like you're reading it to kill time, and a 'zine that can stand on its own as a work, like a good record or a book. Instead of just interviewing Disembodied, editor Eric (who is responsible for most of the stuff in here, in the long-standing tradition of workaholic 'zine writers) tran-

Deadguy show years ago to try to have a dialogue about it (the guy is polite, but sadly brainless in his thuggish commitment to "that's just how the world is, dude"), it's even Atom who is responsible for giving Eric the misinformed perspective on the occupation of Palestine. In addition to all this, there's a little piece on sources of inspiration with responses from various hardcore kids and 'zinesters, a contest giving away free stuff (I lost!), a hilarious humor piece at the end... this is awesome, really. However jaded you are with 'zines, this one will have something to offer you—provided you like to read at all. —b

Eric Weiss, 72-38 65 Place, Glendale, NY 11385

Sampled Silence #1: This is a gorgeous little pocket 'zine that mixes impenetrable poetry and political theory with romanticism in the same way that made the Situationists and Refused so exciting, which others (the Eugene anarchists) have been totally unable to duplicate. I think I need to say nothing more about this than to

a box containing 60 French hardcore kids), is full of great stuff. The CD is a little schizophrenic, with bouncy pop punk songs interspersed with aggressive growly hardcore numbers. As for the 'zine itself, it is interesting and well-written. The letters to the editors are answered by Dorian with exhaustive detail (he responds to everything from criticisms that they accepted Goodlife ads for an earlier issue—if only it were actually possible to definitively settle the debate over what constitutes a fundamental compromise of the DIY ethic!—to a reader's worry that he is a Satanist, and all of his answers are at least twice as long as the original letters if not a good 20 or so times...). There are twelve(!) interviews in here, and while some are very general and not terribly compelling (Awkward Thought, Neck), and that fucking word association thing never ever works, many of them are wonderful. Of course, one can always count on Brian D. to go on and on, especially if one asks Catharsis questions like, "What alterna-

preoccupation with the uncanny accuracy of her predictions for the hardcore scene (which she mentions at least 3 times), I have no complaints at all about a thoughtful, well-written, pro-everything (and provocative, too!, and I'm not talking about Latin grammar...), energetic 'zine. (Except, oh yeah, it's the Dominatrix interview (yay)—and otherwise, it's excellent). Bob from Tilt actually fucking asks if our [his?] perception of Brazilians as being exotic and oversexed is accurate, as if it were a serious question that deserved consideration!) The Vort'n Vis piece, unlike the 'spreads of band photos that I've seen in several other 'zines this time around, is actually fascinating: it is a comparison of that festival with the More Than Music festival in Columbus, Ohio, comparing them on points like childcare, workshops, organizers, stalls, and music (guess who loses out). Also interesting are the surveys she mails out to some of her penpals asking their opinions on a few issues. My only frustration was that to the question, Is it hard to be a vegetarian/vegan where you live? (the respondents were from far-flung places like Brazil, Slovenia, and Malaysia), a couple responded, Yes, it is so hard to find tofu, as if carrots weren't vegan. Not that I think vegans (or vegetarians) should be forced to subsist only on carrots, but I think there are probably greater obstacles to vegetarianism/veganism than the ease with which one can find Tofurky slices for one's sandwiches. Why should vegetarian or vegan food have to be a weird substitute for non-veg food? Also, there's a list and brief description of the ten most important news stories with the most inadequate coverage by the mainstream media in 1998, articles on genetically modified foods and gentrification, and a hilarious interview with God. But most prominent in Synthesis is the feminism, which reveals itself constantly in every element of the 'zine, nor just in the piece on body image or the Dominatrix interview. Laura writes very eloquently about why all the boys out there should embrace feminism, calling not for equality for women, but for liberation for both sexes from the limitations of all kinds that have been placed on us by inherited gender roles. If you don't read this 'zine, you are a fool. Just some friendly advice from—@

Synthesis, c/o Laura, 14 Batavia Mews, London, SE14 6EA, UK

scribes a tarot card reading of the band... in addition to the more standard (still top notch) band interviews (Los Crudos, Indecision, Good Clean Fun, an exploration of why Kid Dynamite broke up, and Ire, who admirably stick to their guns about the oppression of Palestinians even when the interviewer ignorantly suggests this is anti-Semitic), there are interviews with photographers in the general circles of punk rock (an artistic format which receives little acclaim in our community), an organizer of Farm Sanctuary, and a series of mother/punk child interviews (featuring Ian MacKaye, Ray Cappo, and Caithlin from Rainer Maria and their uniformly nice mothers). The ongoing presence of Atom (of the 'Package fame) adds more personality and continuity; he's present in the 7" reviews, giving sardonic opinions, there's an interview and tour report (Eric came with him), a piece in which they approach a guy who beat Atom up at a

reprint this passage: *We like money, because we can embezzle it. We like shops, because we can shoplift. We like banks, because we can rob them. We like cars, because we can steal them. We like planes, because we can hijack them. We like cops, because we can run from them. We like governments, because we can overthrow them. We like time, because we can be late. We like rules, because we can break them.* Without any logic or deduction, that captures a whole book (or more) of theory in a fun little manifesto, offering a modern demonstration of Nietzsche's amor fati in the process. —b

c/o Eight-o-three records, flip basement, 70/72 Queen Street, Glasgow, g1 3en, Scotland

Satori #5/6 (?): This French 'zine (that also means *in* French, in this case), which comes with a CD compilation of 15 French bands (or at least of their songs; unless I'm not special or something, I don't think you can expect to get

tives are there to working?," or ones that begin, "Subject: stealing." But there are also great interviews with Rude, Veg'Asso (a vegetarian activist group), Brent, Watch It Fall, and PH1. I am a sucker for original questions, and anyone who asks a band how they wear their hair, and what relation they think hairdos have to music; or whether they consider themselves professional musicians; or whether they think heroin addicts are victims of social and economic problems or of a fucked up system, or something else..., gets at least a few points in my book. There are also a some articles: a description of the Mad Max movies, a chronology of Black Flag's career, and an essay on Mod fashion's continued presence today, if not in specific clothing styles, at least as an approach to the world. Add to that assorted reviews, a scene report from Croatia (which includes a history lesson and commentary on the scene in lieu of a list of bands), and a lot of

personality, and you're holding a damn good 'zine. —@
Satori, c/o Dorian & Cedric, 32 rue Portalis, 13100 Aix-en-Provence, France

Silent #3: Uh, nobody's gonna be thrilled about this, but the simplest word I can use to describe this 'zine is "emo": it has a pretty, handmade cover, lots of personal wonderings and wanderings and journal entries inside, handdrawn artwork and collages, romance worries written out for the world to see... There's also a reprint of a Noam Chomsky piece on the bombing of Kosovo, an interview with Chalkline (uh, they're kind of "emo" too, aren't they...) and another with Stretch Armstrong, and... well, that's mostly it... —b
Rik Peeters, Duivelsbroek 5, 2400 Mol, Belgium

Truce #1: This is a hardcore kid 'zine, in that long-standing tradition, and as such has the various strengths and weaknesses of the genre. This is much larger and more involved than any little poorly xeroxed 'zine—a fucking lot of work went into this, clearly, and it's awesome to see non-scenester hardcore kids taking advantage of the opportunities this community offers by putting in the work to do a high quality, useful 'zine like this. Drawbacks? Well, the usual moralizing and lack of clear thinking you come across in the straight edge/consumer hardcore world, but to the editors' credit they're not really guilty of this... it comes out of the mouths of others, like the moron from U.S. band Shockwave they interview (maybe moron is a strong word, but his three interests seem to be bragging about how tough his band is, collecting toys, and taking a stand against "evil" things like "free love")—who, incidentally, seem to have a record out on Good Life, surprise surprise. Other (mostly better) interviews include Belgium's Facedown (whose ideas are quite well-thought out, and the interview goes into appropriate depth), Heaven Shall Burn, Ensign (this is mostly a tour diary from a slightly spoiled band on tour, disappointed when only seventy people come to see them!), Spirit 84 (rather than a traditional interview, this is the editors showing the band video clips and asking for responses... one of them is from a pornographic movie, and it's pretty unpleasant to be reminded of that shit in a hardcore context...), and Upheaval. There are hilarious sections (a fake collector's corner filled with parodies, a made-up advice column, etc.) that emphasize the personality of the editors (a crucial ingredient for a good 'zine), and their reviews and column writing are also intelligent. The verdict is that this is already good for its genre, and could be something better if it continues to exist. —b
Jan Albert Veenema, van Munnickuizenstraat 9, 8701 BP Bolsward, Holland

Ugly Duckling #4: This is a spirited, youthful 'zine, interesting and idealistic. Personal and personable. Energetic and energizing. Thoughts in these pages go from the need for more communication in the hardcore community to the editor's solution to the caffeine/straight edge problem. There are long but easy to read, and frequently fascinating, interviews with Lifecycle and Jeroen, who was in Clouded. The only way to describe the rest of this 'zine is to say that it's like being pulled into the editor's head for 40 pages. You can listen in on arguments with pro-life kids, late-night anxieties, rants on various topics, lists of ways to be more ecologically responsible, lists of things the editor finds important ("What I hate in 'zines," "My most precious possessions"). Read over the editor's shoulder as she flips through Time magazine. Listen to a bedtime story. Hell, you can even hitch a ride to the Vort 'n Vis festival. The Ugly Duckling is brash and coltish, but it can also be very insightful. And it's that unpredictable mix that makes it so endearing.—@
Lieve Goemaere, Zwaanhofweg 3, 8900 Ieper, Belgium

The Visible Woman #1: This 'zine is even more awesome for what it represents than what it is. It's the first foray into the 'zine world that I've seen from someone coming from the perspective of middle aged womanhood/motherhood, and it's fucking awesome to read about that perspective in a format I'm so familiar with. This is one of the most important 'zines reviewed here, since it offers insight into a world alien to most of us, and also since (we can only hope!) it may herald the coming of a new era of d.i.y., in which people of all walks of life will make and read and learn from 'zines. Think of the community that could result from that... As for contents: there's some discussion of menopause, the author's relationship to her body, a list ("ten things I know about your mother that you don't") which I consider an instant classic, a story of her interactions with one of her younger friends (and the conclusions she draws), a little essay about how touch is disappearing between people in a simultaneously hypersexualized and prudish culture. —b
406 N. Mendenhall Street, Greensboro, NC 27401

Wild Children: This is absolutely beautiful in its wildly passionate youthful abandon and idealism. That's a lot of praise, but it just makes me feel so good to read stories of young people who break the fuck out and go live as they see fit, articulating how and why along the way. Stories of strange dreams, photos of cat comrades, reading lists (including *Pippi Longstocking*, by Astrid Lindgren, and *HeartattaCk*, "by all of us"—right on!), tales of trouble with police and mothers, informative asides on the effects of radiation from nuclear bomb tests on U.S. armymen, travel adventures, poetic ranting about what life is all about—all written evocatively and eloquently

(except for the cat photo, I guess... well, even in that case, I loved the caption). Yeah, this is good. —b
Scott, 545 Calle del Norte, Camarillo, CA 93010

Willful Disobedience (Volume 2, #3): This newsletter/'zine mixes news reporting and analysis with radically anarchist theory. It covers world events such as the trial of the anarchist comrades in Italy with essays pitting "liberated desire" and Nietzsche references against "the logic of submission." As sometimes happens in this genre, the theoretical stuff is actually more impassioned than the practical information, but I think the overall purpose here is to give the individual more tools to work with for her own projects of liberation, rather than to get her to write letters to her Congressman about the situation in Italy. Personally, I eat this stuff up, as an admitted member of the anarchist community (and thus a person who isn't easily intimidated by what others might see as elitist language, "extremism," etc.)—but as always the real question for the future is how the ideas here can be translated out of this ghetto and into the lives of others outside the anarchist "inner circle." In the meantime, such little publications as this will keep us connected, informed still thinking and debating... —b
Venomous Butterfly, 41 Sutter Street, Suite 1661, San Francisco, CA 94104

Willy-Nilly in Your Kitchen: Recipes! We here at KrimethInc. Kitchens (or is that Kitschens?) were delighted to receive a cookzine for review! The first time we heard from this man, he was in Lithuania, and a lot of his recipes seem inspired by a sort of peasant food aesthetic, market-based in a different way from most things these days (the farmer's market, not the global one...). Somehow we neglected to review one of these in our last issue, but it has turned out all right in the end, as it was full of winter recipes, and the weather is growing cold again right now. Sounds like the perfect time for Hearty Pine Grain Stew (featuring, yes, pine needles) or a Root Vegetable Compote. The only major objection I had is that he offers a recipe for chili without tomatoes, which seemed to me unconscionable, as tomatoes are the essence of existence and to leave them out of a recipe in which they might happily reside seemed to me an unnecessary evil—until Brian pointed out that that would leave more tomatoes for other recipes. The recipes are simple and straightforward, from the ingredient lists (no lemongrass or arugula here) to the cooking instructions. Most of the recipes are vegan or easily made vegan. We tried several and were pleased with all of them. The Lithuanian Groundnut Chowder was delicious, and the Sumptuous Cous Cous Salad divine. Lots of soup recipes, which has been an adventure for a crew that has sometimes subsisted entirely on bagels and rice for weeks at a time. A couple of the recipes can be a little bland, but that just gives you the opportunity to use your spice rack. We weren't big on the Pine Needle Tea, though. Perhaps the winters aren't hoary enough here to be made more comfortable by a mug of bitter pine resins.

P.S. We tried the chili recipe, and it was good, after all. Even without tomatoes. —@

If you know what's good for you, you'll write to *Jack Clang, 26 Lefferts Pl. #6, Brooklyn, NY 11238*

No Longer Blind/United Fury split fanzine: An earnest effort by sincere kids. United Fury is the less polished of the two, containing a couple of band interviews (Standard and Day of Contempt) a personal column on rape and power, one on Amnesty International (of which the writer is a member), some record reviews (in one of which the reviewer actually offers to tape a 7" for people who can't find it, which I think is awesome), a couple of vegan recipes and a fairly straightforward column about socioeconomics and idealism. No Longer Blind concentrates on fellow fanzines in this issue, with interviews with MRR, Slug & Lettuce, Reflections, and United Front, and a couple of essays (done as papers for school!) on what and why a fanzine is. Kind of hilarious, but interesting, to read all the basic 'zine ideology again, but this time with parenthetical documentation! ("Zines, in direct opposition (and usually consciously), are self produced, non-profit publications for cultures that resist the mainstream (Duncombe 1997 pp 111-113).") Then there are shorter essays on various topics that tend to fall under the vast umbrella of hardcore ethics. Violence and straight edge (via the SLC media frenzy), the right of punk bands to have no talent and lots of fun, a call to, well, not arms, but at least action by the nay-sayers and cynics of the hardcore community, and hardcore ideology. There's also one entitled "punk-o-nomics," which, although its ideas are not so ridiculous (trying to put on shows at venues where there is less overhead (as in, for the security guards and bartenders...), and perhaps even charging a little bit more, might generate more money for bands and help them pay for their gas, at the very least), uses such unbelievable facts to support itself on that I can see it sway dangerously in light breezes. A $5 (US$) show 20 years ago, he says, is the equivalent of $30 today. So we are actually giving much less support, financially, to bands now, even though there is a strong community that is supposed to make these things easier. First of all, I am being asked to believe that there has been 600% inflation in a time known for its steadily falling inflation. And more impossibly, since our governments are capable of anything, especially if given 20 years to do it in, I am being asked to believe that alienated, working class punks in the late 70s and early 80s were paying the equivalent of a millennial $30 of their paychecks, if they had them, to see bands play in dives and holes. I think the only band I'd have to pay $30 to see today would be the fucking

Eagles, not Dissemble in my friend's basement. While the inflation point is an interesting one, the numbers given are just implausible. The most interesting thing about these 'zines, for me, is that although they are Australian, the dialect is the same as any American 'zine's. This makes me wonder: do the words evoke concepts that differ in any way at all? Are Australian kids talking about the same things as American kids? Is DIY different for them, or racism, or the Sex Pistols? Even marginally? Or have we really created a worldwide community that speaks exactly the same language? And would that be a strength, or a weakness?—@

No Longer Blind, 74 Gladstone Ave., Wollongong, NSW, 2500 Australia

continued from page 129 **CrimethInc. Special Report**

... and in reality these undercover photos show just how "punk and hardcore" the band really is, relaxing around the pool ...

... but be careful because they still know enough to roughen up unwanted paparazzi.

continued from page 45

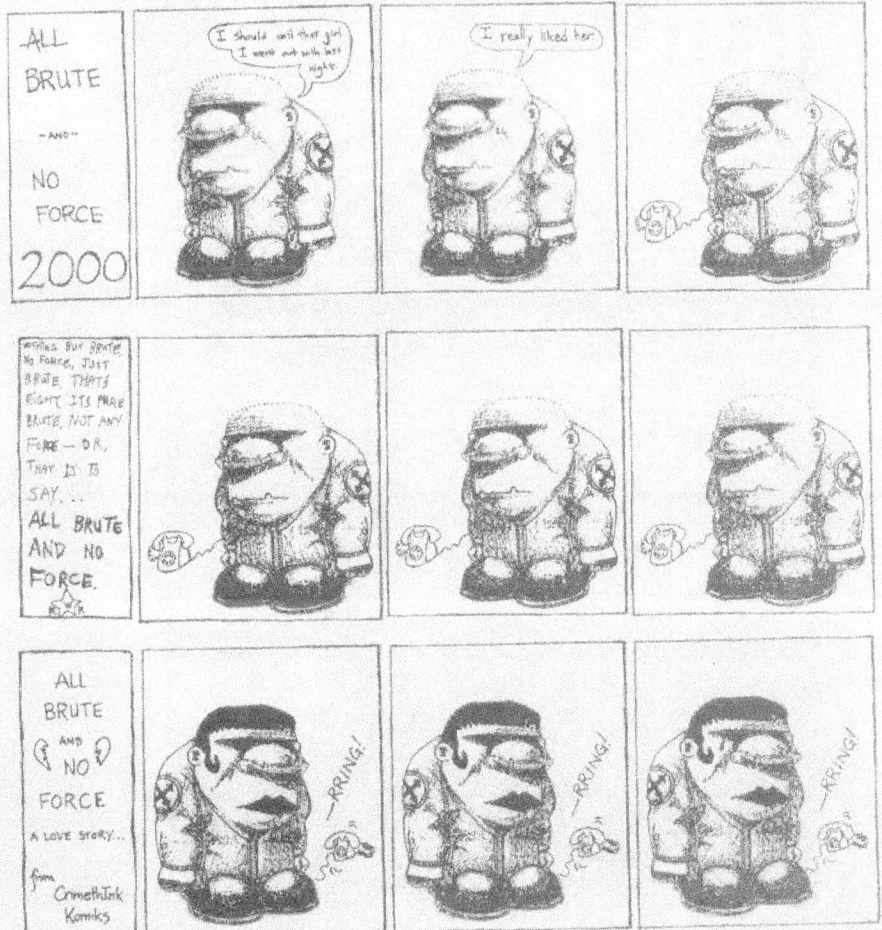

All Brute and No Force is continued on page 152

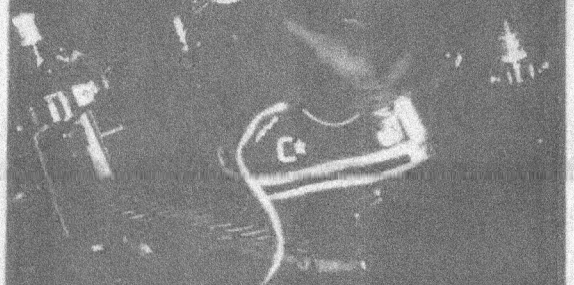

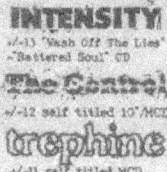

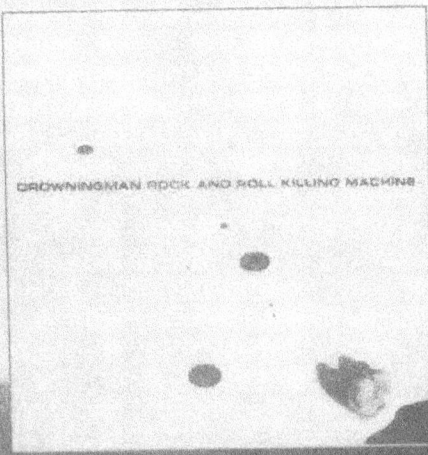

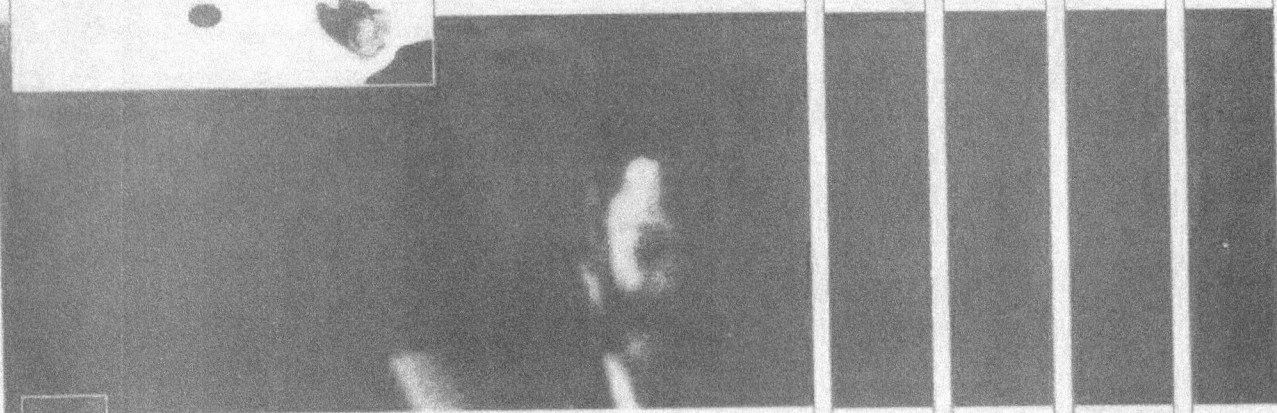

the rewards together. If we don't try, we don't even allow ... ...help us in this fight and hopefully we'll rea[p] make some kind of effort each day of our lives, there *is* that ... ourselves the possibility of success, but if w[e] possibility—and with it, *hope*.

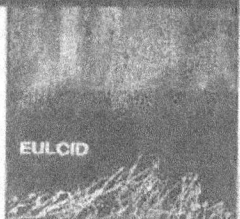

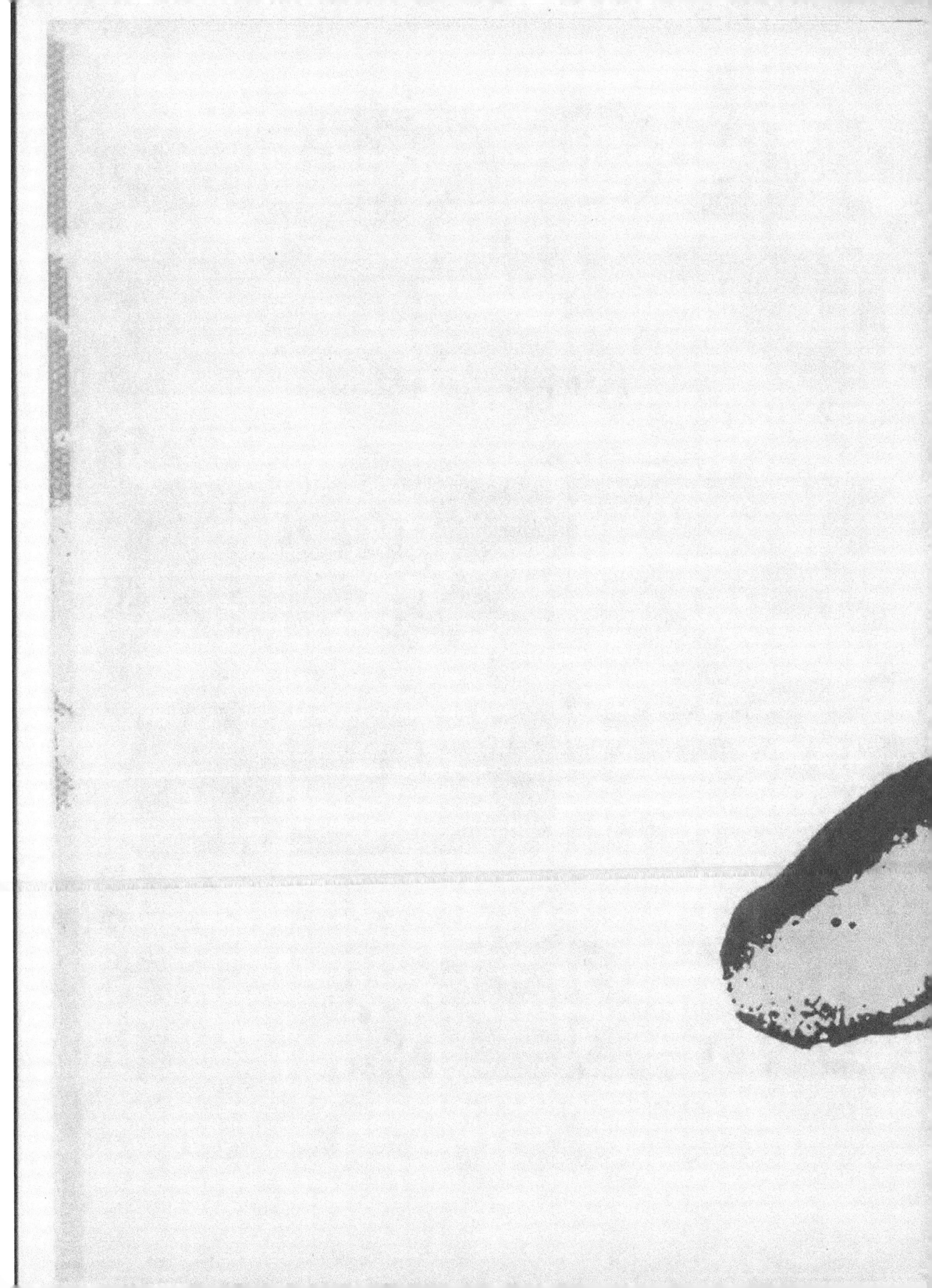

continued from page 137

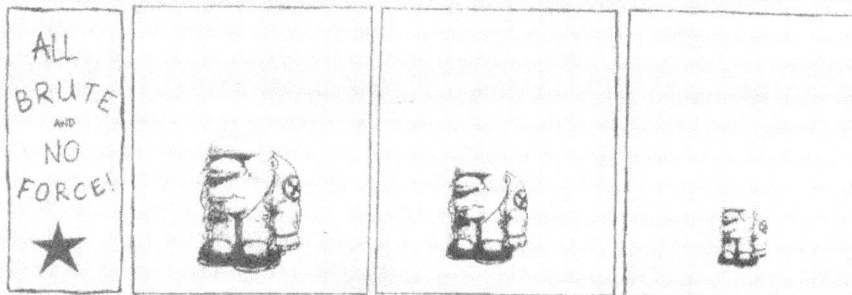

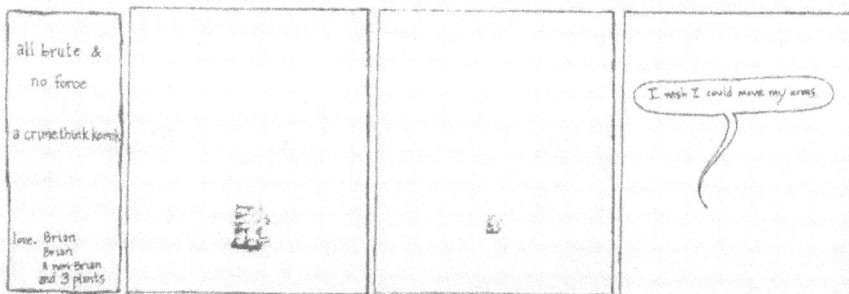

INSIDE FRONT NUMBER 13
COMPILATION CD:

Milemarker "Industry for the Blind"
Newborn "Citadels Burning"
Redemption "Daphne"
Endstand "The Way"
Point of No Return "Casa de Caboclo"
Newspeak "A Nice Talk Between Hollow Walls"
Constrito "Permissividade"
Abuso Sonoro ""
Shank "His Giro Is Gone"
Ruination "Losing Friends"
Speak Up! "Abused Words"
Lariat "Culture"
Memnoch "Consummate Wrath"
Cwill "Darkness"

MILEMARKER
"Industry for the Blind"

This is not conversation. It's just well-wrapped sensation with a mannequin lining to remind you to sign in. It's not altercation, it's just reaffirmation that you're standing on desks shouting at no one at best. You've got to get up to stand up. Don't bother playing dead. Gouge your eyes out. It's better not to see the way things are without a way to get where they should be. The ones who don't were just thinking ahead. They dug this ditch for you, now the best that you can do is lie in it. This is not altercation, it's just well-wrapped sensation, and now you're telling about the chaos you're wearing. The ones who lined in the blueprint to sign in have got you sucking hand over fist. You've got to get up to stand up, don't bother playing dead.

Milemarker c/o Al Burian fan club, 307 Blueridge Road, Carrboro, NC 27510

NEWBORN
"Citadels Burning"

Why are you shouting against certain things, when you just do the same? I can't believe you're so fucking ignorant. Instead of breaking down walls together, you're just raising them high to the skies. Your actions driven by your ignorant arrogance just fuel their fire. And we don't have the time to spark ours. How many words have been said, but nothing came true, how many songs have been sung, but it seems all that we've found are some deaf ears. I just can't believe you're still here at this point. And if you keep doing your pity things, we won't reach forward for the cause. The saddest thing is that you're always having crowds who believe and follow blindly your slogans. But don't expect me to follow you, and don't expect me to believe. I'll be the first one to throw stones at your citadel, I'll be the first one to burn them down. Burn them down. I'll watch your citadels burning, I'll watch them end in ashes. End in ashes.

Jakab Zoltan, H-2120 Dunakeszi, Rozmaring U. 30, Hungary

REDEMPTION
"Daphne"

I knew of spirits who transited as fast as the wind. I knew of men who moved slow through the crowd with enormous weights of skulls. If I stare at my eyes and I search, I know I can find the good angel. Mirror – look well "heart." Angel, I was searching for you by sight. I want to learn how to love, and loving more than myself. Bring like clear river - search and taken I'll be by your sight. Slow I'll go on my without turning back, I'll bring you out of hell "Daphne" and at the sound of the sunset. I will look to a reborn spirit.
I'm not gonna leave you there.
You left me there for a long time.
I will not turn.
Turn around but stay with me.

Redemption is: Perilli - voice • Valentina - voice • Simone - guitar • Livio - guitar • Emiliano - bass • Giorgio - drums • Chiara plays piano in this song • Recorded at The Temple Of Noise (December 99). Produced by Christian Ice and Redemption • Mixed by Christian Ice. Mastered at The Temple Of Noise.

ENDSTAND
"The Way"

POINT OF NO RETURN
"Casa de Caboclo"

Endless nights of persecution
reopening wounds - never healed.

Always willing to suppress our attempts to be free.
Violence is always a tool in so called democracy.
Agents of the state allowed to spread terror, seeking to eliminate sparks of political resistance.

Endless nights of violation
breeding fear - anguished cries.

A blood oath to never surrender.
Committed to the struggle
until all fences are burned.
You'll try the taste of pain we endure every

day.
To quit without resisting would be to live in vain.
Attentive eyes
guard the tents in the twilight.
Women and men
ready to counterattack.
Full moon shines...
The enemy crawls in the dead of night.
No way back...
The masked cops take their final step.

You're trapped.
Surrounded by the mass.
Laws are ignored.
Justice from bleeding hands.

There is a real war across the Brazilian territory. It is a war against hunger, misery and social injustice declared by millions of peasants who joined the Brazilian Landless Workers Movement (MST) - now one of the largest and most important social movements in Latin America. From the past colonization, which fed off all forms of exploitation, very few and privileged people in Brazil inherited a huge concentration of power and wealth, including lands. Nowadays, two thirds of the Brazilian agricultural land are controlled by landlords and by multinational corporations, whereas approximately thirty-

two million Brazilians suffer from starvation and sixty million are underfed. This system of atrocities and inequalities has given Brazilian rural workers no choice other than taking the land by force. Either they carry out occupations in order to have a place where they can live and grow their own food or they starve to death. The MST was then formed to speed up land reform, and achieve social equality. It has investigated unused and unproductive estates and organized landless workers' families to occupy them. Predictably, their actions have faced extreme repression all over the country. Militias have been formed and financed by landlords to suppress and kill members of the MST and there have been frequent violent conflicts involving landless workers, police troops and professional killers, which have always ended in bloodshed. Thousands of peasants have been killed in the last thirty years and MST members have also faced politically motivated trials. Fiction and reality are mixed in Casa de Caboclo as we try to narrate the terrible nights of persecution and torture against the MST. In the middle of the night, the landless workers' tents are suddenly invaded by armed masked people. Children are separated from their parents and shots are fired creating angst and despair. Men are kept naked for hours and are often threat-

ened and tortured. This situation is nothing but an illustration of how violence is always used by the so-called democratic governments that rule this world. It was used during the massacre in Acteal, Mexico, where 45 people were murdered by a military group in December, 1997. That's the way it is in Brazil, too. So far everything is part of a sad reality. The fictitious aspect of these lyrics emerges when the workers, tired of being tortured, decide to react and plan to corner their attackers. This song, however, expresses a feeling, maybe an irrational one, we have rather than some form of behavior we are proposing. In fact, what this song reflects is a position of total intolerance towards the methods of repression used by the State. We would like this intolerance to be present in all sectors of our society. "We are afraid, but we don't use our fear."

Casa de Caboclo was taken from the first Point of No Return CD, which is called "Sparks" and came out on Catalyst Records (www.xcatalystx.com) from the USA and Liberation (www.xliberationx.com) from Brazil. Contact the band at: Caixa Postal 4193 Sao Paulo-SP 01061-970 Brazil valovelho@hotmail.com

NEWSPEAK

"A Nice Talk Between Hollow Walls"

I've found a broken mirror smashed by
expectations
Reflecting privacy violated by the policy of
illusions
Incinerating images of failure and marching
through pacified bodies
I found the gunfire and I keep on telling
myself
Emptiness
We are falling
Silence
We are falling
The lack of hope, the absence of possibilities,
stimulates me to relax and let it go, overlooking everything I condemned myself to look
at forever. Anyway I pay obedience only to
"judge me," and not to circumstances forced
at me by the objects of my hate.
Distance is bigger and now we don't have a
horizon
Makes me want to know where all this blood
flowing through my hands came from
But some guy called "confusion" came first
with opportunities and smiles
And we sit down together eating peanuts and
hiding our knives
We're falling down

Counter-cultural production has always
tried to militantly knock down old myths.
But instead of disassociating with these
myths, dissident music introduced a new
mythology, incarnated in the fantastic idea of
a "day that will come," with the function of
absolving the listener of any responsibility in
the historical process. Thus, protest music
becomes, for many people, a moral support
for their theoretical beliefs. In punk and HC,
this self-patrolling stance became an obstacle
for a bigger (and better) production. Our circuit becomes standardized, and little by little
the questioning and interrogation become
cliché. A hierarchy of values, that indoctri-
nate "rebellion" was institutionalized.
Challenge was mechanized, transforming
something that was once so intensely visionary, into something dated and pedantic. If
we revise the means that we ourselves limit,
we can have a strong instrument for social
action. This latest affirmation may be questionable, but applying a little skepticism, in
the moment when we expose ourselves, we're
socializing our principles. Everything is centered in the scale of absorption, in the number of people reached. And even having a
limited scale, we can't underrate the channels
that remain outside corporate entities.
Therefore, we must use our means of communication ('zines, bands, pamphlets...)
wisely, with a latent spirit of renovation, so
we can plant the seeds of a real departure
from a world that, day after day, takes away
our taste for life.

Newspeak, Rua Juranda 126, 05442-070,
Sao Paulo, SP, Brazil

SHANK

"His Giro is Gone"

My Giro lies by my front door
It was spent before it hit the floor,
Jesus Christ, what a rigmarole
to be in debt, living on the dole

A handful of smash to furnish my dreams
punishment for living beyond my means
my debtors all know it's giro day
but salvation always seems to be a fortnight
away

This grinding eternal now
from which even work won't set me free

You want to experience real fucking
ennui? Try signing on the dole for a year or
two. Living hand to mouth day after day in a
twilight half-life, always conscious that a bit
of unexpected expense might force you to
forgo electricity for a day or two. That bubble of short-lived joy when your giro (that's
'welfare cheque' to our American friends)
arrives every two weeks is inevitably burst
when you calculate just how much you owe
out. And yet, we are supposed to be eternal-
ly grateful to the government for this bind.

I realize that many people around the
world are not afforded this kind of 'safety
net', and I suppose I should think myself
lucky (if you think this kind of enforced
docility can be called luck.) But what really
pisses me off is when the same politicians
who were responsible for cutting back on
my education, turn round and call us 'dole
scroungers' or 'welfare cheats'.

Sorry, but you failed me with your substandard schooling, and now that you've created an unskilled, uneducated underclass,
you want to pin the blame on us? You
trapped us in this Pavlovian cycle - not us.
You seem to forget that welfare was created
as a pacifying strategy - 'three meals away
from revolution' and all that.

If I were you, I have a long hard think
about what might happen when you starting
cutting people's benefits en masse. You
would do well to remember that the most
potent revolutionary forces are compromised
of people with NOTHING LEFT TO
LOSE.

Andy Stick, Flat 1/1, 274 Kilmarnock Road,
Glasgow G43 2X5, Scotland, U.K.

★ **RESISTIREMOS! - Sociedade em descalabro/Afogada em costumes inválidos/Conformismo e inércia/Retardando a insurreição/Condicionada a micro valores/Trabalho árduo por prazeres fúteis/Estresse e violência/São as cartas na manga do Estado/Sim, está uma merda!/As vezes realmente desanima/Temos que convir/Quanto poderoso é o nosso inimigo/Nem por isso vou dar um foda-se/E me entregar ao desalento/Se meu ódio é algo maior/A todo momento/Então que fique bem claro: Nós resistiremos!!!** ★

★ **WE WILL RESIST! - Society on declide/Drowned on unvalid customs/Conformity and inercy/Retarding the insurrection/Conditioned to micro values/Hard working for foolish pleasures/Stress and violence/Are the cards from State/Sure, its bullshit/Sometimes its take us down/We have to realize/That our enemy is really powerful/But we wont turn us back/And bring me to sadness/If my hate is bigger/All the time/To make it clear: We will resist!!!** ★

Abuso Sonoro today are: Juquinha- Drums; Angelo-bass; Rui-Guitar; Arilson-guitar & vocal and Elaine-vocal. They recorded respectively the vocals, drums, bass and guitars live on studio, in the middle month of June'2000.

For more info, friendship, barricadas and resistence, write for this address above : Cx. Postal: 2098 – Santos/São Paulo 11060-970/ Brasil/Latin America.
E-mail: abuso_sonoro@yahoo.com.br
website: http://www.abusosonoro.cjb.net

Constrito

Permissividade
(the title is a combination between two words : "permissivo"
witch means permissive and "passividade" witch is passivity.
So it's a tolerance for passivity, in other words stay quiet in
your home and close all the windows)

Permissividade

Forjar os cadeados e prender as escolhidas
Sugar a energia de seus corpos jovens
extirpando sua inocência
Herdeiras de um legado hipócrita
Patriarcas e mães submissas - violadores
demoníacos com tradições arbitrárias
Negação contínua / traumas profundos
/ segredo de família
De seus lares a imundas alcovas
Começando em casa, indo para as ruas do
desespero
Sofrer!!!
Iludidas na promessa de emprego
Confinadas sob ameaça
Obrigadas a vender-se para sobreviver
Elas sentem a pele em contato com a sua
O fedor do hálito e o suor de corpos
Para quem foge, morte e perseguição
Espancamento para as que voltam
A dor e a terra da vala comum
Sem lamentos ou alguém para se lembrar
A depressão alucinógena cheira álcool
Que os aliciadores sejam empalados
De seu sofrer vem meu regozijo
De no mínimo uma vida salva
Elimine os opressores / liberdade ao corroer
o sistema que se alimenta de destruição
Não posso virar, fechar meus olhos e negar
Um grito mudo explode meus ouvidos a cada vida violada
A ferida aguarda o curativo
A estrada da conformidade leva a cidade do descaso
Junto ao muro da lamentação
Eu busco a elevação da dignidade perdida
Peço que me ouça / considere o meu apelo
O sofrimento deve cessar / grite de suas entranhas
Com a dor dos corpos delas (altruísmo é a ligação)
Seremos uma voz, um instrumento de justiça.

To forge the padlocks and lock the chosen ones
To drain the essence of their young bodies
Striping of their innocence
Heiresses of an hypocrite legacy
Patriarchs and submissive mothers
Demonic violators with arbitrary traditions
Continued negation / profound traumas / family's secret
From their homes to filthy alcoves
Starting to suffer at hearth, heading to the streets of despair
Suffer!!!
Deluded with promises of work
Confined under threats
Forced to sell themselves in order to survive
They feel skin in touch with theirs
The sweat and the stench breath of bodies
To those who run away - persecution and death
Beating for the ones who comes back
The pain and the earth of an unknown grave
Without lamentations or someone to remember
This hallucinogenic depression smells alcohol
Let the executioners be impaled
From their suffering will come my satisfaction
Of at least one life saved
Eliminate the oppressors / liberty as this system
is corroded
That feeds itself on destruction
I can't turn my back, close my eyes and deny
A silent scream blows my ears at each life raped
The wound awaits for the cure
The road of conformity leads to the city of blinds and
to the wall of lamentations
I seek the elevation of the lost dignity
I ask you to listen to me / to consider my call
This grief must end / scream from your guts
With the pain of their bodies (altruism is the link)
We must be a voice, a tool for justice...

The explanation : first of all we'd like to tell you that the translation lose some
of the expressive aspects of Portuguese, so if some parts the lyric sounds strange
it is due to this fact. when the question is about sexual exploitation on women,
Brazil represent itself as one of the leaders in that matter. Because of the 500
years old macho tradition to the enormous profits of sexual tourism the Brazilian
society sees this problem as something that should not be spoken of, "the family's secret".
Even if we are five males and do not suffer directly from this situation we cannot live in this
denial and not defend women rights. We consider ourselves as a feminist band and every
fight in order to reach justice is a fair fight witch needs to be revealed to the public so discussion
will take place and solutions will start to appear.

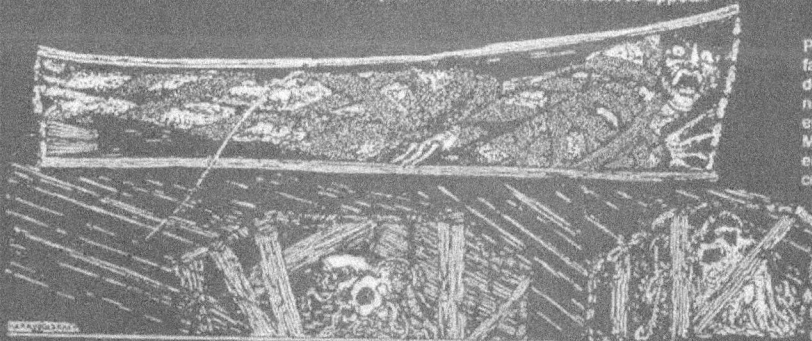

Por falta de espaço e pelo
fato dos leitores deste zine
dominarem o inglês,
não colocamos uma explanação
em português.
Mas para adquiri-la
entre em contato
com a banda:

constrito@zaz.com.br

Cx. Postal 21053 - São Paulo/SP
CEP 04602-970 - Brazil

Ruination
"Losing Friends"

"No, I'm not quite sure just what it is you're trying to rub my face in here, but yeah you've changed, as all things change. If that's your point, it's loud and clear, I think you want me to kick and scream, or try to tell you who to be. I'm still trying to figure out if you're really talking to you or me. Maybe I'm sad to see you go. Maybe I just hate feeling alone. Maybe
I don't know how to take it when it hits this close to home. All we had, the times we shared. We always said it was thicker than blood. I know it's gone, and not coming back, but what IS left? Do we write it off and walk away? See all those years just laid to waste? I can't tone down this life I've found because you've changed your mind. So what we keep and throw away is your call as well as mine."

There is no Inner Circle. Consistency is the exception to the rule. We don't account for changes of heart, and our friendships suffer as we fall into the familiar roles of The nconsistent and the Intolerant. Those of us who fall out have to accept 'our friends' consistencies as much as we'd expect them to accept our changes. Nor should the rest of us have to play down the things we do still care about to save ourselves discomfort. Respect where someone is at, their politics, their lifestyle choices, especially if you've been there, has to be mutual if our friendships are going to see us through our lives and not just our youth. We've all waded through too much shit together to just write it off and walk away.

Recorded on 4 tracks 7.21.00 by Ex-Members of Mike Sutfin in his living room somewhere in Illinois. Ruination is Andy Dempz, Chris Colohan, Ebro Virumbrales and Mike Haliechuk. You can reach us through +/-. Mike is sponsored by Etobicoke track pants and wears exclusively Velcro shoes. Thanks Brian.

SPEAK UP!
"Abused Words"

You're always talkin' to me about love
But the only thing what you want is to fuck
Idealize your instincts and call 'em feelings
Love is what you pretend, is this the end
Your soul is full of filth, guilt
So I don't need you to tell me
What's unconditional loyalty

Rape the love
Abuse the purity
Betray the loyalty

You're hiding behind words
You abuse the words which still mean something
You don't give respect
You come to an agreement with yourself

My love is real!
My love is clear!
My love is true!
I hate you!

contact Speak Up! through Zoli from Newborn

consummate wrath

a steady bleeding on demand
onto the altar of sacrifices
the candle of hope
it never gave me any light
in life

the pain begins in understanding
i'm bathing in anguish and silent despair
finding myself alone in crowded rooms
all we are
puppets in our own naive drama
and our hollow deeds
create a restless nothingness

relieve my torment, kiss me a last
goodbye
i'm dying, leaving it all behind

i feel no regret, can feel no remorse
i found home in darkness
i killed all love, killed all life
i killed my god

inside i'm burning with hatred
the incarnation of wrath
yearning to extinguish, i feel no regret
i found home in darkness
and the pain ends in understanding

she's the perfect victim
her beauty is her guilt
she'll walk on my side
through the gates to hell

her statuesque figure inspires my creation
slivers of moonlight on the blade of steel
i feel no pain now that she's mine
to fulfill my work in flesh and blood

since we are forced to hide or deny our real emotions in every day life there grows the danger of a sick society that one day will violently break out of these chains. passion and desire is considered evil or "uncivilized" and so we pretend to be happy and well-balanced personalities although anger is nothing inhuman. building up this anger is the demon that may develop to such madman like a mass-murderer. these lyrics do not justify violence but we should consider where this brutality comes from before judging such people

"beauty wasn't the treachery he imagin it to be, rather it was an uncharted land where one could make a thousand fata errors, a wild and indifferent paradise without signposts of evil or good."

anne rice

contact:
Roman Schmädig, Florian-Geyer-Str. 32,
01307 Dresden, Germany

phone +49 (0)351 - 4 49 61 98
meinnoch-hc@gmx.de

CWILL
"Darkness"

A dream of darkness
Saved from the burden
Free finally free
What remains is what I love
The only light

Redemption—please save me
Save me from myself

Save me from myself
But I hold back
It's not time yet
Perhaps soon

Endless falling,
Endless redemption
Sleep find the silence
Saved from the burden
Free, finally free

What remains is what I love
The only light I see

A dream of darkness
Endless falling,
Endless redemption
Sleep, find the silence
Saved from the burden

Thomas Vogel, Honggerstr. 18, CH-8037
Zurich, Switzerland

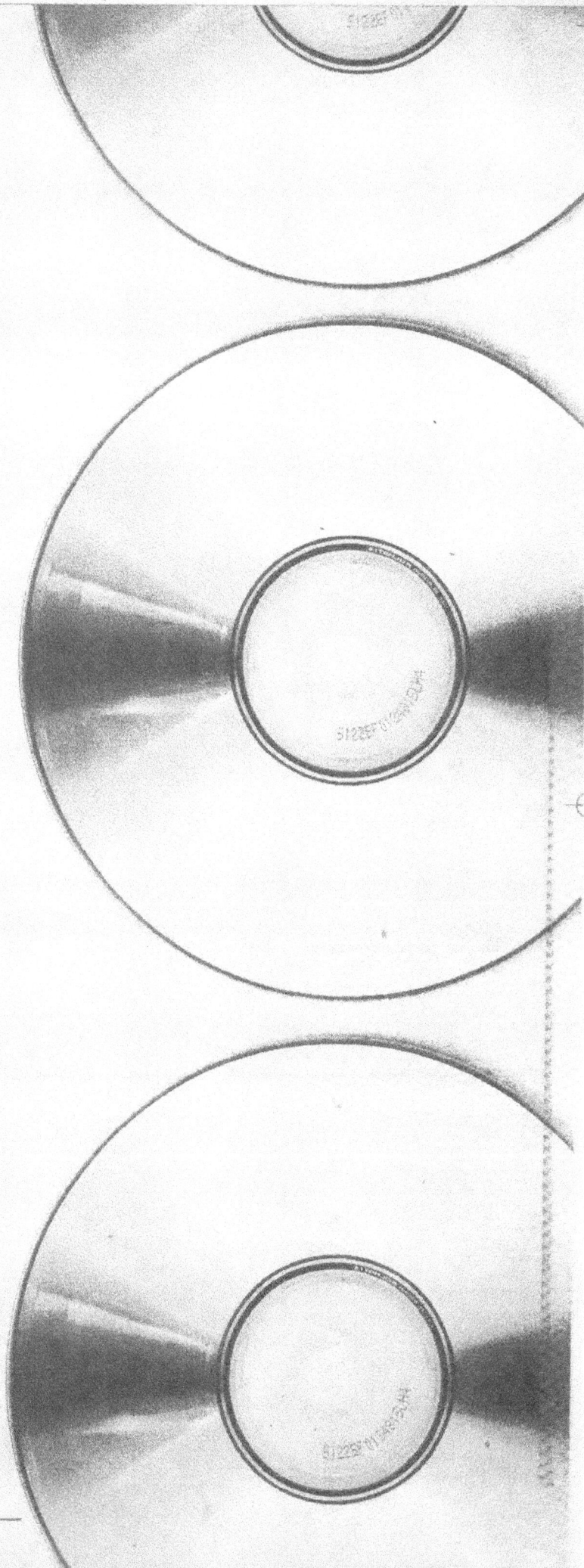

It's been three months of frustrating layout delays and postponements since I wrote the last words of the last review for this issue, and it's ridiculous that this thing isn't out yet [Designer's note: fuck you!]. I guess that's the way it works in the world of 'zines. Now I'm sitting in my lover's apartment (freezing of course, in the Inside Front tradition), listening to Stef's tape of the incredible new Tragedy record, typing the filler for the absolutely final page.

A lot has happened since I first wrote the introduction, of course, and it almost seems naive in retrospect—not because it was too hopeful, but because I didn't have the perspective then to see just how quickly the things I've been waiting for would start becoming possible. This weekend we were in Washington, D.C. to participate in the Un-auguration activities... imagine a world in which the new President of the United States has to ride hidden behind black, bullet-proof windows to get through the Inaugural Parade, as tens of thousands of U.S. citizens scream "FUCK YOU!!" and wave their fists at him from all sides—now check this out: you live in it. Not that this is much help or consolation to the millions still strapped to the wheel of work-rent-television-taxes, but when a march of liberal democrats changes course to rescue a fragment of the Black Bloc trapped and assaulted by police officers, knowing full well that these are kids who oppose voting on every level and are out explicitly for the sake of property destruction, it indicates that a fundamental shift in values is taking place away from the complacency and timidity that make such absurd conditions possible. If this doesn't seem to be taking place in your town yet, hold on tight—or, far better, make it happen.

I spent the week leading up to the Inauguration in Pittsburgh with two friends of mine, establishing a workshop there with which we mass-produced stickers, fliers, and posters to be applied and given away at the demonstration and afterwards. As I described in the features section earlier in this issue, I think that's where it's at for the next stage of resistance—autonomous cells everywhere across the world, capable of organizing their own cheap/free living, propaganda, adventures, activism, taking responsibility for making life something awesome and beautiful...

Here's the bottom line, which I've said a hundred times before, but I don't think it can be said enough—you have to find ways to simultaneously stay alive in this world and make changes in it. Yes, it's hard to live, yes, it's hard to believe in anything when you're filled with pain from childhood abuse or workplace boredom or the simple struggle to get along with the motherfuckers around you—but for heaven's sake don't stop there. So many of my friends are left out of the transformations that are taking place right now because the ways of surviving they found are dead ends—one is an alcoholic like his father, another already dead from a drug overdose, another still working full time to pay for more tattoos, another working at a job he hates to save up money for his next vacation, another spends all his free time working on an intricate model boat. These are all legitimate ways to live—hell, everything is legitimate as far as I'm concerned, and whatever it takes to be able to bear life is right on—but they don't offer open horizons, they don't do anything to put you in a situation where the conditions of your life might change.

If you can tie your immediate needs to pursuits that can create new opportunities for you, you've got a chance to beat the system. If you need to eat, eat in a way that helps others eat too, by working with Food Not Bombs—if you love bicycling, don't spend all your time working to buy new bicycles, new surrogates for adventure: start a bicycle repair collective so you'll have all the stuff around you for free, or go out bicycling across the country, like some friends of mine did to raise awareness about the plight of children in Iraq—if you desperately need a break from the repetitions of the work life, go on tour with a punk band or activist group instead of taking a tourist vacation—if you have to have a place to stay, try to organize a collective housing space, it'll save you money and help you avoid the isolation of a normal living cubicle—if you have children to take care of, there's no better time than now to start working on establishing better day care and school alternatives, especially since your kids are going to have to deal with thousands of other kids who didn't get the benefit of these things otherwise—if you have to work to support your family, work a job where you can join the I.W.W. and help organize your fellow workers—if nothing feels honest and liberating to you except smashing things, you can smash them with the Black Bloc and still participate in making a different world. You don't need do this shit to serve the cause or whatever—I'm just saying that in my personal experience, it feels better. Being a revolutionary is right on just because it's a more exciting, rewarding way to live—I don't recommend it to others because I want "converts" for the "movement" nearly so much as because I'm desperate to see the people around me feel better about things, feel more optimistic and excited to be human and alive.

And the postscript to all of this is that those of us who think we've found ways to do it already have to figure out what it is we're doing that is scaring others off from joining us. Could it be that the greatest obstacle to this revolution is our own self-importance, our desperate need to assert ourselves as the saviors, the knights in shining armor, the assholes who have figured everything out? My personal project for the coming months is to work out how to be less intimidating to everyone else. Anyhow, I'm off, as I hope this 'zine will be to the printers soon—expect to see more from us and of us very soon.

*F*rom here, whatever was worthwhile about *Inside Front* is in your hands. We're not ending our work with the magazine in defeat or exhaustion—to the contrary, we're more involved and active than ever—but rather because it has taken us as far as it needed to; now we find ourselves standing at a vista from which new horizons can be seen, and we have to make new vehicles to carry us to them. This isn't the end of hardcore being relevant to our lives, or of life being relevant to hardcore, or of our contributions to either of those things. But *Inside Front* is now yours, yours to improve on, yours to apply and add to. We're absolutely confident that from these seeds, a hundred greater forces will grow, and we who have nourished this project to this point must simply let go of the reigns to let it become what it must now become—which you can see more clearly than us, we're certain!

Thank you all so much for supporting us in so many ways over the last seven years, which taught us so much—everything we know, really. Hope to see you soon, wherever in the world you are. Yours with love,

Brian and the rest of the C.W.C.

DOWN WITH CIVILIZATION AS WE KNOW IT!!

INSIDE FRONT

INTERNATIONAL JOURNAL OF HARDCORE PUNK AND ANARCHIST ACTION
BACK FROM THE DEAD TO SMASH CAPITALISM

Postscript
Issue #∞

THIS MEANS WAR.

SKULLDUGGERY! MUGWUMPERY! BEDLAM IN BABYLON!

1. Prelude: Our Leader Speaks

First Movement: Foreign Agents

2. Cathode "Stranglehold"
3. The Spectacle "Between"
4. Burn Hollywood
   Burn "Love (as we know
   it) hurts with or
   without you"
5. Carahter "Lider"
6. Bora "Following Rules"

Second Movement: Domestic Threats

7. Countdown to
   Putsch "The Cure is the
   Poison"
8. Dead Things "Education
   Breakdown"
9. Blacken the Skies "Wrench and
   Bone"
10. Witch Hunt "Fed Up"
11. Breed/Extinction "Ashes vs. Leaves"

Third Movement: The Ghost of Punk Rock Past

12. Driven [the last two Driven
    songs]
13. Driven
14. Society of Jesus [the last two S.O.J.
    songs]
15. Society of Jesus
16. By All Means [the last B.A.M.
    recording—a cover
    song]

Fourth Movement: The Spectre of the Future

17. (The Olympia D.I.Y. Percussion and
    Choral Ensemble featuring soloists)
    Herds and Words

18. Conclusion: Dawn

HOW TO NAVIGATE THESE PAGES:

That was our youth, although it had taken a long time for some of us to arrive there. We ate nothing, or garbage, or the most vile of swill, supplied by a religious cult group—apparently the only ones who still saw any reason to keep us alive. Our real nourishment came in the form of letters from far off lands, tales of street riots told around the coals of burnt-out love affairs, a tape of a Finnish metal band with the most melodramatic of pretensions. Often our lives were saved only by a sunny spring day in January, or a book of poetry found on some neglected library shelf and read aloud on the railroad tracks before midnight, or the revelation of a dance move in some obscure band's performance. We carved esoteric slogans into unlikely surfaces, shared photocopies of strangers' secret ambitions and nonsensical demands, composed and destroyed endless drafts of unsendable love letters to impossible subjects of the wildest fantasies we could conceive. Despising documentation, losing journals, lacking resources, we made our bodies the canvases upon which we painted the epic artwork of our desperate lives. We were gods, dispossessed angels singing the arrival of some hidden hermits' paradise on earth; we were bandit queens and pauper kings, led gloriously astray by the fever dreams of our power-mad monasticism. We had nothing—we would be everything. We were invincible, irresistible, ridiculous, and heaven smiled on us from below.

Those precious dreams treated us as we, consequently, treated each other as lovers: the soaring moments beckoning, the beauty longed for, shining from afar—and then when we turned away from everything else towards them, sought to embrace them, to bend every moment of life, every fiber of being to their pursuit, they scorned us, shunned us, left us mute and broken, incomprehensible to the crowds around us who, too, were pursuing dreams, though not dreams of their own. We rejected our crazy dreams, then, furious, broken-hearted; but in their wake, all other plans seemed lackluster, all hopes half-hearted, and one by one we began returning, to soar and burn again.

So here it is, the Inside Front reunion issue, complete with high

door price, lackluster performances, and rockstars drinking beer (provided as per the guarantee) backstage, talking shit about the kids.

This should be a eulogy, a cry for the lost dreams and squandered opportunities and unharrowed idealism of our youth, when, dizzy with enthusiasm and inexperience, we vowed insane oaths— to never work, to overthrow everything destructive and make life a never-ending celebration, to seize those sailing moments of passion and make them last forever—oaths that could never possibly be kept by the living. This should be a lament, mourning the passing of those halcyon, idyllic days when we had no problems greater than mere survival in service of those quests, when life and death were so simple and so precious. This should find me bewailing the senseless surrender of all those irreplaceable gifts to the jaws of time and cynicism, the slow wear of the daily grind—or, worse, declaring, in the centuries-old tradition of the jaded, that real life has come and gone upon this planet once and for all, and if you weren't there to witness it with us you will never be so lucky. At best, this should be the epitaph for a forgotten faction who refused to be turned into slaves and succeeded instead in being turned to dust.

This should be—but it's not. This is the story of what happened when some of us kept those aspirations at the expense of all others, stayed faithful to our muses and missions even when it meant burning up in the wreckage and, harder, living to dwell upon it. Some of us, sworn to fight to the death, haven't died or submitted—not yet! We followed those uncharted paths we swore were ahead of us, we didn't back down, we went for it—and we're still going for it, still struggling to live in such a way that we can be in love with living. This is the story of what we left behind, what we found, what we lost—what we're doing.

We swore to die fighting, and history saw to it that some of us had the chance—that was sobering. Others among us almost prayed for such deliverance, feared we would outlive ourselves waiting for our chance to come. Yet others forswore the whole business as madness or childishness, or found themselves seized by another destiny that had crouched in the shadows awaiting them all along. Holding on to the dream, that we might yet be able to live fighting, that was the hardest thing of all.

Inside Front Reunion issue designed by Jack "Using tabs to begin paragraphs looks stupid" Frost, acting as an agent for the Graphic Violence Artists Group. All layout work done from library computers with stolen fancy programs and stolen fancy fonts.

GRAPHIC VIOLENCE ARTISTS' GROUP

GRAPHICVIOLENCE@CRIMETHINC.NET

Seriously, why another issue of Inside Front?

We thought the old world was about to come to an end—that's the best I can express it.

Back in 2000/2001, I declared #13 the final issue of this magazine so I could have my hands free for what was to come next. It was coming, that was for sure: with the fall of Communism, the old false dichotomy was gone, and people everywhere were starting to recognize that the only conflict left was between People and Power. Explosions were going off everywhere—world leaders couldn't meet without tens of thousands of protesters showing up to interfere, average folks in average towns were starting to get interested in anarchism, punk kids' well-mannered mothers were joining the anticapitalist struggle with their bodies as well as their hearts. There was always something to do, some chance to join the fray, and we were always working on our next surprise, preparing our part for the next explosion, dreaming impossible dreams about what might be possible next.

Here's a little story that captures the spirit of that period of my life. One summer night, I remember, a thunder storm descended upon the small Southern city some of us called home. A soulful hobo folk band from New York were visiting the wrecked punkhouse where I stayed with an assortment of hell-bent revolutionaries and maladjusted pariahs; they'd just left to dumpster a feast for us all when lightning began to crack across the sky. Two of my dearest friends and I set out for the parking deck downtown to get a better view, but by the time we got half way the rain was coming down in such sheets that we were forced against the side of a building. It was torrential, overwhelming, unearthly; one of us said (whimsically, since it was a hot Southern night) "the only way this could be better would be if it started hailing." At that moment, we heard a tap, and then an answering tap, and an instant later white hail the size of golf balls was drumming down before our widening eyes. It filled up the street, smashed out the lights on the skyscraper we so hated for dominating the skyline, proved beyond a doubt that total transformation is always just around the corner. One of us picked up a hailstone and bit into it; we passed it around, tasting the impossible on our very tongues.

That was what it was like every day, whether we were giving out literature and bagels downtown, playing music together, or pelting riot police with stones—or at least it seems so, in the halcyon glow of memory: anything could happen, and all it took to make it happen was to believe in it.

Then came September 11, 2001, of course. I'm not quite paranoid enough to think it was planned or permitted by our government, though obviously it benefited them in their pursuit of total power; I think it's sufficient to remember that this tragedy was simply the blowback of decades of the U.S. training terrorists and committing crimes against humanity across the world. Whether consciously plotted by capitalists or not, it was certainly characteristic of the capitalist program: terrorize and isolate, turn whole nations and peoples against one another, and cash in on the resulting violence as a chance to clamp down and enforce the demands of silent business-as-usual ever more ruthlessly.

It worked, for a while. Activists were scared into silence, everyone else into compliance, and total war began. We all felt powerless. War is what our enemies do best, it's their final recourse whenever people begin to become aware of their own strength: they create another distraction, another dichotomy, one that makes them appear omnipotent, one that scares the public—at least the public you read about in the mass-media propaganda polls—into lockstep behind them.

It took months for some of us to give in to hopelessness and paralysis, but eventually they set in seemingly everywhere. I was gone when the buildings came down—my band had embarked on an insane project, a five-months-straight tour of Europe that almost destroyed us—and when I returned, all my friends were scattered and dispirited, the punk and anarchist and activist communities were all a mess of back-biting and uncertainty, and all the energy and possibility we'd felt before seemed gone. I held it off as long as I could, but as my band broke up, my love relationships fell apart, and my friends disappeared, a serious, deep depression set in. I kept up what activities I could, but as a writer I was blocked, as a lover I was exhausted, as a revolutionary I was stumped.

I guess that's the critical juncture all of us hit at some point in life: events in the world and our own lives alike seem to spiral out of control, and we're left feeling as though we're watching from the sidelines. This is when people cease to think of themselves as having a destiny of their own and go into survival mode, cutting off their feelings, living in denial, no longer hoping. Some are born into this existence, learning it from the sufferers who raise them; others have to be taught it through failure, oppression, defeat. It wasn't what I wanted, that's for sure—I desperately wanted back the feeling that my life belonged to me, and I didn't want to live without it. I only remained alive, honestly, because I knew from previous experience that such suicidal depressions can pass.

And they do pass. Now the tide is turning. Our enemies rushed too fast to consolidate their power ("if you're not with us, you're against us") as soon as they had the excuse—perhaps that power was more fragile than we thought?—and now they've lost all the advantages it gave them ("well, I'm not really with them... does that mean I'm... ?"). As Nietzsche said, a healthy organism can tolerate a whole army of parasites—a dying creature needs a Department of Homeland Security to stave off the inevitable as long as possible. From here on, the lines can only become clearer again: it's People versus Power, once more. After the rush of war is over, as the terrorist threat intensifies (no one needs a government to fund a terrorist action—one only needs hatred and a boxcutter) and the economy crumbles, it will only become more obvious to people that their rulers have been endangering them simply to consolidate their own power. We should not have panicked so fast after that day in September—we're going to need to be prepared to maintain our projects and morale through worse disasters, if we're going to go the distance to revolution. If anything good can come out of that tragedy, I hope it is a new sturdiness in our community: next time the terrorists strike, we need to be ready to respond immediately, visibly offering our perspective and solutions, before the government can put their spin on it—not hide out in doubt and fear. Besides—if we anarchists are right about where terrorism comes from, our doubt and fear can only result in more deaths in the long run.

I'm writing this the night after the United States declared war on Iraq, the night after thousands of activists across the world declared and reaffirmed their corresponding war against tyranny by shutting down freeways, schools, and shopping districts. After the terrorist attacks in the U.S., there was a period when nationalist patriotism owned the streets: flags and jingoistic propaganda lined every window and bumper, and if you didn't subscribe to bloodthirsty groupthink you felt isolated and endangered. Now, whatever their bullshit polls claim, the atmosphere on the streets belongs to us again —and, unlike before the terrorists brought home to the West the destruction capitalism is wreaking across the face of the world, the issues are so close at hand that no one can deny we all must take a stand somewhere. No matter what happens next, even if there are more terrorist attacks, there will be no going back to those days of paralysis and silence. Let's hope there won't be more—but let's do more than hope: we need to disable and eventually overthrow the government that, with their imperialist economic and political policies, is provoking people into killing us.

Forget that slogan "another world is possible"—another world is *inevitable*. The old world is going to come to an end, my friends, make no mistake about that. However much firepower they have, however many crippled nations they destroy, our oppressors and the entire culture that supports them are doomed—the planet itself cannot sustain them or their way of life much longer. But this final cataclysm isn't something we should just await, or fear—it will be what we make of it, and we have to be preparing for it right now. We have to learn how to get along with each other, we have to develop our strength and the support systems in our communities, we have to be practicing anarchy right now, or else the crash that's coming will only make things worse. Fortunately, there are conflicts to be fought, crazy plans to carry out, communities to bring together—excellent opportunities everywhere for us to learn and build for the future. We grew up reading J.R.R. Tolkien and listening to punk songs, dreaming of fighting in the final clash between destruction and rebirth—my friends, it's upon us.

So, once more—why another Inside Front? Because—if you ask me—when everything you're doing almost works only to crash and burn before your eyes, you don't retire on the ruins of your former idealism, you take a step back to what you were doing before the disaster and start from there again. Editing this magazine is something I've done for a decade now, it's something I know how to do, and it's always troubled me how many beautiful songs and books and projects have never entered the world because the people who could create them, by the time they were finally experienced enough to, were too jaded and beaten to do so. This project, however imperfect it may be, exists now—it's no record that was almost recorded or last show that was never played. Too often, we criticize ourselves and our ideas so much that we forget that an idea that comes to fruition, blemishes and all, is always better than one that dies on the vine.

And why punk rock, why haven't we grown out of it after all these years? However small it may be, I think punk rock will have an important role to play in this struggle for a long time to come. However many disillusioned punks-turned-activists, going through their final phase of adolescence, may need to rebel against the crucible of their rebellion, claiming it to be a dead end ghetto, punk rock is still the milieu that spawns them, generation after generation. However insufferable the obvious shortcomings of all subcultures are, we still desperately need places to come together in this isolating world, to get to know one another and get practice working and playing together. Whatever the stakes in the struggle, it's critical we make beauty together as well as fight its destroyers.

Here's another little story to illustrate this. Two weeks ago the Canadian band *Godspeed, You Black Emperor!* played here in the small college town that has often been my home. It was going to be just another mediated performance, the spectators watching the band before departing alone—but we troublemakers had something else in mind. As the concertgoers left the club, bucket-drums appeared from nowhere and were

distributed along with drumsticks, signs, and great banners. Before the local authorities had time to recognize what was happening, two hundred people had surprised themselves by taking over the main street of the town! We marched up and down it for an hour and a half, blocking it completely as the bars were emptying out, and the police, caught totally unprepared, were unable to stop us or even arrest anyone. That tiny triumph gave those same kids the experience and confidence they needed to fill and block the street again at rush hour tonight—and this time, a few hundred people from other walks of life joined us, pouring into the space we opened. Punk rock, a dead end ghetto? Only if we want it to be. Better a breeding ground for revolutionaries!

That's the vision of punk rock and underground culture I've treasured for the past decade, and it's as bright as ever now. We can resurrect punk rock, just as it resurrected us, as a site of escape and resistance and a seed of an utterly different world. Indeed, we *need* to keep punk rock, or something like it, alive: to steal children for the revolution from the families of the middle and working classes, to offer space for those who are alienated by activist smugness but still seek an outlet for their rebellious energies, to be sure we always remember that this struggle is even more about making our own artwork and life stories than it is about resisting those who would destroy them. Punk rock, by whatever name, will be essential until the day all constraints are destroyed and *everything* is music, is togetherness, is adventure.

So here it is, a surprise issue of my old hardcore magazine, as part of my own rejuvenation, in case it can help to rejuvenate our community—and to reaffirm, once more, the worst nightmares of the powers that be: *yes, we're still here.*

Still passionate, still loving and fighting, and, if anything, younger and crazier than I was when I began the first issue of Inside Front a decade ago—yours sincerely, editor B.

"When your friends misunderstand your works and your enemies understand them all too well, when waking up every new morning feels like a defeat rather than a triumph, when the razor blade or the cliff's edge beckons, remember—he is not pretty, death, only well-advertised. Remember what they did to Michelangelo: they waited until he was dead and then painted over all the genitals in his Sistine Chapel—just as Nietzsche's hated racist sister presented him to the world as a proto-fascist genius after he lost his mind, just as Paul used Jesus, and Plato Socrates, and the Communists Durrutti. Give your enemies nothing. Let your tears freeze to stones we can hurl from catapults, screaming. Write your own epitaph and say it out loud, still alive. This life is a war we are not yet winning for our daughters' children. Don't do your enemies' work for them—finish your own." —from a letter that didn't reach Sylvia Plath in time

A gesture of frustration—a letter I'd like to send to certain kids too enamored of their own disenchantment:

Dear ——

So the dreams we celebrated so passionately, so convincingly, have failed you—or, more precisely, you have failed to attain them. Well! In that, at least, we could find a kinship, for the same tragedy has befallen me—far more frequently and painfully than it can have for you yet, I dare say. But it's not kinship you're looking for, is it? Perhaps, instead, this exaggerated disappointment of yours is your roundabout way of claiming a position of righteousness, the same righteousness you must have mistaken me as laying claim to . . . so you have found your own superiority, your own self-importance, but one predicated on failure. As if I was trying to put myself on a pedestal, by proposing all those impossible possibilities—but you, at least, are "honest": it's all hopeless, it's all a scam, all is failure and anyone who tells you different must be out for himself. Bah!

I'll be vulnerable and admit to you—yes, it's hard, it gets so fucking hard to go for it without disclaimers or self-consciousness, when our enemies are still enthroned in all their power despite our every attempt, when all the bands whose youthful idealism and indomitable spirit seemed poised to overthrow capitalism itself grow out of it and into making a career for themselves—when I find out that the moments I felt most free, like we'd all exploded through the shackles altogether, someone else was feeling alienated and angry. So what can I do—what can we do?

Go for it without disclaimers and self-consciousness, obviously! Learn what we can from the critics and critiques, derive whatever constructive insights can be gleaned from them regardless of whether they were intended constructively or not, shake off the rest—forget about it, fuck it all, you're never going to win everyone's approval (was that what your revolution was about?) and tragedies are bound to happen, that's life—and go for it without disclaimers or self-consciousness.

My friend, you're giving up too soon and too easily. It wouldn't be such a stupid, senseless tragedy if we had enough the time to spare for you to loiter in the sullen adolescence of cynicism for a few more years—but we don't, we really don't. Should we let everything we've learned go to waste? We've done a lot, even you have to admit that—you do yourself whenever you parade your former credentials in the course of making your case for disillusionment. Maybe we did it all wrong—now that we know how we'd do it if we had the chance again, why not do it again and do it right? Could you find it within yourself to believe in something again, could you forgive the world enough, forgive yourself enough to fall in love once more? All those things you loved—that beauty you never found words for, the adrenaline rush of risk, the feeling that the fate of the world itself hinged on your actions—they're still out there, they still await you. You're the one that turned away from them—and without you, I'm afraid I can't find my way back to them either. Try this with me, once more. It won't be easy—it won't be any easier than it was the first time. It will probably end in disaster, once again. But it'll be better than the sour grapes of deliberate failure. Suicide would be a nobler option than that.

Your old friend, ——

A dispatch of desperation—a letter I wrote, in a particularly dark period, to my comrades at the San Francisco anarchist bookfair, 2002, but never circulated:

Dear anarchist, beautiful anarchist—

How do I say this, what words are left when we've burned up all our rhetoric on abstractions, glorifying the ghosts we keep close at hand to make this life more bearable?

I had another panic attack tonight, just now, five minutes ago, like I used to in the years before that week in Seattle—I wanted to tear out my eyes so I'd never see another smug, uncontested Starbucks or Shell station, rip off those fingers that might not write the letter (whatever letter it is!) that could set off the next skirmish, throw myself off a goddamn bridge. The worst part is—I feel responsible, responsible now for always having an optimistic, bright vision, to help out in those moments when you might not—even though I know that's bullshit!—but anyway, my fear is all I have to offer tonight, and there's enough of it to go around, so I'll share that.

We make it from year to year, some of us, in this world that denies all our dreams, by believing in miracles—that is the miracle, itself, and it's no mean feat. I've been in that world—spent days in it, weeks in it even—where everything was about to change, was in fact changing. Now when, on those days when I can't find my way back, my companions try to reassure me ("you can't change the world, but you can change one life"—etc., etc.), it makes me fucking crazy—for I know that world of pragmatism and "being realistic" is the counterfeit world, the illusion. If I never again experience what I experienced in those soaring hours, I will go to my grave insisting still that those transcendent moments of possibility were the real world, that this is just a farce, a stand-in world of false fronts until we can get to the next of them. If historians write about me (curse them if they do!) one hundred years hence, noting that I was wrong about what would happen, that will take place in an alternate universe, not the one I believe in, not the one I live in.

I am terrified. I'm terrified that we'll use today just to recruit for our little competing clubs, to argue over trifles and maybe fight for table scraps. I'm terrified that too many of you will have arrived here like I did, not knowing what you will try here or, worse, what direction to go next—and that all of us

will consequently do our best to feel like what we're doing, or not doing, is good enough. I'm terrified we'll find, despite all our swaggering to the contrary, the resignation to survive here—here, in our safe ghetto, with the Palestinians and veal calves dying outside—and die here ourselves, too, even if only by waking day after day to say "I live" and mean it as something other than a victory.

If we were brave or reckless enough for it, our despair—for those of us who feel it sometimes, and I hope we're a small minority—could be a resource as great as any other. It could enable us to do the things our comrades, with their hope and high spirits, shouldn't have to do to make things happen. Otherwise, it is a burden of shame for us to hide, and truly an enemy to fear. Pride would hold us forever in no-win situations, struggling to prove that we can make them work, insisting that we are happy, that everything is going according to plan. We nail ourselves in place here in the same way some pledge themselves to love relationships of mutual misery, trying to prove to themselves they are "good enough" to make each other happy. It takes a ruthless mercy to discard sentimentality and remember all the things that never happened and *still might never happen*, all the dreams that never came true—we can't wait forever, there's not time enough for that. Impatience is a virtue.

Whether or not you suffer these attacks of fear and nihilism, know this: those actions you are considering, that book you're thinking of writing, that hand you might try to extend—we need those, all of us, so badly now—don't you dare hold back out of insecurity or anything else! I've seen too many of my friends die now, driving themselves into living graves or earthen ones, because the world didn't seem wide enough to hold what they wanted. That's what we should be doing here, above all, I feel: widening the world, so the next generation of dreamers can join us, bringing their hope or despair or whatever it is they have to offer; together, we could break down the gates to that other world I talk about, once and for all. I still believe this can happen, is happening, must happen.

Still in love with all of you and the amazing things we can do,
An anonymous and abashed CrimethInc. ex-worker

And, sadly, a eulogy for my beloved, departed friend Emma Berger, a beautiful, courageous woman who did indeed live each day like it was her last—written by another friend of mine who is, let's not take this for granted, still with us as I type this.

Dear Emma,

This is not a eulogy; this is not a eulogy because I will not let you die. Just over a year ago I lost a very important person in my life in a car accident. Emma Berger, 21, deceased. That feeling in your gut when someone tells you they have bad news, the split second that you think about the death of a loved one, the empty feeling when you learn you're right. I had talked to her just the night before, but only for a second; I was on my way to work. They were on their way home, we were going to have a party, her voice was on the fucking answering machine for christsakes. This was my first experience with loss, it was terrifying. People cried and wailed but I just sat there. Stone. Dry mouth and dry eyes. I felt dead. In the days to follow I would go from picturing gruesome, disfigured bodies strewn across the highway to going about my day as if nothing had happened. As the days turned to weeks and we tried desperately to pick up the pieces, I began to remember every little detail about her. Her eyes, her laugh, all those little stories she would tell. Its funny, I had met Emma only a couple of times in the years before, hanging out for a few hours while she was passing through Detroit. Then in October of 2001 she showed up at my house again, this time to stay awhile, and something happened. We connected; it was amazing, unexpected. I don't think I slept for the next two weeks, we stayed up all night talking, telling stories, past and present, hopes and dreams. I don't think I've ever met someone that strong. She dealt with so much, pushed so hard. Of course it weighed on her, but she never let it slow her down. She carried so much on her shoulders but always moved with a light heart, always laughing and joking, inspiring everyone she met. We were supposed to go on the circus tour together, build a metal shop and start teaching people to forge and weld. She could show people how to blow fire, or to lay on a bed of nails . . . I guess things don't always go as planned. It's kind of funny, she would always talk about death; she was thinking about going to mortuary school. It makes sense too, her obsession.

She had been battling cancer for years, she had accepted the fact that she was going to die, maybe even soon, and because of that she refused to be governed by fear, she refused to let beauty slip by unnoticed; the woman had heart. I guess that's what it boils down to; being with Emma, it made me really think about death. It's not just rhetoric—one day, every one of us will be dead, one way or another. We can sit back and watch life drip away, or we can splash it on the walls, write our poetry in our blood and tears. Yes, Emma died, but she is not dead. She lives on in me, in her mother Leslie, her father Terry, and in her sister Blair and in countless other people her life has touched. Her strength is infectious, it burns in me like a fever, and, armed with the tragic beauty of her life and her passing, I greet each new day, because I know I am not alone. None of us is—we all carry with us the memories of the people who went before, those we have lost. Emma knew the price she would pay and greeted it with open arms.

And while I'm sure she had regrets, I am equally sure that if she were alive today, she would still put it all on the line for a friend, for love, for hope. Yeah, life is short. Too short. Too short not to take any risks. Thank you, Emma, for your fearsome beauty and continued support.
With all my heart, CB

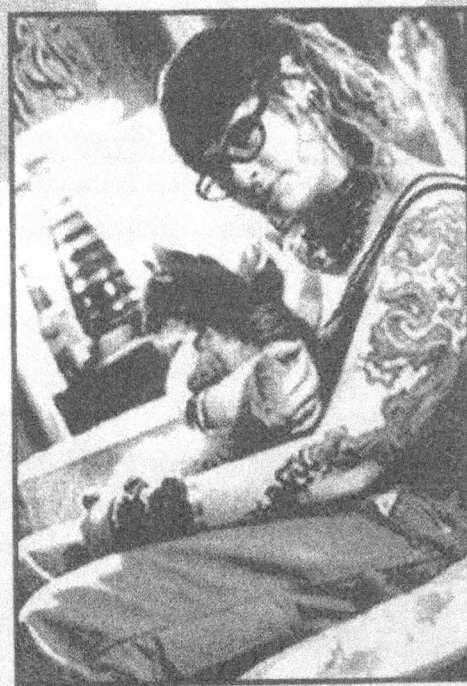

They are playing a game. They are playing at not playing a game. If I point this out, I will be in trouble—I must play their game, that this is not a game, and play no other.

They are not having fun. I can't have fun if they aren't. If I can help them to have fun, I can have fun. Helping them to have fun is not fun—it is hard work.

A little boy comes along and says "Let's have fun." But having fun is a waste of time, because it doesn't help me to help them have fun.

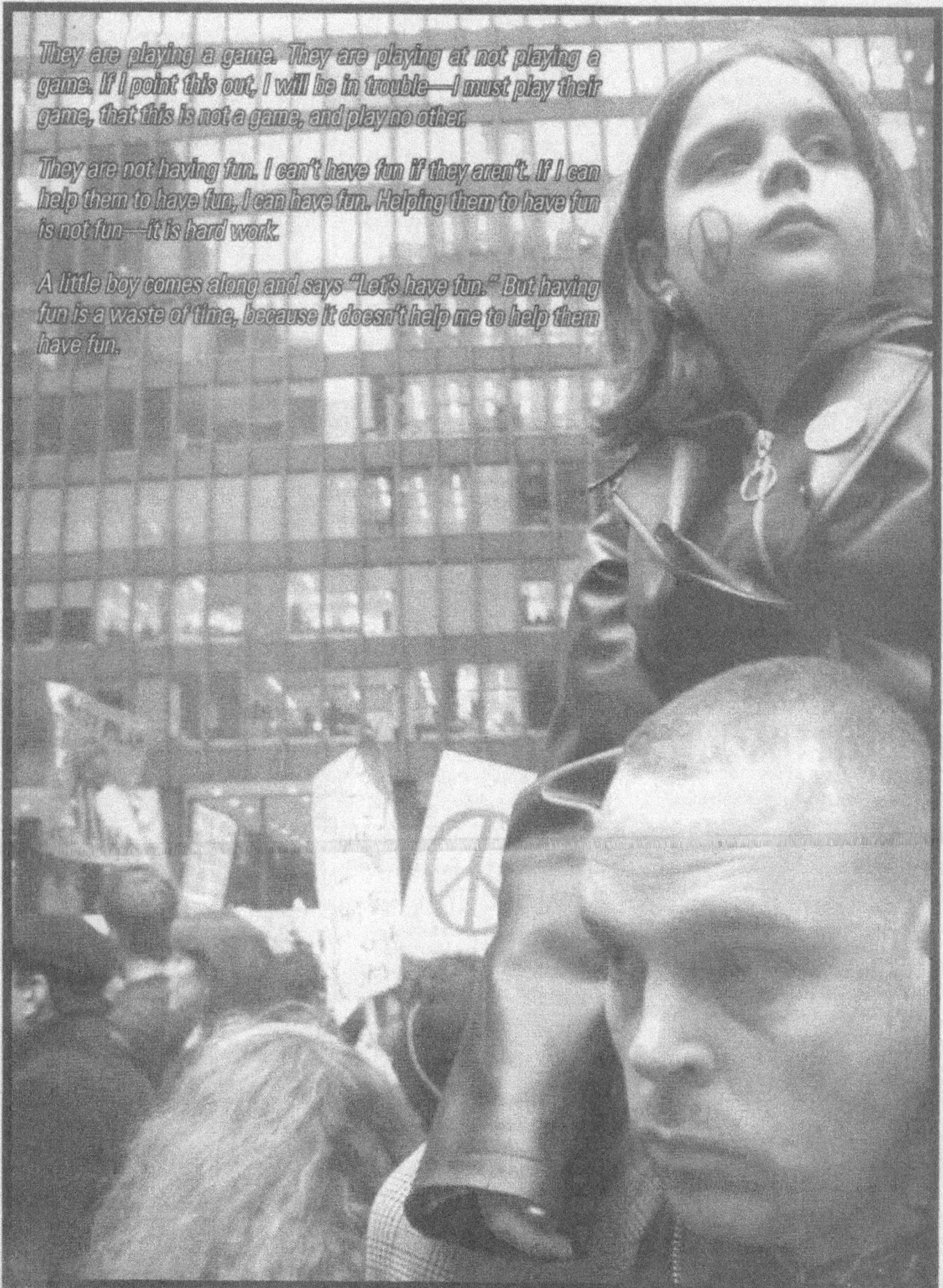

We Have Worked Hard to Improve Activism—now it must be destroyed.

Do you consider yourself a specialist in revolution? Does your heart sing in your chest at the sound of words like coalition, consensus, spokescouncil, social justice, friendly amendment? Is your idea of a good time *a facilitated discussion intended to promote dialogue focusing on anti-oppression work in anti-authoritarian community organizing and movement-building for broad-based social change coming from a place of privilege?* Do you think there's always a good reason to have another meeting—or, in the words of one author, that "freedom is an endless meeting"? Brace yourself, my friend, the diagnosis is grim: it sounds like you have been infected with activism.

Whoa, Nelly! I thought activism was a good thing, was *the* good thing—I thought we were trying to create a new generation of activists, who would, issue by issue and struggle by struggle, finally fix everything! Why criticize activism itself, the knight in shining armor we're counting on to save us all?

Well, for one thing, activism today isn't something we can all participate in. This is obvious, but the next obvious question should be whether it is setting the stage for something we can all join in, or just consolidating opposition as the private domain of experts. There's some of each going on, of course; but, sad to say, activism as we know it is something that seems to attract people who act, however unconsciously, as though they have something at stake in keeping the sphere of social change all to themselves. The typical activist takes great pride in his status as Someone Who Cares, the implication being that those who are not activists are therefore apathists, Those Who Do Not Care; in every conflict, he is "on the side of the angels"—that is to say, as the civilians who are more aware of their own imperfections realize, against all of us. That activism attracts an inordinate number of such individuals, at least during the lulls between revolutionary upheavals, should come as no surprise: except in those moments when it really seems the world is about to change, who but those most prone to fighting and judging would choose to specialize in "fighting for justice"? To quote an

"Activist": A dreamer who has converted to "realism."

old cynic, "the urge to save humanity is almost always a front for the desire to rule."

This is not to say that activism is entirely the province of the self-centered and self-righteous, but rather that we must be careful not to let them—and those aspects of ourselves—set the tone for our efforts. Likewise, we have to be aware of all the ways we can intimidate or estrange others—not least of all, the ways our efforts not to do so can be even more alienating.

Take the buzzwords and sentiments above: regardless of your values regarding the important questions to which they ultimately refer, they either make you feel at home ("I, too, am an activist, Saving The World!") or totally alienated, depending on whether or not you already have (or want) a place as an insider in a certain activist culture. Think of the older homeless guy or factory worker—or, for that matter, the rebellious high school kid!—who comes to an activist spokescouncil meeting, and is impressed with the non-hierarchical atmosphere but finds the walls of jargon and procedure virtually impenetrable. Sometimes these folks do stick around, but we shouldn't flatter ourselves that they do so primarily because we've created a "safe space" with all our complicated processes—if they stick around, it's more often a tribute to their own courage and patience than to our sensitivity. We activists have tried to develop a code of behavior and language that is free of domination, an alienation-free protocol—but protocol itself is alienating, unless one is among those actively developing it. Raised as many of us were by middle managers from the middle class, we naturally tend to take it into our

Despite all our proclamations to the contrary, revolution was still a mere concept for us, a fantasy future—the social revolution, when we would put into practice at last all those abstractions about transforming life; the personal revolution, when we would finally love ourselves as we were and live life like it really was ending one minute at a time. Calling for mass actions in the name of total liberation, we still hesitated to speak to one another about our dearest dreams; defacing diet billboards, decrying patriarchal propaganda, we still put off coming to terms with our own bodies, still wondered if it wouldn't be easier just to lose that weight than somehow persuade ourselves it was beautiful. All those declarations, those fables of revolution—perhaps they were just stuff and nonsense; such concepts spring from the psychological needs of those who trade in them at least as much as from any insight into what is desirable or possible. Looking at the concepts we created, the revolution we spoke of, it seems we needed to be in unreciprocated love with some apocalyptic event (just as many of us were, not coincidentally, with people) at least as much as we actually needed or expected one. This longing suffused everything with meaning, but it also made everything bearable—when we'd once felt, and still continued to insist, that it was all unbearable.

We had found ways of surviving, after all: we, who prided ourselves on our intransigence, who had lived through moments when it seemed the old order was truly crumbling and had pledged ourselves to defend and extend these or die trying; we too found ways to bide time and lose ourselves in routine, albeit a

hands to manage situations even in our attempts to relinquish power and privilege. Yes, it's critical that we make sure that our relationships are free of unhealthy power dynamics, as far as we're able; but when it comes to connecting our little circles to the broader social context, far better that we concentrate our energies on learning how to speak and translate other communities' languages than on developing our own perfect set of oppression-free norms, rules, and lingo.

Yet it's not just that we tend to alienate others incidentally, on account of our cultural conventions; sometimes our most deliberate actions are the most disempowering for others who would fight for control of their lives. If anything characterizes activists as a group, it is that we feel entitled to "organize," to take charge wherever resistance occurs. All too often, when people begin breaking out of the control of the usual authorities, activists assume command: the outraged or overjoyed crowd charges into the street, blocking the intersection, and holds that territory until the activist, negotiating with the police, announces that an agreement has been reached and now it's time to disperse. Activists set the tone and language for discussions, and thus limit the pool of possible participants in such discussions. Activists attempt to rally and direct opposition in communities, and end up setting limits upon the object and scope of that opposition—sometimes disconnecting it entirely from the lives of those who were first drawn to it because it involved them directly. Activists establish themselves as the representatives of social change, and thus alienate from social change itself those who cannot see themselves reflected in these representatives. We have to get a

routine of resistance. We developed our own rituals to commemorate the ghosts of insurrections past, and slowly, famished for something tangible to live on, came to mistake these formalities for liberation itself.

Meanwhile, whether we were paying attention or not, little sparks of revolution continued to shoot through the lives of the civilians around us. Yes, revolution: the electricity would go out on a street, and neighbors who had never met would find themselves marveling at the stars together. Revolution: a child would witness, for the first time, exultant crowds filling the streets after his favorite team won a football game; and for that precious hour, as strangers embraced like fast friends and benches were torn from bus stops to feed bonfires, his world was suffused with a magic possibility that seemed as natural as it was new. Revolution: a couple would fall deeply in love, into the kind of love that makes everything that came before seem like a mere shadow of living—and, gazing into one another's eyes one morning until the solipsism dropped away and the fact of another's thinking, feeling existence became almost palpable, would suddenly be gripped by the wild idea that in an alternate world one might look out across the rooftops and feel that grateful for everyone's existence.

To those who were not fortunate or unfortunate enough to be counted in our ranks, who felt repressed from all sides at once in a way they couldn't even begin to articulate, to whom these restraints seemed to be forces of nature—to these people, as it once had to us, revolution manifested itself above all as a shaking off of reality, a system shock, a cleansing chaos. For those who had lived their whole lives under the burdens of

sense of our own little place in the social cosmos, of the scale of what we can do without overreaching ourselves or interfering with others' autonomy.

The role of "activist" must itself be ended and transcended to attain the ends it exists to pursue. Roles and specialization (i.e. division of labor) are inherent in and necessary to the capitalist nightmare; in this scarcity-based system, those who choose one role do not usually make it more accessible or inviting to others, but less so. If our goal really is to remake a world of universal self-determination, then our primary project must always be to enable others to gain whatever capabilities we have, not to engage in any form of symptomatic treatment for the ills of capitalist society.

So what can we do? We can maintain an awareness of the ways our own psychological motivations for activism become obstacles to its effectiveness. We can focus on exercising, sharing, and reproducing our powers, rather than consolidating them. We can focus on what we are able to do without lobbying or directing others; we might even be more effective, not less, if we concentrated on resisting honestly for ourselves rather than for everyone. We would do well to remember that while we can make revolutions in our own lives, revolution itself is not just ours. We need to be done with the sort of false modesty that enables us to act like megalomaniacs while demurring that "we're not in charge" or "our own processes of self-criticism are never concluded." The real heroes are not activists, but rather those of other backgrounds who are willing to step out of their comfort zones to work or speak with us; it's great when we do our best to smooth

toil, police, self-recrimination, it seemed the aftereffects of this repression could only be escaped by means of a transfiguring experience; perhaps one had to awaken, as the more privileged among us had been lucky enough to, under different constellations, surrounded by beautiful foreigners, to feel ready to revel, risk, revolt. But there were not enough foreign lands to accommodate all the individuals who needed this experience, nor ways to get them there; we would have to conjure them here, somehow, on domestic soil.

Pondering how to accomplish this, I began to suspect that the culture we revolutionaries had developed was not so revolutionary after all, that there might be more liberation going on during one of those power outages than there was in a hundred of our spokescouncil meetings. We had worked so hard to develop ways of interacting freely, had refined a complex system of cultural norms and models of conduct—all this, in order to be free of the old ones! Yet our anarchist protocol could feel as alienating as any other. Perhaps what we needed most was not new mores so much as more volatile situations, seeds which could contain any number of starting points. If someone could create a situation no one could believe, it might do a lot more to create anarchy than any activism by-the-numbers. If someone could do so in an infectious way—well then! Perhaps capital-R Revolution after all!

That revolution is, in fact, taking place today—it is always taking place, though it usually has little to do with our rhetoric. It is simply the rupture point, the fault line running through every society. It is the threshold over which people pass into believing in miracles, for

the way for this, but we don't deserve the credit for it. At best, activists could be a "linking class" between diverse struggles and peoples, drawing on our personal fascination with resistance wherever it appears to help connect disparate resistances (Brazilian landless farmers to punk rockers, middle class mothers to homeless folks, abuse/addiction counselors to eco-warriors)—not to "build alliances" for its own sake (or for the sake of creating a constituency for "community organizers" to "represent"!), but in order that individuals and communities might assist one another in their immediate efforts towards liberation.

So this is not a call for the end of activism for its own sake, either, but rather so it can finally give rise to the revolution we all hoped it would in the first place. In the following fragments we'll address just a few of the aspects of our activism that could use reworking: the predominance of white privilege in certain activist circles (and the counterproductive ways white folks address this in each other), the pitfalls of valuing theory over action (and the useless infighting this can occasion), the ridiculousness of both "lifestyle" (read as: lazy) anarchists and their equally idle critics, and the apprehensions we all have about being seen as "extreme." Have fun reading, and try not to get too defensive—this isn't intended as an attack on anyone by means of ideas, but rather as an attack on ideas for everyone's sake!

lack of a better word—and, in that state of grace, find themselves able to enact them, to change things that were immutable before. Sooner or later, they return from across that frontier, even if they arrive as "committed lifelong activists"—and all the worse, really, for a people to be burdened with a class of activists who no longer honestly believe in miracles! One must be a real romantic, a maniac who trusts in fairy tales more than reality, to remain long beyond that horizon, let alone expect the world to join her there. But that—believing in the unbelievable—is what it will take for our dreams to come true, is what makes such dreams possible at all.

So we would-be revolutionaries, if we would be revolutionaries, must find those fault lines in ourselves and trace them to the corresponding fissures in our civilization. And—more than that—we must live in such a way that miracles are not unthinkable for us. We have everything to learn from the family that experiences an unfamiliar pleasure in responding to a sudden crisis, or the dropout who discovers that pure sailing free joy that human beings are capable of—that is our birthright and should be where the dead stares on the subwaybound daytoilers' faces are. That some yet persist from one day to the next, believing in miracles in a world that denies all magic and mystery, is itself the greatest of miracles: and proof that we can, in fact, do anything.

Here we go again:

Maybe you know the story of the young white anticapitalist who was arrested during protests against the Democratic National Convention in Los Angeles, summer of 2000. After being jailed, he was eventually thrown in general population at the prison, where he remained until his friends and family paid his bail. His first day in, another white guy, sporting some sketchy tattoos, approached him. "I appreciate what your movement is doing out there," the stranger began.

"Oh, you do? That's great," replied our protagonist, relieved. Was this the masses, finally coming around?

"Yeah—I appreciate it, because it's a *white* movement."

This didn't sound quite as encouraging. "I'm afraid I don't understand what you mean."

"Oh, you know what I mean."

"No, I don't," insisted the young activist, torn between outrage, fear, and confusion—he wanted to point to the anti-racist values of his community, the work they'd done to confront the inequalities of the capitalist system, but when he thought about it, all his fellow activists and protesters, all the people arrested with him, they *were* almost all white. Distraught, ashamed, and hoping to avoid conflict, he spent the rest of the day hiding out from the guy with the swastika on his chest.

This encounter brought up a lot of difficult questions for the boy who lived it, as it still does for our community. It's no secret that, even though the subject has become more widely discussed over the past few years, white activists as a whole still have a lot of progress to make unlearning our role in the system of white supremacy. There are now some good dialogues going on about this, and one of the main reasons the subject hasn't been addressed before in Inside Front or other CrimethInc. materials is that we had little to add to the perspectives others were already offering. But at the same time, this issue is occasionally addressed in ways that are ultimately counter-productive—that obscure the real issues, or even alienate the people who most need to hear and listen to these critiques. Who's ready to rethink the ways white activists have been addressing the question of their own (and, more to the point, each other's) privilege? Who dares to risk saying anything about such a sensitive topic?

Yet there's no getting around it: we have to consider not only how we can unlearn our racist programming, but also how we can encourage other white folks to do so who don't necessarily place political consciousness at a premium. Currently, the dialogue about race, class, and privilege is limited to the more political fringes of the punk rock scene; elsewhere, punks go on ignoring the issues, believing them to be the private domain of the vindictive and guilt-ridden. We can blame this on the general apathy and defensiveness of the white middle class; but all the same, if we don't do our part to make a critique of white supremacy common outside our oh-so-right-on anarcho-punk ghetto, we have only ourselves to blame for it.

Is there anything we're doing in presenting these issues that is needlessly alienating? Considering that we white folks have been raised to specialize in alienating others and each other, and that even the most vehement anti-oppression activist is still infected with the lust for power this society teaches each of us, the answer is probably yes. We don't need another generation of white activists wallowing in guilt complexes, or attempting to create them in others—we need to focus on making actual progress towards overthrowing white supremacy. Considering one's racial privilege should appear to the public as a useful way to enhance one's relations with others, not simply a pastime for neurotic masochists. In the worst-case scenarios, white activists actually use the race issue as a way to get the upper hand in power struggles with other white activists: competing to speak "on behalf" of the ones not involved in the discussion, throwing around accusations rather than helping each other improve, we only hinder the struggle against white supremacy. In light of this, I propose we step back and reconsider some of our assumptions about race, privilege, and how to address them in our community and struggle.

Let's start with the classic question: why is there so little racial diversity in the North American anarchist movement? I can only address this as an insider, being a white kid myself, but I've got some hunches about what's going on. First, I want to point out that the question itself is slanted: the more homogenous the circles the inquirer travels in, the more he will answer with an alarmist negative. There are in fact anarchists of all different ethnicities, colors, and classes active in the United States (whether they use the word "anarchist" to describe themselves or not), and the suggestion that there are not reflects as much on the speaker's narrow experience as it does on the conditions he purports to describe—asked this question, one might reply: *which* anarchist movement? Second, there are plenty of reasons people of color are hesitant to get involved in predominantly white anarchist movements. Historically, we white activists are fuckups—every time a struggle has gotten really intense or the government has really come down on some

Punk, Activism, and White Privilege

From one white punk kid from a middle class family to another

organization of color, we've been nowhere in sight (John Brown is pretty much the exception that proves the rule). Even today, most of us have made so little progress challenging our own racism and self-importance that I can only imagine how difficult it is for others to work with us; and even if that wasn't the case, it still wouldn't mean that the projects people in our community tend to take on, or the tactics with which we proceed, are necessarily relevant to folks from other communities—as I'll discuss further below. These are all points that others in our community have taken great pains to emphasize, about which others can be more eloquent than I can.

Now let's try a follow-up question that is often glossed over: given that our communities—especially the North American punk rock scene—are disproportionately white, in what ways is this a problem, and in what ways is it not necessarily one? Certainly, by keeping to mostly-white social circles, white folks miss out on a lot of the perspectives and challenges to our comfort we need—not to mention hoarding for ourselves the power our privilege gives us. On the other hand, trying to figure out how to get folks from other backgrounds to join *our* movement is self-centered, if not imperialist: who says we have the answers to everyone's problems? Who says our tactics should be everyone's tactics? To the extent that people of color didn't participate in direct action against the World Trade Organization in Seattle because white activists created an uncomfortable environment, we have a problem we have to solve; but if it is also true that great numbers of people of color didn't participate because they thought they had better things to do, we should trust their judgment. This doesn't mean that we're necessarily doing the wrong thing by protesting there—it may be good for everybody in the long run if we do—but that particular fight may be our problem, our responsibility. Before we assume that everyone who isn't there with us is just doing nothing instead, we need to educate ourselves about what they are doing in their own communities. That knowledge will prove very important.

And speaking of communities, let's not throw out the baby with the bathwater—if punk rock appeals to a mostly white demographic, that's not necessarily a problem. The fact that, this being the case, punk rock will inevitably offer limited perspectives on the world and limited chances for white folks to learn to interact outside their comfort zones *is* an important factor to consider at all times; in view of this, punks will hopefully make an effort to look beyond the walls of their subcultural ghetto for insight and education, and take great pains not to be alienating or insensitive to those of color who are involved in punk. But the homogeneous nature of the punk scene (or, to be more specific, some punk scenes) is not necessarily an argument against its existence or value. In fact, if the punk/anarchist community was somehow transformed into a foundation upon which a reliable, predominantly-white revolutionary movement could be built that deserved trust and showed solidarity with other movements, that would be as worthwhile a purpose as any radical subculture could ever hope to serve.

Many concerns about the overwhelming whiteness of certain activist movements center on the issue of representation, which I think is something of a red herring. For democratic, socialist, and communist governing structures, which are supposed to wield the disembodied power of the community at large, representation is an important issue, perhaps the most important; but anarchists, on the whole, do not believe

in "representation"—we don't believe in giving our power to others, we prefer to represent ourselves. Some democrats and communists seem to think one black person can represent all black people on a board of directors; anarchists don't believe that any individual can represent a group, or that any group, however similar the members may be in terms of ethnicity, gender, class, etc., can be summarized. Accordingly, anarchist structures are not intended to represent any person outside them, nor to wield power over others, but rather to enable those who participate without disabling anyone else. Assuming they succeed in this tall order, then, a lack of diversity does not necessarily imply an imbalance of power; the important question becomes, instead, whether the group is proceeding in a way that enables it to have the diversity it needs to accomplish the purposes for which it exists. For example, if a Food Not Bombs is intended to serve the needs of folks from diverse communities, it's stupid to have the cooking take place at a private house belonging to white people, where people from other backgrounds are less likely to feel comfortable; on the other hand, if you book a punk show in your basement and everyone who comes is white, that doesn't *necessarily* mean the event is consolidating power for white people at everyone else's expense—provided you're not gentrifying the neighborhood and driving your neighbors crazy, that is!

All this is *not* to say it isn't important for activists from predominantly white movements to develop relationships with people from other backgrounds. It *is* important, very important, and it's something that rarely happens—so I want to talk about one way white activists can foster this, since the responsibility lies on us to make this possible. Again, it's not realistic or right on to expect people of other backgrounds, with different interests, to join a project once it's already started and the goals, procedures, and tone established—especially not if the ones you're hoping to attract have been oppressed by people who look like you their whole lives. Projects that are to cut across ethnic lines have to be multiracial from the start, so they can develop with everyone involved having their interests respected and thus feeling a sense of ownership. But why would anyone of color want to start a project with white activists, anyway? If we want to work with people from other communities, we first have to build trust, establish actual friendships that common causes can be founded upon. To do so, we need to learn what revolutionary projects people of color are

undertaking that we can get behind, and support these, following their initiatives in the process rather than seeking to impose any leadership of our own. This is right on, anyway, since we white folks have a lot of resources that it would be senseless to keep to ourselves. In the process of working together, people will get to know each other, and the next project, or the one after that, can be initiated together—provided you always keep an eye out for where your privileges can be applied for everyone's benefit, and where your conditioning is interfering.

I want to add a few proposals that I hope can assist our community in making more progress with these issues. First, let's do our best to avoid framing discussions of specific cases in terms of whether a person, group, or tactic is "racist" or not—this approach immediately establishes a polarizing conflict complete with accusations, denials, all the makings of a long-term community-fracturing feud. It also provides an easy out for those not accused of racism to avoid reflecting on their own behavior: "I'm not one of the racists," they can say to themselves, "we already purged all of them." Instead, let's approach every discussion with the assumption that, as we were all raised in a racist society, we would all do well to consider constantly how we can improve our conduct and consciousness. In such a context, discussion can focus on offering practical, constructive advice and perspective, rather than bogging down in debates between people who each believe that their subjective experience is the objective truth. Forget about whether you're "a racist" or not, "objectively" speaking—if someone else subjectively feels that you are behaving in a racist or insensitive manner, you should value their perspective enough to focus on listening instead of defending yourself.

Second, let's make a distinction between activities that *utilize* privilege and actions that *abuse* or *reinforce* privilege. Simply having privilege, or doing things that those without your privileges cannot, neither of these things alone is unjust. After all, we all have privilege to some extent or another: some have white privilege, some have the privilege of an able body, etc. The problem comes when individuals take their privileges for granted, or feel entitled to more privilege than others, comfortably accepting the advantages a hierarchical, discriminatory society has accorded them at others' expense rather than challenging these iniquities. But individuals possessed of privileges can take advantage of this to undermine the system that conferred them: the U.S. citizen staying in a Zapatista village so the Mexican army will not dare attack it is an example of this, the upper class dropout who spends her trust fund on rent for a community center may be another—assuming she doesn't behave as if she owns the place. If it is not the case that privilege can be applied for good, if simply having privilege in the first place is itself evidence of guilt, then the reactionary morons who characterize our politics as a race to the bottom in pursuit of the righteousness of total victimhood are correct in their analysis. Therefore, it makes little sense to criticize, for example, white shoplifters for taking advantage of the fact that security guards pay less attention to them; the real question is, can this power be used in a way that helps in the struggle against the system of domination, or does it necessarily reinforce that system no matter how it is applied? And assuming it can be used in such a way—say, by white kids stealing spices for a multi-racial Food Not Bombs—how can those white kids be persuaded to do so, rather than alienated by accusations of white privilege and guilt? From now on, we have to be very specific and very nuanced in all our considerations of the issue of privilege, not just throw the term around dismissively.

Finally, to ensure that all our discussions of this issue are more productive than vindictive, I have a suggestion: every time someone brings up white privilege in the punk/activist/anarchist community, they should give concrete, reproducible examples of approaches they have tried or at least heard about that have successfully addressed it and worked to dismantle it. This will ground discussions in the important question of how to change things, and circumvent the twin pitfalls of mudslinging and wallowing in guilt. I think that many people in our community really want to fight white supremacy in all its manifestations, but have no idea where or how to begin; the more examples we have to work from, the easier it will be for each of us to figure out how to get going. Hearing too much about problems without hearing about possible solutions can be overwhelming and immobilizing, anyway; it's always best to aim for a ratio of 50% critique to 50% proposition.

In that spirit, I'll conclude with a story from the small Southern city I sometimes call home, about an instance in which some punk rockers connected their activities to an issue affecting others outside their social stratum. I think it illustrates well the way activists can be a "linking class," making the things different social groups do anyway into effective resistance tactics simply by linking them to each other.

An innocent young black man was injured in a car accident; the police showed up before the ambulance did, and one of them shot him to death. Such a senseless murder is typical of racist police violence, but unfortunately that isn't the end of the story; when the parents of the murdered man called the police officer who killed their son a murderer, the police department sued them. Members of the activist community engaged the parents in dialogue, and they said they wanted to make a fuss about the murder and call attention to it.

This is where the punks come in. Black-clad, patch-wearing punk rockers, the kind uptight activists and liberals often deride as alienating on account of their wardrobes alone, lived in this city. They didn't have a lot of money to help with the court costs, and they didn't have ties to any voting bloc that could be called upon to pressure the local government; but they did shoplift and screenprint and spraypaint a lot. Normally, these skills were only used to affirm their subcultural values in isolation from the larger community, but soon the parents of the young man had a closet full of screenprinted shirts to sell to raise awareness and legal funding, and the walls and sidewalks of the city came alive with graffiti: *Gil Barber killed by Deputy Gordy, Deputy Gordy=Murderer*. There were demonstrations organized, and great numbers of punk rockers and their friends turned out to show support for the parents and opposition to the police. All these combined to exert force back on the police, to make their callous court case cost them public support and let them know they couldn't expect to get away with murder.

Nothing we could do could restore Gil Barber to life, or make up for this tragedy; but the case against his parents was dropped, and now our communities are connected. Gil's mother, radicalized by the injustice done her but also by her good experiences with young folks in funny outfits, is now involved in other ongoing struggles, as others are in hers. It's a humble little story, but perhaps an example of what could be possible on a much grander scale.

Just for the sake of Argument...

DRAMATIC DEBATE

"CAN THE LAW BE ENFORCED?"

SUNDAY JUNE 6th

8:00 O'CLOCK

"If you want to immobilize a person, ask him to speak more on a subject. The more he speaks, the less immediate his need to act will be."

–Bill Gates, inventor of the internet discussion forum

There are times when no distinction need be made between speaking and acting—in such situations, speaking is itself acting. And there are times when action is not yet called for, when discussion, deliberation, and planning must take place first.

There are other situations, though, in which people talk—or, more frequently, argue—instead of doing. Ideas and theories become commodities, extensions of their owners' egos, like the dogs at a dogfight; like the dogs at a dogfight, they are pitted against each other, each against all with the owners' rhetoric for claws, logic for teeth, and quick wits for reflexes. The glory of winning a debate, the gratifying knowledge that one is smarter than others, the righteousness of being right, these are exhilarating and addictive drugs—and when one has given up hope of ever effecting or experiencing real change, pursuing these consolation prizes can be a very seductive surrogate activity.

It is the nature of commodities that while they appear to increase the wealth and power of the one who possesses them, in fact they represent his dispossession—since, in capitalist society, one must give up parts of oneself (control over one's time and the products of one's labor and invention, faithfulness to one's conscience, the possibility of a life based on cooperation rather than competition) in return for the power to purchase substitutes for them. It is no different with ideas: when they become competing commodities, when there's not enough rightness and righteousness to go around and people struggle against each other to "win" arguments instead of benefiting from each other's perspectives, the ensuing competition can only maintain the dispossession of all involved by interfering with their power to find common cause or at least establish mutually beneficial relationships.

There are anarchists who "develop their theory" with the same obsessive energy others put into collecting and restoring fancy automobiles, who exhibit and defend their theses with that same fervor and combative spirit. In these contests of egos disguised as debate, whenever one wins an argument at the expense of good feeling everyone loses. It is just as important that we foster good relationships that can form a foundation for putting our ideas into practice as it is that we foster the ideas themselves. Theory serves the interests of no one as end in itself, though the personal gratification one finds in vanquishing a rival theorist can almost make one feel as though the revolution is that much closer. Theory is only one of many resources which must be developed socially—that is, in a way that promotes respect, affinity, and trust—in order to arm individuals and groups to liberate themselves and protect each other. Anarchy isn't just a good idea in a vacuum—it is dialogue and mutual aid empowered to enforce the conditions which make them possible.

Some theorists whose bark is more frequent than their bite would defend their predilection for hostile, confrontational rhetoric and/or endless abstraction by arguing that, as the development of theory is never finished, it is folly to call for solidarity, outreach, and action in place of further discussion. But finished or not, we must constantly act on our theories, as much as we think on them—otherwise our thinking will be ill-informed, to say the least. Theory is not some retirement fund one can work to cultivate and then finally cash in—theory is thought which informs ongoing action, or else it is thought without teeth. To misquote the famous buffoon, "a theory can only describe the world—the point, however, is to live in it." Or, in the words of a more recent wiseguy, "any idea which is allowed to flow into action is a spell cast for more of the same"—what spell are we casting when we get caught up in endless debates, instead? And how are we to act with the power we can only have among friends, if our endless debates alienate us from each other?

We must once and for all discard the academic's notion that there is any real distinction between thinking and action: even the most silent actions speak volumes, and every articulation of thought is itself an action—even if it is merely a wordy opting for inaction. As actions should be evaluated according to whether they are good ideas, so articulations of theory should be evaluated according to their effectiveness as actions. The best-sounding theory is worthless if it results in no practice; the most educated debate is meaningless if it does not produce a change for the better in at least someone's life.

To make this concrete: Please, please, all you brilliant anarchist theoreticians, stop fighting amongst yourselves and figure out how to accomplish together the goals you have in common. No matter how smart you all are, your current squabbles are doing no one any good, not even yourselves.

Do you still insist that we answer your favorite question, that we declare what brand of anarchists we, which suffix we prefer to use to ghettoize ourselves? All of them, we will reply: we are anarcho-syndicalists on the shop floor, anarcho-primitivists in the forest, anarcho-communists when there's something to share, social anarchists in our communities, individualists when you catch us alone, insurrectionists when the shit hits the fan— above all, we are revolutionary anarchists, we are anarchists who believe that, as life and culture are essentially matters of context, it is up to us above all to challenge and transform this context and be prepared to start from scratch afterwards. Therefore, we don't waste much time prognosticating or constructing vast systems of protocol. We act now to change what outrages us and pursue what attracts us; we will reevaluate and act again later. We don't want to mistake our analyses for the world, nor mistake critique for liberation itself; we try not to get too comfortable with our ideological positions—they are chiefly tools with which we work towards change, not masters commanding it of us. We choose our individual strategies for enacting change based on our individual characteristics and preferences, as much as on abstract strategizing which may or may not prove accurate; we don't expect our theories and

"In the end, our most dangerous enemies are not the subversive operatives themselves, who can be isolated and exterminated if it becomes necessary; they are, rather, those who offer constructive criticism of their efforts. Fortunately, such criticism can be buried beneath an avalanche of hostility and impertinence.

Make every discussion into a debate with two opposed sides, pro- and anti-. This distracts attention from the ideas and subjects in question; it also compels all parties to entrench themselves in rigid positions. Always ▓▓▓▓▓▓▓▓▓▓▓ refer to your opponent's ideas as if they constitute a fixed, disembodied ideology; always address your opponent as if he is an automaton serving this ideology, not a complex being with a life history behind him. Never approach involved persons with questions; always take your criticisms directly to the public. Do not offer any strategy other than your own the benefit of the doubt. Focus on the very simplest, stupidest, weakest ▓▓▓▓▓▓▓▓▓▓▓▓▓▓▓▓▓▓▓▓ material; points in any ▓▓▓▓▓▓▓▓▓ emphasize these. Disregard subtleties. Pick a simple accusation and stick with it, repeating it over and over until everyone is so fed up that they leave the entire arena of discussion ▓▓▓▓▓▓▓▓▓▓▓ to escape your negativity.

Make your objections simpler than your target text or tactic; it must be easier to be against it than it is to understand and interpret it. Unblushingly judge books by their covers. People should be able to take a stand with you without having to learn anything about the subject. Make it a style to dismiss as a style; make it a trend to accuse of being a trend.

Attack egos, exhaust patience, be as incoherent as possible. Make it impossible for anyone to derive anything positive from your tirades, despite their best intentions and efforts to get past your aggressive tone. When speaking of aspects of their work which make you feel alienated, for example, be as alienating as possible yourself. Defensiveness is what you want to provoke, above all-- it discredits like nothing else.

Whatever ▓▓▓▓▓▓▓▓▓▓▓▓▓ demographics your opponent is reaching successfully, demonize. Utilize hot potato terms such as "sexist" and "classist"-- use them over and over, with as little specific reference as possible, until it is impossible to have constructive discussions about the important issues these accusations raise. Assume you can represent the views of individuals from backgrounds other than your own--especially demographics that "need" representing, as if they cannot do it themselves. Refer to bona fide representatives of these demographics, when they appear in positions you ▓▓▓▓▓▓▓▓▓▓▓▓▓▓▓▓▓▓▓▓▓▓ didn't expect, as "token."

Lower the level of discussion with pointless personal attacks, sarcasm, and self-righteousness. No depth is too low to stoop. Become obsessed with your crusade; calculate your blows to hurt feelings and offend bystanders. Everyone who has grown up in this vicious world has built up a certain amount of frustration and resentment; utilize this, learn how to trigger it in others. In every discussion, ▓▓▓▓▓▓▓▓▓▓▓ set negative energy in motion and make sure it wins out over constructive thought and respectful dialogue. Even if no one is persuaded by your arguments, this creates an environment that frightens off all outsiders.

Above all, be afraid. Be afraid of your own well-hidden doubts and vulnerabilities, and of others' reputed superiority-- and spread that fear, that shame, that guilt and resentment like a plague. Paralyze yourself and everyone else with blame for supposed imperfections. Hate yourself so much that you can only find respite in attacking others."

Point your guns in the right direction

The would-be revolutionary seeks criticism, above all—she relies upon this to refine her strategies, to learn from others' perspectives, to maintain her humility. She knows that evaluations of her efforts are of the utmost value to everyone involved in the revolutionary project, and so she is the first to insist that these efforts are far from perfect.

The most effective way to undermine her work is with *unconstructive* criticism. Harried by idle faultfinding, name-calling, petty attacks and personal vendettas, she eventually becomes deaf to all feedback—and thus frozen, neutralized.

Trust that your comrades are sincere about changing the world, and approach them with input as gently and supportively as you can. We're going to *win* this revolution, sooner or later, so there's no sense in taking out our frustrations on each other— but we're only going to win it together. Save the offensive for your true enemies—the ones with whom discussion solves nothing.

strategies to be relevant after the next big transformation—indeed, we hope they won't be. Whether our ideas are objectively "right" or not matters much less to us than whether they actually succeed in improving our lives.

And which ideology do we endorse, what brand of tactics do we extol as the One True Way? Organized federations or networks of friends, direct action or "community organizing"? These distinctions are dangerously distracting, if not outright false dichotomies. We defend the right of our comrades to organize and act however they want, and, more importantly, we won't waste everyone's time criticizing others for choosing different models than we do. We're grateful whenever others try something we wouldn't—it saves us the trouble, since every strategy for resistance must be tried, until something works! Whether some strategy is platformist or lifestylist, individualist or pacifist or adventurist is of little concern to us, so long as it is directed at genuine liberation and carried out with a modicum of respect for those trying other strategies. We didn't get involved in revolutionary politics because we liked sectarian infighting, or sports competitions, or politics for that matter; no, we simply wanted—and still want!— to get more out of life, to make it sweeter and fairer for all.

Being anarchists, aspiring to reorganize society on a cooperative basis and so studying the ways in which people can get along and support one another, we seek not to outsell the competition— whether they be capitalists, evangelical Christians, or other anarchists—but to hone our own abilities to foster harmony and mutual aid, and offer tools for this project to whoever wants them. Solidarity, not as unquestioning unity but rather as the ability to build mutually beneficial relationships with others however different they may be from ourselves, is of the utmost importance in this undertaking. When we say "solidarity," we mean neither simple allegiance to those who agree with us nor willingness to compromise ourselves in mutually unsatisfactory unions with those whose purposes run counter to ours. No, for us solidarity is a practice, a way of approaching every situation—it is almost a verb. Deeds are worth more than any words in this struggle, and actual cooperation is worth a million theoretical treatises on it.

A Letter to the Editors of Fifth Estate

September 2002, courtesy of the C.W.C. Anti-Squabbling Squad

"Just for the sake of argument—" I've just returned from the supermarket dumpster down the street, backpack full and graffiti pen empty, to a house from which CrimethInc. propaganda is distributed.

My friends look up from the piles of pamphlets and papers and posters they've been stuffing into boxes since morning, and cringe. "You know it's not going to be good," says the one with the beard—"when someone wants to talk 'for the sake of argument.'"

"Yeah," I allow, "that could have been an alternate title for that piece in the last Harbinger, 'Infighting the Good Fight.' All the same—I've been reading this piece in the new Fifth Estate, in which one Pono Bonobo endeavors to rescue pacifist anarchism as well as CrimethInc.—whatever the term means in that context—from those indignant class war anarchists, and I've been wondering: in point of literal fact, can't one actually use the master's tools to dismantle his house?"

"Well, yes, you can," he rejoins—"but you can't use the master's tools to dismantle his tools."

"Fair enough—what are you supposed to dismantle his house with instead, I wonder?"

"We've all been trying to figure that one out," laughs the one with the pigtails, folding a poster around a book. "I guess it's OK for everyone to try different things, so long as the house ends up dismantled and the tools in the ground."

"Yeah . . ." I'm unloading perfectly good bananas and mangos, as two of them seal up a huge package to Puerto Rico. "Bonobo and this 'Ashen Ruins' person on the internet have been hashing it out over which approach, violent direct action or nonviolent stuff like naked marching, is more appealing to the masses and so on, but I don't personally see why we can't have a movement with a place for both, in which they complement each other."

"I've found both rewarding and effective, at different times," offers my pigtailed friend, as she reaches for the tape.

"Some people are going to gravitate to one, and some the other, anyway—why not accept that and focus on how to integrate the two?" Beneath the bananas are big bags of salad greens. "And that brings me to my other question: I appreciate the editor's gesture of solidarity in rebuking anarchists who attack our projects, but I'm not sure if I think it's a good thing. I mean, it feels good for my ego, but that's usually a sign that something's dangerous."

"If we're being defended on the same grounds as we're being attacked, it's not so good," suggests a fourth voice. "Contrary to some charges, I don't see us as being 'lifestylist' at all—I've never seen anything with the CrimethInc. name on it urging people to 'drop out until the system collapses.' We've published stuff about some ways people from the more privileged classes can survive without working, but I always thought the idea was to use that liberated space to wage war for everyone's liberation. Revolution has to happen, somehow, and to have time to work on it, some of us will have to get our lives out of the work economy." She goes back to answering a letter.

"What's this 'we,' white man?" jokes back at her the smiling woman at the computer, deleting the orders for free papers that have been packaged this evening.

"The way I see it," the bearded one begins again, hefting a bundle of tabloids, "the last thing we need is to be defended from our critics in the anarchist community. First off, if we're serious about focusing our energies outwards, to those who could be involved in this struggle but aren't yet"—he takes a marker and begins addressing a box to a kid in Texas—"rather than inwards, for more struggling of anarchist against anarchist, then it just perpetuates the internal conflicts for other parties to take sides. Clarifications of misunderstandings, apologies for mistakes, those things we need; more bad energy, more battles between egos, we don't. Second, I wonder if it's occurred to the people at Fifth Estate that we might not mind these attacks—maybe it's our role to say and be things that are unpopular. Maybe for some, we can be most helpful as an enemy, something to rebel or react against."

The woman looks up from the computer again, more serious. "It seems to me that we actually have a symbiotic relationship with the class war anarchists. Their diatribes can serve to bring the same things we're talking about down to earth—I've learned things from them before. And, especially if someone does misunderstand our efforts as 'lifestylist,' that critique needs to be there to clarify what our literature did not. Our tactics don't and shouldn't work for everyone, and the Class Warriors are there to provide an alternative—viciously attacking us in print is just their way to let the world know it, and responding with insults of our own wouldn't improve anything. It's not like they interfere with our activities in practice."

"Yeah, the last place Evasion needs to be is the Wooden Shoe bookstore," agrees the pigtailed one. "Everyone shopping there already has points of entry for other approaches to radical organizing and living."

I'm finally unloading the potatoes at the bottom of my pack: the class warriors are right, we can only hope, that we scavengers will have to find other sources of food once the revolution comes; but for the time being it's sad and absurd that they aren't here to help us share this vast bounty with hungry families around town. "If anything, I'm annoyed by the way our anarchist critics all seem to read the texts so carelessly—like in that piece on the internet: 'Flipping through their first book speaks volumes,' or the other guy who brags that all he has to do is judge our book by its cover. I'll quote that Zapatista letter to Green Anarchy"—I rummage through the 'zine rack and find the issue—"here it is: If these "critiques" had included a detailed discussion on our tactics with reference to our history and current positions in the world, it wouldn't have been a big deal, nothing that we don't do constantly within our own organizations.' Without that, it just seems like they're looking to make enemies."

"But that's just my point," replies my bearded companion. "As long as we are getting that kind of constructive critique from some, we don't need every anarchist to read our work thoroughly, let alone praise it. We have to keep our eyes on the prize, as it were—keep focused on getting useful resources out to people not already involved in any anarchist community. That's the project we've taken on in this house, at least, right?" He gets a can of spray paint out to test a new stencil. "Anyway, that's why I wish our comrades at Fifth Estate, being well-versed in our materials and what has worked in our tactics to date, would focus on pointing out ways we can improve. We don't need defenders—or advertisers, at this point. We need insightful, creative critics."

DISPATCH FROM C.W.C.. CENTRAL COMMITTEE FOR IMMEDIATE RELEASE:

Quitting your job was about having more time to do what needs doing, not just isolating yourself from the rest of humanity—wasn't it?

If one makes propaganda extolling what is revolutionary about shoplifting, one is not necessarily trying to get would-be revolutionaries to shoplift so they can be "more revolutionary" [obviously a stupid approach if there ever was one—although exploring the tactical benefits of shoplifting for a class of people looking to do less buying might make sense]—one might instead be trying to identify for shoplifters what is already insurrectionary in their actions, so they can broaden their analysis of their own lives.

Crimethought is not any ideology or value system or lifestyle, but rather a way of challenging all ideologies and value systems and lifestyles—and, for the advanced agent, a way of making all ideologies, value systems, and lifestyles challenging. It is not crimethought just to survive without a job by dumpstering, squatting, and hitchhiking; it is crimethought to realize that this lifestyle provides resources that can be used to revolutionize demonstration activism, or underground literature. It is not crimethought simply to distribute propaganda attacking the monotony and limited options of traditional employment; it is crimethought to create situations in which both workers and ex-workers benefit from each others' different experiences, and consequently discover new options and new adventures that were previously obscured.

The Stalinists, Surrealists, Situationists, and even Southern Baptists all had their bloody purges and internal dissensions, so why can't we, too? Having no membership should be no obstacle: we can still hold exclusions from time to time, just to be sure everyone remembers. These are festive occasions for us weathered

politicos, analogous to the subtextual backbiting at the dinner parties of the bourgeoisie or the witch trials in the Salem, Massachusetts of old. But first, before we get into the fiery self-righteousness of the thing, some background.

It's been nearly a year now since I went through my entire proofing copy of the *Evasion* book in the dark back seat of a Greyhound traveling by night, with only my trendy activist headlamp for light. Even then, we knew already what the greatest drawback of publishing it in book form would be: all the general ideas in *Days of War, Nights of Love*, the inspirations and analyses and especially the rhetoric calculated to encourage revolt, would now be summed up in some minds by the specific formula spelled out by the stories in this new book. Even though *Evasion* is not a work of political theory, or a prescription of tactics, but clearly a personal account, a memoir—even though we've maintained from the beginning that there is no single strategy for insurgency, but that everyone must

ALL TRAVELER KIDS PURGED FROM CRIMETHINC. MEMBERSHIP

invent and reinvent their own—it was inevitable that we would be misunderstood by some, and we accepted that in publishing the book.

In publishing it, we wanted—to articulate this for the thousandth and last time—to introduce an account (one of many) of work-free living to a wider readership, and thus challenge conventional notions about the sanctity of property and the misery of material poverty. With this cultural warfare, we hoped to do our part to expand the anticapitalist movement. Sharing particular scams, extolling the lifestyle of the scam artist, these were secondary goals at best. The 'zine had already been produced and distributed on as massive a scale as the infrastructure of our d.i.y. underground allowed, to the demographics who would be most likely to utilize its scams and emulate the author's life choices; we printed the book version to see if this narrative of refusal and adventure could sow other seeds outside its native environment. Some of the feedback we've received from beyond the existing activist and anarchist communities suggests that it has; but now it's time to shake off whatever success we've achieved, as one must always do to make space for new attempts.

And to speak, for the last time as well, of how our efforts, with this book and other projects, have been misunderstood. There is a certain kind of reader who,

of these readers, by producing material that was too simplistic or too complex; perhaps this kind of reader is simply too rampant today to be altogether avoided by even the nimblest of propagandist's pens. One certainly can't say enough, though, that nothing in the world is one-dimensional.

So while this, too, has been said a million times, perhaps it will do some good to say it again in this context: the traveler kid lifestyle is not in itself at all revolutionary. It may surprise some to hear this from us—that shows how little they've been listening all along. Shoplifting, hitchhiking, scamming, unemployment—separated from a program of life- and world-transformation, all these are merely alternative tools for survival, a survival which makes do with and ultimately accepts the status quo. Yes, it *is* better, however infinitesimally, to steal products than to give money to our executioners—but it's not enough! Three millennia of shoplifting now, and the exchange economy is still thriving. If it's life we're after, not mere survival, as the old dichotomy goes, we can't just sit tight now in our squats and punkhouses, eating dumpstered bagels and selling our shoplifted wares on e-bay; we have to keep on risking everything to challenge the system that denies us the *rest* of the world, if for nothing else at least to continue challenging ourselves.

Nowadays, one who would think freely is in need of crimethought. But one who crimethinks is especially in need of anti-crimethought. And, to serve its purpose, crimethought must be forsaken, still more so anti-crimethought.

though you do your best to bring out the subtleties and ironies, will always focus on the most superficial, controversial terms in your works, and interpret your complex critiques as simple dismissals and endorsements ("paying=bad," "shoplifting=good"—or, far worse, "=anticapitalist"). Whether he professes to be your adversary or accomplice, it is best to avoid him altogether, for he will lower the level of dialogue on any issue to his own low denominator—and at that elevation, little of value can be discussed or achieved. Perhaps we can be blamed, in part, for creating some

For the record, and to briskly repudiate every imbecile who has used "CrimethInc." as a synonym for scamming and freeloading, we've never been interested in being or being seen as partisans of any lifestyle; we've always insisted that being radical involves subverting all possible lifestyle choices, all traditional strategies and identities. Revolution occurs when some part of the social equation changes: when apolitical workers initiate a wildcat strike, when middle-aged mothers start to show up in the black bloc beside their

sons and daughters, when vagabond dropouts integrate themselves into local struggles for affordable housing. The letters we receive from adult secretaries who have used CrimethInc. literature to inspire themselves to change their lives are infinitely more encouraging to me than the scores of teenagers reading *Harbinger* as they set out on the hitchhiking excursions young folks always have. Not that there is anything wrong with being a hitchhiking teenager—but to be a *dangerous* hitchhiking teenager, you must do something more than simply hitchhike, and interpreting anticapitalist texts as glorifications of your hitchhiking doesn't count.

I hopped my very first train just a few weeks ago, after nearly eight straight years of unemployment and anticapitalist agitation. For most of that time, I was never much of a hitch-hiking, train-hopping, scam-pulling traveler kid, and neither were most of the individuals I collaborated with—there are, believe it or not, a wide variety of other lifestyles that are equally conducive to such endeavors. The historical intersection of the latest wave of youth nomadism with the propaganda groups like ours have been spreading is, in some ways, unfortunate; it has had some good effects, but it has also made it easier for people to dismiss some radical ideas as the alibis of a new youth trend—or, worse, to believe that they are being radical simply by joining such a trend!

The creation of subcultural ghettos, the reinterpretation of subversive acts as promotions of some alternative lifestyle—these are processes by which opposition and subversion have been repeatedly neutralized over the past four decades, if not centuries. Yes, it is critical that we build new communities, with new cultural values and approaches, and that we not belittle these as "mere subcultures" when they do arise—for it is in these communities that we can develop and sustain a resistance, and create a context in which to lead free lives. It is also critical that we keep challenging these communities, that they do not become stagnant or self-satisfied: for as long as we are all under the great thumb, freedom is always for all or none.

CrimethInc., and for that matter (and far more important) crimethink, are not membership organizations, anyway. Subverting is not something you *are*, it's something you *do*, and must find new ways to do in every attempt. Let's not rest at expelling the traveler kids—hell, we're *all* expelled, time-tested CrimethInc. agents first and foremost! Even the most experienced of us insurrectionists must start from scratch every morning to foment insurrection, shaking off the inertia of the past to see anew what the current context calls for. When we succeed in doing this, we can change the world, for it is inertia above all that keeps the wheels spinning as they do. If we cannot, we are done for—we will be more anachronists than anarchists, and our activism mere retroactivism.

And so now we turn away from the past, from all explanations and justifications and apologies, to face the future and the experiments we have in store for it. Doubtless, they will occasion comparable storms of controversy and misconception, if we are ambitious enough to keep pushing our own limits and hazarding schemes crazy enough to work. So, all would-be crimethinkers are hereby expelled from CrimethInc.—whoever can discover the strategies for the next offensive, set the terms for the next infectious revolts and heated debates and social upheavals, let them claim it for themselves! Expect our next book, or one of them, to be a liberation manual for middle-aged mothers, not another youth's chronicle of willful indigence. In the meantime, let's us traveler kids stop congratulating ourselves on how free we are and start using that word, *free*, as a verb, not an adjective.

"On one point we are in unqualified agreement with our critics: it is of the utmost importance that CrimethInc. be absolutely and categorically destroyed. Unfortunately, for this to be possible, it is necessary to overthrow capitalism and Western Civilization in general. In this endeavor we wish them well, and will assist them where we can."

the sound as a co

COMPOSED AND ILLUSTRATED BY TWO GRADUATES
OF THE CATHARSIS COLLECTIVE

When it works, you'll lie with your companions, crowded fifteen onto an apartment room floor, listening to the unbelievably loud snoring of the one who always falls asleep first, and it will be the sweetest sound you've ever heard. You'll ride into a new town each day, fearless and all-powerful in your certainty that together you will transform everything you touch. Your songs of healing and destruction will echo off the walls of trailers in Mississippi and squats in Italy, or, better, will transform your own home town into the Paris of May 1968, and

you'll embrace in mutual gratitude and wonder. All the petty disputes and anxieties that made daily life such a miserable chore will vanish, and you'll know you are living as human beings are meant to live: in tribes of shared desire, where the logic of coercion and compensation falls away and magic is wrought nightly. The world itself will tremble before the forces you unleash as you discover what you're capable of together. That's when it works.

When it doesn't work, you'll lie awake plotting revenge on your closest

friends, you'll marvel in terror that something supposed to be fun could be so much more agonizing than day labor was, you'll even think, in the bleakest moments, you've found the proof that the anarchist revolution is a pipe dream after all.

This is about that critical foundation for world revolution through d-beats, circle pits, and patches—getting along with your friends and bandmates. Without that, nothing is possible; with it, anything is.

WHEN IT WORKS...

...AND WHEN IT DOESN'T

It's distressing how many avowedly anarchist groups, who evangelize publicly in favor of non-hierarchical blah blah blah, are plagued by authoritarian and coercive internal dynamics. On the other hand, considering how much trouble even the best of us can have getting along with each other in relatively stress-free circumstances, it's really phenomenal how many punk bands, composed largely of emotionally disturbed young people suffering from mental illness, have all the same succeeded in working together long enough to record artistic masterpieces and even tour the globe repeatedly. Anyone who's tried either of these things knows how emotionally taxing they are—especially without any social support system or financial means to speak of.

The art of cooperating closely with a few comrades under pressure is probably the most important skill the hardcore punk milieu can foster. When they function, affinity groups such as the punk band are notoriously capable of achieving triumphs out of all proportion to their small size—and not just in the realm of rebellious music, either; additionally, they function as a scale model demonstration of how an anarchist society operates. Besides—

if we can't make three, five, and eight person collectives work, how are we supposed to succeed in overthrowing capitalism and making a world where we all get along?

So without further hoopla: some of the various strains of band pathology, and how to treat them.

Specialized Roles, Ideological Centralization, and the Provisional Dictatorship of the Singer

One pattern especially seems to recur over and over in the case of the "political band": the singer versus everybody else. Who's to blame for this?

Division of labor means that every member becomes specialized in his or her instrument—and, often, in the accompanying role associated with that instrument. Bassist jokes[1] aside, the one most deeply affected by this is usually the singer. Already likely to be outgoing and expressive by temperament, the singer finds herself/himself in the role of using words and thoughts to represent the whole band. Lyrics and accompanying song explanations are expected of her/him, interviews tend to be directed at her/him,

bandmates will count on her/him to introduce the songs while they fine-tune their instruments. All this serves to reinforce her/his inherent authoritative tendencies (let's not kid ourselves—we all have some), and soon being the spokesperson comes naturally.

The best analogy to use here is the Communist State—the singer has become The Party, whose White Man's Burden it is to educate the Masses, starting of course with the Proletariat of his own band: the other members, the ones who actually manufacture the useful product (the music, without which there could be no band). He, of course, is only giving voice to the politics they already hold unconsciously—he is the Vanguard, and this gives him the important responsibilities of managing their labor, representing their interests, issuing statements on behalf of the group, etc.

Being able to express one's feelings in words, to speak one's mind publicly, to articulate complex ideas on the spot, all these are valuable skills to have—the problem is not that the singer exercises these, but that the way the band tends to function develops them in this one person and not in the others. The singer may well be saying and organizing things that need saying and organizing,

[1] Q: What do you call that person who hangs out with the musicians in a band? A: The bassist. Q: Why did the bassist spend the night on the porch? A: He didn't know when to come in. Q: How many singers does it take to change a light bulb? A: One—he just holds it and the world revolves around him. Q: How many bassists does it take to change a light bulb? A: Who cares?

and he or she may for that matter be the one who takes the most responsibility for important matters such as the relationship between the band and other people (thanking people who lend equipment, being personable with hosts and other bands, etc.)—but this specialization is not usually sustainable, and never healthy. Tensions develop between the different class strata of the band, now that they have different interests according to their different roles. Seriously, how many bands have broken up because the dissensions between the singer and the rest of the musicians became unbearable?

In a worst case scenario, your Singer will metamorphose into a Dictator. Responsibility and responsibleness alike tend to flow in one direction once a pattern is established. The more one person does, the more she or he knows how to do, and feels invested in these things getting done—and the less everyone else does. Worse, that person can thus become unwilling to trust others with responsibilities, just as others cease to be aware of how much work there is to be done and what it takes to do it. The Dictator blames others for not taking on responsibilities they don't even know exist; the others blame the Dictator for hostility and resentment they lack the context to understand.

It's worth clarifying here that The Singer in question may not actually be the singer, strictly speaking, of the band—it might be a guitarist, tambourine-player, even a bassist (!) playing this role. Hell, the actual vocalist of your band might be the most tight-lipped, antisocial, irresponsible person in the group. The phenomenon of The Singer is a social affliction that tends to take root in singers but can appear elsewhere (just as even in interactions between women, it can happen that one plays The Man). An instrumental band might end up with a Singer, despite themselves—that's the danger of division of labor of any kind, even the most informal or accidental. For that matter, one member might play The Singer for some time, and then another member slide into the role.

So how do we protect ourselves against this cancer? There's the reformist approach: try to keep your Singer in check with continuous feedback, constantly apologize for the position of privilege and power you hold as Singer, etc. And then there's the radical approach—change the structure of the band unit itself: eliminate The Singer as a musical or organizational role, rotate the

THE PROVISIONAL DICTATORSHIP OF THE SINGER

NOT UNITY, BUT HARMONY

role from member to member, form bands in which everyone sings. Neither strategy can work without the other, really: no radical restructuring of band format could by itself undo the effects of the decades of hierarchical conditioning all of us have already undergone, and at the same time it's foolish to think people in structures that are conducive to specialization and centralization can behave differently just by deciding to.

Harmony, Not Unity

Many political punks approach band-forming with the idea that to work together, be (seen as) sincere, etc., all members of a political band must share a specific political platform, a certain lifestyle, and a strict code of conduct. And you thought the pressure to conform was bad in high school! Once again, "radical" ideologies that neglected to do away with hierarchy (such as Communism) have historically demanded such standardization from their ranks, and have ended up with consequently sterile movements, artwork, and societies; anarchist thinking, on the other hand, suggests that diversity is necessary to any healthy ecosystem or organization.

Greater diversity gives you a wider range of inspiration and ideas to draw on, and makes for better music; and since human beings are always different, even when they try to homogenize themselves, any value system that encourages conformity can only spawn dishonest and superficial relationships and projects.

A collective of would-be clones can learn to do one thing well, at best; a circle of unique individuals can do many differing things that complement each other. The best bands are the ones that engage the sum total of all that the different members have to offer, not the ones who limit themselves to what they have in common. Some of the really great moments in punk rock have come when bands that "should have" broken up over ideological and artistic differences stuck together long enough to make one more beautiful, eclectic masterpiece. Let your drummer bring in techno remixes, your bassist design matching costumes, your guitarist expound on the post-Marxist implications of improvisation, and see what happens—that Conflict record you admire for its seeming political and artistic

single-mindedness has already been recorded.

Starting from diversity is as important as fostering it. Everyone is unique, of course, and it can happen that there is more divergence of personality, skills, and experience between two people of the same background than between individuals from differing demographics—but that said, it sure can be a great thing for a band to include members of different genders, social classes, ethnicities, cultures. When people from such differing backgrounds learn to understand and respect each other's perspectives, complement each other's strengths and weaknesses, and form symbiotic relationships on the basis of their differences—that's revolution in action, even if it's just a handful at first.

Almost needless to say (in these pages, at least), bands composed of members proceeding from widely differing conditions of privilege will have to work extra hard on learning to interact as equals. Oppressive patterns—middle class people tending to take over the organizing, working class people to do the physical labor, men to make decisions in ways that exclude women, etc.—come with us into our bands from the hierarchical world that raised us; let's make these bands social laboratories in which we learn how to break these patterns, in preparation for breaking that world.

Make Those Autonomous Zones Expandable!

Achieving supportive, non-hierarchical relations inside of your band is great, but it's not much use to the world unless it helps others do the same. Here we must address the role bands, even punk bands, play in the society of the spectacle.

Let us return to The Singer. Watching a band play, audience members tend to unconsciously identify themselves with the singer, the same way a spectator in a movie theater identifies with the hero on the screen, or a reader with the protagonist of a novel. This explains why so many people willingly shell out their hard-earned money for recordings of hip hop artists bragging about how much they earn from record sales—the listener identifies with the MC rather than as the victim of his money-making scheme, at least while the album is playing. This displacement of agency is at the root of the powerlessness of today's average Joe: the power to be creative is projected onto the successful novelist, the power to play sports onto the basketball star, the power to make history onto the politician.

The question for the anarchist musician is how to enable rather than disable listeners. That's tough, because what we're dealing with in the case of the punk band is a specialized, perhaps technically proficient, group creating what is essentially a spectacle, a "show." Keeping these shows small-scale, so the performers and spectators can interact as individuals rather than only as people playing those roles, is one solution; creating performances that demand or provoke audience participation is another. Maintaining humility, and keeping your eyes on the prize of extending whatever powers you develop for yourself to everyone else, are essential. Ultimately our goal should be to make the punk community something like an extended open mic circle, in which everyone has a turn to receive attention for their creative efforts.

Finances

Capitalism plays into the division between artist and audience too, of course. A punk band trying to operate under capitalist conditions needs to have a clear analysis of the challenges they're up against, and which compromises they're willing to make, if they want to be anarchist in deed as well as word. That's why we punks have always tried to keep our record prices low and our door costs sliding-scale, and scorned the pursuit of mass popularity.

The aforementioned hip hop artists are not the only hip hop artists, of course; they're just the only ones who have time and other resources to focus on their art, since everyone else is too busy earning money to pay for food, housing, and—their records. We punks have developed an anti-consumerist, anti-rock-star ethic to ensure that a greater proportion of our numbers can engage in creative pursuits; but it's still expensive to buy, maintain, and transport conventional musical instruments, and that money has to come from somewhere.

Your band will need a collective fund to pay for this stuff. That fund will probably have to be started from a pool of your own private capital, and will hopefully come to sustain itself as you get established enough to break even. Try to resist the temptation to solve all your problems by making a lot of money off the band—remember, there's not all that much money in the punk scene, and the more of it you get, the less others have access to for their own projects and needs. You don't need to make a living off your band—you need to develop a lifestyle that enables you to play in it. Seek out other ways to meet your needs—dumpstering food, sharing living quarters, having fun playing music or writing graffiti instead of going to the movies. You'll probably need to make some money in short bursts of wage labor—medical studies, crop harvests, working and quitting, whatever—to pay for your needs and remain free to go on long tours.

It may seem crazy, voluntarily choosing poverty, perpetual uncertainty, exclusion from mainstream economic and social relations just to play music; in the bleak moments, it will feel like you've exiled yourself from the whole world for nothing. But you are investing in something that will pay off, too, something much more reliable than the material wealth of today's erratic market. You're building relationships, community, shared resources ("social capital")—the foundation for a good life no full benefits package could ensure.

Commitment

Commitment is the bedrock social capital is built on. When you give up all the false riches and reassurances of the capitalist nightmare, you'll need this from each other more than anything else.

The world we live in, or rather, what world we live in, depends entirely upon our investments: we go on living in this world of sales, wages, rent, and cages because every day, everyone wakes up and—seeing no other viable option—invests their day's activities in surviving within its structures, thus perpetuating them. If you can somehow invest all your energy in creating and perpetuating another world, that world exists at least to the extent that you exist—that's the logic of living a radical lifestyle. Now, one person alone living and believing against the grain can barely survive, let alone make a real impact; but a small tribe of people who reinforce and sustain one another can thrive, and help

others open doors to new worlds of their own.

The anarchist punk rock underground, at best, is a network of such tribes, all trading support and inspiration with each other and helping plant seeds that could grow into new realities. At worst, it's just another messy, unhealthy social scene. The most critical, decisive element in the struggle between these two incarnations of punk rock is commitment. A group of people who are ready to go, ready to go through whatever, who know they will be faithful to each other and their dreams through the hardest of times, need not be perfect; as time passes, they will learn what they need to learn and improve where they need to improve.

All that energy that goes into making skyscrapers, writing computer programs, and strip-mining mountains comes from us and folks like us. Even something as simple as buying groceries or gas is an act giving great power to the corporations who maintain the status quo. That same great power is ours when we invest our energy in shared projects instead of dictated routines. Even being at liberty to try this option, no matter how difficult it may be in the trying, is a rare privilege in this society—but that's all the more reason to do so, for everyone's sake, to whatever extent you're able; and playing in a punk rock band is a well-tested model for such an experiment.

When you're considering which people to form a band with, characteristics like musical proficiency and access to equipment should be secondary—a person who has neither but is possessed

PRIVATE CAPITAL

by a burning desire to play can acquire these. The most important question is—are they down? Likewise, if you want to get anywhere playing punk music or working in cooperative groups of any kind, the most important characteristics you can develop in yourself are commitment, dedication, reliability, responsibility. Don't let your friends down in a tough situation. Let them know, through your actions, that they can count on you for everything you undertake together.

Three of us can share and minimize rent and food costs, make heart-breaking, riot-starting music, and tour the globe; ten of us can grow vegetables, home-repair vehicles, and set up a long-term housing project; one hundred of us can establish a permanent commune, organize city-stopping demonstrations, and fan out across the country to share those skills with ten thousand more—but it all comes down to commitment!

Don't Be a Fucking Jerk

I wish this didn't need saying, and you may not think it does—at least not until pursuing your visions of punk rock revolution to the ends of the earth lands you and your best friends in your first, or fiftieth, really trying catastrophe.

If you raise your voice at your bandmates, apologize explicitly as soon as you can, and try to work out the reasons you lost your head so you can avoid it next time. If one of them raises his/her voice at you and then apologizes, make it clear you accept the apology and

DON'T BE A FUCKING JERK!

harbor no grudge, and ask if there is anything you could do to help avoid this happening again. If no apology is offered, approach your bandmate in a non-threatening way and make it clear how important it is you receive one. Check in with each other consistently—daily, on tour, and not just in formal meetings, in which some members may feel intimidated—about how you're communicating and making each other feel. Solicit constructive criticism, and take your companions' needs very seriously—your band depends on this.

Shouting at your bandmates is abusive, coercive behavior. Such

SOCIAL CAPITAL

behavior comes in subtler forms: sulking, sarcasm, insensitive teasing, refusing to participate in discussion, dismissing others' perspectives or needs. Forcing others to be the responsible ones (always being the one drinking, never considering others' needs until they remind you, etc.), or to patiently absorb the stress of your outbursts because you're too volatile for dialogue, these are also coercive. If you find yourself thinking it necessary to "get tough" with your

what your bandmates are going through or need support in—or even that they're going through anything at all—just by watching from a distance; you have to be someone they know they can come to for support, someone they will want to come to no matter what's going down. This is important between all people, but especially so for a small group undertaking long-lasting, high-stress projects in close quarters. Don't get too comfortable in the role

so much if the promoter isn't able to scrape up as much gas money as you'd hoped.

Translating

To repeat it once more: communication is central to collective activity, and it's a voodoo art if there ever was one. No two people speak the same language the same way—different words, gestures, actions always mean different things to different people. Don't

bandmates by raising your voice or acting in other ways that make them uncomfortable—or for that matter thinking that they somehow deserve this treatment for something they have done!—then make no mistake about it: you are becoming an authoritarian. Join the fucking cops, get married and raise some kids you can beat the shit out of, whatever, but get the hell out of punk rock—or get your act together.

Make yourself accessible and approachable for dialogue at all times. You may not be able to tell

of supporter, either—you need to be just as comfortable seeking support as offering it; and if you're offering support, you'd better be sure you're receiving it from somewhere too.

Lastly, above all—make sure you're doing something you really want to be doing. This will make you more accommodating and good-spirited, not to mention the fact that needing "compensation" to justify your activity, as you did when you were waiting tables or washing dishes, will now appear ridiculous. If you really love the music you're playing and the people you're with, you won't care

get angry and self-righteous about communication breakdowns—there's no "right" way to communicate, no One and Only Way to handle things; anyone who tells you different is trying, consciously or not, to impose their personal system upon the cosmos. On the other hand, some ways do work better than others—ultimately, the only thing that matters is that your group finds a common speech or method that enables you to figure things out with each other.

Something else not to forget: whenever the composition of

TRANSLATING

It's been a knee-jerk reaction of punk consumers to judge a band's or label's integrity according to their prices since I got involved in this community. This is short-sighted and superficial: sure, having low record prices makes a symbolic statement against the high prices of profit-hungry record labels, for those who witness the statement (do punx, who already hate sold labels), but it also ensures that the labels (and, also, their communities) never have the capital to achieve much besides keeping the wheels of alternative production/distribution/consumption turning in their corner of the underground. Break-even prices—this is something often forgotten—mean that the label doesn't get its original investment back until months after every single record has sold—assuming they all sell—when the last distributor finally pays up—assuming they do all pay. And there are so many hidden production costs in making records—so many labels (yes, there are a lot!) forget to factor in all the unforeseeable expenses in their hurry to prove how pure and d.i.y. they are. They end up burning up all their energy as well as resources in a handful of releases or less, and giving up, while the capitalist scum on the fringes of our community continue to rake in punk money and even establish careers for themselves.

We should be thinking of who our prices benefit and how, for one thing. Flat record prices are like flat taxes: they are hardest on the poorest. If you want the prices low so the records will be more accessible to people without much money, then why not sell them on a sliding scale? The band I'm in has done some tours in hardcore communities outside the wealthier nations: we sell our records at higher prices in those richer nations so we can sell them significantly cheaper in poorer ones. Sure, some people in the former countries are poorer than some in the latter, but it's easier to give them cheaper prices or trades, too, and still break even ourselves, when the price for those who can afford it is somewhat higher than break-even.

your group shifts, or even when it remains the same but the people inside it go through changes (as we all always are), you'll have to figure everything out all over again. Even the addition of a new roadie may throw off all the dynamics you had come to rely on; and when you have a new band member or two, don't assume that you can simply march forward according to the plans and procedures you'd worked out before.

Band Dynamics: A Round Table, Not a House of Representatives

Imagine the relationships in your band as a system that can be diagrammed: support and information pass between some members more than others; pair bonds are formed, tighten, loosen. All this is inevitable, and fine enough; but the general shape of the system has critical effects on the way it works for those inside it. Some bands have circular systems, in which communication takes place between all, or, if two members are not interacting as much, they are linked to each other by everyone else; other bands develop linear systems, in which at some point in the chain of relationships there is one person who alone connects one group or individual to the rest. The circular system is healthy and durable; the linear system is risky and fragile.

Linear dynamics may not necessarily be accompanied by hierarchical power structure—but at the very least, they tend to encourage power

GOOD DYNAMICS: A CIRCLE, NOT A LINE

unhealthy and disempowering; the politicians who claim to "represent" our interests in this so-called democracy inevitably fail us, for one can only learn one's own interests by representing oneself. Even if the linking member earnestly makes every effort to represent the needs of two parties to each other, he or she does a disservice to both by enabling them to avoid figuring out how to communicate directly. Additionally, the stress this representing imposes on the linking member, especially if one or both sides are being aggressive, can be extremely difficult

to bear. This stress, like all stress in a band situation, is inevitably passed back on to everyone else again—so don't try to be a hero, solving everyone's problems and carrying the whole group forward on the strength of your diplomacy.

The linear dynamic is a classic problem for bands (and entire touring groups) in which two members are involved in a love relationship, since in our society people in such relationships are encouraged to isolate themselves from others and form one unit, the

polarization. As in the case of the singer-vs.-band dynamic, the skills and needs of the people occupying the two (or more) ends of the line evolve independently of each other, and the resulting specialization of interests can lead to conflict.

Communication, which ordinarily would resolve such conflicts, is especially difficult in a band that has linear dynamics, because the one

person who links the two "wings" of the band has to represent them to each other. Representation is already recognized by anarchists as

joint interests of which are then related to the group by one of the two. Blame monogamy monoculture for this. We don't necessarily need to stop fucking and sucking our bandmates and vanmates, but when we are we need to be especially aware about keeping communication mutual and representation to a minimum. Non-monogamy, not in terms of sex so much as relationship expectations and dynamics, has a lot to teach us on this subject.

Avoiding linear band dynamics is as easy, and as hard, as solving every other internal band problem: watch out for bad patterns, keep lines of communication open, don't be a fucking jerk. Remember not to carry someone else's load when it comes to communication, any more than any other responsibility; remember also not to be so difficult to approach that others avoid you.

you won't get infuriated at the kids putting on their first basement show for not knowing how to make your vocals loud enough; have extra maps in the van in case of bad directions. Feel confident enough in your instincts to be able to say a gentle "no" to the drunk gutter-punk who creeps you out when he asks to borrow your amplifier—you don't want to have any more bad experiences than necessary, since you'll need to feel comfortable lending that amp

of anyone else. Higher record prices in the d.i.y. community might thus, believe it or not, be in the better interests of the less wealthy kids: sure, records would cost a little more when you buy them instead of trading for them or taping them, but on the other hand, if you could borrow enough money from your aunt to release one, you wouldn't have as much reason to fear being unable to pay her back.

Now, I hope you've all trusted me enough up to this point not to misunderstand and think I'm suggesting labels need to make more fucking profit on their records for their own pockets. No: all it seems to me that, if we're trying to supersede consumer-friendly capitalism as the model of punk economics, we should sell the records for a bit more and put the extra money that will come back towards things that CAN'T fund themselves: free literature, activist projects and legal support, cooking pots for Food Not Bombs. Let's put our money where our mouths are, not keep the records cheap so the kids can buy more fancy vegan snacks after the shows! If we have to make consumer products, they should make it easier for us to accomplish our anti-capitalist projects. Otherwise we'll be treading water forever, or at least until we get burned out and sell out.

The existing precedent we have for this is benefit records and benefit shows. There's something to be said for these—at best, they provide a channel through which financial resources can go to worthy causes from a community that wouldn't otherwise be able to get its shit together to support them. At the same time, there's a difference between giving a handout to someone else trying to deal with a problem and working yourself to create a sustainable strategy for solving the problem—and I have to say the latter, in my experience, is almost always more effective. Our experience with Crimethinc. is central to my argument here, and if it turns out to be unrepeatable, then you can throw out my thesis, but I don't think it will: like many d.i.y. labels, we started with only a few hundred hard-earned dollars, astoundingly bad organizational skills, and a couple decent recordings.

It may well happen in a crisis situation that one member will retreat into isolation from the rest of the band, fearing or resenting all of them except perhaps the one who knows best how to communicate with him or her. This situation will not be resolved until the others can recognize his or her needs, and the individual can feel support coming from all of them. As the success of any collective project depends on everyone involved, this should always be possible, somehow—it had better be, since in the long run no shortcut or substitute will suffice.

Protect Your Idealism

Part of being an anarchist is not setting yourself up to be disappointed. Your faith in other human beings, your trust that they can be responsible for themselves and each other, is more integral to what you're doing than anything else—so whenever possible, don't give people unnecessary chances to let you down. Carry toilet paper with you, so when there's none in the bathroom at the squat you won't hold the whole punk scene accountable for it; learn how to operate a P.A., so

to other bands for many years to come. Know what you need, and ask explicitly for it as far in advance as possible, but be self-sufficient and durable too. Enjoy developing these qualities in yourself, so you can consider it an exciting challenge, a final exam of sorts, when your show turns out to be in a one-outlet barn barely above freezing[3]—instead of feeling yourself a martyr crucified by the laziness and stupidity of an unfeeling world.

Ultimately, you should be able to thrive in any kind of environment or cultural context (being on tour is all about learning not to need to impose your own), and to be grateful for whatever people have to offer you, no matter how humble it may be—since in the d.i.y. community, where we've done away with notions of debt and duty, everything given is given only out of generosity. Approach everything in this way, and you'll be easy for everyone else to work with—not to mention you'll have a better time yourself.

PROTECT YOUR IDEALISM

by our friends' hands. Unlike some other labels, we always had the intention to do something more than release records, and aimed for that from the beginning. We priced our records like our enemies did, the smaller but still profit-oriented hardcore labels, rather than like the d.i.y. punk labels we admired, and after a year and a half, we had enough money to print thousands of copies of the first Harbinger, a free radical paper. We kept investing the break-even money we got back in more projects, spent the profits on free publications and similar projects, and eventually found we were accomplishing a lot of the things we'd only fantasized about before, without having to borrow money as frequently. Admittedly, this has been easier for us because most of us are fortunate enough not to work to have financial needs, living instead through the usual tricks (contrary to popular belief, none of us have trust funds—if anyone does meet the much spoken-of something, kid with a trust fund, could you introduce us to her or him, please?), so we've been able to put in a lot of hours of work without needing money or whatever back ... still, I can't believe we're the only punk kids who can do that—I've seen hundreds of others living the same way, with a lot of energy just waiting to go into something!

I would love to see others duplicate our experience with raising money from record sales to go into political work. I believe it's important for us punks not only to support other political projects going on out there, but also establish our own sustainable foundations for projects of our own [we know a couple of us accomplish with $25 what one of those Non-Governmental Organizations would need $3000 to do]. As a long-term goal, punk labels would do well to aim to take the private capital that they end up with from doing business, and feed it into public capital, that is, use it to fund show spaces, community resources, projects from which everyone could benefit whether rich or poor or punk or not. From each according to her means [record sales are voluntary, you know!] to each according to her needs, that old ideal. Sure, we can keep selling the records at low-as-ever prices and passing around the [not-so-silent pocket change when one of us goes to prison, but ... well, isn't that

When Times Get Tough...

Remember, as long as we live in this cutthroat society, troubled relationships are going to be inevitable. That's why we're fighting in this revolution! The dynamics within our groups and ourselves mirror the patterns of strife in the larger world around us, and we can't expect them to be much healthier than it is. The struggle to heal one is the struggle to heal the other, and neither struggle will be concluded until both are. The good news buried in this conundrum is that whatever you discover that does work within your small circle may well also work to change the world at large.

It might help, when things get really bad and you start to feel ashamed of your group, like you're all a bunch of phonies and have nothing to offer the world or even each other, to consider all the other beautiful, important things that anarchists like yourself have accomplished—that great Amebix record, the resistance in the Spanish Civil War, the millions of meals served by Food Not Bombs.

You can be sure all those feats were only barely snatched from the teeth of internal dissension, resentment, and pessimism. Everything good we achieve, we achieve because we're willing to engage in projects that are imperfect—and to forgive ourselves and our relationships for that imperfection. The only thing that is perfect is nonexistence. Hold out a little to see what good you might still be able to accomplish, however flawed, before you opt for that.

Fallout and Aftermath

Sooner or later, even with the best

At the risk of sounding like a maniac, I'll own that on the last tour we did, during which we played in a number of unheated squats in the middle of winter, I carried a thermometer with me and distracted myself on many a cold night by comparing that night's temperature reading against other nights'. Make the hard things into a game, whenever you can—don't take your sufferings too seriously.

internal dynamics anticapitalism can buy, your band is going to break up. That's inevitable, just like death (and the eventual abolition of taxes, god damn it). Things may well end in emotional drama and disappointment. Don't beat yourself up over this—learn what you can, and move on. Again, none of us are perfect, and recognizing that, being comfortable with it, is as radical and positive as our efforts to improve ourselves.

too proud to admit it's not working). Seriously, who wants to end up touring with the same songs into old age, like the Rolling Stones?

So don't get demoralized—take every lesson you learned, every skill you gained, every idea that has yet to see expression, and make that capitalist system regret it ever let you get out alive. Hope to see you in the basements—hope we'll take it to the streets.

makes it necessary for everyone to be perpetually packed into whatever indoor space is available (the van, the basement, the promoter's tiny apartment), and thus it can be hard for band members to get the space and time apart they need.

* It's best there are at least two people who identify as women in every touring group, if possible. An all-boy group will inevitably lack certain important perspectives and input, and a lone woman in a group of boys

Dear working card?

I understand that in making this proposal, I'm placing a lot of emphasis on trusting the people doing the labels—and that is an Achilles' heel for the whole idea. It's true, especially since the more money anyone makes, the more they want to make it, whether it turns out being for a good cause or not. At the same time, losing money to keep consumer prices down, as I've pointed out, hasn't been helping our community progress much, either. I guess this is above all an appeal to anarchists and activists who are already considering releasing records, a suggestion of how to create a synthesis between punk and activist work that isn't often achieved. Also, as a side note—organizing labels as collectives, with discussions as to how resources should be deployed and attention paid to the wishes of the larger community, can really help to keep them on the right track.

To conclude—this is no set of rules. I'm not saying to tell you what to do. I'm just bringing up one thing that's like, so important to the whole world. I hope you're recognizing my reference here, that it seems to me could be done differently. When or if you are others trying something different, don't write them off immediately—talk to them, figure out what they're working towards. Maybe they're actually doing something more right on than the label that sells 12"s for $5!

Always saying what nobody wants to hear, [a] member of the CrimethInc. Work Shirkers Collective

All this is to say—brace yourself, before you turn to our catalog in the back and see our new prices! Uh, just joking...

The fact that it comes to an end doesn't have to mean you were doing the wrong thing, either. It's like the objection people sometimes bring up against non-monogamous relationships—"Oh, I know some people who tried that, but they ended up breaking up." Being able to have a healthy relationship includes knowing how and when to conclude it: the conclusion is not necessarily an indication of inherent problems. Not being able to conclude, on the other hand, might be (think of the miserable monogamous marriage that drags on forever, the inmates

Send requests for band counseling, bitter denunciations of your bandmates, and videotapes of shows we played (that would be swell!) to Punk Rock Retirement Plan, c/o C.W.C.

Some final hints:

*Touring in winter (north of the equator) is much more difficult, emotionally and socially, than touring in summer—not only because of the emotional impact of the weather itself, but also because the cold

is going to have to deal with a lot of frustration on her own. All-woman groups, on the other hand—well, our scene could use more of them!

*When a new member is going to join your band, don't make too many plans for the time after she or he is to join without her or him involved in the decision-making process.

*Plan time apart from each other, and time together that has nothing to do with the band, into both your tours and the rest of your lives. You won't regret it!

PEERING THROUGH THE FOG BEHIND HIS EYES, HE SAW AN ALCOHOLOGRAM: A WORLD OF ANGUISH, IN WHICH INTOXICATION WAS THE ONLY ESCAPE. HATING HIMSELF EVEN MORE THAN HE HATED THE CORPORATE KILLERS WHO HAD CREATED IT, HE STUMBLED TO HIS FEET AND HEADED BACK TO THE LIQUOR STORE.

ENSCONCED IN THEIR PENTHOUSES, THEY COUNTED THE DOLLARS POURING IN FROM MILLIONS LIKE HIM, AND CHUCKLED TO THEMSELVES AT THE EASE WITH

Wasted

Sloshed, smashed, trashed, loaded, wrecked, wasted, blasted, plastered, tanked, fucked up, bombed. Everyone's heard of the arctic people with one hundred words for snow; we have one hundred words for drunk. We perpetuate our own culture of defeat.

Hold it right there—I can see the sneer on your face: *Are these anarchists so uptight that they would even denounce the only fun aspect of anarchism—the beer after the riots, the liquor in the pub where all that pie-in-the-sky theory is bandied about? What do they do for fun, anyway—cast aspersions on the little fun we do have? Don't we get to relax and have a good time in any part of our lives?*

Do not misunderstand us; we are not arguing against indulgence, but *for* it. Ambrose Bierce defined an ascetic as "a weak person who succumbs to the temptation of denying himself pleasure," and we concur. As Chuck Baudelaire wrote, *You must always be high. Everything depends on this.* So we are not against drunkenness, but rather against drink! Those who embrace drink as a route to drunkenness thus cheat themselves of a total life of enchantment.

Drink, like caffeine or sugar in the body, only plays a role in life that life itself can provide for otherwise. The woman who never drinks coffee does not require it in the morning when she awakens: her body produces energy and focus on its

WHICH ALL OPPOSITION WAS CRUSHED. BUT THEY, TOO, OFTEN HAD TO DRINK THEMSELVES TO SLEEP AT NIGHT — IF EVER THOSE VANQUISHED MASSES STOP COMING BACK FOR MORE, THE TYCOONS SOMETIMES FRETTED TO THEMSELVES, THERE'S GONNA BE HELL TO PAY.

Indeed: Anarchy & Alcohol

Ecstasy vs. Intoxication: For a World of Enchantment, or Anarchaholism?
Excerpted from Guy Debord's famous work, "Insobriety and the Spectacle"

own, as thousands of generations of evolution have prepared it to do. If she drinks coffee regularly, soon her body lets the coffee take over that role, and she becomes dependent upon it. Thus does alcohol artificially provide for temporary moments of relaxation and release while impoverishing life of all that is genuinely restful and liberating.

If some sober people in this society do not seem as reckless and free as their boozer counterparts, that is a mere accident of culture, mere circumstantial evidence. Those puritans exist all the same in the world drained of all magic and genius by the alcoholism of their fellows (and the capitalism, hierarchy, misery it helps maintain)—the only difference is that they are so self-

abnegating as to refuse even the false magic, the genie of the bottle. But other "sober" folk, whose orientation to living might better be described as enchanted or ecstatic, are plentiful, if you look hard enough. For these individuals—for us—life is a constant celebration, one which needs no augmentation and from which we need no respite.

Alcohol, like Prozac and all the other mind-control medications that are making big bucks for Big Brother these days, substitutes symptomatic treatment for cure. It takes away the pain of a dull, drab existence for a few hours at best, then returns it twofold. It not only replaces positive actions which would address the root causes of our despondency—it *prevents* them,

as more energy becomes focused on achieving and recovering from the drunken state. Like the tourism of the worker, drink is a pressure valve that releases tension while maintaining the system that creates it.

In this push-button culture, we've become used to conceiving of ourselves as simple machines to be operated: add the appropriate chemical to the equation to get the desired result. In our search for health, happiness, meaning in life, we run from one panacea to the next—Viagra, vitamin C, vodka—instead of approaching our lives holistically and addressing our problems at their social and economic roots. This product-oriented mindset is the foundation of our alienated consumer society: without consuming products, we can't live! We try to buy relaxation, community, self-confidence—now even ecstasy comes in a pill!

We want ecstasy as a way of life, not a liver-poisoning alcoholiday from it. "Life sucks—get drunk" is the essence of the argument that enters our ears from our masters' tongues and then passes out of our own slurring mouths, perpetuating whatever incidental and unnecessary truths it may refer to—but we're not falling for it any longer! Against inebriation—and *for* drunkenness! Burn every liquor store, and replace them with playgrounds!

Spurious Rebellion

Practically every child in mainstream Western society grows up with alcohol as the forbidden fruit their parents or peers indulge in but deny to them. This prohibition only makes drinking that much more fascinating to young people, and when they get the opportunity, most of them immediately assert their independence by doing exactly as they've been told not to: ironically, they rebel by following the example set for them. This hypocritical pattern is standard for child-rearing in this society, and works to replicate a number of destructive behaviors that otherwise would be aggressively refused by new generations. The fact that the bogus morality of many drinking parents is mirrored in the sanctimonious practice of religious groups helps to create a false dichotomy between puritanical self-denial and life-loving, free-wheeling drinkers—with "friends" like Baptist ministers, we teetotalers wonder, who needs enemies?

These partisans of Rebellious Drunkenness and advocates of Responsible Abstinence are loyal adversaries. The former need the latter to make their dismal rituals look like fun; the latter need the former to make their rigid austerity seem like common sense. An "ecstatic sobriety" which combats the dreariness of one and the bleariness of the other—false pleasure and false discretion alike—is analogous to the anarchism that confronts both the false freedom offered by capitalism and the false community offered by communism.

Alcohol and Sex in the Rape Culture

Let's lay it on the table: almost all of us are coming from a place where our sexuality is or was occupied territory. We've been raped, abused, assaulted, shamed, silenced, confused, constructed, programmed. We're badasses, and we're taking it all back, reclaiming ourselves; but for most of us, that's a slow, complex, not yet concluded process.

This doesn't mean we can't have good, safe, supportive sex right now, in the middle of that healing—but it does make having that sex a little more complicated. To be certain we're not perpetuating or helping to perpetuate negative patterns in a lover's life, we have to be able to communicate clearly and honestly before things get hot and heavy—and while they are, and after. Few forces interfere with this communication like alcohol does. In this culture of denial, we are encouraged to use it as a social lubricant to help us slip past our inhibitions; all too often, this simply means ignoring our own fears and scars, and not asking about others'. If it is dangerous, as well as beautiful, for us

to share sex with each other sober, how much more dangerous must it be to do so drunk, reckless, and incoherent?

Speaking of sex, it's worth noting the supporting role alcohol has played in patriarchal gender dynamics. For example—in how many nuclear families has alcoholism helped to maintain an unequal distribution of power and pressure? (All the writers of this tract can call to mind more than one such case among their relatives alone.) The man's drunken self-destruction, engendered as it may be by the horrors of surviving under capitalism, imposes even more of a burden on the woman, who must still somehow hold the family together—often in the face of his violence. And on the subject of dynamics...

The Tyranny of Apathy

"Every fucking anarchist project I engage in is ruined or nearly ruined by alcohol. You set up a collective living situation and everyone is too drunk or stoned to do the basic chores, let alone maintain an attitude of respect. You want to create community, but after the show everyone just goes back to their rooms and drinks themselves to death. If it's not one substance to abuse it's a motherfucking other. I understand trying to obliterate your consciousness is a natural reaction to being born in alienating capitalist hell, but I want people to see what we anarchists are doing and say "Yeah, this is better than capitalism!"... which is hard to say if you can't walk around without stepping on broken forty

New World by the murderous European colonists.

But this is just a story, speculation. Let's consult the history books (reading between the lines where we must, as these books come down to us from yesteryear's conquering killers and their obedient slaves ... that is, historians!) to see if it lines up with the evidence. We'll start in the early years of agriculture, when the first tribes settled down — in the fertile lands around rivers, where wheat and barley were easy to grow and ferment in mass quantities.

The Domestication of Man — by Alcohol

Enkidu, a shaggy, unkempt, almost bestial primitive man, who ate grass and could milk wild animals, wanted to test his strength against Gilgamesh, the god-king. Gilgamesh sent a prostitute to Enkidu to learn of his strengths and weaknesses. Enkidu enjoyed a week with her during which she taught him of civilization. Enkidu knew not what bread was, nor had he learned to drink beer. She spoke unto Enkidu: "Eat the bread now, it belongs to life. Drink also beer, as it is the custom of the land." Enkidu drank seven cups of beer and his heart soared. In this condition he

washed himself and became a civilized being.

—The first written narrative of civilization, the Epic of Gilgamesh written in 3000 B.C., describes the domestication of Enkidu, the primitive, by means of beer.

The oldest authenticated records of brewing were fashioned over 6,000 years ago in Sumer, the oldest of human civilizations. Sumer also had the first known state-organized religion, and the official "divine drink" of this religion was beer brewed by priestesses of Ninkasi, the Sumerian goddess of alcohol. The hymns of Ninkasi were brewing instructions! The first collection of laws, the Code of Hammurabi of Babylon, decreed a daily beer ration in direct proportion to social status: beer consumption went hand in hand with hierarchy. For example, workers received two liters while besotted priests and kings got five. (For an interesting thought experiment, ask yourself how much alcohol you get now, and what that says about your position in society.) Historians pondering the primacy of alcohol in these ancient lawbooks have even conjectured that the original function of hierarchy was to permit some men to hoard mass amounts of alcohol while ensuring that a sufficient labor force (pacified by their meager alcohol rations to discourage

revolt or escape) was always at hand to keep farming and brewing. Kings used a golden drinking straw to sip from the giant containers of beer that were always at hand, a tradition that has been preserved in plastic throughout the Western world. The pivotal role of alcohol in this first hierarchy is easy to recognize, even from a cursory reading of these records: as in every authoritarian regime, "justice" was a cardinal concern, and the punishment decreed for all who violated any of the laws governing beer was death by drowning.

Though it was yet newly-invented, beer influenced every single facet of emerging human civilization. Before the invention of money, beer was used as the standard item of barter ... a money before money! In Ancient Egypt, a keg of beer was the only proper gift to offer to the Pharaoh when proposing marriage to his daughter, and kegs of beer were sacrificed to the gods when the Nile overflowed. As civilization spread, so did beer. Even in regions as remote as Finland, beer played a crucial role from the moment civilization struck: the Kalevala, the ancient Finnish mythic cycle, had twice as many verses devoted to beer as to the creation of the earth. Brewing could be found wherever civilization was, from the rudimentary villages of

bottles. I've never considered myself straight edge, but fuck it, I'm not taking it anymore!"

-Personal Reflection by yet another disillusioned anarchist...

It's said that when the renowned anarchist Oscar Wilde first heard the old slogan *if it is humiliating to be ruled, how much more humiliating it is to choose one's rulers,* he responded: "If it's humiliating to choose one's masters, how much more humiliating to be one's own master!" He intended this as a critique of hierarchies within the self as well as the democratic state, of course—but, sadly, his quip could be applied literally to the way some of our attempts at creating anarchist environments pan out in practice. This is especially true when they're carried out by drunk people.

In certain circles, especially the ones in which the word "anarchy" itself is more in fashion than any of its various meanings, freedom is conceived of in negative terms: "don't tell me what to do!" In practice, this often means nothing more than an assertion of the individual's right to be lazy, selfish, unaccountable for his actions or lack thereof. In such contexts, when a group agrees upon a project it often ends up being a small, responsible minority that has to do all the work to make it happen. These conscientious few often look like the autocratic ones—when, invisibly, it is the apathy and hostility of their comrades that forces them to adopt this role. Being drunk and disorderly all the time is *coercive*—it compels others to clean up after you, to think clearly when you won't, to absorb the stress generated by your behavior when you are too fucked up for dialogue. These dynamics go

two ways, of course—those who take *all* responsibility on their shoulders perpetuate a pattern in which everyone else takes none—but everyone is responsible for their own part in such patterns, and for transcending it.

Think of the power we could have if all the energy and effort in the world—or maybe even just *your* energy and effort?—that goes into drinking were put into resisting, building, creating... Try adding up all the money anarchists in your community have spent on corporate libations, and picture how much musical equipment or bail money or food (-not-bombs... or, fuck it, bombs!) it could have paid for—instead of funding their war against all of us. Better: imagine living in a world where cokehead presidents die of overdoses while radical musicians and rebels live the chaos into ripe old age!

German barbarians to the god-emperors of ancient China. Only those human beings that still lived in harmony with wild nature, such as the indigenous peoples of North America and some sectors of Africa, remained alcohol-free — for a time.

The "classical civilizations" of Greece and (of course!) Rome were as soaked in alcohol as they were in blood — the entire ancient world was lost in a collective hang-over. This must have helped the nobles and philosophers to gloss over the fact that their "enlightened democracy" was based on the subjugation of women and masses of slaves. The greatest work of "classical" literature, the Symposium, details a drinking party starring Socrates, whose claim to fame as a philosopher was enhanced by his inhumanly high tolerance for alcohol. Studying his glorifications of the abstract over the real (provided these weren't falsely attributed to him by his mendacious pupil, Plato), one can still catch a whiff of the sour breath of a drunk.

Brew and State

In life he I called Gambrinus, King of Flanders and Brabant, who first have made mash from barley and so conceived of the brewing of beer. Hence, the brewers can say they have a king as the first master brewer.

— The Patron Saint™ of beer was a monarch, of course.

The Roman Empire finally collapsed, as all empires eventually do (including this one, god damn it!), after a generations-long drunken orgy of decadence and degeneration. The two most influential survivors were beer and Christianity. Brewing had once been the domain of women — but with the rise of the Catholic Church the monastic orders seized that domain for themselves, destroying one of the last bastions of primal matriarchy. Monks, washing away in prayer, relied upon the drink to ease their miserable religious fasting — and so, not surprisingly, the consumption of beer was not considered a violation of their vows of non-consumption. Beer consumption in monasteries reached unheard-of levels, as monks were allowed to consume up to five litres of beer a day. Both the popes and early emperors such as Charlemagne would personally supervise

the brewing process, hoping to create the perfect drink to obliterate both their consciousness and the consciousness of their subjects.

The birth of capitalism and the nation-state began with the commercialization of beer. The monasteries, overflowing with more beer than they themselves could consume, began to sell it to the surrounding villages. Monasteries doubled by night as pubs, and these men of God created some of the first well-managed profit-making enterprises.

With the weakening of the power of the Church and the rise of the modern nation-state, kings and dukes moved in to close the tax-exempt monasteries. They began licensing out brewing to the rising merchant class, imposing a heavy tax that hastened the centralization of power and wealth in these nations. Beer became the focus of every night and the mainstay of every celebration. Christmas "Yuletide," for example, derives from "Ale tide." To pacify women on their wedding night, an extra-potent "Bride Ale" was made, and so our word bridal. Everywhere the triumph of drunkenness, everywhere the triumph of God and State.

Sobriety and Solidarity

Like any lifestyle choice, be it vagabondage or union membership, abstention from alcohol can sometimes be mistaken as an end rather than a means.

Above all, it is critical that our own choices *not* be a pretext for us to deem ourselves superior to those who make different decisions. The only strategy for sharing good ideas that succeeds unfailingly (and that goes for hotheaded, alienating tracts like this one as well!) is the power of example—if you put "ecstatic sobriety" into action in your life *and it works,* those who sincerely want similar things will join in. Passing judgment on others for decisions that affect only themselves is absolutely noxious to any anarchist—not to mention it makes them less likely to experiment with the options you offer.

And so—the question of solidarity and community with anarchists and others who do use alcohol and drugs. We propose that these are of utmost importance. Especially in the case of those who are struggling to free themselves of unwanted addictions, such solidarity is paramount: Alcoholics Anonymous, for example, is just one more instance of a quasi-religious organization filling a social need that should already be provided for by anarchist community self-organizing. As in every case, we anarchists must ask ourselves: do we take our positions simply to feel superior to the unwashed (er, washed) masses—or because we sincerely want to propagate accessible alternatives? Besides, most of us who are not substance-addicted can thank our privileges and good fortune for this; this gives us all the more responsibility to be good allies to those who have not had such privileges or luck—on whatever terms *they* set. Let tolerance, humility, accessibility, and sensitivity be the qualities we nurture in ourselves, not self-righteousness or pride. No separatist sobriety!

Have a drink, it's on me—because consumers are what makes capitalism work!

for a lucid bacchanali

Sedated

Revolution

So anyway—what are we going to do if we don't go to bars, hang out at parties, sit on the steps or in front of the television with our forty ounce bottles? *Anything else!*

The social impact of our society's fixation on alcohol is at least as important as its mental, medical, economic, and emotional effects. Drinking standardizes our social lives, occupying some of the eight waking hours a day that aren't already colonized by work. It locates us spatially—living rooms, cocktail lounges, railroad tracks—and contextually—in ritualized, predictable behaviors—in

ways more explicit systems of control never could. Often when one of us does manage to escape the role of worker/consumer, drinking is there, stubborn holdover from our colonized leisure time, to fill up the promising space that opens. Free from these routines, we could discover other ways to spend time and energy and seek pleasure, ways that could prove dangerous to the system of alienation itself.

Drink can *incidentally* be part of positive and challenging social interactions, of course—the problem is that its central role in current socializing and socialization misrepresents it as *the* prerequisite for such intercourse. This obscures the fact that we can create such interactions at will with nothing more than our own creativity, honesty, and daring. Indeed, without these, *nothing* of value is possible—have you ever been to a bad

party?—and with them, no alcohol is necessary.

When one or two persons cease to drink, it just seems senseless, like they are ejecting themselves from the company (or at least customs) of their fellow human beings for nothing. But a *community* of such people can develop a radical culture of sober adventure and engagement, one that could eventually offer exciting opportunities for drink-free activity and merriment for all. Yesterday's geeks and loners could be the pioneers of tomorrow's new world: "lucid bacchanalism" is a new horizon, a new possibility for transgression and transformation that could provide fertile soil for revolts as yet unimaginable. Like any revolutionary lifestyle option, this one offers an immediate taste of another world while helping create a context for actions that hasten its universal realization. No war

as being slave-owning aristocrats, were all brewers of beer. Coincidence?

The foundations of colonial genocide bear the stench of a long and protracted alcohol-induced nightmare — nearly every indigenous culture the Europeans encountered was destroyed by European alcohol and disease. The spreading of "firewater" among indigenous populations of North America went hand-in-hand with the distribution of lethal smallpox-infested blankets. Many of these cultures, without the experience of thousands of years of civilized alcoholism to draw upon, were even more subject than the Europeans to the ravages of "the civilized brew." Between alcohol, disease, commerce, and guns, most of them were quickly and utterly destroyed. This process was not unique to North America — it was repeated throughout the world in every European colonial endeavor. While the drug of choice varied (sometimes it was opium, for example, as in the "Opium Wars" Great Britain waged to control China), alcohol was judged in many countries to be the most socially acceptable tool of pacification.

The Industrial Revolution was hastened by the prospect of brewing beer yearlong, since the temperatures needed for

brewing occur naturally only in winter. The steam engine invented by James Watt was immediately applied by Carl von Linde to enable artificial cooling, allowing those with the infrastructure of civilization to brew anytime, anywhere. Contrary to popular belief, Louis Pasteur invented pasteurization for beer-making, and only later was it adopted by the dairy industry. Yeast, which is found naturally in the air, is no longer even used in that state by modern brewing, as scientists have isolated a single yeast cell and induced its artificial reproduction for brewing. Following the invention of the assembly line, beer has come to be mass-produced on an ever larger scale. Over the two centuries since, the alcohol industry, like all capitalist industries, has been consolidated under the control of a few major companies controlled feudally by families like the infamous Anheuser-Busch beer syndicate — infamous for its connections to right-wing groups and religious fundamentalists. As for other links between alcohol and far-right/fascist activity — perhaps the reader will recall where Hitler initiated his takeover of Germany.

Resist Capitalism — Desist Drinking

It's no exaggeration, then, to say that alcohol has played a key role in the epidemic of fascism, racism, statism, imperialism, colonialism, sexism and patriarchy, class oppression, ungoverned technological development, religious superstition, and other bad stuff that has swept the earth over the past few millennia. It continues to play that role today, as the peoples of the whole world, finally universally domesticated and enslaved by global capitalism, are kept pacified and helpless by a steady supply of spirits. These evil spirits squander the time, money, health, focus, creativity, awareness, and fellowship of all who inhabit this universally occupied territory — "work is the curse of the drinking classes," as Oscar Wilde said. It's not surprising, for example, that the primary targets of advertising for malt liquor (a toxic byproduct of the brewing process) are the inhabitants of ghettos in the United States, people who constitute a class that, if not tranquilized by addiction and incapacitated by self-destruction, would be on the front lines of the war to destroy capitalism.

Civilization — and everything anxious and baleful it engenders — will crumble when a resistance movement

but the class war—no cocktail but the molotov cocktail! Let us brew nothing but trouble!

Postscript: How to Read this Tract

With any luck, you've been able to discern, even through that haze of drunken stupor, ha ha, that this is as much a caricature of polemics in the anarchist tradition as a serious piece. It's worth pointing out that these polemics have often brought attention to their theses by deliberately taking an extreme position, thereby opening up the ground in between for more "moderate" positions on the subject. Hopefully you can draw useful insights of your own from your interpretations of this text, rather than taking it as gospel or anathema.

And all this is not to say there are no fools who refuse intoxication—but can you imagine how much more insufferable they would be if they did not? The boring would still be boring, only louder about it; the self-righteous ones would continue to lambaste and harangue, while spitting and drooling on their victims! It is an almost universal characteristic of drinkers that they encourage everyone around them to drink, that—barring those hypocritical power plays between lovers or parents and children, at least—they prefer their own choices to be reflected in the choices of all. This strikes us as indicating a monumental insecurity, not unrelated to the insecurity revealed by ideologues and recruiters of every stripe from Christian to Marxist to anarchist who feel they cannot rest until everyone in the world sees that world exactly as they do. As you read, try to fight off that insecurity—and try not to read this as an expression of our own, either, but rather, in the tradition of the best anarchist works, as a reminder for all who choose to concern themselves that *another world is possible*.

For more preposterous treatises, or to send an angry, inebriated repartee, please contact the CrimethInc. chapter of Alcoholics Autonomous.

PREDICTABLE DISCLAIMER

As in the case of *every* CrimethInc. text, this one only represents the perspectives of whoever agrees with it at the time, *not* the "entire CrimethInc. ex-Workers' Collective" or any other abstract mass. Somebody who does important work under the CrimethInc. moniker is probably getting sloshed at the moment I'm typing this—and that's OK!

appears that can dam the flood of alcohol immobilizing the masses. The world now waits for a temperance that can defend itself, for a radical vision unclouded by drink, for a revolutionary sobriety that will return us to the ecstatic state of wild nature.

Our Anti-Authoritarian Heritage: Teetotalers Fighting Totalitarianism

It's not widely remembered that strict vegetarianism and abstinence from drink have been common in radical circles for many centuries. One need only thumb through the history books to amass a long list of heretics, utopians, reformers, revolutionaries, communitarians, and individualists who adopted these lifestyle choices as essential elements of their platforms. We'll leave that list-making to the enthusiastic reader or obsessive critic—let it suffice to say that examples range from old white guys like Friedrich Nietzsche, who eschewed even caffeine while extolling the kind of ecstatic bacchanalism described herein, Vachel Lindsay, the visionary hobo of Springfield, Illinois who traversed the early United States to share his poetic appeals for temperance and willful unemployment, and Jules Bonnot and his fellow anarchist bankrobbers, who invented the getaway car together, to

Malcolm X (of course), and the E.Z.L.N.—who prohibit alcohol as per the counsel of Zapatista women fed up with men's bullshit. (The capitalist government of Mexico has tried to undermine revolutionary activity by importing beer into villages like Ocosingo; in that city and others, Zapatistas have responded by setting up barricades and fighting the soldiers who would enforce this "free trade" upon them.) One of Public Enemy's best songs attacked the role of alcohol in the exploitation and oppression of the African-American community. You can bet anarchist Leon Czolgosz was stone cold sober when he shot U.S. President William McKinley to death. Oh, and—could we forget?—there's always Ian McKaye.

On the other side of the coin—can you imagine how much more progress we would have made in this struggle already if anti-authoritarians such as Nestor Makhno, Guy Debord, Janis Joplin, and countless anarcho-punks had focused more energy on the creation and destruction they loved so dearly, and less on drinking themselves to death?

Enough History! Let the Future Begin!

Perhaps so much talk about faraway times and peoples leaves you cold. Sure, history can be dead—and the history of

triumphant armies and mass-murderer Presidents is indeed a history of death. All the same, we can learn from the past, as from each other, if we apply our imaginations and a keen eye for pattern. Professional historians and their fellow slaves of slaves might call this account subjective or biased, but then—which of their histories isn't? We're not the ones whose salaries depend on corporate sponsorships and patronage, anyway!

Even if you do decide that this history of alcoholism is "the" truth, for heaven's sake don't waste time looking back into the past for some long-lost state of primitive sobriety that—for all any of us knew—may not even have existed. What matters is what we do in the present tense, what histories our actions create today. History is the residue—no, better, the excrement—of such activity; let us not drown in it like yeast, but learn what we must and then leave it behind. Let nothing stop us, not even alcohol, as ingrained in our culture as it is! Those drunken despots and beer-bellied bigots may destroy their world and smother beneath their history, but we bear a new future in our hearts—and the power to enact it in our healthy livers.

WHY, VEGAN?

HOW PASSÉ!

Why we should bring back Veganism

If we can consider reclaiming straight edge as a "revolutionary lifestyle option," there's no reason to stop there—why not bid on veganism, too?

From Vegan to Freegan

In the mid-nineties, it seemed all my friends were vegan and self-righteous about it. I was hanging out in a mixture of straight edge and political punk circles, at the high point of Earth Crisis's fame, so this wasn't unusual—although, to be fair, I wasn't vegan myself, so it was probably more the case that I was defensive than it was that they were self-righteous. Whatever was going on, I remember one of the things that alienated me most about their dietary habits was the amount of money they spent on fancy vegan treats: I was already a couple years into my no-work experiment, and could barely afford rice, much less bourgeois-bohemian soy cheeseburgers—and besides, funding the non-meat "alternative" foods industry, a mere subdivision of the whole evil corporate food monster, didn't seem much more right on to me than buying from the more obvious bad guys in the same market. It seemed to me that my friends' money would end up, at best, funding some "free range" chicken farm, where the captives got an extra foot of space to pace until they were killed. I've since been proved essentially correct in my suspicions about the whole "voting with your dollars" approach to animal rights: the vegetarian/vegan trend has helped cement the iron grip of friendly-faced, evil-hearted corporations like union-busting Whole Foods over their own new niche, the bourgeois feel-good "organic" market, thus driving community co-ops and mom'n'pop

shops into even worse straits, and closing down far fewer animal-exploiting corporations than more direct-action-oriented approaches have.

Anyway, I decided my own food activism would be to stop buying from the bastards altogether. In my case, this wasn't much of a change, as I couldn't afford to in the first place; but as I started to get a sense of how much food went into the dumpsters every week, and how much money my friends were wasting on their fancy diets, it became clear to me that—fuck consuming "cruelty-free" products—those of us who could should just drop out of the economy, period. I imagine a lot of people were going through something similar to what I was, because a couple years later, the term "freegan" was in use, and people were starting to talk as much about where what they ate came from as what was in it. At first, this was still a minority position in reaction to a veganism that had claimed to address animal rights without addressing capitalism: eating dumpstered cheese pizza was a big fuck you to middle class vegans who thought their hands were clean just because they stayed out of the dairy aisle.

From Freegan to...?

Nowadays, it's almost hard to believe that freeganism appeared as a reaction to (and a reinterpretation of) veganism—in punk circles, it seems to be much more prevalent. This, of course, may simply be my limited perspective—but whatever

strikes me as being most prevalent is the thing to react to and reinterpret, in my book! Now that freeganism has replaced veganism as default setting for punks, it's time to look at the vegan diet and figure out what might be good about it, minus the consumerism that alienated some of us from it in the first place.

First, back to my own story: for years after becoming freegan, I figured I'd just starve to death if I began limiting my choices in the already limited world of free food. I ate cheese, even meat, whatever. Eventually, I started having doubts about it, though—I noticed that I would eat meat or dairy others had paid for when I had the chance, and that was really compromising my position. I decided to find out if it really was impossible for me to be vegan as well as freegan (that is to say, to eat only food that was both vegan and free); it wasn't, and soon I was eating a strict vegan diet. In fact, it turned out that I went one direction when everyone else went the other: pretty soon all my formerly-vegan friends were freegan, while I became the last of the uptight, ingredient-reading vegans.

I hate to say this, but the next step for many of my friends has been a relapse into omnivore apathy. For a while, they only ate meat if they dumpstered it or found it dead on the road; now they're the ones buying "free range" chicken, buffalo patties, whatever. You have to travel in pretty sheltered activist circles to think you're being rebellious by doing something everyone in mainstream society does! Sure, sure, what you eat is a matter of personal choice, and one kid's diet isn't going

YOU CAN PRY MY DUMPSTERED DOUGH-NUTS OUT OF MY COLD, DEAD HANDS.

...to feel compassion living in earshot of the sweatshops, the stadiums, the slaughterhouses, with the scent of blood cheap in the air...

to make or break an industry; but aside from the question of economic complicity, aside from the excuse to be self-righteous, even aside from the health issue, there is a little-discussed reason for strict veganism that has turned out to be really important to me.

Desire as Medium

For me, the most important thing about veganism is that it provides a concrete example of how we can transform our own habits and desires, how we can revolutionize ourselves. I figure we need to practice personally what we want to do on a global scale, if we are to have the knowledge and momentum to do it one day.

As the old sage once said, *in a world turned upside down, the true is a moment of the false.* Another way one could put this today: *in a life of suffering, pleasure is a component in a system of pain.* Here's an example, lest the philosophizing get too murky: a man comes home from the job he hates, exhausted, and turns on the television to unwind. Watching television is actually a fundamental part of his dispossession, but he experiences it as a pleasure, a reprieve. Here's another example of the same thing: *mmm, hamburger.*

In a world in which our own desires are turned against us as agents of our own oppression and the oppression of those around us, real indulgence, true hedonism, must therefore be a *contesting* of our desires, as well as a fulfilling of them. To experience joy and pleasure, not as a momentary reprieve from a miserable life, but

as a total, gratifying *way of life*, we must subvert our own habits and tastes, we must challenge and reconstruct ourselves outside the template of our programming.

One of the best examples of this in action is veganism. I'm not talking about those vegans who go around complaining about how much they miss yogurt—that shit drives me crazy: if your politics are about self-denial, you need to reconsider your whole approach. No, I'm talking about the transformation that takes place in a person who has not eaten meat for a year or so, who slowly stops looking at meat as being food at all. Remember, the omnipresence of flesh isn't just about sales and profit; it's also about desensitizing us to slaughter, getting us to look at our fellow living things as commodities. The fact that I can pass a McDonald's now and see the corpses of tortured animals rather than a selection of tasty lunchtime delights is, for me, a little victory. It means I've brought my desires a little further back into connection with reality (as I perceive and construct it), and it suggests that, given enough time outside—to choose another example—patriarchy, I might also be able to unlearn the objectifying that was programmed into my sexuality, or the striving for domination programmed into my social behavior.

One friend of mine once chided me for making even dinner into a symbol, but that's backwards: those hamburgers are, in fact, the dead bodies of cows raised in factory farms—it's capitalism that presents them as "symbols," as products with exchange values rather than

individual lives. I think that if we are to pursue happiness with some chance of success, we all have to be in touch with ourselves, not blocking any of our emotional responses. Doing what it takes to feel the tragedy of the factory farm holocaust whenever you pass a butcher shop is simply part of seeking to be a complete person, to be sensitive enough that you can experience joy fully, too, when you have the chance.

Perhaps one day, when animal-exploiting, environmentally destructive techno-industrial society has collapsed, I'll hunt deer in the woods, respectfully killing and eating my fellow creatures as my ancestors once did. In the meantime, I'm on strike. They can't sell me their products—I can get my hands on what I need for free—and neither can those products brainwash me into accepting genocide and exploitation as a part of everyday life. Every time I turn down some corporate animal product, however it reaches my low place in the food chain, it feels better to say FUCK YOU to our enemies and their war on us all than it ever could to eat steak or drink milkshakes.

So, erstwhile freegan, if any of this stuff about liberating your palate as well as your grocery budget makes sense to you, perhaps you'll reconsider your diet. You and I can hang out cutting up vegetables while everyone else eats dumpstered doughnuts and roadkill. Maybe veganism will get so trendy again that we'll have to rebel against it once more! See you behind the supermarket, Editor B.

DISASTER AND THINKTANK

"In a thinktank, a specific amount of time and space is set aside explicitly for the attainment of a specific impossible goal." –Manifesto on Concentration, 1914

During the second world war, Colditz Castle, a one-thousand-year-old fortress near Dresden, was chosen by the Nazis to serve as a high security POW camp. Colditz was prison to the most dogged allied escapers, and as a result it became an elite school of escape.

After several failed attempts involving such standard tactics as hiding places, disguises, and ropes, the prisoners' "escape committee" approved a plan to depart by air. In 1943, the prisoners began building a glider that was to be launched from the rooftop of the castle and piloted to a field across the nearby river. Over the next year, the glider was assembled entirely out of parts of the prison: floorboards, bed sheets, improvised fasteners, adhesives and tools. Just before the craft was ready to fly Colditz was liberated by allied troops. The voyage was never attempted.

A Nova documentary, entitled *Escape from Castle Colditz*, offers a nostalgic and dramatic presentation of the story. The documentary comes complete with a "re-creation" of the original Colditz glider--purportedly constructed following the original plans. At the conclusion of the documentary the glider is successfully flown for the witness of a vanload of octogenarian Colditz vets. It's a breathtaking moment.

Dubious congruency between the original glider and the simulation notwithstanding, the need of the documenters to answer "the big question"—would it have flown?--just misses the point.

What was the point? First, consider that, regardless of the flight-worthiness of the glider, it was an absolutely terrible concept for getting POWs back to the front lines. It took years to build. It required a huge amount of resources and the energy of dozens of prisoners. For all that exertion, the glider was to carry just two prisoners. Worse still, assuming a flawless flight, the escapees would have landed in a field just 1000 meters away. Such a position was far from escape. Earlier attempts had clearly established that the walls of the prison were a minor barrier compared to the navigating of hundreds of miles of enemy territory.

So in the terms of standard escapes from standard prisons, the Colditz glider was a ridicules scheme. The plan looks different, however, if we adjust the notion of what constitutes prison. If prison is not a singular condition of spatial confinement but a spectrum of confinements ranging in concreteness from iron bars to endless peacetime suburbia, what qualifies as a successful escape can diversify as well.

Whether the escape is from a high security POW camp or the high security of a living room sofa, the best plans succeed not because

' For a definition and thorough discussion of the "thinktank" approach to concentrated activity, consult the features section of Inside Front #13.

they cross a demonstrable line from "not-free" to "free" but because they play with and within the terms of confinement. What changes one's relationship to confinement more than a secret plan? The Colditz story is a perfect example. Because the glider plan was so far off the map, it was able to fly below the radar. It did succeed, at least in its penultimate goal, but I argue that it also claimed its ultimate goal: to re-create prison (both literally and figuratively) on the terms of the prisoners. With the glider, the soldiers escaped the prison of awaiting rescue and the prison of escapist routine (double entendre intended). Also, as much to their chagrin as to their longevity, the soldiers escaped the confinement of the terms military conflict and service had imposed on their lives since the beginning of the war.

Crisis Chronicles

Popular culture is full of crisis stories. These stories work in different ways. Colditz is an example of a kind of bourgeois crisis story. In this type, moderately- to highly-empowered protagonists experience a loss of power or choice, which exposes atavistic capabilities or freedoms.

Stories of contingency cannibalism are an extreme example of this. Cannibalism is one of the "fundamentals" that separate "civil" humans from a notion of uncivil humans and animals. Such stories are case studies proving the negotiability of even the most fundamental taboos — they are coded maps to loopholes in the social contract, if you will.

In the film *Alive*, a rugby team's airplane crashes in the Andes — and we witness an experiment we could never produce. The hypothesis, that certain fundamental morals separate civil humans from uncivilized humans and beasts, goes unsupported when the survivors begin eating the

casualties. The story is a convincing counterpoint to the moralism of fictional heroes like Odysseus who would starve to death before eating Apollo's sheep.

A scenario like the one represented in *Alive* calls all manner of lesser rules and morals into question. The film's airplane can be viewed as a symbol representing civilization, institution, government; it is a system that offers a service or a measure of protection in exchange for compliance to its rules. A contract exists between the passengers and the plane: the plane safely transports the passengers, the passengers behave within certain limits. But when the plane crashes it is not too long before the passengers adjust their behavior to suit a new arrangement. This is the refrain of the bourgeois crisis story: when protection is withdrawn those who were protected stop paying tribute.

Emergency Liberation

I am not suggesting that instances of contingency cannibalism expose a hidden desire of humans to eat one another. These stories simply describe an upper range of the adjustments that socialized humans are capable of making.

In crisis stories, barriers between human and nature break down, class becomes irrelevant or just silly, and the dispossessed or complacent become active. What appears to be going on with the popularity of crisis stories is a latent anarchist curiosity. The crisis story is a thought experiment. It wonders out loud what it would be like to live with radically different rules.

The story of the Swiss Family Robinson, while certainly an idealized tale, implicitly contains a notion of disaster as a kind of liberation. This liberation is not a utopian end-to-struggle or a glorified primitivism; it is a liberation from the notion that meaning and well-being are

inextricably linked to civilization. At the point of crisis, the family's connection to civilization is severed. When the their ship wrecks, traditional modes of power, choice, security, and luxury are lost; yet, as the story develops, happiness and meaning are retained. Furthermore, a kind of urgency and adventure take over, and we marvel at the ingenuity and cooperation that result.

Thankfully, those most attractive elements of the crisis can be detached from the crisis itself. There is no need to pray for the ambiguous good fortune of the Swiss Family Robinson. The desirable aspects of crisis are even commonplace — an easy example is the snowstorm or blackout that temporarily halts the normal flow of life. This could mean you finally meet the neighbor that has lived beside you for a year — and the two of you sit around all day trading stories, eating food from defrosting freezers.

Crisis Programming

Crisis stories almost always show an institution or symbol of an institution being destroyed and the subsequent triumph of something human. Considering this, what could be more dangerous to institutions than a popular fascination with crisis? The circulation of propagandistic "crisis spectacles" is one way institutions divert or defuse such subversive interests and desires.

"Reality" television is a prominent spectacle that serves this function. In the typical mode of the crisis story, many reality shows represent characters in eccentric scenarios working with novel rules. Of course, such shows are not designed to inspire people at home to experiment themselves, but rather to continue watching as actors[2] perform skits about such things.

Consider the "reality" teevee show, *Survivor*. It would be wrong to think of *Survivor* as an updated version

[2] Yes, let's not kid ourselves, these "real (people" are actors, just like "actors" are real people! What's an actor, anyway? Survivor contestants are carefully cast for their rolls. They perform their character for a camera, on set or on location. After filming, a director selects from the footage to create the desired characters and stories.

of *Gilligan's Island*. The *Gilligan's Island* "crisis" is a cooperative and funny respite from class, law and luxury. *Survivor*, on the other hand, is a total inversion of that premise. The characters contend in a winner-takes-all, losers-take-none scenario of scheming and backstabbing. Apparently, the free market survived the show's hypothetical shipwreck! This isn't the survival story we are used to; this is the capitalist survival story as celebrity feud or sporting event. Instead of selling soap, *Survivor* employees sell the citizen-testimonial that life without sofa, television, hierarchy, capital, cops, etc. is a life of even more conflict, misery, and destructive competition than we (the privileged) currently experience.

To complete the image, *Survivor* adds the justice of Uncle-Sam-style Democracy to the story. So, although the reasons that a particular character survives (wins) seem petty and arbitrary, the whole selection process is run by vote. Indeed, the losers who go home with nothing do so by voting for the winner. For the winner, the prize is the very cat in whose (supposed) absence the mice did play: a one million dollar

check that fortifies against a single additional day of "survival." Here, crisis fetish, with all its anarchist underpinnings, is being reigned in and re-presented as aggressively as possible. The embarrassing magnitude of the lengths to which the programmers have to go is quite inspirational—can our yearning for trouble be that dangerous to them?

Thinktank and "Reality" [Television]

The thinktank experiments certainly feed off of the same desires for alternate systems that are vented in reality TV. Ultimately, however, they undercut these spectacles, because those participating in their own projects are not watching, reading, or purchasing products, not buying into passive participation.

It certainly seems that contemporary media must walk an increasingly fine line in order to both display "real people" doing interesting and eccentric things AND discourage

(ostensibly the same pool of) real people from following suit. People sometimes ask, when they hear about our latest thinktank project, if we are emulating our favorite television shows. I only wish I saw *Survivor* or *Junkyard Wars* and said to myself, "Well, hell! We can do that." No, sad to say, I actually came to think-tanking through unmediated brainstorming and barnstorming with friends. But if television programmers ever actually mess up enough to bump a few customers from spectators to participants, that's just the kind of slippage I can get behind.

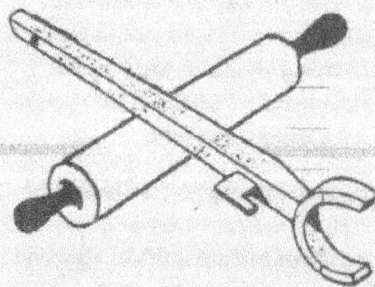

Auto Revision—and to Answer Your Question

The Automobile Revision Project[1] was a tabletop crisis, a bench test. The primary characteristics were all there: limited choices, inspired work, unity of purpose, sparse amenities. But the most important characteristics were our locally determined rules. Our central legislation was the discarding of volumes of legal and social code governing the uses of a car. As with many crisis situations, what had been product became a material, what had been solid became fluid.

To our interest, our visitors could

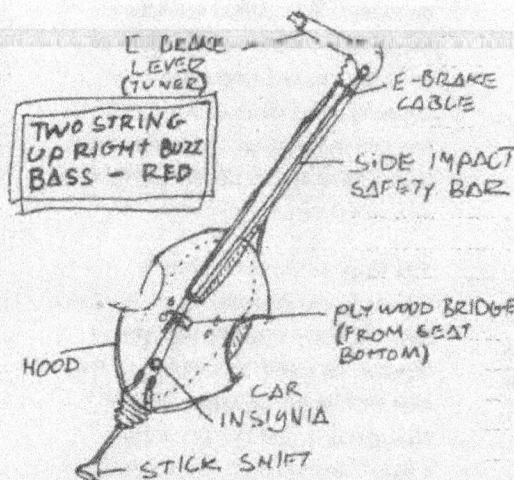

rarely be shocked by us breaking the rules of car nation. But the broken rules of sanitation and privacy were a different story. For all the strange things that one could hear and see through our window, visitors' concerns were concise: number one, what do we do about poo, pee and bathing; number two, "Aren't you killing each other in there?"

The questions seemed so strange. Was it "reality television" that naturalized the idea that humans just don't get along with one another—or is that a central myth underpinning our entire civilization? Do we really owe what little harmony we have to smelling fresh, flush toilets, mobility, privacy, and distance communication?

For me the Auto Revision was a

[1] In this project, a small team of folk-scientists locked themselves in a squatted garage with an automobile, which they proceeded to deconstruct and fashion into a variety of musical instruments. For a detailed account of this notorious thinktank, consult the pages of the first issue of Hunter/Gatherer, available from most CrimethInc. cells.

Thinktank in Action:
Kitchen Renovation Theater.

Between March 1 and March 14, 2003 five researchers continuously occupied the kitchen of an abandoned house in Pittsburgh, Pennsylvania. Over those two weeks, the investigators deconstructed everything, both tangible and intangible, they could get their hands on or wrap their minds around, and reassembled the pieces into props, sets, puppets, musical instruments, ideas, and scripts for a series of performances. When the two weeks were up, the cooks exited the kitchen to present their inventions and discoveries in a series of performances in a number of cities.

counterpoint to all that. For two weeks, we didn't shower or change clothes, we slept on the ground, and we used a bucket as a toilet. Those things caused no stress. For two weeks we couldn't check e-mail or talk to anyone at a distance. We also couldn't talk privately about anyone else in the room. Those

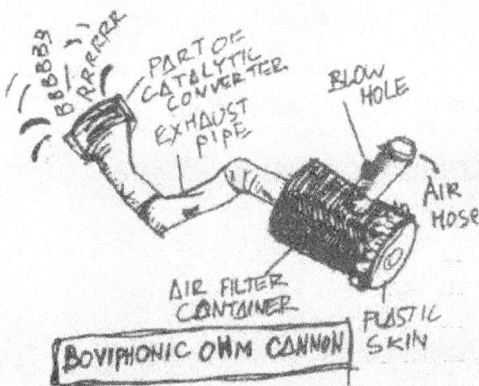

BOBBBB BARRRRR
PART OF CATALYTIC CONVERTER
EXHAUST PIPE
BLOW HOLE
AIR HOSE
AIR FILTER CONTAINER
PLASTIC SKIN
BOVIPHONIC OHM CANNON

1. Recipe: How to Turn A Kitchen Into a Puppet Show[2]

A variant of a food long known to the ancient elders of (fill in your favorite romantic indigenous culture), this recipe makes a sturdy and nutritious dough that can be easily altered to taste. Keep your kitchen stocked with the basic ingredients so you can whip up a batch whenever you feel your blood or other humors getting thin.

Basic Ingredients:

-Time (We used a heaping two weeks)

-Kitchen (An abandoned kitchen is best—we found ours in Pittsburgh)

-Participants (5 is ideal, although we found that 4 1/2 can add an unexpected effervescence)

-Food (Enough to eat healthily for the period of the project, but should also include silly food: marshmallows, pickles, seaweed, coconuts, etc.)

-Solitude (Nothing in, nothing out once the door is closed. Like a souffle, this recipe will fail if it comes in contact with the outside world before it has fully risen.)

Tools (depends on the interests of the cooks, but strong suggestions include):

SNAP! SNAP! SNAP!

"THE CLAM"
MADE FROM DOOR HANDLE RECESS HINGED FACE TO FACE

things acted to eliminate many standard collaborative stresses. For a visitor to see what was going on in the micro-culture of the Auto Revision she/he had to see through the surface of restrictions into the world those restrictions revealed.

This was a world in which we couldn't run errands—but we also "couldn't" sit

in traffic. By design of the project, all of the solutions were right before our eyes. We worked at interesting activities all day, without interruption. We cooked for each other every evening, and talked about new ideas as we ate. Every evening, we played the instruments we had made that day. Every night we fell asleep totally exhausted. That is to say: things were great, so great that we began to turn the question around—asking visitors, "Aren't you killing each other out there?" And, of course, the answer is, "Yes, even with showers."

"If I am captured I will continue to resist by all means available. I will make every effort to escape, and to aid others to escape. I will accept neither parole nor special favors from the enemy." -Article 3, U.S. Military Code of Conduct

[2] *Remember that puppets don't have to made of socks or papier mache. Anything can be a puppet: a hardboiled egg, a potato peeler, a beet, a plastic grocery bag, a piece of celery, a yellow plastic glove, a clothes pin, or your own precious and irreplaceable self. You've heard of puppet governments, haven't you?*

On Day 17 I found myself alone in the kitchen for one rare moment. We were packing up and getting ready to go; the kitchen was nearly stripped except for a jar of Beth's sprouts and some burnt toast on the windowsill, and a few last banana peels, shrunk down to the size of vanilla beans, hanging on the clothesline over the stove—the stove and oven themselves non-functional because the gas company had forgotten about us. We didn't actually care about the gas since we cooked our meals and deep fried our puppets on a Coleman stove set on top of the white enameled range, and heat was easy to compensate for with sweaters and bathrobes. The fact that the phone company forgot us as well was a bit more of a problem since the only information exchange—not so much exchange as monologue—we had with the non-kitchen world flowed through our crabapple-sized webcam. We had solved that problem on Day 4 by lowering a note with a quarter taped to it out the window, asking a passing stranger to go into the coffee shop below us and call a friend to call the phone company, which both the stranger and the friend generously did. After that we were on-line, although still without phone since Noel had gutted the telephone and made a kick drum pedal out of the hang-up mechanism and an ocarina out of the receiver. We didn't miss the phone; we didn't miss the world, which felt increasingly remote and constricted as our kitchen expanded. In two weeks the kitchen had gone from an inert and arbitrary container of air to an entire continent criss-crossed by our hunting and gathering, freighted with the histories we had brought in with us and the histories we had created. I stood on a chair with a damp sponge in my hand and unscrewed the light bulbs.

The kitchen light had been burning non-stop since Day 11 when Mark pulled too hard on the chain. That was during one of our nearly-every-night performances for each other, this one at the end of the day when we had agreed not to speak for 24 hours, a day of comforting, comfortable silence. Justin had come up from the coffee shop—he was considerably younger than the rest of us, less sure about two weeks of

confinement. He redefined his own kitchen to include the coffee shop beneath where he went from writing angry poetry at a small table to getting a job washing dishes behind the counter. Our only knowledge of the coffee shop was the music that traveled up through the water pipes behind the compost bucket and the limited gossip Justin brought us; the coffee shop became a land of conjecture at the edge of the map of the world, an alien culture with a single ambassador. Justin came in with a loud sound of foot stomping and the smell of late winter air. He chided us for our silence: "You've got to communicate to get anything done," he said, and went out again. We went back to our silence, listening to Noel pluck heartbreakingly sweet notes on the egg slicer under the cabinet.

We hardly noticed the light on after that, since by then we had only four days left before our first performance. The kitchen itself was an extended affair—actually a small abandoned apartment, its white walls grimed to the color of melted coffee ice cream, nothing but a tiny kitchen, a kind of dining nook, and a living room that opened off the dining room through a handy proscenium arch: the kitchen, the auxiliary kitchen, and the outer kitchen. We did have a bathroom and one other room, a chilly, remote bedroom down the hall where we kept our bedding during the day and where no one liked to go—too far out in the wilderness. We preferred to be in the human warmth of the kitchen where the walls expanded to accommodate our expanding understanding of each other. We slept all over the place—sometimes in the living room, sometimes on the kitchen floor all bunched up like puppies, sometimes in a corner half out, half under the table. We ate on the floor in the dark; at the table by candlelight, the candles held in place with wrenches or melted onto pieces of toast; standing up. On Day 3 we agreed that we hadn't fully explored the variations on eating so that night we held our soup spoons with salad and toast tongs, levering the spoons upward towards out mouths like herons. Afterwards we outlined the splotches on the tablecloth with markers and dated them, a record of our passing as casual and rare as dinosaur footprints. As dinner ended someone lifted a pair

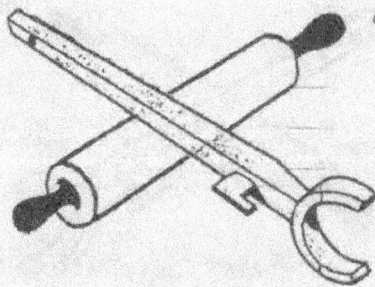

the inner meat, and spice to taste. Perform for audiences in children's museums, punk spaces, art galleries, coffee shops, community centers, and church basements (may be varied infinitely). Keeps well if preserved in video and 'zine form.

Soup pot
Screwdriver
Drill
Skill saw
Rubber bands
Duct tape
Bamboo skewers
Knife
Can opener

Mix together the basic ingredients and apply tools. Set a task, preferably a performance. Tell stories, laugh, play word games, sleep, saw things, take things apart, look out the window, cook, feed each other, find the slumbering music in telephone receivers, egg slicers, cabbage, wine glasses, pot lids, sifters, and wooden spoons. Peel off received identities, functions, utilities, and rules. Mince, puree, chop, parboil, deep fry, and mash

...and another version of the same prescription...

2. Recipe: Kitchen Renovation Dinner Theater [Thinktank 18]

2 weeks of time free and clear

5 organic free range strangers born in at least three different decades

1 kitchen squatted or borrowed

of tongs and clashed the jaws together lightly and we all joined in, a delicate whispery percussion that filled the whole candlelit kitchen and drowned out the sound of traffic on the street.

One day we saw snow fall outside our window; one night we heard a gunshot in the street and watched the reflection of the blue lights of the police cars slide across the toasters and coffee pots lined up on the floor. We wondered sometimes what kind of world we would find when we came out of the kitchen, what state of war or almost war the world had tilted over into. Other times we laughed so hard we felt dizzy. In the morning I would wake up in a square of sunshine and listen to breathing. On Day 9 Beth cut my hair in the kitchen and trimmed back Noel's curls; she kept the hair in a measuring cup on top of the cabinet and from then on we measured our morning coffee water with a teacup. Beth and Mark discussed shaving off their eyebrows but they never did. On Day 3 I got out my iron and began fusing plastic grocery bags together into billowy lengths of gauzy tissue. I made a ball gown for myself, a butcher's apron for Beth, and a pair of pants for Justin, who had invented a new sport called cabinet boarding to compensate for the fact that his skateboard was locked in our car on the other side of Pittsburgh. Mark filmed him jumping over saucepans and catching the cabinet board in tongs; Noel composed a frantic soundtrack on his computer to the steady scratching of sliced cabbage.

On Day 1 Beth and I had taken down the torn and stained roller blinds from all the windows; one of them hung for two weeks from the light fixture over the table where Beth had suspended it for her first night's performance in which she retrieved a rubber glove with an electric mixer and twine. On Day 5 she unscrolled the other two blinds and cut out giant silhouettes of a fork and a spoon; she filled the spaces with more ironed grocery bags fused with cabbage leaves and beans. The two banners hung over the sofa for the duration of the kitchen universe. On the night of Day 7 Noel and Mark performed a show for us

on top of the kitchen cabinets among the cans and jars, advancing and retreating an argumentative carrot and a conciliatory piece of celery skewered on the slats from the bottom of the blinds. On Day 8 Noel drilled holes in one of the aluminum rollers and made it into a flute. Our world pulsed with abundance. There was too much wealth in the kitchen to mine in just two weeks: blenders we never took apart, colorful wires kicked to one side because we didn't have time to make them into jewelry, can lids that never got snipped into stars. We were busy from the moment we woke up every morning until we shoved aside the drills and microwave parts and unrolled our sleeping bags well after midnight.

By Day 14 there was no sleep. Mark was the first to leave in the early minutes of the last day, sent out into the world to bring back wood and more tools. Noel and Beth and I stood in the lighted doorway, listening to Mark descend into the dark. We hovered at the threshold but couldn't bring ourselves to cross quite yet. The world we had created was as temporary as the first intensity of love—we knew that—we just didn't want it to end. Our world inside the kitchen was infinite; the world beyond was hedged with constraints and habits, with too much information. In the enormous kitchen everything shimmered with possibility; the world outside seemed narrow and static. We left, of course, in the end. The bombs fell across the ocean and on the screens of a million television sets. We hadn't changed anything—we hadn't set out to change anything. We had simply tethered ourselves for a few weeks in a world that kept changing all on its own, that was so rich and so vast and so full of delight that it would have taken a lifetime to understand. And we spent a lifetime there, a two week lifetime. I wondered as I unscrewed the last light bulb if I should have waited for everyone to stand and mark the moment with me, but it was too late for that. The light had gone out in the kitchen as soon as we opened the door, or rather had moved on to another place, been swallowed and digested and become part of our gristle and bone.

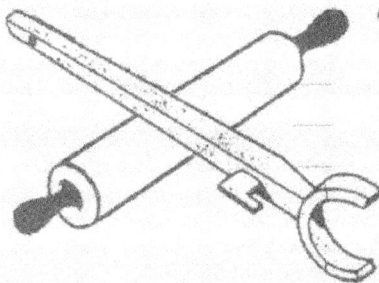

100,000,000 unnecessary, poorly designed, poorly built, dangerous, ugly, downcast, abandoned or ignored kitchen tools marching through our lives on their merry way from bad idea to landfill

6 buckets food, food promises, food hang-ups, food imperatives, food traditions, food tragedies, food fads, food scares, food miracles, food allergies, food color, food poisoning, food for thought

1 freezer-full of documentation equipment (very optional)

1 can opener

1,000 Chance operations, games, recombinations, lists, inversions, vague notions, questions, tools, thought crimes, enzymes.

Spread news of an unlikely activity that will result in an as-yet unknown performance. Arrange for as many places to perform as time and resources allow.

Enter kitchen and lock the door behind you. Agree as a group that no one will leave for two weeks. Get to work. Recklessly feast on all ingredients. Hold gatherings every night in which participants or pairs of participants present the day's thoughts and work in the form of ad hoc performances. On Day 10, start reconsidering performances and objects made so far. Choose what you would like to serve to those outside of the kitchen. Rehearse, add, subtract. Open door. Serve leftovers.

For more information about this and other thinktanks, write TankthInc. c/o CrimethInc. Headquarters, or email iamtheyeast@hotmail.com or hobbldhoy@aol.com or visit www.tankthink.com

white shark tales: anarchy in the u.s.a.

The strength of capitalism lies in its ability to make us be still. Where there is stillness, there is the danger of being chained down. It slips upon you like a thief in the night, tip-toeing past your defenses. It first appears in many guises—careers, expectations, degrees, promises . . . parents, neighbors, children, employees, students, rent, mortgages, plans that we never had a say in and futures that aren't ours to possess. Yes, the capitalist thief moves quietly in the night, and the thief is efficient. The thief takes everything, and leaves you nothing but a shell, a cheap imitation of the life you really want. However—can the thief rob your house if you don't have one?

Yet how can you have no house, no possessions, nothing to your name but the clothes on your back? Simple. You must always be on the move.

There are many paths that leave this world of poor-paying jobs and unfulfilling lives. To each her own path—it would be arrogant to attempt to tell you what your path is out of the mundane humiliations of everyday life. In sheer physical terms, there are many ways to be on the move. You can just walk to the side of the road and stick out your thumb, and a stranger will pick you up and take you on the road. For those of you who enjoy the usage of your legs, you can always just walk through the woods, relying on wild berries and the kindness of a stranger farmer for a bowl of porridge in the morning. Some may enjoy hopping on the underground railroad, modern-day hobos criss-crossing the country on the forgotten industrial skeleton of our most digital of societies. For me, it was a White Shark that stole my heart. Nothing much, just a normal white van, of cheap make and dodgy American build. I'm not sure how it all came to pass, how the Shark was released upon the country to wreak innumerable acts of utter piracy, revolt, and complete lack of regard for all capitalist values (except excessive gasoline consumption). I remember only that there was nothing left for me where I was. There had been too many horrors, too much failure—glorious failure, but failure nonetheless—and I felt like a ghost in my own hometown. It occurred to me that maybe I needed a change of surroundings, so I grasped my best brother-in-arms Ishmael by the shoulder one lonely night and told him we should do it, just leave it all behind. We met with an elite group of co-conspirators gathered in the wreckage of the former anarchist compound amongst the slowly creeping kudzu. We decided to leave right then and there the ruins of our youth, and we gave little heed to the future. All we had was a few ideas, a few dates and events, a few scraps of a plan, and an atlas. Being a generous soul, I volunteered my old van, purchased from one of my neighbors whose mother had recently died, for transport. After all, we had to make it to these events on time, and train-hopping and hitch-hiking are notoriously unreliable. Little did I know we were releasing a monster, a monstrous shark the like of which I have yet to see again.

None of these stories are fictional, despite their ludicrous nature. Indeed, all have happened to me. However, names have been changed to protect the innocent (or, to be precise, the not-so-innocent), and the chronological order of events has been changed to throw off the fucking feds! Also—these adventures haven't been written down to glorify the last year of my life, but to bear witness to the possibilities all of us have before us. Indeed, there are many adventures of grander scope than mine in this world, but I still hope these tales warm some lonely soul . . . and cause her to quit her job, jump in her van, and never look back.

in which a boy and his van set out to liberate each other...
by Secret Agent Captain Ahab

Only a Manner of Time Before Banks.

Somehow, the White Shark had swallowed Isabella from Brazil, although exactly how was somewhat of a mystery. Perhaps it was because she had just been arrested at some demonstration in Philadelphia (and I'm sure the paranoid Philadelphia cops were shocked by her passport—the international conspiracy of anarchists manifesting itself!). Perhaps it was because the white van had carried the CrimethInc. troupe to a presentation in Worcester where we complemented her video with a band made purely out of dumpstered metal scraps we had found around town the day before. To be honest, I have no idea. The White Shark is a magnet for discontents and malcontents with absolutely no respect for borders, and its siren-song is hard for anyone to resist.

One problem about the White Shark is you have to feed her to keep her happy, and she takes no other food other than gasoline, occasionally garnished by oil and transmission fluid. We had made our way to Maine after ending the North American Insurrection Tour in New York City (due to unfortunate circumstances, but mostly just having been around each other for so long we just hated each other!). Now, with every single member of our merry crew utterly and completely broke, how we were going to escape the ever-pleasant woods of Maine was going to be a problem. The obvious thing to do was to just steal the gas, which we had done a few times before. However, in the words of Ishmael, "Sometimes you gotta keep the small laws to break the big ones," and given that the White Shark currently carried one recently arrested international and at least one felon, getting caught brazenly stealing gas would be amateur. Also, one key to stealing gas is having multiple escape routes, and Maine has really only one highway. There had to be an easier way to get money. After considerable deliberation at our secret log cabin deep in the woods of Maine, we took out maps and decided we were going to do a raid at a Wal-mart shopping center in the port of Augusta. Ishmael had protested its construction years earlier, so at least one of the company was familiar with the territory. We decided the most cunning path would be for us to into the shopping center and steal everything we could get our grubby hands on, getting money to feed the monstrous hunger of the white van from various cryptic return scams and shady pawn shops.

Filling the van with dumpstered chips (Maine seems to specialize in Frito-Lay dumpsters!), we left with enough rations to make it to the next port of call, and came up with a scheme on the way. We would walk into a very expensive and over-priced yuppie store that was known to be exceptionally vulnerable to return scams. Given that it was a small store, an advance squad would distract the few employees with various requests, while one guerrilla warrior-thief would walk in—cool as ice—and fill a backpack full of loot, then run out, to be intercepted by the Shark who would be waiting obediently outside. We should have known the best laid schemes of sharks and men can go awry.

As a member of the advance squad and perpetrator of innumerable thieveries, even I was shocked by how easily the two employees were hoodwinked into leaving their positions unguarded. We went in, dressed the best we could as yuppie shoe-shoppers, and demanded new shoes. Both employees simultaneously left the cash register and disappeared into the mysterious netherworld of shoes that must have been somewhere out of sight in some closet in the store. The guerrilla came in, grabbed a backpack, and with a smile on his face began throwing all manner of loot into his bag. It all appeared to be going well when, to our dismay, another customer walked in! This ordinary bourgeois customer immediately noticed that something was not right with this shop, and yelled for the employees. The guerrilla, ever quick, fled the store full backpack in hand before the employees bumbled from their closets of shoes. Not sure what to do, we decided to delay the employees, questioning both of them as regards the whereabouts of our demanded shoes, denying the existence of the shoplifter that the other customer saw race through the door. After several minutes of complete confusion by the employees, they decided that something weird definitely was going on and called the police. We kept up a whirlwind of utter lies and ridiculous demands upon the employees till the bitter end, but when they picked up the phone to call the police, we felt we might be suspected of collusion with the more obvious criminal elements of our enterprise. We politely made our farewells and fled the scene of the crime ourselves. Quickly I made it back to the helm of the White Shark, where a wanted political criminal who had wisely avoided participation in the crimes of the day reminded me we had to get him away from the scene of the crime, and whispered that he had grabbed the loot the criminal had wisely dropped near the Shark on the way out of the store. The White Shark bucked, and we ran behind the store complex, hoping to outrun the police and find our erstwhile guerrilla friend. Unfortunately, he wasn't there, and, seeing the police car roll into the shopping center, we quickly sped away through another exit.

Making very quick decisions, I decided it would be best to get all possible criminals (except myself!), felons, and recently stolen goods out of the van. However, we couldn't leave our friend in the claws of the police. Quickly, I grabbed Isabella and told her that she should exit the van and begin a search for the guerrilla thief, and if he was seen to tell him to hide away as far in the woods as possible. She was to meet us in front of the shopping center and inform us of his general location, as soon as she communicated this to our companion. Not feeling entirely right for dropping off a South American revolutionary in the middle of a desolate shopping center that was currently being occupied by the police, the van sped off. I wondered what a parallel situation would be in like Brazil—what if a group of Brazilian anarchists left me as a scout in the middle of Sao Paulo? After getting a few miles away from the site of the crime, the more criminally wanted of our crew jumped out the van with the loot, and fled far into the woods after a few minutes conversation about the various bird-calls and honks I should use to announce the return of the Shark. Quickly, the White Shark sped back around and headed back into the mouth of the enemy. Indeed, the police car was right outside the recently robbed yuppie-store, and Isabella was walking about the complex looking nonplussed about the entire situation. I rode up and she jumped into the van, informing me that the police were still in the store questioning the employees, but she had not seen our missing guerrilla. In complete panic, the Shark prowled around the parking lot looking for its missing servant—and out of the corner of our eyes we spotted a shirtless vagrant in the woods on top of a hill! It was our guerrilla, shirt torn off, looking like some strange escaped Cro-Magnon man gazing upon the concrete landscape of an encroaching alien civilization.

Now, the mind of a thief works in strange ways, and whenever I see a young man with his shirt off in the woods I know he is trying to escape the cops. Obviously, the first thing someone is going to tell a cop about a criminal is his clothing description. So, the bright criminal is either going to change clothing, or, lacking a spare change of clothing, just take the shirt off! Myself, I wasn't sure exactly what the cop would do if he saw a young and shirtless man in the woods. I recognized the dire situation, and the van pulled up as near as it could, as our young guerrilla charged headlong into the open maw of the shark. Fellow pirate safe and no cops in pursuit, we rolled back to the mysterious spot in the woods where we had dropped off the rest of the crew. Unfortunately, in the heat of moment I had completely forgotten where exactly I had dropped them off. As night approached, it was beginning to look like we would never find them again. I started honking the horn wildly, driving like a madman up and down the street. Out of the corner of my mind I thought I recognized the spot where I had dropped off my compatriots. Jumping out of the car, I heard what could only be the sound of semi-automatic weapons! After fiddling with the bird-calls for a few minutes, I just began yelling for them. Within minutes, the criminal underclass reappeared from the woods, scared out of their wits. "They're shooting fucking guns, I don't know who they are but these fucking woods are being pumped full of metal!" Recognizing the perilous nature of being stuck in the woods with gun-toting Mainards, we jumped back into the safety of the van and sped off into the distance.

I looked into Isabella's eyes, trying to give some semblance of an explanation to our behavior in the last few hours. I didn't know what other types of activists or revolutionaries she had been hanging out with beforehand. How did this compare to what anarchists did in Philadelphia...or Brazil? I imagine most of the circles in Brazil put our petty crime to shame. I fumbled for words, trying to explain what we were doing. "We're not exactly activists you know...we're anarchists...we're sort of cousins to outlaws, but we have a mission in life, you know?" I could see the gleam in her eye. She knew. Welcome to the States!

Revolution in the Heartland

The van drove and drove and drove. To all of us in its depths, it soon became obvious that this was not just an ordinary van, but a van with the heart of an animal. Very quickly, small parts of its machinery of lesser quality soon fell apart. First it was a tire, then a strange part of radiator, then yet another unnamable piece of metal. Like some ungodly monster, sometimes it appeared as if the van was reducing itself to the very minimum needed for the trip. Four of us in a van, keeping each other in good spirits with stories and memories, dehydrating in the summer heat. Sneaking in and out of campsites without paying, attempting to find back-roads into the Badlands, running out of gas in the middle of the Badlands, a kind indigenous family providing us gas from their own personal store. Clearly we were slowly going mad in the van—I was even struck down with blindness due to poison ivy in my eyes! Yet the White Shark kept chugging along, ruthlessly plowing across the country all night. Ishmael

drank cup of coffee after cup of coffee, and the black liquid of darkness fueled our madness. Many a lonely gas station was left short of food and gas, and many an anarchy symbol scribbled on a bathroom wall.

Small towns appeared before us, and in every one we found a little cell of anarchists plotting the destruction of civilization as we know it. No town was safe from the rapacity of the White Shark. We would pull into the parking lots of shopping centers, walk in without a cent, and walk out our pockets full of fruit and vegetarian sushi—and if we were feeling lucky, one of us would run out with a full shopping cart of wine and soy cream! In one small town, the girlfriend of our host called to tell her boyfriend that some strange vagrants had walked into the store, clearly stole large sums of food, and walked out—and every employee knew, but no one could be bothered to stop them because it was so humorous. Laughing, our host told his girlfriend to come over and meet the culprits. We created anarchy anywhere and everywhere, yelling revolutionary manifestos in coffee-shops in Des Moines, organizing discussions with Christian straight edge kids about abortion rights, rioting—and throwing donuts!—against cops on the streets of America's largest suburbs, cheering our hip hop comrades the Insurrectionists as they spun poetry that mixed equal parts relativity theory and John Brown practice for crust-punks in warehouses and hip art crowds in New York City. We even played basketball with kids outside church, and then snuck in to steal their food! Everywhere, not just anarchists, but anarchy itself.

It was soon obvious that we were in no mere van, but some strange animal hell-bent on destruction. We imagined—or did we?—a large fin rising from its white roof; and did not the grill of our vehicle appear to be a gaping maw? The white van clearly had been hiding a secret identity from us the entire time. Like some bizarre automobile superhero—our van was actually a White Shark! Despite innumerable tires blown, arrests for mob action, being late for our own shows, and alternating between loving and hating each other, the van— by now clearly becoming more and more animal— finally made it to the Earth First! Round River Rendezvous in Wyoming. H. Rap Brown (who, I might add, our government has framed for murder and thrown in jail!) was only partially right. Anarchy is as American as apple-pie.

The first night at the rendezvous, rumor broke out a local bar was offering, I kid you not, one hour of free beer. Immediately, dozens of smelly anarchists piled into the belly of the white shark, arms and legs sticking out at all possible angles from every possible orifice—window, that is. Barely able to move, I somehow drove the mad creature down to the local bar. When we entered it, we were quickly surrounded by cowboys: huge men with giant muscles, tight jeans, and mighty mustaches that would make Emiliano Zapata proud. As everyone sat down and drank beer after beer, it quickly became apparent that the anarchists had wandered into the wrong bar. The largest cowboy with the most terrifying visage of all of them began to systematically harass the smallest woman who had come with us. The largest anarchist amongst us, a mighty redneck himself from the wild woods of Maine, inserted himself into what appeared was going to be a brawl between the local working class and the anarcho-eco-warriors. The night could not be going in a worst direction, and the cowboys were much more well-muscled than ourselves.

Luckily, at that moment a local folk singer, himself sporting a mighty beard, rose to the stage. The anarcho-redneck, realizing the fate of the Movement itself lay in the balance, called out for some Folsom Prison Blues:

I hear the train a coming, its rolling round the bend, and I ain't seen the sunshine since I don't know when, I'm stuck in Folsom Prison, and time keeps dragging on, but that train keeps on rolling, down to San Antoin...I shot a man in Reno, just to watch him die...when I hear that whistle blowing, I hang my head and cry

The cast of Eugenia and Wobbleo prepare to give the performance of their livces

As if by divine intervention, the crowd all began singing: cowboys, anarchists, roughnecks, eco-warriors, rednecks, eco-warriors, and hippies, all dancing like the devil himself possessed them. Every single one escaping their own personal Folsom prison, grasping shoulders and swaying to a man who could only be Johnny Cash reincarnated. Nothing could stop the crowd, and the man sang for hours. In fact, in the heat of the moment a train-hopper with a banjo jumped on stage and began playing with our cowboy singer. As soon as the cowboy singer stepped off the stage, the entire Dumpster Country Ramblers—a wild anarchist old-time music band if there ever was one!— jumped onto stage themselves, and began playing their hit single: *"With a Banjo and an AK-47 by my side.".* The cowboys kept going wild, and soon everyone was intermixing, talking about how much they hated politicians, kissing their sweethearts, and sharing stories about the mountains and woods. America, there is hope.

After a series of entertaining workshops, the highlight being How To Kill With A Mag-light, we decided it was time for CrimethInc. to manifest itself in a way it never had before, in a way that would be utterly entertaining, yet as relevant as it could be to the mangy hundred-odd anarchists and earth warriors congregating: we were going to throw a musical.

There have always been raging debates amongst the more intellectual of our brethren about what exactly things will "look like" after the revolution, despite these conversations doing little to nothing to bring anything even slightly resembling a revolution about. Of these debates, one of the most vicious and irrelevant has always been the "green vs. red"

anarchism debate...and we let our imaginations go with the flow. What if there was a Revolution and folks really divided upon those lines? What if Ted Kaczynski was freed from jail to lead the dread-locked green anarchists to victory against syndicates of red anarchists who controlled the manufacturing plants of Carhartts and Mag-lites? What if the daughter of Ted Kaczynski, Eugenia, fell in love with the young magnate of the One Big Union, Wobbleo? Yes, we had a plot for a play, and were going to call it Wobbleo and Eugenia.

Soon, we had gathered a horde of anarchists from every corner of the United States, with the dreadlocked greens putting twigs through their noses and reds bedecking themselves in full-length bright red pajamas. While the cleverness of the drama can never be conveyed to those who were not there, at one point the greens and the red anarchists, involved in a gang fight over the various interpretations of May-day (as either a pagan festival or celebration of workers rights) began singing to the tune of a fairly well-known boy-band song, My Way:

I want to have a class war, I want to see industrial collapse, I never want to hear you say... I want the revolution my way!

Soon, the green anarchists, engaged in acts of excessive pot-smoking, were infiltrated by the young Wobbleo, who wooed the beautiful Eugenia with his ode of how "he works everyday, and there's nothing that I own..." She let down her dreads and the burly Wobbleo, red cape and all, climbed into her tree-sit for a night of hanky-panky. And as soon as Ted Kaczynski found out about her love-making with the enemy he quickly scolded her: "Don't you know that the Industrial Revolution and its consequences have been nothing but a disaster for the human race!" Soon, war broke out between the feuding anarchists, and as Wobbleo and Eugenia desperately hopped trains to have their child in a safe haven, the greens and reds began hacking each other to bits to the tune of Michael Jackson's "Beat It."

"You dumpster-dive to live, that ain't primitive, so beat it!" "We wear bones through our nose and we'll cut down your cell phone poles!"...until one green anarchist reveals a dirty secret: "I got a trust fund and I got an SUV, it's parked over there right next to a tree.". A hushed silence fell upon the collected forces of Earth First! For a second, we thought maybe our satire had hit a bit too close to home for some of those in attendance... but then the crowd burst out laughing. Surrounded by the dead bodies of their overly-ideological anarchist opponents, Eugenia gave birth to their green and red love-child—Plaid! Soon, the entire crowd began singing:

Why, why did the all anarchists die, was the theory too heavy and the logic to dry? If we dump the ideology and bake a new pie, maybe this won't be the day that we die, maybe this won't be the day we die..."

The Shark versus The International Monetary Fund

Of course, the Shark soon began looking for larger targets than yuppie shopping centers and greater dreams to host than traveling anarchist circuses...the Shark was straining at the leash. The Shark decided that only the largest of international financial institutions would sate its eternal hunger for blood. Before even I knew it, I was driving with a small crew of anarchists to the hotel where the International Monetary Fund was meeting in a few short months. The hotel resembled nothing more than a nightmare of modern architecture, a veritable Death Star of comfort and luxury for the rulers of the world in the new millennium. Huge towering glass doors, giant towers and escapades. Yet, with all their might and power, how were we going to get in? There is always something to be said for walking through the front door.

Four smart but still black-clad anarchists walked right into the hotel where the International Monetary Fund was going to meet, without any of the staff even giving us a small blink. Quickly, we looked around—and it appeared that we were about to crash a party, a party named for some strange corporation with one of those oh-so-fashionable names to inspire investor confidence, like DigiCorp or NeoTech. Quickly realizing we were strangers in a strange land, we ran up the nearest stairs we could find, desperate to camouflage ourselves with any thin veneer of legitimacy. It appeared as if by magic: four mostly empty wine glasses left idly by. We grabbed them, and soon had metamorphosed from anarchist secret agents to slightly drunk and bewildered employees at a company party. Indeed, we heard loud pumping music below, and, never ones to forgo a dance party, we made it down the stairs and into one of the largest halls I have ever seen. A huge screen towered above hundreds of drunk employees in neat white shirts, with an image of a woman with perfectly manicured hair across an a sky so blue that it could only be digital. She spoke, and it was if God or Big Brother himself was speaking: "Welcome to the future..."

Aghast, we looked up, only to see a giant green dinosaur being slowly deflated by dozens of angry computer programmers and bureaucrats smashing it with giant rubber hammers. The future was apparently going to be very strange indeed. Although I was sorely tempted by what appeared to be free food near the sagging dinosaur, we thought actual employees, even if slightly drunk, might ask us which division we worked and so give us away to the authorities. Hand in hand, we fled upstairs.

Wandering throughout the halls of the future meeting place of the IMF, capitalist waste manifested itself as it always does at the most opportune of times. The halls of the hotel were lined with leftover room-service food that the chubby programmers and fat bureaucrats couldn't even finish. I immediately began a one-man mission to eat every last morsel I could. Half-finished martini in one hand, decadent half-eaten ice-cream in the other, I was unstoppable. We wandered floor after floor, and went up ten whole stories of sleeping chambers and wasted food. Whenever a hotel employee would appear and ask us what were doing, we would leer drunkenly at him using our best acting skills and ask where some random room number was. "Oh, I'm so sorry...I thought I was on the fourth floor!" The security system completely compromised by four anarchists armed with empty wine-glasses.

We became bolder and bolder as night ticked on. Soon, even the drunkest of the employees of the computer company were going to bed, and the hotel became virtually empty...and all ours! We found strange staircases that went down into the depths of the hotel, walked down endless corridors and found doors to empty rooms and storage chambers. We conjectured that if we had been a bit more prepared and had brought a few months supply of food, we could hide in one of those rooms and come out in the middle of one of the meetings of the International Monetary Fund with our guns blazing. Using napkins found on silver platters found outside hotel rooms, we scrawled maps of the entire complex. Eventually, as we got deeper and deeper underground into service corridors with 'Employees Only' written on them, we would occasionally hear what sounded like an employee coming around the corner. Panicking, we would run around corners hold our breath, jumping into elevators and hitting any button we could to escape. Occasionally, we would have to confront some bored night employee late night. They would always be very perplexed by the appearance of four anarchists holding wine-glasses in a corridor which no one in their right mind could possibly have wandered into by accident. Yet we would hold to our story: "Oh, we must have walked down the stairs instead of up them to our rooms! What were we thinking?" Human beings, if given implausible situations, tend to accept even the most irrational of explanations as long as it lets them reconcile whatever is before their eyes with their internal conception of reality.

As dawn starting creeping up on us, we had actually scouted one of the largest hotels in the world completely out, and we decided to leave. On the way out, as all scouts are supposed to do, we checked door knobs to see if they were unlocked. Right next to the exit from the hotel we found a unlocked door that led straight to what appeared to be some ludicrously fancy, and completely closed, hotel restaurant. In every hotel restaurant there is a bar. And in every bar there is beer.

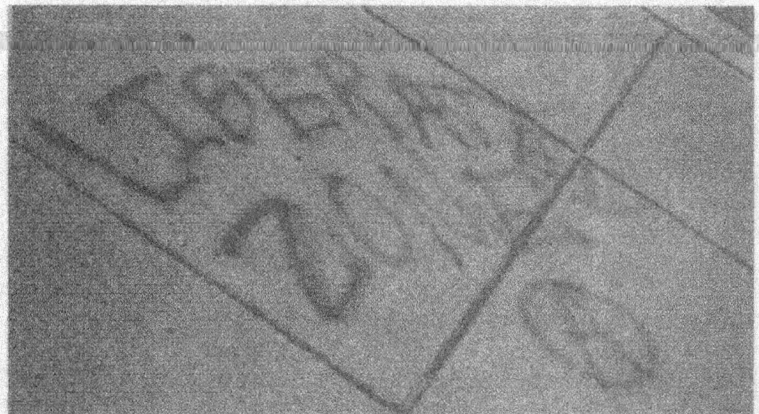

Where's the next liberated zone? Can we break into the oval office and nap there next?

Our logical chain complete, we jumped over the bar in the restaurant and started trying to open all the locked cupboards.

While the last employee at the restaurant had been bright enough to lock the wine-cupboard, they had left a giant case of iced beer and liquor completely open. Inside, it was like a treasure trove of beers with strange German names and liqueurs the like of which people of my social class aren't even supposed to know! We quickly stuffed our pockets with cans of the finest beer and peppermint schnapps, only to realize that there was no way we could carry it all out. After peering out the door, all four of us scampered out of the hotel and to the van, unloading our liquor on the way. Personally, I began feeling a bit paranoid, and thought that maybe this act was taking it just a little too far, that now we were dealing in pure hubris. However, the first beer run had only whetted our appetites. Grabbing our backpacks, we meandered right back into the hotel, walking through the front door, straight into the bar, and began filling our rucksacks with alcohol. In we went, and out we went, and in again, and out again...until every last beer was gone! In an act that can only be considered complete chutzpah, we had stolen the IMF's beer!

As we loaded up the white shark and our one other vehicle with the beer, we came to the realization that we had no idea what to do with the excessive amount of alcohol we had just stolen. The White Shark, drunk off its latest victory, seemed to be smiling upon us. Suddenly, a member of our jolly crew had a brilliant idea: We should give out the beer free at Food Not Bombs! Although it would surely be breaking one of the bylaws of the International Network of Food Not Bombs©, anyone who had to spend their nights hungry in DC at least deserved a beer to keep them warm. We drove it back to our secret anarchist hideout in the depths of the Capital itself, and, as we opened the back door, one of our compatriots came stumbling out of bed, red dreadlocks flying. When he heard the idea, he grinned. It was going to be one hell of a Food Not Bombs. Some may call it stealing, but as every modern-day Robin Hood knows: it's not theft, it's redistribution of wealth.

Intermezzo

The relationship between the driver and her car is hard to understand. Relationship is a dry word, a word used by dating guides in cheap newspapers and half-hearted people who are afraid to commit themselves to anything greater than a life of romance novels bought at supermarkets. The love between a car and her driver is hard to understand. The lines between us and our methods of transportation become fuzzy, and we melt into our own machinery. No words can express my affection for the White Shark: it feels more like home to me than any house I've ever lived in, and my sleeping bag has more fond memories associated with it than any floor the world over. Words cannot describe the many nights I've spent living in her metal shell, never able to stretch fully out—so leading to my habit of curling up like a wolf even when I sleep in a bed[1]. The White Shark transformed with me, from a respectable minivan in which a mother might drive her child to a soccer match, to a torn up, smelly, vengeful, dark vagabond of the night. The paint started chipping, the white began to be encrusted with dirt that no amount of washing could fix, strange liquids continually leaked from its shadowy crevices. The tape player, often the only thing holding my sanity together in the darkest hours of those nights, even that turned cannibal, eating the

tapes we put into it. Yet despite all her flaws, and perhaps because of them, I loved the White Shark. You can have your fancy red Mercedes, yuppie scum—I'd rather spend the night with my old dirty van any day of the week. Rich and arrogant bourgeoisie of the world, behold the White Shark! Behold your future executioner!

The effect the White Shark had upon its inhabitants was positively insidious. Nothing could describe the effect of watching ordinary people, disillusioned with crappy jobs or boring lives, jump into the van and, before my very own eyes, be transformed into anarchist warriors at the beck and call of any good cause within driving distance. At first it started out as petty theft, money for gas, a few bites of food. As the distances and the glorious heights of the plans increased, everyone in the belly of the Shark slowly got more grizzled, their bodies more gaunt, and the mad look of a pirate entered in their eyes. Defending tree-sits in Ohio, offering eco-defense workshops in poor neighborhoods in Baltimore, defending indigenous lands in the highlands of New York state, fighting for squats in Manhattan...the White Shark made me believe in knights errant again. When you needed us, you just needed to get in touch with one of the associates of the White Shark and the fucking cavalry would be there the next morning.

Cars, like friendships, need maintenance. And so I descended into the inner depths of my vehicle, exploring its nooks and crannies. I knew her limits and she knew mine. I also befriended an anarcho-mechanic, the father of one of the members of the Company of the White Shark, who helped me maintain her. He repaired the cars of all the local street kids and neighbors in his own garage, and for far less than any auto-shop. He knew all the shadiest auto-parts dealers in town, and all the honest ones as well, and his word was as good as gold. As I returned again and again, after strange adventure after even stranger adventure, we bonded over the White Shark. He would tell me tales of his adventures in New Orleans and Mexico, and I would tell him of stealing food from hotels in French Canada and fighting cops in Philly. He taught me what a gasket was, what weird part of some strange metal piece connected to some other piece. In between inspecting one weird problem of the White Shark after another, he would mutter things like "That Ariel Sharon's a bloody butcher..." Indeed, both the shaggy-haired anarchist and the auto-mechanic with a family in the outskirts of the city agreed that Western civilization was headed straight towards its doom, and the President George W. Bush was a madman at the helm of sinking ship. Because of these things, our anarcho-mechanic continued to repair the White Shark, and I continued to drive the distance with the wild beast. We hypothesized that the beast would keep on going until there was nothing left but a whirling engine, a dying transmission, and a rusty metal frame, and then I would drive her into the ocean, lighting her on fire and giving her a proper Viking funeral.

In the Hands of Our Enemies

The White Shark is a wild beast, and while I may recount some of its nefarious adventures here, I can only recount those I know of. For the White Shark has been on many adventures that even I, its monomaniacal Captain, don't know of.

---

[1] *Editor's note: Only in punk rock circles can you find people who approach sleeping as an extreme sport!*

The White Shark does not just aid and abet thieves: the White Shark plans full frontal assaults on the foundations of capitalism itself, with a vengeance that would put most people to shame. The White Shark makes plans, and it sticks to them. As just related, the White Shark has a personal vendetta against the global financial system, especially the International Monetary Fund. Not too long after the beer had been stolen from the IMF, the attacks on the World Trade Center and the Pentagon happened, and took even us aback. All the same, the White Shark was first and foremost a van of action, and while most of its activities after September 11th are too dark too recount in the light of day, it did successfully ferry us away from danger. However, its hunger for blood is insatiable, and before we knew it, it was driving us right back

but me and one of my most perceptive partners in crime noticed that such a huge banner was going to completely impossible to carry. After all, it was larger than most anarchists, who by nature tend to be a short lot, and offered about as much tactical defense as a wet blanket. The wily White Shark, ever to the rescue, took us to the nearest home repair store where we began a brutal campaign of return scams to get a large amount of PVC pipe. With much PVC jutting out of the back of the White Shark, we drove back to the Anti-Capitalist Convergence Center and spent the entire night transforming the large banner into a formidable defense barrier by reinforcing its corners with plastic pipes. Our task done, we slept barely a wink before having to mobilize ourselves for the protest. As we wandered back into the Convergence Center, one of the organizers ran up to us and told us that there was a serious problem: there was no way to transport the banners, including the marvelous pipe banner, to the actual site of the protest. Would the White Shark come to the rescue? But of course!

This was clearly going to be one of those sketchy situations. The black bloc had assembled, several hundred strong, in one of the small central parks in DC. They were just waiting for the banners. The White Shark parked behind some decrepit gas-station and released its scouts to check the situation out. When they returned noting the huge number of pigs but the clear passage-way for vehicles, the White Shark realized the time to act was now or never. The White Shark drove up maniacally right in front of the Black Bloc and released its doors. Out from its bowels came banner after banner, pipe after

The banner that nearly cost the White Shark its life!

to the meeting of the International Monetary Fund, which, despite the attack, had gone on. The White Shark dropped us off back at our secret anarchist hideout in the Capital, and we began preparing for what seemed to be one of the most frightening protests of our lives. It was clear this protest was no ordinary protest—and it wasn't going to be the North American version of Genoa we were all hoping for. No, this was testing the waters after a major terrorism attack and subsequent reactionary scare. The results of this test could be fatal as well, for now it was clear our government felt threatened and was looking for someone to lash out against. The bombing had just started on Afghanistan, and it was clear that one of the next things on their 'To-Do' list was to rid the world of those pesky anti-globalization protesters, especially the troublesome anarchists.

However, when the going gets tough, the tough rise to the occasion. As the White Shark landed in DC, tons of CrimethInc. propaganda (produced for free at our local Kinko's) in the wings, it became clear that the work was to be done. A huge banner was being constructed in a haphazard fashion by a contingent of artists in the convergence center,

pipe, flag after flag. As the Captain, I kept an eye on the cops, and they had definitely noticed this bit of maneuvering by a mysterious white van, as they started marching towards us. Panicking as the last banner was dropped off, I put the petal to the metal and the White Shark sped away, down one road after another. Finally, we parked off what appeared to be a road in a residential area, carefully backing our van into the parking spot to have the license plate to the wall, and jumped out. I took all of the money I had to my name out of my pockets, a good crisp two hundred dollars in the form of two hundred dollar bills, and afraid they would get nicked by the police in the protest, I hid them in the ash-tray. Also, as I was living in the van at the time, all my possessions from my record collection to my two or three pairs of marginally clean underwear were in two huge black containers in the car. Throwing my bandana around my neck, I exited the White Shark and made a sprint to join the Black Bloc.

By the time I got there the banners were fully erect and ready to roll. In fact, the main black banner was simply too large—it towered over the heads of everyone in the Bloc except extremely tall people like myself. Small eye-slits were cut into the banner so people could see out of it, and then it began advancing. The police, not entirely sure what to do with the giant black thing reinforced with pipe advancing towards the street, just let it go. Soon the Bloc had occupied the street and began a relentless march towards the Building of the International Monetary Fund. The march made it to the monetary fund almost without incident, but as soon as it got there the police tried to hem us in and everyone feared a mass-arrest. The giant banner, having served its purpose as a giant police-repelling shield, was dismantled and, much to my surprise and joy, the various pieces of PVC piping were re-commissioned as cop-beating clubs. Escaping the grasp of the cops through a charge, I met up with my former lover who I had noticed earlier carrying the banner. I was overjoyed to see her; we split up from the main group of the protest and leisurely strolled over to the Food Not Bombs that was serving in Malcolm X park. Spending hours reminiscing with her, I completely lost track of time. As sun down approached, I ran to get my van from its parking spot...and it was gone!

I was horrified. Never being known as someone with an excellent memory for where I parked my car, I suspected that I had merely misplaced the old Shark. I patrolled the neighborhood, but nonetheless it became abundantly clear that the van was indeed missing. Seeing as I was currently living in the van, and that all my money was in the van, I was as stranded as any castaway. Not knowing what to and fuming with rage and confusion, I ran to the secret anarchist hideout, and, using the same phone that had been used as the legal support number the day before, called the police to report a missing car. They told me they would need to talk to me personally to file a report. Now, I had not changed out of traditional Black Bloc gear since the protest the day before. I had my steel-toe black combat boots on, a black hoodie, a black bandana, black fingerless gloves and black fatigues on. No 'anarchy' patches, but definitely not a normal citizen. Even worse, since I had been on the road for a few months, my hair had grown extremely wild and shaggy, and a scruffy beard had developed, along with a body odor that in most circles of society would identify me as homeless. Lastly, the anarchist painters' bloc that had painted the banner I had reinforced and held yesterday had used non-drying red paint on banner, leaving my hands a various parts of my body covered in a strange red substance. I wasn't sure how the cops would react to me. What if they recognized me from the Black Bloc the day before? And I sure didn't want them driving up to the not-so-entirely-secret anarchist hideout and ringing the doorbell. Panicking, I gave them the address of a building down the road and told them I would meet them outside.

In a few minutes, surreally enough, I was for the first time in my life being driven about in the front of a cop-car, not under arrest. In fact, the police officer was completely ignoring my appearance and smell and was instead cheerfully chatting to me about "those kids who steal your car, drive it around for a day, and park it right back..." After about an hour of driving about in cop car (mentally taking notes, having never been in the front seat of a DC cop car!), we finally surrendered and the cop wrote the car down as "stolen." In the pits of deepest despair, I went back to our anarchist secret hideout and began maniacally trying to figure out what I should do. What if the cops had stolen the car? After all, it was the banner-mobile, and maybe this meant the cops were looking for me? The behavior of the cop I had just met had been friendly enough; however, the many heads of the capitalist hydra sometimes

If we must raise a flag over our town, let it be black.

doesn't talk to each other, so maybe I had just been lucky. In a fit of complete paranoia, I called a friend from a desolate northern state and told him that my situation. In a spirit of complete generosity, he offered to buy me a plane ticket to his snow-bound home. Since September 11th, plane tickets had noticeably fallen in price, so a ticket to his place was actually about as expensive as the gas to get back to my small Southern stable. Not thinking through the possible advantages of hitch-hiking or train-hopping, or the obvious disadvantages one would face security-wise at the airport at this point, just wanting to go somewhere where I would be fed and housed indefinitely and off the map, I agreed to go.

As my friend dropped me off at Dulles airport, I immediately recognized this was a mistake. First, I was still in complete Black Bloc gear without anything except an ID and a

make decisions in ways that exclude women, etc.—come with us into our bands from the hierarchical world that raised us; let's make these bands social laboratories in which we learn how to break these patterns, in preparation for breaking that world.

Make Those Autonomous Zones Expandable!

Achieving supportive, non-hierarchical relations inside of your band is great, but it's not much use to the world unless it helps others do the same. Here we must address the role bands, even punk bands, play in the society of the spectacle.

Let us return to The Singer. Watching a band play, audience members tend to unconsciously identify themselves with the singer, the same way a spectator in a movie theater identifies with the hero on the screen, or a reader with the protagonist of a novel. This explains why so many people willingly shell out their hard-earned money for recordings of hip hop artists bragging about how much they earn from record sales—the listener identifies with the MC rather than as the victim of his money-making scheme, at least while the album is playing. This displacement of agency is at the root of the powerlessness of today's average Joe: the power to be creative is projected onto the successful novelist, the power to play sports onto the basketball star, the power to make history onto the politician.

The question for the anarchist musician is how to enable rather than disable listeners. That's tough, because what we're dealing with in the case of the punk band is a specialized, perhaps technically

proficient, group creating what is essentially a spectacle, a "show." Keeping these shows small-scale, so the performers and spectators can interact as individuals rather than only as people playing those roles, is one solution; creating performances that demand or provoke audience participation is another. Maintaining humility, and keeping your eyes on the prize of extending whatever powers you develop for yourself to everyone else, are essential. Ultimately our goal should be to make the punk community something like an extended open mic circle, in which everyone has a turn to receive attention for their creative efforts.

Finances

Capitalism plays into the division between artist and audience too, of course. A punk band trying to operate under capitalist conditions needs to have a clear analysis of the challenges they're up against, and which compromises they're willing to make, if they want to be anarchist in deed as well as word. That's why we punks have always tried to keep our record prices low and our door costs sliding-scale, and scorned the pursuit of mass popularity.

The aforementioned hip hop artists are not the only hip hop artists, of course; they're just the only ones who have time and other resources to focus on their art, since everyone else is too busy earning money to pay for food, housing, and—their records. We punks have developed an anti-consumerist, anti-rock-star ethic to ensure that a greater proportion of our numbers can engage in creative pursuits; but it's still expensive to buy, maintain, and transport conventional musical instruments, and that money has to come from somewhere.

Your band will need a collective fund to pay for this stuff. That fund will probably have to be started from a pool of your own private capital, and will hopefully come to sustain itself as you get established enough to break even. Try to resist the temptation to solve all your problems by making a lot of money off the band—remember, there's not all that much money in the punk scene, and the more of it you get, the less others have access to for their own projects and needs. You don't need to make a living off your band—you need to develop a lifestyle that enables you to play in it. Seek out other ways to meet your needs—dumpstering food, sharing living quarters, having fun playing music or writing graffiti instead of going to the movies. You'll probably need to make some money in short bursts of wage labor—medical studies, crop harvests, working and quitting, whatever—to pay for your needs and remain free to go on long tours.

It may seem crazy, voluntarily choosing poverty, perpetual uncertainty, exclusion from mainstream economic and social relations just to play music; in the bleak moments, it will feel like you've exiled yourself from the whole world for nothing. But you are investing in something that will pay off, too, something much more reliable than the material wealth of today's erratic market. You're building relationships, community, shared resources ("social capital")—the foundation for a good life no full benefits package could ensure.

Commitment

Commitment is the bedrock social capital is built on. When you give up all the false riches and reassurances of the capitalist nightmare, you'll

secret anarchist hideout were now completely sure I was mad; stumbling back into their house, which was currently engaged in a raging party featuring one of the locals rocking out the Smashing Pumpkins on acoustic guitar, I announced that the White Shark had returned! Determined to leave DC as soon as possible before the White Shark was either kidnapped or ran off yet again, I offered any of the plethora of traveling kids currently staying there a ride South if they so desired it. One dreadlocked hippie agreed, and as she jumped into the van, I suddenly realized that when I got back to my small Southern town, I had no place to stay...and hoped she might have an idea.

All dressed up with nowhere to go...

Whatever foul force had seized my car had cleaned out almost all of my personal possessions, but had in sloppy fashion left my 'Aesop Rock' tape in the cassette player. As we drove manically through the night, only the incessant mad poetry of hip-hop kept me vaguely sane. We rolled into my small Southern town, and I announced to the anarcho-hippie that not only did I have little funds, but that at four in the morning I could think of nowhere to spend the night...except the ruins of the old anarchist collective house mentioned at the beginning of these tales. She agreed that it would be better to sleep outside in fresh air than in the van, so I drove down the dirty road to a house I hadn't seen in months. It looked like a wreck: the windows were smashed out, the ever-creeping kudzu had slowly taken over the much of the broken TVs and bikes and other strange junk that littered the front-yard, and the crazed house appeared to be barely standing, laying somewhere on the strange edge between reality and madness, between enchantment and accursedness. I parked, and walked up to its spray-painted walls: stabbed into the front door was a knife, with a strange note beneath it. The note said, in a scrawled hand-writing that seemed familiar: Here is the ruin of our house, a place where we tried to live the Revolution that we all want. We have all left, so please come in and make your

Reclaim the Streets breaks it down!

home. The hippie was absolutely shocked, having never seen an abode, even of anarchists, so utterly magical and yet utterly ruined. "It's like an magical anarchist hill-billy shack in the middle of nowhere..." I smiled and nodded. However, the inside of the house was so littered with broken fridge doors, yellowing books, and broken glass that we decided to climb upon the roof and sleep on top of it. From the roof, I looked down upon the valleys of kudzu that stretched out before me, and as the birds began to sing to greet the rising dawn, I felt implacably at home. I held her hand, and we fell into it, like a fever, like a dream.

The Shark Goes Back To Its Native Waters

Within a few months of losing everything, all our possessions, our lovers, our homes, our sanity, and nearly the rest of our lives to prison, Ishmael and I sat at a corporate bookstore drinking the finest of coffee and eating ridiculously decadent chocolate cakes. An atmosphere of doom prevailed. We always knew we had hit rock-bottom when were at the corporate bookstore. Other people may drink forties on street corners, lay in their beds all night and cry, but we would always fall back upon the easiest of scams: stay up all day in the bookstore drinking bourgeois coffee, plotting the next step in our revolutionary schemes. Still, it was depressing. Yet, maybe it was the carrot cake, maybe it was the autobiography of Bill Ayers we were flipping through, maybe it was the double shot of espresso in my white chocolate mocha, but the conversation between Ishmael and I became exceedingly animated. So animated, in fact, that the strange, rotund black man with an elegant mustache who was sitting next to us turned around and said, "These people, these people," flipping his wrist at the yuppies and students sipping their lattes all around us, "these people do not interest me. But you, you interest me." Within minutes we were engaged in a conversation with someone who spoke not in mere sentences, but in well-crafted paragraphs with clear theses and dialectical development. The conversation soon turned from the depression of myself and Ishmael, to the grand heights of Kierkegaard and Aristotle, and then returned to ground itself in an analysis of the political economy of global capital. The man, named Sherlock, was originally from Jamaica, but had been educated among the ivory towers at Oxford, and for some ungodly reason had moved to the second circle of hell we called home to teach high school. It was amazingly reassuring, for it would have been almost impossible to imagine backgrounds more removed, yet this man clearly echoed our sentiments—capitalism, civilization itself, is sick and we're all headed straight towards apocalypse, it is the responsibility of ordinary people with the barest thread of decency to fight back with all their might, we must never, never surrender. There is hope, even in the lounges of soulless corporate bookstores, and there are allies in the most unlikely of places.

Inspired, the entire process began again. We picked out the largest, cheapest, most fucked up house we could find in town, and, through an act of sheer willpower, transformed it into an anarchist collective. While at first we were worried that we wouldn't be able to find enough anarchists to fill the house, soon there were more people living there than humanly possible—over twenty rocking people in every little nook and

corner, three of us (including myself) in the attic! The White Shark went mad, and my former home soon became the most rapacious and ruthless of thieves. Every night the White Shark would ride into the dark night, stomach empty, and return with all sorts of plunder. Anything that was not nailed to the ground was taken. Chairs, trashcans, cement, woods, nails, soil. We walked into the philosophy department at one of the local universities late at night, and, while no one was looking, grabbed a chalkboard right off the wall, fleeing down a fire escape into the ever-waiting maw of the White Shark. We would spend entire days prowling about the city, looking for strange items that our house needed, thinking of places to run scams, and then entire nights rolling about in the White Shark. The White Shark was a pirate ship, constantly moving from port to port, raiding the soft underbellies of suburbs for all they were worth. Within a few weeks, our collective house was well-stocked. We spent some time engaging in other adventures, starting bands, drinking and carousing, engaging in acts of personal drama and infighting. It soon became clear what this town and house needed more than anything else was not just survival against the capitalist machine—we needed to go on the offensive.

There we were, sitting in the living room of our collective, plotting the night away. There were, even in our most small and isolated of Southern towns, other anarchists, some quite formidable ones at that. The local kids had thought of the idea a number of years ago. We were going to have a Reclaim the Streets on the main shopping street of town, on the street where I myself had wasted my youth in drinking, begging for just another few dimes so I could bribe some local to get me a forty. The street that everyone hung out on, and cursed afterwards for offering "nothing to do." The street where everyone from the local businessmen to the cops knew us by name. It was a completely mad plan, but we have never denied being madmen and madwomen.

The White Shark began its nightly prowls yet again, searching the night for items that could be useful for a Reclaim the Streets. Paint, both for banners and faces, was stolen. Surgical strikes were conducted on party-favor stores, with noise-makers and costumes taken by force. Our friends working as employees at a warehouse of scrap cloth winked as we walked out without paying, helping us select the choicest scraps. Thousands of stickers and posters were printed by the good graces of the local university's lack of regard for printing quotas. Giant banners were constructed to redirect traffic, and huge poles of bamboo were cemented into plastic buckets to physically force the traffic. Other anarchists began spreading the news first by word of mouth, and then by wheat-pasting every square foot of the entire city with flyers proclaiming the upcoming "Street Party." Whispers, plots, schemes, allies were gathered, and before I knew it the anarchist collective house had stopped drinking and started buzzing with activity.

Everybody throw your lighters up,
Tell me y'all gonna fight or what?
Everybody get your shit started...
It's y'alls motherfucking party!

In an act of musical intervention, the Coup came to rock out the night before the Reclaim the Streets. Anarchists converged from the mountains, from the ruined industrial cities further up north, from the swamps to the east and from the soulless suburbs and tiny rural towns. The forces

The Transcontinental Killing Spree

The problem with having sprawling adventures is that, when they are complete, you are left with no option but to surpass yourself, to make even wilder plans involving even more impossibilities, even more undiscovered continents in which to plant the black flag. As we sat in our musty attic, we laid down an atlas. Earlier, a mysterious old women had approached me as I was repairing computers in the local infoshop, and offered a simple proposition: the Zapatistas needed computers, and all I had to do was to gather them and get them Chiapas. A simple plan, and as Ishmael and I sat discussing it, it became abundantly clear we had many other things to do as well—protest global financial institutions, eco-defense on the West Coast, meet friends at yet another Earth First! Rendezvous...so like the professional composers of adventures we were, we strung together harmonies of actions, triads of locations, rhythms of travels. Trainhopping across the northernmost wastes of Canada, hitchhiking up and down the West Coast...driving the White Shark up and down the East Coat, and then to the fucking Lacondon Jungle! Yes, we were going to criss-cross the entire fucking continent of North America, from Alaska to Chiapas and everywhere in between, with no stops, no holds barred, no gods and no masters. Such a journey could only deserve one name: The Transcontinental Killing Spree.

We offered seats to anyone who wanted to come along, although the ability to speak Spanish was preferred. Only one mysterious e-mail from a professional adventurer named Hibb on the West Coast answered us in the affirmative. The White Shark was getting weary. We had put on tens of thousands of miles on its already straining hold. Everything was breaking down, bit by bit. Radiators in Texas, fuel pumps, everything except the core of engine and transmission. Deep in my heart, I still felt that the White Shark was going to make it this time...though the White Shark's transmission was making a high-pitched whistle that could be its death-knell, we still had our own mission, and the White Shark had not a mere mortal engine of gears and oil, but an engine of pure destruction. I took it by the anarcho-mechanic for one last check-up. Oil changed, tires rotated, filters placed in, new gaskets. The White Shark was readied for its final and most glorious ride.

Our merry band had to drive across the entire country, dumpster-dive some computers, and then take the White Shark and drive the electronics to Chiapas. Nothing could be easier. There were problems, the first being not having any computers. Never to let something as dreary as reason curb our enthusiasm, we began to pray to the ever-shifty patron spirits of thieves and hobos to deliver unto us computers. As soon as we began to seek the computers, they

were surrounded, with the crowd yelling "Shame!" and "Let him go!" The cops, terrified with their backs against the wall, began reacting with brutality against the festive party-goers, swinging clubs and releasing pepper spray. The crowd stormed up to the cops, and chaos ensued. Before anyone knew what was happening, the local Indymedia reporter was thrown against a police car, screaming. It was completely mad. Local hoodlums who had spent years dodging the cops while trying to hustle a bit of green were now throwing down with the pigs, grabbed and kicking. Acts of both extreme heroism and cowardice were taking place—women kicked cops twice their size as they charged at them, young men kicked themselves free of cops' clutches, crowds yelled and terrified the police, police reacted by pepper-spraying innocent young children. In the chaos, a friend of mine ran up and grabbed the Indymedia video camera that was still running. As the madness engulfed the street, our little quiet town was filled with the closest thing it had seen to a riot in years. As the cops fled the scene with our sisters and brothers in the backs of their paddywagons, one member of the crowd took initiative and, black flag of anarchy held high, began marching the entire party straight to the prison. The cops, by attempting to stop the Reclaim the Streets, had caused the crowd to do exactly what they had most feared—the march to the prison had shut down downtown.

As the crowd rallied outside, the cops inside the prison panicked, and one by one our compatriots were released. Fifteen arrests, one felony. The Reclaim the Streets had been both far greater than our expectations and far worst than our nightmares. We had never wanted our brothers and sisters to go to prison, and the White Shark began to creep away, to retrieve from a downtown that the poles, the banner, the stereo, all the evidence. All the evidence must be destroyed. Yet for one moment, the impossible, the marvelous had broken loose. In the most unlikely of desolate Southern towns, for absolutely no better reason than "we could," we, with no spokesperson, no message, and no leaders, had brought to life the biggest party ever seen. The media was utterly baffled. We had brought down the house, and with it the Police Chief and the feelings of despair that had choked these streets for our entire lives. It was a breath of fresh air—and it hurt.

incarnated themselves in answer to our prayers. A group of semi-professional activists were willing to donate some old computers they had been given by a non-profit group that trained home-free[2] folks to build computers. Of course, by the time we sorted this out, we were in eastern Canada and they were on the West Coast. Without fear, a brave fellowship of companions rose to the occasion to get there and bring them to Mexico. With little in the way of possessions, no money (as usual), and absolutely no grasp on the fundamentals of rational planning, we hopped trains across the coldest reaches of Canada, reaching the West Coast by surviving purely on one large pack of oats. Arriving on the West Coast, we promptly gave away our oversized bag of oats to an indigenous family that was hitch-hiking to Seattle to see the world. Not just traveling kids, but a traveling family.

We picked up the computers from the non-profit, and then realized to our dismay that we, without a car, had no way to transport them down the street, much less to Chiapas. Again, our lack of planning seemed to doom us! We couldn't carry them by hand to Chiapas, and the White Shark we were hoping to drive there was taking a brief respite in the woods of Maine, on the other side of the United States. Luckily, a group of anarcho-primitivists were passing across the West Coast on a tour to promote the destruction of civilization, and, although we reasoned that computers were surely included under the category of civilization, we asked for help anyways. After all, the computers were for guerrillas! Despite the irony of the situation, the anarcho-primitivist gang was more than willing to help the Zapatistas, and strapped the computers to the top of their van that was driving to Texas, taking them with them one step closer to Chiapas. In search of our long-lost White Shark, we got a ride across the country in yet another heroic automobile known only as the Duster, funded purely by an orgy of gas-thievery and, by last estimate, over a thousand dollars in scams, until our ragged crew—fueled by a bizarre combination of stale pizza dough and organic energy bars—returned to the fair woods of Maine. After nearly a month vacation, and against all odds, the White Shark revved up again, loaded with even more computers from a shady inside job at a major Washington, D.C. corporation, and began its slow journey to Texas, getting in two major breakdowns and one near wreck, almost flipping due to the amount of computers loading it. One of the computers was even bartered to a car mechanic in rural Georgia for a used axle!

The problem of the border presented itself as nearly insurmountable. After all, you're not supposed to truck a vanload of computer parts into a foreign country and not expect to have questions asked by the border guards. But within a few weeks, the primitivists dropped off the computers, a group of Quakers funneled them to a friendly church, who then, in collaboration with an autonomist sweatshop workers' union, maneuvered them across the border without a problem. Computers in tow, we drove to Chiapas triumphant. The truly remarkable feat was that we, who had no resources besides our unemployment and mania, had, with the aid of the legend of the Zapatistas, helped create through mutual aid a network of friends that crossed an entire continent, a network of as diverse backgrounds and ideas as imaginable, a network ranging from young balaclava-clad anarcho-primitivists to middle-aged Mexican sweatshop wage slaves and elderly Christian pacifists: a network

of friends capable of doing the impossible for an armed indigenous rebellion.

The drive to Mexico City was, even by the high standards of the White Shark, a new record in non-stop driving. Our new friend from the West Coast created a magical talisman for the tiburon blanco. Ishmael took it upon himself to merge his body and soul with the machinery of the White Shark. Coffee in one hand and wheel in the other, he drove without rest through deserts, through the megapolis of Mexico City, right through all possible physics of time and distance. It became hard to tell who was really driving, the White Shark or Ishmael, or if there was any difference between the two. Our anarcho-mechanic had regaled us with tales from his youth of being stopped on the Mexico byroads and having all his money stolen by bandits, and even our shoplifted *Let's Go Mexico* warned us of two guerrilla armies (the ERP and ERPI, although most likely defunct in my opinion) operating in southern Mexico. Not surprisingly, the only real bandits we encountered on our journey were the cops. Cops in Mexico are even more blatantly corrupt than those in the States: they will just pull you over, vaguely complain about the hassle they would have to face in writing a whole ticket out for whatever your fictional offense was, and suggest you just give them the dineros right there so they can "forget" about the matter. Bribes in hand, funded by medical experiments to which we had sold ourselves, we passed without incident through both shady encounters with the police (although once we used furniture to blockade ourselves in the union base where we were sleeping, due to fear of police reprisal!) and even military checkpoints. Dressed in our finest possible tourist clothes, we were always "going to see the ruins," which just happened to be in the middle of Chiapas. To be honest, the fiercest threat the White Shark faced was the danger of the infamous Mexican speed-bump, the topez. While speed-bumps in the States seem to be mainly aimed at slowing a vehicle down, in Mexico the topez is designed to stop the vehicle by whatever means necessary. The White Shark vibrated as its undersides were torn and grimaced as its speed was suddenly stolen from it, but, resolve unshaken, plowed ever onwards towards whatever fate awaited us in the jungle.

Once in Chiapas, the White Shark broke all the rules of safe driving. It was finally among equals, for the Mexicans in the mountains had just as much a deathwish as the Shark did. Flying up and down mountains, through rain and mist, through darkest night and with barely any gas, the White Shark never rested. Zapatista children would peer from around corners at the strange internationals and their white steed, and would draw strange pictures in the dust that caked on the White Shark's windows. We found ourselves driving down roads with no names, to deliver strange aids to Zapatista villages which, in acts of cartographic imperialism, the government refused to put on the map, due to their refusing to acknowledge the mal gobierno. Once, while standing outside at the gates of a Zapatista village to track the movements of military, I tried to explain to one of the Zapatistas (who was busily scrawling down military truck numbers on his hand as I wrote my notes down on a pad of paper) where we were from and how the tiburon blanco had transported us in. My shaky knowledge of Mexican geography, combined with his lack of knowledge of the geography of United States, led to me scrawling in the dirt a giant map of the Western Hemisphere and mapping out the adventures of the White Shark. As we swapped stories in a

---

[2] For those who don't know, "home-free" is the politically correct term for those the capitalists call "homeless."

strange pigeon mixture of Tzotzil, Spanish, and English of fighting cops and neoliberal globalization from the farm fields of Chiapas to the streets of the Capital, he smiled and told me that if the military stopped threatening his land and the mal gobierno was destroyed, he and his children would jump in the belly of the Shark and visit us in the States.

Words cannot express my awe of what the Zapatistas have done. While Marcos and the balaclavas are definitely sexy, the real strength of the Zapatistas lies in their autonomous and self-organized communities. Everything we anarchists in the States only talk about, the Zapatistas have actually been doing—shared land for community farming, free schools teaching revolutionary history in which the pupils help design the curriculum, hospitals based on natural remedies, preventive medicine, and everyday health, amazing food, coffee, and art co-operatives. And not a single fucking cop. Hell, the police and the tax collectors weren't even allowed in the village—yet I felt safer in Zapatista villages than I do on the streets of any city in the States. The warmth and kindness of the Zapatistas, despite their poverty and the continual threat of attack by the military, radiates and fills their villages with an atmosphere that can only be described as enchanted. Although I barely could speak their language, I felt strangely at home behind the giant black and red gates of the Zapatista villages. So different, yet so similar to what we are trying to do in the States. Giant murals of balaclavas mixed with the huge mustache of Zapata, the circle 'A' mixed with Mexican flags and indecipherable Mayan symbols, everywhere children, chickens, and scruffy dogs. It even smelled like some of the wilder collective houses we had back home, but on a scale that we could never have possibly imagined in our wildest dreams. If people ever tell me that anarchy can't work, I'll just tell them to get in a car and drive four days south, and see revolution with their own eyes.

As if emerging from a dream, it came to us that we had to leave Chiapas and return to our home in States. After all, despite the temptation to live the revolution with these mountain folks, we had to continue our own struggle amidst our own people. Besides, Ishmael had a court case coming up. The White Shark began its final ride home, and we looked on a map and saw what appeared to be large highway straight to Minatchitlan from Tuxtla, the capital of Chiapas. So off the White Shark went, bidding fond farewell to the free air of the Zapatistas, and down the highway. We should have expected trouble as we entered the highway, as a large toll or military blockade (somewhat hard to tell the difference in Mexico) had been set up, but we drove right through it without pause, leaving only the guard with only a confused stare. We drove miles and miles, completely alone on the road, upon what appeared to be the finest road in Mexico. As the sun set behind the mountains, we found the situation to be strangely eerie...yet the road continued ever onwards. Or so we thought.

Out of nowhere, a giant lake appeared on the horizon, and the road went right into the lake! Throwing on the brakes, we realized that the Mexican government had been optimistic in placing this particular highway on the map. Not knowing what else to do, we turned around and drove back to Tuxtla, sorrowfully noting that we had wasted a whole day driving on a road to nowhere. As darkness set in, the poor White Shark starting having the automobile equivalent to the tremors before a heart attack. The overheating of the engine is a dread phenomena in all cars, in which, rumor has it, the engine can

be utterly destroyed, so we pulled off to the side of the road and let the White Shark simmer down. The White Shark simmered a bit, but when we starting driving again, the air conditioner mysteriously stopped functioning. Then, after a few more minutes, the engine started over-heating again and, to our increasing horror, the lights went off. We pulled off to the side of the road, and let the White Shark rest again. When we started the White Shark once more, it made it a few yards to a nearby gas station, and suddenly, in a truly surreal moment, the gauges all started moving backwards. The speed, the heat of the engine, everything starting going to zero before our very eyes. The engine refused to inject fuel, and, paralyzed with shock, we coasted into a gas station that was full of cops wielding giant machine guns. We quickly backed into a strange parking spot, and then opened the hood to see if we could deduce what was going on. The heat coming from the White Shark's insides was scalding. We opened the oil tank—it was fucking empty! We ran into the station and began desperately pouring oil into the White Shark, trying to revive her. It worked—we restarted the engine, and the White Shark's lights came miraculously back on. Yet, we drove it only a few yards from the gas station, and in utter exhaustion, the White Shark collapsed again, dead. Quaking in terror and avoiding looking the cops in the eye, we walked into the gas station and pleaded with them to let us stay the night. Confused, the clerks merely shrugged and smiled. We got the White Shark back into the gas station parking lot. Ishmael looked me in the eye, and said "You know, I normally try to stay hopeful with these things, but I bet fifty to one the White Shark is dead." I nodded in somber agreement. How were we going to get rid of the corpse? I didn't even have legal registration! Our options were limited, we were thousands of miles away from home (no, wait, we had no homes), and the only way to dispose of the White Shark was to drive it off a fucking cliff. In bleak despair, I told Ishmael that a captain always has to go down with the ship, as I fell asleep in the driver's seat.

In the morning, we woke up and had one final idea. We were going to call the hometown anarcho-mechanic. We went to the nearest payphone and called him, and described the symptoms. He mulled over it, and within seconds came up with a diagnosis for the White Shark. Over the length of a thousand miles, his wise words told me to open the hood and see if our engine belt was still there. Putting down the phone, I walked over, followed his advice, and—behold, the anarcho-mechanic was right! It was just missing, it must have fallen off somewhere on the highway! Apparently, once the belt fell off, the engine couldn't work the alternator, so one by one everything inside the White Shark died as the battery drained. Leaping in joy, I heaped a million blessings upon our dearest anarcho-mechanic, and walked down the highway until we found, surrounded by vicious barking dogs, a tiny little automechanic shop. A man who resembled nothing more than a Mexican leprechaun emerged, and as we explained the problem to him as best we could, he smiled and drove us back to the beached White Shark in his truck. He jumped inside the metallic bowels of the White Shark, and after some messing around, attached what appeared to be giant rubber band correctly to the engine. We restarted the engine, drove it around for a test drive, and received a final wink as we handed him twenty dollars worth of pesos. The White Shark was back on the road—its crooked grill, positioned over a crooked bumper, smiling a wicked shark smile.

Back on the road, we did a maniacal drive straight back to the States, matching in furious intensity our earlier trip. Our funds slowly dissolved, and eventually I was left with barely enough blood money to make it back to my hometown; Ishmael had only a single dollar to his name. After recrossing the border without incident, I dropped Ishmael, Hibb, and our brave and intrepid translator (who had jumped into the White Shark at a moment's notice on the West Coast, and whose services had proved invaluable) at the Greyhound bus-station. We all hugged, and, looking each other straight in the eye, Ishmael and I promised each other that we would meet again for even further adventures. I felt like I was losing my family, and as we bid each other farewell, I felt strangely alone.

As I drove the now-empty White Shark on the final leg of its trip, the anniversary of September 11th rolled around. The radio waves were jammed with our so-called President's hate-filled and patriotic speeches cursing our enemies and proclaiming our "freedom," songs about attacking innocent countries, and flag-waving. The radio stations, ever ignorant, began playing "Born of the Fourth of July." These war-hungry madmen filled the airwaves with their calls for vengeance from their comfortable chairs in the White House, pasty bureaucrats whose children would never die in a war, plump God-fearing politicians who feel no guilt for raining hellfire onto families in the name of security and a quick buck. Their hypocrisy stank to the high heavens. At least the murderous Al-Qaeda had the courage to fly the plane into the World Trade Center themselves instead of pushing buttons from behind a screen. I struck back the only way I could, with an act of kindness towards a stranger. A grizzled hobo stood beside the highway in Alabama, thumb proudly stuck up in the air. So, tired and sick from caffeine, I picked up the man, who jumped in White Shark's belly. He gave me a cracked smile, and before long we were chatting up storms, telling story after story. It was like a Thousand and One American Nights, each one of us telling stories like our very lives depended on it—which they did, since these stories were the only thing keeping me awake as we headed inevitably north. The strange hobo, twice my age at least, started telling stories of fisking, of growing up in the wilds of rural Louisiana, of his stint in the military. Slowly, it came out that we both hated the government with the intense passion that most people reserve for their lovers and family, and we loved our lovers and family with a love that most people reserve for God. The hobo had a child in Virginia he wanted to visit, and I had my own tribe in my small, Southern hometown that I missed as well. Finally, too exhausted to drive any more, I pulled off to a deserted rest station in Mississippi, and, as the crickets chirped away, the hobo took a bottle of whiskey out of his tattered rucksack, the White Shark's lights dimming as I turned the engine off. I took a sip to calm my tattered nerves. I began thinking of new adventures, new horizons, new chances to fight for everything I held precious in this world. Yes, the White Shark had to retire with the anarcho-mechanic, if only for a time. But she would ride again. As the traveler and myself sipped whiskey in the warm Southern night, we promised each other that we would hold onto our stories. We would never forget.

And Nocturnes

In the end, the power of capitalism does not lie in its ability to make us be still. Stillness, a certain measure of quiet and solitude, is needed. Some things can only be done in one place. Some communities are too big to fit in the back of van. Hell, sometimes all your band equipment won't even fit in your van! A van has limits. It is merely an enclosed square of steel, fueled by a vicious combination of modern technology and ancient fossils that will surely have no fate other than causing the utter destruction of life on this planet. Yes, automobiles are evil. But how can we look ourselves straight in the eye and call ourselves "revolutionary" unless there is no evil that we cannot subvert, no means we cannot turn towards our ultimate ends? How can we call ourselves free if we cannot carry the stillness we need inside of ourselves, if we cannot find it wherever we lay our heads and plant our feet? The answers to our woes are not movement or technology. It's not that freedom happens to you. No, freedom is something that happens because of you: Freedom is something you live, you act, you do. It's both as possible and impossible as getting that real fucking crazy plan—the one that no one would ever believe you capable of—in your head and doing it. In a twisted way, it is moving that even in America, a land of unending horizons paved with highways of gold and fueled by the blood of the world, a teetering architecture built to collapse beneath our wheels, a van can be a vessel of freedom. If even a lowly automobile can become the leaky raft of a castaway band of escaped wage-slaves, we must ask: where are other underground railroads, other avenues of escape, other possibilities of freedom, other vessels of adventures? Our civilization is an anachronism, or, as one of our favorite bands sings: a speeding car, and nobody's driving! Unless we seize the wheel...

...Which may be impossible. There is a good possibility that's true. Maybe nothing we can do could ever save this world, and we're all fucking doomed. But must we only accept our imminent demise? Let us love our doom. With all faith in the future lost, anything becomes possible now. We can make love in the back of dingy car-vans, eat rotten vegetables from filthy hands, make mockery of their laws, steal beer from international bankers and give it to the homeless to offer them the warm nights our so-called civilization won't, throw tear gas back at cops—and when the canisters run out, throw donuts!—lie, cheat, steal, fuck, and do it all over again, but this time when they aren't expecting it! Hold each other's hands as we sweat from our darkest fears, kiss tenderly beneath the dying birch trees, cry flash-floods of tears that we've been holding back all these years, and drive until motherfucking dawn. When the sun rises, and the first rays fall upon the endless horizon, our futures are painted in colors that we never even dreamed of in the night, and the fate of the White Shark becomes apparent. The van is not to be confused with us, our smiles, our memories, our skins, our flesh, our bone, our sweat and our lives. The vessel is only the backdrop, a thread to hang stories together with. We are alive, and we're not going down with the ship. Not tonight.

This isn't actually what happened:

Everyone is counting on the band to start playing—waiting on this next step in the night's ritual to begin, they stand around, gossiping about so-and-so's deteriorating relationship or simply shivering in an advanced stage of social phobia—but the band won't start. The drums are set up, there's a wind instrument somewhere, along with a few typically pretentious props (a giant papier-mâché head, a potted plant), and it's high time for the set to get started, so everyone can get home and shower or check email and get enough sleep for tomorrow, but the musicians—are there really only two of them? aren't there supposed to be precisely three, four, or five?—are studiously ignoring these, creeping around the audience in ridiculous outfits, gibbering and mumbling, looking the audience members in the eyes one by one. Spectator by spectator, the room falls silent, opening a space where the performance can get started and, thus, eventually finished.

But they still won't go near the instruments. Finally one of them starts reciting some philosophical treatise—is this theater, then? that could be neat, some of those in attendance have seen avant garde theater before—but stops quickly. Now there are simply two people, one dressed as a sitcom jailbird and the other as a human puppet, staring at the audience, and the audience staring back. This goes on for minutes, minutes which seem to stretch to hours.

The tension becomes unbearable. When a pop punk band plays or an anarchist author reads, one can lose oneself in the show, even if only in the boredom of sitting through the same old shit; but here everyone is painfully conscious that they are standing in place, absurdly staring at two other people who are also standing and staring, and the effect is agonizing—something has to happen or else everyone here must be certifiably insane. Attention has been focused, a ground has been set, but there is no figure to fill it, no action. The world is a vacuum, an empty, meaningless void.

At length, partly out of boredom or desire for attention, and perhaps partly for the sake of psychic survival, a boy in the audience picks up a flier off the floor and rips it down the middle. That noise is enormous in the silence which has descended upon the room. He tears it again, and everyone is conscious of every contour in the sound of separating fibers. The performers do nothing, still staring straight ahead, almost drooling. Another spectator takes a piece of the flier and begins tearing, and then another does; now there is a form against that background of silence, a rustle and whisper of movement. The first boy begins to crumple his torn sheets; that crackling is like oil in a frying pan.

Someone further back in the room sings out a low note. Another answers. Maybe she has been in situations like this before and believes this to be the appropriate conduct, maybe she's been waiting for a chance to debut as a singer herself, perhaps she simply likes to sing; but here, when she sings, a third voice, more hesitant, perhaps inexperienced in song, joins hers in a shaky harmony. And then others—soon the room is filled with a soft humming, and a tentative melody is being worked out, like the motions of joined hands upon a ouija board. More voices join in, and the first ones become more confident—the song gathers strength, the harmony deepens, and now it is as if everyone were borne up upon a flying carpet of sound, the notes in others' throats reverberating in every skull.

Finally, almost forgotten by the others, the band members come back to life. One of them picks up a clarinet and begins to play along, within that sound, within that space of possibility; and those few familiar notes sound like the sun rising over the garden of Eden, chillingly unfamiliar, wildly beautiful.

WORDS

The performer who would abdicate his role and depose himself, destroying and activating the audience in the process, is analogous to the anarchist who strives to ignite a self-managing revolution. The artist who would cast off the entire history of art to make a moment with no inertia, no influence, is analogous to the mystic who would, by means within this world, depart to experience other worlds.

A song is descended from the music its composer has heard her whole life like a poem is from the language the poet has spoken: it is made up of terms, i.e. sounds that can be identified as music because they have appeared in others' compositions. The combinations work because of the history shared by the musicians and the listeners.

To make an alien music, one must...

But wait, perhaps that's not what Herds and Words are trying to do at all.

Inside Front: Let's start with your name, Herds and Words. Where does that come from?

John: Well, words—that's what we first found we had in common, playing with words. I would do that with my brother,

before—just say words, pass them back and forth, see what developed.

Robert: And herds—we met when we were both working as cashiers, and all the people coming in and out—herds.

J: That's something in German—das Herden.

IF: Is that a term that represents a particular concept?

J: Just—herds. People.

R: We were cashiers.

IF: So let me ask—it seems to me, what's happened at the last two shows, that what you're trying to do is to make moments—

R: Make moments? We're not gods, we're not special. The moments are already there.

J: Yeah...

IF: OK, I understand—but I guess, in my case at least, to be really in those moments is another thing entirely. Often I feel like the history of the world, and my own history, is all one great obstacle to recognizing the possibilities of a moment and really experiencing it. If I don't do something to jerk myself out of the chain of events and routine that's already in place, I'll just end up experiencing the same things, on autopilot, default setting. I think that's the secret of what's going on in a lot of situations—punk shows, dances, special events in every circle of society: people make these unreal moments happen just by bringing their expectations that something will happen, something magical... and

those expectations, that projected energy, is enough to make it take place.

R: OK, yeah.

IF: So is what you're doing about your experience, or the experience of the people at the show? Do you think about what you want to make people feel, or just about getting yourself to that place, just about what you're feeling?

R: Well, we don't talk a lot about what we're going to do—

J: —Like, just before we start, I'll say a sentence, and that sentence will be what we do—

R: —Or I'll say that I'm going to tell a story, and then just start... telling.

J: For me, I follow what I'm feeling, and I look for vibrations from other people, and... like at that show here in Olympia, the other night, I just had my eyes closed, and I was making my way through the people, and I found that guy, and we were speaking nonsense back and forth, just like:

"BSFIEWNWWW!"

And I had my eyes closed, which helps—like, I had my eyes closed, and I was totally there, but when I opened them for a second, he was looking right at me, speaking nonsense, and I wasn't quite there the same way, so I closed them.

IE: I think things like that, like closing your eyes, or dimming the lights or setting up the equipment or whatever, can be things we do to disconnect from 'normal' reality, to set the stage so something else can happen. To get together in a dark room, late at night, and close our eyes and dance and scream together, that's one thing—but to be able to create that same feeling, at eleven a.m. by the checkout line in the supermarket, that's another thing altogether... So how much does what happens at a show depend on the audience? Totally?

J: Yeah.

R: Well, we don't... we're not playing in a vacuum, like most—I don't want to say most bands, but a lot of performances you see, you see something from the past that they've put together in their town, in their space, and then they bring that product, and play it for people. We work with the environment that people—

J: —or even just driving into the city, like how we drove into South Dakota—

R: —Pierre—

J: —and having the meal before the show there, everything led up to what happened...

IE: What happened there?

R: Wait, this isn't Pierre, this is Olympia... but this is an example of what we're talking about. Here, we talked beforehand about a part: "we'll play this section, bass clarinet and drums, and then we'll stop and hum the same tune that the bass clarinet is playing in the first part." In our minds, or at least in mine but I'm pretty sure it was collective, in our heads it was just: we play that part, we sing that part, John and I, and we do it for a while, see how it feels, and then go into the next part. But the audience, the people there took over, and totally transformed what was happening, joined in, and made it—

IE: That was the best part, for me—suddenly the whole room was alive.

that, I'm not conscious of that. When we play, for me—we start, and then we're done. I forget most what happens.

J: Yeah—all of it.

R: John and I talk afterwards, and he might remember a part, and relate it to me, and I'll be like "Oh yeah! I forgot about that!"

IE: Is that a good thing?

R: It's an amazing thing. It's something outside of just our selfish selves.

IE: I've always thought about that—you know, the worst moments of my life I can remember, crystal clear, but the best ones are all blurry, opaque. What's going on when you're living without memory? Does that mean you're totally present in the moment, or does it just mean you're in a trance state? Or does it mean—

J: Nothing.

R: For me it's like, I don't want to say refuge, but it's a different place that feels totally natural, because it is of the moment. If someone else does join in, it's like a bonus, it's on top of that—because already I'm satisfied with playing, and doing it, and that's enough.

J: How could you expect something if you want something new? I try to stay away from intentions, to not want anything... except for just, strap it on, strap on my bass clarinet and just...

R: It's not good or bad, it just is.

IE: I have a question. Have you ever done something like this without it being a show, without fliers and stuff? Have you ever walked into a supermarket at eleven in the morning with your bass clarinet: "All right, this next hour is going to be one I won't remember!"

R: I can say—not with a bass clarinet, er, for me... but, without instruments, we'll have moments where we're just sitting in the van and, I don't want to say freak out, but we just get into life and it's, it would be as if you were watching us perform.

IE: Now is that a way of living, of experiencing life that you think can be extended past minutes into hours, into days?

R: When someone sees us doing that on the street, they're not willing to accept it because of whatever social constrictions they have, so they're not open to... the nonsense. But if you see it in a forum where people go to watch something, they are more open to it, and it turns into a ball from there—and whatever they get from it, is theirs.

IE: So do you feel like there's a difference between shows you play where people are open to what you're doing and respond, and ones where they don't? You can't plan for the unexpected, but you can think about the effects, about different situations. What's the difference, for example, between performing in Des Moines [at the convergence of the CrimethInc. flying circus tours, August 2001] for a bunch of ready-to-go crazy motherfuckers, and then in another place where people are less open?

J: In Des Moines, we still didn't expect anything but anybody, but... going back to our beginning, when we first started playing, we just had music, and we'd play it, we had a set—we might have improvised a little, but we didn't run around the audience. As we've gone on, we've lost our expectations of what we could do...

IE: You've been trying to shake off expectations?

J: It just happened.

R: It was just music, when we started.

IE: You were "just a band"?

R: No, you know I never believed in that word! But it started with us playing in the basement... it was always loose, there was always a level of improvisation, but in everything else—the words that we say, the actions that we do when we play, it's all like our lives becoming more a part of this—having it be less of a performance, and more of... the world.

J: Yeah, I can think of one time we played in North Carolina—Raleigh—we had this set, and we played it through, and then we lost each other at the end—and all of a sudden we just stared at each other, like this, for a long time. We were both waiting for one of us to come back into it, to get back into it so afterwards we could say "OK, we played that part"... but we just ended up staring at each other, and it just turned into us messing around, and we started laughing as hard as we could, and that turned into... It just grew into something like: we could laugh at ourselves when we're playing in front of people, I can say "oh, this sucks, we're outta here, we're not a band—what are you doing, why are you looking at us?" So that's how it's grown. We lost expectations of ourselves being musicians, and of people being audiences...

R: That thing, that was one of those moments ... and to us, it was a part of our song going on a tangent—

J: It was the song, you know, that was it.

R: Yeah. We could name—you know, how people title songs—we could title every night something different, have a different name for it.

IF: And yet the few times I've seen you you've been playing the same couple tunes, when you played at all—it was the context you created for them that was totally different each time. So when you're performing, are you trying to get other people to start doing things, are you trying to get other people to take the reins out of your hands?

R: No.

J: Well...

IF: Sometimes!

J: I don't think about that... well, maybe just one time, I might be, one single moment. But the initial intention is just to do what I feel, and not expect anything out of the audience.

IF: Do you care either way? Not when you're in the middle of the show and you're not thinking about anything except that moment, but other times: when you think about your role as performers, do you care whether the effects of what you're doing are that everyone starts singing or doing whatever, or that everyone just stares at you and afterwards says to themselves "that guy was crazy"?

J: No.

R: You know, every day, we have twenty three hours where we're not playing; and for those hours, I'm conscious of the hours, I'm conscious of time. And when we play, it's a break from

---

IF: That doesn't happen to every band, though—a lot of bands just try to write better songs, get a better record deal—

R: That stuff isn't, like...

IF: I'm not surprised that stuff isn't where you're headed, but I'm always curious what the difference in evolutionary forces is that makes different people and different groups turn out the way they do.

R: This is really elementary for us—it's about letting go. The freedom... which is what everybody wants...

IF: That was something I was thinking about, with your band—now when it comes to the question of freedom, there's anarchist organizing, on the one hand, the whole history of what anti-authoritarianism has been and so on ... and actual bona fide chaos, on the other. Talking about letting go, talking about freedom—there's a difference between the freedom of actively letting go, of shaking off expectations so anything can happen, and the kind of freedom that is supposed to take place in a vacuum: like if you walk into a room and just say "We're all free, we can do whatever we want," people will just keep doing the same thing. I feel like freedom is something you have to... win—

J (soulfully): Yeah...

IF: —by, say, going into that room and setting yourself on fire and throwing yourself through a plaster wall... and then if you shout "You're free, motherfuckers!" it's something totally different. Or maybe on the other hand, they'll just say "I'm from New York, you know, I've seen that a hundred times—I'm not free."

R: I think what it's about is—you know, you can walk into a room and say in a complacent voice "you're free, do whatever you want"... but I think it's a matter of building something after you've recognized that freedom, building a feeling or creating a crazy room or whatever you consider building, however you define that. It's a matter of making something new after you destroy whatever confines are there.

IF: I think you have to demonstrate what freedom is possible, demonstrate that freedom is possible, for it to be possible. If you're able to do something outlandish, people may say to themselves "I didn't expect that. I wonder what else is possible?" That's something I do consciously try to do, myself—sometimes—is to create situations in which I don't know what is going to happen. And for me, at least, creating those with other people—it's not better, necessarily, but it's different. It's different—like the person from New York in my skit a minute ago, he's seen crazy things done by "performance artists," while everybody watches... and that experience, that's a problem, if you're trying to create situations without expectations, because people then have expectations about "crazy" things, too.

J: Yeah, we play totally different to those people.

Every day, we have twenty three hours where we're not playing; and for those hours, I'm conscious of the hours, I'm conscious of time. And when we play, it's a break from that, I'm not conscious of that. When we play, for me—we start, and then we're done. I forget most of what happens.

R: OK, here's an example: Boston, Massachusetts. I don't remember the day, but we had fifteen minutes to play—you know, fifteen minutes, what's that? What's time when I don't know how long what we're doing lasts? I mean, one of our songs, one of our sets, it could be thirty seconds, or it could be... But anyway, we're there, ready to play, I'm messing with the sampler, making some fuzzy noise—and everyone's in the back, drinking a soda or whatever, and all of a sudden I just start:

R: On a side note, New York City was one of the best shows that we've played. I didn't know how it was going to go beforehand, either... but it was the first show that I can remember the audience, people there besides me and John, totally clapping and

... like, I was playing the drums, and my high hat came undone. I was still keeping time on the rim of the snare, and I looked at the person standing next to me, watching, and he was already nodding his head to the beat, so I was like "Clap! Clap! Just clap!" He started to clap, and then the next person, and then the next thing you know everyone's clapping. I just put down the drumsticks and jumped up and yelled "Yeah!" You know, I totally forgot about that instant... right now to then is connected in the weird world, that we don't see.

IF: So, talking about that world... going to that place that you can go there for an hour and you come back unable to remember anything, or you go there for—what seems like five days... Is that a sustainable place? Is that a place to try to be, more? Can you attach any kind of value to it, to going there?

J: If you start to think about it too much, it won't come...

IF: Like the story of the goose and the golden eggs.

R: I'm not even saying it's real, I'm not saying anything. Just because I'm talking about it doesn't mean it's a real thing. I mean, it could be—but I'm not going to say.

IF: Stuff that you've done yourselves, to surprise yourselves, to shake off your own expectations of what's going to happen—have you experienced that you try something like that, and it works, and then it stops working?

R: You know, level of expectation... some people might think: you have this crazy thing, this wild thing, this extreme thing, and the only way to defeat it is to keep going and making it crazier and wilder. But the way that we've been handling it... it isn't necessarily a reaction against that, but—creating a balance. Seattle we played to some people, and we were pretty wild, came out with masks on, yelling... and it

turned into a more fast-paced thing. And then the next night, to surprise ourselves, we started out the opposite way, with me telling a soft story in the dark, and then starting a smooth, slower tempo song. That's a balance that we... more than pushing ourselves to surprise ourselves, we're balancing.

J: I think the best, some of the best times I feel when we're playing is when I say a sentence, and I just let it go, to be... however absurd I want it to be—

IF: "Let it go," repeat it over and over again?

J: No, like, let it go out into... nowhere. That's how I surprise myself. It's just a matter of acting, and letting the act just take over... take one step after the other. And of course—I have every right to stop, too. Well, not every right, but... I can do it.

IF: Now, you're talking about things being different every night... I think the opposite of that is folk music, like certain kinds of punk rock now. When I was younger I was totally against tradition, of any kind, but now I've been listening to music with d-beats for half of my life—and that feels good, when another band plays a d-beat, and we all do our dances that affirm that we're alive, that we got through all this shit and we're celebrating with our traditions, traditions we made. I'm not sure I think that's a bad thing anymore. Can that coexist with trying to do something different every night, or with just letting something different happen every night?

J: Yeah... that's how we play music. We throw the music in there that we've done...

IF: The musical themes are the same, right?

R: We do have parts that we habitually play. But at the same time, if you listen to some of our parts, it's not... you have to go back to the '60's, or the '40's, or... I guess I'm going to say it, to jazz music. I'm not going to say we're a jazz band, but—our music itself is not a brand new thing that's never been heard on the surface of the earth. It's not common in punk rock circles, but...

Sometimes I think of—a thousand dead people, I'm possessed by them, and we're here to raise the dead.

IF: Well, people playing music or singing together or doing rituals to get everybody out of their heads, that goes back to the beginning of time.

R: Yeah, you're talking about these punk songs or these folk songs as universals... where you can go to Chicago and you can hear a punk band, you can go to New York and hear a punk band, and it makes you feel comfortable having that security, that home—it's like a net or something... but—

IF: On tour, Mark and I would talk every day about what the difference was between that security when it's life-affirming and when it becomes an incarceration... we didn't come to any conclusions, though.

R: I'm not saying we're not that—I'm about to say we are that. Because if you listen, what we play can get really primal, and that goes beyond, that's at the heart of everybody—banging on a drum, banging on a bucket, yelling, that's in the woods, that's cave man music. That's universal, we're playing that.

IF: You have done a lot playing, though, a lot of playing musical instruments...

J: When you talk about roots... we met in Philadelphia, a lot of black musicians have come out of Philadelphia, and we've been around black culture a lot, and we do—we sound black, we have that in us. I've been increasingly interested in African percussion, and that is primal—you know, humanity came from Africa. We use clapping, we use all those forms... sometimes I think of—a thousand dead people, I'm possessed by them, and we're here to raise the dead.

IF: A lot of white musicians have talked about what you're saying before, in the 1950's and 1960's, placing African traditions in opposition to Western civilization, and trying to desert Western civilization and learn instead from this other tradition...

J: Yeah, and—I mean, before, when we started this, I was like "I'm sick of this white boy shit." You know? I guess I do feel like that's kind of a bad thing, to just say fuck you to all of punk history... but that, too, sprang out of the work of a lot of American black musicians that didn't get a lot of credit for what they did.

IF: Yeah, that whole history is invisible behind—

J: And that's been argued before, too—black people can be way more articulate about that than I can, but it's something that I feel, and when I say we sound "black," I don't want to limit it and omit anything else that we could sound like or that we have hints of, but... I think it's very important that we came from Philadelphia, and that's how ... we are.

IF: That's a controversial thing, though—when you talk about "sounding black," is that something that you can do without having the actual life experience of being a black American? Or is that something that can transcend race and ethnicity? How do you define... ?

J (emphatically, determinedly): I think I just have to say that—we sound black. We sound more than that, too, but...

R: Well, I... wait, why do you feel that you have to say that?

J (serious): I can't explain it, dude, I don't know. We came from Philadelphia. We are from there.

(a minute later)

R: I want to clarify something that John was saying—we don't sound like we're black like we are black, that we have that personal history, or we go through things that other people do... but there's another part of the history of music or American history that's ignored, pushed to the side. And we respect that, we have learned from that more than maybe from rock and roll or punk rock. He's not saying we're from that race—it's more like, instead of "jazz," the term "black classical music." That's where that term comes in, the word "black"—it's not, we're not, I mean, race is a fiction, and that's exactly where we're coming from... but that word, in this interview, should be clarified.

IF: OK, before, we were talking about departing from expectations—and then we were at the opposite end of the spectrum, tying into this long-standing historical tradition. You seem to be drawing a distinction between the tradition of expectations, and a more "primal" (?) tradition... maybe you're not doing this consciously, but that's what I got out of what you're saying, like there's a tradition of constricting expectations, and then a tradition that is—a more primal force, that you can be possessed by. Like you talked

about being possessed by a thousand generations of dead people...

J: I feel like that's right, but that connection has totally been unconscious.

IF: That's just one way to construct the whole thing. I wanted to talk about—a folk tradition of violating tradition, a movement of denying movements, a history of evading history—like the Dadaists, some of the more theater-oriented stuff that you do reminds me of what they were doing, and then... OK, there's jazz, and then there's free jazz—

R: Well, there's a million different kinds...

IF: A friend of mine is an African-American historian studying the history of jazz in this country up through Sun Ra, and he wrote in his dissertation about free jazz that what the musicians were actually trying to do was to make a music that could escape the inertia of jazz, the ways that jazz had been colonized and occupied by Western, white capitalist forces, bought out and the musicians addicted to capitalists' drugs and so on... and like I was talking about before, when you spoke about balance, how a ritual that was a means of escaping expectation can give rise to new expectations... anyway, in that text he argues that the more precise way to put those words together is "jazz free," that they were trying to make a jazz-free music, a music that escaped from everything that had been jazz. They would practice playing together and hitting the notes that everyone expected least, the most fucked up notes, and doing the shit that nobody was ready for, that would make the white critics and other vultures uncomfortable, that would create a space where nobody knew what was going to happen.

J: I do listen to a lot of black classical music, but I don't have much of an academic background, I couldn't be a historian... I think I should get into it more, get more points of reference, just so I can grow. I think those guys, they felt natural doing that... and the way we have the music and the words coordinated, that's how we feel natural, you know. Like running across a room, and saying... nothing—it could be silence, and I could step, and just be frozen. And that feels natural, and at the same time comfortable, too. I don't want it to be some kind of war with criticism, somebody establishing himself as a critic... you know, when we

played in Seattle there was one guy, who was just sitting in his chair like this, he was a critic. And of course I ignored him, but he kind of got to me after we'd played and he was still there being this cynical guy. I don't want it be like that—not too much thinking about it, just being human. That's maybe why people do join in. That last show at the bookstore in Olympia, I saw this girl, she was leaning against the bookcase, and I walked up to her—we were singing that tune, I think, and I just started to go "ûlûlûlûlûl," to just move my head, and that vibrato... and then she, all of a sudden, starts making noise. And I kept on doing it... eventually I left, but—that felt totally natural.

R: I forget—you said something that got me.

J: A war of critics?

R: Yeah—

IF: Are you saying that when there's a "critic" present, somebody who's just thinking about things intellectually—

J: Well, I'm not usually aware of the crowd, as much, but I just don't want things to be...

R: This isn't our product that we made, that's out there for people to weigh against everyone else—because it's not against everyone else...

IF: That's a good line!

R: ... it's a part of everything, you know? We're doing this with everybody. And—you asked us before—instead of for others or for ourselves, it's with, it's with them. And I think what we do—I don't want to say it's an example, but it's definitely with people, and if you've seen us play and you've been there, then you know that.

IF: That sounds... a little more deliberate, a little more out of the closet than what you were saying before about not trying to have any expectations at all. It sounds like there is some sort of feeling about what would be good for your interactions with people to be.

J: Well, I was just saying... how we just like to feel natural, you know...

R: What we actually do, and what I think of critics... are two different worlds. This is coming out right now, from me. When we play, those ideas are in my body, in my head—but they're not—they don't affect what we do.

J: I just meant, like—the "natural" aspect, that's the no-plan.

IF: You're saying "doing what feels natural," but in the story that I offered earlier, doing what feels natural can be a problem because it can be nothing but what's expected. To create a situation where I'm not doing what comes naturally, but doing something else, sometimes that can be really liberating. But maybe this is just semantics.

J: I think we're going, I think we're on the right track but we're using the wrong words. Because that's what I mean by "natural," just—doing the weirdest things. I can't, I can't throw words on that.

IF: So I'm—there's a part of me for which the best thing in the world is when nobody knows what's going to happen, and I'm in a place where everything is up in the air. I've tried to found my politics, my engagement with society—I mean the deliberate aspects of my engagement with it—on pushing for that, you know, instead of pushing for some anarchist ten-point platform, or more reformist demands like "better management of the workplace" or whatever. But I'm straddling these two worlds, there—the world where you don't want to put a name on anything, you don't want to try to repeat anything, or set any goals, at all—and then the other world, which is deliberate—

R: I, this is something I've been thinking about, and I'm in the same place that you are, with weighing these options, like which way to go.

IF: I've been just trying to combine them, but there seems to be some kind of tension there.

R: This is something that I've... in more than just playing music, in my life—when I'm thinking about something that I want, or something that's going to happen, instead of having an ideal, exact picture of the end, that goal, the act is the goal. And you completing that. You have the idea, you act, and just the act is enough, as the goal, instead of having this—finishing picture. And that's the medium that I'm working with right now.

IF: Perhaps it's like you were saying to me a minute ago, John—you don't want to put a name on something, or elevate it to an

end, or a desired thing, you don't want to be like "freedom from expectation is the goal, let's create a strategy to attain that goal"... because that freezes everything up. But at the same time, for me at least, it feels like if I don't do something to get myself there, I'm not going to be there.

J: Yeah.

IF: And I, personally, I enjoy being there with a lot of other people. It feels like the energy is multiplied by everybody else who's in there. The difference between two people performing for a bunch of critics who are just sitting there, and a whole room of people all just surprising each other constantly...

R: I think that just as much as people who see us are surprised, I'm surprised by people watching us.

J: Yeah, no shit!

R: The truth... the truth.

IF: Yeah, that's totally what I want...

R: I mean, I'm surprised that this is happening, right now.

IF: That's been the paradox and the challenge for me over the last few years—how to be a partisan of chaos, or whatever you choose to call it, without... freeze-drying it.

R: More than a matter of trying to create something, I guess it's... coming to an understanding...

J: I guess maybe if you have a—I'm thinking "will," but I don't know if I could define that will. Some openness...

R: It goes with what I said a few minutes ago. Instead of trying to attain something that you already have defined, just being—like a being. Just being a being and being.

J: (struggles to remember a passage he thinks is from Sartre's St. Genet)... It's about the nature of somebody, and once they feel—OK, so this person has a new consciousness, they have a new life. And they have new commitments... I wish I could remember it. Once we feel that we have this new consciousness, that we're on this new path—"once one feels that he's entering the world from a new point of view, with new commitments, believes he's gone beyond what was before, he realizes that he has returned to his starting point."

R: What he's talking about sounds like an evolution of circles, one after another—

J: "To adopt a mental attitude is to place oneself in a prison without bars."

[whatever you believe imprisons you]

IF: We were talking about words... a lot of the expressions we've been using sort of point to things rather than representing them, and it may be hard to transcribe this interview in a way that makes sense, with all those generalizations. But that abstractness can be a way to protect yourself, too, to resist the legislation of nouns.

R: I don't disagree with words or labels, but you have to know that reality and life is here, and words are just on top of that—and we can play with them.

IF: It seems to me, if you want to talk about freedom, our lives are made up out of these words...

R: You have to make that distinction, I think, to feel comfortable with either. You have to know that you're living here (gestures in one direction), that you're living this life, and these words are here (gestures in another direction)—and that's what they are, they're words.

IF: Are you saying they refer to themselves rather than to life?

R: I'm saying you have to know the difference. Wait—what did you say?

IF: Is the whole world of language is a separate world from the world of experience?

R: They're—different things, but they're obviously connected, because you know what I mean when I say... if I say "tree," you know what I'm talking about, you can walk to that object and touch it. (pause) I hope that served... ha, I hope that what we said just now served—

IF: —the purpose of pointing to the thing that it's about?... Hm... I think about ... you know, if our lives, the expectations in our lives, are made out of words—this (pointing at the tree next to us) is a tree, which you cut down and make into toilet paper, or else it's something you hug, and lock yourself to—you can't just decide not to speak anymore, if you've been raised on language, because those words will go on delineating and denoting inside your head.

But you can play in the language—"tree... tree, tree, tree" (singing)

R: ... and then you have Herds and Words!

IF: ... until you give it some other kind of meaning.

J: "To adopt a mental attitude is to place oneself in a prison without bars. One seems able escape from it at any moment; and in point of fact, no walls or bars can prevent thinking from going as far as it likes. But actually, at the very moment this thinking believes it has gone beyond this chosen attitude, and that it is entering the world by a new path, and with a new point of view and its new commitments, it has become aware that it has returned to its starting point." And that's like—you know, where do we go from here, with surprising ourselves. Because we have full control, and then when we realize that we're in this new place, we're like—"oh shit, I'm in control... I'm back where I started."

R: Is there anything left!

IF: These are all just points of departure ... I guess the one thing we didn't talk about is how the skill level, the proficiency that you have as musicians, as performers, people who aren't afraid to do crazy stuff, how that intersects with creating these spaces of freedom—like, does somebody have to be an expert to create that space?

R: Definitely not.

J: He started playing drums...

R: ... a year ago. Seriously. The drums I use I got a year ago.

J: I started playing bass clarinet half a year ago.

R: We played together before that using different instruments.

IF: But are you more capable now than you were a year ago of using the drums to make a situation that is... out of control?

R: It's not about how good you are.

J: No!

R: It's not about how good anyone is. We're there, and we do what we can do.

J: Yeah, we're not—professionals, at all.

R: I don't have these limits of talent, or limits of—anything. I just play how I play. I'm not going to say it gets better, but it can change. I feel comfortable, and that's what matters.

IF: All the other skills and proficiencies aside, it's the feeling comfortable that's the real resource. The fifteen-year-old kid that a lot of us have been, that's playing his first show and is just terrified—the chief resource that he or she is lacking is that comfort, that knowledge that whatever happens, it's OK.

R: At the same time that whatever happens is OK, I still get that gut excited feeling sometimes, that I initially got when I first played my first show... back in the '90's. (laughter) Why I think that might happen is that—we keep saying this, but we do something new every night, or we throw a new element in, and I'm excited to see how it turns out, like when I was younger, playing a show, I wanted to see how that would turn out.

IF: So you don't think, as far as the importance of what's going on, that there is a difference between when the fifteen-year-old plays his first show and he's terrified, and when...

R: It's relative... I mean, he's him.

J: I don't... when I first played shows, I felt this detachment from my mind, or just—from my hands, that I had to be outside myself, and watch myself. I hardly ever feel that feeling anymore.

IF: So is that something that you've built up, an ability you've developed?

J: Yeah.

IF: So in that sense, is that a sort of a skill that is required for what you're doing?

(both): well...

J: Sometimes I do become conscious of the whole situation, like I have this invisible person observing me and everything else... and that's usually negative for me.

IF: For me... deliberately trying to create situations where everybody feels that comfort level, my experience is that it often takes somebody who feels that comfort level to bust through, and everyone can follow through the space, the hole that she leaves. But that goes back, again, to going to lengths to create these situations without expectations, that sometimes that's something you would have to plot like you would plot a murder.

R: A reality heist.

IF: But really, I think anyone can do it, can create a crazy situation or play an amazing show or whatever. A lot of it depends on the context, not the individual. I think having more experience, coupled with good momentum, just raises the probability that you'll succeed in doing it when you try in a given situation. That's a good reason to go on tour, to get that experience busting out of different situations.

Robert wants everyone to know they can contact him for tape duplicating.

morethandrums@yahoo.com
www.angelfire.com/scifi/mnstrattacks

Word Herds
759 W. Bridwell Street
Glendora, CA 91741

Simply
put,
Tragedy
is my
favorite
band
playing
punk
music right
now. I'll admit
that the sheer fact that
they're still doing it, that
they've been playing and recording and
touring for as long as I've been active
doing the same things, is an important
part of it for me: seeing them play, still striking distorted chords and counting
off on the drumsticks and believing in it, is an affirmation of our durability not
only as a musical and cultural movement but also as individuals—we've endured
starvation, humiliation, tear gas and terror, many of us even jail, prison, or mental
hospitals, and still are able to sing. That's the theme of this issue, anyway—surviving to fight another
day, burning up in the wreckage and pushing on to build anew. The fact that their music has, if anything,
only gotten better over time is itself a sort of vindication: perhaps we haven't yet succeeded in remaking the
world entirely, but in the meantime if there is a way to live in this fucked up world and remain human, this is it.

TRAGEDY

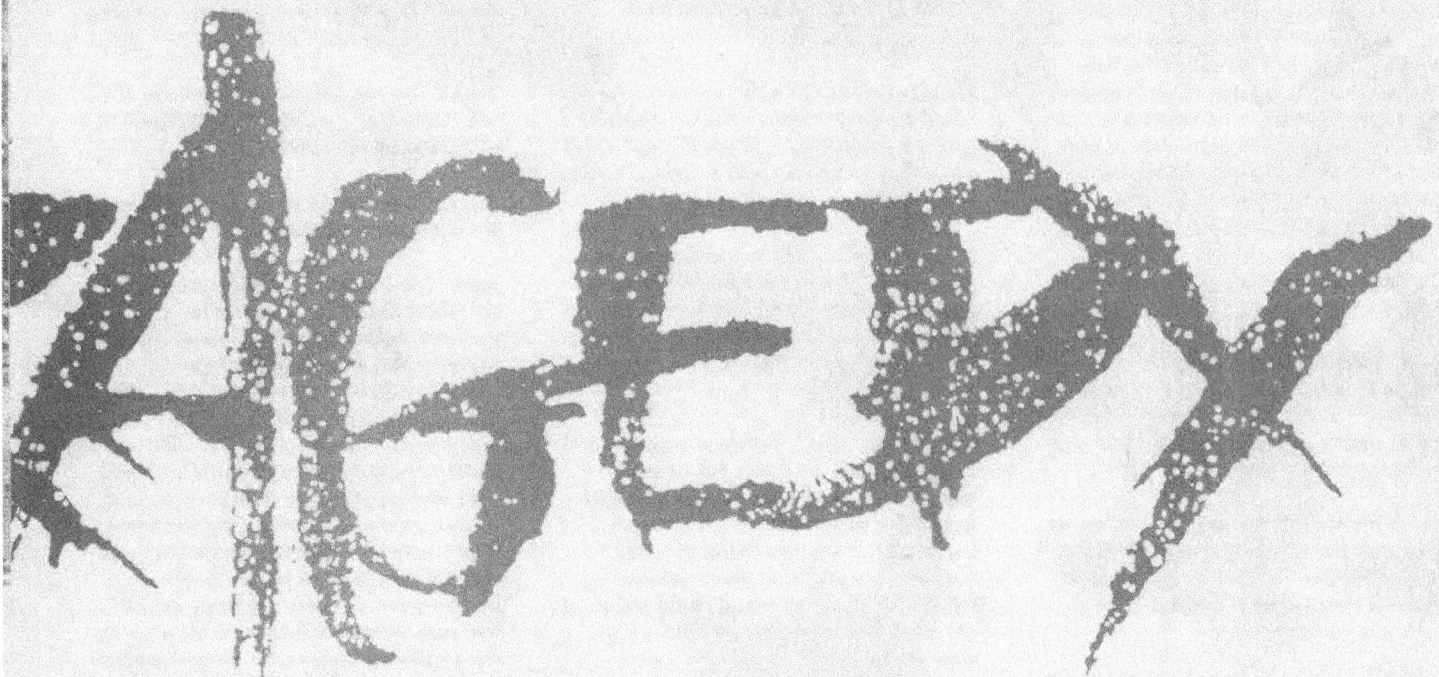

I stopped by their not-so-native town of Portland, Oregon in Spring of 2002, and asked the three of them who were in town (bassist Billy was out on tour with other punks... see "The Punk Band As Anarchist Collective" for bassist jokes) some questions. The tapes wouldn't play in the stereo I was using then, but almost a year later I finally got them to work and transcribed this sometimes-contentious conversation.

Inside Front: All right, the first question I wanted to ask is... how you feel about the d.i.y. music press. I've done a lot of these interviews, and I often feel when I'm doing interviews or writing reviews that I'm using the band as a sort of screen onto which to project all the things that I, the journalist, want to get across. Do you feel like 'zinesters are a bunch of vultures, or...?

(stony, uncomfortable silence)

Todd (finally): It's horseshit. (relieved laughter all around)

Yannick: (says something about the importance of d.i.y. media in the infrastructure of the d.i.y. community, which the tape recorder picks up as a muffled rumble of low frequencies)

Paul: No, I think it's inherent in any media that it's going to be biased in favor of whoever is conducting the interview or review, or whatever reference point is involved... so I don't think there's anything necessarily strange about that. I think maybe if you have perspectives from different reference points, it can offer some sort of balance to really understand what's being described.

Todd: It's always annoying when you do an interview with someone who wants to ask you questions just so they can state their opinion about the said question. But then I'm just kind of relieved because, you know, I don't have to talk as much. But I guess we end up doing so many interviews on tour that it's like... um, I don't really remember what the question was.

I.F.: That's fine, it was a broad topic. Here's something I wanted to ask you: do you think of yourselves as artists or artisans, in terms of the music you make? Are you, like, working people creating a product, not a product in the sense of a commodity but a product as a part of a folk culture—or are you artists, creating unique self-expressions?

Todd: If those are my two choices, I don't think I'd go with either one. I don't really consider myself an artist, or us as a band... to me, playing music is what we do, it's our reflection of what's around us. Actually, I was just reading this Henry Miller book where he was talking about writing, saying that writing is only necessary because our world is so far removed from true experience that you need writing as an attempt to be in touch with that... it made me kind of think of music in the same way, that music is the same thing. If we were living in a more sane world, maybe that world's own creations would sound more like music and music wouldn't be something that people have to make to try to save themselves or feel better about what's going on around them. But, given the way we live, that's how I see music, for us—that's what comes out, the product of our lives and what we do. And I think that music and the feelings that music releases in us make our lives more tolerable, make us feel a little bit more sane—and hopefully make other people feel that way, too.

Paul: Just to add on to that, I basically agree—when I go too long without playing music, I actually, physically and mentally, feel a tension build up that it seems I can only release with music. But—though I wouldn't say I think of myself as an artist

or our music as art—in this particular band, I think we tend to think of everything that comes out in the end as a whole, rather than writing some songs and fitting words to them or whatever. I think the primary reason behind that is what Todd said—it's a product of who we are and everything around us, so it makes sense that everything comes together as some overall statement.

Todd: When it comes to doing tours and making actual artwork for records, that's something that we have to try to do, and organize ourselves to do, but the actual act of playing music isn't something we actually have to try to do or set out to do. We get in a room together, and music... comes out.

Inside Front: You all play in other bands, and this one seems to be the one that you take the most seriously as a chance to do things that would be called artistic by some people, in the sense that you (Paul) were talking about, being really conscious of how the final product fits together... maybe this is off base, but though obviously you don't consider yourselves artists in the bourgeois, uptight sense of the term—the elitist sense of the word—there's a sort of tension in the music you've made between innovations and doing new stuff on the one hand, and being a part of this long-standing punk rock tradition on the other. So are you setting out deliberately to do innovative things, or...?

Todd: I think I can tell what you're asking, and my answer would be that—I don't think we ever try to do anything different, as far as "let's try to make hardcore music sound different than it sounded before"—not that we even did that, but...

I think that what happens is, and I think that what's beautiful about punk music, is that anyone can do it and you don't have to be specifically musically talented by some standards or whatever. What's most important is that when you're making the music, it's real and it's coming from the combination of people that are making it. And if you're trying to copy someone else or sound a certain way, even if your whole goal is to sound like nothing else, then you have a preplanned thing that molds you—to me—molds you into sounding... I don't know.

Paul: Maybe that obstructs your ability to make music that is actually a product of the four people, rather than... because even for those four people to agree on it being a certain thing, you'd have to all have the same idea of what that is.

Yannick: We don't want to be innovative, but we definitely take from our influences and try to add something instead of just going through the motions of writing songs in the same style that wouldn't be interesting...

Todd: Well, my point is, if I write lyrics, I normally don't sit down and say "OK, now I'm going to write lyrics for this song"—the lyrics I end up writing, usually a thought comes into my head and I end up writing it down and then it develops into lyrics. So I can say those lyrics came from a true thought that came into my head, for whatever reason, based on my surroundings—therefore it tends to not be as much of a pre-planned thing. And the same with the music—when I think of a song, a lot of times it just pops into my head while I'm walking down the street, I go home and figure it out, maybe next time we practice I play it. Maybe it's a variation of some song I'd just listened to that morning, that somebody else wrote...

Paul: But I think the key there is that the element that distinguishes between art and production is... passion, however it's derived, even if that be passion as an influence from some particular music you listened to, at least that passion is pushing whatever you make to come from within you—even if you are influenced by the outside world. Maybe that's the case, to some degree—part of it is that we're all music nerds, what we like is all over the place, and I think if you were really well-versed in music you could probably see that in our music. But I think maybe the key there is what Yannick was referring to, that extra element that makes it something more than just going through the motions: even if we're influenced by other music, playing together has the feeling and the joy of... wanting to create something, rather than just recreate something.

Todd: I'd like to think that if anybody ever thought than anything we did was innovative or different or whatever it would be because we are four individual people who create something together, and therefore, I guess, technically,

it shouldn't be like anything else, with that combination of people.

Inside Front: So that's not a conscious thing, it's something that just comes out of the way you approach things. How do you decide which riffs, which ideas, go into this band as opposed to some of the other bands you've done?

Paul: I mean, we don't limit ourselves, and we don't try to be avant garde either, but I'd say at this point we have, to some degree, some sort of style that we can stick to, to some degree. I mean, some things we try, and they're just too far out there...

Todd: I mean, nobody ever comes to practice with something totally out there... but sometimes, somebody will come to practice with something that's a little bit more melodic, or a little bit less melodic, or whatever, and we try it, and sometimes it works and sometimes it doesn't. Usually, if it comes naturally, if we play something and it feels like—it feels right, or it doesn't. We throw out tons of stuff.

Inside Front: But you write pretty fast, compared to some bands I know.

Todd: Yeah, I guess we're used to playing with each other.

Inside Front: What are some of the more far out there influences or sources that you've ripped off, that people might not notice?

Todd: Me, I have no far out influences... as far out as I would go would be '77 punk, but... (here comes the wind-up a for a joke they must tell a lot) I pretty much listen to both kinds of music: punk and hardcore.

Paul: I'd say that's probably far out for people who listen to our music, in general. We're definitely very influenced by '77 punk and early '80's punk, and there are elements of musical styles that we sound nothing like that we take and use.

Inside Front: So the stuff you're drawing on is pretty much all in the punk tradition, is that what you're saying?

Todd: Pretty much. I mean, we could say that we stole ideas or riffs or feeling from New Model Army or something like that—that'd be about as far as we could go.

Yannick: I'm probably the one who listens to the most wide-ranging music—

Todd: He likes Pink Floyd, stuff like that (laughter). I mean, I can't say that it's influenced your songwriting at all—

Yannick: That's what I mean, but I did realize that we have a straight up AC/DC riff.

Todd: If anything, I would say the music we take riffs directly from is stuff that doesn't sound like us, but that is punk related.

Yannick: Sometimes you get an idea for a change or a transition from something...

Todd: I actually have a little book, and if I'm listening to something I'll hear the way a band goes from one part to the next part, and I'll just remember that, and write it down. And when I'm trying to figure out something, and I need that one part, then I remember it. It's kind of ridiculous to be like "that band is an influence," because we sound nothing like them. But I think that's what happens when you listen to music all the time... and while I can't say that my musical scope is really broad, I'm also obsessed with punk and hardcore music from all over the world, so... to me, that alone is a huge scope of music that—from the outside, I'm sure people would say that it all sounds the same, but the more you look into it the more it all sounds different, and the bands from each country have their own feel to the music, their own language.

Paul: I had a friend who was making fun of me the other day, he was in my car and he was like "You really don't listen to anything but punk music, do you?" And I was like, "Yeah, I listen to hardcore too." But—I thought about it, and I do listen to a few token non-hardcore bands, but I'd say the reason why I don't derive much influence from anywhere else and I'm not terribly interested in lots of other music is that—that connection, whatever that feel that comes from punk music that I can relate to, I just don't really find elsewhere. I mean, there's a few random other records of different styles that I like a little bit, but it's all really token things that might work... in the right mood, or something like that, whereas punk music—it's broad enough that every mood you can think of, there's a song for.

Yannick: There's just so much, to keep you interested in it. There's no moment when I really tire of punk.

Inside Front: I guess I wonder—OK, punk is a folk music tradition, because people play it, not an elite, and we've been playing punk rock for twenty five years. That's different from the kind of music you hear on the radio, where it's supposed to be different every year, new and improved products and progress. I guess classical music was or is an example of that demand for innovation in music, too. At the same time, I wonder when the final possible combination of notes with a d-beat is played, what happens then—do we go back and start with the first one again, or...?

Yannick: Yes. (laughter)

Todd: Well, like I said, I think it happens naturally—things evolve, and music changes naturally. If you read things from early hardcore

I have no far out influences... as far out as I would go would be '77 punk, but... I pretty much listen to both kinds of music: punk and hardcore.

bands, or look at a band like the Bad Brains, like the early stuff they wrote, if you read what they were listening to—they weren't listening to music that sounded like what they sounded like. But somehow they made this music that was totally raw and fast and sounded almost like nothing else that had been made. Or Minor Threat, even—if you read about Minor Threat, they were talking about listening to the Jam and Wire and stuff, and they were making this music that was totally different...

Paul: Well, they ripped off the Bad Brains.

Yannick: That brings up where we're heading, what's the future...

Inside Front: That's what I'm saying, yeah.

Yannick: Because we are only listening to pretty much what we're playing. Of course, we're adding something, which goes back to the last question, but it wasn't culled from various far-fetched things, just—

Todd: No, but they weren't pulling from weird things, they were pulling from rock music, which evolved into punk, which evolved into hardcore—

Yannick: Yeah, but there was a definite step there. There was a definite step from the Jam to Minor Threat.

Todd: Yeah, but somebody who dropped out of hardcore eight years ago would probably think that a lot of the bands now sound like they've taken a step, too.

Paul: I think that question's pretty unanswerable, the future's unresolved...

Yannick: I didn't mean we could see the future, but since we do listen to stuff that's so close to what we come up with I wonder how much... where we'll derive the creativity from, or if we'll just give it...

Todd: But—to me creativity isn't just finding some new weird chords, it's—you write your own words, and put your own ideas into it, and your own feeling. I mean, talking about folk music, I'm not that educated in folk music, but my assumption is that folk music, like acoustic folk music, probably hasn't evolved—people are probably playing the same open chords on acoustic guitars, and that doesn't mean that, for people who like that kind of music, that people aren't making new songs that are good to them.

Paul: Right, and the point there is that folk music doesn't serve the role so much of trying to create something new so much as to answer to the needs, or reflect a certain culture—that's why it's folk music. I think punk music can do that to a certain extent, endlessly, though it might peter out as far as how many people want to keep listening to the same d-beat songs over and over again. But maybe that d-beat genre is a good example—you

pretty much have to be a total nerd, into that style, to want to have every record by every band with "Charge" or "Dis" in its name. I mean, there's some really great stuff that's all like that, but it answers to a pretty limited audience. Punk as a whole, there's so many genres that you can keep doing that for a while. I guess ultimately the question is—is it to become something which is simply answering to itself, reflecting itself, or does it... does the culture evolve with the music, or vice versa? I guess that question asks whether our culture is evolving.

Inside Front: Right. Are we trying to be part of an evolutionary culture, or a cyclical culture?

Todd: I think it keeps changing. I don't think it has to get more technical, more out there, more experimental, more anything.

Yannick: As far as styles go, if rock and roll or early punk or whatever was superseded by something else, we can assume then that punk is eventually going to be superseded by or evolve into something else, or be a catalyst for it. Just like in the early '80's, something will change, and punk will be a relic, still alive in some sense, but we can't assume that it's just going to be an endless cycle.

Todd: No, what I'm saying is I don't see it as a cycle—

Yannick: Yeah, OK—

Todd: I don't think—I mean, I don't want to name a certain band, but if you just think of a certain band that's putting out records now, that you like, you can't really say that they sound completely like another band from five or ten years ago. If they're good, they have their own thing that's a little bit different in some way.

Paul: But I think if you think about when those changes happened, they didn't just happen musically, they exploded because, in 1977, there were a lot of pissed off youth that had just come from a generation that was supposed to change the world, and when it didn't, there were a bunch of disillusioned people, and then punk rock exploded. And then you could say in the '80's, there were a bunch of, again, disillusioned, angry young—suburban kids, essentially, and that exploded into what early '80's hardcore was. Like, Black Flag wouldn't have been Black Flag if there hadn't been a bunch of fucking angry southern California fuckups. And that's why every kid in the early '80's listened to fucked up music and went around on a skateboard and was considered a vandal; in answer to what was going on at the time. I think you have to look at that in a larger perspective; what happens culturally is that eventually that becomes swallowed up, and that anger becomes quenched, and the problem is that it's like one of those little twisty balloons—you squeeze it one place, it's going to pop out

somewhere else. The question is—is that going to be within punk culture, or maybe punk culture, once it's squeezed, just becomes cyclical within itself. Who knows when another moment is going to come along when that anger or that particular thing can explode on a mass scale where there's thousands and thousands of people, or whether that will ever happen again.

Inside Front: I guess the way that I see it... Some bands are always bringing in new changes, new variations on beats or whatever, while other types of music spin off and become these cyclical folk culture genres, where people actually aim for being something like the other bands, and it does come out that way. I guess you're refusing to associate yourselves with either of those two options... ?

Yannick: I definitely think we're doing the cyclical thing, in that case, because we're not trying to reinvent something...

Todd: And I mean, that's just musically—punk, as a culture, has definitely evolved, and changes so much... the network, and the d.i.y. culture as it is, is so much different even than it was five years ago, let alone fifteen years ago.

Paul: One of the ways that's obvious is—when you see someone who dropped out ten years ago, they look at what's going on now and they think that it's nothing like the punk they were involved with. So often it's the case that it's evolved beyond what they related to so that they don't understand it anymore.

Todd: While we're used to that, because we live in that culture—we don't see how it changes.

Inside Front: So, along the lines of what you [Paul] were saying, what's the relationship between anarcho-punk music, and that tradition, and anarchist, punk rock activism, squatting and all that? If you're interested in that kind of action, that activism, that whole community, is there an imperative to keep the music that it's been based around alive?

Paul: I think one really rests so hard on the other that I'd think that if someone was really involved in one, whichever one they wanted, they probably would stick with it. However—I'd say that for the most part, it's more of a soundtrack for a culture, in which case, sure, the music is important as long as... From a social perspective, as long as someone continues to get something good out of it, then it's important. From a musical standpoint, if anarchism or whatever, that lifestyle, continually pushes the music in some artistic sense, then sure, I'd say it's important—but I think that generally, it's more the other way around, that there are a lot of people who are just into the music, into the

...If there are any slogans in the lyrics it's because they sound good, they fit well, whatever, but it's not to try to force things into people's heads and make them think "oh, yeah, this is bad, and this is good..."

sound, and maybe they relate to the politics of anarchism in a very loose way.

Inside Front: How do you see yourselves, as far as what you're trying to do with your music? You were saying it's about self-expression as a way just to try to survive...

Todd: Well, I think that would be the point. Like I said before, I don't think we're trying to do anything. We play music, and express ideas, and create something that we like and we want to share with other people. And in terms of vision, ideals, I don't think we have a larger goal outside of that.

Inside Front: So you make music in the d.i.y. community...

Todd: I think we just present something, and whatever people get from it is up to them.

Yannick: That's definitely what I would say, but I thought—a few months ago you were saying that you were going for something, not forcing, but you were trying to convey a message—

Todd: Yeah, but we never got into that. I assumed that you and me were on opposite ends about that, I don't think we necessarily are, but...

Yannick: I've always... felt like, yeah, like you said.

Todd: But what you were saying then was that music is entertainment, and that's not how I feel about it.

Yannick: That's not what I was saying.

Todd: OK. Well, we probably didn't understand each other anyway, because we got cut off, I think we ended before we even got into it. But I think, even from a lyrical standpoint, if there are any slogans in the lyrics it's because they sound good, they fit well, whatever, but it's not to try to force things into people's heads and make them think "oh, yeah, this is bad, and this is good..."

Yannick: We disagree on so much stuff that it would be hard to come up with a coherent plan or agenda.

Paul: I think there is power of propaganda in music, if you want to use that, but I definitely don't think we're the type of band that has any particular message. I had this conversation with someone the other day, they were asking if I knew some pop singer and I didn't know who they were, and they were like "oh, you must be kidding, you're pretending" and I was like, wow, I guess I just forget that I live in such a bubble. She just didn't get the fact that I'm such a dropout I don't know what's going on with Britney Spears and all this bullshit. So I think to some degree, the politics are inherent in our music when our music is so wrapped up in our

lifestyle. I think that there can be an effect based on that—it's not like we're changing the world, we don't have a political agenda we're trying to spread to the masses, but definitely within any media, music or print or whatever, there's power, to influence. Sometimes it's kind of frightening to think what that might be, but I just—the only level of conscious direction in that is knowing that we don't want our music to be just baseless, or our content to be just baseless. We would rather reflect the things that we do feel strongly about.

Todd: Yeah. I'm definitely not saying there's nothing there, I'm saying that what's there is not so black and white—because for me what's there when we play music, the anger and frustration that I put into our music is real, and it comes from a million factors that have gone into my life, and that's nothing that I can completely explain in a song or a million songs. Realistically, people get into punk for so many different reasons that—I wouldn't expect people to get that as the point of the music... but I'm sure that there are people who came from, or arrived at, feelings and frustrations similar to my own. But—that's not the goal of playing music, to get someone else to think a certain thought or feel a certain feeling. Some people are just going to like the music because it's fast and loud or whatever. We have friends that might like it just because they like us as people, or there are people that might like the stuff we sing about, who'd like us lyrically, but musically it's not their thing.

Inside Front: Do you think it prostitutes music to try to make it serve some propaganda end?

Todd: It depends on the way you do it...

Paul: It happens, sure. I think the power, if there's any power in what we do, it's that one person's reality, or one person's common thoughts, or someone else's revelation, some things that might seem... I mean, some of the ways in which we exist and have existed for a long time, at one point, were revelations to us, from the way someone else existed. That's the constant process of thought, that's what keeps me inspired, learning new things, is that constant process of having new revelations and ideas. Perhaps the reflection of where we're at, at this particular point, could serve to do that for someone else. Again, that's not the intention, but I think that's probably the most powerful point in what we do—I mean, there are very few bands that I've ever listened to that had a specific message that really changed me, maybe bands singing about vegetarianism—but there were bands that would sing and with a certain element of anger or a certain reflection on their lives, and that influenced me to feel differently about myself and the world.

Todd: Sometimes much more than the actual lyrics. But really, honestly, I play music to stay

sane, and anything that anyone else gets out of it is like a bonus, but it's an extra thing to me. I do it for mostly personal, selfish reasons, to stay sane and attempt some kind of satisfaction, happiness.

Paul: To answer what you said, I think when bands prostitute themselves for a message they completely annihilate the power that I was just referring to. In doing that, you reach specific people: you reach the people who are looking for answers rather than ideas. To me, that's so much less powerful—those people aren't going to stop thinking like sheep just because they have different answers now. If there's anything I would ever want to promote to people, it's to think more deeply about things, come up with your own answers. To me that's just one of the fundamental principles of free thinking or whatever.

Yannick: Some of the great propaganda bands, like Conflict and CRASS, were obviously out to send out a message and try to change the world—

Todd: Oh yeah, those bands changed my life, for sure, but I don't think we're one of those bands.

Yannick: I know, I know, but he (the interviewer) was speaking generally, not just about our band. I think bands like that definitely... I mean, it helped a whole social group that at the time was huge, hugely influenced... so the power of that propaganda can't be discarded.

Todd: I've said before in another interview that Conflict probably had—arguably had more influence than any other band, ever, just for the fact that probably thousands and thousands of people were awakened to animal rights and became vegetarian through... bands like that.

Paul: I would argue though that the power there was at least partly from the knowledge that those people were living what they what they were saying—minus—(name withheld out of common courtesy), that ol' (laughter)

Yannick: I think it's safe to say that none of them were living it! (laughter)

Todd: Actually my point in that other interview was actually the opposite—where people say "oh, they're hypocrites," or "they don't live up to what they sing about," and that undercuts everything. The propaganda of what you do comes out through your own individual lifestyle. What you say, the ideas you promote, can be more of a fictitious thing. What you actually do with your own life...

Paul: You know, for me, I was influenced by knowing those CRASS records people had a collective, had their own thing going on. To me that was more inspiring than any of the words they were singing. I'm sure there are people who are more academic, so they read lyrics like information, and that information processes in their brains in some logical way, and they're like "oh, this is the answer," but...

> **The propaganda of what you do comes out through your own individual lifestyle. What you say, the ideas you promote, can be more of a fictitious thing.**

Inside Front: Next question: you deliberately keep your music in the d.i.y. sphere—and you seem to be moving more into that, rather than less, which is the opposite of the progression that usually takes place. Is that just because that's where you're most comfortable? Or is that something you consciously think about, the way you produce and distribute music and the way that fits into what's going on in the world?

Paul: Talking about moving in a more d.i.y. direction, or...?

Inside Front: I understand what Todd's saying about making the actual music and lyrics as a response to personal experience, but there's the question of how you introduce that music into the world, and you haven't sold yourselves as artists to some record label—that's a very deliberate choice. I guess that grows out of the context of the lives you've chosen to live, but it's still a deliberate choice.

Todd: I think a difference is—with a lot of bands, they get a little bigger, and then they attempt to get bigger, and they think about what they could do to get bigger... but I think with us it's gone the opposite way. Honestly, I don't think we ever cared how so-called popular we were in the scene, or how many records we sold, but at a certain point we had to think about that, because we were doing things... and I think it was kind of the reverse, how do we react to the fact that we can sell a lot of records, by those standards? What do we do about it? Because if we don't think about it, then someone else who doesn't give a shit is going to pop out of the water and try to get control.

Paul: I think the point in there is that we're influencing, in the practical sense, which I'd say is as important as in any ideological sense. It makes sense that we do it this way—everything else about our lives is about being dropouts, living in this bubble that we live in—to some degree, it's a lot nicer to have fewer people to deal with... though the people that we do deal with, I'm not disrespecting them in any way. Things aren't black and white, sometimes you have to make decisions which don't fit the d.i.y. template or whatever. But I think we've always been conscious of doing things in a way that was comfortable for us.

Todd: I think it all comes down to financial stuff. If we had the finances, I don't think we would even do... I mean, we'd go through fewer steps, fewer other people. We don't, so...

Inside Front: How about the way you do things inside of the band? I know that you are always trying to...

Todd: It's called disorganized organization. It's kind of like my Slingshot organizer over here—it's in about thirty pieces, it's scattered all over the place, but it works.

Inside Front: Well, I know a lot of bands have a serious division of labor problem, in which there's one person sort of telling everyone else what to do, or there's a tension over who's responsible for what.

Paul: I think the most fucked up thing about division of labor in general is when the hand that feeds is separated from the mouth. I think people get caught up in, like, a cooperative consensus mentality that means that everyone has to be brought down or up to the exact same level, and everyone has to be doing the exact same things. We've had frustrations with that to some degree, but I see this happen so often with people who are in this mindset—they want to start a group, and if someone's excelling and doing too well in one direction, that people start going "wait a minute, you're not listening to me." I think there has to be some balance, I think everyone has to be included so you feel like you're not totally distanced from the hand that's feeding you, so you at least feel like it's your hand to some degree—but there are certain things that make sense. Yannick does a lot of business stuff because, in some senses, he's already been dealing with record stuff for years and years and years. When it comes to fixing a van, I'm the dude in the band that knows how to work on cars... I think within our band sometimes it's a matter of figuring out how to balance that so that everyone knows what's going on, and one person isn't doing too much of the stuff, but I think when one person does something particularly well, there's nothing wrong with that.

Todd: We haven't figured it out, by any means, it's something we're always talking about and trying to work on.

Yannick: We've gone through crises, back and forth...

Todd: Where someone's not pulling their weight, or someone's pulling too much...

Yannick: ... and ended up butting heads for a while...

Paul: And I think that is the process of cooperation—there's never a template that you can put down. Though I think that's what a lot of these people want, that I was referring to before—they want the rules according to which you

THE BOLD PULL QUOTE

> The most fucked up thing about division of labor in general is when the hand that feeds is separated from the mouth. I think people get caught up in, like, a cooperative consensus mentality that means that everyone has to be brought down or up to the exact same level, and everyone has to be doing the exact same things.

cooperate. You have to put your thumbs up at the right moment, to say the right thing at the right time, everyone has to speak in the same tone of voice. That's not the way people work. People have different ways of speaking and interacting, that's the whole concept of dynamics between people. I think that's one of the problems we've had, is the dynamics between us are different, we're different. That's the hardest thing we've had to deal with, that...

Todd: We're four really stubborn people, really opinionated.

Inside Front: I think, like you're saying, that the organizational structure has to come from the people who are trying to work together, not people imposing a model of organization upon themselves. It's amazing to me that any bands, or groups of people who are really stubborn, are together at all, after a couple years of fighting.

Paul: But I think that any band that does do things on a cooperative basis, which means that there's not one person that's playing a bunch of puppets, which happens—I think that's a great model for the way real cooperation should work, in that it directly answers to the needs of the people immediately involved, whereas you see groups pop up all the time in left culture that are like "let's do a group to save this," or whatever, and some of the times the inner functionings of those groups come to outweigh the focus on whatever it is they're actually trying to do. When the main focal point is where you're trying to get, and everyone agrees that that's what you're doing, then I think the other things tend to work themselves out—definitely with a lot of bumps in the road, but at least that's... the focal point. I think with a band, the whole point is you're playing music and you have to work things out—you're working things out because you want to play music, not because you're attempting to cooperate. The cooperation part is something that follows.

Inside Front: How about the responsibility, or the relationship, of the band to the larger punk rock community—do you feel like, aside from making music, you have responsibilities to the people you make the music for, or around, or with?

Todd: Not by choice.

Inside Front: Do you feel like you're public property in that sense?

Todd: Yes.

Inside Front: Is that good, or bad?

Todd: Bad.

Yannick: I mean, we do what we do, we play music for ourselves, and consequently we have to...

Todd: I just know, my personal life, this whole thing has pushed me into being more and more antisocial, more and more of a recluse. More and more guarded, because of being in this small little circle, being in some kind of public eye, being defensive, and other people being offensive—that whole thing's definitely changed my personality, I can't deny that. I don't feel a responsibility like "it's my responsibility to do this, for the scene," or whatever, but I also am, we all are kind of socially dysfunctional in our own ways, I'm not the most extroverted person, and a lot of times if someone approaches me I'm not like "oh, hey, great, how ya doin?"—that's not my personality. So someone who doesn't know me might not know how to take that, and when you're on tour, and people want to talk to you, you... I feel like I have to use extra energy to be more personable, because people don't know me, and don't know how I react and express myself, so...

Yannick: Does that mean you have to do that?

Todd: ... that's like a responsibility.

Yannick: It's not a responsibility for you to be nice to everyone. You just do it because that's your personality.

Todd: But no, I do because that's how the punk scene works, that's what's kind of special about our subculture, that if people like your music, that might not be enough for them to respect what you're doing. If they meet you and—I mean, you know how it is, if people think that your band are shitty people, assholes, then people might not like your music, just like that. I mean, if you care about that anymore.

Paul: I think there's only a certain degree to which you can care about that, but—I think the point is, we do what we do because it's what we want to do. But at a certain point, you have to recognize power, whether you wanted it or not. And if you're in a band—I mean, I don't care what band you are—when you're on stage, there's a power differential that has not been broken down, as much as we may try to say it is when we're playing on basement floors. The band can say things, it can influence people in a way that people on the other side of that differential can't... especially if you're a band that starts to get a little more popular or whatever, that power exists and it definitely influences—to some degree, it ends up affecting how you act.

Yannick: But it's not a responsibility.

Paul: No, it's not a responsibility, but it's—it's relevant to that question.

Todd: Ahhhh, it almost is a responsibility, though—with us being four people who do think about things and are trying to be conscious, if we put out a record that was completely substanceless, I would think that would be irresponsible.

Paul: That goes back to what I was saying before, about bands.

Todd: If we made six thousand pieces of plastic with cardboard around them, that had nothing to them, I would think that would be irresponsible.

(Yannick, indecipherable on the tape recorder, presents what appears to be a counterpoint; the others bring up a time when he seemed to take the opposite position; they work it out amongst themselves.)

Inside Front: OK, another tension I want to ask about between different themes in your band is between, on the one hand, seeking high recording quality, not to mention using at least decent equipment, and on the other hand, being highly critical of technology itself. How does that play out, how do you resolve the tension between being a high-tech-recording band and an anti-tech-idea band?

Paul: You mean, like, we play a show and say something about technology and somebody's like "dude, your amp's on!"?

Todd: Like why aren't we just banging on rocks, or singing a capella or something?

Inside Front: Well, specifically, not just playing the amps but—you have a mastery of the technology you're using, you're pushing for that. Some people who say "fuck technology" are like "yeah, I use whatever."

Todd: One thing I will say is—when it comes to recording, we heavily favor analog recording, which is becoming more and more a dinosaur of sorts. At this point it's an extremely primitive technology, in the face of the high technologies that exist and are being created on a daily basis. That's our favored method of recording.

Paul: If you're saying that technology is bad, and you're picking and choosing between certain kinds of technologies, implying that you're trying to promote a certain direction, that's like saying that missiles are bad and then picking between two particular types of missiles. The difference being that a missile is something that you can have a choice to deploy;

If you're saying that technology is bad, and you're picking and choosing between certain kinds of technologies, implying that you're trying to promote a certain direction, that's like saying that missiles are bad and then picking between two particular types of missiles. The difference being that a missile is something that you can have a choice to deploy; and I think that we're entrenched in technology that we're unable to just shed off our shoulders.

and I think that we're entrenched in technology that we're unable to just shed off our shoulders. Sure, guitars and amps could easily qualify as that—I don't think that was ever the intent of our statement—

Todd: The thing is, unless we're living on the land, in some kind of sustenance lifestyle, basically human life has "evolved" to the point that we make different combinations of technologies, are surrounded by different combinations of technologies, and use those to do whatever we do with our lives. Using the broad definition of technology—I mean, everything you do is—we're always using things somebody else created or invented. Whatever you can make do with of what's there is... I mean, this is an old argument, but we never at any point said "fuck all technology," that's pointless, it's like saying "fuck modern life," like fuck everything. The point is just trying to increase awareness, for people not just to jump head first into every new thing that comes along, for people to remember that ten years ago there was no www-dot-whatever, and now we can't even imagine a world where you wouldn't look around and see that on every billboard, wrapper, label, every single thing—that's like science fiction, to remember that ten years ago there was no such thing, not even on a punk record, and now it's everywhere and we can't imagine life without it. As a band, I think that was our whole intention, to increase awareness and to continue to promote free thought.

Inside Front: To restate the question, in a better world, would there be no recordings? If that's the case, why are they necessary here? And if they are necessary, why are "better" recordings, more high-tech recordings, better?

Todd: Maybe that's kind of like the Henry Miller thing I was talking about. At the point we've come to, we're adapting to what is around us, to make do the best we can. That's the point I was making before—maybe in a less confusing world, music wouldn't be such a separate thing, or wouldn't sound the way it does.

Yannick: Then this all leads to our differences over the internet and so on. Since the internet is now so entrenched and part of everything in the world, how do you see that?

Todd: I mean, I don't think that high-tech recordings are great—

Paul: I think the difference is the perspective you're looking at it from. I don't think the internet, from a technological viewpoint, is largely different from telephones. Telephones completely shaped and altered not only our culture, but the way in which we think, the reality in which we live. We now know that you can pick up this little thing and immediately talk to someone, while normally you would have to spend time traveling to see them. So they not only altered the way our minds think, they altered the dimension of time itself. I think the point is, with the internet, it became another technology that did that—it completely altered the way we think about our connection to the rest of the world: you can get on the internet and send a message instantly to someone in China. To me that completely abstracts the distance, and everything else. But all of that is a matter of intellectual thought or whatever—whereas, to me, there's the matter of the actual, physical effects of doing things that affect the way you think and the way you spend your life. Personally, there are certain technologies that I know affect my life in a way that I don't feel so good about. There are people that we give shit for riding around in a car more than necessary—I decide I should stop, and ride a bike. It's a decision that I make—I know riding in a car changes the way that I think about my life, as opposed to riding on a bicycle. To me the internet is just one of those things, where I occasionally use the internet to get information or do email or whatever—I don't see it like "I'm getting my hands dirty," because the rest of my life is involved in these decisions. But to me, staring at a computer screen for too long alters the way that I think—I'd rather be staring at sunshine, or rain, or whatever—things that are more important to me. So to me, that makes it an important personal choice, along with the rest of the personal choices that I make.

Todd: I'm saying—I don't think we as human beings needed that invention, just like we didn't need most of the inventions. And that one in particular—I don't care to have it in my life, and so I'm stubborn.

Yannick: But the question, specifically—recording is a few steps further along the line, it's past the point of the invention of recording stuff instead of just keeping memories. Now it's so part of the way we live that we don't see it that way... of course it changed everything the same way that telephones did—but what I'm saying is that now the internet is fully entrenched in everything that we do. Whether you as a person uses it or not, it's there, and it's there to stay, or to be superceded by something else down the line—

Todd: I don't have the illusion that I'm making it change by not using it. But that doesn't mean that I want to use it just because it's there.

Paul: There were people who resisted recorded music, simply as a lifestyle choice. There were people who thought that taking a photograph was—stealing your soul, or something like that. There were people who—they knew what music meant, to be able to see it and feel it when it was actually played—and to be able to hear it played back on a phonograph, there were people that freaked out when they heard that.

Yannick: So much of our old argument with His Hero Is Gone was based on the righteousness or

whatever of refusing the internet, and technology as such, and I think it was kind of misplaced to try to push that. I think we spoke more as if we had a platform, rather than just personally. I agree with the attack, that you may not want the ways the internet changes the way you live...

Todd: Yeah, but I think it changes the way everybody lives. And I thought that before, but I never had a platform, I never told people "you should stop using the internet—everyone, you should resist."

Paul: I think that self-righteousness was more perceived than spoken.

Yannick: I mean, I was involved just as much in it in the discussions...

Todd: As a person, and as a lyricist, and whatever, I definitely encouraged resistance to technology and rejection of it, and I still do, as a person.

Yannick: Yeah, so do I. The point is, we tried to approach it as a platform, rather than just saying it was a personal thing from our perspective.

Paul: Maybe, but I think there's power in that. Whether it was spoken or perceived, I think there is power in saying "this is something that is happening right now"—because it's only at that moment that you can really say that. Even though we witnessed the introduction of the internet, it's so ingrained in our lives now that it's hard to remember that moment at which it broke. It's right at that moment when a new technology is increased that you can scream your lungs out about how it's affecting you and sound self-righteous or whatever. At some point that argument just becomes null.

Yannick: But we were screaming at a car that was far gone, that couldn't hear us.

Todd: But I also personally enjoyed the fact that it was such a controversial issue that I never thought would be controversial—at that point I enjoyed the fact that saying "fuck this stuff, reject this stuff" would piss people off.

Yannick: The thing is, I still agree with everything you said, but I think more from a personal viewpoint than—trying to talk people into it.

Paul: Yeah, I guess I can see that too, I think... Maybe I can use an analogy that I've made before to someone when I was trying to get them to understand my point of view about understanding these things, understanding technology but also, to broaden it, living in a world which is uncontrollable, which is a perspective that people think is cynical. The analogy is—if you suddenly

awoke in a room with no doors or windows, waist-deep in shit, the fact that you exist in that room amidst that shit—you're not being cynical or pessimistic to say that you exist in that and have no choice but to exist in that. To me, true—I hate to say optimism, because I think it has bad implications—but true living, that can possibly happen in an existence like that, has to come from a recognition of where you actually are. I think if there is any personal salvation, in our own hopes and desires or in anything in this world, it either comes from having that understanding or being so completely blinded that you can just walk around with a smile on your face and pretend that the world is a happy little flower or something. To me, that's the primary point of trying to bring about recognition of these things.

Todd: But going back to your question, to me recorded music is a documentation. In a lot of cases, it's the only proof that something existed. If I pick up some record from some kids in Brazil that somehow recorded a 7" back in 1983, of course I know that this record can never represent the lives these kids lived or what they did when they made this music, but it's the closest thing that I can get to it. Just like I recognize that, to relate it to technology, when I make a phone call, it's not the same as seeing someone in person and having a conversation with them—but it's the closest thing I can get to it sometimes. For me, recording—it's not a substitute for life, it's a documentation of life.

Yannick: But that's assuming that music needs to be documented.

Paul: Yeah. The evolution of technology, if you follow that backwards, philosophically or anthropologically, you could find a point at which the need to capture moments began. If you follow that back, you come to that point which we call pre-history, which, the anthropologists are telling us now, that was the point when humans started doing something different. It seems to be at that moment that everything changed, and there became a need for history, there became a need to pass things down. To say, at any point over the last century, to say that it was fucked up to want or need to capture music to listen to later, I think was a null argument, in the same way that every time someone criticized something that came along that was building upon that same crutch that happened somewhere behind us in that evolution of technology, that was a null argument. Except that—each individual that made that argument was arguing from the point of view of their life having been altered. But all we're doing is continually building layers upon layers of fucked-upness, all—possibly, possibly—stemming from some point in time behind us when our lives became so fractured that we needed to be able to tie down moments, tie down seconds.

Todd: Possibly there's some kind of human conditioning—whether it's conditioned or instinctual—that makes us want to leave a mark in some sense... and most of the marks we leave, obviously, are horrendous and unforgivable, but

...All we're doing is continually building layers upon layers of fucked-upness, all—possibly, possibly— stemming from some point in time behind us when our lives became so fractured that we needed to be able to tie down moments, tie down seconds.

I think there's something to be said for wanting to leave a mark that maybe goes against the other things.

Yannick: But how do you see us to be doing that... or what about not leaving marks...

Todd: Well, that's what I mean, like, leaving a mark in a less literal sense than destroying things.

Inside Front: It does seem to be characteristic of human beings in the West that we feel that when life happens, it's unreal, but when it's recorded, it's real.

Todd: I don't even necessarily mean physical things—

Paul: I don't even think it's necessarily Western. I don't want to start sounding like I'm talking primitivist bullshit or anything, but I would take it a lot farther than just Western. I think there's a certain cultural perspective that, from the literature I've read at least, didn't exist in peoples that lived other ways, nomadic peoples for example. This is up until about thirty years ago that there were peoples living this way. They didn't need to make that mark, because they were happy with their existence from day to day. I don't put too much weight in what scientists have told me about these things, or people who have gone and studied them or whatever, but it's interesting to me—to think that humans existed for thousands and thousands of years making virtually no mark on the world... whereas everything that's happened in the last ten thousand years has made not just marks but scars. I think that's an astounding difference.

(Todd leaves)

Paul: I think a lot of that stuff started to sound pretty philosophical and intellectual. I'm simply trying to say something that seems to explain something that is a part of me, something I can relate to. And I can't relate to intellectual or philosophical things that don't, in some way, answer to that.

Inside Front: That don't connect to you, your experience, your feelings in some way, you mean.

Paul: Yeah, maybe it's just that I don't give a shit about things that don't connect to me, which is in some ways abnormal in the human psyche as we know it. But—I'm not intending to say those things as some far-fetched intellectual theory, but simply that, when I talk about these things that we're talking about, I like to at least try to think about where these origins might have come from and how that might be relevant.

Inside Front: OK, so—being in a punk band, you're—well, things aren't always so easy, are they? I know when I saw you in Sweden, the singers' voices were all fucked up, and you (Paul) are always sick... when we were in Belgrade, my friend there told me when you were there you were so sick you were about to die, and a friend somewhere

else told me the same thing about when you were there, and I know the same thing has happened to me on tour. Todd was talking about leaving a mark—I wanted to ask him about where you draw the line between trying to make music to stay sane, and when it becomes something that—the whole process of doing it, getting along, being able to do this despite all the difficulties, emotional and physical and whatever—where you draw the line between trying to make a mark, trying to stay sane, and then the mark it's making on you, so to speak. When the music creates more problems than it solves...

Yannick: Yeah, but I don't know if it does. We obviously get something out of this, or we wouldn't do it.

Inside Front: You wouldn't do it otherwise, if you didn't actually enjoy it.

Yannick: Yeah. In fact there's so much stuff on personal levels, musically, and certainly financially—there's no way I'd do something like this if it wasn't something that I thought was awesome.

Paul: Yeah, by normal people's standards I do nothing out of responsibility, besides the things I do to survive. By those standards, I'm pretty much as far out of the cycle as it gets. Meaning, when I wake up—if I don't have something that moves me to do that day, I'm depressed. Yeah, that's a result of living in the culture we live in, and having to do those things rather than just being happy with existence—but the point I'm getting at is that I don't do things unless they move me or mean a lot to me, and no matter how much I could think about what something should mean to me, if it ever lost its significance to me I wouldn't even think about it. I don't have enough time in my life to do all the things I'm obsessed with or passionate about. I don't have time to do things I don't want to do, to do shit for no reason.

Inside Front: So that explains why you still do it. But you've played punk rock for a lot longer than a lot of people do—what do you think is the difference there?

Yannick: As much as we tried to say we're not trying to do something new or innovative, I think it's changed for us. Even if we're not playing the same music we were, but something similar, it always changes, the circumstances, things just change to be something new every day. Tour, it's all always something new, even if it's not new music it's new experiences.

Paul: Interestingly enough, there's something that I get out of—and I'm not talking about music or lyrics, here—there's something I get out of the actual experience of touring that I think benefits my life in a way similar to how I said if I didn't play music I'd explode. Because—my mind shifts from that waking up and needing something to be passionate about to get me through the day, to... being on tour, I think the constant motion changes the perception of time, and you lose sight

of whatever's at the end of the tunnel because you know that the next day's the same thing. Me, I get in a mode of thinking where I become much more peaceful, I'm just—being, wherever we are. I can spend hours doing nothing, just riding in a van, reading a book or looking out the window, and be totally happy, however slow or fast time is going by. That's something I can never achieve at home, because I think that—to live in the busyness of a city, the time frame of the city, jobs, these kind of things, I think for me after tour my life always kind of shifts back into that gridwork within a certain amount of time, no matter how dropped out I am from normal life. That's something I get out of touring that—maybe you could just get it out of traveling normally, but to me it's irreplaceable, who knows what I'd do without it.

Yannick: When we get back home—none of us really work that much, none of us really have responsibilities or are used to the time frame in the city. I think all the responsibilities that we have and that we do deal with are...

Paul: Granted, it's not the nine-to-five that we come home to, that's not what I'm saying—but even when you just live around the nine-to-five, there are some ways it makes its way into your life. Like if you need to go to a store to do something, you have to do it within certain hours. I usually go through a period when I come home from tour when I'm depressed, because I don't know what to do with myself, and don't know where I'm going. The fucked up thing that happens to me is that I feel like I have to be doing something or something's wrong. I have to be accomplishing something, or something's wrong. What that says to me is that I can't be happy just to be alive—and I don't fight that when I'm in the city, because to me all that matters is being happy, and I think it's great to find things that I'm passionate about. But it's something I'm very conscious of, and ultimately I think that other goal of existence is more important to me, I'd like to live in a place that was quiet enough that I could be happy with whatever I was doing. Accomplishments, stuff to keep us busy, all that shit is ultimately meaningless. We live, then we die, and what matters is that we should be happy in between. What you accomplish or whatever is only a means of achieving that happiness.

Inside Front: So you do what you do because it's the thing you think you can do that can bring you the most happiness in the world, out of everything you could choose.

Paul: It's not the thing, it's a thing.

Inside Front: Got it.

Contact Tragedy at:
2336 N. Killingsworth
Portland, OR 97217

LACK sOngs Of PROtEst AnD LOvE

Haggard, but satisfied by a tasty vegan stew, I waited for another show to begin. I was in a squat in Oslo, Norway, and going on about the 60th show in two months. Hanging out by the literature table, I caught a glimpse of the first band setting up and saw that their singer was writing out all his lyrics on giant posters and hanging them around the performance space—my attention was snagged enough that I inched forward to watch them play. I watched those four lads, Lack, play their hearts out that night—everyone in a swirl of movement. At one point the singer started break-dancing—what a gift to bring such a beautiful thing to the hardcore scene (later that evening I asked him where he learned to break-dance and he told me that when he was younger he had been a B-boy in Copenhagen—of course!). Their performance that night was something so refreshing and essential to the lifeblood of punk rock; it is through such rebirth that we are stripped down to what matters. Thomas and I talked of this in our interview below. What is critical, more than any sound or politic or thing, is the realization of possibility: that, in the face of impossible inertia and despair, the shake of a hip—a scream, a note—can indeed turn the world upside down and send you spinning.

I had the good fortune to travel with Lack the next couple of days and witness them play a couple more times in Sweden. Before we parted company Thomas, the singer, took the time to write down in my journal a lot of the lyrics they were working on for the upcoming LP (Blues Moderne: Danois Explosifs, reviewed elsewhere in this issue). It was a great pleasure to receive the CD in the mail a year later and hear those lyrics realized and shaped with beautiful, painful, intense music. It's been quite a while since that record was released and Lack has been through a fair bit as a band and as people. It's exactly bands like Lack that keep posthumous issues of Inside Front coming, and we thank them. Below is an interview with Thomas conducted just recently from Copenhagen.

As my words have grown more hateful, so has my love gone wilder and untamed / And if I slit any wrist let it be not that of my own, but of the me I am expected to be

Bruce: When Lack works, what makes it work?

Thomas: Musically it works when we manage to take a musical idea and built a structure for it that somehow expresses the essence of the idea; when we exhaust an idea for its useful potential in a way that "works" for us. Personally I think we are best when we create tension primarily through the use of chords and their internal relations, through melody, rather than through the use of rhythm and violence. Because with rhythm you can only go so far in terms of, say, extremity, but with chords and melody (which obviously involves rhythm, but not primarily) there is no limit to how far you can go in your creating expressions.

Furthermore, I think Lack works when lyrics and music complement each other and form a flow, when they support each other. When a certain lyrical point is emphasized or translated by the music (and vice versa) I am happy because I feel a sense of accomplishment, a sense of having mastered chaos, given it form and a consistency that function.

Finally, I think Lack works when we collectively manage to do something we haven't done before. When we play a show and it just works and everyone is working together, playing together, collectively letting go, collectively becoming expression, then I feel something I rarely do—momentum. When Lack creates that for me, then I think it works.

Bruce: Do conceive of yourselves as a particularly "Danish" or perhaps "Scandinavian" band?

Thomas: If Refused had not made their two last records, Lack would not have sounded as we did on Blues Moderne LP or the Sisyphus 7"—and the same goes for Breach and their It's Me God. Those bands meant a lot and they were both Swedish. In fact, the whole Swedish rock thing has had a rather big influence on us. But apart from that I don't feel like being a Scandinavian band, musically.

In other ways though, we have experienced what it means to be a Danish band—equipment is extremely expensive, van renting is economy-breaking, rent is devastating, food prices are depressing, recording prices are absurd; the underground is underground and small.

When we wrote mails to people in order to book shows it sometimes felt like writing "Danish" sort of disqualified us from being interesting. In Europe there is hierarchy as well—the west over the east and the north. Just like Americans who 'intuitively' disbelieve that a European (or non-North American) band can offer anything valuable at all—besides being maybe "exotic." So we have experienced that being Danish meant something. But primarily in the beginning of our "international adventures."

In terms of culture and politics, then I think there can be found some elements of being Danish, since we deal with subjects that are particular and related to where we live. Not to say that they can't be translated or be relevant to people who live in other places since I think our songs are relatively easy to relate to, but they are created in our milieu. As an American reader you are not used to living in a genuine welfare state with all its goods and evils. A welfare state which is kind of socialist because of the high taxes and the access to free education with state support and health care, but which is still capitalist because it maintains the right of private property and extremely high prices on everything. There is a rather big labor movement, which used to achieve a lot in the past, but these days they seem so immobile, inactive, and monolithic that you almost suspect that they have cut a deal with their friends in the private and the public sector. Very little is actually happening in the realm of the worker. It is as if the workers' unions are satisfied with the wage system and the whole 40 hours a week rhythm, because they are certainly not doing anything to change it. So people work much more than they have to actually. This makes it rather depressing, because most people are so entangled in the whole career/job thing that there is very little room for anything else.

Denmark is also a country with a very strict sense of what you can do and what you can't. Not only in terms of morality which is actually rather laid back (Denmark is a protestant, almost atheist country, which makes moral systems up for debate in most places), but rather in terms of envy and small-mindedness. It is a little hard to explain, but there is a kind of unarticulated social code which states that you are not supposed to be too much of something, too famous, to believe that you are better than others, that you are worth something. It is an cultural ethic of being humble, and you see it everywhere, even in the punk community. A band plays a lot of shows, they get known and suddenly people think they're rock stars, or idiots (I am not talking exclusively about my own band, because this is rather general). The problem with this kind of ethic is that it keeps people in their places, because everyone is so eager to make sure that everyone is not "doing-too-much." It is hard to explain, you have to experience it. But ultimately, this kind of ethic stands in the way for attempts at social change, because people are afraid to believe in themselves and what they actually want for themselves and the world they live in. It creates apathy.

So perhaps, in some aspects we are a Scandinavian band.

It's like being buried alive when our masks become our faces/ It's like being buried alive when our ideals become our tombstones/ Life is too short to die/ Turn away to live again/ In the name of every fallen hero that ever sold out, show me the next exit and I'll be the first to take it

Bruce: What is the role of a collective of artists making music in the revolution?

Thomas: First, I don't think any of us believe in the revolution, but rather in revolutions. Mostly because revolutions happen all the time and revolution doesn't. But also because the revolution has an implicit totalitarian, fascist, tendency to it: you are either for the revolution or you are against it. The wildest revolutionaries in the revolution are either first against the wall or the ones pulling triggers "after" the revolution. But there are multiplicities of revolutions, they happen everywhere and all the time — micro and macro, bad ones, good ones.

Feminists can have revolution now, while Marxists have to wait.

To make a long story short, then, I think the role of the artist is to do what she does as good as she can. To create new feelings or to express old feelings in a new way, to give expression to something unexpressed, to create new worlds and people. I have left shows, movies, books, affected. Sometimes those effects have revolutionized my life and made me make decisions and act in ways I had not thought I ever would. I think the role of the artist is to create affects, to create momentums and to affect us all to create momentums of our own and in our own lives. Ultimately, the artist's "role" is to show that in creation the negative and the positive collide, and once you create you are never "safe"—you must risk... just like in "real" life.

Bruce: What about the danger, in the context of the traditional hierarchical performance, of being "creative specialist" vis-à-vis a mostly "passive" audience? How has Lack worked to alter this? What sort of space does Lack seek to create at its shows?

Thomas: My biggest fear is that we contribute more negativity than positivity. Adorno & Horkheimer said that workers read Donald Duck to learn to live with humiliations, violence, and all the other bad things connected to being of working class. In the same way I fear that Lack can become a medium for accepting despair and hopelessness, because we emphasize these feelings so much in our music. I am a very pessimistic person and since I am the vocal person in the band, both lyrically as well as the one talking in between songs, I often present a very negative approach to the issues we present. And this, I fear, may just create more despair and hopelessness. But, maybe we take ourselves too seriously here... I don't know.

But to answer your question somehow: we try to create a friendly space first of all, because we want people to feel good during the event, a relaxed and open atmosphere to counter the tense and pained atmosphere of the music. It doesn't always work and sometimes we even end up playing hostile shows—but usually not on purpose. Simultaneously, we also try to make the space one of focus, energy, and excitement,

maybe even drama, basically a space for people to indulge in and get lost in. We try to create a passionate space, in order to show that we are as much at the mercy of our passions as we master them—not just the band, but also everyone at the event.

All these ambitions don't always manifest themselves, but sometimes they do. And that is when people react, act and respond, when they "break" the crowd silence and become participants. They may not seize an instrument, but they participate and through that they create a whole new event. When that happens the event becomes a participation-event, instead of a spectator/spectated-event. But this is all very idealized, because mostly we don't even master ourselves when we play, so to master transforming the entire event on our own is almost out of our hands. But we do pay attention to the whole cliché-ridden formula of "rock band rocking out on stage" and the fundamental boredom implicit in this spectacle that we have witnessed again and again.

More concrete initiatives: we have postered the lyrics on the wall behind the drums for everyone to see, thus making the vocalist as much an interpreter of the words as the audience; we have addressed people directly without microphone, which only works in small crowds, but creates a more intimate space; we have made fun of ourselves—"over-posing"—thus adding irony to the dead seriousness of the whole event. Small stuff...

Bruce: How would you define the tension between Lack as a live performance and Lack as a pre-recorded commodity, a CD to be bought and sold?

Thomas: We sound better on record. But, of course, there is much more vitality and immediacy in the live performance, much more intensity. But most important, it is unique, whatever happens only happens once—even if you tape it, in which case you only get a mediated, translated version of the event. It happens here, now! And we better pay attention because in a while it is gone, and that is it! Just like life. A recording is much more of an object. An object you may have a detailed and rich relation to, but an object nonetheless—a thing.

This does not mean that a thing can't affect, it can, and sometimes you can even create exactly the expression you want with a studio recording, because you can work on it until it's there—undisturbed by drunk idiots, sound problems (oh, the sound problems), breaking strings, lacking electricity or just the static electricity biting your lips as you approach the microphone.

But then there is another danger: what is the "true" version of a song—I always tend to compare a recorded version with a live performance (or the other way round). I remember watching Snapcase destroy their own intensity and songs in a live performance, and

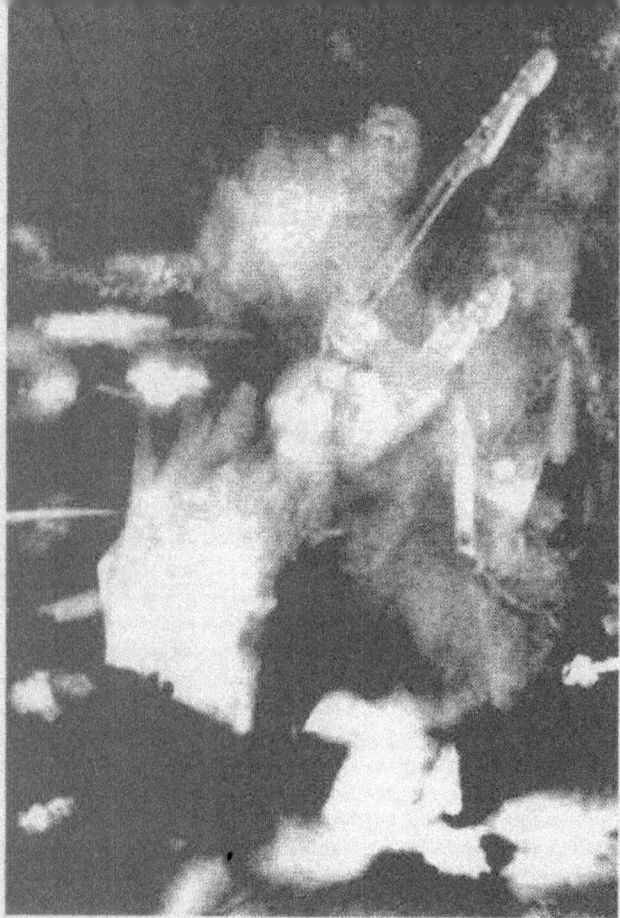

it really made me sad, because I had expected so much from them. If you can't live up to your own recording you endanger yourself—or conversely, if you rely on performance and volume, your recordings are going to lack. I often try to imagine a band that refuses to record—how would that work out?

Bruce, you once told me that you watched a movie so good that had you known this and prepared yourself for it, it would have been the last movie you ever saw. I sometimes get that feeling with a live show: "tonight could have been the last time—I could have walked away from it and not looked back. Because it was so perfect." I never get that feeling with a record. Never.

When the most honest of emotions turns into a commodity, this can't be a surprise/ This can't be/ No/ But I never stopped demanding/ I am more thirsty than ever/ If this shall make my heart the loneliest: so be it

Bruce: What role do pessimism and hope play in the struggle of everyday life, in attempting to change the world we live in?

Thomas: Hope is treacherous, but perhaps necessary. Treacherous because when it comes to radical politics it is often focused on non-existent things, say the Revolution or "someday someone is going to do something" or "someday this suffering will end" or the "what I am doing is very important" activist kind of thing. Hope can create illusions. But worst of all, hope can break you, because if you have

a deep-felt hope in something and it doesn't work or happen, your hope will die and then what have you left? You can either create more hope in something else or you can just give up and become a realist. Get a job in the bureaucracy. But hope is very important at the same time, because it is a drive, a motivational force. Hopeless people need desire, desperation, or pure despair in order to act, because you need something to make the machine function. If there is no hope at all, then what is the point to try at all?

Pessimism is the feeling of anticipating the worst or seeing in everything only confirmations of the notion that everything is fucked up. I have been a pessimist my entire life and I still fight it as hard as I can. I don't think it has any positive role to play in a struggle except draining energy and imposing the realist, defeatist attitude. But again, if things are fucked up then it is very easy to become pessimistic. But it is important that you learn to leave that feeling behind or it may prevent you from acting because "it doesn't matter anyway, it's all fucked up, it's too late, it has always been too late, we are already dead."

Bruce: What might Lack's escape plan look like?

Thomas: I have no clue at all. The anarchist liberation of desire founded on a gift economy and mutual aid?

Bruce: Is punk rock still a legitimate medium?

Thomas: Yes. But only if it refuses to be fully signified and captured by repetition, boredom, commodity fetishism and capitalist machines. Punk rock is transformative, expansive, it follows a line of flight when it is most ambitious and daring and this gives it continuous potential to be an alternative. Refused was a line of flight for a while (until they became a fetish), because they dared to defy definitions and rules. Punk rock is legitimate to me, because of its relentlessness, because it doesn't care, it doesn't want to be understood and accepted, continuously becoming flight. The creativity of punk rock makes it a legitimate medium for me, not necessarily because of the punk rock aesthetic, which is often boring, but rather because of the explosive, intense blossoming all over the place. The fact that you can start a punk band, or any band basically, without any pre-established musical capabilities, start playing and do things without having to suck up to anyone, is still a valid justification for punk

in my book. The whole DIY network—that you can play music or whatever without having to surrender to mechanisms of "big business" is another valid justification as well.

Of course there is bullshit in punk, and lots of it. But these days, I prefer to look on the positive, creative aspects of the whole "movement" instead of focusing on bad, negative, useless aspects. It's like a dialogue based on association instead of discussion and "conflict": you create something, someone else is inspired by it and creates something else, which again inspires someone who suddenly inspires the first one back. A flow instead of dead ends. Punk rock's biggest asset is the emphasis on the possibility of the impossible and if nothing else, then this makes it valid for me, because that is exactly what we need these days: to experience that we CAN do things differently and the impossible does in fact happen. And very often indeed.

Bruce: What is the next step for Lack?

Thomas: I don't really know for sure. Music wise, we are definitely finished with the whole Blues Moderne vibe. I don't think we can ever write a song like those again and we don't want to either. We are just so worn out by it by now. Not that we don't like it, we just desperately need to readjust our creative focus in order to do anything at all. So we have begun writing new stuff and it is definitely an interesting process, because we are working with different musical tools than what we are used to. It is very challenging and exciting. So far we have written some songs that we are actually pleased with.

I think we will record another full-length someday, and then we will probably do the tour thing—maybe try to avoid all the catastrophes this time. But when exactly is very open. We might have a secret record coming up.

We played with the thought of having a small book to compliment the next record, but we are extremely lazy so let's see if it happens. Personally, I want to emphasize the political content of our music in a different way than the usual "speaking between songs" thing, which doesn't always work that well. I think that all of our songs are basically political, but I want to emphasize this even more in the future.

Numbed by what you call your life/ Show me you're alive.../ To my generation: I dare you to give me something more than this/ Or have we given in?

You can contact Lack (Jacob, Kasper, Jakob, and Thomas) at:

Lack c/o Thomas Buro
Flensborggade 33 1 tv
1669 KBH v
Denmark

lackdk@ofir.dk
www.lackattack.dk

THE DENIA[L]

The reader is encouraged to recall to mind Greg Bennick's (juggler, filmmaker, former singer of Trial) column in the last Inside Front on an Iron Maiden show he had just attended and his skillful, smooth transition to his then-recent reading of The Denial of Death, discussed below. The Iron Maiden anecdote made us laugh, and his eloquent discourse on death-driven anxiety sent us to the sofa, face down, to weep.[1]

Since his reading of The Denial of Death, Greg has taken these ideas and run quite a ways in the last three years. It was my intention with the following interview to follow the trajectory of Becker's ideas first germinating in Greg's head to his auspicious meeting with Patrick Shen, who went on with Greg to make their film Flight from Death: The Quest for Immortality, a documentary based around many of the ideas Becker discussed, to the completion of the triumvirate with the meeting of Professor Sheldon Solomon. It was with Prof. Solomon that the World Leaders Project was formed, in which Becker's ideas were given radically pragmatic shape and taken out into the world, literally to its leaders, to discuss and understand their consequences in our everyday lives.

I highly encourage anyone interested in the ideas to track down any of the books we discussed and especially to keep on the lookout for Flight.

[1] It is known, from inside sources, that Greg originally intended to write that issue's (#15) column on the sinister and widespread rhyming of the words "fire" and "desire" in the last century's go at pop music. In this airing of our dirty laundry Greg was going to roast our own house band, Catharsis, for yes, their unashamed rhyming of these very words and mercilessly compare this action to any number of pop acts from the past. And in 2003 the recent top ten hit "Your Body is a Wonderland" rhymes, you guessed it, these same menacing words! Greg, perhaps sensing the already condemning Al Burian "No Sun" review of Catharsis's Passion LP, later in the same issue, tactfully dropped the fire/desire controversy in favor of waxing hilarious on his love of metal.

Sunrise, reading, Trial tours, Filmmaking and Death Anxiety

What's so bad about the fear of death?

The terror of death. The terror of knowing that one day, from unforeseeable circumstances, you shall die. You shall perish from the Earth never to exist again. You inhabit a dying, decaying body—a machine processing matter—eating, digesting, shitting. Animals, bleeding, mating, suffering, dying. No—this is not the sum of your existence, you are a human! You are valuable, your life has meaning. You are in possession of a soul, of Reason. You can conceive not only of this world, but a cosmos—a new life, a better world. You, human being, are a duality, possessed of your withering dying body with a finite number of seconds left before decaying to dust, and of a unique ability to imagine the world outside of that body, to imagine eternity, transcendence. What are the consequences of this duality? What is born of the tension between this tragically temporal descending and eternal longing?

In the early 1970's a cultural anthropologist, Ernest Becker, attempted to tackle and understand this duality. In his monumental Denial of Death he examines the fear of death as the root cause of all of humankind's actions. However, Becker concluded this fear of our death is too much for most to bear on a daily basis, so we create all sorts of systems and means of drowning out the terror of reality. Becker understood this in terms of immortality-striving. Architecture, religion, ideologies, governments, works of art, social interactions, raising children, wars are all in some way manifestations of our need for permanence, our need to transcend the sad temporality of our existence. Becker even proposed the chaos of a menial job as the perfect "forgetting" of the unmanageable, true chaos of life[2]. This fear of death is so encompassing in every movement of our lives that often it seems it isn't even there. Becker wrote, "even if the average man lives in a kind of obliviousness of anxiety, it is because he has erected a massive wall of preparations to hide the problem of life and death. His anality [his denial of all that is bodily] may protect him, but all throughout history it is the "normal, average men" who, like locusts, have laid waste to the world in order to forget themselves."

Humankind, as far as we know, is unique in its realization of its inevitable death and likewise unique in its reach beyond it. Everyday life is characterized by our attempts to manage the wild chaos of the world with a series of small fictions known as "self." We create a structure of limits and fabricate an order of who we "are" onto which we can function; a denial that simultaneously allows us to live and denies us so much of what might be possible in our lives. Otto Rank, a disciple of Freud, who later broke ranks with his school and was a central inspiration for The Denial of Death, wrote, citing Rousseau, "every human being is equally unfree, that is, we create out of freedom, a prison." Immortality-striving or our immortality projects, whether writing a book or buying a house, are a defiance of our finite existences, they serve on a psychological level to soothe our sundered being. Though it would seem correct to ask first if these immortality projects are positive or negative in nature, it is more critical to realize if we identify at all with what we are doing.

Understanding these basic concepts of our fear of life (its chaos) and fear of death (our end) creates a picture of the extremely fragile means humans use to navigate

L OF DEATH

the world, for all around us are "competing" immorality projects on all levels, from the personal to the cultural. Anyone that differs to an extent from our own is a threat. If they worship a different god or they believe anarchism is intrinsically flawed and doomed to failure and you think it the salvation of mankind—one of you is wrong from a relative point of view. This is the crux of the matter, because this very conflict leads to violence: if I deride you, if I cannot convince you of my point of view, if I cannot in some way accommodate your view to mine, to render it harmless—then I must eliminate your point of view, lest my conception of self and my claim to the eternal be shattered. And so often our point of view is simply dictated from a position above and greedily received. Self-definition, which so many of us need in order to cope with life, is offered ready-made, with minimal effort on our part, from leaders—statesmen, priests, authorities on revolution, intellectuals. The lure of accepting these definitions, the surrender of believing oneself to be "presto" an American or a Marxist, with an incredible array of leaders and ideological frameworks and consumer goods to back it up—this denial of our own potential and denial of life,

this pseudo-protection from the terrible reality of our existence—for this so many are prepared to do untold violence again and again.

Bruce: I want to start off by mentioning the story you told after the screening of your film in New York City of how The Denial of Death was put in your hands along with two other books, Man's Search for Meaning...

Greg: Yeah, that was by Victor Frankl and Art and Artist by Otto Rank...

B: Otto Rank, who Becker is so fond of...

G: Yeah, absolutely.

B: What I'm curious about is the process it took for you to finally read The Denial of Death and begin to make connections to other ideas in your life already present in the Hardcore Punk scene, the activist scene, and your own personal ideas, etc. How did all this match up with The Denial of Death and finally to the point where you are thinking: I need to make a film of this?

G: First and foremost, the film was originally the brainchild of Patrick Shen, who is from Los Angeles, which I'll tell the story of in a moment. But after reading The Denial of Death—and I quite clearly remember when I finished reading it—I was in the Trial van, on tour, packed in like a sardine in the back of the van somewhere near Reading, California, driving north to Seattle from San Francisco on the highway. I remember the Sun coming up and I had been reading by flashlight all night long—I read the last lines of the book as the Sun rose. It sounds quite poetic—the Sun has crested this hill, everyone is asleep in the van, I'm by myself reading—it's fantastic—it would have been perfect if I had been reading some Barbara Cartland love novel—but poetic regardless. I remember it clearly. But after reading the book I remember immediately starting to make connections to different areas of my life and to different things I was experiencing. One thing I was really thinking of from the start was that

Becker through his writing and academic career constantly reminded readers not to turn him or his ideas into some sort of icon. He was always critical of himself in that regard and I took this to heart at the end of the book. And I tried not to take everything he said that spoke truth to me and apply it to every aspect of my life. I definitely made some strong connections: the ways in which people strive in our particular society to achieve wealth and fortune and examining those things from the perspective that they were possibly—and I say possibly, not to say Becker was absolutely right—representative of that person's desire to achieve immortality, that would allow them to live on past their physical body. That suddenly rang true to me. And so looking at world leaders, for example, and the positions of people in power and the dynamics between them and people who don't have power—these things came into sharper focus as seen through the lens of: these are the means people are using to achieve symbolic immortality.

B: Did you make immediately the connection to being an artist, in the terms that Becker lays out in the book?

G: Absolutely, and not to kill the book for anybody but at the end of the Denial of Death, Becker wraps up the book by speaking about crafting ourselves, our lives, or an object as art, making our lives as art and offering that, so to speak, to the world at large, or to the "life force" as he says. ("The most that any one of us can seem to do is to fashion something—an object or

[2] Editor's note: I can't restrain myself from pointing out that, if this is indeed Becker's primary explanation of why people work low-status manual labor jobs (I don't know for sure, as I haven't read him), he was suffering from an acute case of class-privilege-induced blindness.

from Death. Greg and Patrick's film (see the contact details at the end of the interview). The final edit is finally almost ready with Hollywood actor Gabriel Byrne (End of Days, The Usual Suspects) narrating. It's a beautifully conceived documentary, sharp, accessible and timely. I saw a rough cut at a showing of a slightly earlier edit (with a different narrator) in a lofty apartment in Manhattan last fall, with about forty-odd other people crowding the room (there was a second showing later that night). The skillful presentation of Becker's ideas and examination of violence in our world intended for a widespread audience, without diluting their power, is an excellent example of what can be done by artists driven to create, even in the obscenely constrained and costly world of American film.

Some Recommended Reading:

The Denial of Death by Ernest Becker (The Free Press, New York) Becker's masterpiece is largely accessible, readable, thought-provoking, and even quite entertaining in places. However, he covers some ground that muddles his brilliant ideas; for example, his re-working of Freud's psychoanalytical language and ideas has value, I'm sure, from the point of view of the psychological community, but hinders the overall effect. His long chapter on the Scandinavian philosopher Kierkegaard, though interesting in its own right, has the same consequence. Still, don't let either of these put you off from tracking down this book and engaging with some of the more important ideas of our time.

Art and Artist by Otto Rank (Agathon Press, New York) Rank's illuminating book on the motivations and psychology of the artist and

the "creative urge." This book, first published in 1932 in the US from the ex-communicated disciple of Freud, was the foundation for much of The Denial of Death. In fact I believe that at one point Becker states that he is simply trying to make accessible with his book some of these much-neglected ideas of Rank. If you enjoy the sections on the role of the artist in The Denial of Death you would do well to follow up with Art and Artist. Plus my edition has the bonus of a forward by Anaïs Nin!

Man's Search for Meaning by Viktor E. Frankl (Touchstone, New York, Etc.) The first half the book is made up of a narrative recounting his survival of a German concentration camp in World War II, in which his entire family perished save his sister. He originally wrote this part of the book just months after his release. It's an important account of how he managed to piece together some meaning amidst suffering and, even more chillingly, how the camp represented an intense pared down and focused study of industrial life. The second half of the book is the fleshing out of his ideas in the narrative in what he calls Logotherapy. Conceived 20 years later it is quite detailed and systematic in its approach. A good companion to The Denial of Death, especially for those looking for some more tangible answers to the problems raised in that book than Becker sought fit to present.

In the Wake of 9/11: The Psychology of Terror by Tom Pyszczynski, Sheldon Solomon, and Jeff Greenberg This is an excellent recent book examining Becker's ideas in a modern context. All three of the authors (I believe) are interviewed in Flight from Death, especially in their scientific approach to Becker, and the validation of much of his ideas on death anxiety through thorough social experiments.

I spoke with Greg by phone from his home in Seattle.

ourselves—and drop it into the confusion, make an offering, so to speak, to the life force.") I connected immediately to that as an artist. For example, at the time we were touring on the Trial album, which had just been recorded and released, and I connected to the idea of creating something that was absolutely representative of my thoughts feelings, beliefs and ideals, along with those who were playing music with me as a collective and offering that to the life force. What did that mean to us? What was its significance and on how many different levels could I analyze that significance? One of the most profound ones was that playing in the band and playing shows and creating art was doing something for me on a psychological level and I had never thought of that before. And by psychological, I don't just mean, "Wow, that made me happy," rather it was soothing me, quite literally to be thinking, "I am contributing something that I feel has worth to this world." And in doing so that is making me feel good about my existence and my potential to be "remembered." That's such a superficial way to describe Becker—but something was going on.

B: I think Becker is interesting, too, in that he seems to waver a bit in his evaluation of the artist. For a while he says the ability to create is unmistakably valuable and "in this sense, objective creativity is the only answer that man has to the problem of life." But then he says essentially, well, you know, most people don't have any real talent for art and that's the problem. Too bad. Besides, the artist is trying to swallow the whole world, and I don't know if that is going to work. Becker seems to pull back and hesitate about creativity as a "solution."

G: I think Becker may have also realized that creativity doesn't necessarily mean that you create good things. Creativity leads

human violence, how it leads to wanting to one-up one another, to destroy one another, be the victor, the one who survives—amid the field of corpses lying around us, to be that one who stands strong. He was working on this film and heard about the World Leaders Project, which we can get into in a bit, that I was undertaking with a professor friend of mine in New York, and wanted to do an interview with me for his film and when he called me and we started talking, I realized: Wait a minute, you're doing a film about Becker? And when he heard about the World Leaders Project he said: Wait a minute, you're going to meet face to face with world leaders just to talk about Becker? And so we just instantly hit it off. We decided to help each other out, so that's how I got involved in the film, which was originally Patrick's film, which over the course of the last 18 months got to the point where we were co-producing it, co-writing and working on it in equal shares. It came together because we realized there is much more to Becker than realizing that "Hey, we want to be famous because we recognize that being immortal would be a neat idea." There is a dark underside to the work as well that we wanted to cover in the movie.

B: I don't know if it's going to become a standard question at the Q&A at the end of the film: "So this your immortality project, right?" When someone asks that, and some did at the New York screening as I recall, it presents us with this: Here is something we might consider a "positive" immortality project, not proclaiming to be "the truth", despite all disclaimers, be it your film or Becker's book we nonetheless react in such a way that we are saying to ourselves, well that's not the truth, I know better.

G: That's what's interesting, and again while I say what I'm about to say, I would

way we can communicate otherwise? I believe that there is, but how do we define that? That sharing, reciprocity?

G: I think people need to do this. One thing Becker seems to be saying is, that we're saying in our movie, is that this just isn't something that you get over, that we end, that we do away with. The 'this' being immortality striving and trying to be the one who last and lives longest. Becker's point was that the human animal lives in constant fear of death, at least on some subconscious level. Or rather the human animal is constantly aware of its own death. Keep in mind that we are always working against that or using that information to guide the course of our actions. Becker's suggestion is that these little warfares that go on throughout the day, from the little kid—he uses as an example the kid who says, "Mom, he got a bigger piece of candy than me"—to "You tried to kill my dad, Saddam Hussein, therefore you are next on my list," all of these things can be traced back to death anxiety and that all of them are part and parcel of who we are as people. We are reacting based on the psychology of being a human being. These things are inescapable. I guess the point of Becker that we, as producers of the film Flight from Death, have tried to encapsulate in 90 minutes is that all these little pieces of warfare that go on throughout the day and all these huge wars that go on across the world are quite possibly inescapable, but an awareness of these things can help reduce the aggression and hopefully the pain that is associated with them. And again, that's somewhat up to the interpreter. Meaning that there are those who think that pain for a specific cause is quite a fantastic thing. I guess I am representing a majority who would suggest, as a general rule, that hurting or killing others is bad.

B: I believe that in our increasing awareness

...Quite possibly our actions are motivated by a subconscious, innate fear. That creates interesting conversation and I would argue absolutely allows for change of behaviors, or at least less violent and destructive ones. Up until now, with Flight from Death, I don't think these ideas have been popularized nearly as much as they could have been.

you for example to do an interview which contributes to what hopefully will be an excellent magazine. But creativity can also mean "Wow, if we all have box cutters and we all get on the plane at the same time we might just be able to fly it into a building." I think Becker realized that striving for immortality isn't always necessarily a good thing. It leads to a lot of issues and problems, terror and violence in the world. It also leads to, dare I say, interesting hardcore records being made!

To finish the answer to the initial question. What the connection was to the film was: Here we have Patrick Shen in Los Angeles. Patrick read The Denial of Death completely unassociated with the punk and hardcore music scene. He was blown away by what he read and thought "I need to make a film of this"—he was a filmmaker in L.A. He wanted to make a film looking at the negative effects of striving for immortality. Of how it impacts

like you and your readers to keep in mind what I just got done saying: don't apply Becker to every aspect of our lives, we would just go nuts—"Why am I buying the vegan chocolate candy bar, it must have something to do with immortality" We could look at the person who ask the question: "Isn't this your immortality project?" with that cocky air, we could look at that person asking that question as living their own immortality project, because in doing so they say, "Well, I obviously know more that you and when all these other idiots are dead and gone, including you, I'll still be around due to my acute sense of thinking and amazing intellect." We could look at this from a million different angles.

B: I find that such an interesting situation. Is that not how we interact in the world? Trying to achieve our immortality on some level through these petty exchanges throughout the day? Is there a real, valuable

of these underlying motivations, the very first simple step of saying, "Hey," "nudge nudge", "there is this denial of death thing going on," is so important before you make those larger connections. We're not all yet walking through our day thinking, "Hey, I exist in this duality of my creatureliness and my immortality-striving!"

G: One thing we wanted to do and one thing that we have argued throughout, and I'm not sure at which of the New York screenings this question was raised, the second one I think: "What good does this do in terms of the world at large? What good do these ideas actually have in changing the course of human behavior?" Our answer was, ultimately, just having these ideas on the table helps. Meaning that, granted, we are not going to get rid of the daily battles, we're not going to get rid of people beating the crap out of each other or treating each other unfairly. But realistically, having the thought on the table, just for discussions, out there for everyone to see. That quite possibly our actions are motivated by a subconscious, innate fear. That creates interesting conversation and I would argue absolutely allows for change of behaviors, or at least less violent and destructive ones. Up until now, with Flight from Death, I don't think these ideas have been popularized nearly as much as they could have been. Ernest Becker was suppressed throughout his entire career because of his relationship to Thomas Szasz and those who worked with Becker were ostracized from the psychology community for associating with Becker.

B: Who is Thomas Szasz?

G: Thomas Szasz at Syracuse University—and as I understand it, readers would do well to research on their own and correct me here, he was against the medicalization of psychology. And I think that what happened was that Szasz was arguing against going toward a space where drugs were prescribed for everything. Which of course means less profits for psychologists. If psychologist can prescribe fancy medication they can drive fancier cars. And get rich. Szasz I think, was saying we need to be looking at psychological problems from a psychological perspective, not medical perspective. And a psychological perspective that looks at the human animal on a social level—almost veering into anthropology. I know that for Flight from Death, we interviewed one of Szasz's and Becker's friends, a psychotherapist from NY and he told pretty much the same story, that Becker and Szasz were ostracized and continue to be frowned upon by the psychology community. And I guess that the end result of that is, that Becker puts out this book, The Denial of Death, which is no piece of trash, it won the Pulitzer Prize and how many people have even heard of the book? We've encountered a handful, 20 or 30, who have come to us over the last year and said, "Oh guys, you're making a movie about this? It's a great book, I read it in college." But we've talked to thousands of people.

Stomach Cramps, Faith, and James Bond

B: Becker pokes fun at himself at the beginning of the book, writing that all the great ideas already have books about them. How dare I throw another book in there, another weighty tome no one will read?

G: Exactly.

B: He's obviously hopeful that that won't be the end of it.

G: Of course it's honorable of him to say, I'm writing this book, but don't give it a second glance, it's nothing. I'm sure that Becker knew however that this was going to be a colossal piece of work and a discussion piece for generations to come. His own immortality project. And it doesn't take anything away from the people who encounter these ideas as new and are incredible advancements on ideas they maybe have heard before.

B: In terms of the everyday results of these fears, near the end of the book Becker cites a haunting story told by Otto Rank

of this woman who comes in with stomach cramps, with no apparent medical cause, to Otto Rank's office. Rank questions her: She lives with her married sister in this cute alpine village, has no great love, great passion, but has a "good" life. However she has a vague feeling that she is missing out on something. But things are good, you're happy, you spend the summer in country, Rank tells her. And then he suggests, Hey, let's not figure out what's causing those stomach cramps. Whatever revelation about those cramps we happen upon will probably make you more miserable. There is a certain amount of pain we must endure in order to live in this world. Maybe we shouldn't solve this one problem, maybe this is the price you are paying to go about your life in this tolerable manner? That reminded me of a thing Becker wrote earlier in the book, where he wonders how these workers survive in chaotic restaurants or hectic factories or travel agencies in tourist season. Then he says the answer is obvious. This chaos resembles life, but the job is a manageable chaos. Rank I think was insisting on the same thing: your stomach cramps are a manageable pain—what we would uncover if we really stopped to consider the problem, the chaos of life or your undisclosed loss, might be too much. The question that raises for me, especially in the context of our revolutionary project, our desire for change, is how much do we ask of people? How many of these stomach cramps do we really wish to cure? What would we unleash?

G: Meaning what would we unleash if all these things were gone?

B: What are we asking of people when we are asking them to give up their stomach cramps? Becker notes that if you are going to remind people of an unmediated joy, you must also remind them of the terrible despair that can accompany that joy. It makes me question the refrain of "Hey, everyone, there's this great thing going over here! Quit your crappy day job—there is joy out there!" It's not that simple, but I wonder what happens then.

G: It reminds me of what anyone in the course of my life has ever said to me when talking about ideas like Becker's or the example of "Hey, consider quitting your job and pursuing your passion." And that example is just an example, certainly not the key to your salvation. Using that idea, people rejoin with, "Well who's going to sweep the streets, wash the dishes, scrape the elephant cage?" What else do we create when we create this "heaven" on earth? Becker hints at it throughout the book, when he's talking about "whose

heaven on earth?" One thing that's come up when making this film, is that we're saying people can strive to create a better, more beautiful world by being aware of their own immortality project. Doesn't that simultaneously open the door for people to say, "Hey, you're right, let's all die for a cause and kill tons of people because what we're trying to do with our belief system is the 'right' thing to do and it's going to create a beautiful world and a passionate world, and I don't need to work anymore!"? Yeah, we potentially open up a huge can of worms, I don't think there is such a thing as a perfect, an ideal world, where we're all living passionately and beautiful. And that is sort of ominous and upsetting. To be honest I don't there is any example of a life that is completely passionate and without sadness and a heavy heart at times, or without tragedy or terror or horror. I think that's what keeps the human animal in balance and moving forward. I think it's almost healthy in a way. The ultimate question for me becomes, How do we take all that, and instead of ending up on the floor, a quivering blob of protoplasm unable to function, or knife wielding maniac running through a shopping mall—how do we take that information and create an existence for ourselves that is nurturing, and that isn't destructive toward other people, and is fun and enjoyable and gives something beautiful to human existence? Again it's all a matter of interpretation.

B: There was some criticism at the Q&A that you were portraying religion in this terrible light in the film—that you just showed that all religions universally contribute to the denial of death and the seeking for immortality in this very fanatical, harmful, way, the repression of others. In the sense of everything having a positive and negative shadow, when you were making the film and examining religion and ideology, trying to understand this really negative affect that it has had, what was the positive shadow of religion? Becker seems to come to a lot of religious conclusions, despite the scientific rigor of his work. But connected to the film...

G: We had to be acutely aware of that the whole time. Neither Patrick or I connect strongly to any particular religion and in fact I have a strong critique of religion, on a personal level. But in making the film, we didn't necessarily want to define our film

by our personal belief systems so much as we wanted to look at the larger picture. And the larger picture turned out to be: Let's look at religions critically, but let's not look at them critically exclusively. Let's look at them critically along with all other institutions that are similar, look at them all in the same light. Instead of saying, Religion is something to be really aware of because of it's contribution to violence, let's look at all these institutions that we engage in our culture and take a look at their contribution towards violence and their effect on human psychology on different levels. What do they all have to contribute? In doing that, we leveled the playing field. We made religion and capitalism and all the others that we covered, equal players in this world, in this social construction. And in terms of looking at religion in that regard, we were able to say, what religion does is it gives people a sense of self worth, of hope, faith in something greater than yourself, soothes that part of human beings that quite possibly fears that this abstract existence is really ridiculous and meaningless, which is almost too much for most people to bear. Religion soothes that part of the human psyche, but taken to another level, it causes people to react and do crazy things, to suppress other people. As Becker suggests in the book, and as we explore in the film, it causes people to want to beat the crap out of each other. Ultimately, and I'm drawing on the work of Sheldon Solomon, my partner in the World Leaders Project—if there's somebody of belief system A in a room and somebody of belief system B comes into a room, well, the two of them can't both be right. So who ultimately wins out? There has to be one that wins, because neither will except that they are both wrong. And that's the underside of religion. What we were doing in the film was saying, yeah, but that's also the underside of patriotism, of capitalism, of communism, of all of those things.

B: It seems that part of a possible solution to achieve a more desirable existence—and I don't know if there is a real solution—but Becker seems to conclude that faith plays a large part of it, something higher than yourself. He goes on to describe Kierkegaard's "knight of faith". I wonder if we must view this faith, whether in god, an idea, or a "life force", in terms of subservience to that idea, ourselves as part of a greater whole? I feel like Becker was understanding that ideal of faith in terms of subservience. Is faith necessarily a subservient action?

G: Becker, over the term of his life and the book, seems to be pretty atheistic. Becker at the age of forty nine was diagnosed with stomach cancer, and he died relatively quickly. On his deathbed, he was interviewed by Sam Keene, who was at the time working for "Psychology Today" magazine, and Keene is actually interviewed in our film as well, we met with him California. To Sam Keene he says that he had returned to Judaism while he was dying. Patrick and I actually visited Becker's grave in Massachusetts and there is a Star of David on it and the words on were definitely indicative of a man who was born and who certainly died a Jew. I think that quite literally Becker might have gotten scared toward the end of his life. And said to himself, Wow, what if this academic approach I've taken is

right, and all we have is this psychological construct of some type of future and that doesn't offer much solace. I imagine that he saw some good in subjecting oneself to a higher power and went for it—and if it soothes the dying man in the painful throes of cancer, then that is a great thing. But I don't think he necessarily said that we have to be subservient to it. I know that when Patrick and I were trying to draw a closing to our film, we looked at Einstein who said that science is going to drop you on the doorstep of religion at some point. And here's a guy who examined every micron of the universe. He still found more and more questions, and less and less concrete answers. I think that Becker, along those same lines, realized that there are no definite answers, in terms of what do with our faith, as long as we continually remember our humanness, our immediate worldly existence and don't just blindly step into that faith hoping that it's going to take over and answer all our questions for us. Becker was pretty aware that you can be soothed by something larger that is out there. But always remember that you are a human as well and there are very human issues going on here.

B: It seems what Becker wanted to make room for in the world, next to faith, is the

things about my life, and not my life as different from anybody else's, but my life because it's all I really know, is how much is fucking hurts to be me sometimes, and simultaneously how blissful it feels to be me sometimes. How sometimes those things are as intertwined as two people making love. How close the gut-wrenching pain and the absolute bliss are intertwined. That's part of the deal. Once you pop out into the world, that's what you get, that simultaneous pain/bliss. Joseph Campbell said that life is like an opera—imagining the power and passion of an opera—except that the opera hurts and we are in it, neck deep. That's what we get for being living people. In the last couple of years and the more I work on the film, I find it more and more potent to think of my life in those terms. When I was working on the lyrics for the Trial records, that just came up constantly, all the journal entries, the heartbreak, coinciding and clashing and working in absolute symbiosis with all the joy, happiness, and triumph.

B: That seems to connect to Becker's idea of Heroism. Becker understood much in these terms. In the introduction I really like something he seemingly just drops in—"The urge to heroism is natural and to

B: I think he was much more sympathetic to the basic urge toward heroism, rather than encouraging the idea that people should be James Bond. I think he wants us all running through the streets, that sort of thing, drunk on life.

G: Absolutely. Realistically, at the expense of offending Vaneigem or anybody who's read him and got really excited about it—I did for one—a fulfilled life doesn't necessarily entail living every passion. I would be satisfied if everybody on the planet lived a little more passionately. I would be satisfied if individuals would just get a little more in touch with the things they want to do, a little more in touch with the psychology of what makes them tick and behave the way they do. I think that would be a huge colossal improvement over the status quo. Even individual examples of that make me really excited. In terms of the punk-activist community, yeah, absolutely, the options are all there. What about in terms of other subcultures that are perhaps not as inundated with examples of passionate living and artistic expression? I would love to see people in those cultures say I can improve my life immensely by doing *this*. Whatever that thing might be. As Patrick and I were talking about who our audience is, we made the decision to

that relationship about? I was listening to a lecture given by a guy named Sheldon Solomon, who ended up being a terrific, amazing friend of mine. Sheldon made reference in his lecture—this was during the whole Bush/Gore vote scandal and mayhem—that maybe we should let Bush and Gore know that their striving to get the most votes was a good example of their striving for immortality. He intended it as a joke in his lecture. I went up to him afterwards and said, "How about we write to Bush and Gore and how about we write to every other leader on the planet and suggest that we would love to give them insight into the nature of leaders and the nature of followers." And using that insight, that insight of death anxiety, that people often enjoy being leaders and followers, and how that might help diminish violence worldwide, being that the leaders are often the folks guiding policy over the majority. The World Leaders Project absolutely stemmed from reading Becker. From trying to apply something real-world. You know, and your readers know, we all know in the punk/hardcore music community that risk we run is just shouting, screaming, hitting guitars, and making sounds that fulfill the needs of the ears, eyes, and minds of those who expect those types of sounds, without making anything happen. By happen I

Joseph Campbell said that life is like an opera—imagining the power and passion of an opera—except that the opera hurts and we are in it, neck deep. That's what we get for being living people. I found that in the last couple of years, and the more I work on the film, I find it more and more potent to think of my life in those terms. When I was working on the lyrics for the Trial records, that just came up constantly, all the journal entries, the heartbreak, coinciding and clashing and working in absolute symbiosis with all the joy happiness and triumph.

---

idea that there is mystery in the world, whether that mystery is in Judaism or an idea of a living Earth.

G: When he says we create out of art or our lives an object and drop it into the confusion, make an offering of it to the life force, I don't think he's imagining the life force as some little deity with a beard running around in the clouds. I've interpreted it as the collective existence of living things and the collective experience of being alive, its awesomeness. We craft this interview and throw it out there and see what it does. And if turns out that people read this interview and run out into the streets and kill each other, well, then we look at that and ask ourselves, "Why is this going on?" We might look at it throughout the lens of death anxiety and adapt our behaviors accordingly; to at least use that idea, that lens as a means of making the world a better place.

B: That quote from Becker that you just cited (offering our creation to life) reminds me so much of Nietzsche's dancing star line from Thus Spoke Zarathustra: "I say unto you, one must still have chaos in oneself to give birth to a dancing star. I say unto you: you still have chaos in yourselves." The idea that, essentially, there is something to give to the world.

G: That idea that you talked of earlier, that it might be born of a state of chaos—I think that one of the most beautiful

admit it is honest; for everyone to admit it would release such pent up force as to be devastating to societies as they are now." That idea reminded me of Raoul Vaneigem writing in The Revolution of Everyday Life how much sympathy he had for this man driving home from work and at each light he is imagining himself some sort of hero or another, James Bond, etc. This is going on all around you, people yearning for a sense of heroism and meaning, even if in such bland terms as James Bond. I wonder if we are standing on the brink of people granting that to themselves.

G: I would hope so.

B: I think Becker is convincing in arguing that so-called primitive societies were successful in structuring themselves in such a way that people could feel satisfied in that urge toward heroism and meaning. And hopefully in our activist and punk and all the greater cultures are also developing ways of interacting that can give people voice and space for those yearnings.

G: Or even non-punk and non-activist subcultures. I think that ultimately striving for the heroic doesn't dictate Vaneigem's example of imagining that they are James Bond. You don't have to be James Bond and having sex with Halle Berry to be a hero.

get this into the hands of as many people as possible, because we, like you, saw that Becker was on to something. And while we shouldn't encase it in a solid gold ark, we feel people across the board could benefit from what he had to say and from reflecting on his ideas.

The World Leaders Project

B: The World Leaders Project (WLP), was that something that stemmed out from your reading of Becker? Or was that something that had been brewing and those ideas are what made it grow?

G: As someone who has looked upon the structure of politics as something a little bit weird, that hundreds of millions of people elect one little person to represent them—a little weird. I'm saying "just a little weird" so we don't have to go into what's the right system of politics, blah blah blah. A little strange. Just the idea that somebody else speaks for me, a little weird. When I started to read Becker I wondered, what is the death psychology of a leader? And what is the relationship to the follower? And what are they doing for each other? Not just the leader saying, "Followers you make me feel like a god." Rather, each of the followers saying, 'Wow, it feels really good to be a follower.' There are so many other followers and I don't need to stick my neck out, that guy over there is doing it for me. Because I elected him." What's

mean, and no pun intended, cathartic change, some feeling, action or change, real change. Not just people jumping around—which of course could be real change for some folks—but I wanted to take the ideas of Becker and take them out of an academic arena and say okay, let's put him in the political arena and let's not just put him in the ideological political arena, let's go talk to some folks. And have those folks be world leaders and meet them face to face. And hit them with these ideas and share these ideas with them and not just from the perspective of, "we have all the answers," but put them on the table and see what happens. Our meeting with the president of Guyana was unbelievable because he actually listened to us.

B: You and Sheldon had written him a letter—and Patrick...

G: Yeah, we wrote every leader in the world. Sheldon and I wrote the letter. And Sheldon, Patrick, and I wrote a document that described our ideas, that we sent out to all those who responded. Meeting with the president of Guyana was fantastic, because he listened. I think it would be naive to think that he would walk away from the meeting and went out and bought Denial of Death and went to flightfromdeath.com and watched our trailer for the movie and pre-ordered the DVD. That would be ridiculous. All I wanted for that meeting was to go in and say, here are a couple of books, here are some thoughts to think about. Tell us a little bit about Guyana, what goes on down here? How's life down here? What is existence like here? To be totally honest, living in Seattle I have no idea. And Patrick, he was filming the whole time, but living in LA, he had no idea and Sheldon living in New York had no idea. Tell us about Guyana and how can we help each other to create a better place? A place where suffering isn't as widespread. Again we are not going to get rid of suffering, but there is a lot of suffering and violence that don't need to be there. So how can we diminish violence in our two cultures by looking at it through the lens of Becker's ideas? Tremendous, to have that conversation was just fantastic.

B: And what did he say initially? Was he stumbling or what?

G: No, no. He agreed with us, looking over the document, human beings being motivated toward violence because the fear of death was quite possibly part of the problem. He added that racial relations and economic issues were at the heart of much of their violence. We talked a bit about his. By the end of the meeting though, it wasn't a situation where he where he smiled through his teeth and said have a nice day, goodbye, but actually invited us back and said that he himself would set up a speaking engagement for us at the University of Guyana. So Sheldon and I are going to go back and lecture something this year. We're in the midst of working out which dates, then we will get in touch with President Bharrat Jagdeo and make it happen again. It was awesome for me after preaching to the choir for years and years, to take the ideas in a very non-traditional way out into the world. And see what happens. Again, craft something and offer it to the world and see what comes of it.

B: That experience of taking yourself out of your familiar surroundings, what you saw

band and gave me your record and I never listened to hardcore and I don't really like the music but it made me think about this time in my life when... fill in the blank. Some experience in their life, whether their girlfriend was raped or their parents died in a car crash. Whatever made them happy or sad or terrified, that by some crazy method of that record getting to them, it changed their life. I thought to myself, it changed their life, and on some small level we have a great conversation. I thought to myself, with the WLP, okay, we hand these books to the president of Guyana, he goes on with his day and has 40 more meetings, let's say. He goes on with his year and has 40,000 more meetings. Well, what happens at the next CARICOM meeting, where Caribbean leaders talk about economics? What if, what IF he rubs elbows with some other leader that triggers something in his brain about something that we talked about and introduced him to and those two guys get into a conversation. Or what if by whatever freak incidence, the G8 leaders are getting together and the president of Guyana happens to be there and rubs elbows with George Bush or one of the other global political heavy-weights, and they share ideas based on this conversation. You know, what IF. And to be totally honest, to see this have happened again and again and again with Trial I thought to myself, what's the difference between the president of Guyana and a punk rock girl in North Carolina? What's the difference? There's no difference in that they are people, experiencing life. Maybe in individual ways, but also in the same sorts of ways: They want to understand the world. And they want to understand their lives and make them better and they are going to encounter other people and work together to make those things happen. I thought to myself, this is brilliant! Again, I'm not saying that I'm the brilliant one, you would have to put that in Becker's hands for getting all those notes down. The

of Terror. What we would like to do is tour, Patrick, Sheldon and myself—and I mean tour. Ultimately, I would like to tour from colleges to the palaces of presidents and prime ministers, Sheldon speaking about his book on terror and Patrick and I showing the film and integrating all of that; since Sheldon, Patrick and I have become this WLP triumvirate, we would like to share these ideas all at the same time. Granted, when we get our next meeting with a world leader, whoever that might be, we're not going to be in a situation most likely where we can show a 90 minute film, have them read a 100-plus page book, and talk about it. But at least we'll have those kinds of ideas in mind.

B: Where does the film stand now in production? Is the final edit done?

G: Near done. Patrick is working on it as we speak and we have spent this week that we are interested in having narrate the film. [A Hollywood actor, Gabriel Byrne, was brought on board for this task in March.] We have a whole list of folks we are pursuing. We are utilizing a number of contacts we have made in the last year to get screenings and to find a distributor. Between Patrick and myself, we have managed to arrange a few more screenings. This year we'll be in Edmonton, Alberta, at a conference called Culture and the State, which is going to be in May of 2003. We'll screen it in Seattle in March in conjunction with a lecture by Robert J. Lipton. We'll screen most likely in Houston as well. Also, in Michigan, there will be a weekend long series of events: Sheldon, then our film, then all of us talking collectively about Becker. We have gone that route in terms of trying to set up individual screenings, but also utilize the contacts we have made to set up distribution for, hopefully, national and international TV releases and movie theaters.

There was one stretch of 20 days where we slept between one hour and half and three hours a night to finish this thing. One day we worked quite literally 22 and half hours on our film. State of mania. Since we got the rough cut finished, since the NY and Seattle screenings, I was able to kick back a bit and focus on some other stuff. I am always of course doing juggling and entertaining stuff, which is my true passion in life, I love it. I'm going to be doing some speaking dates on my own at some colleges on the East Coast. That's stuff I love, too, talking to audiences. And it's actually quite fun doing it without a band, there aren't nearly as many things to worry about. But I'm also neck deep in trying to help the Western Shoshone Nation with whatever I can, helping to resolve their land dispute with the US government. A dispute that has been going on for about 150 years or so now. I just got back from a trip, an interesting trip when you look at the clash of cultures through the lens of Becker. Native Americans and Euro-Americans are a great example to look at when belief systems and ideology clash. I was very fortunate to be able to drive a van load of Shoshone elders to Rapid City, SD for a meeting between them and Lakota tribal officials to form alliances on various political issues. The first time, as I understand it, that Lakota and Shoshone officials have met since the Battle of Little Big Horn in 1876. An awesome experience heightened by being inundated with all this immortality thinking and belief system clashes. I got to ponder first hand, Wow, what's the effect of a dominant invader? What do people do in response to it? What questions can we ask in terms of fear of death and the systems they create to maintain a sense of lasting permanence? Fascinating. Throwing fire machetes and bean bags around, helping the Shoshone, movies, and talking to world leaders. That pretty much keeps me happy.

...What's the difference between the president of Guyana and a punk rock girl in North Carolina? What's the difference? There's no difference in that they are people, experiencing life. Maybe in individual ways, but also in the same sorts of ways: They want to understand the world. And they want to understand their lives and make them better and they are going to encounter other people and work together to make those things happen. I thought to myself, this is brilliant!

there, then coming back to your home and Seattle and saying to yourself, what next? Has it made you push for more or see how things that were done before might not have been working so well?

G: Push for more, absolutely, I would say since summer of 2002 I have been relentless in terms of wanting more and getting more. Getting more—I'm not talking about cars and diamond rings, I'm talking about seeing how far I can go in terms of creativity and developing ideas and talking them out of traditional, for me, realms and modes of thought. The World Leaders Project blew the doors wide open. I think just to have on the table those ideas, in the President of Guyana's hands, reminded me of all the times that after working on the Trial record for a year, recording the album and putting it out into the world—times where somebody would come up to me after a show and say, you know, my friend's brother is into your

brilliant thing is, this could really work. The effect that we desired in terms of bringing about some change and the lessening of violence was that this trickle down effect could happen on the scale of world leaders. You know what, if I am naive to think that, so be it. I was also naive to go out and waste my voice almost to the point of not ever being able to speak again in hopes that it would help people deal with rape or sexually transmitted diseases or the loss of a spouse through punk rock: and I saw that time and time again, a hundredfold. That's just one kind of channel, one ray of light opened to me, through the success of the WLP.

B: Your strategic plan with Flight from Death: is that something that is becoming intimately connected to the WLP?

G: Sheldon has just put out a brilliant book, In the Wake of 9/11: The Psychology

B: Is there going to be a DVD release?

G: Absolutely. We are going to finish this film. For frame of reference in case someone picks this 'zine or interview up in 2012, I'm talking about this film is done, March 1st 2003. When we secure all the money to do all the things we like in terms of packaging and extra things on the DVD, we'll do a release as soon as possible.

B: I'm really curious what else you have on the table? I can see how these things would dominate your life, but do you have any other projects?

G: Those are the main things I do. Flight from Death in the second half of 2002 took on an entirely new focus and dedication. In August, September, and October of 2002 Patrick and I were working so hard on that film I actually ended up in a doctor's office. I thought I was dying of a heart attack.

I know I want as much out every second of my life as I can possibly get. Because one of the things that reading Becker has done to me is to make me acutely aware of the fact that yeah, I'm going to die. Just a matter of time before I'm worm food. The past year has just made me intense in terms of wanting more and more and more out of life. Limitless passion—all the stuff just gives me a sense of being alive that in my own life is unprecedented.

For more information on the worldwide web:

www.flightfromdeath.com: watch the trailer, get production updates, find out where it's playing next!

www.wordsareweapons.com: Greg's site, where you can find out more about the Western Shoshone work he does, the World Leaders Project, and much more.

Or write to Greg Bennick c/o Inside Front.

HUMOR:
Burn Me in a Fire, You Are My True Desire
Greg Bennick

A few years ago, I was up in beautiful Vancouver, B.C., Canada to attend a punk rock show. I try to head up to Canada as often as possible because I think it to be the greatest country on the planet, based on the friendliness of the people, the wide variety of vegan eats available, and the lack of firearms. Of course, my superlative about the country is declared with no offense intended to Poland, which of course has Warsaw—also one of my favorite cities—where my old band Trial was once fed a meal fit for kings by the local punk/hardcore kids. Or should I be saying a meal fit for punk/hardcore kids, served to us by kings? Why should the kings get all the good entrées? But already, I digress. I was in Vancouver (which I might have already mentioned is one of my favorite cities) and while hanging out with my friend Ivan outside the punk show, we overheard some young punk kids talking to one another and poking fun at each other. We didn't pay it any attention until one kid called his friend "gay." Now, Ivan and I assumed that the kid's first name wasn't in fact Gay, and we assumed also that the kid was using the term as a pejorative. We decided to approach him and confront him on what

he'd said. I have to say we would have felt pretty dumb starting to yell at the kid only to have his friend pull out a driver's license and prove to us that his name was in fact "Gay" Smith. You have no idea how many times people have called out to me during my shows, "Hey juggler... you suck," only to be embarrassed later when they learn that my legal name actually *is* Hey Juggler You Suck. I had it changed just to avoid confusion. Anyway, thankfully for Ivan and me, it didn't go down like that. Ivan and I approached the young punk, and engaged him in conversation. Ivan took the lead and offered a brilliant example of how to deal with the situation. He identified what we'd heard, and asked the kid why he'd said it. Of course, the kid just shrugged his shoulders, laughed a sort of "Don't be a dork, old man" sort of laugh, and said, "I dunno... whatever." Ivan asked him why he'd used that particular word, and the kid again had little or no answer. Ivan then asked the kid, "What purpose does language serve?" At this point, the kid realized he wasn't getting out of the situation easily, and actually started to pay attention. He looked up at Ivan. Ivan asked, "Wouldn't you agree that the purpose of language is to convey meaning?" The kid agreed. Ivan said, "Well, if the purpose of language is to convey meaning, what meaning are you conveying through the use of the word 'gay'?" The kid had no answer, for to answer honestly and say that he was trying to

convey that his friend was a homosexual—and that the comment was intended to be an insult—would have made him look like a moron. Ivan and I suggested to the kid that using words uselessly, especially when they have the potential to insult or hurt others, is a waste of time and breath, and is evidence of ignorance. We offered that he could have insulted his friend far more creatively and intelligently, and then we left him to think for himself as to what those venomous barbs might be. Overall, it was a great experience that reaffirmed to me the importance of language. Language defines us as individuals and also defines our cultural constructions. It creates and conveys meaning at the same time. As we communicate and use language, we are developing a narrative that gives meaning, literally, to our lives. In this process, there is little need for useless talk.

One can extrapolate from this that the same importance rings true in lyrics, prose, and poetry. There are no extra words. There isn't room for them. As a writer, I strive to achieve potency, though it could very easily be argued that I fail miserably. As a reader, I find myself wanting that potency from the lyrics, stories, or poems I encounter. The idea of not wasting communication, or maybe more to the point, of making our communication as creative and as potent as is possible (and *beyond* what we think is possible!) is at the core of the human experience. We have to connect with each other somehow, someway, *any* way, in this disconnected and superficial society... so why not make that connection as vital and intimately expressive as we can? When our speech and text truly convey the intent that we are trying to express in the words we've selected, then we truly have accomplished something significant.

Literature is full of examples demonstrating high achievement in terms of crafting writing to convey meaning. Take, for example, these words from Goethe, "He only earns his freedom and his life who takes them every day by storm." Or these lines of poetry from John Greenleaf Whittier, "For of all sad words of tongue or pen, the saddest are these, 'It might have been.'" It becomes easy to see how language can be used effectively when we have examples of brilliance. What is harder to determine is what happens when things go wrong in the use of language. The example I used before, of the young punk rocker insulting his friend, was a blatant example. Others are more insidious. You might ask confusedly, "But Greg, how can we isolate the problem of misuse of language? How can we prevent ourselves from diving headlong into the traps that ensnare aspiring writers and leave them wallowing in useless unintelligible babble?" I sympathize with your question, and can offer a concrete response. To avoid falling into these traps, we must follow simple rules of development that allow us to create a relationship with the words we craft. Following these rules will result in writing—both for prose and poetry as well as for lyrics—that is potent, interesting, and connected. The rules are as follows, and there are three of them. Rule #1: Always write in a voice that is your own, and stop at nothing to drag the deepest truths from yourself and onto the page, no matter what you are trying to express. Rule #2: Utilize the limits and full expanse of your own creativity and ability to describe images, and pursue each word and line as if your very life depended on it. Finally, but most importantly, is Rule #3. Never, under any circumstances, even under threat of torture or death, rhyme the words "fire" and "desire."

These three rules apply to any type of writing. When we speak from a combination of the heart and mind, and when we do so without restricting ourselves by convention or by outside opinion, we unlock enormous potential to connect with a reader through our texts. The third rule applies mostly to lyrics, and as most people reading this article are at the very least music *fans*, I will assume that you recognize that this rule has relevancy. Rhyming

fire and desire on the part of a lyricist is, without a doubt, the worst possible crime against humanity. It is evidence of a deeply rooted psychosis. Those guilty, and the list includes Jimi Hendrix, The Eurythmics, Bananarama, Zegota, and Sir Mix-Alot among others, should be forced to undergo extensive psychological tests before their sanity and safety to the general public are declared. I will leave it up to you to explore and apply the first two rules, and will choose to spend my time here exploring Rule #3, the "Fire/Desire Rule" (as it is called in most collegiate texts), giving examples of what can go wrong if you defy this rule, and ultimately offering examples of other routes you can take in your writing.

One of the most common things that can happen when you join the ranks of the linguistically insane and ignore the Fire/Desire Rule, is that your grammar will deteriorate dramatically and quickly, leaving you essentially unable to communicate. There is no medical cure for this, and your readers will be left stranded in a literary wasteland without nourishment or shelter from your ongoing assault on their minds. Take for example Bruce Springsteen. Bruce, to his credit, started off as a writer struggling against profound disadvantages. Aside from being from Asbury Park, NJ (Try to name one other quality writer or lyricist from Asbury Park. Go ahead. Name one. What was that? Oh... Jon Bon Jovi got his start in Asbury Park? Really? Let's see here. You are trying to justify quality writing by using Jon Bon Jovi as an example? A man who wrote the lines: "I'm a cowboy / on a steel horse I ride / I'm wanted dead or alive"? I rest my case.)... as I was saying, aside from being from Asbury Park, Bruce Springsteen suffers from denim poisoning caused by wearing only one pair of jeans every single day since the release of the "Born in the USA" album in 1984. Regardless of the hardships Bruce has faced however, the fact cannot be denied that his grammar suffered tremendously as soon as he engaged the vicious mate of fire and desire. As evidence, I offer his song "I'm On Fire" in which he writes *"I'm on fire / I got a bad desire / I'm on fire."* Got? Bruce 'got' a bad desire? Funny he should mention it, because I got one too. I got a desire to not buy any of his insane, fire and desire exploiting records at any price. Bruce's grammar difficulties get worse in his song "Fire." The denim seeping deeper into his brain, he stops using nouns and verbs completely in the second part of his lyrical phrasing. He writes, *"You say you don't love me, girl you can't hide your desire / 'Cause when we kiss, Fire."* Aside from the fact that I ask why Bruce is kissing someone who says she's not interested in him, I wonder what happened to all the verbs? And why

the sudden capitalization? "When we kiss, Fire."? I have a better suggestion. How about, *"When I listen to Springsteen, Kill me."*

Another shocking example of the effects of using fire and desire is that the use of these words together will cause you to call your loved ones by nonsensical names. Your relationships will deteriorate faster than the fame of an "American Idol" finalist. The members of the rock band Kiss made a fortune by painting their faces to look like psychotic clowns and then playing songs filled with sexual innuendo. Talk about a genius marketing gimmick! Why didn't I think of it? Evil looking sexual space clowns. It has millions of dollars written all over it. A sure bet indeed. Regardless of their marketing brilliance (the effect of which was expressed quite clearly last year by bassist Gene Simmons who said in an interview "Kiss is not a rock and roll band. We are a rock and roll BRAND") the band lost their minds completely in the song "Heaven's On Fire." In the song, Paul Stanley (vocals/guitar) used a pet name for his lover that made the ultimate lovers Romeo and Juliet spin like dynamos in their literary graves. He wrote: *"Paint the sky with desire, angel fly / Heaven's on fire."* I have to say that I love my girlfriend with every cell in my body. I have covered ground with her that lovers worldwide wish they could experience. I cherish her and she cherishes me. We are beautifully whole together. At the same time, the thought of calling her "Angel Fly" has never once crossed my mind. I have thought to call her a hundred different pet names, many more ridiculous than the next. I actually *have* called her many of these things. But "Angel Fly"? What the hell is an angel fly? Why is it a term of endearment? And would you really want a space clown with a boner calling you "Angel Fly" as he chased you around painting the sky?

Now, you might be wondering, "Are these misuses of language dangerous? Might they lead to actual physical harm?" In fact, I am sad to report, the answer to you: I suggest that these misuses can actually be life threatening. Breaking the Fire/Desire Rule can result in you starting to carry extremely dangerous items as you walk around publicly. As proof I offer U2's song "Desire." When Bono is not running around the globe making peace and solving the world's problems, he is actually endangering the lives of others. In the song, he sings: *"Gonna go where the bright lights / And the big city meet / With a red guitar... on fire / Desire."* Need I say more? I wouldn't even carry a burning match to where the bright lights and big city meet... and this idiot is carrying a flaming guitar? Someone could easily be burned or killed! Bono is a madman and he must be stopped before he strikes again. I suggest a pre-emptive strike. I will arrange an international coalition, or the fragments of one. Bono must be disarmed and removed from power at any cost.

For some, use of fire and desire causes disorientation and lack of focus. Having, and being able to act, with freewill is a large component of being human. Without the ability to decide and act on a course of action, we lose the fullness of our ability to imagine and to create. For the group The Backstreet Boys, it is far too late in this regard, due to advanced fire/desire addiction. Life for them has become very sad indeed. The Backstreet Boys did the unthinkable: they used fire and desire in the same song, not once, but *twice*. May God have mercy on their souls. The result of this lyrical atrocity was the collective loss of the few cells of intellect they had to begin with. In the song, and resulting entirely from their overuse of the fire and desire combination, they make declarations and then contradict them immediately. They leave the reader and listener feeling dizzy and ill. I offer you their smash hit, "That Way": *"You are my fire / The one desire / Believe it when I say / I want it that way / Am I your fire / Your one desire?"* At first glance, all appears normal. But look deeper, my friends, look deeper. Here is where things get perplexing. After blatantly stating that "you" are in fact the "one" desire, they then offer themselves to be not only a second desire, but a fire as well! This is extremely intense, and very confusing. If "you" are not in fact the "one" desire, then does it stand to reason that there are in fact multiple desires as yet undiscovered? And if there are in fact multiples, might we then consider for a moment just where we are going to find fires to match up with these desires? The mind reels at the thought. Thankfully, now that The Backstreet Boys have no career (largely, I would suggest, the result of their lyrical indiscretion), they will have time to help us look.

Please be advised that coupling fire and desire will also affect your use of metaphor. Metaphor is, of course, one of the most potent tools in a writer's box of potent writing tools. Metaphor is a window that can be opened on the world. Now, wasn't that just clever? In describing and defining a metaphor, I actually *used* a metaphor! Delightful. Keep in mind, while you sit there, blissfully enchanted with my wordsmanship, that metaphors can have a dark and seedy underbelly as well, whatever that means. When used incorrectly, metaphor becomes the season of the finger of death. Metaphor can be a drowning sand clam. It can appear as a playful rodent,

and then instantly turn, developing wings while being reborn as an alien toenail. I think you get my point. This problem can be avoided however. You can actually cheat fate. Simply avoid the union of fire and desire, and your metaphors will remain well defined and intact. Look what happened to the 80's band The Cars. They slipped up only once, but the effect was immediate. To tell the truth, they didn't even get out of the verse before an attack of horrible metaphor cut them down. In the song "Let's Go," the band sings: *"She's a frozen fire / She's my one desire."* A frozen fire? Is that anything like the U.S. military's term "friendly fire" where people shoot their own comrades? Given the course of The Cars later years in music, I might have suggested this to be a better alternative for the band.

Finally, and I am sharing this last point of warning with you because I care deeply about your personal well being, allowing fire and desire to become lyrically one, can help you give life to inanimate objects. It is true. While this may sound exciting—after all, who hasn't thought about what it would be like if scissors could talk—it does open up an entire world of problems. The band Silverchair found that using fire and desire together allowed their body parts to begin to think for themselves. This has profound and potentially horrific implications. In "Anna's Song," they sing: *"Open fire on my knees desires / What I need from you."* Now, I am all for the exploration of desire and for encouraging others to explore their own desires. However, I would have a very hard time being convinced that my knees have desires, and an even harder time being convinced as Silverchair suggests, that those same knees then deserve to be fired upon for expressing their desires. If my knees actually do have desires, or if they acquire the ability to have them, then I believe wholeheartedly that they should be able to express them as they see fit, without the threat of violence. Anything less would be entirely oppressive. Kneeist, if you will.

I seem to have painted a dismal picture. Amid these shocking uses of fire and desire and their profound effects, we might ask in terms of language and its use: what other routes can we take? How can we avoid the monumental problems mentioned in this article? How can we avoid having to carry flaming guitars through areas of town with which we have limited familiarity? What are we to do to stop kneeism before it starts? How might we settle on the pet name "Sweet Potato" or "Honey Bun" rather than "Angel Fly" for those we love? My suggestion is simple: follow the three rules, and pour your heart into all of your writing. Create every song lyric and every line of text as if it was an epitaph, applying

the same importance to those words as you would apply to the last statement you make to the world. Now, given that I have to be on a plane in six hours to travel to Michigan, I hope that I have not created a self-fulfilling prophecy here. In case you didn't know, I hate flying. It doesn't make sense to me. There is no doubt in my mind that those who invented modern day flying listened to The Backstreet Boys. How else could they possibly have justified spending money on research to develop flying tubes of metal filled with hundreds of people? Only a fire/desire fan could have conceived of such madness.

Given our sound bite world, in which everyone seems to have an attention span of four seconds or less, we can either work to oppose that trend—actually creating vital communication by taking the time to conceive of and then actualize potency[1], no matter what the cost—or, we can play to the lowest common denominator and not challenge ourselves, or our listener/readers, at all. The end result of the second option doesn't strike me as a communicative realm that I want to be a part of. I want a world in which we express ourselves effectively and efficiently, a world in which I can be assured that the ideas being expressed in the words I read and hear are as much an artistic creation as the music, painting, sculpture or other forms of art that might accompany them. Anything less just wouldn't set my heart on fire, or fulfill my burning... well... forget it.

Thanks for reading. I really appreciate it, and would love to hear from you too. Write me anytime: xjugglerx@yahoo.com.

MEMOIR:
Incendiary
The tale of Fucked Up
Chris Somerville

The bars on my window were thin shafts of black iron. They were mounted to the outside so we couldn't touch them. You see, anything we could touch we could use to hurt ourselves and naturally the entire room was designed with this in mind. There were no real corners anywhere. From the headboard of the bed to the bottom of the table legs, smooth, rounded edges.

During dinner, someone had told me there were cameras in our rooms. Even though they checked our pockets after every meal for cutlery stolen from the dining hall, even though we were denied access to electric razors and dental floss, even though we were at arm's reach from a crew of attendants stationed day and night to open our doors

[1] *Editor's note—when reading this column, imagine Greg teaching it to you as a writing seminar: "Actualize Potency."*

and check on us repeatedly, still they hid fucking cameras in our bedrooms. I scanned the room viciously and upon finding nothing, I thought about what it would mean if the cameras were really there.

I wondered if someone was watching me at that very moment and as I sat there on the windowsill, hugging my legs, resting my eyes against my bent knees because it was the only comforting thing I could do, I wondered what a stranger would think, I wondered what a stranger would feel when she looked at me. I turned away from this thought, faced my window, saw only thin shafts of black iron.

A knock on my door. "Chris! Hey Chris!" I knew that raspy half-whisper, it was Marie. "Come on out man, we're gonna jam!" I opened the door and saw Ben and Marie smirking at me with mischievous glints in their eyes.

"What do you mean *jam?*" I asked, instantly infected by their mischief, "Jam with what?"

"With my guitar," Marie gleefully retorted.

"Your *WHAT?!*" I had been away from my guitar for six days now and could already feel my fingers begin to atrophy. Naturally my mind was stagnating as well.

Playing music, even with the sub-basic understanding I had then, was a way for me to flush my volatile, caustic emotions through a medium. Destruction, even self-destruction, is a form of creation.

Nothing was for keeps in those days. I didn't "write songs," I just played. My guitar was my journal, my confidant, my cardboard box to bash with a baseball bat. It was my door to slam, my emotional release and without it I could not possibly be expected to behave in a rational, socially acceptable manner. Although I suppose that was decidedly a non-issue in this place.

"Come *ON!*" Marie tugged me by the sleeve down the hallway to the attendant's desk. She blew past the desk clerk, reached behind the counter and withdrew a black nylon gig bag that was obviously filled with guitar.

My jaw dropped. I stood motionless, transfixed on the object, eyes bulging. "I... I don't understand... how is this possible?"

"My mom brought it here for me. Now *LET'S GO!*" We ran back down the hallway, tromped halfway up the stairs to the

fulcrum point where the flight changed directions. There was one of those wide pentagonal steps, big enough for the three of us. We sat in a circle facing one another, beaming.

"Okay, are you ready?"

I couldn't speak. Slowly, Marie unzipped the gig bag, threw it open and there, in the middle of our circle, lay a yellow imitation fender telecaster. It was almost as ugly as my guitar at home and the mere sight of it filled me with fresh light. I was exalted.

"Alright you guys," began Marie, suddenly very serious, "Tonight, we are a band."

"A band..." I whispered in disbelief.

"What should we call ourselves?" Ben mused.

Marie picked up the guitar. There was a pick wedged behind the nut and she pulled it free with a *plink!* She looked up at us from underneath thick, dark eyebrows and played the most dissonant tinny awful chord ever to bounce off those white walls.

BRANG!

"Live from Four Winds mental hospital, we are... FUCKED UP!!" DA-NA-NA-NA-NA!

"Yes!"

"Fucked Up! We're Fucked Up!" I shook myself spastically, startled by my own excitement. And just then something, perhaps the sound of a door closing, snapped me back. I looked down the stairs and remembered where I was.

"But, Marie," I murmured, pointing in the direction my concern was now drifting, "Aren't they afraid you'll..."

"... hang myself with a GIT-ar string?"

"Yeah!" said Ben, "It'll be just like that Beck song!" But I could feel the night attendant's ears prick up. They didn't understand, I was serious.

"Don't worry about it, man," Marie assured me in earnest, "As long as I don't take it into my room we'll be fine."

"Okay," I said, gradually returning, "So if we're a band, we need to have songs." They both looked at me, grinning widely.

"Let me see that guitar." Marie handed me the instrument, which I immediately tuned to drop-D. *JUN-JUN-JUN-JUN!* I chugged swiftly up the neck and sighed deeply with relief. *At last...*

"So, what do we write songs about?" I inquired. Ben and Marie looked at each

other and shrugged. "Oh COME ON! We're on Suicide Watch, there has to be *something* we're pissed off about!"

"Hhhmmmmm... what about the meds line!" A brilliant suggestion from Ben, we all agreed. You see, every day, twice a day, we had to wait single file, on a line that led to a split door that led to a dominating, stupid, insensitive fucking nurse who would give us medication, make us stand before her so she could watch us take it, then check under our tongues to make sure we had swallowed it.

Ben *hated* taking meds. He just hated what they did to him. Hated himself when he was on them. So he was really good at hiding his meds and everyone knew it. The nurse would thoroughly inspect his mouth with a flashlight, *and* make him empty his pockets, thereby forcing him to swallow those fucking pills every day, twice a day. "Fucking bitch..." he murmured to himself.

"Right!" I said, now driven and determined, "the meds line it is!" I burst into my favorite four-chord Riot Grrrl riff and Marie let out a mocking call met by Ben's bitter response: *DA-NA-NA! NA-DA-NA! NA-DA-NA! NA-NA-NA-NA!*

"Time to take yr medication now."
"FUCK YOU! YEAH! YEAH!"
"Wannanother cuppa water?"
"FUCK YOU! YEAH! YEAH!"
"Now let's check under yr tongue."
"FUCK YOU! YEAH! YEAH!"
"C'mon now, swallow it!"
"FUCK YOU! YEAH! YEAH!"

We collapsed all over each other, quaking with uproarious laughter. Ben almost fell down the stairs. We collected ourselves, reformed our circle and stared rabidly into one another's eyes. There was a ferocity inside all three of us, a wildness that could be given no voice within those walls. Medicated, silenced, walking single file, they tried starving it out of us. Strapped down, sedated, a breakdown alone in the Quiet Room, they tried beating it out of us. And when the scowls from our eyes, the bile from our mouths showed them that it just wouldn't die, they gave us "outlets," "drama therapy." They told us to scream our guts out at the folding chairs, pretending they were our parents. And we scoffed at this hollow gesture, laughed out loud in their faces at how ludicrous it was. Cursed ourselves later for not doing as they asked, for not drawing on our rage, our most deeply seated *fucking hatred*, letting it pour out of us and into the place it truly belonged: *INTO THEM.*

For yes, we hated our parents, and yes, we hated ourselves, but we hated them more. And we saw their mission to make us "safe"

for what it was: to strip us of autonomy, to cut us down to size, to protect us from ourselves. But that night as we sat in our circle on the stair, as we looked into each other's eyes, brimming with ferocity, the wildness they sought to starve, to beat, defile, desecrate, we could feel it pulse from every pore.

Reveling in our rebellion, tiny though it was, the threat of consequences had no power in our hearts. A separation contract (we would speak only in secret), banished to the Quiet Room (we would not speak at all). The tools of their control, in that moment, *decimated*. For the flame they had thought sensible to snuff was once again ignited, all because we stole away for just one moment, ran away just one click beyond surveillance, just one inch beyond arm's reach, to draw in one breath that was *ours*, sing one note they couldn't silence, draw a circle 'round ourselves for just one moment in Our World.

And for this we risked everything—punishment, imprisonment, the ever-looming threat of an ever-longer stay within their walls and in their lines, waiting to be pacified. Another flashlight in my mouth, another pocket inside out, another confiscated butter knife, another night alone. We risked everything for *THIS*: To feel alive.

To feel alive.

HISTORY:
A Brief Introduction to the Cynics, Greek Punk Rockers circa 400 B.C.

on loan from Crimepensée™

We're not in this alone and never were. The status quo and the circulation of power and domination both rely on our isolation, whether it is spatial, communicational, or historical—but we are everywhere, all of the time, out of the time.

The cynics of yore were the converse of today's cynics; rather than simply accepting their role as complicit complainers, they broke every rule and dictum in the then-nascent social contract. It was thus that they earned their name, for "cynic" comes from the ancient Greek for "dog"—their critics said of them that they were shameless as dogs, and they agreed, cackling.

As of today, the cynics are the oldest bad-asses we know. Our forefather Anthistenes was born 25 centuries ago; he spit in the faces of Alexander the "Great" and Plato. Diogenes, his pupil, followed in

Editor's note: It's all Greek to me!

the 4th century BC. He lived in a wine cask, scavenged all his food, and wrote approvingly of cannibalism and incest. Exiled from his birthplace, presumably for defacing the local currency, he took "deface the coinage!" as his motto, implying that the standards of his day were corrupt and should be marked as such by being broken. He was followed by Crates, who renounced all his wealth to become a couch-surfing cynic, and Hipparchia, a proto-feminist who refused the role of the Greek woman working the loom to focus on educating herself instead.

It's said that once, on a sunny day, Diogenes showed up with a lit torch in one hand, claiming he needed it in his search for honest human beings, and a pilgrim's staff in the other, with which he said he would beat the debris who answered his queries. We carry on Diogenes's torch and staff, but this time with a different plan in mind...

The Cynics' Nine Point Program to Destroy Civilization

1. Contrary to peripat(h)etic philosophers, the cynics consider animals as their model, perfect in their freedom. They recognize themselves in the wandering dog, ferocious yet dignified. They only bite their friends—they are the only ones who deserve it. They defecate, eat, sleep, and masturbate in palace and garbage dump alike, or wherever else they feel the need to. They bite, piss, and shit over the subhumans who hide behind the masks of power—that is to say, impotence: for every chain of command works both ways.

2. Facing falsified life, the cynics falsify all contractual and conventional values. They find security in danger, wealth in absolute poverty, happiness in independence and autonomy, and wisdom in the derision of habit.

3. The cynics reject hope as an escape. Hope is the virtue of the slave. The cynics merge the means and the end: no anti-chamber of freedom is acceptable. No end can justify the sacrifice of the moment. Their lifestyle is liberation and liberating. They yield to the instant without compromising the totality.

4. The cynics are cosmopolitan: they belong to no city, to no home. Beggars, vagabonds, living from day to day, they belong to nature; they submit to it, only the better to master it.

5. The cynics have nothing to do with the obedient camel or the lion's negating roar.

GIBBERISHISTORY:
The Situationists Come As Fuck!

I receive the luxurious album of Laurent Chollet: *The Insurrection Situationist*. Again history of young people who, after this war, assimilated the surrealist revolt and who want to make incandescent all the cantons of the life, individual and daily, political, social—i.e., and that starts always thus since Dada, by saying shit to the literature, painting, and the usual forms of the language. Lettrisme will have its heroes, picturesque like Isidore Isou, pretentious like Maurice Bismuth (says Lemaître), sympathetically unforeseeable like Gabriel Pommerand. They do not live all as tramps, but put into practice all this slogan: "Never work!"... graffiti on the walls of the Sorbonne with this other, quite as difficult to assert: "Enjoy without obstacle!"

Guy Debord becomes the thinking head, the federator of what is neither a federation nor international, of what will take the name of "International Situationist," and, in the final analysis, it will only be found, after the autodissolution in 1971. "The Situ" made speak about them, and not only in May 1968. They counted painters now known, poets and agitators of high flight, writers like Debord itself, Raoul Vaneigem, they "essaime" in Italy, in Germany, in Holland, in England, and as far as Australia.

After the autodissolution, they are the drifts: brigandage in Baader, brigades red, terrorism, the delinquency, drug, after the "Proletarians of the all the countries, cherish you!" the profitable pornography industry. The company of the spectacle of Debord in book of pocket, just like the handbook of good manners of Vaneigem, remain excellent breviaries for a youth from now on revolted to good measure—but is, even revolted?

Like children, they dance and juggle with existing conditions—perpetually inventing new possibilities for life, making short work of habits and conventions, calling new styles and new forms of expression into existence.

6. The cynics shit on subcultural mechanical intellectualization and afferent sophism to leave room for acts and life. "It is of no use to know by heart the pentatonic scale if one's soul isn't tuned."

7. The cynics spit in the face of seriousness and pharisaism. A cynic, once taken prisoner by slave sellers, answered thus a buyer who asked his abilities: "Managing men! Is anyone looking for a master?" This somersault won him his freedom. The cynics' subversive methodology is irony, sarcasm, provocation, even insult. They play with the language to undermine and subvert. Their Maieutics is mediated by abortion[2].

8. The cynics push scandals to their paroxysm. They spit their freedom in the faces of others, to purify souls. They advocate zoophilia, incest, cannibalism, open and public sexual relations, and the refusal of any kind of burial, in order to demonstrate that taboos are social constructs.

9. The cynics reject all forms of power and domination (except over themselves). They see solipsism as the only truth and find excellence in virtue. They spit upon gods and masters. They do not advocate any sub- or anti-culture, but instead a counterculture.

Spit down your throat by the Crimepensée™ special force for "elitizing the masses." For more information about the cynics, agoraphilian sex, the bibliography of this piece, or whatever, write to info@crimepensee.org, or try www.crimepensee.org

HOW TO:
Sybarites of the World... Unite! Or, How to Give a Badass Massage
by Adam B., Licensed Massage Practitioner

Feeling worn out after a long, hard day of sticking it to "The Man"?

Does your body ache upon coming home from the shit job you force yourself to wake up for?

Tired and sore after a night of walking; searching for something this world we've carved out for ourselves has to offer, searching for just one dignified face?

Massage exchanged amongst friends can be a great way to counter such maladies, among others. Here's how (really condensed and incomplete as fuck)...

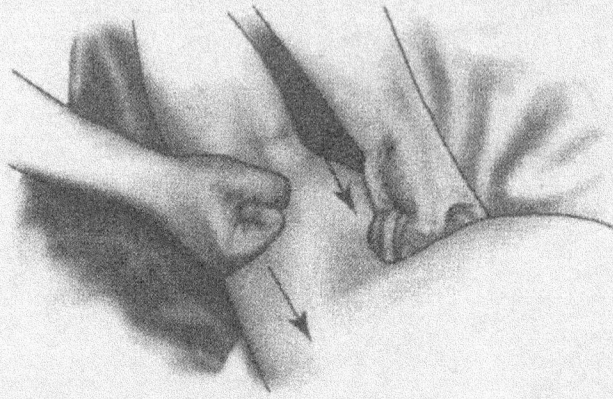

FIGURE 8-6. Deep effleurage to hamstrings using fists.

Obviously, you can massage somebody anywhere, but if you want to get fancy, find something for them to lie on that is about the height of your knuckles if you make a fist and hold your arm to your side. Have the person you're massaging get as naked as they're comfortable with, cover them with a sheet, expose the body part you're going to work on, and start rubbing!

For lubricant vegetable or almond oil works fine. If you're interested in scented oils, fuck the stuff you can get at over-priced horrible stores—make them yourself! *The Art of Aromatherapy* by Robert B. Tisserand seems like a good resource to me. When applying oil, use the minimum amount necessary to allow your hands to flow over the body without pinching.

Here are descriptions of the three main Swedish massage strokes, and a bit about how to execute them:

Effleurage is the first and last stroke used on a body part in Swedish massage, as well as being used to transition between other techniques. It is a long, gliding stroke. The first couple passes serve to spread oil as well as introduce your touch. Pour a little bit of oil into your hands, rub them together to warm it, and gently spread the oil on the skin, keeping your hands loose and melded to the contours of the body part. After a few light strokes gradually increase the pressure. Physiologically, this moves blood, lymph, and interstitial fluid (the fluid in spaces between cells), thus improving local circulation. To execute effleurage you can use open palms, knuckles, forearms, elbows, fingertips, or thumbs depending on the

desired pressure and result.

So say you're massaging the back of the leg—what you want to do is, starting at the foot, keep your arms *straight* from your shoulder to your wrists and use your legs to push your hands up the leg. Keep your legs in a lunging position and lean forward with your body to apply pressure (try to keep your back pretty straight as you do this). The pressure and strength of the stroke should be coming from your legs and use of body weight—NOT your arms! Always apply pressure towards the heart and gently glide back down the body part.

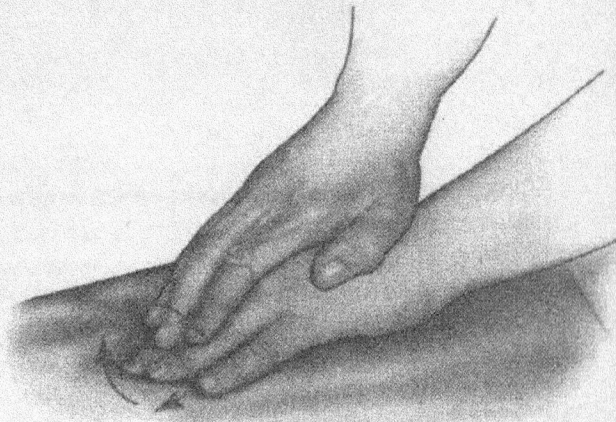

FIGURE 8-1. Circular friction along erector muscles using fingertips.

Pressure going away from the heart puts undue strain on the one-way valves in your veins which help move deoxygenated blood back to the heart.

A rad variation of effleurage is called a C-drain. Put your thumbs and fingers in a position so they form a "C." Then alternately stroke up the body with each hand, always leaving one hand in contact while the other is lifted. This is an excellent technique to use on someone with poor circulation, as it moves fluid like a motherfucker.

I usually close a body part with nerve strokes. This is simply lightly brushing your fingertips over the skin.

Petrissage, or kneading, is the second stroke of a Swedish massage. Petrissage lifts tissue from underlying structures. The motions of it serve to "milk" the tissue of accumulated

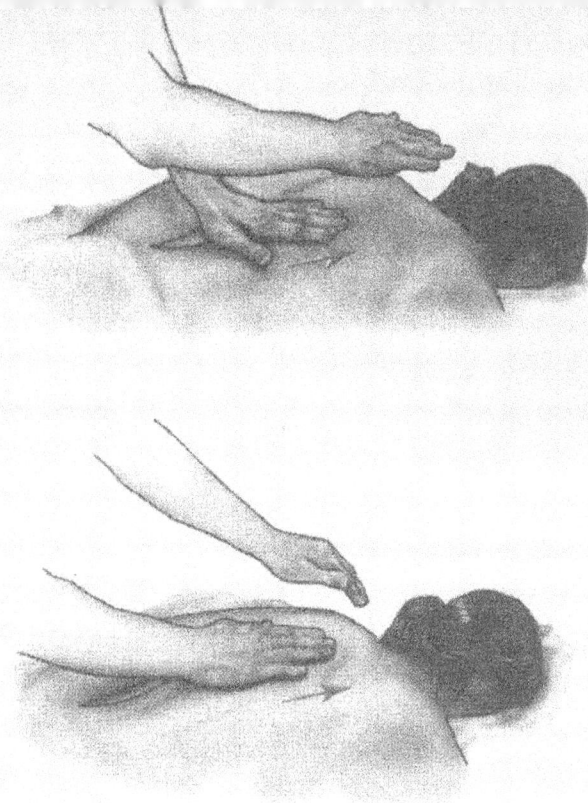

FIGURE 8-4. Shingles effleurage with hands parallel to the spine and to the direction of movement.

waste products, increase local circulation, and assist venous return (oxygen-depleted blood going back to the heart).

Probably the easiest variation is two-handed kneading. It's performed by lifting, squeezing, and then releasing tissue. Your entire hand should be in contact with the tissue. The movement is lifting muscle tissue away form the underlying bone.

The variation I use most often is called bilateral petrissage. Say you're working on the back—stand facing the receiver from the side with your feet spread far enough apart to allow you to comfortably move your hips from side to side. Start on the far side of the back by the hips. Grasp tissue with one hand, and, using your thumb as a nearly immobile base, bring your fingers up towards the thumb while still grasping the tissue (be careful not to pinch). As you complete this motion, slide your other hand onto the same area and repeat (remember—lift the tissue!). Continue this all the way up the side of the back. When you get up towards the shoulders move your body so you are facing the top of the receiver's head and do some work on the trapezius muscle (the muscle that is at the top of the back) and the neck. When you've finished with the trapezius and neck keep up the petrissage while moving so you are facing the other side of the receiver's body and continue down the other side of the back. On legs and arms work from thigh to ankle

and shoulder to wrist. As you apply the stroke sway your hips in the same direction that pressure is being applied.

Petrissage, and especially the bilateral variation, is probably the hardest massage stroke to master as well as being hard as fuck to describe with words only. When I'm doing it I just think "lift... lift... lift" in my head, as well as making sure my hips are moving along with the motions of my hands. The most important thing is to grasp and lift as much tissue as you can and working to maintain an even, soothing rhythm.

Friction is applied after you've sufficiently warmed up tissue with effleurage and petrissage. Make sure there is not too much lubricant remaining on the skin when you are ready to apply friction. The intention is for the receiver's skin to move over tissues underneath, rather than just sliding your thumbs, fingers, etc. over the skin. When applying friction always check in with

the person you are massaging. They should not at any point be in pain. Just as with effleurage, when performing friction to legs and arms always apply pressure towards the heart.

Friction is also similar to effleurage in that you can use open palms, knuckles, forearms, elbows, fingertips, and thumbs to execute it. The difference between the two strokes lies mainly in the amount of pressure applied and the speed of them. Basically, you can never go too slow with friction. Even keeping friction stationary works great in some areas. For example, if the receiver is lying on their back and your are working on the back of their neck, you can just curl your fingertips and let gravity apply the pressure. Whatever part of your body you use to apply friction, remember to be mindful of how you are moving. Make sure all the joints from your shoulder to fingertips are as straight as possible and that pressure is coming from your body weight combined with the movement of your legs and torso—not your arms or hands!

One of the most useful aspects of friction is its ability to break up adhesions. With lack of movement, or stress or trauma to an area, muscles fibers can stick together or tendons can stick to tissues they come in contact with. Deep friction can help separate such tissues and keep bodies moving smoothly.

Really, massage is the sort of thing you have to practice a lot to become good at, rather than reading a bunch of books, but hopefully this gives you some good ideas and information. Remember that the intention you give to your touch and the state of mind you are in is much more important than how many fancy techniques

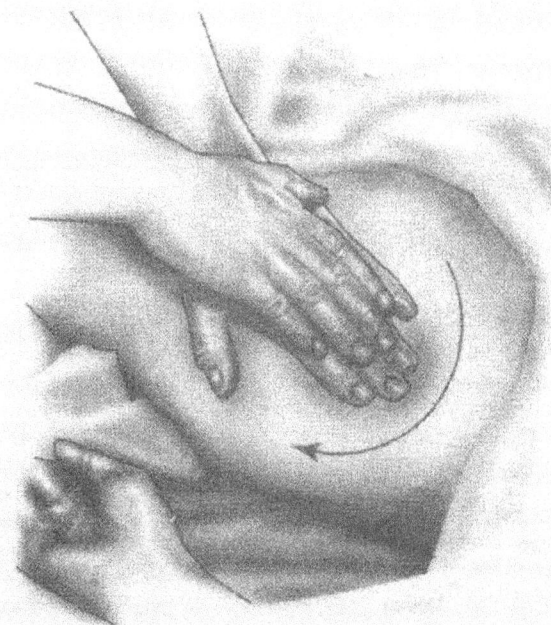

FIGURE 8-5. Deep effleurage to the gluteals using reinforced fingertips.

you know. Just stay relaxed and in tune with what your receiver is feeling, remember to breathe (both massager and massagee!), maintain contact and a steady soothing rhythm and you'll do fine.

—An excellent book on massage/bodywork is *Job's Body* by Deane Juhan. It explores how the body's physiology is affected by bodywork. Even better, it describes in fascinating scientific detail why it makes no sense to discuss the "mind" and "body" as separate, distinct entities.

—If you have any questions about anything I've written, or desire more specific information, feel free to write to me. Really, all you people should just write to me anyway, for anything, and I do mean anything, at all. If you happen to live somewhere near Tacoma and want me to show you some massage stuff in person, or just hang out or something, I'd be happy to.

—I'm working on a vastly expanded version of this article, and hopefully will be able to put together a whole zine about these matters. I'm going to try to get it done by the summer, but we'll see. If you'd be interested in having such a zine, get in touch.

Adam, P.O. Box 208, Kapowsin, WA 98344, USA (dot_4strings@hotmail.com).

Re-Code Your Own Price!

RE-CODE.COM is a free web service that allows its customers to share product information and create barcodes that can be printed and used to re-code items in stores by placing new labels over existing UPC symbols to set a new price—participating in an act of tactical shopping. RE-CODE.COM at its core is a shared database, updateable by our customers. Participation is free and requires no special membership agreements or software download. After entering the website, customers can choose to search and view information in our database currently or add their own collected data to the system. Using our custom Barcode Generator application, barcodes are drawn in real time and made available to the user.

If you like to save money, you've come to the right place! Our unique process of shared database building based on preshopping, recoding, and postshopping, enables you to pay only what you are willing to for the name brand products you want. In the process, we save our customers millions and millions of dollars! Here's the inside scoop on how our revolutionary "Re-Code Your Own Price" service works.

Our customers and community members travel to their local chain stores to collect information about the products the stores carry, when possible noting major brands and their generic equivalents. Using our convenient downloadable Data Collection Sheets, RE-CODE.COM customers are able to easily note UPC ID number, name, product packaging, and price. This information can then be easily added to the RE-CODE.COM supercomputer to help build a shared database. The process of adding original item UPC's and prices to RE-CODE.COM is known as postshopping. Postshopping is critical in building a large database of products for each area of the country. A database which is both ours and yours!

It's a simple concept, but recoding a product's original UPC barcode with another item sold at the same store's code, and with a much more acceptable price, enables tremendous savings for you the customer. By planning your store purchases in advance, and logging on to our website, you can engage in the process of preshopping. Preshopping's value is determined by you the customer, as you search our database for the prices you want to pay at the stores you plan to shop at. Be sure to take note of packaging materials for each product to make the recoding process simpler. Either generate product barcodes on the fly using our custom Barcode Generator application, view search results and cut, copy, and paste resulting barcodes into any graphical layout utility, or find a Pre-formatted Barcode Sheet for a store near you. After locating the codes you want

in one of these three ways, simply print your barcodes at home onto label paper available at most office supply or electronics stores and cut out your codes in preparation for re-coding. We encourage our customers to re-code brand name items with generic item codes. Through this process, the customer pays a more reasonable price for what is a quite similar product. It is best to make only slight adjustments such as these to avoid the notice of our competitors—the chain stores and the major brands they carry.

Checking out is simple. Many stores even offer self-scanning checkouts. This is of course the easiest way to scan your re-coded items undetected. In situations where this is not available, cashiers will assist you through their workplace boredom by only listening for a beep as they scan your item rather than noticing the product name which their register might display. Again, if recoding brand name products using their generic equivalents' UPC codes, it is likely that the registers product name displays will not appear all that different. In one test, both Kellogg's Frosted Flakes ($3.39 US) and Better Valu Sugar Frosted Flakes ($1.69 US) appear with the word Flakes in their name at the register. This helps the cashier to remain focused on the beep rather than the product name as they scan away your savings. Of course, this requires some flexibility on your part, but this is what allows you to save up to 40% on brand-name products every day.

www.re-code.com

Contact: press@re-code.com

Promotional Video:
www.re-code.com/videos.html

Disclaimers: We in no way endorse the theft of products or services. Re-code.com was created as satire. We intend only to call attention to the prevalence of barcodes, and begin a critical discussion about what their pervasiveness means. This is not a product designed to be used in any malicious or illegal manner. Any such use is strictly prohibited. You should not use any of the barcodes available from this site for any illegal activity. They are here for your amusement only.

BE FREE, AT NO FEE, SMASH TOURISM!

Atrophied letterbomb to the editor disguised as prologue to the Scene Reports[1]:

Tourrorist Attacks Increase
U.S., Japan responsible, claims anarchist group

a travelogue supplied by little Marko Polo, age 15. overseas correspondent

Dear friends,

I'm stuck out here in Norway with my parents on this stupid vacation. God, it seems like I could go to the fucking moon with them, and it would still be like being home in New Medford. These people make everything petty and dumb, even fjords and Viking longboats. I know I should feel lucky to be out here—most of my friends back home will never get the chance to see this place, and that's just another level of how fucked up everything is—but this isn't even like *being here*, it's just more being with my family in the fake fucking world they live in.

They share this pathological spectatorship with the rest of their class, as far as I can tell—looking around at all the others here like them. Coming from a milieu where values of *owning* and *appearing* have replaced those of *feeling* and *acting*, these bourgeois vacationers seek diversion in the symbolic possession of parts of the world other than those they normally occupy—a possession they establish by the act of *looking*, "sightseeing." This is the true meaning of the all the photographing and videotaping: the pictures may not be important later on (except for those insufferable

slideshows to which one imagines conquering Roman emperors would have subjected their courts, had they possessed the technology), they may not be taken with any artistic application or intentions, but they serve to establish the tourists as *collectors*—they collect images, just as others collect butterflies. This is the only way the unreconstructed bourgeois family knows to relate itself to foreign things[2]: the beautiful and the wild are quite scenic, but lack meaning until they are hunted, captured, pinned.

The hastily snapped images are preserved, as if in formaldehyde, and the family congratulates itself on knowing "all about" Norway, and/or Sweden, France, Italian architecture and cooking, the wildlife of the Pacific Ocean, the struggles of the first Polar explorers, the troubled childhood of Van Gogh ("and that," intones the tour guide of the slideshow of photos taken from behind a rope under the direction of another tour guide, how's that for post-modernism, "is the very room he spent his first six years in!"). Even more importantly, the lenses never leave the eyes of the tourists in the course of their vacation, literally or figuratively. This mediation is also integral to the tourist experience.

The modern tourist arrives at his calling from a world of control mania, already an expert at protecting

himself to death. The bourgeois insist on being safe wherever they go—not just from actual danger, but from everything not already anticipated, comprehended, controlled. The travel guides and guidebooks, the painstakingly planned itineraries, the safe bubbles of tourist bus and museum and hotel, the armies of salesmen who cater to every fabricated need—all these combine to ensure that being in Oslo or Zimbabwe actually is the same as being in Oklahoma. And yet beneath everything, tourism is still a desperate bid to experience something *different*, something "exotic," which is to say—something not quite as lifeless, meaningless, tedious and banal and insipid as daily life under the tyranny of the hair dryer and the cellular phone[3].

And so the worst tragedy is that tourism destroys the observed as it maintains the alienation of the observers. Just as in the course of their exploits explorers have cut wider and wider swaths through the natural environment (until all that remains of it in some places are fishtanks in museums), the tourist crushes beneath him exactly that which he seeks. The human being in the bourgeois man needs variety, danger, adventure, but the bourgeois in him channels these needs into surrogate enterprises and hedged bets: traveling to France, he still wants to speak English; rafting the

[1] *... or is it the other way 'round?*

[2] *Witness ecotourism—essentially the idea that a little fragment of an ecosystem deserves to be left alone as long as it is entertaining to the bourgeoisie. They go on vacation to ooh and aah at exotic wildlife when they won't even recycle bottles in their own kitchens. They speak about "special" places that should be made parks and reserves, neglecting the fact that the very ground they live on was once just as wild and beautiful, before it was destroyed by the lifestyles they refuse to question.*

[3] *Indeed, when one listens closely to the ghost stories shared by bourgeois kids on the summer vacation backpack/hostel circuit, about kidnappings and stolen kidneys, it becomes clear that they are practically fantasies, legends of something real and endangering—engaging!—happening to someone just like you, told in desperate faith that something crazy and new is still possible in even this world, and couched in the only terms at the disposal of bourgeois youth confronted with the unfamiliar: terror!*

rapids, he still needs a release to sign and an "historic path" to follow (as all meaningful experience is held hostage in the past, or in the exotic lives of other peoples); landing on Mars, he would look around for a sign announcing the next guided tour. Wielding the power of the new angry god, Dollar, he is able to compel everyone he encounters to provide him with this safety net of chains. Wherever the tourist tramples, soon little remains but the manifestation of his own creative and cultural bankruptcy (visit Cancun, Mexico for proof). Whole cultures have been annihilated in his wake—tourism is, as the venerable master points out, the descendant not of ancient quests and pilgrimages but rather of colonial imperialism.

In the absence of the real thing, the tourist is left with simulation. Even the most wild and crazy travel handbooks ("Europe on twenty cents a day!" "Antarctica for hitchhikers!") are just museums of fossilized adventure by the time they go into circulation—as if there could ever be such a thing as a "guide to adventure," when adventure is precisely that which happens off the map. The most the daring tourist can hope to find is the cooling trail left by the *real* adventurers before her, the ones who embarked without maps. The others have to make do with monuments and museums and theme parks, forever asking rhetorical questions ("I wonder what it was/would be like to...?") without connecting their own lives to the possibilities they unconsciously raise. Perhaps they buy more guidebooks, seeking characteristically to purchase the solutions to their needs embodied as products—rather than shaking off the alienation and doing something to find them.

The common quality that unifies all tourists is *disconnection*: they are totally uninvolved in what they see, pursuing as they do the sight alone without all the entanglements and liabilities that come with real life. They can passively vote on their favorite place or painting, or, at most, develop some paternalistic, picturesque Hallmark sentiment that "exotic" environments or cultures should be "protected,"

but it never occurs to them that they *are interacting* with the worlds they would view with the same detachment one watches television—thus they are unable to take responsibility for the role they play in eradicating them, or for that matter, for their own spiritual malaise and restlessness. They could be at home—or even where they are—*giving* themselves to something, becoming involved in some part of life, acknowledging their own wishes for the world and believing in them, holding themselves answerable for the effects of their actions and in so doing making changes in the world deliberately for once; instead, they vacation in the never-never land of disconnection, extending their own alienation to the furthest corners of the globe. This alienation replicates itself there, driving them to ever more expensive ocean cruises and souvenirs in a listless addict's pursuit of stimulation—when all it would take to break the spell would be for them to commit themselves to some value or dream, one that would drag them into danger and heartbreak and ragged glory and all those other things one must experience to live an engaged, fulfilling life. They could do that without ever booking flights or packing suitcases. The fact that they are able to maintain their distance from life ten thousand miles from home as easily as they can in the midst of the inertia of their daily routines is a testament to the total and global triumph of universal self-estrangement. Capitalism, oppression, colonialism, though responsible for creating this state of affairs, are mere superficial problems beside it. Ultimately, tourism is not a leisure activity but a *way of living*, an expression of the vacuum at the heart of consumer society. What the executive does in the Louvre and the Himalayas and Jamaica is what he does in his own neighborhood when he drives past woodlands being cut to make way for new gas stations and condominiums. What it will take to snap him out of this trance—to make him relate himself to the others around him, and the transformations taking place constantly in the world—well, the fate of the planet relies on us discovering that, doesn't it.

To do so, we have to follow the leads in our own lives, locate the parts of ourselves that are not yet totally detached, the loves and longings that still stir within us. The truth is, I do long to travel—my heart still leaps at the thought of dropping everything and setting out free and empty-handed across this unfamiliar landscape, and I don't think this is simply the bourgeois spectator within me. Travel is fundamental to human liberty and romance: it was the original state of our species, and we still long for it. It is in traveling that we can shake off our old selves and hunt down others that have been waiting in alternate worlds—it is in travel that freedom is possible, for without new horizons we would simply repeat the well-practiced choices we have already made, in thrall to inertia if no other master.

So, with all the world standardized under cultural/corporate imperialism and technological/industrial capitalism, when we bear the seeds of these poisons within our own unwilling, colonized breasts, where is there left to go? How are we now to travel? The answer is: *in place*. The adventures of the future will be created, not by Westerners who destroy worlds in their desperate bid to escape the Western one, but by people who seize familiar parts of this planet and make them unfamiliar. Washington, D.C. could become Paris, 1968 overnight, if a group were ready to make the right adjustments; a sense of one's own importance and capabilities can transform even a suburban bedroom into the setting of the greatest of real life epics. Really, this was always the case: one either regards the world passively, or approaches it as a participant—all things hinge on this, whether you are at home or at the bottom of the sea. In traveling in place, we can rediscover that art of *participation* which is essential for any adventuring... and with any luck, my children will never have to write an article like this about me.

Hey, send me some mail, it'd be cool to find it waiting for me when I get back—write to Spoiled Brats c/o CrimethInc. Trust Fund Army

Walk down the streets of Durham or Quebec City today; chances are you'll find it hard to imagine that anything is possible there other than buying and selling, impatience in traffic jams, the petty business of everyday life that consumes all time and energy. Resistance to routine is shut up, shut out, shut in, shut down in order of the danger it presents (sure, you can still pose as a threat, but that doesn't make pose a threat, let alone really pose one). No one in sight is suffering—the homeless and poor have already been hounded out by the police—and for those who remain, it's out of the question; suffering here, for something one really cared about, would be a triumph, unimaginable in these circumstances. That is to say—for the modern law-abiding citizen, hell is overhead.

But this isn't the only reality, the only possibility. Just a few months ago, tens of thousands of us were fighting the police for those same streets, to get a little space and time to prove that—and, for a few hours and blocks at least, we did. It's the nature of status quo that it appears unassailable; but don't be fooled, disturbance is brewing, and will be back again... one day to liberate the place you are reading at this very moment.

Uproar is our only music.

News from the Front

quebec city

EYEWITNESS ANALYSIS:
FREE TRADE AREA OF THE AMERICAS
[F.T.A.A.] SUMMIT APRIL 19-22 2001

WHAT HAPPENED IN QUEBEC?

In short, a handful of autonomous, cooperating groups took to the streets and fought the pigs until practically the entire city was fighting with us in autonomous, cooperating groups of their own. This is an unprecedented event in the recent history of the anti-capitalist struggle in North America.

In this report, I'm going to concentrate on how and why this was possible. If you want to know specific details about the F.T.A.A., the summit, or the events that transpired before and during it, there are plenty of other sources that can give you that information. Here I'm assuming you have already found access to that information, and also that you already know what you have at stake in resisting global "free trade"... and capitalism itself, for that matter.

THE CONDITIONS THAT MADE THIS POSSIBLE

Quebec, the French-speaking region of an otherwise English-speaking nation, has a long-standing independence movement, and natives harbor some resentment against both their government and the cultural standardization imposed by the nearby United States. This proved to be really decisive in the events of the weekend, though few demonstrators saw in advance how important this would turn out to be.

The Canadian government, fearful of another demonstration like the one that took place in Seattle during the World Trade Organization meeting,

had a concrete wall with a chain-link fence atop it built entirely around the center of Quebec City, and closed off the space within it entirely to everyone not possessed of a resident's card. The wall was built at great expense to Canadian taxpayers, and trained riot police were sent in from other regions of Canada, armed with water cannons, new stun guns[1], tear gas, etc. All this infuriated the locals: not only were a group of foreign leaders invading their city to discuss matters of "free trade" (which, it's an open secret, is sought by the rich so they can become richer at everyone else's expense) in a working class region of Canada, but their own city was being taken away from them for this purpose, and they were being treated like illegal aliens in it.

In addition to local outrage, another important ingredient was the presence of a great number of protesters from a wide variety of backgrounds. Because thousands of the protesters in attendance were seen as coming from a center-left position (i.e. being "mainstream," according to the old myth), and the media in attendance had not already stigmatized them as marginalized extremists, the police forces had a stake in being seen as restrained. The protests at the presidential inauguration last January took place in similar conditions. Then, as now, this made it possible for the small minority who were prepared from the outset to use confrontational tactics to do so without being immediately subdued by police violence and arrested—and this time, thanks to local outrage and the fact that no one else was offering an approach that actually contested the source of everyone's frustration, these tactics were soon appropriated by practically everybody there, even locals who hadn't thought of themselves as "protesters" at all.

THE ORGANIZING

To my knowledge, this was the first major demonstration on this continent in which a large part of the organizing was done according to anarchist procedures, including a sympathy for what was referred to as "a diversity of tactics." For a thorough discussion of this subject, consult the CrimethInc. report from the demonstrations in Sao Paulo, 2000, which appeared in the previous issue of Inside Front as *The Violence/Non-Violence Question: How (and Why) to Transcend It*. In Quebec, the "diversity of tactics" included property destruction, provocation

[1] It's interesting to note that while Canadian police have been required until now to test their stun weapons upon themselves, so as to personally know their capabilities and effects, this requirement was waived for the new weapons they received for this event—explicitly on account of the weapons being "too dangerous"! And—let's not forget—these are the same police who were captured on videotape only a few months earlier using Q-tips to apply pepper spray to the eyes of protesters who were already locked down and unable to move or protect themselves. "Protect and Serve" indeed!

and aggressive self-defense. The two French Canadian groups organizing for the protest, C.L.A.C. and C.A.S.A., that accepted this approach, took a lot of heat from the more traditional, cuddlier and cuter, more liberal and authoritarian organization, S.A.L.A.M.I., which, predictably, reserved the right to tell protesters exactly what to do and how to do it. We'll discuss in a couple paragraphs what the results of this kind of organization were for those who permitted themselves to be so controlled.

C.L.A.C. and C.A.S.A. took the wise approach of separating the demonstration into different actions and areas according to level of risk: green for no danger of arrest, yellow for some danger of arrest for nonviolent civil disobedience action, and red for tactics of deliberate provocation (such as attacking the police fence). The green and yellow areas were charted on a map of Quebec, affinity groups at the spokescouncil meetings identified themselves as taking green or yellow approaches (no one spoke about red groups or actions, for obvious reasons, until the action was taking place), and this helped to reassure everyone involved that they knew exactly what risk they were incurring. As it turned out, most people were ready to go a lot farther than they'd expected once the possibilities of the situation were clear, and the police violated their own commitment to respecting the green zone, so the color-level categories were pretty much meaningless by the time the demonstration got going; but they served their purpose ahead of time by making everyone comfortable with setting their own level of involvement and risk.

Because the organizers declared in advance that they were ready for and supportive of "diversity of tactics," most everyone in attendance came prepared to accept this, too: first, those who came knew what to expect, and second, the fact that the organizers were comfortable with this helped others not to be

uptight about it. It only happened a couple times at the spokescouncil meetings before and during the demonstration that some stubborn loyalist to left-wing authoritarian tradition brought up the issue of whether it was wise to "allow" people to use their own judgment about what tactics to apply; and both times, thanks to the fact that C.L.A.C. and C.A.S.A. had already established that they saw this as a non-issue, everyone was able to simply ignore the interruption and concentrate on practical matters.

Planning for earlier demonstrations has often been characterized by endless, pointless, symbolic debates about whether or not organizing committees should "give permission" to protesters to use direct action tactics like property destruction. This time, a lot of time and trouble was saved by acknowledging from the beginning that demonstrators were going to do whatever they believed was right, sanctioned or not by self-appointed authorities, and that the role of organizers should be simply to help coordinate cooperation between different groups. That the demonstration proceeded without any of the tens of thousands of demonstrators present doing anything really stupid to hurt the interests of the others there, despite the fact that there was no "official organization" issuing rules and mandates, is important—it simply proves that anarchy works. And if there are still some who believe that anything other than obedience to rules (*their* rules!) imposed by a centralized power constitutes "ineffective" demonstrating (let alone "violation of their rights"!!), this just shows that some have yet to understand that actual democracy means giving up your "right" to command others.

C.L.A.C. and C.A.S.A. deserve accolades for the hard work they did to make everything possible—they did speaking tours across the continent to raise awareness, helped U.S. citizens work out schemes to cross the Canadian border (a few even got married just to give wedding-invitation-clutching U.S. activists a legitimate reason for entry), arranged for food and housing for the tens of thousands of people converging upon their city. The housing was especially important: at many earlier protests, like the I.M.F./World Bank protest in Washington, D.C. a year ago, traveling activists who had no place to sleep were arrested before the action began for sleeping in their cars or on the street. One indispensable center of activity was the university campus, which hosted thousands of demonstrators in the gym (the sight of so many bodies stretched out across its vast floor in the half light was surreal and beautiful), and lots of important organizational meetings as well in other buildings. Hecate only knows

how those kids persuaded the university to receive all these travelers who had already been branded enemies of the state before they arrived. Individuals from C.L.A.C. and C.A.S.A. were also not afraid to embrace illegal tactics openly (as they did on Friday night at the spokescouncil meeting after the first day of action, when they supported the idea that the next day's actions should concentrate on attacking the fence)—a few of them landed in legal trouble for this, and they deserve our support for the risks they have taken.

Finally—the remaining crucial contribution of the C.L.A.C. and C.A.S.A. organizing was that the march and day of action they organized fell the day *before* the march organized by the more "mainstream," well-behaved S.A.L.A.M.I. Summer of 2000, at the protests around the Republican National Convention in Philadelphia, the day of direct action came after all the other events had ended—so the only activists left in the city were the ones already perceived by the police as "terrorists" (even if they were only armed with puppets!), and the mass arrests and police violence that followed came as no surprise. This time, holding the [first] day for direct action before the main event meant that the events of that day set the atmosphere for the next.

BLACK BLOC PREPARATION AND ACTION: PROVOCATION, OR SELF-DEFENSE?

This was the most organized, best armed and equipped, and, as I've explained above, most broadly supported Black Bloc I have ever witnessed. Considering that many of those in its ranks were in a foreign country, some of them illegally and even with outstanding arrest warrants, I was amazed at how confrontational they had prepared to be: people had brought bolt cutters (for the hated fence) and similar tools, projectiles such as hockey pucks, slingshots and marbles, helmets and homemade body armor, larger shields, and similar equipment. It turned out to be the right decision.

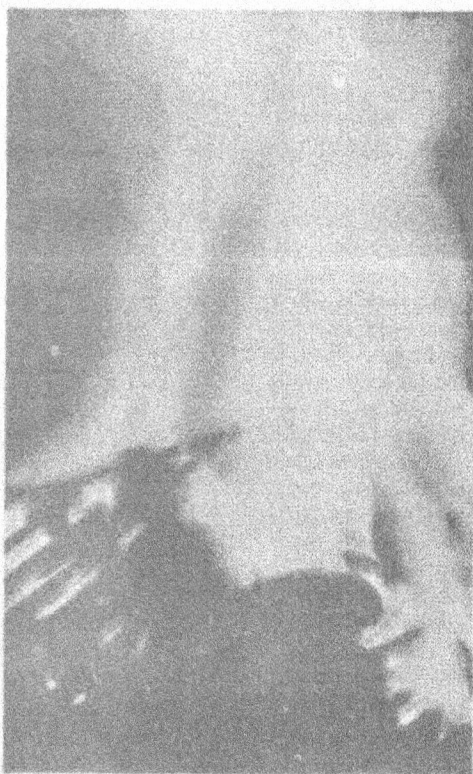

Friday's march began at the university, neither accompanied by nor—strangely enough—harassed by the police, who remained concentrated around the fence both Friday and Saturday (this was fortuitous, for it meant we could move around the rest of the city without serious fear of arrest—which has not been the case at many earlier demonstrations). The Black Bloc was dispersed among the crowd, already disguised but not clearly identified as a group.

Shortly before the march arrived at the fence around central Quebec, those (few, as it turned out) who wished to remain in the green sector split off from it.

The others proceeded on, and as soon as they arrived at the broad square which bordered on the fence, the 'Bloc came together and moved immediately to attack the barrier. Within seconds, a wide section of it was torn down—something not thought possible by most of the protesters in attendance—and a few passed through it. The police quickly appeared in greater numbers from within, firing tear gas; the rest of the day and following night was given over to back-and-forth struggles between the police, who sought more to hold a line than to advance, and the confrontational activists who threw projectiles at them and were reinforced by the numbers of less confrontational activists.

A few might describe the Black Bloc tactics as deliberate provocation, and blame them for embroiling the others at the protest in more violent conflict than they were prepared for, but I would describe what happened differently. First of all, had the wall itself not been challenged, the protest would not have been given any attention by the police, the media, or the locals—furthermore, it would have been unclear what there *was* to do instead: the experience of wandering around all day holding signs in a designated protest zone, ignored by the rest of the world, would have been demoralizing to everyone. Some of those who did attempt pacifist actions such as lockdowns in other zones of downtown Quebec that day related that evening at the spokescouncil that their actions had seemed pointless—the delegates to the summit were already inside the perimeter fence, and had they not been, they could have been delivered with helicopters even if all the roads had been blocked. This was the reasoning of a number of participants in the Black Bloc, too: since it was not possible to stop the summit by keeping the delegates out, they undertook instead to make the whole experience as inconvenient as possible for the heads of state and their lackeys. The next day, in fact, the summit had to be called off until Sunday, because there was so much tear gas in the air around downtown Quebec that it entered the duct system of the building in which the meetings were taking place. So as it turned out, the somewhat antiquated tactics of street fighting turned out to be the most effective for this situation.

But back to the provocation question: clearly the Black Bloc were not the only ones interested in attacking the wall—after the first day of action, at the spokescouncil meeting Friday night, when there were few if any participants present from the 'Bloc, it was decided, by people who had earlier seemed much more timid about doing this, that the next day's actions should concentrate on again attacking the wall. Thus the 'Bloc helped protesters to feel more confident about doing what they already wanted to do, by showing that it was possible. The chief functions the 'Bloc served, thus, proved to be not provocation, but rather *defense* and *demonstration*. *Defense*, because they formed the front lines that protected everyone else from the police. The police, if my experience is correct, had not just assembled tear gas, water cannons, concussion grenades, plastic bullets, and such devices for show—they intended to use them to break up whatever demonstration took place. They were prevented from doing so precisely because the Black Bloc was so organized and ready to fight: every one of hundreds of tear gas canisters shot at the crowds was immediately thrown back in their faces by an initially small number of courageous gas-masked 'Blocers, to such an extent that sometimes one could only tell

"THE ANARCHISTS WHO THREW SNOWBALLS AT ATTACKING RIOT POLICE ON RENÉ LÉVESQUE, WHO FOUGHT THE BATTLES OF THE BARRICADES AROUND THE LATEST BERLIN WALL AND CHOKED BY THE TENS OF THOUSANDS UPON THE TEAR GAS OF THE TOTALITARIAN REGIME, REFUSED TO CONFINE THEIR REVOLT TO THE PRIVATE WORLD DESCRIBED BY PUNK ROCK LYRICS OR THE PUBLIC WORLD DEFINED BY LEFTIST PROPAGANDA. THEY DEMANDED JURISDICTION OVER THEIR OWN HEARTS AND HEADS, INSTANT GRATIFICATION AND PERMANENT REVOLUTION... LACKING THE BOURGEOIS PROPRIETIES OF THEIR INSTRUCTORS AND LABOR LEADERS, THEY TURNED THEIR UPRISING INTO A FESTIVAL OF SPONTANEITY, PLAY, AND SOLIDARITY." –GNOME CHOMSKY, A PEOPLE'S HISTORY OF THE UNITED STATES (AND TERRITORIES)

THAT IS TO SAY—REVOLUTIONARIES MAKE LOVE AND WAR.

where the police lines were by the cloud of poison surrounding them; the police feared to close in for arrests, because of the constant shower of rocks, glass bottles, broken concrete, and even molotov cocktails that the streetfighters maintained. I suggest that the other role of the 'Bloc was *demonstration*, because the tactics they used were available to everyone who recognized how effective they were. As I'll discuss in a couple paragraphs, the Black Bloc began as a couple hundred people, and ended up being thousands only a day and a half later.

Mainstream media always praise the pigs for their "restraint" at demonstrations like this, which seems to me to be sheer stupidity: the pigs are fucking *employees*, they do what they're told (especially in front of the cameras!), they don't deserve credit for anything they do—that's what is so disgusting about them. In a situation where everyone else present was taking responsibility for themselves, acknowledging their part in what goes on in this world and acting accordingly, the pigs were the only ones present who were still using the Nuremberg defense to do whatever their masters ordered, even when it meant shooting searing tear gas canisters at the heads of unarmed, non-violent middle-aged mothers (I know this because I witnessed my good friend, an unarmed, non-violent, middle-aged mother, get hit by one such deliberate police attack). If anyone should get credit for "restraint," it's *us*—we always show good sportsmanship, we work willingly with vastly inferior technology (seriously, marbles versus plastic bullets?), we give everyone a David against Goliath show just to demonstrate how much more courageous and intelligent we are. I'm sure of the thousands of people at the demonstration, at least a couple hundred were gun owners—but we didn't ever defend ourselves with lethal weapons, even though they were attacking us with unprovoked violence that would have given anyone cause for armed self defense in a court of law. That's because we're nice people, responsible to each other and even merciful to our enemies, and they're lower than fucking worms. Watch the way they move their bodies in those Halloween costumes and you'll see the murderous machismo of power-addict slaves. Anyway, back to the subject.

Saturday was the "official" protest day for the more "mainstream" organizers, principally the Canadian unions (the "other government," I've been calling them since that day), who demonstrated just how absurd it is to organize anti-authoritarian protests in authoritarian ways. They arranged a giant union march, departing from a place in Quebec City away from all the action and moving through the empty industrial areas, where there was no one to even see them marching, to a

dead end in a park where a small band was playing. The tens of thousands who participated in this march couldn't have felt more like they were wasting their time—even the mainstream newspapers reported that it was all the union marshals could do to keep the workers marching in line away from the real action, let alone chanting along with the monosyllables blaring from megaphones attached to the cars in which their "leaders" rode, resting their precious feet. Anyone could see the difference between their approach to politics and ours by comparing the amount of freedom available to their marchers to the open relationships between autonomous demonstrators on our side of the city.

Meanwhile, we kept up our street war in central Quebec, strengthened by new numbers now surrounding and attacking the wall from all sides. Those who had thought they only wanted to hold signs now backed up masked kids tearing apart the sidewalk to make projectiles. Now, I've always been critical of violence, because it's something that you can turn on but you can't turn off; even more than other tools, it tends to control and manipulate those who apply it. But this somehow didn't feel like violence: everyone who was involved, everyone who was participating, valued the various contributions of the others present, whether they were setting police on fire, providing medical attention to the injured, or simply watching from a distance—everyone felt united and safe with each other. The violence directed from all the human beings present at the only ones there who still refused to be human didn't contaminate us.

PIVOTAL MOMENT

Then, in the middle of Saturday afternoon, something happened that was of pivotal importance, which probably went unnoticed by almost everyone else there. During a lull in the streetfighting, a segment of the Black Bloc proceeded to a multinational bank and smashed all its windows in. At this point a large number of local street kids had congregated, not as protesters, but simply to watch the unfolding events; these locals were sympathetic to the foreigners fighting the police, simply because they were fighting the natural enemy of street kids everywhere, but they were still suspicious of the activists on the grounds that, like the delegates and the pigs, they were foreign invaders. Nothing the protesters had done until this moment raised their wrath—but, having no prior experience with the rationale of property destruction, the sight of a bunch of foreigners smashing up windows in their city enraged them. They followed the 'Bloc all the way around, uh, the block, picking up weapons and threatening them². A couple 'Bloc members tried

² At this point, something occurred which is too funny to disappear into history untold. The locals, following the 'Bloc and harassing them in French and with the little English they knew ("fookers!"), passed by an older liberal guy with a beard, who took great pains to explain to them: "No, they're not fuckers, it's just a bad tactic." Appropriating what they must have misunderstood as a term of more biting abuse, they continued following the 'Bloc, shouting "bad tak-teek! bad tak-teek!"

ONE ORDINARY WEEKEND IS MORE BLOODY

to reason with them—the language barrier proved insurmountable, as did the machismo barrier, and both of them got punched in the face.

These two kids are the ones most responsible for the success of the demonstration, though nobody knows it. They had the humility and focus to turn and simply walk away when this happened, which is fucking amazing, especially considering the reputation the Black Bloc itself has for machismo. If they had not done this, the whole weekend would have been ruined, and direct action activism would have been set back a decade—for the visiting activists would have ended up in a riot with the locals, and every possibility of something positive happening would have been lost.

Given some time to cool off, the locals sent a couple of their number to speak to kids from the 'Bloc. It turned out they really wanted to fight the pigs together with these foreigners, and they respected what they [we] were doing, but needed an assurance that these kids weren't just here to trash their city. This given, on the conditional terms which any anarchist has to speak in when "representing" a larger group, the episode was over and everyone could focus again on the real enemy.

I'm not opposed to property destruction, of course—if it were up to me, every corporate store, office, and factory would be burned to the ground by tomorrow morning—but it was critical that the 'Bloc kids recognize that, under these circumstances, it was an ineffective tactic, because the locals did not understand what it was intended to do. Had they insisted on sticking to 'Bloc dogma, catastrophe would have resulted. Instead, everyone returned to the front lines, and the action reached its heart-quickening climax.

ESCALATION

As the sun set over Quebec, the police slowly pushed forward to the north, until they were stopped in a standoff at the foot of a freeway overpass. At this point, practically everyone had their faces covered, for protection from the tear gas that filled the air; at the same time, people who had been timid before had lost their fear—from two days of watching police hit in the

head with bottles, of seeing supposedly impregnable walls torn down with ropes, of breathing tear gas until it no longer intimidated them. It was impossible to tell now who had been from the Black Bloc and who had just joined the struggle: formerly apolitical Quebec street youth manned the front lines, throwing back tear gas canisters and rocks as they had seen the activists doing, thrilling in the feeling of reclaiming their city from the powers of police and capital. They hid behind makeshift barricades, running up close to the police line to throw molotov cocktails into it, showing superhuman courage in the face of the riot troops that had had them terrified twenty four hours earlier. Behind these kids, over three thousand people of all ages and backgrounds stood on the freeway, beating out a deafening rhythm on every surface available in support of the street warriors. The street signs, which only two days before had told them where to go and how fast, became sounding boards for their frustration and their conviction that this conflict was worth fighting; the concrete, which had cut them off from the soil beneath their feet and reinforced the corporate propaganda on every street corner proclaiming that the only possible condition was capitalism, competition and cultural standardization and mind-numbing work—that very concrete was torn up to become hammers to play that music of revolt, or else be thrown, carried on the echoes of that percussion, into the faces of the insect-like riot pigs across the road. A piece of North America had been transformed into Palestine, a first world Intifada now raging such as only the most idealistic punks and radicals had dared dream of—and immediately comprehensible and worthwhile to all present.

Below the freeway, in the activist camp that had once been part of the green zone, free food was shared, hundreds danced joyously in circles; spirits were higher than they'd ever been for parades or holidays. People who had never been exposed to the do-it-yourself values of sharing and self-determination immediately apprehended what was going on. It seemed the entirety of the old world was about to puncture and collapse.

Who among us has not spent hours, weeks, whole years of life that, at the end, left its nothing to show but the physical fact that we survived, that we lived through them? This moment justified even those sad, squandered years—even those weary ones among us who had slogged through decades of tedium and absurdity were vindicated: we had finally arrived at this, the first threshold of childhood. The past behind us that had seemed so senseless, the future ahead unknowable and all the more menacing as we made out handcuffs on the belts of the police, all this was worth it, justified into eternity, so we could live this danger, this freedom, this feeling of breaking through the skin of the world.

There is another world, a secret one made up of all our unlived dreams and unacted impulses, all those parts of ourselves which find no point of entry into the one that is—it waits, simmering, ready to boil over at six billion different pressure points. When it did, that afternoon, we drank tear gas with gratitude and abandon, we were energized as people sometimes are when the power goes out or hurricanes come—neither plastic bullets nor water cannons could daunt us, for we were living as we had always known we should. The music we made together, beating out our own cadences on the sheet metal of the city, was the eruption of our individual longings into the material world; united in their singularities, they formed a symphony no composer could have authored. It surrounded us, deafening, greater than ourselves; when we closed our eyes, it sounded like singing, like a vast unearthly choir above us.

I would have liked for that song to have gone on forever, to have been our lives. Editing this, now almost two years later, my ears are still ring with those rhythms; perhaps they are just ringing, as ears do after great noises... or perhaps the beat goes on.

That day, for the hours we traded in the currencies of courage and conviction rather than cash and compliance, we were able to cast off all consideration of exchange in our *bodies*, and the space we moved through, as well as our minds: we saw capitalism incapacitated. Better we should see it decapitated!

THE VALUE OF WHAT HAPPENED

We didn't, it's true. We almost did, though, and anyone who tells you different wasn't there like we were there. For a world revolution to take place, there would have to be events going on in every city at once, twice as intense as those taking place in Quebec City around nightfall on April 21st. That probably won't happen for another decade or two. So—let's talk about what was valuable about what *did* happen.

Well, first of all, it got the F.T.A.A. in the news—duh. Not that the corporate-controlled newspapers are ever going to tell the truth about it or "free trade," for that matter, but at least those who read the newspapers have since had the concept in their vocabulary, and we, thus, a starting place from which to raise the questions we need to. Second, we got some great experience to employ in future demonstrations. Third, we didn't suffer quite as crushing a tally of arrests as we have at some demonstrations, thanks to the defense on the part of the Black Bloc—this means we had less to recover from, fewer hassles to drain our energy and attention.

All those obvious things out of the way—the important thing is that everyone there, the local non-activists especially, got a demonstration of what anarchy is, how it works, how individuals can work together in large enough numbers to overpower the forces of control marshaled against them. The "revolution" isn't some far-off single moment, anyway, it's not the crux of history Marx talked about—it's a process going on all the time, everywhere, wherever there is a struggle between hierarchical power and human freedom. In Quebec, I was part of the largest-scale manifestation of mass cooperation and struggle against control I've ever experienced; I've seen this before, hundreds of times, I've chosen a life of pursuing it, so this particular weekend may not have been as absolutely transforming for me as it was for those who hadn't recognized such a thing going on before—but it was still something amazing, which I will remember clearly until I go to my grave, even if I live through "the revolution" itself first.

In moments like this, living becomes something like music is for the musicians who improvise together: everyone contributes their own theme, but rather than a conflict, a cacophony, the different elements combine to form something much greater and more compelling than the sum of the individual parts. In this sense, the weekend in Quebec was important to me above all because it was a sort of pilgrimage, to a moment of anarchy as irreplaceable as all such moments are.

That's all for the memoirs—now it's time to get out there and create new adventures, touch off new confrontations with our oppressors. Until capital capitulates, yours—C.W.C. Rioters' Bloc

See you on the streets!

THAN A MONTH

OF INSURRECTION.

genoa
G8 PROTESTS, JULY 2001

[Editor's Note: Tragically, this is only the first half, in unrefined draft form, of the more massive scene report my friend was going to submit to this issue. The second half was to cover this person's Bakuninesque flight through the Alps to escape the police crackdown following the demonstrations, including idyllic hiking scenes and a life-threatening thunder storm atop a mountain peak. But, shortly after the following text arrived, when I was clamoring, as we editors are wont to do, for the rest of it, I received an unnerving email from my friend with references to police investigations ("I'll write you back if I'm still free after this week—they've invaded the house, and...")—and then, nothing, no responses since, and I haven't been able to get any more information. Let's hope my friend is safe, somewhere, and has merely sworn off email or something like that... As for you, dear reader, who may want to participate in the same level of resistance but not under any circumstances to risk being "disappeared," fear not: the more of us take the step of action, the more difficult it will be for them to identify and apprehend each of us. I hope we can one day look back to the trying events in Genoa as a difficult coming-of-age for the new generation of anti-capitalists.]

"I've often wondered if the urge to destroy is really the desire to do away with a way of living that does not bring us joy"—Derrick Jensen

"...[T]heir protest will continue because it is a biological necessity. 'By nature,' the young are in the forefront of those who live and fight for Eros against Death... Today the fight for life, the fight for Eros, is the political fight."—Herbert Marcuse

As the needle descends onto the circular vinyl, I'm resurrecting the memories that were once scored one and a half years ago in the streets of Genoa. The music I'm playing is the new Godspeed You Black Emperor! record, and as the effect of this record escalates, its sound waves remind me of the effects of tear gas, the sound of breaking glass, the sound of people, the image of death, life and fire, the feelings of danger. Accusations of a desire to be associated with the romance of insurgence and insurrection can be forwarded to my address, and after all, as they say, "Love can be found at the end of a gun."

The memory I am referring to occurred in the summer of 2001 in the Italian city of Genoa; where the autocrats of Western Civilization gathered to make yet more decisions on our behalf. This is my story of events—they may or may not be true, but I think it's important to settle rumors, discuss tactics, and ultimately see where we can go from here; and hopefully this account will be appropriate for this. (For another account from the affinity group I was part of please refer to the chapter "The Tracks of our Tears" by Jazz in the book On Fire: The Battle of Genoa and the Anti-Capitalist Movement.)

July 2001—We catch the train from the UK to the French town of Nice and sleep in the street for the night. The following morning we're on a train heading towards the France/Italy border, anticipating the border guards' usual antagonism, but thankfully after a brief delay we arrive in Genoa. We dress accordingly, trying to blend in to as "backpackers" to avoid the eyes of the Law. We then manage to find our way to the Genoa Social Forum convergence centre (GSF—the GSF would by the end of the week win my "liberal enemy of the week award"). As the bus drives through the city I feel like Spartacus approaching the Roman Empire; I glance out the windows—I see fences being erected, police patrolling the streets in squads, helicopters, armored vehicles, and cars. It is all my nightmares of a police state that could only exist in the most pessimistic of science fiction novels actualizing themselves in my reality.

The GSF advise us to stay in a park about a 2km walk along the promenade; a park that has been designated a campsite for the duration of the summit. We set up our tents, wander, acquire some food, talk, and rest. I people-watch the others in the park-cum-campsite; a gathering sense of surrealism interests me in the locals that use the park to walk dogs, lounge in the shade and sun and play tennis.

That evening a meeting is called to organize camp security (not from ourselves, but from the Italian pigs). We discuss why we need to be prepared—especially after the Stockholm police tactic of storming the places where people slept; a gate rota is sorted out, iron bars collected to secure the gate, and an alarm decided upon in case of a raid. (Although there were small groups of people that said that the State could not possibly raid us!)

We meet several English-speaking anarchists, and begin to work out how to achieve our intentions in Genoa. Stories and lives are shared on the beach as we begin to formulate our plans. We form an affinity group of eight of us, all ready to be black-clad.

The most exciting part prior to the weekend of action was the meeting up and networking around the city, where we had to find quaint streets so as not to be stopped by cops (we just didn't want to be unnecessarily harassed), and then met other anarchists to get our tactics understood so we were all fully aware of the affinity groups' intentions. I met many people, probably some of whom I'll never meet again, but just the feeling of a connection because of our desire was an unquestionable moment. We eventually had some idea of how the day of action on Friday was going to be constructed. Some groups would attack symbols of capital such as banks and the rich, some would deliberately attack cops to draw away and concentrate their forces, and others would attempt to pull down fences and attack the "Red Zone" (à la Quebec City actions). We decided ourselves to head towards the Red Zone. That evening, when many people had gathered for social functions, in the cover of darkness and Mediterranean storms we did our best to gather wooden posts, ropes, iron bars, body armor and anything else to "complete our mission." To this day I will always remember the rain storm. The rain was heavy and loud enough for us to carry out everything that we wanted to, but the heat of the local climate created the kind of rain that you could only want more of, how it seemed to find its way into every part of your body, how it dropped into my eyes from my hair. The following day was a relaxed affair of chatting, cooking food, scouting maps and sun bathing. In the evening was the first mass demonstration, against the EU laws on asylum seekers and border controls. It was the first time we would get to estimate how many people were gathered here. We found our way into the menagerie of green, black and red flags and began our tour of Genoa. The mass of people must have been into six figures, and the anarchist bloc was a massive turn out, around 6-8,000 participants—and part of me was wondering whether this was everyone. The demo ended without conflict; it was really a wander in the streets.

The next morning I awoke to start making makeshift body armor that would fit beneath my clothes. I used a cut up sleeping mat and drainage pipes, and many meters of duct tape. All being well, it wasn't my intention to have to use it—I was relying on predicting the situations, and the speed at which I can run—it was more precautionary than anything else. I think in the future, skate and BMX pads are a better solution for this kind of body armor; I did have a bike helmet, and many people had invested in motorcycle helmets. Each affinity group had one person go to a "camp meeting," and then it dawned on me. I looked around. The majority of people that were staying in the camp site were indeed a portion of the Black Bloc, and to this day this was one of the best coincidences I've ever been in. Our intention as a camp was to join in the COBAS demo (a European group of revolutionary Marxists), and then go and do our separate things from there. After some delay we left the camp en masse. We were amazed that this many people dressed in black did not get one ounce of police attention, and we were deceiving the Law. As we descended into the town, calls of "No Justice No Peace—Fuck the Police," "No Borders No Nations— Fuck Deportation" rang from the streets. Once in the town center we realized that there was very little continuity anywhere, no organized marches that we could join, there was just a mass of people, and the only conclusion was that there was already a riot in full flow. This was damaging to our plans, but there was nothing we could do—and perhaps people had already started attacking the cops? In order for our affinity group not to separate we used a word that we would call out if we all needed to come together, think of something uncommon, for example we used the word "Moose." The section of the Black Bloc that I was in got split up at this point; once we regained our bearings we decided to try and make our way towards the Red Zone. With us we had a marching Black Bloc band, and many affinity groups. The sun was hot and unrelenting, I was drinking water faster than I could find some fresh, and on a day like this all shops were shut. So what are the alternatives? Looting. We came across a supermarket, and the next thing we know we are trying to pull off the door shutters, and eventually they came off, and we had the whole shop to our delights. I ran in and got as many cartons of fruit juice as possible, and bags of crisps and light snack-type foods. The sprinkler system triggered itself, and visibility was reduced, as I was running out.

I tripped and smacked my right foot on an abandoned cash register. (The pain slowly released itself for the duration

of the day). Once refreshed our affinity group had a re-think and we decided to de-black ourselves and find a quicker route to the Red Zone.

We found ourselves in a park square, where summer bands were playing, people drinking Italian wine, and children were playing. We sat and calmed ourselves in the peace that became a much needed breather; it was almost like being in a fairy tale with Orpheus. I decided to try and find recent news and wandered the street; I met another affinity group, they said "the prison is being trashed, and a fragment of the Black Bloc will be here soon." So with that news we all got back into our other identity. It was not a moment too soon. I looked to my left and there was a barrage of riot cops, and without hesitation they tear gassed the whole area. At this point it was too late to put on my gas-mask, but I could neither retreat to find clean air as in front of me were children as young as 5 screaming, crying and panicking. I did my best to get them behind us and clear the area of tear gas canisters. The gas was overwhelming; once the children were safe I ran in a "safe" direction, at this point I couldn't breathe, see or think—all I could make out was the shape of one of the members of our affinity group. Luckily he was twice the size of me—he picked me up after I called his name and he flushed the gas from my face, eyes, throat. We were safe for the time being, and all of us were fucking furious at the level of disregard shown by the cops for the children that were in the area; in my own mind I declared myself in a state of war.

We decided to head into the city center and join anything going on there. Genoa is a hilly city, so we could see across the horizon and see tear gas and black smoke billowing into the sky above, and hear the continuous firing of "anti-riot weapons" by the Italian State. We eventually found ourselves next to a train station where the road was a dual carriageway with what looked like thousands upon thousands of people. We headed gingerly amongst the crowd as we were expecting hostility because of our dress code, but there was no conflict. I knew a British friend of mine would be in Genoa, but I had no idea where he would be, and as I was walking in the road I heard someone call my name, it was my friend. I was wearing a mask, sunglasses and baseball cap and he still recognized me, and we somehow managed to meet each other at this moment in the space-time matrix! I got chatting to him and he took us closer to the "front line." We equipped ourselves and I put on my gas mask, saying to myself it's now or never. One of the most significant moments, for me, was seeing how many people were suffering the effects of tear gas but not knowing what to do—some were ignoring it, some washing water straight into their eyes, and others using lemon-juice solution! I saw a middle-aged man in a bad way, his eyes massively swollen and looking in pain. I approached him to assist him in his situation. I was anticipating daggers, but he was very warm and welcoming of my assistance, considering I was dressed the way I was and had a full face gas-mask on. We connected. He thanked me in his best English, and when I waved goodbye, he raised his fist and smiled.

Down at the front line many people were dodging the "mortar bomb"-style tear gas grenades. I've never seen anything like them. When they landed they deposited very dense gas, but didn't get hot and were easy to handle. The cops obviously witnessed how easy it was for us to throw them back. So instead of launching them at a 45 degree angle, they decided to fire them at head height. If you were hit by one of these the effects could be life-threatening. We gathered as much ammo as possible from crumbling walls and pavements, and began disposing of them towards the cops. Things were at a stalemate, no one moving back or forward. We assisted each other in dodging the large tear gas canisters, and we began to hold the cops at bay. We looked around to see if there was anything that we could build barricades out of, but there was nothing. I went back into the crowd and met members of the affinity group, and refreshed myself on chocolate and water. The heat of the day was extremely unforgiving. We went back as a group and momentum had built up on our side; we were pushing the cops back at such a rate that we were able to pick up the stones that we had previously thrown. A supermarket trolley was adapted to transport stones. Things were going well and at a very quick rate of speed. I felt no angst, no remorse, no sadness—I was so focused on the job at hand of watching the air for missiles, trying to breathe in the gas mask, and monitoring cop movements that the whole event was a series of explosive events. The foot that I damaged was the bane of my day, so I had to go and rest. I sat on a doorstep on the side of the street, and waited to regain my energy. It wasn't a moment too soon, I was jogging back to the front line when my ears were subjected to the noise of mechanical screaming; there was an armored vehicle driving straight forward into the crowd of people. People ran. I ran. I looked across the road and saw

cops running with it hitting and pummeling anyone, and in the other lane a water-cannon was doing its best to shoot down people who were running away from the scene. I turned around and saw the nozzle of a water-cannon pointing at me—I tried dodging it, running in a zig-zag, but it was too late, the next thing I knew I was been blown across the road like a tumbleweed into a crowd of people. I got up and managed to get back into running. A woman fell flat on her face in front of me, I helped her to her feet and I saw her face of terror and absolute fright. There was so much tear gas in the air you couldn't even work out what direction was the best to go in. I lost the affinity group and was on my own. I darted up a narrow street doing my best to get out of tear gas- and water-laden clothes whilst still getting my breath back. A group of people who I thank to this day gave me water and carried my rucksack whilst I gathered my mind, body and energy. They were so accommodating and helped me go through all the back streets to where we were camping.

All I could do now was to wait for my friends to get back. In my waiting I heard plentiful rumors, some depressing, and one rumor became truth. The state murder of Carlo Giuliani. It haunted me, and still haunts today. I later found out that the street battle we were in was very near the scene of Carlo's death. Eventually my friends arrived back as smaller groups or individually. Then, like a sudden storm, another rumor. We heard that the GSF had held a press-conference for the Italian Media, and that they were reported of saying something along the lines of "...The violence today can be solely blamed on the anarchists, the violent majority of which can be found" in the campsite where we are staying. This knocked us all into a temporary state of shock, almost waiting for the first blow to the head by a cop's truncheon. We decided that we should sleep somewhere else that night. In darkness we packed our tents, got ready, and decided how to escape to the GSF car-park where we would sleep in the open with many other people. We dissolved ourselves into an "Official GSF Lawyer Accompanied Group" (the only way you could get this "protection" was to be a member of the GSF!).

The next morning I awake with a sore foot—I probably couldn't run if my life depended upon it—and in circumstances such as these, that wasn't the best thing that could have happened. So we decide to see how the day pans out, and what we can do. We sit at the side of the road and watch the Saturday march go by, but we never did see the end of it, there were that many people! Then we see along the promenade the movements of the riot cops. People begin to move back from where they came. Above us, a helicopter drops tear gas onto anyone. The police offensive is massive, and we have to "retreat." We have no idea what we are going to do, and my friend suggests we head out of Genoa as "scared tourists" on the train somewhere. (We had no intention of leaving this early, but after reading a newspaper report that refers directly to the city we are from back in the UK as a source of troublemakers, we decide that we'd best not have a conflict with The Law.) After walking for many hours we arrive at a small Italian beach town, and the waves beckon our visits. I hadn't washed in over a week; the water was so refreshing, just to swim amongst the crashing waves was a stark contrast to the whole week's worth of events.

We are now on a train heading out of Italy to the Mediterranean coast of France, and are exhausted. I feel good, but my mind has been overworked. Still, deep down between the superficial pain and angst I know that this whole experience has given me that feeling that the risks we took somehow were worthwhile; we fought for our lives, and our desires defended.

I later hear about the cop-raid on the school where many people were staying after the Saturday night march. It was in a British newspaper that I picked up in Nice that reported that a few of the individuals that were beaten were members of the affinity group, and subsequently close friends. Tears shed, and shock lets itself be known around my body. I'm thinking "...that could have been me... but they are my friends!" I managed to get in touch with them, and met them only two weeks later at the Earth First! Summer gathering; thankfully, they weren't injured as heavily as I first thought. The other day I managed to watch the Indy Media video called Genoa—Red Zone. I'll always remember what one of the victims of that raid said: "I thought I would never hear the sound of my own bones breaking inside my own skin..."

One and a half years on I read the UK Direct Action bulletin "Schnews" (www.schnews.org.uk) and see the following: "It's clear that not only those who materially took part in the devastation should be prosecuted, but also those who facilitated the acts or gave strength to their purpose. These people should be prosecuted even if they didn't conduct any material act." - Italian judge, Elena D'Alosio.

Is it me, or was this exactly the kind of future George Orwell predicted in 1984? The very idea of "thought police" is now a very real concept that is being used to justify state repression. House raids, arrests, charges, state and police repression are happening under the aegis of Berlusconi Big State Business Crew. The hardest part for me is working out exactly where can we go from here. The pathology of civilization seems unrelenting, and there seems no escape even to work out how it's possible to live. Will the cracks in the Empire finally break all the way open? Will we see a downturn of some description in our lifetime? All I know right now is this machine can't carry on unchecked, and for the sake of life's necessity we have to dismantle it. Like they say, "Revolutions always happen, don't they?"

Cited texts and further reading:
Against His-Story, Against Leviathan - Fredy Perlman
Eros and Civilization - Herbert Marcuse
A Language Older than Words - Derrick Jensen
Empire - Michael Hardt, Antonio Negri
On Fire: The Battle of Genoa and the Anti-Capitalist Movement - Various

argentina
DESTINATION: ARGENTINA; PERIOD OF TRAVELS: JULY 1-AUGUST 5, 2002

A travelogue of someone who set out to discover the beauty of the world and the sincerity of the people.

All addresses of the places and names marked with an asterisk are listed in the appendix.

ARGENTINA ARDE!
MAY ARGENTINA BURN!

A slogan and a demand appearing, among many other places, on a lot of house walls throughout the country, especially in the larger cities near Buenos Aires and, of course, in Buenos Aires itself. Fuera Duhalde, chau Duhalde, FMI arde, etc. The country is in a state of awakening.

First, some words concerning the basic situation in the south of South America: hunger, unemployment, death, fighting. In short, the economy of the nation has been totally ruined by the demands of commercial money-lenders, as represented by the rapacious International Monetary Fund. During the period of his time in office, the former president Menem pushed through plans to sell many Argentinean institutions to private owners, in obedience to their pressure. In late 2001, rebellion and revolts began to occur more and more in

response to the economy and the policies of the government; these culminated in the well-known events of the 19th and the 20th of December 2001, when in some areas of Argentina, many people were killed. (Two dates similarly known in Europe are the 20th and the 21st July 2001, the days of the killing of Carlo Giuliani and the assault and the massacre at the DIAZ-school during the protests in Genova, Italy, against the G-8 summit).

Demonstrations, lootings, street fights in some cities, blockades, militant fights against the Riot-Policia and other special units of the government, and a tremendous rise of awareness among the people, as well as their attempts to organize themselves: all of this is a result of the calamities. Mr. Duhalde, the current president, is the fifth president within the last eight months; during this period, 38 people lost their lives because they fought in the streets against these conditions. (The last three presidents before Duhalde had to replace each other within 10 days).

Meanwhile, all these problems spread to Uruguay, one of Argentina's neighboring countries, and showed similar effects: hunger, unemployment, and street-fights in Montevideo—this was some of the news I heard during my last five days in Buenos Aires before I returned to Europe.

My trip started in Madrid, my stop-over on the way to Buenos Aires from Austria: I spent a joyful day there accompanied by a friend who showed me, among other things, the book and record store*(1) of the "Sin Dios" people.

The seriousness of this trip was emphasized by the news of the killings of two Piqueteros, Maxi and Dario, which had happened during a street blockade only a few days before my journey. I really had no idea what was waiting for me in this country.

Moreover, I had no idea where I would sleep in Buenos Aires—but through friends, I got some addresses of people living in Argentina who welcomed us (my travel companion and me) like old friends. The candor and the warmth of the people in South America deeply touched me. Suddenly, the edge was taken off many things because of the simple but very important certainty that I *always* would have a roof over my head and people near me who could help me if there were any problems. A heavy load had been lifted from me.

At the same time, it gave me a really bad feeling to realize once more how privileged I am as an EU-citizen. This can be seen in so many areas that it makes me feel sick. The mere fact that I was there, in that place, already proved it; just like the fact that everything was so "cheap" for me: food, public transport...

The safe-guarding of the capital is immediately apparent, not only during demonstrations but also in other areas: the large banks, for instance, are not merely protected by wood boards, as they were for instance in Genova. No! The windows are covered on both sides by heavy metal sheets that protect the glass from breaking, and which, moreover, cannot be used to set the building on fire. This "protection" was noticeable in most places during my stay there, depending on the intensity of the protests. But here too, traces of the fighting could be seen—the sheets bore graffiti or dents and deformations from the sticks of demonstrators. All these were signs of deep rage against the government, police and FMI (=IMF = International Monetary Fund).

In general, there is a lot of graffiti and painting on the walls. It's common to see demands for Duhalde's death, or the death of the FMI or of other politicians; sometimes, however, these "only" announce various demonstrations, or assemblies (Asambleas). All of these wonderfully-decorated walls reminded me of Euskadi, the Basque region of Spain where the walls are also covered with information, critique, and anger.

On the day after my arrival, July 3rd, there was a demonstration, the first one I was able to participate in. The reason for it was police repression. The deaths mentioned above of the activists Maximiliano Kosteki (23) and Darío Santillán (21) turned out to have been murders, most likely planned and carried out in cold blood. Memories of the military dictatorship in this country in the late 1970s and early 1980s came back to many Argentineans. After some considerations, the daily newspapers printed the photographs which had been taken. They showed that Darío had tried to help Maxi, who was lying shot on the ground. Darío himself was shot dead in cold blood over the severely wounded Maxi. The openness with which this took place was scary. Some of the uniformed killers looked directly into the camera and could easily be recognized on the photos. These actions reminded me of the assault on the DIAZ school in Genova, which was also carried out with a cruel openness that suggested a background support by the Italian government.

These killings took place as a reaction to the blockade of a very important bridge, a major entrance to the center of Buenos Aires. The people who blockade the streets are known as Piqueter@s. (This use of the @ is seen in critical Spanish; it is an attempt to address the sexism built into the language. Piqueteras—feminine—and Piqueteros—masculine— are combined into one word, in which the a and the o become @. This way of spelling may be compared to the English word "wimmin.") Blockades are a very common and important form of action in Argentina, and efforts are made to link the various activities in a network.

This demonstration went from the train station Avellaneda, the square where the executions took place, via the above-mentioned bridge into the centre to the Plaza de Mayo, the best-known square in Buenos Aires. The demonstration lasted for about four hours in chilly rain; similar to Italy, and in contrast to Germoney and Austria, marches are not surrounded by police escorts at all times. There were only two accompanying police—and special units posted along the route of the demonstration, one by the bridge (military police and riot police, some with sharp weapons!) and one for guarding Casa Rosada, the building of the government of Argentina. At the checkpoint by the bridge, some demonstrators were allegedly wounded.

The Casa Rosada is completely sealed off during the demonstrations by very strong iron-bar, about 2.30 m high, behind which there are many riot cops armed for the street fights and for defending the Casa.

It was striking for me, coming from the climate of Austria and Germany (which is rather cold and dispassionate as far as human relations are

concerned), how differently the people in South America act. About 70,000 people participated in this demonstration, which took place in continuous rain. Although there was no street fighting, things were pretty lively: people danced and sang their death-wishes for the government, the FMI, and the police with some very militant words. They were accompanied by numerous drummers who beat time tirelessly and kept the hearts of the demonstrators beating hard. When these people dance, their whole bodies move; they jump with their arms almost flying free of the chest, in a movement that continues into the fingertips. Two or three people start with this beautiful form of protest, and all the people around let themselves get caught in this dance which shakes the ground—and, all of a sudden, there are hundreds moving, and a tremendous strength coming from the mass.

Very often such protests against the government and the FMI are combined with a nationalism that reminds me of the nationalism of the Basque liberation movement. Many people in Argentina come with flags to the demos; this is seen as a criticism of the government and the police units who are not considered to represent Argentina—an idea I found strange, just as I did the singing of the Argentinean anthem after the demonstration. First all this criticism, and then no thoughts on how things really could change and get better—after all the difficulties from the capitalist programs, after military dictatorship, after the government selling the public industries to private owners, after police and military repression, murder, and after millions of indigenous peoples have been dispossessed by imperialism...

The anarchists here too will have to face a lot of enlightenment.

During the next days in Buenos Aires I was able to contact two Asambleas: one of them meets in the northern part of Buenos Aires every Thursday, and the other one every Wednesday closer to the centre in the squatted (occupied?) house Tierra del Sur*(2): Asamblea Parque Lezama Sur*(3). The information for the first Asamblea was given to me by a journalist who originally came from New York. She has lived in Argentina for 10 months and has created a web page in English calles Argentina Now*(4), which reports on what is going on there.

"EL PUEBLO EN LAS CALLES CONSTRUYE SU PROPIA HISTORIA" OR, *THE NEW DISCOVERY OF THE WHEEL*

The *Asambleas* were started as an answer to the situation in the country, a response to the repression, the murders. Many people simply got together in public places, parks, or churches to discuss what could be done to improve the situation, and which activities could be used for resistance against the government.

There are about 200 Asambleas in the metropolitan area of Buenos Aires, which are now in permanent contact with each other. Rotating delegates are sent to the "head meetings"—the "Interbarriales" (barrio = district). These delegates may be authorized to make decisions for their Asamblea. It is moving to see how this autonomous administration works.

The Asambleas show a wonderful strength and sow a great amount of solidarity into the hearts of the people. What makes these Asambleas a wonderful weapon is the fact that people from very different levels participate, from the two-year-old toddler to the 70-year-old grandmother. *All* of them take part in the Asamblea, able to share their ideas, problems, and wishes without any hierarchies—at least, that's what I saw.

Many of these ideas are really beautiful, and these ideas need space to be developed. Therefore, these people made plans as to where they could make a cultural centre. And as the buildings of the "Banco Mayo" stood empty because of bankruptcy, the idea was near at hand to squat them.

This happened two weeks after my arrival in the district Barracas. The people there told me that this was not the only building of this bank-group which had been squatted. It indeed is a strange feeling to spend some time in a squatted bank, to sleep there, to watch children playing and being creative, simply to make living space out of this deadly building. What a change has happened there!

What is next? What comes after the squatted villages in the Basque country? What after these banks? What after the factories? Streets, woods, embassies, offices, trees, hearts... How many people meet in these places for the first time, where there is a feeling of community? Which friendships start here, which projects? Which dreams are dreamt here which people will later realize together?

At a concert addressing the death of Carlo Giuliani (20.07.2001), a friend of mine spoke thus: *"Not until every police(wo)man has a relative who also protests in the streets, will these uniformed people cease to fire their weapons."*

All of a sudden, it seemed to me that this could take place in a different way, even without force. Take the cultural centre of this Asamblea Lezama del Sur, the squatted bank: because of the many activities organized for children, it might happen that the son or daughter of a policeman found his/her way into the bank, into this self-governed building, and made friends inside it. How could such a policeman think of evicting his own child from such a daycare centre?

The police came three times, as far as I recall, and asked what was going on there. But after some people explained that this was now a social centre, they went away without giving them any trouble. In my talks with the squatters, the people of the Asamblea, it turned out that the police acted in such a discreet way because it seemed unwise to clear a squat like this one when the political situation was so vague and the solidarity of the people with each other so overwhelming. This is so important: solidarity within the Asamblea. The police would not just have to fight against a few marginalized squatters, but against a huge mass of people—mothers, fathers, children, grandmothers, grandfathers, etc.

As for solidarity: Directly after the squatting, a man working across the street in the office of a leading Argentinean telephone company offered to supply them with electricity. The nearby grocer immediately offered them a discount when he learned they were buying food for the Asamblea.

THE COMPARISON WITH SPAIN IN 1936?
AND A PERSONAL ACCOUNT OF THE CACEROLAS DEMONSTRATIONS IN BUENOS AIRES.

The friend in Buenos Aires who introduced us to life in the metropolis told me such wonderful stories about those now infamous days of December 2001.

The people had had their fill with all the events—the crash of the economy, the widespread hunger. It thus happened that a few began to stand in the streets, each armed with nothing but a cooking pot ("cacerola" in Spanish) and a tool to beat on it. They did not really know why they did it, but it seemed to be a way of protesting, and they found themselves laying claim to the streets, giving voice to feelings shared by so many others...

The sound of the banging cooking pots echoed through the streets, and others heard it and were touched. They laid down their work, took a cooking pot with a spoon as an instrument of protest, left their flats and joined the people in the streets. All of a sudden, there were thousands of people running, shouting, and banging through the streets. The destination seemed to be clear to all of them: the Plaza de Mayo with the Casa Rosada at one end. Soon, even the president had to leave the "Casa" by helicopter.

I don't know if it is possible to make a comparison with Spain in 1936, and I shall never know it, but I think that everything that is happening in Argentina is something very special (let's help make it something usual!) in the present situation of the "New World Order": All these revolutionary movements, all the struggles from the Piqueter@s' street-blockades to the self-organizations in the Asambleas, from the power of the Cacerol@s to the mass demonstrations, graffiti, lootings—all these activities can lead to more, and the future is as always uncertain and exciting. Perhaps it is not necessary to compare the conditions in Argentina with any other situation in the world or its history; it is important in its own right.

WEST TO MENDOZA *"I hope you win..."*

We left Buenos Aires to travel by bus across the whole latitude of the country, from the Rio Plata to the foot of the Andes. I was happy to see a wonderful sunrise, the snow-covered mountains dipped in pink before me and the rising sun behind me. I experienced this after a night ride on the "Colectivo" (bus), the usual way of traveling in Argentina since almost all the trains have been stopped due to lack of money.

Once again, we stayed with people we had gotten to know through friends, and again we were received with the wonderful candor I experienced there so often. This time we were accommodated by the artists of the "Argonautas," a theatre group in Mendoza. Once again, the presence of children fascinated me. In Argentina, children occupy a totally different place in the social fabric than the one I am used to. The children there hardly ever experience a feeling of being excluded, and they are allowed to participate in many activities; whereas, in Central Europe, it's my experience that children always are "sent to bed," and thus, against their will, excluded from social life. The "Argonautas" people told me that there was a squatted cultural centre in Mendoza, although unfortunately I didn't manage to visit it; however, I was told that the emphasis there was also put on work with children.

"I hope you win," the man behind the counter said when I told him why I just had spent three and a half hours before the Internet PC, and in what kind of work (anti-capitalist) I am involved. "I hope WE win," I answered, and he knew exactly what I meant.

This little encounter reveals the spirit that thrives throughout the country, a spirit often called solidarity. For me, it was like finding a well of water shortly before dying of thirst. The chance to tell so many different people what I do and what my work is about, and to be congratulated for doing it by a man entering my life as a "normal" worker in some place or other, gave me a lot of energy, especially for my life in my usual surroundings in Europe. And the idea of joining with so-called normal people in our struggles, or at least letting them in the know, is something very beautiful; if we anarchists all began to tell everyone we encounter what we are working at, at least in rough outlines, it could be very effective. In order for our efforts to endanger the ruling system, even the so-called normal people have to discuss change, not just the "left elite."

THE WAY OF PROTEST BY THE PIQUETER@S

Once, I was at such a street blockade: first, tires are laid down across the street and set on fire. Then all kinds of things are put on the street in order to

erect a stable blockade which is then protected by people. Depending on the situation, of course, there are different ways of proceeding. It is interesting and inspiring to see the militant appearance of the people marching towards such blockades; they are masked and armed with iron rods.

During the last months, there was even a movie made in Argentina: *Piqueteras*. In this film, various Piqueter@s' activities are shown and Piqueteras(!) are interviewed. The militant behavior of the blockaders can be seen here, too, as well as the procedure of the police and the special units against the blockaders; these reports come from rather rural areas: Cutralco (province Neuquén), Mosconi (province Salta) and Plaza Huincult (province Neuquén)—Piqueter@s fighting the riot police who attack with tear gas, water cannons, rubber bullets as well as some live ammunition, and are answered with slingshots and stones. The determined proceeding of these protesters is immensely inspiring for the fights in other parts of the world.

This is a viciously abbreviated version of a much longer report by ReCistencia. To read it in its entirety, contact wc_prelude@everymail.net

Appendix:
1. *La Idea-Difusión Libertaria*, C/ Sta. Bárbara, 7 28004 Madrid (sindios@nodo50.org)
2. *"Tierra del Sur" Centro Social*, Olavarria 1293, Buenos Aires (tierradelsur@latinmail.com)
3. *Asamblea + Casa okupa-Parque Lezama Sur*, Suarez 1244, Barracas, Buenos Aires
4. *Argentina Now* http://argentinanow.tripod.com.ar

More contacts:
5. *Biblioteca y Archivo Histórico Social, "Alberto Ghiraldo"* Paraguay 2212, 2000 Rosario, Argentina (ghirald@hotmail.com)
6. *Federación Obrera Regional Argentina-F.O.R.A.*, Coronel Salvadores 1200 LaBoca, Buenos Aires
7. *Federación Libertaria Argentina-F.L.A.*, Brasil 155, Buenos Aires

and always very hot:
http://argentina.indymedia.org
http://uruguay.indymedia.org
http://www.indymedia.org

colombia
A REPORT FROM COLOMBIA: CORPORATE GLOBALIZATION BY FORCE

(Hey, North American/European punk kid—this is for you, if you'd like a little more perspective on why it's important that you show up at actions against the World Bank/I.M.F., W.T.O., F.T.A.A., and so on.)

The imposition of corporate globalization requires the initiation of structural reforms. These measures, promoted by the World Band and the IMF, are the conditions for the inclusion of Latin American countries in the Free Trade Agreement of the Americas. With these reforms, capitalists propose to diminish or annihilate all the people's achievements over the past decades. Latin America is being confronted with

demands for labor "flexibility," privatization of public enterprises, acquiescence to cultural imperialism, suppression of environmental regulations, and other concessions which enable the exploitation of land, life, and labor by multinational corporations and their networks.

In this way, Latin America is being shaped into a massive market where the lords of capital are the only beneficiaries. However, strong resistances have emerged around the continent: MST and MTST in Brasil, EZLN in Mexico, MAS in Bolivia, "los Piqueteros" in Argentina, indigenous communities in Ecuador, a whole network of social struggles that have been shaped in the last couple of decades. These groups are fighting against neoliberal reforms, and most of them are organizing collective economies and alternative ways of life which defy the order imposed by capitalism. In Colombia, the multinationals' CEOs are not only facing the diverse action of social movements, but also the guerrillas, who are seen by some as the armed wing of the resistance. Although the guerrillas' political propaganda is not a great worry for the establishment, its military force is a dangerous threat that must be defeated by the promoters of corporate globalization.

But in this conflict between the forces of oppression and resistance, we are faced with a new blow from the right wing with the election of the current Colombian president, Alvaro Uribe Vélez. After massive propaganda promoting order and authority, Uribe obtained his victory in the first round, and declared "State of Seizure" August 7, 2002. To the uprising of the people—the rebellion of men and women who do not want to see their lives reduced to merchandise, people that refuse to be subjugated to economic variables, who recognize that this new phase of capitalism is leading to absolute misery—the president answers with military measures that have been incorporated into our everyday lives. The State's fight is not only against guerrillas, but against all those social movements who continue to offer opposition. Declaring every antagonist force "terrorist" and thus illegal, the government attempts to silence the screams of the multitude for freedom and equality.

Some of the military measures being implemented in the current State of Seizure include searches without warrants, detention of people on suspicion alone, "rehabilitation zones," interception of communications, and the creation of a whole network of informants who get paid for notifying the police of "irregular situations" and possible "terrorists." The National Strike was harshly repressed by the police last September; similarly, a Youth March was forbidden and surrounded by military forces, the "Permanent Assembly for Peace" (a Non-Governmental Organization) was raided October 25, the "cleaning" of some neighborhoods in the city of Medellín was used as an excuse to arrest various community leaders, and the National University was closed a week before Colin Powell's visit. In the same manner, right wing paramilitary activity has increased considerably in the past year. Last September, some farmers were killed, and there exists an ongoing persecution of teachers and leftist militants, including the detention of the president of the Trade Union "USO" with charges of rebellion and the recent disappearance of one student at the Industrial University of Santander.

The State of Seizure smoothes the full initiation of Plan Colombia. This plan was developed secretly by the US and Colombian governments, and has an estimated cost of US $7.6 billion, of which US $3.5 billion must proceed from international aid. This Plan hides behind the war against drugs in order to commit dangerous and random fumigations, escalate the internal war, and violate human rights. The US argues they are fighting solely against narcotraffic, but the reality is that Plan Colombia does not attack the great drug lords responsible for the narcotics market, but assaults almost exclusively the farmers who cultivate and transport the leaves. These farmers are situated in the lowest stage in the whole drug chain, and receive insignificant profits from the drug traffic. The farmers are now the perfect attack targets, not only for their resistance, but also to smooth the way for the new agroindustrial plans of the capitalists. This is why we are experiencing the erection of new military bases with US personnel, the purchase of helicopters and weapons from warmongering multinationals, and the constant menace of an international invasion that would only benefit the national and international oligarchy. US intervention in Colombia is not presented in its spectacular display of military power as in Iraq, but as a war of "low intensity," aided by the paramilitaries and the fascist president who controls public opinion through nationalistic propaganda.

This last issue can be confirmed by the example of an upcoming referendum that is being presented by the President as the direct legislation of the people. People are being asked to vote to combat political corruption, but the referendum includes neoliberal structural reforms, such as tax and labor policies. With this referendum, the President is asking Colombian citizens to vote their own death: with this vote, people will make legitimate the fascist policies of the current government. However, strong opposition is rising from a united left, that is presenting an abstention campaign as the only solution against the referendum.

ANARCHISTS IN COLOMBIA

Although the anarchist movement is fairly small compared to other left movements in Colombia, people continue to organize collectives and coordinate networks in order to gain ground in the struggle against capitalism and towards the formation of a free society. After some years of forums and demonstrations against FTAA and WB meetings, anarchists are mostly interested in working directly with the people. This is why some collectives are doing direct contact in neighborhoods, universities, and schools, among other possible spaces. There is an ongoing link between anarchists and independent media centers, as well as a steady participation of activists in national demonstrations and theoretical work.

There is a great need for people to realize that the whole nationalistic discourse is just a weapon used by the State to maintain its order; anarchists are trying to address this issue by involving themselves in antimilitary causes, antipatriotism, and abstention campaigns against the referendum.

The majority of known guerrillas in Colombia have a Marxist-Leninist background which clashes with anarchist ideas. However, there are libertarian militants who prefer to work with a minimum base of agreements in order to unite forces against capitalism. In this way some libertarians have joined their ranks.

HARDCORE AND THE COLOMBIAN SITUATION

The recent contact with other South American scenes, and the current conditions in our country, have caused a revaluation of hardcore's role as a countercultural manifestation. Many bands continue in the whole "street and unity" NYHC thing, but several bands and labels are now denouncing the economic and political circumstances, and some are taking direct action.

Shows are now far more diverse, and you can attend gigs in different neighborhoods. There are also benefit shows, and some are done in universities or public spaces. Some kids are starting projects with displaced people, and others are forming countercultural collectives. One clear example is the CrimethInc. Colombian Cell, "Crimental." They recently released 1000 copies of "Heraldo" (Harbinger) and organized a couple of shows with expositions and videos about Seattle, the FTAA in Colombia, and the MTST in Brasil.

Last year, along with various punks, we organized the first Colombian anarcho-punk congress. We prepared presentations and discussions about "Plan Colombia," the FTAA, straightedge, DIY, antimilitarism, counterculture, feminism, and vegetarianism. It was a four-day gathering where meals were collectively prepared, where we were able to share opinions and learn among other hardcore/punk kids about the situation in our country and the different activities against capitalism emanating from hardcore. We finally made some future plans of organizing the Colombian anarcho-punk federation.

Right now some kids are concentrating on putting on shows to collect money for anarchist collectives and to exercise propaganda against the above-mentioned referendum. In a general sense, there seems to be an increasing relation between hardcore and the diverse Colombian social movements.

Montag (*xmontag5x@yahoo.com*, www.banderasnegras.8m.com)

isle of skye

INSIDE FRONT SPECIAL REPORT: IN SEARCH OF THE BARON

by CrimethInc. Private I Marlowe

Some of them went on to form Zygote, their drummer now plays in Muckspreader, and their singer lives in isolation on the Isle of Skye, as a blacksmith forging medieval weapons—no joke!

-Inside Front 11, Amebix retrospective

By hook and by crook I had found myself in Edinburgh, Scotland, of all places. While the details of that journey are too twisted to tell here, one day while idly checking my email at the local library I remembered I had heard a rumor (from *Inside Front*, too!) that the Baron, the lead singer of the infamous Amebix, had moved to the Isle of Skye off Scotland. I suddenly realized that I was only a few hours' journey from the Baron himself! Action had to be taken. I surfed the Internet for hours, reading old Amebix interviews, and finally came upon the Baron's human name: Rob Miller. The first clue! Then, searching Google for "Isle of Skye," "Rob Miller," and "Sword," I found the name of the current location of the Baron, the aptly named "Castlekeep Forge"... specializing in hand-made swords, without modern technology! Suddenly, I realized it was my divine (although the Amebix would have preferred *infernal* to *divine*) mission to retrieve a blade from the Baron.

Getting to Skye was easier said than done. I frantically emailed Rob Miller, attempting not to sound like the deranged and psychotic Amebix fan that I am, but instead a friendly sword aficionado who only, on the side, happened to be mildly interested if this particular Rob Miller was indeed The Rob Miller, aka The Baron, of the Amebix. His response proved my research correct: "Ay, that's me."

Earlier, I had spent some time trying to track down the mysterious Degsy or "Deek," the singer of Oi Polloi. When I had first got to Edinburgh, most of my impressions of this town had come from brilliant Oi Polloi songs such as "Bash the Fash." To be honest, I was a bit disappointed that I was not fighting fascists on the streets with Oi Polloi. Although apparently every member of the rather small Edinburgh punk scene with the barest inkling of musical talent had been in Oi Polloi at one time or another, currently his whereabouts were mysterious. There was a rumor he was either living with one of his side-project bands "Fucktheirsystem" (whose first record has the brilliant title "Fuck their Fucking System"!) in Finland, doubtless riding motorcycles with Umlaut with the Lapland Popular Front, or studying Gælic, the ancient traditional language of Scotland, on the Isle of Skye. Imagine, maybe Degsy from Oi Polloi was hanging out with the Baron. Maybe on that remote island they were plotting to create the greatest crust-punk record of all time.

Now there was the problem of getting to Skye. While apparently Skye was something of a tourist destination during the summer, it was nonetheless a remote island that absolutely no one visited during the dead of winter. Having just got to Scotland, I had only the vaguest clue how to get to the Isle of Skye via public transportation. I didn't even know if any roads went there, and I had lost my atlas! While miserably contemplating this situation in the local anti-capitalist coffee shop (to be exact, a coffee shop that, while owned by a capitalist rat, had a staff who displayed remarkable liberties with their coffee and food that would make any CrimethInc. agent proud!), one of the employees revealed that he was actually from Skye! When I asked him how Skye was, he would respond with odes to its mountains and strange remarks about fairies. Mountains and fairies! He also gave me the web page and schedule of the

BLACK MEDICINE ARMY FACTION PLOTS TO VISIT THE BARON HIMSELF IN SECRET ANTI-CAPITALIST COFFEESHOP IN EDINBURGH

ferry that took one from Mallaig, the closest town to Skye one could reach via land, and was off. There was apparently some type of bridge and a bus one could also take there, but why take the bus if one can cross via ferry!

At the last minute I had my doubts. It seemed much more sane to go sometime in spring when the buses were operating and things on Skye were open. There were also rumors of a blizzard coming from the South. But one friend I had told about the trip got even more excited than myself, so, not wanting to be left out, I went along with her. The ride up to Mallaig was beautiful, and as we got further and further outside Edinburgh the land became wilder

HITCHING A RIDE ON THE BOAT OF EWAN THE MAD

and wilder, the mountains larger and larger, and my expectations higher and higher.

The train tracks literally ended in Mallaig, a small, sleepy little fishing town. I had somehow left my schedule at home, but remembered the ferry only came twice a day, once in the morning and once before the evening around 5 o'clock. Looking at my watch, I had only a few minutes left. We jumped off the train and ran for the dock, only to be greeted with a wide expanse of ocean where the ferry should have been. Clearly, something had gone awry. I ran to the office of the Calmac Ferry Company, and asked them where the ferry was.

"The ferry doesn't run on weekends."

Definitely an ill omen to begin a journey.

"When does the next one run?"

"Monday morning."

Not good at all. The last thing I wanted was to spend my weekend in small town in the freezing cold of northern Scotland, where I didn't know a soul, especially when I could be tracking down the elusive Baron. Still, five miles of churning ocean lay between

us and Skye. Suddenly, our collective hobo instincts took over: Let's hitchhike by boat!

Mallaig is a fishing town, and right next to the empty ferry dock was a fishing dock. It was approaching evening and most fishermen were coming home. Storm clouds were clearly rolling in. Not being exactly sure how to hitchhike by boat (I mean, do you just stick out your thumb on a pier?) we decided to talk to a group of fishermen who were getting off their boat.

"Hey, do you know of anyone going to Skye?"

"Ay, at this time I don't think anyone is going. The weather's been shite all day and getting worse. You'll have to wait till Monday. Well, crazy Ewan might take ya..."

However, no one saw Ewan around. Immediately, despair set in. No one could even hear us scream for a ride on the pier, since most of the fishermen were inside their boats. Luckily, a stout and magnificently mustached man suddenly appeared out of nowhere, merrily trotting towards a little boat. We immediately stopped him and inquired if he was Ewan.

"Ay, I'm Ewan."

We were saved! While Ewan wasn't planning on going back to Skye today, he seemed impressed with our determination and perhaps more impressed with our willingness to give him a bit of hard cash in return for the favor. Finally, after long deliberation, he agreed to take us on. He told us to wait at the bottom of a creaky and rusty ladder than descended more or less straight into the ocean. We climbed down, and then a little tugboat pulled up, the *Old Grimsley*. We threw our backpacks straight over the water—praying they wouldn't fall short—and jumped into the boat. Ewan waved us aboard and the boat took off erratically.

Nothing had prepared me for this trip. Ewan was no ordinary man, but a St. Francis amongst fishermen, surrounded by a bevy of animals. He went through great pains to post a sign up in Skye looking for his pet cat Wee Jimmy, who he carried pictures of in his pocket. His good mate Sammy the Seagull would fly manic circles around his boat and perch himself on the helm, and swoop dangerously close to your head—and Sammy followed the boat the entire trip! Lastly, he admitted he was not only a Jehovah's Witness but a former alcoholic. It was going to be one hell of a ride.

As soon as we got out of sight of land, he offered us some coffee. We agreed, with very cold rain pelting down on us. I quickly threw my waterproof jacket over my backpack to defend its contents from the storm, but it was too little too late and I was getting soaked to the bone. As he was busy preparing the coffee on a decrepit stove he had in his cockpit, and while we were occupied barely avoiding an increasingly hungry and irritated Sammy the Seagull, he started not paying any attention to actually driving the boat. As the boat became increasingly erratic in its behavior, large waves started coming over the boat, soaking me. Things got even more hectic when Ewan started trying to serve us coffee, as the boat shook so much as soon as he got close enough to hand us the coffee, the boat would rock, causing the coffee to spill out and burn our hands. Finally, I managed to get the coffee in my hand and shovel it down my throat just as I noticed I was starting to get seasick. Ewan began revealing his deep dark secrets, confessing of his deep hatred of alcohol, his enduring love of his cat, and the fact that he had lived in his boat for a few years. We swapped stories about living in various strange forms of transportation. Ewan also bemoaned his inability to get a proper wife, being a poor fisherman, and I told him how my life in the back of a van presented insurmountable problems for romance. I still wondered how much he really drank, as our drunken boat barely escaped capsizing a number of times. Grey mist descended upon the boat. A mobile phone my friend had lent me for "emergencies" was now completely destroyed by salty brine. Yes, the home of the Baron destroys all technology.

We approached the distant Isle of Skye, and, as if timed perfectly by the crust-punk gods, a giant rainbow crossed from the mainland to the Isle. The Baron must have had some hand in it. Ewan waved us off as we climbed yet another rusty and treacherous ladder towards shore, into the mysterious village of Armadale. Being frozen and wet, we decided to attempt to get into the nearest warm place—but the entire town was closed! All the tourist shops, all the restaurants (well, all two restaurants—Armadale was more a village than a town), everything was closed. No one in sight. Finally, an old man walking a very skinny dog came down the road, and we asked him if anything was open and warm. He seemed more than a bit shocked we had come to Skye in the middle of the winter. He pointed us down to the Armadale Hotel where we could get warmed up and get a place to stay the night. However, the Armadale hotel was just as mysterious as the rest of Skye. As we walked in there was absolutely no one there! Skye was a ghost town! So we walked inside the hotel to warm up in the lobby. Suddenly, a strange voice said from out of nowhere, "Hey, come over here and play some pool." I peeked around the corner, and the next room over was a bar filled with several drunken Scots.

THE RAINS AND WAVES NEARLY KILL YOUR POOR AUTHOR ON THE BOAT, BUT SKYE APPROACHES IN THE DISTANCE!

"You wanna dram?"

I had no idea what a dram was, to be honest. I figured out, being at a bar, it had something to do with alcohol, so I refused. However, this was taken as violating Skyian social taboos, so when they asked yet again I hesitantly agreed. As I lifted the strange clear liquid to my mouth, my taste buds were greeted by one of the harshest alcohols I had ever tasted—even more harsh than some of strange homebrews and moonshine I had tasted in my reckless youth in North Carolina. The locals smiled at my reaction and immediately offered another. The bar at the Armadale Hotel was a truly fascinating and stunningly egalitarian bar. There was apparently no 'bartender' per se, but every one of the locals seemed to take turns serving each other endless amounts of "drams." As we waited around, the bar soon became *the* place in town to hang out. One strange old man after another would maneuver inside and sit down, chatting in a strange mix of Gælic and Scots that was mostly indecipherable to me. One of the most interesting characters was an ancient old man with a cane, who was obsessed with whistling John Denver's "Country Road, take me home, to the place I was born..." I befriended him by knowing the words by heart. Also, a large amount of the Armadale winter residents were students at the Gaelic college, and they all knew Degsy from Oi Polloi, who was studying Gaelic in Skye! Unfortunately, no one there actually knew where the Deek was that weekend. Also, my friend was getting quite drunk on the drams, and when it was revealed in the course of conversation that we were not dating, an entire bar of male-small-island-trapped sexual frustration came simmering to the surface. One large man started hitting on her, mixing his romantic aspirations with various insults at her for being "a terrorist," since she was of Indian descent. Luckily, the rest of the bar residents were against blatant racism and war, and soon the bar became involved in a heated argument—and

my friend easily defeated her single conservative opponent verbally.

I stayed out of it, just trying to figure out where we were sleeping, and managed to phone up an older man named Jim Fraser who would let us stay at his place. I was also very hungry, and being well-versed in the art of starving to death in America, had brought a large amount of stale—and now wet—bagels with me. When I hid in a corner and starting munching down on my bagels, a large man came up and angrily told me to put my bagels away. I soon figured out he was the owner of the hotel, and he was upset that I had violated the sanctity of his kitchen by bringing in stale bagels. I decided it was time to hit the road and find Fraser's crash pad. As I walked into the bar I heard a scream.

The large and drunken pro-war bastard had jumped on my friend! Normally, I somehow manage to cover my deep-seated insanity with a thin veneer of rationality, but a history of having my female friends victims of violence combined with my Southern heritage caused me to flip out. Using some of my knowledge of ju-jitsu, I quickly slid my arm around the larger and more physically imposing fat man's neck, and within a second had choked him. He fell down to his knees, and the rest of the

bar stood by, aghast at my act of violence. The fat man scampered off to the bathroom to hide, and I realized that despite my good intentions I had just done something completely socially unacceptable and should exit the bar immediately. The rest of the bar began quickly apologizing for the fat man's behavior, and I just smiled: "I think it's time to go." We had just gotten kicked out of the only warm place we knew of in Armadale. Later, when we got to Fraser's place, a kindly old man with no small obsession with Scotch and beautiful Goethe quotes, he gave us a warm bed for a bribe. That night my friend berated me about what she viewed as all-too-typical male violence, and I apologized for my quick temper and even quicker reaction-time. Honestly, I wasn't sure how I should have dealt with that situation—I mean, anarchists shouldn't just choke people who are hitting on their friends too hard—but what do you do when your friends are confronted with physical violence? I went to bed feeling sick.

The next morning I realized we were going to have a problem. First, it had started snowing. Second, we knew that the Baron had his forge somewhere between Broadford and some other place named Elgol, but that was at least fifteen miles away and no buses were running Sunday. Lastly, no one was driving around, leaving us few hitchhiking options—and due to my act of violence, the only warm place in Armadale had kicked us out. Clearly, it was an emergency. I found a public phone on the dock where Ewan had dropped us off, and called my friends at the anti-capitalist coffee shop in Edinburgh. Within a few other calls, I found the phone number of a chef who was a friend of my friend from Skye at the coffee-shop. She said we could stay at her place and she was going to pick us up after she got off work. We wandered aimlessly in the snow and rain through various strange castles and deserted gardens (Skye is simply full of at least two castles and innumerable beautiful vistas, but during winter the tourist attractions are all shut down and the locals, like locals everywhere, pay them no attention) until we finally gave up on our friend-of-a-friend and just starting trying to hitch out of Armadale. The first person who drove by picked us up, a kindly old fellow. I asked him if he knew the Baron, and he replied that not only did he know the Baron, but he would go out for drinks with him on occasion and that he was "a fine man." However, he was only dimly aware of the Baron's murky past, knowing only that a long time ago the Baron had indeed been in "some rock band." We were getting closer. Just as he went up the one road going from Armsdale to Broadford, our friend appeared out as if out of nowhere. We switched cars in the middle of the road— and soon we were off. I tried hurriedly to explain to this good Samaritan about my plans to visit the lead singer of my favorite rock band and have him forge me a sword. She seemed mildly amused and, for fun, drove me down the road where his forge was. As it was getting dark, I only had the luck to glimpse the sign "Castlekeep: Medieval Swords and Celtic Jewelry" before we had to turn around and drive back. I was so close I could almost smell the Baron—a smell mixed of motorcycle oil and blood.

One thing every visitor to the Isle should know is that hitchhiking is a long and honored social tradition in Skye. We suspect this is because if you're driving in Skye during winter (as the tourists invade in summer—so be warned—this may only be seasonal!) and someone is hitchhiking, you probably know them. If you don't know them, they probably know your parents. As we were leaving the Cuillens, the breathtaking mountains on which the Baron makes in his home, a giant shadowy figure loomed out into the distance with a huge thumb pointed squarely in the air. We pulled over to pick him up, and after five minutes of conversation in thick Skyish he revealed that he indeed was the good friend of the father of our driver, and had known her as a wee baby!

Back at the house of our host, we cooked a large meal of eggs and spaghetti to feed her and her fellow housemates, and luckily I had brought a secret weapon in my front-pocket all the way from Edinburgh—a fiver's worth of weed. Yes, I realize the potential political and moral compromises of giving out weed as a way to help earn favors from complete strangers. Yes, I am a horrible example to future generations. However, when in Skye, do as the Skyians do—and in Skye weed is hard to get, since few enterprising drug dealers make the journey this far from civilization. Personally, I felt like I was Marco Polo exchanging noodles for fine spice. The weed was gladly accepted, and soon myself, my friend, and a bevy of sundry women working temp jobs in Skye were off to a pub to celebrate. The snow was falling a bit harder and the roads were icing, and after walking for ages a hotel, on some small island off of the coast of Skye, appeared from the mist.

Inside the hotel it was a different world. Like most of Skye, this hotel skirted the fine line between a capitalist enterprise and an anti-capitalist potluck. Sandwiches and beers were passed around with little regard as to whether anyone was paying. We were also, I might add, the only people in the pub. The waitress sat down and regaled us with tales of her adventures in the States and her great love of country music. She, a woman from a semi-rural island, had somehow traveled almost everywhere I, a semi-professional hobo, had over the last year. She even brought out her prized country boots from Nashville and placed them, without any regard for hygiene, on the kitchen table. A maid named Rock-around-the-clock Kate came in. A thoroughly ancient woman, at least eighty years old, she lived up to her nickname. She drank whisky dram after whisky dram, plotting her next journey to Amsterdam, and then began singing "Rock, Rock, Rock, around the clock..." It was going to be one of those nights, yet again.

The next morning I woke up with a severe headache. Stumbling down the stairs, I looked out the window... only to see a huge deluge of snow before me. The blizzard had struck. In fact, the blizzard had not just struck, but was *striking*. I was snowbound, in a

remote house full of people I barely knew, and my only friend, while being very polite about the mad premise of this trip, was doubting my logistical abilities. Soon, the entire house of girls was hovering around the television, and much to my horror and their delight, the newsperson announced that more or less everything was closed. I silently screamed—now I would never seen the Baron. Gripped by terror, I ran out of the house into a good foot or two of snow, and up the hill. The roads were definitely all snowed in. In mindless fury, I hiked a few miles till I got to a major road that, while icy, seemed drivable. No cars in sight.

I shambled back to our snowbound house and then completed the

THE BARON HIMSELF!

next part of my plan... I called the Baron. A voice answered, and it was not the Baron, but a man known only to me as Garth. He said that the Baron would usually be dropping his kids off for school at this point in the morning! However, given the huge snowstorm, school was cancelled—and he was going to be in the forge! If the Baron could brave this storm, so could I! When I told my friend this, she started to doubt my sanity openly. She noted that the last ferry back to the mainline left at five, and, as it was about noon, I would have no time to get back to the mainland if I hitchhiked out to see the Baron. While it was a good point, I have never let good points stop me before. I felt horribly guilty when I realized that we had to take separate paths, and she had to hitchhike by herself back to Armadale to catch the ferry—and hang out at the bar where I had strangled someone just a few nights ago! I wondered what the locals were going to do. Still, sometimes you either have to get on the road or go home with your tail between your legs. That means you have no choice but to hit the road.

So, there I was, with a giant backpack, a bag full of wet and now icy bagels, and a thumb. Since the road was covered with ice, no one was going to pick me up any time soon. I began walking. After about an hour and a half, I made it to the edge of a road that was dangerously icy, but not completely covered in snow. As the snow started pelting me harder, in the

distance I heard the familiar sounds of... a car. Lo and behold, what was clearly an SUV pulled beside me. A pleasant-looking fellow, who was either an aging yuppie or a degenerate aristocrat, with an English accent (quite different than the variety of Scots/Gælic accents everyone else so far had!) told me to hop on in. Soon, my savior and his wife, also an elegant English woman, were driving me straight to Broadford. I impressed them with my tales of being a lost American on Skye and my deep love of its natural beauty (all the time carefully disguising our clearly differing positions within the class struggle), and they chatted about photography, the coming war on Iraq, and Skye. Like any good bourgeois couple, they were not going to let a good foot or two of snow, nor icy roads, stop them from shopping, so they dropped me off in Broadford at the local grocery store. I began walking towards Elgol, and again put my thumb out. After a good half an hour of walking, an SUV again came roaring from behind me! My yuppie saviors had arrived yet again, and they pulled over! I must have made a good impression.

I told them about the Baron (not the singer-for-a-crust-punk-band part of his life, but the swordsmith part). They were immediately fascinated, having lived on this island for years and never heard of him. They were looking for a gift for some American cousins, and what better than hand-forged jewels! Now that I had enchanted my hosts, they speedily made it across death-defying mountain roads and suicidal sheep by means of their all-terrain vehicle. The mountains were getting higher, the snow was falling quicker, the sheep were multiplying, and the world was getting wilder. In these subtle changes, I detected the presence of the Baron. In the distance, I could spot the strange stone building on the mountainside that was Castlekeep, the forge of the Baron himself. We pulled over a precarious walled-in driveway, and, after clambering through the gate, I entered the Hall of the Baron himself.

Inside, it was a giant medieval hall, the kind that one would imagine Vikings drinking in after ruthlessly plundering a monastery and skewering its monks. Crossed swords hung over the rooms, and other medieval chain-mail and helmets hung about. I peered in, and then a long and haggard, yet strangely familiar face appeared from the darkness. The Baron.

The Baron looked a bit surprised that visitors had actually came in the middle of a blizzard. I don't know what I looked like, but I was definitely frozen and wild-eyed. He looked at me quizzically and asked me if I "would like a cup of tea." In complete shock, and recovering from the cold, I agreed and sat down at nearest table. The Baron disappeared behind the door, and appeared carrying a large pot of tea with a multitude of cups and piles of sugar on a giant steel platter.

From inside, a stout man with a long beard, who resembled a Nordic warrior (or Gimli) strode in, and announced himself as "Garth." Garth immediately seized the yuppie couple who had just wandered in into his land of precious jewels.

First thing about the Baron is he looks like a man who has lived through hell and came back alive. He's got an incredibly tall, terrifyingly skinny frame and wears thin, black glasses. His hair is shaggy and wild, but the entire time I was with him he kept most of his mane beneath a small woolen cap. His smile is a bit craggy, and his manner very gentle. I have found through years of experience that people who have lived lives that are truly unimaginable, who have eaten shit and pissed their own blood, are not psychotic in their social relations, but instead incredibly soft-spoken, as if to make up for the rest of their existence. At first, I had no idea what to say. I didn't want to appear to be a crazed punk rock fan who had traveled halfway around the world to see him. I wasn't sure how seriously he took his life in punk rock now that he was a swordsmith, and if he had any idea that people had had their lives changed by his old band's music of despair. Did he know that we had sung "Arise" from the deepest, darkest pits of a Philadelphia jail, when we had little hope of being released? Did he know that while hopping trains in the bleakest colds of northern Canada, to keep our spirits warm we sang each other "The Darkest Hour" as we fell asleep, perhaps never to wake again? Could he understand that we had listened to "Chain Reaction" over and over again while driving through the mountains of Mexico to aid masked guerrillas? Could he imagine that we had stowed away in luxurious hotels, humming "Drink and Be Merry" all night, hoping for a free breakfast in the morning? Would he approve of us putting the Amebix on a mix tape with Lynyrd Skynyrd, since we did leave off "Sweet Home Alabama"? Could he possibly understand that as we had starved, stolen, fought cops, and drunk tear gas, *his band was the fucking soundtrack?* I had no idea what to say.

I decided to blow my cover as a Amebix-crazed anarchist punk. After all, I didn't have a single piercing and my circle-A tattoo was covered by my clothing, so for all the Baron knew I wasn't even an Amebix fan, just a deranged sword-fan. The Baron knew me only as some weirdo who had sent him a few e-mails, and had on the side asked if he was the singer of Amebix.

"To be honest, Rob, I don't know much about swords. I definitely want a blade of some type, and I really don't even want it for myself as much I want it for some of my friends in the States who are having hard times right now. I didn't come to get the sword from you because you're the best swordsmith. I want you to forge a blade for myself and my friends because you were the singer for the Amebix and that music means a lot to us."

I didn't say we wanted the dagger to kill cops. Felt it might be impolite.

With the mention of the Amebix, the Baron's raven-like eyes lit up with a spark.

"Ahhh... yes, the Amebix. I always felt we broke up just as were on the verge of doing something great."

Well, I had broached the question. It was like going out with someone you had a crush on for years and then finally asking him or her if they liked you. *One thing I've always wondered about is if punk rock is relevant, ten years after your band—who lived out of dumpsters, starving, freezing, stealing, and playing some of the most heart-rending music ever made—breaks up, you have children, and start forging swords for a living. Does is still fucking matter anymore? Was it fucking worth it?*

The Baron's eyes were still alight. "Yes, yes, we were really about to do something great. We ran out of chords to play though. You know, it's all just A and E."

I had conjectured so myself. "You know, when we were playing, we weren't really all that good. It was like, hit the big string, now hit that string." With an almost apologetic attitude towards Amebix's musical prowess, he continued. "Well, the music just sort of happened, you know, from what we were living..." Yes, the music still mattered to the Baron. More importantly, he still saw some value in what he had done. It was in his eyes.

I started telling him about myself, about how people still listened to Amebix in the States, and how his music kept us alive during dark times. He nodded, but how did he get from Amebix to Skye?

"Yes, we all went our separate ways. You know, Spider's still the same as he was back then... living in squats, playing in bands. I didn't really know what to do with myself after the band broke up. I hadn't really thought about it that much, so I got on my motorcycle and wandered off across Europe. I did that for a while, and then got in an horrible accident, and I fucked my arm up so that I couldn't even ride my motorcycle. I didn't know what to do after that, but I had some folks in Skye so I went to live with them."

So the motorcycles stories were true. I also started telling him about my life, about how much anarchism meant to me, about how once I had spent all my time just listening to music about not bowing down to any gods or masters, and now I had spent the last few years living it. How his music helped me understand

the annihilation that is before us, that is with us, to come to terms with it and then fight to overcome it. We were reminiscing about our old friends, our lives, our adventures. In the meantime, the cups of tea seemed to last longer and longer, and the yuppies also sat down with their cup of tea. Having done their role in bringing me here, I thanked them profusely and continued telling stories of anarchy with the Baron. The yuppies, definitely realizing that their friendly hitchhiker had a secret identity as a raving mad anarchist, and this friendly swordsmith secretly had an identity of a rock star, decided not to reject this strange meeting of worlds but merely continue upon their own, and after their cup of tea, returned to inspecting the jewelry without a bat of their eyes.

Of course, this still left unanswered the question of how one transforms one's life, how one metamorphoses from being the Baron to Rob Miller the Swordsmith. I mean, it's not exactly what most people would call a normal career path; your high school career counselor couldn't give you any advice on it.

"I worked a whole lots of crappy jobs, you know, mostly in bars and hotels. One day I wanted a sword. So I asked my friends where to get one. And then, no one knew where to get a sword at... because no one actually made them anymore. So, I decided I might as well make them, as I was interested in swords. But there was no one to teach me, so I kept working these jobs in hotels, and by night I taught myself how to make swords. I just got the books and read them, and got the equipment slowly, and starting making swords. For years I just would sell them by the side of road with a sign. Never made much money out of it, to be honest. Then one day my Garth here told me about this house he wanted to get, and set up his shop in, and he asked me to join him. So, I did."

Yes, it's true. The Baron taught himself how to forge swords, all by his fucking self. Do-it-yourself sword-forging! Not only that, but his passion for forging blades was like a fire that must have been kindled out of the ashes of Amebix, because he's damn good at it. World-class. The only swordsmith in Scotland, he makes his blades without modern technology, using ancient and rekindled techniques. His eyes lit up with same intensity when he talked about swords as they did when he was reminiscing about the Amebix or his motorcycle.

The Baron does not make mock swords, he makes real swords. Fully forged blades that no one can match. These swords are huge, giant steel affairs capable of killing men in a single blow. I know it sounds like I'm kidding—I'm not. It's just amazing. He taught himself an entire art, and it's almost proof that if you really struggle, if you have nothing left at all, if even your motorcycle's gone and you can only study overdue library books by candlelight in a squat on a remote island, you can learn to do anything. The Baron is living proof. He can do anything with a sword, a knife, a dagger... anything. Just ask him.

Soon, I realized my time was up... I had only an hour and a half till the ferry left for Armadale, and if I didn't get there in time I would be stranded on Skye in the snow, with nowhere really to stay. I mean, by this time I had sort of burnt out my welcome in the few places that had let me in with my mania. As I mentioned to the Baron that I had to go, he smiled and offered me a peanut-butter cookie. Another mysterious woman appeared out of nowhere, and a pile of peanut-butter cookies manifested themselves. That cookie was the only thing I had to eat all day. Now that the yuppies had left, the hall of Castlekeep transformed from shop into a feast hall, a merry snow-bound island of humanity in the middle of a blizzard. I gobbled the cookie down and in thanks gave him the only thing I had as a gift for him. It was a copy, albeit nearly destroyed by the waves of Ewan's completely mad trip across to Skye from Mallaig, of *Fighting for Our Lives* that, like the Baron himself, looked like it had been through hell and back. I gave it to him, and he looked through it with a smile, promising to read it. He seemed a bit worried for me, although he noted with humor the facts that I was clearly losing my sanity and my friend was waiting for me at a bar where I had choked a man two nights before. After a quick tour of the Baron's forge, which looked like a truly mad collection of weird metal scraps and half-created blades, we shook hands, and I walked back into the snow, thumb in air.

It's damn refreshing to meet someone like the Baron. He gives me hope. After all these years, all these opportunities for cynicism, opportunities for selling out to capitalist values, for drinking himself to death, for just giving up the fight, he's still there, still staying true. Sure, he's not vegan or a political activist. However, life's not about lifestyle choices, record collections, political victories, or any of that. It's about staying true to what you love, living a life you can love. Even when the entire world looks at you and says you're completely off your fucking rocker, even when they try to prove it to you by making you work horrible jobs, starving you if you quit those horrible jobs, trying to make you believe in anything but yourself, giving you a million options of consumption, narcosis, and—most of all—submission... even after all of the shit you have to live through every day just to survive, you can still stand there, alive and defiant. Staying true to your feelings, to your life story, to your past, your friends, the mountains, and yourself—that's staying true in a more powerful sense than anything I've ever heard on any second rate punk record. It would have been deeply disappointing if the Baron had really given up on it all, had given up on his music and his words, if he had thought it was all just youthful indiscretion or a complete waste of time, if he had become just another cynical swordsmith. He didn't. You could tell by the look in his eyes. He still loved the Amebix, motorcycles, and all of it, the starvation, the freezing, the anarchy—it was all worth it. And now he was doing something that was on some level just as crazy as being in the Amebix: forging swords on a remote island, surrounded by friends and giant snow-covered mountains. Yes, it's a small business, but the Baron isn't making swords to make money. He's making swords because he fucking loves to make swords. Remember, he taught himself to make swords for no other reason than he wanted to, than he could. The Baron is staying true.

Yes, there's hope. Yes, it's all worth it, every last moment. As for where we all will eventually end up, well, one can never know. As for the Baron, we can only aspire to such a fate.

I never directly asked him if his swords could kill cops. However, I did tell him that we might need them to be very sharp, and that we wanted to really use them, and that we were anarchists. The Baron

smiled, and he answered all my questions, including some I never asked him.

And now the road goes on forever... and the sun will always shine... one day we'll be together... when we cross the final line... if I turn to you... when all is said and done, will you meet me on the other side, seven million miles beyond the sun.
—The Amebix

la luz, tx

THE US/MEXICO BORDER FROM BOTH SIDES

by Gloria Cubana

I felt underdressed as soon as I saw Flaco. I was suddenly very out of place in my casual clothing as he strode out of the house in a cowboy shirt and tight jeans accented by a wide leather belt with a large buckle. I listened as he persuaded his father to let him wear his cowboy boots, and they hopped around in the dust of the yard as they traded shoes.

We rode to the *jaripeo* in the back of the pickup, bouncing out of Crespo (pop. 2000) on the main road. Carolina, Miguel, and Blanca all wore *charro* outfits, too, and my sister and I hunkered down in the bed of the truck and listened to them talking animatedly. On our way through Celaya, we passed some boys hitchhiking by the side of the road who turned out to be cousins, and they all jumped in the back of the truck, too, perching on the sides as we barreled down the road toward La Luz, TX.

La Luz, TX, is about 4 hours northwest of Mexico City, in Guanajuato state. Not, that is to say, in Texas. The humble town of La Luz became a boom town when many of its male inhabitants left for the United States in search of better employment opportunities, and mailed money home for their families and to build houses there. Because of the way Mexican immigrants rely on a network of already-immigrated relatives and friends when they begin their new lives in the US, they tend to stay in the already established communities that have grown up there. Most of the residents of La Luz had ended up in Texas, so they'd renamed the town. We joked that Crespo, which is at an earlier stage in that economic upswing—it's still a town under construction, many of the houses being expanded and remodeled with money from the US, while La Luz has settled down more—should be called Crespo, NC.

A *jaripeo* is a bull-riding contest, and the parking lot outside the *plaza de toros* was filled with hundreds of vehicles, many of them American ones probably belonging to Mexicans working in the US who had come home for the holidays. I didn't spot any Texan plates (the name may be more whimsical than factual at this point), but I did pause to feel sorry for the man from this dry place, hot even in late December, who ended up living in Minnesota.

The inside of the plaza was even more crowded than the parking lot. It was packed to a degree that would certainly violate the most generous of American fire codes. There was a dirt floor down below beside the ring where people stood to watch the bull riding, and a spread of concrete bleachers up above for the faint at heart. I ended up sitting on one of the concrete terraces next to a man who told me that he had lived in Raleigh, NC—about 60 miles from my home—for two years. When I asked him if he had enjoyed living in the US, he said, "Well, my life there was working, and my life here is living." Talking with this *ranchero* from a rural Mexican community who had lived for two years in a foreign country made me think about how limited the American perception of the Latin American immigrant experience can be. Since immigrants to the US frequently have little formal education and are from poor families, we tend to think of them as having little experience or understanding of the world, when they have often seen more of the world than the average American.

We associate a person's socioeconomic status with a particular level of travel, and the immigrant confounds those assumptions. It does not occur to us that immigrants have crossed thousands of miles of distance to work in the United States; that they may have lived in several American cities, from Los Angeles, CA to Yadkinville, NC; that they may follow seasonal agricultural work or construction jobs all around the country. This very un-American disjunction between class and travel is strange to us, as travel for most of us is a leisure activity, something done as a vacation from work, not to find it in the first place. My sister found herself struggling to reconcile these two approaches to travel when she and Flaco's older brother, José, decided to travel together. She was convinced that José, who has lived in the United States for 13 years, would be transformed if he had the opportunity to travel the way she is used to—the way she had found her own life transformed. Is it just from the vantage point of bourgeois privilege that we can believe that staying in a hotel in a foreign country might be a life-changing experience? Or was my sister right to think that José had missed out on some vital element that is deeply a part of her kind of traveling? Is our tourist-style travel a diet version of the cultural immersion that immigrants experience? And to what degree are Mexican immigrants, who tend to remain within established and tightly knit immigrant communities, actually immersed?

While the immigrant communities themselves are embedded in the larger culture, and inevitably interact with its cultural and social currents, the individual members of the communities frequently remain isolated to varying degrees. José lived in Los Angeles for 8 years and learned barely any English. It was only after coming to North Carolina, which lacks (although increasingly less so) that well-established, intricate network of resources and employment for Hispanics, that he began to learn the language. In addition, the focus of many of these immigrants on work to the exclusion of all other things—as I heard from my neighbor at the *jaripeo*—limits their ability to explore the culture that they have entered. It's much more important to earn money to send back to the place that you consider your home than it is to try to make a home of what is basically, well, a very extended stay in a foreign hotel. So my sister may be on to something when she insists that José's world would open up if he got to see more of the world, because it's not the "more" she's focusing on, it's the seeing.

José, on the other hand, was frightened by the idea of a trip of that sort, which my sister and I found incomprehensible. This man had crossed the US-Mexican border illegally several times, crawling dehydrated through stretches of desert and nearly freezing at night, moving with the pressures of poverty behind him and of the INS patrols all around him. How could he be afraid to do the comparatively undemanding (and completely legal) wandering that we were used to? Part of it seemed to come from a sense of guilt, from a feeling that, however much he might want to do it, that sort of travel was something that rich people did, and that his was not the sort of life in which that sort of travel belonged. He was only tangled in that internal struggle because of encountering my sister's and my privileged expectations about what the world might offer *our* sort of life. Traveling, for him, meant being irresponsible to his family and to himself. Also, he was intimidated by the idea of traveling in Latin America (which we found surprising, having assumed he'd be more comfortable there). He was anxious about finding himself out of place in a part of the world where he presumably should feel relatively at home. But the part of his fear that fascinated my sister and me, and the part we found most startling, was that he felt the same kind of anxiety that people feel when contemplating their first major travel experience, in spite of his frequent border crossings and long residence in a foreign country.

It was in discussing our incredulity that my sister and I discovered that we had both independently imagined going down to Mexico and hiring a *coyote*[1] to take us across the border. It sounds ridiculous to admit this. As José was considering, with some trepidation, embarking on the kind of trip that for him was a shirking of major responsibilities to his family and to his own sense of self, my sister and I were contemplating making adjustments to our own style of travel, wondering if it would be possible to buy ourselves an illegal border crossing, like a more dramatic safari. Were we just fantasizing about being Extreme Tourists, about taking our travels one crazy step farther than most people dared—and if the *coyote* abandoned us in the desert[1], that would be the ultimate travel adventure, right? I'd rather think it came from somewhere sincere, not from an overdeveloped sense of backpacker one-upmanship, and I don't think I'm just deluding myself in believing that. It came from a real desire to understand what it must be like for someone to make that dangerous trip, even knowing that we could never hope to actually replicate the experience of someone crossing into the US illegally. Even if a *coyote* could be persuaded to take us across, the dangers would be mostly absent. We would have none of the driving motivations, and if the border patrols were to pick us up, we'd be sternly and thoroughly questioned, and perhaps fined, but our passports would probably protect us from any greater punishment. We would not feel the pressure to make the journey wearing high heels, or with far too little protection from the sun, so as not to look too suspiciously prepared to cross.

Still, we could certainly be accused, if not of any actual crime, of exoticizing illegal immigration, of reimagining the desperation and bravery of those who make the dangerous crossing as a sort of dashing adventurousness. In some sense, though, that silly desire was a variation on our standard approach to travel, a way to bridge cultural gaps, a way to expose ourselves to an entirely different life experience. The closest we had so far been able to get to immigration, and to its effects on the social landscape of Mexico, was on buses crossing the Mexican countryside, listening to itinerant musicians in the aisles playing Los Tigres del Norte songs about immigration to the US, amazed that there is an entire subgenre of songs dedicated to the phenomenon. With a *coyote* at our sides, as long as he remained there and didn't fade into the desert with vague instructions to head toward a distant highway, we might be able to get a bit closer: not all the way, of course, in the same way that people who follow pilgrim trails as a travel experience cannot hope to replicate all the fervor and spiritual intensity of a pilgrimage, but closer. We both realize, however, that this is one gap all our earnest wishing will not close.

It's easy to dismiss our style of travel as a mere dabbling in culture, a poor substitute for the real cultural immersion that an immigrant faces, but that's not necessarily a useful way to look at it. It's true that often, since they live abroad for so long, even though they intend one day to return, Mexican immigrants to the United States don't feel quite at home again in Mexico. They find themselves caught between the assumptions of the two cultures, and never manage to reconcile them. In the best of circumstances, where they still feel strong ties to Mexico, and plan to live there in the future, they remain unable to make a living in the place that they consider their home, estranged from their own culture by economic circumstances. Mexican women have told us that many women go with their husbands when they cross the border to look for employment, but then never come back, even when their husbands do, since the strictures on gender tend to be less intense in the US. (The prevalence of domestic violence in rural Mexico feeds into this dynamic.) Our museum-heavy jaunts through foreign places rarely expose us to that kind of cultural dissonance. But it was our kind of traveling, the bourgeois, boring kind, that led us to La Luz, TX, where a quick game of count-the-gringos in the crowd came up with us and one other man next to the bullpen.

Both my sister and I had our worlds broken apart and glued back together in a larger and more wondrous form when we did our first bits of middle class tourism. It became a world in which the man sitting next to me in a crowded *plaza de toros* might also have been a neighbor in a world a couple thousand miles away. It became a world in which the economic conditions of a small town in rural Mexico can be both a trigger for and a reflection of social and cultural changes in my own country. It became a world in which I and a man from that Mexican village could have different ways of traveling, and share them with each other. It's unlikely that I'll ever be forced to look for jobs in another country because the only ones available to me in my own can't provide enough money to live on, and José will never feel like two years of his life would be well-spent being a dilettante abroad. Nevertheless, it's not enough to say that our ways of moving through the world complement each other, or even that either way is valid: it's important for me to be aware of the cultural dynamics that foster that difference. It will be as good for me to understand the kind of privilege I enjoy as it may be for José, who flew to Brazil last week, to feel free to lie on the beach in a foreign country, instead of propping up its economy with his labor. This shouldn't mean that I have to renounce all the advantages given to me by this privilege, though, so if anyone knows a good *coyote*...[2]

---

[1] *A coyote is an immigrant smuggler; people pay them thousands of dollars to lead them safely over the border into the United States. Leading them safely can apparently be too much of a pain in the ass, however, and some coyotes have abandoned their charges, leaving them to wander around the desert alone, sometimes many miles from civilization. Thousands of immigrants have died in the past ten years while attempting to enter the country, many of them because of negligent traffickers.*

[2] *Relax, you idiots, she's joking.*

africa, india, pakistan

GREATEST HITS, 96-01

supplied by Volvo, CrimethInc. Travel Agency

I'm the first one to admit that adventure can be found right around the corner. However, if you're somewhat fortunate, and can manage to save up some money for an airline ticket, I recommend you go beyond your known horizon, because there is a world to discover. Travels in far off countries can prove to be nasty, brutish and short, but also mind-bending and truly exhilarating. I've picked my brain for some stories that I hope could serve as an inspiration...

1. HITCHHIKING ACROSS THE SAHARA DESERT
"You can't go there, there are no roads..."
~ My local travel agency

THROUGH OCCUPIED TERRITORY

I boarded a bus in the town of Laayoune, where I'd spent a night, and was just as happy to see some familiar faces on the bus as I was to leave this dusty godforsaken town-turned-military-outpost behind. Laayoune is the heart of the Moroccan annexation of what was formerly known, and is still recognized by the U.N., as Western Sahara.

When Spain evacuated the phosphate-rich region of Western Sahara, which they called Spanish Sahara, in 1975, partly because of harassment from the Polisario, a rebel group fighting for national liberation, both Morocco and Mauritania raised claims to the sparsely populated desert territory. Mauritania dropped its claim in 1979, after the Polisario had crippled their economy for several years, in exchange for Morocco renouncing any historical right to, and dropping plans to absorb, Mauritania. In November 1975, King Hassan II orchestrated the infamous Green March: about 350,000 Moroccans, mostly civilians, marched into the territory to stake out their "historical" right. In the late sixties it had become clear that the native inhabitants, the Sarahavis, wanted independence. The Popular Front for the Liberation of Saguia al-Hamra and Rio de Oro (Polisario) embarked on a long guerrilla war against the new Moroccan overlords. Polisario scored occasional successes against their far superior enemy but as they lost Libyan and Algerian backing and the Moroccans erected a 1600km-long sand wall to hamper their movement, it become clear that they were losing the battle. The U.N. brokered a ceasefire in 1991, under the understanding that a referendum would be held to settle the issue one and for all. The ceasefire has largely been holding up but the referendum keeps getting postponed and has yet to materialize. The referendum has been postponed due to bitter disagreement of who would be eligible to vote. The Polisario, rightfully, wants only those registered as citizens before the Green March allowed participating, but Morocco naturally wants to include many of the region's new inhabitants. A lot of these inhabitants have been enticed to move into the area with the help of tax-relief and prospects of employment. Morocco has also strengthened its hold on the territory since the ceasefire, by investing in infrastructure and expanding the city of Laayoune.

A lot of these improvements have to do with the fact that they need it to support their mining and military activities as well as to accommodate new settlers. Recently the U.N. made clear that they support a "frame-work agreement" with a limited autonomy for Western Sahara within the state of Morocco. This proposition is not only a concession to Morocco and a slap in the face to the 165,000 Saharavis living in refugee camps in Southern Algeria. To add insult to injury the camps are also having their food supply slowly cut off, most probably to make them more prone to swallow any deal. However, the Polisario is not accepting the agreement—but the chance that they will get the territory, which according to a ruling of the International Court in Haag 1975 belongs to them, looks small at the moment.

Seated on the bus with big smiles plastered over their faces were two other travelers I bonded with in the Moroccan capital of Rabat while we were all trying our best to acquire the visa for Mauritania. This tedious process ended up involving fake airline tickets, exchanging currency on the black market, and a bit of legwork, but finally we had it within our grasp and passport covers.

Local custom dictates that you offer food you devour while traveling to the surrounding passengers, and in exchange for a banana passed back an aisle in the bus I struck up a brief friendship with a man on his way to visit relatives. At a brief stop the man, and his traveling company, treated me to the traditional tea ceremony, involving three progressively stronger and sweeter cups of tea, while I was trying to sit cross-legged on a carpet on the floor. Most of the other people in the room were sitting by the tables on the chairs provided, and I figured that my newfound friends who preferred the carpets on the floor were Sarahavis, so I brought up the subject of Polisario and was hastily quietened down under the pretext that the "walls have ears" and "the only free debate takes place on the internet."

We arrived in Dakhla a couple days before the next convoy was due to leave for Mauritania, and tried to find a suitable ride. After registering with the army, which leads the bi-weekly convoy to the Mauritanian border, we managed to secure a ride with two French guys in their cars. They had done the trip a couple of times before, every time bringing cars with them which they sold once they got them through the desert and arrived in the capital of Mauritania, Nouakchott. At first they were reluctant to bring us along, due to the extra weight—but on the other hand, we would be more people around to help with the digging and pushing once the cars got stuck. The convoy consisted of Mauritanian traders in over-packed jeeps, some other travelers in beat up vehicles, nicely robed men with turbans in shiny BMWs, and an English guy on motorcycle.

IN THE HANDS OF THE REAPER

The convoy left Dakhla in the afternoon, and as the car I was riding in overtook all other vehicles at a neck-breaking speed it slowly dawned on me that my benefactor at the wheel, Richard, was more than a little crazy. We later dubbed him Minus and his more rational counterpart Olivie, Plus, because Minus sometimes drove the car into pieces before reaching the destination, quite purposefully, and lost all his money on the trip. This time he didn't have

OUR GUIDE KHALITA, AND PART OF OUR LITTLE CONVOY ACROSS THE SAHARA

any to start with either so Plus had put down the money for both cars and hired him on as a driver for one of them. This seemed like the worst possible set-up so naturally I asked Plus why he would chose Minus over any other sane person to do the job—to which he replied something to the effect that "it makes it more interesting." While most other people eased along trying to minimize the impact of the road, which gradually deteriorated, we were way up ahead flying past camels and the odd sand dune. Minus's English wasn't top notch, but he was eager to learn; so while we were pressed to our seats, flying over "roads" one wouldn't be able to bike on, he popped a tape into the stereo. We were shooting like projectile through the desert into the unknown adventure, and "Bombtrack" by Rage Against the Machine came blasting out of the stereo, which made me feel so intensely alive that I got goose bumps and screamed at the top of my lungs. Minus, the driver, on the other hand, let go of the steering wheel and fished out a handwritten note with the lyrics and started following along and make out the words, asking questions about some of them and generally not keeping his eyes at the road at all, which pushed another couple of ounces of adrenalin into my bloodstream. This became a common occurrence...

At nightfall, we arrived at the end of the road, literally, where the last Moroccan army post is, and camped there. In the morning we were waved off into the desert, which in that area is filled with landmines. We crossed our fingers, cranked up the stereo, and stuck to visible tracks and the odd pieces of dirt road here and there. The traders and their jeeps defected from the herd well before the first Mauritanian border post, in order to avoid taxes and scrutinizing eyes. We in our trusty, dusty old Mercedes hit the border first and were greeted by camouflaged soldiers, who crawled out from a dilapidated shelter.

I ponder their situation being posted out here, fully exposed to the merciless sun, landmines, heat, the constant blowing of sand. When we were filling in our personal data in a big ledger I noticed that one young soldier's shirt, sticking up from under his uniform, sported a collar embroidered "Tupac." He might be dead, but he is still everywhere in Africa—although few people seemed to know that he was a musician, let alone dead.

We tried to get airborne on a sand ledge, which was blocking our path, and stopped further down to see how they others were making it over. The English guy on the dirt bike got some air, but his front wheel sank deep when he landed—he ate shit and got his bike over him as a dessert. We ran back to aid him—and while lying motionless in the sand, his face white as a sheet, he gave us his diagnosis: the femur broken in two places. This was corroborated later. We pooled our skills and tranquillizers, and managed to put the leg in a splint. He was then put in the back of the fastest jeep, and sent ahead with a soldier to speed up the process at the different checkpoints. Considering that he'd nearly fainted from excruciating pains when he was lifted with utmost care, nobody envied his position in the back of that jeep, bouncing for hours through desert before they reached a hospital—if there was one. We later heard through the grapevine that by some incredible luck he was taken in and operated on by a hospital attached to a foreign mining company—he survived.

After a number of irritating and seemingly unnecessary checkpoints, we finally arrived in the first town in Mauritania, Noadhibou. The fun doesn't stop here though, because after all, you are in Mauritania, and there is no road or reliable tracks that lead through the desert to the capital, Nouakchott.

THE END OF THE WORLD AS WE KNOW IT

Mauritania gained independence and started to build their capital, Nouakchott, in 1960. This Islamic republic, ruled by former nomads or their descendants, has since been ripe with military coups and racial tension. In the late 1960's, 83% of the population was still nomads, but desertification and persistent droughts have only spared the 10% that is still officially nomadic. Today, the country is a complete desert and only 1% of its area is fertile enough to sustain crops. This infertility of the landscape might be a plausible explanation for the female beauty standard of the Bidan caste of the Moors, which is to be plum and fat. Supposedly, some of them even feed their daughters a special diet of milk and peanuts so that they will grow up to be desirably colossal. Some members from a differing and lower caste, like the Haratin Moors, are probably happy if they get fed at all—because they might be slaves. In 1980 Mauritania declared slavery illegal, as the last country in the world, and it's estimated that there were an about 100,000 Haratin slaves within the country's borders at the time. To declare it illegal doesn't equal the eradication of the practice, and a lot of slaves didn't really have any options. Therefore it might not be all hearsay when some sources report that people are occasionally still bought and sold in the Adrar area, northeast of Nouakchott.

After checking in at a primitive hotel, our French drivers sought out a reliable guide, and we scraped together a raggedy lot of people and cars to share the cost. A guide is a must-have unless you desire to turn into toast somewhere in the desert after getting lost or breaking down, something that happens all the time. His name was Khalifa, he looked like a character out of a fairytale, and he was well versed in navigating the stretch from being an old guide for the camel caravans that used to cross the vast plains before some of the trafficking was taken over by trucks. He didn't speak anything besides the local dialect of Arabic, Hassaniya, but communicated with signs as he was riding shotgun and leading the way with his hands. At tricky passages he walked in front of our small caravan and checked after strands of firm sand. With my limited knowledge of Arabic I later managed to find out that he had 37 camels out there somewhere (he pointed to the horizon), which made him a very wealthy man in this neck of the woods. Our little caravan consisted of the Frenchmen and their two cars, two Germans in a minivan, and three Spaniards with one car each. After stocking up on water and food—mostly that French type of bread that goes rock hard in fifteen minutes—we left town in the afternoon. We managed to squeeze through the military checkpoint without parting with any of our money, and, after picking up a hitchhiking local couple, we were off.

DESERT WITH MIRAGES

I had imagined the Sahara desert to be one picturesque sand dune after another, but it was actually a very varied landscape with everything from enormous plains made up of sand or little rocks to what looked like a savannah. The common denominator, though, was the constant maelstrom of sand that traveled with the winds over the infertile surface. A thin film of sand covers and permeates everything; after a while we had more sand in our eyes, food, cameras, sleeping bags, and cars than you can find in any urban playground sandpit. The first day passed in a joyful bliss and even the digging and pushing of the vehicles that got stuck was a novel experience. When the daylight disappeared we camped in the shelter of a croissant-shaped sand dune. The local people slept on the ground wrapped in their roomy attire and I got down into my sleeping bag. The weather during the day wasn't unbearably hot, thanks to the breeze from the nearby ocean, but at night it got pretty cold. I woke up almost covered in sand that settled on me during the night, had some sandy bread with sandy water, and we were off again. We continued to traverse the landscape; most of the other cars kept getting stuck, due to poor drivers'

A MINE WARNING SIGN SOMEWHERE ON THE BORDER BETWEEN MOROCCO/WEST SAHARA
MEDITERRANEAN

ONE OF THE ZILLION TIMES WE HAD TO BAIL THE CAR OUT

skills or weak engines, while our cars were doing circles around them. We also chased the odd camel at the horizon and did some roof-top surfing to pass the time. It was an amazing feeling to hang on to the sunroof while Minus was trying to set new speeding records on the vast sand plains. We took a little detour, although we had no way of telling, to drop our hitchhikers off at a Bedouin camp in the middle of nowhere. A beat up Landrover in their camp was the demarcation between this century and the last one and as we entered one of the tents, a sight greeted me that to this day I have tattooed in my retina. In the middle of the tent, cross-legged on a big carpet, sat an old man with a huge white beard and turban in front of an enormous and very old looking holy Koran. He also had his eyes generously encircled with blue eyeliner, which would have produced laughter in any other situation, except for this one: being face to face with an infamous Tuareg. The Tuaregs are historically known for being fierce warriors and skilled traders or raiders, though robbery was considered an honorable occupation. However, they were more or less forced to abolish their old lifestyle when the French put an end to nomadic movement and abolished slavery. Most of them turned to herding and had to leave the desert in search for greener pastures; but some of them still follow their traditional nomadic lifestyle. They are easily recognizable, due to their fair skin and indigo-blue robes or shawls wrapped around their heads to protect them from the elements. We were offered diluted camels' milk prepared by the women, and before we left we reciprocated their hospitality by exchanging some of our bread for ancient arrowheads, remnants from early human habitations that came to an end when the desert started spreading about 10,000 years ago.

UNDER A SHELTERING SKY

We had expected to arrive the same night, but some of the cars started to give trouble—and the very same cars, more than often the Spanish driven ones, repeatedly got stuck. As the day progressed, joyous acclamations turned into curses, loose objects into car parts, and bushes at the horizon into houses with attached swimming pools. The guide Khalifa got

more and more opportunities to kneel towards Mecca and brew tea in his little teapot. We on the other hand were digging, cursing, and pushing the cars, which returned the favor by wasting our drinking water with their coolers. Minus wrecked the whole steering apparatus in our car by hitting some big rocks in a restless stupor, which disabled us to the extent that we could only turn left. We were literally driving in circles before the problem got fixed with some rope and a chain. The good mood was gone and so was our food. We seriously, and deliriously, thought about leaving the two most faltering, haltering Spanish cars behind, with or without their drivers. The night was getting closer and we had to change our plans and head for a little fishing community by the ocean. We towed the two Spanish cars and arrived half-starved in the little village before nightfall, where we took a well deserved bath in the ocean and went hunting for food. The only available meal around the huts was some meat-based dish so I retracted into the car with some canned vegetables and some bread that I managed to acquire. The next day I was happy to leave because the little village had an eerie feeling to it and the villagers were doing their best to exploit our precarious conditions to extract as much money as possible from us. We had to leave the two cars behind because towing wasn't an option anymore, due to deeper sand and the extra stress on the leading vehicle. Several times during the day we had to cross over some real dunes; at first glance this looked impossible, but we pulled through. In the afternoon we reached the last stretch before the capital, which you drive on the beach at low tide. We reached some amazing speeds on the hard-packed sand, while dodging jackals and stranded boats. At one point I remember that the three Spanish men, packed into their last car, overtook us and I egged on Minus to retain the pole position. He replied that he paced himself because "behind one of these corners there are rocks which you can't see on beforehand" with that priceless French accent, while he stepped on it and brought the trophy home. Minutes later we turned a corner at full speed only to be met by huge rocks all over the beach, and I screamed as we were launched off a big one. I swear that we got fully

A BUTCHER AT THE SMUGGLER'S BAZAAR IN PESHAWAR

airborne before we crashed with a thunderous noise right off the shoreline, water splashing everywhere. While I did a check of all my limbs, the others in our caravan turned up and were flabbergasted. Miraculously, we could continue driving as soon as we backed out of the water. We arrived in the capital, Nouakchott, where the roads to the rest of sub-Sahara start, at nightfall. I took some time regaining my strength and sanity before I continued my adventure, with my traveling partners, on public transportation—but that is another story...

Recommended reading:
The Sheltering Sky, Paul Bowles
(A beautiful novel concerning love, hardship, and traveling in the desert)
The Nomad or *The Vagabond*, Isabelle Eberhardt
(Amazing writing from this female vagabond who traveled the area disguised as a man)
... and anything on the conflict in Western Sahara.

2. A BRIEF SCENE REPORT – PESHAWAR

"Power springs from the barrel of a gun." –George W. Bush

"Ladies and gentlemen, Inshallah (God willing), we shall soon be landing in Lahore," announces the authoritative voice loud enough for me to wake up and ponder my destiny, now apparently in the hands of God. Slumped in a seat onboard a plane belonging to Pakistan International Airways, which has the dubious task of flying very used equipment around the world's most hostile aviation environment, I find I'm kind of nervous, being not only an infidel but also an atheist. Seemingly safe on the ground, I greet this magnificent country while exiting the terminal as the warm weather embraces me to a backdrop of the commotion you'll find in any travelers' hub in this part of the world. Pakistan has had a rich and sometimes turbulent history that would be just as hard to condense as it would be boring to read. The teeming

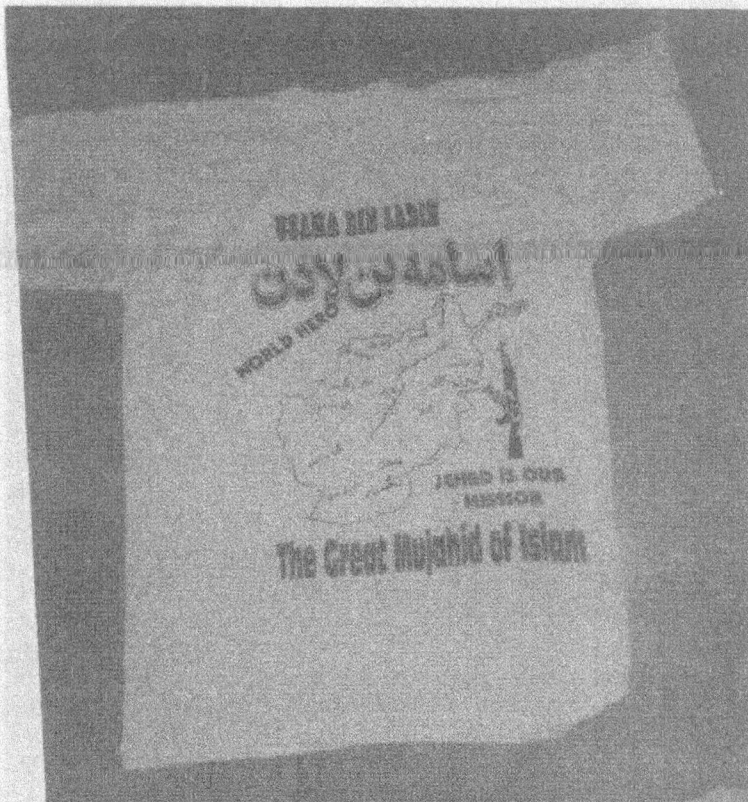

LOCAL MERCHANDISE IN PESHAWAR

population of Pakistan is as diverse as it is large. Its population of about 130 million is made up of several different ethnicities, and the while the country is officially Muslim, with both the Sunni and Shiite strand represented, there are people of most religions thrown into the stew. The pot is not only melting but occasionally also exploding as well, in outbursts of sectarian, political and social violence. Even if this is what makes headlines around the world, the country has so much more to offer—and the mind-bending landscape with its deeply hospitable people is bound to leave some long lasting impressions, as it did upon me. Here are some of them...

Politics on the Border to Theatre

On my first day in the country I traveled to the border between Pakistan and its neighbor India, some twenty minutes west of Lahore. I went to witness the daily ceremony surrounding the closing of the only open land crossing between the two enemies. India and Pakistan are arch-rivals and try to outdo each other in everything from cricket to a nuclear arms race, and the spectacle at the border was no exception. After paying the 4-cent entrance fee we hurried over to what looked like a construction site, which I realized would serve as a grandstand. The Indians already had one, which was now filled to the brim, while we on the Pakistani side had to stand on the ground. We lined up beside the road that led through the border gates, with women and men on separate sides. I barely had time to study the soldiers, displaying their best, although worn out, uniforms before the ceremony began. Suddenly the soldiers from both countries started screaming while they performed a well synchronized ritual which eventually led to them hauling the flag. One by one they stormed forward towards the iron gate with a stride reminding me of Charlie Chaplin's impersonation of Hitler. The arms were pendulating all the way around the shoulders and the legs were lifted so high that their noses seemed to be in danger. But it wasn't the nose that was at stake, but the country's honor, so every move was made with both grave seriousness and precision, all while the audience applauded their respective side and its maneuvers. I had to bite my tongue in order not to burst out laughing while every soldier marched forward and performed his patriotic duty. Every soldier slammed his feet down really hard, which looked painful, in order to create a noise that he complemented with shouts and loud theatrical sniffs, directed at the infidels on the other side. The Indian soldiers at the other side did likewise and they even had a big sign directed towards Pakistan saying "India – The largest democracy in the world." A not so subtle jab at Pakistan who has had more dictators than elections lately. After the flag was hauled the men of both sides gathered by the gate and the festive atmosphere was gone, replaced by a shouting match. Although this took place at a time when the relations between the countries were better than they'd been for a long time, I got a little bit worried. Luckily it didn't turn into a new shot in Sarajevo but merely died down as the men reunited with the women and children. A lot of families went out along the fence to a stone that marks the actual border and snapped some photos for the family album.

Lahore

The Old City of Lahore, which consists of a maze of narrow roads and alleys, is surrounded by a moat and filled with bazaars and people—a lot of transactions take place here, some of questionable nature. Defying warnings by exploring it alone, I was pretty wary at first; but after the first day I found nothing but a friendly reception and scenes out of the Arabian Nights, although with small polluting cars and plastic merchandise added. Shaking hands seemed to be a prevalent custom among men and during my stay in Pakistan I probably shook more hands than an American presidential candidate. One day while drifting in the endless bazaar somebody suddenly pressed my hand and when I directed my eyes to the man in front of me a chill went through my spine.

DARA ADAM KHEL: ONE OF THE COUNTLESS HOLE-IN-THE-WALL SHOPS...

A GUN MANUFACTURER IN DARA ADAM KHEL, WORKING AWAY IN HIS SHOP

In front of me was a man with a knife through his throat and another one through his wrist whose still attached hand held a wad of money. Judging by his smile, and the fact that he was smiling, I assumed a closer inspection would cost some money so I quickly moved along. The knife through the throat was most probably a fake, but the one through the wrist looked darn real—but I didn't want to learn and at the same time encourage people to self-mutilation in order to eke out a living.

HOLIDAY IN OTHER PEOPLE'S MISERY

After a couple months of traveling in nearby countries, I returned to Pakistan to lick my wounds in a comfortable setting, and I found myself back in Lahore due to my connections in the city. It was late spring and the mercury was going through the roof. I started to get some travel fatigue; the enchanting bazaars and street life in Lahore lost some of its luster in the heat. After being fortunate enough to recover and catch my breath for a while in the crossfire of two air conditioners, I set out to experience a truly mythical place, Peshawar. I boarded the train in the evening, found my designated bench, hidden under a thick layer of dust, and added my sweaty body. When the train sped into the darkness, gusts of air from the window saved me from the assault of the heat outside, where temperatures were hovering around the 45 degree Celsius mark (115 Fahrenheit) on a daily basis. I came to think of how lucky I was in comparison to the majority of the people in Pakistan, of whom about 80 died as a direct result of the heat during the week I spent in Lahore. As the Pakistani writer Moshin Hamid declares in his critically acclaimed novel, Moth Smoke:

"There are two social classes in Pakistan," Professor Superb said to his unsuspecting audience, gripping the podium with both hands as he spoke. "The first group, large and sweaty, contains those referred to as the masses. The second group is much smaller, but its members exercise vastly greater control over their immediate environment and are collectively termed the elite. The distinction between members of these two groups is made on the basis of control of an important resource: air conditioning. You see, the elite have managed to re-create for themselves the living standards of, say, Sweden, without leaving the dusty plains of the subcontinent."

The

A DOGON VILLAGE BENEATH THE ESCARPMENT

reality is much worse, though, with more than 35% of the population living in poverty, a relative concept defined by an inability to meet the most basic needs for food, clothing, and shelter in any weather. Despite the indescribable hardship and suffering, many people could still afford a smile or a hospitable gesture. Many times I got invited to share a cup of tea in the street over some small talk—and, in contrast to a lot of other countries, there was never a catch involved. The poverty remains a great tragedy, though, and I'm not sure what infuriates and saddens me the most—the fact that it exists, or the knowledge that the majority of people in the industrial world is not hard at work obliterating it. This was a sidetrack—but if I return to my story, I wake up as the train is coming to a halt in the city of Peshawar.

A MERCURIAL PLACE

The city of Peshawar, which was founded over 2,000 years ago, has had almost as many names as rulers. The proximity of the famous and strategically important Khyber Pass, a vantage point for would-be invaders of the subcontinent and a vital route for traders, made the area a melting pot for different conquerors and civilizations. The footprints of the Mongol invaders, the Chinese pilgrims, and the Tajik traders are still visible. Today Peshawar is embedded in the unruly North-West Frontier Province (NWFP) of Pakistan, bordering the Khyber Pass Tribal Agency, one of the seven autonomous tribal areas in the region. The tribal areas were never fully conquered and subjected to outside rule by Alexander, the Moguls, the Sikhs, or the British back in the day, and neither are they today by Pakistan. They are populated by a number of tribes of Pashtu ethnic origin, none of which is known for a pacific nature—hence, it's one of the world's most lawless places. However, The Pashtus must abide by the Pashtunwali, their moral code, and the decisions of its application by the jirga, a council of elders, or they typically get their house burnt down and face expulsion from the tribe. The code, together with a fondness for arms, has made the area ripe with prolonged blood feuds

over *zar*, *zan* or *zamin* – gold, women, or land. A declining quantity of drugs is still grown and refined in the area, although nowadays it works mostly as a conduit for the stunning volumes coming in from Afghanistan. It seemed like an interesting place, but when the tribal vendettas and clashes between smugglers fail to keep the inhabitants busy enough, the entrepreneurial spirit easily turns their legendary hospitality into kidnapping—so I decided it wasn't really worth the trouble to holiday too much in the area.

THE AFGHAN CONNECTION

Given the proximity to Afghanistan, it's not surprising to learn that the countries are intertwined in more ways than ethnicity (Pashtus have always lived throughout the area, regardless of national borders). When Afghanistan was occupied by the U.S.S.R., it become home to a senseless war. The Afghan guerrilla force, the Mujaheddin, who courageously fought the Soviet aggressors, received money and weapons from a number of countries, among them U.S.A. The goods were funneled through Pakistan's secret service (I.S.I.) and changed hands in the area around Peshawar, where a lot of the military training also took place. The US committed some four to five billion dollars between 1980 and 1992 in aid to the Mujaheddin. However, the C.I.A.-I.S.I. arms pipeline favored the more radical groups, which naturally radicalized others, who were to liberate a country that so far been pretty moderate. Among other things, the U.S. provided the Mujaheddin with some 900 Stinger anti-aircraft missiles in 1986-87. After 1992 the C.I.A. launched a clandestine but unsuccessful buy-back operation to try to retrieve those Stingers not utilized. It's not hard to imagine the harm these easily-operated missiles could do at a civilian airport somewhere in the world—and they were floating around a largely failed state. After the U.S.S.R. withdrew in 1989, leaving more than 1.5 million dead and millions of landmines behind, Afghanistan plunged into a civil war in which several different warlords mercilessly fought each other while terrorizing the civilian population.

Later, and partly as a reaction, the Taliban movement originated in the many *madrassas* scattered around Peshawar, Quetta, and other Pakistani towns along the Afghan border. A *madrassa* is an Islamic theological school, hence the name of the movement though *talib* means student of Islam, and they offered the only opportunity for Afghan refuges and poor Pakistanis to receive a semblance of an education. The leading Talibans were all veteran Muhajeddin warriors who were dismayed by the moral corruption among their peers. They saw themselves as cleansers and purifiers of a society gone wrong, and the Islamic way that had been compromised by excess and greed. They recruited young students, mostly Afghan refugees and Pashtus, in the *madrassas*, who were disillusioned with the formerly idealized Mujaheddin commanders who now pillaged their country. These were literally children of the war: growing up in refugee camps in Pakistan they hardly knew their own country or history. The young rootless boys seemingly without a future studied little but the Koran and Islamic law as interpreted by barely literate Mullahs, religious teachers. Most of them had never fought before—but, like all Pashtus, they knew how to handle a weapon, and the prospect of returning to their homeland and implementing a just society based on the teachings of the prophet Mohammed filled them with a sense of direction. The specific background of these young men and their seclusion from women while growing up in the *madrassas*, together with their Pashtu tribal traditions, have a lot more to do with the draconic policies of the Talibans, especially the ones targeting women, than with Islamic fundamentalism alone.

When I walked around Peshawar the shadow of Afghanistan was evident in every corner, mostly symbolized by women in blue head-to-toe *burqas* and Afghans begging. I was less of a novelty here as a foreigner here, since several hundred foreign N.G.O.s (Non-Governmental Organizations) working to address the misery in Afghanistan and the natural result, refugees, have their headquarters in the city. About six million Afghans have been forced to flee their country as a result of more than twenty years of war and the last couple of years of drought, and they now reside under horrible conditions in refugee camps in Pakistan and Iran. Peshawar is surrounding by dilapidated camps like Jallozai, where 80,000 people are sheltered under primitive tarps, generally trying to survive under the most desperate conditions. This must be one of the greatest humanitarian catastrophes at the planet today. I was in Peshawar six months before September 11 and Pakistan was still supporting the Taliban. The reason was probably the large Pashtu presence in the military and the fact that Pakistan dearly wanted stability in the region, so that they could start trade overland with the Central Asian Republics. Stability was also the keyword that provided the Talibans with backing from the powerful trading mafia whose smuggling and transporting activities were obstructed by the presence by the many small and unpredictable warlords. After twenty years of war a majority of the population also welcomed the Talibans, who had disarmament programs and generally promised security and peace. When their breach with traditional Afghan values like tolerance, their ethnocentrism, and later their failing discipline became apparent, their stocks plummeted. Soon they had a very limited support, of maybe 15% of the population. In exchange for supporting the Talibans, Pakistan got more refugees, extremism, and contraband.

SMUGGLERS' BAZAAR

It isn't only people that are spilling over the border on donkeys and overcrowded trucks and putting a

ANOTHER DOGON VILLAGE

dent in the already stressed Pakistani budget, but also goods of all kinds. Through an arrangement Afghanistan is allowed to import goods tax-free through Pakistan. Due to the lack purchasing power in Afghanistan, most goods do a u-turn in the desert and are smuggled back into Pakistan. I took the chaotic local bus out of the city and jumped off at the end of the road, which continues, into the Khyber Agency Tribal Area. Here lies Karkhani Bazaar, or Smugglers' Bazaar, which is a more colloquial and appropriate name. As my guidebook to the region proclaimed, and I confirmed with my own eyes, it wasn't a matter of some windswept tents where men in turbans sold dusty antiques, but Hong Kong in miniature. Small stores housed alongside weird concrete buildings were jam-packed with TVs, computers, soaps, household appliances, clothes, and everything else imaginable, and beyond. Among the small vendors selling toiletries and other products for more intimate use, I found my favorite article. It was a small tube of "breast enlargement cream" which promised growing breasts after generous application in the region. At the end of the market, where the tribal area starts, there was a gate guarded by the tribal police and huge signs forbidding foreigners to enter. On the other side of the border the commerce continues and the goods are largely made up of arms and drugs. I talked to other travelers at my hostel that managed to sneak around the gate in the company of local friends sharing their devotion for drugs, and they testified about the mass quantities of hash and heroin that are put up for sale. The drugs come sewed up in sheepskin sacks, and big blocks are openly sold for ridiculously low prices. With a pale complexion and without local knowledge and company you might be mistaken for a D.E.A. (the American Drug Enforcement Agency) agent, which needlessly puts you in grave danger. It's estimated that the value of the trade with smuggled goods, without accounting for arms and drugs, is about 2 billion dollars—and this is said to be the spine of the Pakistani black market sector, which is estimated to be about 55% of Pakistan's G.N.P. (Gross National Product, the annual sum of all goods and services within a country).

HAPPINESS IS A WARM GUN

Along with some other raggedy drifters, I also took a trip to the town of Darra Adam Khel, arranged and lead by the old and authoritative owner of the hostel where we stayed. We kept a low profile in the back of the truck through the checkpoints and villages, while our guide for the day did the talking and lined his pockets with our money. Finally we came to a halt on what felt like another planet, one where Charlton Heston surely would go apeshit. Darra Adam Khel is an unkempt town, situated in the tribal region of the Afridis, hence beyond Pakistani law and somewhat closed to foreigners. We disembarked in an alley, like so many others in the town, which was bustling with activity. The alley was lined with small shops where men were busy doing what they, and their forefathers, have done for a century: namely, making guns. Despite primitive tools, the Darra gunsmiths, estimated to number 3000, are capable of making a working copy of any known firearm. A Darra gunsmith can duplicate a rifle he's never seen before, making the first template in less than ten days; each additional copy then takes between two to three days to finish. We were taken around the little shops by the best guide money can buy, the local tribal police officer. The craftsmen who were sanding, drilling and carving either acknowledged us with a smile or by proudly showing off their finished products. A wide array of weapons is manufactured in the town: Kalashnikovs, M16s, most varieties of handguns, shotguns, hand grenades, rocket launchers and even anti-aircraft guns. It was a surreal experience walking through the little alleys, meeting fierce-looking men with arms casually slung over their shoulders, all to an accompaniment of constant firing, emanating

A DOGON VILLAGE IN MALI, ON THE DUSTY SANDPLAIN

from everywhere a gunsmiths happened to be trying out finished products. While we were drinking the customary cup of tea, a small arsenal was circulated at the table, and we negotiated the prices for trying the different weapons. We went around a house and shot Kalashnikov at a nearby cliff, as well as pistol at a pile of bricks, while little kids ran around to collect the shells. The area has grown into one of the largest unofficial arms markets in the world. It might be worth mentioning that the majority of suffering due to weaponry originates in official markets, despite the sometimes glossy packaging (as described by John Pilger in *The Hidden Agenda*). A copied Kalashnikov started off at about 80 dollars and handguns about half of that. We were also showed a 22-calibre gun disguised in a pen, engraved with the name of the town, which was selling for 8 dollars. It's estimated that between 400 and 700 guns are finished in Darra Adam Khel every day. A lot of them used to cross the border into Afghanistan before the Afghan warlords found other benefactors willing to fuel the fire. Nowadays most of the arms end up within the borders of Pakistan, especially in the tribal areas, but they are readily found throughout the society.

From Peshawar I traveled north in search of greener pastures and a more mild climate, which was to be found where the three great mountain ranges meet. There among the Himalayas, the Hindukush, and Indus mountains I found my Shangri-La.

Recommended reading:
Moth Smoke, Moshin Hamid (*An interestingly written novel about the decadent life of the upper class in Lahore*)
Taliban – Islam, Oil and the New Great Game in Central Asia, Ahmed Rashid (*A good introduction to Taliban, the struggle over the oil in the region and its geopolitical implications*)
Danziger's Travel, Nick Danziger (*An account of an exciting journey through the region during the Afghan war with the U.S.S.R., with Nick paying little regard for borders, visas, or money*)

3. THE FUNERAL SHOW

HOLD YOUR PANTS

I'm relieving my bladder as I'm watching the sun setting over a mesmorizing landscape from my position behind the last train carriage. I figured it was safe to get off the train after watching some other passengers crowding around a nearby well in order to wash themselves before evening prayer. Meanwhile others were eating dinner provided by the many crafty locals that sprung out of the nearby village with a veritable restaurant on top of their head. It was yet another unexplainable stop in the middle of nowhere on the only railway route open for passengers in that end of West Africa. It's something very mythical to be looking out from a train window and be graced with the picturesque image of the vast African savannahs while having the repetitive beat of the sills to soothe your ears. I can't really find the words to describe it but I think Hemingway got it right somewhere, even though I wouldn't know, because I haven't read a word he's written. Lost in thoughts, now as then, I buttoned my fly when suddenly the train whistle cut through the serenity and the train started moving as rapidly as unexpectedly. It accelerated faster than ever before,

with me running frantically behind, trying to catch up with the last carriage. I managed to swing myself up at the last door, with the aid of friendly hands and that vertical handle, like I was the star in a bad western movie. We pulled up some other runners but a majority who foresaw their defeat threw up their hands in a desperate gesture and screamed. I was extremely relieved to be onboard and not left in the middle of nowhere without even a sweater, let alone the rest of my luggage. The next train wasn't scheduled to pass until after a couple of days, assuming it didn't derail. The train driver didn't seem to bat an eyelid, and we continued to gain speed with every meter along a trajectory that took us further into the impending darkness and the country of Mali.

BAMAKO

It took the capital in the fifth poorest country in the world for me to swallow my pride and take refuge under the cross. I checked into a primitive hostel run by a convent and some stern catholic nuns in order to escape from the chaos. It's plausible to think that the capital in a country like this would be a sleepy affair but nothing could be further from the truth. When I first arrived at night I teamed up with some other travelers at the train station while trying to find some kind of accommodation. We walked into the dark night on streets that were lined with literally thousands of people sound asleep on the pavement. I couldn't possibly have felt smaller and more vulnerable walking those streets with only a little switchblade knife as possible defense if someone would try to take more than my wallet. At last we found the hostel before bad luck found us, and when we woke up the next morning the city didn't look quite the same—it was bustling with activity that would put any anthill to shame. Thousands of busses, mopeds, and cars chased the impending accident on roads of differing quality. I think that the majority of the roads were gravel as opposed to tarmac. Every available inch of the pavement was covered with people and vendors hawking their products. I didn't find God in the hostel, just some other travelers, among them some female volunteers on a break from their stationing in Mauritania. We were heading towards the same area, the Dogon country, and decided to go together as well as sharing the cost of a guide to the area.

DOGON COUNTRY

The Dogon people of Mali are famous for their art, distinctive adobe architecture, colorful masked dances, and ceremonies. Their culture is based upon animistic religious beliefs and is being preserved through a tightly knit social structure with intensely cooperative group behavior. The Dogon have made their home along the remarkable Bandigara escarpment, a 200-kilometer cliff face which runs like a wall across the desert. Their picturesque villages scatter the foot of the cliff, which is at places perforated with little caves that served as protection from marauding groups and slave raiders for hundreds of years. On the rocky rubble below and in the sandy plains and fields stretching out from there, the Dogon, who are skilled agriculturalists, raise millet, onions, sorghum, and other crops, despite the inhospitable environment. Communal labor, collective action, and group responsibility are characteristics of Dogon village life. They are very hospitable, something which may be a factor undermining their culture and cohesion. The contemporary visitors don't take or buy slaves, but culturally important art objects, as well as risking distorting the traditional village life. On the other hand, the little trickle of tourists have also become an important resource in ensuring the survival of the Dogon and their culture by providing them with an income when other sources dry up. Hence we decided to go with a guide that came highly recommended, to minimize our impact and make the encounter somewhat mutually beneficial to both parties. Working as a guide has become a lucrative business, attracting a lot of people without the necessary knowledge, discretion, or ethnicity. After wading through offers including impostors we finally met our man, David, in the village of Sanga. We left for our trek the next day and our guide David negotiated our passage through homes and villages, by paying fees and distributing the *kola* nuts as required, on top of explaining every cultural trait under the sun as we went along. The kola nut is a purple-colored nut frequently used as a gift to and among the Dogons, who chew on them. They're supposed to give you a mild intoxication but I came halfway through the chestnut sized devil before the extremely bitter taste threw me off so I can't tell you what it's like.

The Funeral

We got back to Sanga after spending a couple of days trekking along the escarpment and staying in the little villages, and I was starting to feel really sick. There was a funeral in a nearby village and our guide David asked the village elder if our little group could attend. We were given permission to attend a ceremony that lasted for at least two nights. The first night I felt too sick to move and while the others went, I laid on the roof of our primitive hotel like a fish on dry land, gasping for a gust of cool air. I slept quite a bit on roofs all over West Africa for that reason, but I didn't really bother with mosquito nets, which is probably what made me sick in the first place. Later that night the others came back all excited and gibbered incoherently about all they had witnessed. I wasn't sure whether it was just another feverish dream because it sounded pretty unreal. The next afternoon I joined them and we all walked over to the village for the second day of rituals. When we approached the village we were greeted by a large mob armed with spears and antique rifles who ran along the village perimeter while shouting and screaming. The first thought that flashed through my mind was that we were on the menu that night, but our guide David explained that they were circling the village in order to ward off all the evil spirits that settle after the somebody dies. All the villagers were gathered in the little town square and we were assigned some space on the roof of a mud hut overlooking it. The epicenter of the square was a dead cow, which had been slaughtered sacrificially and adorned with various fetishes, sacred objects and the deceased man's shroud. The women were gathered in a colorful and improvised choir along one side and they sung and clapped to the beat of African drums. Most of them were wearing the traditional African dress, although some sported an odd sun bleached clothing item of foreign kind—the very same clothes people in rich countries donate to aid organizations who ship them over there. It was an enchanting and surreal musical carpet to the events that took place. In front of us the men were gathered and most of them were armed with ancient looking rifles. They took turns doing a little dance around the corpse of the dead cow before firing into the air to ward off the evil spirits. They on the other hand seemed to be in good spirits and it was a festive atmosphere, no doubt fueled by the reunion with their kin in the village and home-made millet beer. Most young men were sporting more modern clothes and were more cosmetically adorned, with some small traditional clothing item. This is probably due to the structural male migration that is common in Africa, and other societies marked by economic dualism, where young men leave for the cities in order to find a job and make money. I don't struggle with romantic notions of cultural purity, but it was truly weird to see a young man ceremonially dancing with a rifle while being dressed in a traditional garb complemented with modern sneakers and sunglasses. I did however struggle with my grip on reality, partly because of the heat and my sickness, but mostly because of the incredible scenes that were played out in front of my eyes. It never felt like a dream, though, since the dreams I had at the time were all really horrible stories induced by my preferred brand of malaria prophylactic. After a while the ceremony was crowned by a group of men dancing while wearing the incredible masks that the Dogon people are famous throughout the world for sporting on special occasions. The masks, which are kept in a sacred cave for most of the year, are colorful and very elongated. The longest ones extended for several meters over the wearers' heads. The group of men bearing the masks, as well as some other amazing clothes and bijouterie, were performing dances in which they were letting the long mask sway back and forward in front of the enthusiastic audience. I felt privileged to be immersed in such a scene and celebration and it was truly a Kodak moment, if there ever been one, but we weren't allowed to take pictures. After the ceremonies were over the whole village seemed to be fermenting with joy, as was the millet beer in everybody's stomachs. This brew taste a little bit like German wheat beer, but my already weak legs prevented me from joining in and putting the Munich October fest to shame. Although fatigued, I was happy as a clam when I walked back to my mattress on the roof to write the next chapter in my history book, largely dealing with the continued illness which later forced me to cut my trip short and return home.

Recommended reading:

Dogon – Africa's People of the Cliffs, Walter Beek and Stephanie Hollyman (*Large book with nice pictures and informative texts*)

stockholm
(International) Noise Conspiracy
Video Shoot

Respectfully submitted to HeartattaCk by freelance gossip columnist B. Dee

Mercilessly bootlegged and reprinted here by CrimethInc. assholes bent on getting in even more trouble than they have already.

It's a scene out of a Fellini movie. Three and a half years after I first saw Refused reinvent punk rock as a pop culture molotov cocktail that left me sobbing and soaring with new, unrealized dreams of revolution, I am pursuing a budding and already doomed bohemian love affair at the insular, insulated artists' collective where their former drummer lives—and I tag along with their former roadie to see their former singer's new band, who are shooting their latest video for MTV. Dennis, said singer, insists that this new band is an equally subversive project, intended to create and encourage revolutionary desires in the masses. Perhaps inconveniently, I take him at his word about their intentions, though many of our mutual comrades now assume their politics to be a purely aesthetic aspect of a pop music career. Now I show up to be the token hardliner at the "radical" band's video shoot, sullenly taking notes in the corner as my "less committed" contemporaries are primped and preened by cosmetics girls for the harsh light of the cameras ("you should write to HeartattaCk about this," jokes Dennis, and I laugh). It's a familiar dynamic—I refuse to get my hands dirty by participating in the day's events, but as a friend from way-back-when I still expect to be fed, in exchange for parading my intransigence on the sidelines. I'm the "street cred" flown in from the U.S.A., the ghost of punk rock past lingering in the MTV studio, here to spread revolutionary guilt and cash in on a free meal in return; I'm the anarchist on the guest list: everything is free for me because—well, just read my manifesto. I'll spend the breaks in shooting critiquing my friends' tactics and credibility, and assume I'm doing everyone a favor.

Well, be that as it may. We arrive at the location, a shell of a house in the richest neighborhood of Stockholm, and the inside is done up in 1970's retro decor, including vintage typewriters and musical equipment, a couple old posters for demonstrations, and a hammer-n-sickle or two. The director in his casual denim suit and professional-free-spirited-artist's curls is bustling about with the film crew, scorching lights are being adjusted, and the youth in attendance are all picture perfect in those nauseating retro fashions that express nostalgia for the television shows of yesteryear. The rouged and mascara'd women especially provide quite a contrast to the unshaven, Rubenesque feminist I spent the previous night with. If I didn't "know the band, dude," it seems certain a boy like me would only be here if he sneaked in to raid the buffet—which I can't find anywhere, incidentally.

Dennis explains the plotline to me: they've bought the rights to some kitsch 1970's action movie in which police surround a house of outlaws. Thanks to splicing, the police will be outside, while inside the music fans and radical band are partying in defiance of them. Quite a fine fee—upwards of ten thousand dollars—has been paid to use the film and techniques

of that bygone day, so the video will actually appear to have been shot back then. Let's waste no time here, gentle reader, considering what social tendencies are expressed by retro chic and what role they play in the "society of the spectacle" Dennis has read so much about. The point is—well, we're here to smash capitalism by having a good time, aren't we? That's what the video is about, anyway.

There will be subtitles in the finished version—the police lamenting that the kids are having that fun "outside the structures of commodity relations" and must therefore be stopped. I joke that the chief pig should instruct his henchmen "If you can't arrest them, at least put them on MTV!" and Dennis likes the idea—maybe they'll use it. I resist encouragement to get powdered up and appear in the video myself, clinging to the antiquated notion that when none of us are on television, it will cease to exist. Dennis, for his part, politely declines to wear my KROSSA USA! (that's Swedish for "smash the U.S.A.") shirt, since the bandmates are all dressed in matching uniforms (my shirt *is* black, though, just like the one he's wearing), and emphasizes the "fun" aspects of the video; he doesn't want to undermine these by specifically mentioning the police shootings in Gothenburg, showing people actually fighting the pigs, or otherwise stepping over the line.

The director assembles the band and their friends before the cameras, and in the moments prior to shooting, Dennis warms up a little, prancing like a Swedish Mick Jagger—it's something he does well, though it's still ambiguous whether he has learned the pop language of his enemies in order to subvert their hegemony over culture production, or just been colonized, bodily, by their standards of hipness, their fashion "consciousness," their images of youth and style. The director yells the Swedish equivalent of "action!" and everyone is dancing about, trying hard to look like they're having the "good time" Dennis spoke of.

At this moment, looking on, I profoundly miss the environment of a good basement punk show, where this good time is real and not representation. If nothing else, if it does no more to liberate the masses, at least there one aspect of the equation is decidedly real and unambiguous. Here, watching my comrades acting out that "good time outside the commodity system" to make an advertisement for a commodity, it's difficult to tell where—or if—the pose ends and reality begins. And I can't stop wondering—when do we eat? Is there a buffet anywhere in this building?

Admittedly, it's early (it turns out work starts at 8 a.m. in the rock-n-roll world, too... coincidence?), and the film crew can only add to the overdeveloped self-consciousness of Swedish middle class youth, but I expected to see a little more enthusiasm. The d.i.y. punks of D.S. 13 seem to be struggling as hard to enjoy the one-liner irony of their participation as everyone else is to enjoy posing for the cameras sincerely. I can't shake the feeling that no one here, not the d.i.y. punks nor the pop radicals nor their various hangers-on, harbors any real conviction that Things Can Change, that this or anything will jerk the capitalist world out of orbit. "We are up for sale, everything that we know is up for sale" keens Dennis' voice over the stereo, and it sounds, here, like a statement of fact, not the bitter, furious challenge it should be.

seconds or so. i read and wrote in my journal, and we eventually began to inch away from kiel. "finally," i thought, "no turning back."

light-years later, it was 1 a.m. you know you're tired when you blink and have trouble reopening your eyes. i had been doing this for a few hours, my only sanity found in writing about this whole fiasco, and picturing stockholm and my brother's new life there. i was weary from constantly challenging and overcoming my shyness and complacency, and my only rations consisted of 9 slices of dutch bread, dutch appelstroop, and the ever-present punk-traveling-companion belly-filling getting-old-quick (dutch) peanut butter. there was a WC (toilet) just across the room, and i planned on resorting to sleep there, in the dried piss of the small stretch of tile. sleeping out in the open was an invitation to the question "so, why are you not sleeping in your cabin?" to which i had no wits to conjure a decent response. i denounced myself for not finding out more about the operations and formats of the ferry before getting on. it was 2 a.m. now, and time for me to move spots.

i had been on my couch for pretty much 8 hours and people were beginning to wonder about me. earlier, one asshole who i had asked if he could take me onto the ferry stopped and dared to question me: "did you pay for a ticket?" "no, i just got on." "well, you have to pay." "um, yeah, i'll probably pay when i get off." "ok." "ok." i really HATE people like that. mind your own fucking business. you have your way of doing things and i have mine. and mine is FREE!!! the scary staff people (who were obviously a bunch of former bodybuilders and army boot camp drill sergeants) began coming by and locking things and cleaning things, their jingling keys becoming the sound i link to a certain humiliating death sequence. i went to the WC and started wondering if they would be cleaning it like everything else for the morning crowd. so i called an emergency reevaluation meeting with myself.

we concluded we would instead go sleep in the car decks under a car, or find a place there somewhere. so, risking being spotted and sure death, i raced down the corridors and steps to the LOCKED door to the car areas. "baaahhh!," the sweat screamed from my bewildered body, from an already dehydrated punk kid just trying to save a buck and catch some zzzz's in the meantime.

i turned around in amusement at the submission hold now had on me by the ferry goddesses, and my eyes happen to rest on the place where i was to lurk for the "night": a dark corner under the stairs, just barely out of sight from most viewpoints. it was crazy enough that it just might work, and this was the ultimate gamble—a much heavier wager than those made above me on the casino tables. i cuddled with the wall and my beloved bags in the fetal position for 5 hours, from about 2 a.m. until 7 a.m. now, this was some shit. i can't sit in a chair without sitting upside down in it after 10 minutes, so hiding here took the most exhaustive abandonment i have ever undertaken.

throughout those hours, the time was so thick i had to chew it before swallowing. the seconds were so slow i could've named each one, and pleaded with it to PLEASE hurry up. i cramped up and my butt was numb after the first 12 minutes. i heard footsteps above me. i froze. the jangling keys, they are coming. i watched like an owl as each control person came

and went, without turning around to spot my bulging eyes between the 5th and 6th step. there was one every now and then, but i really couldn't tell (i had no timepiece, a pivotal contributor to my apparent madness). some looked around, and some unlocked the door to the car deck, where i was glad i didn't go. i dozed in increments of 5-15 minutes, but i was always somewhere between an REM comatose and a clockwork-orange-style forced awakeness. they never found me, and the angels rang at 7 a.m.: "(soft music)... (blah, blah in swedish and german)... ladies and gentlemen, it's 7 am, the café and breakfast bar are now open..." i figured there were angels, but i didn't think they would speak through the Stena Lines PA.

i emerged, cracked my bones back into place, and they echoed through the stairwell. it took me a full 3 minutes to re-boot my memory and locomotion systems and for my heartbeat to return to normal. lifting my head, i felt like i had earned something, something that I'd known i would earn some day, but didn't know what. i smiled and became a person who had slept under the stairs on a ferry to sweden. i had come that much closer to really knowing myself and my capabilities. i had shed old skin, and above all, i now know where to never, ever hide again.

walking was fun. walking up the stairs was even more fun. i found my couch just where i had left it, and i celebrated with a cup of coffee. 30 minutes later i had it: freedom. i just walked on off. "i win!," i screamed, but all the other passengers who paid couldn't hear me, didn't know me, didn't know what i was feeling! i think i actually floated off the ramp! i guess all they cared about was drinking the cases upon cases of freaking beer they were toting around on their luggage dollies all the way from germany.

i passed through another kontrol and a drug-sniffing dog (where a sign told me i was supposed to have my boarding pass ready for someone—and this gave me one last heartattack before i realized it was nothing), and into the arms of the fresh swedish morning air. no more boats. no more running. i win.

EPILOGUE: i take the final few hundred kilometers by 25 dollar bus, and make it to the Box 4 hours before moe, who took a train for the last leg (we both sold out, i know). i still win.

but i haven't yet gotten my cup of coffee.

[Editor's Notes: For the uninitiated, an "Evasiontank" is presumably a Think Tank (see Inside Front #13, among other sources, for thorough discussion) applied specifically to the project of getting away with stuff. Also—I can't help but add this observation from experience, which will probably only heighten readers' enjoyment of Will's tale of tribulation, but may well make him shake his head and sigh: I've ridden at least one ferry on that route before, and there were a few people—our band, for example—who had opted not to pay the extra expense for a room, and just slept, bandanas over our eyes, on the floor in the main hall while those folks with key rings Will feared so much walked about. Perhaps there were no roomless passengers on Will's ferry besides him, but unless something has drastically changed on that ferry line, I think he could have just hung out wherever and he would have been fine! Probably the stress and exhaustion, and the difficulties of being in a brand new situation with no context, heightened his paranoia *to dangerous levels—I've certainly experienced the same thing. Your friends find you hiding out under the stairwell, shaking and sweating, after a night's direct action gone awry, and can't persuade you no matter how hard they try that it's safe to come out and hang out with everyone else. Maybe one day all us scampunks will lose it and move in under the stairwells for good. Let's hope the revolution comes and the ferries are all free before then!}*

savannah, ga
MAY 31 2002 GREYHOUND TERMINAL, SAVANNAH GEORGIA

Today was beautiful. Sometimes, my head says "live, don't document." Today, I'm willing to take up the pen, feeling good and relaxed, ending this little trip with a ride on the hound, no photo finish this time. *"Patience makes the hobo strong."*

It takes a while to relearn patience after being in the City for so long—all subways and epic walks through the canyons of culture and architecture. I'm on different time here, road time, hobo time in the American south, the humidity hitting its stride the deeper I go.

I'm looking forward to the farm, if for a few days of sticky contemplation. The world ends here: at the heart. The sunset is righteous in Savannah today, its pale blue and silver lined clouds; last night was even more magnificent—Carolina ablaze, all oranges dashed with pink. I took a few snapshots from the piggyback, but the train gods snatched them away this morning, along with my Bolivian pasamontañas: all in exchange for free passage, no hobo humiliation, no overnight stay in the Williamsburg Co. jail, no premature end to my teaching career. A batch of snapshots and that beloved knit cap, even trade I guess for my freedom; summer is coming, I suppose I'll have to get a new look.

Savannah! Deep with history, fat tourists, fat harbor, fat heart of the American south—love it until I die. I woke up this morning in Kingstree, South Carolina, seat of Williamsburg Co, one of the poorest regions in the state, so says David of the Marcus dept. store: a jew and fine conversationalist, his family fled Brooklyn in the late forties; Kingstree had one of the few synagogues in the area, though they had to go 80 miles to Charleston to get a kosher butcher. Kingstree population 3000 or so, drops a little every year.

I woke up in that sleepy town this morning to the rough static of the police radios: "okay, the train is stopped, we'll find him." Fuck. Yep, that's me, guilty as sin, all bundled up in a sleeping bag, uniformed cop and rail employee less than fifteen feet away. "You go up, I'll go down" the cop says, my freedom passing before my eyes, dead center of Main street, Kingstree, got its name three hundred years ago—not far away, the masts of the British King's ships were cut from the mighty forests.

The railroad man nods to the cop and looks dead at my car, cramped up beneath the giant wheels of the trailer truck, hoping for a 'deus ex machina' style reprieve, and the guy chuckles 'yep, gonna find us a hobo' seemingly to me not five feet away. He passed my car and I grabbed my bag, and casually, like I was

rolling out of bed, jumped off the train, slowly, deer-in-headlights-like, walking in the opposite direction. No gods from the sky, just me, incredibly, walking away somehow, amid flashlights blaring everywhere against the radio static. They never found that hobo, though I did enjoy waiting in the high weeds behind the nearby Piggly Wiggly for the next five hours, awaiting dawn, not more that 100 yards from the scene of the crime: two shooting stars assuaged my nervousness, and I swore to myself I'd get on the first bus out of town. 18 hours ago, fugitive heat, fear and excitement. Now, a cooling memory, and yet another travel story.

More to come. Florida bound, D

olympia, wa
ALLEYWAY PARTY, APRIL 2002

I was thinking of you so much last night, when the kids of the town took over an alley in the midst of a boring "art" festival. We paraded through with a giant festive vagina, then set up a generator and P.A. in the alley between a bakery and a record store... the walls got covered with graffiti in a few minutes, and the ground strewn with flowers; an altar was erected to Sampa Mayka, goddess of garbage and alley-dwellers, and before long the music started—and the dancing. And yes, there was the usual stand-offish self-consciousness... but there was also rampant silliness, discarded pride, even glimpses of absolute abandon. As it got dark and the moon came out, rumors kept spreading (as always) that the cops were just about to shut it down—making it the perfect time for pounding drums and a fire show. So we burned up the parking lot with dancing and the cops stayed away and it was one of those beautiful circles where you look at the faces around you and know that you are all right there, for those moments, in the same place and on the same plane, and that space is free.

It went on that way. Just a few things I think you would have appreciated (I did): The kid crowdsurfing *in a fucking alley!* The kids from up the street totally rocking out on Nirvana covers and nothing but—and two thirds of the crowd wailing along into the mic with them—one of the mics was just out in the crowd, nowhere near the band. Finally, Nervous Chris wildly making out, in the midst of the dancing crowd, with some girl who just grabbed him. He stopped kissing long enough to ask "What's your name?"—then dove right back into it. Then and there I knew this was liberated territory.

Oh que vida, que pena... Keeping afloat on a raft of coffee and hope. Yours with love, H--

It felt as if we'd left the bad old days for good—just a few minutes before a rainbow appeared to us all in the middle

FLYING CIRCUS

of the night, to confirm that we had entered fairyland by sheer triumph of camaraderie, someone said to Mark: "you know, we don't actually have proof that this isn't going on everywhere in the world right now"... and I felt so good I could even believe it might be!

Crimethinc.

HOW TO GO ON TOUR WITHOUT A PUNK BAND...

In spring of 2002, we announced that that summer various CrimethInc. cells would form do-it-yourself flying circuses and travel the country performing in a variety of settings, with an emphasis on appearing in cities outside the usual anarchist circuit. These tours would make radical perspectives visible again in the wasteland of paranoia that remained in the wake of the terrorist attacks of September, 2001; they would share skills and stories among longtime anarchists and civilians alike; they would offer a chance for a new generation of potential revolutionaries to "run away with the circus," and in the process become both more experienced in rabble-rousing and more connected to the international web of resistance culture. We sent out a call for others to form circuses of their own and go on similar tours, and organized (well, perhaps that's a strong word for it) a convergence of all the touring groups to take place at the climax of the summer, in Des Moines, Iowa—the center of nothing-ever-happens America.

Here follows a selection of texts we circulated before the tours, to share what skills we already had with other touring groups. We reprint them here in hopes that others might apply them, too, on future anarchist circus or barnstorming or skillsharing tours! After all, if you're going to travel, you might as well engage the world in give and take as you go.

CrimethInc. Folklore/Folkwar Tour Class of 2000 Advice to Upcoming Circus Tours of 2002 *courtesy of Barely Anonymous*

This is a brief introduction to some of the experience my friends and I have had undertaking projects like the ones that will occur this summer, and a short summary of my current ideas about what could be possible this time.

First, one vision of what these traveling circuses might do: my experience on previous such tours, both with bands and performance groups, is that whenever we spent one night in a town, by the time we left we were just barely getting to know all the exciting things going on there that we wouldn't get the chance to explore; on the other hand, when we spent a few days in a town, we often ended up feeling paralyzed and left out, since we didn't know what to do with ourselves in an alien environment when we weren't focused on performing. Solution: spend two or three days in each town, with different activities planned for each day.

The first day could be the traditional performance/punk show event, since those are always good chances to keep in contact with your community and meet newer people who are just getting involved; the second day could be a day to connect with the creative/activist community, to trade workshops and share skills and resources (circuses should bring some useful knowledge to share, but also can learn more and more to share as they travel from town to town if locals are willing to teach); and the final day could be set aside for doing something in a public space: staging guerrilla theater in Wal-Mart, setting up a strange interactive tool in the park to start conversations with strangers, wheatpasting Main Street in Romulus, Alabama with the kids you taught the recipe the night before.

The three-day approach requires three times as much from the organizers, of course, than the one-night show, so be sure, if you want to try this, that the people organizing the individual events are ready to go the distance. They will know far better than you can what is possible and valuable in their community, so work closely with them in advance to figure out what they should set up and you should prepare for. Also make sure in advance that everything is clear about how food and lodging will be arranged; and if you do think others may join you in the course of your trip (offering a chance to "run away with the circus" is an excellent social service, as long as it doesn't cripple the circus or the escapees' communities...), make sure to provide for this possibility. [1]

MENTAL RESOURCES

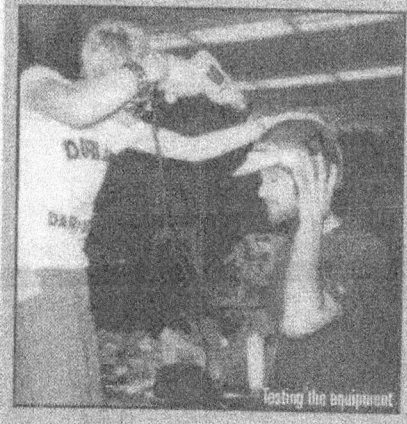

Testing the equipment

Think about what the skills you have to share are—especially the unusual ones, ones no one would think of sharing!—and bring what you need to help others pick them up. At the least it couldn't hurt, especially if you're going off the beaten track, to bring the raw materials necessary to show interested young people how to do their first screenprinting, or something like that. That could be a whole day's exciting and worthwhile activity right there. Also, bring your own curiosity, since you'll have constant chances to learn.

Be as prepared as possible to provide for your own needs: if you are traveling in an automobile, for example, make sure someone knows at least something about car repair. Try to form a team of individuals whose strengths and abilities complement each other, e.g. one who is good at organizing shows and keeping up with them and likes to drive, one who enjoys public speaking and has some expertise in diplomacy, one who perhaps is shy about public performances but can do amazing practical work with her hands and keeps her head in emergencies. At the same time—try to rotate responsibilities as frequently as possible!

CrimethInc. North American Insurrection Tour Class of 2001 Advice to Upcoming Circus Tours of 2002 *by Secret Agent Bartleby*

What is happening with the CrimethInc. Tour this summer is an exercise in imagination, and like any worthwhile adventure will be difficult. Perhaps a few rumors have circulated around the short-lived CrimethInc. North American Insurrection Tour last summer... what happened, what worked, what failed, and what went up in fucking flames. Flames are—after all—what we want.

You are not a rock band on tour

In a band you are traveling with a few people you know, who all have preset roles—"drummer," "singer," "lead guitarist"—who all do a certain thing together, like "play a show." You do this on a regular basis, usually at a "club" or "house." You do this once a day, sometimes twice, and survive by taking a piece of the proceeds at the door or selling "merchandise."

None of this applies anymore.

[1] *Note from the Graphic Designer: Despite possible appearances, this piece isn't a horribly incomplete rant—the rest of this it has been cleverly hidden in the grey boxes.*

Anker reciting poetry in the tent

Try to utilize as many of the five senses as possible at once, not to mention other faculties, the more the better, as long as the different media don't interfere with each other. Read manifestos backed by mood music performed on the spot, add visual aids, sound effects, appropriate scents if possible. Compose a rock opera to be performed by your puppets, while they toss fortune cookies to the audience. If you want people to join in on the chorus, hold up placards with the lyrics on them. Utilize undercover agents in the audience to keep things coming at people from all sides.

Try utilizing a variety of formats—not just puppet shows and discussion groups. Try interactive games, pull off your whole show as a staged accident in front of the show space as people are arriving unprepared, invent unthinkable religious ceremonies, hold a wedding between corporate and political interests in the middle of the shopping district and then carry off the environment in a coffin right through the Gap.

It's been my experience over and over that it's better to bring a "toolbox" of skills, ideas, and materials to draw upon than one highly evolved organism that will either thrive or perish in each different environment you enter (a punk band is a perfect example of the latter). Have a fall-back plan, yes—a few of them!—but be able to adjust constantly to circumstances, so as to render your project relevant to any and every space. If you can, arrive in each situation in time to make plans tailored specifically to its possibilities and challenges. Assuming you have the good energy in your group that will be critical to your success, continuous revision and expansion of and experimentation with your projects will give you something exciting to do between shows. By all means brainstorm insanely as you're driving to each event, and practice shouting out the lines to your new skit over breakfast. Bring a notebook of ideas each and talk constantly about how to implement or combine different ones. That said—practice as much as you can in advance. There's no reason not to try things out at home before you leave; you're going to have to shake off that shyness at some point, and a couple disasters ahead of time can only be a blessing in the long run.

Again, in my experience—the best presentations are interactive, but only after a certain atmosphere has been established to ensure that whatever people do together will be different than what they would do "normally." We all need circuses and bands and so on because we depend on such things to snap us out of the expectations and routines that we fall into otherwise. If you can raise anticipation and excitement to a high enough level, people will be ready to do exciting and courageous things themselves—but they're probably counting on you to set the scene. Yes, of course it's bad that people approach these events with a spectator mentality, but like it or not, if that's going to be shaken off, you probably have to

You are going to be traveling with a completely unknown number of people, without any funds, and you will all have no idea what you're doing. This can be utterly fucking exhilarating, but it can also lead down the path to apathy (a path littered by beer cans, I might add!) and inability to actually do anything. In the beginning of your tour, not knowing what you are capable of is an advantage—for example, a member of your merry troupe formerly known primarily as someone with foot rot and great shoplifting skills can let their inner Shakespeare out. However, someone you also thought was a gentle, kind, and caring individual could also let release his inner Mussolini. Things like this will happen.

That's is why it is important to have a plan, although in all likelihood you will light it on fire and throw the ashes out the van window within a few days of beginning your tour. It may not prevent personality problems, but it will at least give both Mussolini and Shakespeare a common goal. A plan sets the tone and timbre of the whole fucking trip, so you should do everything within your power to make it at least an uplifting plan, and a good one. Write a manifesto. An important part of CrimethInc. is inspiration—if you can't inspire yourselves, how do you think you're going to inspire others? Without any plan the tour will devolve into wandering and drinking in short order. Even if the entire group read *Evasion* and realizes the lack of revolutionary potential in drinking, the tour will just devolve into wandering and shoplifting instead, making a mockery your pretensions of doing something extraordinary.

You know you want to do something historic, but you will have no idea what that will be—at all. The most effective approach is

start the shaking process. Put a bunch of kids in a room together and shout "You're free! Free to do whatever you want! The world is yours, you godlike motherfuckers!!" and they'll probably just talk about who's dating who and when the 'Tragedy show will be; set yourself on fire, do a wild dervish dance, sing a mad hymn to love and war and then shout the same thing, and the results might be different.

Connect your activities to whatever is going on in the rest of the world: be a news source about the arrestees from the last demonstration or current events in occupied Palestine, spread information about what the I.M.F. actually is (and how that connects to what happened in Argentina), be sure to present interested people with possibilities of what they can do next.

And connect your activities to your own life—this is really important! Draw on whatever unique experiences or stories you have—those are your greatest resource, and the one that you can be certain no one else can provide if you don't. What you do has to be challenging and exciting and involving for you, first of all, if it is going to be for others, so make sure you're doing the things you most need and fear to do.

Try to make sure whatever you do can't easily be placed and classified. DO NOT add more fuel to the fire of popular stereotypes (the myth that CrimethInc. is essentially the religion of traveler kids especially has to be smashed—this isn't about glorifying a certain lifestyle, but subverting all of them, right?) If you wear Carhartt and hop trains, fair enough, there are decent enough reasons to do both those things, but challenge people, surprise them, don't let them brush you off as a recruiter from another social clique; maybe you should consider doing something other than blowing fire. To this end, it would be good to involve people from as far-flung and varying backgrounds as possible. A bunch of punks will probably tend towards starting a d-beat band (or at least a puppet show about drunken pirates), however much they want to do other things; a punk, a folk-artist sculptor, a macrobiotic chef, and an addiction/abuse counselor, on the other hand, might have a hard time doing anything together but unique projects. Try not to limit your ideas to what you have in common, but instead approach everything in a way that brings out the differences and even contradictions within your group. The more ingredients, the more tensions, the sweeter the pie.

to look at your resources and think what the current situation needs, and then try to fucking do it. From our experiences last summer—if you're at a gathering of wild eco-warriors in the woods who all know what "CrimethInc." and "Anarchy" are, but are spending far too much time infighting, maybe a comic musical about a love affair between a "green" and a "red" anarchist would work. If you're in a town where people are complaining that "nothing ever happens," go wheat-pasting with the locals under the cover of night, and make sure to leave the recipe and copies of the posters. If you're stuck with a bunch of pretentious white artists in New York City who recently opened a show space in a working-class Latino neighborhood, have the common decency to fire-bomb their show and drive them out of town. Don't underestimate your abilities: if a fire-bomb is called for by circumstances, then fucking do it!

On the Highway to Heaven or Hell

Put as much time as humanly possible into the places you visit—and be on time. Being on time to a show is utterly impossible when dealing with the logistics of maneuvering train-hoppers, hitch-hikers, vans that break down, shows that last too long, people who get caught shoplifting or arrested throwing tear-gas canisters at police, and so on. It is our job to do the impossible.

To add to earlier recommendations of three-day stays, I would recommend putting at least a whole day between each show as the "traveling day" (regardless of physical distance, which has little to do with traveling time), and having the day before each show devoted to scheming the next show and nothing else. Practically, bring along someone on the tour who knows something about repairing cars, a triple A membership (someone should have it, doesn't have to be person who owns vehicle), and a spare tire. If you have some sightseeing or relaxing to do, devote a whole day to it. Also, if people are feeling exhausted, make sure to have a day of relaxing. At the same time, beware of starting to relax and then forgetting that you're on a world-wrecking tour that is fighting for the survival of life itself. And—if people are too slow, leave them behind. They wanted adventure, right?

Never forget survival: it takes time. Last summer, we crossed the country with nary a cent, thanks to continual dumpster-diving, shoplifting, the Home Depot scam, donations, and the kindness of strangers. Shoplifting will play an ambivalent role as a double-faced dark god in your weeks on the road. You will have no money and be hungry, and like some strange deity shoplifting can provide for many of your material needs in return for your faith and continual participation in its foul rituals. Like any god, though, worshipping shoplifting leads straight to slavery—in a van it becomes just too easy to just drive around new places and shoplift continually, assuming you have the white privilege and the clean clothes to do so. In our last experience, as the tour progressed and we became increasingly bedraggled, shoplifting became (to borrow the words of the Unabomber) "a surrogate activity," one that simulated creative activity and excitement under the pretense of survival while taking up way too much time. Shoplift only when necessary, and try to make money by having benefit shows beforehand, selling books and records, putting out donation jars, robbing banks. Learn how to siphon gas.

Finding Spectators—and Destroying Them

As said before, people who call themselves anarchists and live in a thriving scene are some of the last people that need a "CrimethInc. tour." Anarchist outreach is not about reinforcing John Q. Anarchist's belief that what he is doing or believes in is just swell and dandy. We could be more useful reaching those people who are discontented with their lives and the world, and fanning the embers of that discontent into flames. Driving people over the edge straight into the abyss, past the point of ever returning to the "normal routine,": that's fucking important. Those people are everywhere—with the possible exceptions of punkhouses and infoshops. They're on street corners at midnight

EMOTIONAL RESOURCES

Positive energy: most of all, you'll need to do this with people you love and believe in and trade inspiration with constantly. It will be that energy that sustains you on your adventures, as well as everyone you come into contact with. Most of the really intense moments and months of performance and intervention that I know about came out of love affairs of one sort or another. At the same time, make sure your love affair isn't too fragile, or you might find yourself in the ashes of your project half way through.

Diplomacy: fuck, this is important. Being cool-headed, ready to talk out conflicts inside and outside your group, not practicing that childish and counter-productive escalation of aggression some people do when arguments break out... without this, you'll be hard-pressed to have a good time or survive challenges. Practice being smart, nice, open to others' perspectives, goal-oriented rather than vindictive and petty. Think hard about whether you're ready to do what it takes to get along with others in all circumstances before you undertake something like this—that is perhaps the most important question. Make sure everyone in your group is thinking about this, not just one babysitter.

Babysitters? That brings us to... responsibility! If you tell people you'll arrive at 5 p.m., be there, at all costs, or else you are doing your part to destroy the d.i.y. community and prove that all these crazy dreams will not work after all. Seriously! A larger project like this depends on the blind trust of a wide number of people; betray that trust, and it'll be twice as hard for people to do something like it next time. Sure, sure, there's always some excuse, but there's always a way to make things work, too. In the d.i.y. world, everything you do you do by virtue of others' generosity and goodwill. Be constantly aware of their needs and feelings. Wash the dishes you use at their houses, clean up your mess, thank them for every favor, be understanding when things go wrong.

Menstrual Health Workshop in the park

Programming the drum machine

It seems to me that the wisest way to organize something like this, that involves a lot of people doing independent projects, is according to the "autonomous cell" model. Get together a tight affinity group of people who know how to work well together; be prepared to function on your own in all circumstances. Like a big demonstration, this project will sometimes put people who don't know each other in situations where they have to work together and depend on one another; it's best, in those conditions, that people are organized into small units that can present their needs and intentions to other such groups in a simple fashion, and can work things out for themselves in emergencies. Be prepared, also, to respect and support what other groups are doing, and see diversity as an opportunity for each to reinforce the efforts of the others, not for competition and infighting.

Talk in advance about how to handle some of the disasters that may befall you: interpersonal conflicts, sexual harassment, arrests, financial crises, private tragedies. Things are going to go wrong. Maybe really fucking wrong. Make sure in advance you're as prepared as possible, so this can be a good experience in the long run no matter what.

selling drugs, they're trapped in boring high-schools, they're drinking coffee before going to work.

Many small cities and towns across the U.S. are developing wild and wooly anarchists of the most unlikely stripes. These are the people that I want to do shows for—not the latest anarcho-hipster from Portland, but the kid doing a literature distro from the basement of the church in Appalachia where they hold shows for traveling bands that rarely come. That church deserves to host some guerilla warfare disguised as guerilla theatre! Realize too that some people will be openly hostile to "CrimethInc"—most likely not the police, but other anarchists who fear that "CrimethInc." is on a mission to contest their self-identification as the only true and correct anarchists. Just give them Harbinger #4 and encourage them to read "Infighting the Good Fight"; tell them that the first step to becoming a member of the CrimethInc. Ex-Workers' Collective is to reject the CrimethInc Ex-Workers' Collective.

Some of the best shows of last summer were spontaneous shows done at coffee-houses and public parks, where people

who had never heard of "anarchy," much less "CrimethInc.," were exposed to them and enjoyed themselves with us. If there is some important event going on that requires you to ditch your show—for example, a black man accused of trying to kill a cop in self-defense is going to trial and needs support—always feel free to drop the CrimethInc. act and just help out. From cleaning the dishes at the place you were staying to providing the shock troops for some demonstration, almost every community needs a few productive anarchists to do some task or another. Whatever it fucking takes!

Days of Performances, Nights of Soap Opera

All sorts of vagabonds, runaways, and others will join on the tour as it continues. Soon you may have multiple cars, be doing shows with people you didn't know, and be more excited yet more exhausted than you ever thought possible. First, greet all with open arms, but be very careful with letting your adventuresome band spiral out of control and lose track of its purpose—revolution! For example, if room in the van becomes scarce, make sure that you don't overload it with people. Obvious points like that are often overlooked. I would personally discourage anyone from joining an ongoing tour unless the current tour feels very comfortable with the person; instead, try to persuade people to form their own tours, if possible.

Try to have large group check-ins, but avoid them devolving into semi-formal meetings. Instead, try to keep the group small enough that you can work out everything face to face as friends, without a ludicrous official facilitator. Any more than about ten people will probably lead to self-destruction, in my opinion. If people desire to join the tour mid-way, you should discuss with everyone already involved whether they want to travel with this person. Of course, you probably won't find out the true colors of the person till much later in the trip, so it needs to be clear that the whole tour is dynamic and ever-changing, and it may be necessary for people to leave the tour. Don't let problems fester, don't skirt around issues of sexism, racism, boredism, alcoholism, laundry, lack of productivity, and so on. If problems do fester and spiral out of control, always remember that sometimes you have to tear all the maggots out of rotting flesh so it can regenerate.

Your relationships will stretch to the boundaries and probably break. If you have a group of people in a small space going on wild adventures, people in short notice will start mating in all imaginable combinations. Soon, the trip may resemble a syndicated soap opera. Leaders will emerge, with pecking orders, and those on the bottom of the pecking-order will attempt to exterminate each other. These things can be prevented with balanced distribution of authority, and a firm commitment from everyone in the trip not to let their hormones rule their human faculties to such an extent

*Bring exciting ideas (driving games, trails of graffiti to leave in every neighborhood, whatever) for in between performances and events, too, so things will always be fun. Not a single moment should feel like work.

*Don't be intimidated about everything you don't know! Someone does. Just ask. A band can give you a contact to book a show in that town, a volunteer at the infoshop has the experience you need with paper mache, a relative knows how to build a loft for your van.

*If you have the chance, take your circus to places no one goes! There's already a lot of good things going on in Philadelphia, and a fair bit of knowledge being shared there; and everyone knows New York is painfully glutted with cool stuff. Go to West Virginia, to Maine, to Oklahoma, to Kansas, to places where no popular bands bother to go. People there are ready to rock, too, when energy comes in from somewhere— and without all the stress and distraction of being in a "cool town," they might be better equipped to focus on doing good things with the inspiration they pick up.

*There are plenty of records of earlier experiments like the ones you're undertaking. It couldn't hurt to look back at them for ideas about what might go wrong or right. One (of a million) examples is the book Autonomedia (and, er, Bloodlink) published a few years back about the Nomadic Festival tour. Better yet, read about "real" circuses, street performers, and hobos from a century ago, to unearth forgotten secrets that took generations to work out and shouldn't be denied to new hearts.

*For fuck's sake, you herd of idiots, don't needlessly alienate. A banner that says "Work is for Bored People" might be exhilarating for a crowd of rebellious teenagers, but to a gathering of older people it might appear that you're flaunting the privileges they don't have. Another example—if you're performing at a macho hardcore show, unless there's no alternative, try to find a way to tap into whatever radical tendencies are present (you know, "we mosh because we love to be intimate with other boys, because it makes us feel alive—the same way I felt that night I..."), rather than just telling everyone they're a bunch of dumb sheep. The latter tactic is only useful in emergencies, when a line has to be drawn immediately so the people in the middle will see just how important it is that they distance themselves from the ones you are picking as opponents. We had to do that with Earth Crisis, maybe we have to do it with the Socialist Workers' Party, too, but there's no fucking reason to make everyone our enemies. Show the people you interact with that anarchism is about mutual support and respect for differences and all that jazz. (OK, ha, can you tell now that the first sentence of this paragraph was intended to be ironic?)

Above all, good luck. You'll learn on your own skin what you need to, if you're ready to go through the fire. See you at the conclusion of all this in Iowa—Imagine all the stories we'll have to share with each other there!

that the tour is destroyed. Most problems shouldn't wait for the next group meeting. Waiting for the next "Group Meeting" is like waiting for "The Revolution." Instead, at the moment a problem begins, all those involved should talk to each other about it face-to-face. If it's best for people to separate, it should just be done. There's room enough in this world for a million tours, CrimethInc. or otherwise.

CrimethInc.: The Legend

The strangest part of a CrimethInc. tour is that people will continually ask you "Who wrote the book?" or "What's the next book?" and, most frequently, "I don't believe that quote on the back of the Evasion book!" It's frustrating, but simply be honest while maintaining the mysterious nature of crimethinking: "I don't know who wrote the book, but it sure as hell wasn't me—and goddamnit, I didn't write that fucking quote either!" There's no need to give the full names, addresses, and phone numbers of every person ever involved in a CrimethInc. project, or at the other extreme add extraneously to the CrimethInc. mythology (hopefully the tours will do that merely by existing!). As independent autonomous cells are producing CrimethInc. propaganda and actions, no one actually does know exactly who did what and who is planning for their next project. Tell them about your life, how you got involved with revolution, what your next projects are. Then ask them about their lives, what they love and hate about CrimethInc., and what their next projects are. Be very open—anyone can use the CrimethInc. logo for anything, and anyone can distribute CrimethInc. literature for whatever purpose they have without any need to contact the CrimethInc. Central High Command Committee for Decentralization or e-mail Paul F. Maul. CrimethInc. isn't a logo, it's a challenge, a mood, a moment. If you need it, use it. If not, don't. Quite simple, really.

After the Tour

The tours are happening for multiple reasons, and everyone is going for their own. What is important is that these tours be used to build something even greater for the future. The tours should help strengthen bonds within our own communities, and build alliances with new ones. We don't need just another list of contacts for booking shows, an anarchist version of *Book Your Own Fucking Life*. We need fellow revolutionaries, lovers, fighters, dreamers, and friends. These friendships that are being built should allow us to do even greater projects nationally and even internationally. Our tour last year went out with the express purpose of helping decentralize Harbinger distribution (a plan that was cancelled post-tour, too!), but in the process we made many allies, nearly died in a desert, inspired people to make their own CrimethInc. flyers, websites, and so on... we also threw donuts at the cops, barely escaped an orgy, met astounding people, met people we wish we never laid eyes on, were brutally assaulted at a coffee-shop, put on musicals despite our inability to sing in key, hated each other, loved each other, and in the end went our separate ways unto even greater things. Some of the people on the last tour now live in a collective house, work together on a garden, have started writing poems and books together, and beyond. We'll destroy the whole world together!

We are the modern day refugees of Louis and Clark, who, turning our backs on their quest to map out the wilderness for exploitation, now turn the wreckage of American civilization into a new wilderness. Let's remember what we see, the strange tribes we encounter, our adventures, our knowledge. In the end, through our travels, we shall collectively know the United States in all its majesty and all its madness as well, if not better, than the government itself does. It is always useful to know one's enemy. With love in our hearts, AK-47s in our hands, and a new world being born beneath our very noses... aim beyond the stars, Agent Bartleby'

Note from the Editor: My comrade took this temporary nom de guerre in honor of Herman Melville's famous character, Bartleby the Scrivener, a clerk who moved into his office and refused to move out, because the night he wrote it we all broke into his workplace to use those empty offices for ourselves to get things done. When I was a little kid, adults read me stories of the goblins and fairies who would come out at night and mess with things while humans slept—I didn't figure out until that night, with my feet on the desk of my friend's boss and my texts-in-progress on his computer, that "goblins and fairies" was just storybook shorthand for—anarchists!

Part I: The Tour

So what did we do? How did it go? I can only speak for the circus I toured with, but we had an amazing month. It started out just two of us, myself and my friend Mark, an inventor and yoga student with whom I have been having adventures since we met as boy scouts nearly two decades ago; by the end of the tour, we were eight, including a spoken word artist, a Poi expert organizing for protests against the International Monetary Fund, a freestyling M.C. of amazing capabilities, and two specialists in the "anarchist ice cream" scam. We began with a 200 pound d.i.y. drum machine, among other instruments and props; by the tour's end, standard drumsets seemed foreign. We finished assembling and testing our 38-foot-diameter inflatable circus tent only hours before our first show, for 200 4-H campers in rural West Virginia; we also performed at a wedding for many hundreds of guests, for four people behind an art gallery, and for mixed audiences of bearded anarchists, amiable parents, and restless children in assorted public parks, theaters, infoshops, and basements. We learned how to shut off the gas at fast food franchises, and made a 'zine with the instructions, and various other texts we'd composed during the tour, to give away. We taught the radical history of puppetry with puppet shows, we screamed out manifestos and recited original-composition children's stories to ancient folk songs. We held round table discussions to introduce anarchist ideas to teenagers—and their families. We got heckled by punk rock clowns with clown paint tattooed on their faces, who thought we weren't circusish (or drunk?) enough.

Other circuses had more mixed results. One disappeared, one had to cancel practically its whole tour, another group arrived in Des Moines having driven all the way from the West coast with no licensed drivers in a quickly dying automobile. The Northeastern circus arrived with more than twenty members, many of them newly joined, and mentioned that many others had passed in

CREATING OUR OWN MYTHOLOGY—MYTH #1 CIRCUSES ARE LIKE COCKROACHES—IF YOU'VE SEEN ONE, WATCH OUT.

Our home-made inflatable big top.

From our first show in West Virginia, the totality of the Circus Tour was just a myth—but it was a myth we spread. Every night we would remind the audience, not to mention ourselves, that in six locations across the United States, six circuses were performing, skillsharing, or at least stuck by the side of the road swearing. It was something to think about now and then; but none of that seemed real until our convoy came to a weary halt in the parking lot of the campsite, a state park in Indianola, Iowa.

The group I was traveling with included contributors to several written projects published under the Crimethinc. moniker. We assumed, but more accurately feared, that we knew of the majority of active Crimethinc. affiliates.

So when we hopped out of our cars at camp and were greeted as welcome strangers by a member of the NE circus group, she may not have known that it made my entire day. As more and more circuses arrived, our fears dissolved. No group was less gorgeous, inspiring and excited than the next. We began to figure out that each group had arrived with the same fears as us. As the week spun on we were amazed at the differences in the groups, each one a strange planet with its own culture, concerns, aesthetics, tactics.

Since I returned home, the myth of all I experienced has been more important than ever. I am back in a familiar place, now feeling there is a thread behind my dreams and activities that is present in one hundred more places than I imagined. I have a feeling that every minute I spend cooking up ideas (or dumpstered veggies) is multiplied. Now I have to do my best to keep up with the brilliance of a new universe—not play small or shy so as not to scare one away.

I have harbored a version of that myth, even cared for it as my own. But during our circus travels this summer I saw it publicly shamed and exiled.

Our circus elected to avoid large cities in favor of smaller cities and towns. We also tried staying in towns one or two extra days to share what we had and to learn what we could. What we learned is a list too long to recount of the most breathtaking nobodies in the world. Families with children, sharing direct action tactics and spreading information on community building that will let them quit their jobs and feel like their children are cared for. Young kids running would-otherwise-be-disposable punk houses, with long-term plans to fix roofs and stop developers. Rural West Virginians who taught us rookies a lesson or two in anarchy and pet care.

Backwards indeed! I realized that Power has a vested interest in everyone believing everyone else to be hopelessly stupid. Isn't it obvious, for instance, that Power could have chosen any number of presidential puppets, puppets that middle class intellectuals would think well (enough) of, handsome and intelligent-seeming puppets?

But no, in an absolutely brilliant moment of inspiration Power stopped short. They choose George Bush—that lovable pooch—to entertain the small minority who, through misinformation, elected him. Then they sit back and watch the rest become crippled with despair because a "majority" (as implied by the media, and the sheer fact that he is president) of their fellow citizens must drink him up like the milkshake he is.

"Obviously," smacks the regular at the coffee shop, "this is a nation of imbeciles!"

What this nation is, is a vast majority who feels unrepresented by and simultaneously fearful of a majority, actually a minority, who only appear to be represented. It's easy to catch that myth because it is broadcast so thickly by the media that an antenna in your liver could pick it up (that's fucking true by the way!). It's easy to keep because it helps justify that second latte and another blasé political analysis. [God, I used the accent-e button twice in one sentence!].

But out here, in America itself, we saw this myth to be one more façade, a false front disguised as a castle wall. When we storm our rulers' gates, when we really do it instead of muttering amongst ourselves about it, our fellow-serfs will be at our sides.

and out of their group in the course of the tour. The Southeastern circus started out their pre-tour organizing as a group of ten, and arrived in Des Moines as a twosome able to do the work of twenty.

It was definitely in our favor that our particular circus group was built on the bedrock of my friendship with Mark and our experience doing such things together. It took the pressure off the others who joined us, and established a positive, energized atmosphere that colored everything we did or encountered. Our best shows were definitely the ones in the less-traveled regions; in cities like Chicago, people are so jaded that it's hard to get them to take booking a show seriously even for a well-established touring group, but just a few hours away in Springfield, locals roll out the red-and-black carpet for anybody that comes through.

As I mentioned, we finished building our famous circus tent, having no idea if it would work or not, less than twenty-four hours before our first show—and then started wondering what we'd do at the show. We wrote most of our skits in the next few days, struggling to compose lines on the way to the following shows. This improvisation and intense ongoing development gave our early performances an immediacy that could create real magic ("OK, this is a poem I wrote and memorized one hour ago—") and a disorganization that could totally sabotage that (imagine me stopping in the middle of that poem, mind blank, just when everyone's pulse was beginning to quicken, and finally being forced to search for my notebook). It was indeed a lot of fun to spend every day's drive helping each other to memorize our lines, but I imagine that if we hadn't already been tried-and-tested working companions the extra stress of this would have been one more straw on the proverbial camel's back. I wish we'd done more general preparation in advance, and then done the improvising around details and additions as we went. At the end of the tour, when we were finally really good at everything we were doing, I regretted we hadn't started out that good and improved from there... but, you know, I'm a perfectionist. The southeastern group prepared a great deal in advance, and did little improvising, while the northeastern group did little else.

Was it all a success? Over forty cities hosted radical events of some kind over a period of less than a month, whether that meant a hundred people dancing naked together or six kids talking about what the alternatives to college might be. Everyone ended up with a lot more skills and experience to be applied next time, and the sheer

If the tour our circus undertook drove anything home for me, it is how important it is for us anarchists to be visible in every community we pass through, how important it is for us to travel and trade information and inspiration openly with everyone we can. Punk rock shows and touring bands were crucial for radicalizing the demographic I come from, and although not everyone can or should be a punk or a traveler, we should never underestimate the strategy dissidents have used for centuries: roving bands of entertainers and organizers crisscross the land, planting seeds and conveying information from one entrenched resistance group to another—in person, the way human beings have always interacted best. Yes, for the last time, the majority of us at any given point should be located in a community we know and belong to, so we can have the stability and

Our first show after the wedding is on a hilltop between the forests and farmlands outside Wheeling, West Virginia. It's a far cry from those lifeless rituals that big city shows can be at their most cliquish—a pre-punk, post-apocalypse scene in which a motley

crew of rural folk mill around tables of free food set out on the gravel road, confused proto-skinheads sit in a field debating patriotism with teenage whiz-kid anarchists, and a solitary maniac can be heard playing scorched-earth electric blues from the barn. We run four hundred feet of extension cords all the way up the hill to inflate our giant d.i.y. circus tent, and one of our hosts four-wheels our equipment up in a big country truck. After the show, Norma, the matriarch responsible for this venue, known by young people in the area for sometimes appearing at shows in her dominatrix ensemble, drives it back up to help us get our stuff.

"I knew y'all would want to be on this hilltop. My daughter said you'd want the barn, but I knew it, that you'd choose the hill. This hilltop here, this is a special place. You know, I get those corporations coming to me every week, telling me they want to buy all these trees off me—and I say, you listen: every single tree here, every blade of grass is a living thing, and you're not touching a one of them! They're not used to that, you know, I'm probably the only fifty-one year old black woman they met who owns hundreds of acres of land, and they think I'm going to turn it over easy, but—well, I'll tell you what, I don't want you to think I'm crazy,

fact that this happened hopefully gave hope to others that their own grandiose schemes might also be possible. And—if future tours are easier and better thanks to the experience we gained, then every problem, every misadventure suffered this past summer, will have been worthwhile.

commitment to build support networks and long-term projects—but some of us should be out there in the world, too, building geographical links as well as local ones, making possibilities visible where they weren't before.

Part II: The Convergence

If the tours had ups and downs, the convergence at the end was something else entirely. None of us have really tried to capture it in writing or words since; we all seem to agree that the joy of the experience went beyond anything mere words could capture.

We gathered at a campsite a couple dozen miles from Des Moines, and alternated activities for ourselves there with activities in downtown Des Moines. Staying out in nature, most of us sleeping outside, helped us feel connected to the earth and focused on ourselves and each other; after a few

disappointed by), a majority of the people there had arrived after weeks of traveling with projects of their own—and even those who hadn't been on tour had usually had some crazy adventures trying to get out to convergence, whether they were riding their bikes across the country or hitchhiking. This meant that the spectatorship, and attendant dichotomy between organizers and onlookers, that mars too many gatherings, was absent from the beginning: everyone there had something to share, and knew it.

This created an atmosphere of total participation. Everything worked because everyone was down to contribute their share of both practical and creative input: fuck the books of theory, this was anarchy in action! The fact that there was no formal organizing, and thus no set distinction between organizers and organizees, made it easy

but I have a thing for dirt. Dirt—you know, huge trees grow from this stuff, isn't that a miracle! That's not something to sell to anybody, no way. We come up here on this hill, we have dinner on this hill, watch the sunset, drink up here—I have sex on this hill, I come up here and get naked, and look at the stars! I say—you haven't lived until you've felt the wind in your crotch under the stars! Well now—y'all are anarchists, I hear. Tell me, what's anarchy about?"

Days later, in Springfield, Illinois, we set up the tent in the parking lot next to a community space just opened by our new friends here. Most of the people who come to the show and the skillshare the next day are significantly older than us—many of them are part of an "unjobbing" group that meets here to trade skills for cutting back expenses and escaping from the employee/consumer cycle. This is really inspiring to see, to be reminded that we're not the only generation engaged in the struggle for liberation— still, we're a little anxious about how our more militant masks-and-molotovs rhetoric will go over.

But just as it happened when we performed for a mix of teenage punks, college radicals, facially tattooed anarchists, nicely dressed parents with young children,

and local journalists in Athens, Ohio, and they all seemed equally entertained by our antiauthoritarian theater and rhetoric—just as it reputedly happened when Stef and Ben performed their puppet tutorial on molotov-making in a Louisville public park, and the mothers present sent their children away while continuing to watch avidly themselves—these women and men turn out to be thrilled to hear about how anarchists fought the pigs back in Quebec City, to learn direct action techniques they can apply locally, to cheer poetry celebrating full-scale insurrection. It's almost unnerving. We were wrong, Mark confides to me in the truck afterwards, to fall for the propaganda in the papers and on television about our fellow U.S. citizens: people everywhere in this country are fed up with business as usual, desperate for adventure and intrigue in their own lives, suspicious at the very least of the powers that be—if not already eager to work towards their demise. All that's lacking are approachable, supportive local faces of revolt, and the secret army will start to come out of hiding—we just have to show our confidence in what we're doing, our certainty that it is normal and neighborly to want the utter destruction of capitalism and capitulationism, and everyone can drop their masks.

days there, we were in tune enough with the land and climate that the changing weather seemed to express our own moods back to us.

Unlike just about every other conference or convergence I've been to (and, frequently, been

to avoid any barriers to participation like hierarchy or laziness. When we got there, nothing had been planned out for the coming days; but within hours, there were events scheduled, fliers for promotion being copied and distributed, meetings taking place, tasks picked and handled. Every day we met at noon in a circle, to discuss what we would all like to do, and how things were going; people volunteered to be in groups that handled the acquisition of food and cooking, which went surprisingly smoothly (if always a little behind schedule, as is customary everywhere outside the corporate pale)—and there was always enough to eat, somehow. When it came to performances and workshops, almost everyone had something to offer, and we could have gone on forever listening to and learning from each other. The supportive atmosphere this created made it easy for people

From a postcard sent from one circus participant at the convergence to his relatives

Guerilla theater

Thursday night, an informal, unexpected drum circle began under the shelter in the middle of the campsite, and instead of dying down after a few minutes it just kept gathering and gathering momentum, until all of us were dancing or beating out rhythms, and one by one we felt the atmosphere change: magic appeared in the air, it was suddenly like we were living a dream. People began singing or screaming, spinning and spitting fire, spontaneously yelling out poetry that was lost in the noise now bigger than all of us, like that noise some of us had heard in Quebec when thousands tore down the street signs to make percussion instruments. At some moments, we were all singing together, and it was intoxicating to hear in our ears the feeling of tribal unity already thrilling our hearts. Soon, dancers began taking off their clothes, until a number of women and men were dancing naked, which felt absolutely natural and unaffected. At this moment, I looked over and saw, at the edge of the circle, two men from the nearby neighborhood, standing and watching, beers balanced on their paunches as if they were at a football game. Looking back at my fellow dancers, I marveled that we had created a space so safe that boys and girls who had been terrorized all their lives by the culture of insecurity and fear could dance and sing naked and free without fearing each other's gaze—or the gaze

who I think would never have come forward in another environment to do so; it also made it much easier to be a creative or vocal person, because you didn't have to fear that you were hogging the spotlight.

The head count at the daily circles hovered over thirty and under one hundred. I think altogether, counting all the people who were part of the group at some point between the beginning and the end, that probably a little over one hundred and fifty people came in and out of the community staying at the campsite. This meant that by the end of the event, even though some of us (like me, for example, believe it or not!) had arrived knowing almost no one, we'd all gotten to know many or most of our companions. It was a perfect environment for getting to know others quickly: there was a lot to do together that really opened people up, and a common understanding that we were there to build friendships and community. Incidentally—I've been in many "radical" environments in which people were supposed to feel validated and secure enough to be open to receiving serious constructive criticism, but this was the only one in which the love in the air was palpable enough for me to feel that such a thing could really work.

What did all this mean for The Struggle? Traditional uptight class war anarchists might not think that

us of how beautiful life can be and pushes us to push for that at the same time as it helps us purge the bitterness of unsatisfying survival from our weary systems. I know witnessing this kind of energy for the first time left a deep impression many of the locals who were there, some of whom did in fact quit their jobs and transform their lives immediately thereafter. The connections we made with each other, the skills and ideas and inspiration and hope and faith we exchanged, will make us infinitely more dangerous to the capitalist beast. In those hours when we entered Des Moines with all our fearless, unfetterable energy, dancing in the middle of intersections and starting serious political conversations with strangers, I could almost imagine that all it would take to change the world would be for us to start together in this one city, expanding our numbers every day as we

of outsiders with no context for what we were doing, and no commitment to respect. That safety was a show of our strength together—that we could not only make magical spaces, but also knew we were secure in them together, come what (or who) may.

Driving up en mass to Des Moines from the campsite Friday evening, our convoy of cars stopped at a corporate supermarket to use homemade coupons to pick up vast quantities of vegan ice cream, which we gave away on the streets downtown a few minutes later. As we were waiting in the parking lot for everyone to get ready to go, dancing to the music on someone's car stereo and enjoying Joe's freestyling ("here we are in the place to be, forty one anarchists and me"), the manager came out to tell us that he "appreciated our business" (ha!) but we "had to get moving." Joe answered him smoothly in freestyled rhymes—something the guy was totally unprepared to deal with! He retreated into the supermarket, and the lot was ours.

That night we descended upon downtown Des Moines in several small groups—some

The new noise

went individually, from door to door, starting conversations with locals about radical politics, with surprising success; others paraded and played drums; others looked for a good place to set up our d.i.y. drum machine, climbing up lampposts in

a few days like this could make a difference one way or the other, but I see it so very differently. Tasting the world we want to live in, living it, is an antidote for all the misery and powerlessness of the world we're trying to escape: this taste gives us something to fight for and stay alive for, it reminds

reveled publicly in our love of life and each other, and push slowly across the country, transforming every intersection, every interaction, every city as we went.

Hey Y'all,

Let's have another circus tour! If we do, I promise I'll have my lines memorized better—and I'm already working on a teleprompter for 2004! Also, I'll remember not to run out of gas. And Fluffy, please remember not to leave my gas cap on the top of the truck. And you—motherfucker in the BMW—remember to swerve two thin inches to the right so my gas cap doesn't smash into a hundred bits right before my teary eyes.

I'll remember to shave my butt, too, so I'll feel more comfortable about shucking down. And I'll do some Nordic-Track or something beforehand, so my little heart can keep up with my Big Heart when the NE circus performs. Yo NE, y'all are gonna do that thing again right?! For real though, NE told me they'd do it again but they'll be using body doubles for all the nudie scenes—so maybe I'll just bring my strap-on butt.

And can we get a committee together? We seriously need a better name than "The Convergence"—something with a "Z" in it, I say. One day it will get so large that it'll break free of the "DIY community" and spread to the "I'll-go-DI-for-someone-else-to-get-some-money-so-you-will-come-DI-for-me community." I know it's still a few years out, but we might want to talk about charging $150 at the gate so newcomers can have the awesome experience of being as broke as those mythic pioneers of old were when they arrived.

When circus tour finally eats itself enough times to be fat and safe, we can sell the event, and its new Z-Name, to Fluffy. By that time he'll be rich off the six dollars he invested in the market instead of buying me a new gas cap. Fluffy and I will stand in the skybox looking out over our minions. I'll say, "Fluffy, things are getting a little out of hand out there." Then, in a desperately nostalgic move, we'll hire security guards to kick everyone's asses. Fucking kids!

After the revolution, [nothing but maze-working maniacs] will be on television.

search of a working outlet. Suddenly, unexpectedly, all the groups converged, and a spontaneous Reclaim the Streets broke out in the middle of the bar district! A rhythm, reminiscent of the one from the preceding night, was struck up on the mailbox and found-object percussion on hand, wild dancing began, and soon a woman, towering on stilts, was blowing fire in the middle of the street. Locals on their way to the bars stopped, amazed, and some began to dance with us; a man tried to seize the U.S. flag that some of us were happily trampling, but was backed down by cool-headed kids while the other locals, surprisingly, looked on in disapproval of his macho stupidity—even in this post-September 11 world, they didn't mind us stomping on the flag, as long as we were smiling!

Stepping back, gasping for breath from the dance, I realized that our numbers had magically doubled. We had pulled off one of the most successful Reclaim the Streets actions I've witnessed, by sheer accident!

Saturday late at night, just before I went out to sleep, I was saying goodnight to my friends in the barn, when I noticed a young man bedding down with them who was wearing a cow costume for warmth in that chilly night. Double-taking, I realized it was the local guy in the Dr. Who shirt who had run into us in downtown Des Moines the night before, having no former exposure to punk or anarchism, and joined us in the street party! Then I recognized him as one of the individuals who had participated in that day's discussions. It turned out he had called off working for the weekend and come to camp out with us, avidly learning all he could and joining in our activities! Walking to my sleeping bag, I wondered if others like him—or perhaps: how many!—were among our numbers, in other corners of the campsite; and wondered why we'd all waited so long to make a space like this where people could

Hey, let's not have another circus tour! Let's cultivate the connections we made. Let's spread the myth in the twinkling of our eyes and the poetry of ripped off zines. Let's allow the impossible magnitude of our experience to force us to be better storytellers. Let's remember what is possible in our lives, so we'll have that to think about during moments when nothing seems possible.

Most of us left Des Moines saying "let's do this again." I said it too, and goddamnit, I meant it. But for me "doing this again" is not necessarily about converging in Iowa, traveling "circuses," puppet theaters, or even midnight rainbows. This was about swallowing deep and committing to the shakiest-sounding idea I had heard of in a long while (hard to imagine from this perspective). Doing it again will be the same.

So let's not make a magic potion out of all this, a set of instructions that we swallow again hoping to get just as big. Rather, let's think of new plans that are as beautiful,

maniacal and impossible as the one we just pulled off. After all, if that convergence taught me anything, it's that what we ask for, we get... so long as we ask for everything!

Loving, and missing, and still with you all, Mark

join us and experience for themselves what we meant when we said freedom!

During Joe's freestyling workshop on the grass downtown on Sunday, the local homeless men who had walked up to see what we were doing felt comfortable enough to treat us to some of their rhymes.

Returning to the campsite from the workshops downtown, I saw ten, then fifteen great fireballs explode into the air at once, as Stef and Jane led their firebreathing workshop.

Sunday night, after the formal performances were over, when people were shooting off firecrackers and dancing and singing together and spirits were so high it felt as if we'd left the bad old days for good—just a few minutes before a rainbow appeared to us all in the middle of the night, to confirm that we had entered fairyland by sheer triumph of camaraderie—someone said to Mark: "you know, we don't actually have proof that this isn't going on everywhere in the world right now"... and I felt so good I could even believe it might be!

At the final circle, on Monday before we went downtown to liberate a block for one more afternoon, we spontaneously began sharing poetry, songs, confessions with each other,

celebrating each other and the tune we'd shared. It was a space in which all of us felt safe enough to be vulnerable and passionate and naked before each other, and the beautiful things that came out were breathtaking. It felt as if we could go on forever, reveling in that trust and freedom, like we should just put down roots in that space and plant gardens in that field and live there together as one clan, all in love.

DOWN WITH REVIEWS!

After the show in Sarajevo, we split up into little groups to stay in the small apartments of different locals. Rob, Stef, and I went with the tall, older guy to his place, high up in an apartment complex overlooking the river. From that height, we could gaze down upon the snowy rooftops of many different centuries of beautiful architecture—and upon some of the wreckage and ruins left from the war, still waiting to be cleared away these years later.

As usual, I was mute, Stef was withdrawn, and Rob was self-absorbed, so we didn't make particularly good company for our host. He was a few years older than me, sociable but serious, with lines already carved into his face; he'd spent his life here, and since the early 1980's he'd followed the invention and extrapolation of punk rock at varying distances, depending on the political climate. We were the foreigners coming through from far away, so he was hoping we'd have stories to tell, new bands to play him, perspectives to trade on older bands—but after three months of non-stop tour, and with another tough two months ahead, we just wanted to be left alone.

At the show I'd received a deep gash in my forehead which had only just stopped bleeding—many if not most of the kids in attendance had grown up in refugee camps in the middle of Europe's worst ethnic conflict in decades, so it wasn't strange they'd express their frustration in extremely violent dancing. I'd been making my way into the middle of the crowd as I sang, to try to break up some of the aggressive energy, when someone's fist accidentally struck me. I still remember standing there pointing to the blood streaming off my face, screaming *"look at this! look! is this what you want?"*—and the kids staring back at me, as if to say they were sorry, but it was beyond their control. Now I was in the bathroom, cleaning the last crusts of blood off my brow and checking to see how the new safety pin tattoo on my chest was healing, and Stef was putting out our sleeping bags on the couch. Our host, therefore, was trying to engage Rob in conversation.

He was going through his records, trying to figure out what Rob was interested in—"you like Casper Brotzmann Massaker? Einsturzende Neubauten?"—but Rob was at least a decade younger and didn't know any of these bands. "Throbbing Gristle?" Finally, it became too uncomfortable for me to listen to them misunderstanding each other, and I stuck my head out of the bathroom to nod encouragingly at this last one. "Aha, yes, I have Psychic TV too—" he began, but with my voice thrashed all I could do was nod

my head, so pretty soon I gave up again in vexation and retreated to the bathroom to brush and floss my teeth[1].

He gave Rob a try once more, with some newer bands: "How about Korn? Do you like Korn?" At this, Rob made a face: "No, I don't really like them." *Korn?* I could read in his expression, *you like Korn? Everyone knows they suck!*

I was done in the bathroom, and tried to make my way past them to lurk inconspicuously by the window; but our host, finally weary of trying to squeeze water from the stone that Rob was, followed me to it. "This direction," he explained to me, as we looked out, "was the front, the fighting, just a few hundred meters away."

I followed his gesture out into the night. "This meant that I had electricity, here, when the rest of the city did not. I had radio equipment, so I could pick up the international radio shows, and that was when I heard this new music coming out of England and the U.S., bands like Korn, Tool. I was interested. I would tape their songs from the radio and sit here and listen to them as the shooting was going on down there."

I could only nod, still, and so he wished me a good sleep and went to bed. For Rob, Korn was a terrible MTV rock band marketed to adolescent boys to cash in on their gawky angst and antagonism. For our host, their music had been his only connection to sanity in a nation gone crazy with violence and hatred; their songs had been a secret world he had discovered and retreated to in order to survive when everyone around him was killing or dying.

A half-decade ago, in the introduction to the reviews in Inside Front #11, I speculated that one could compose a song that, like Ice-9 in Kurt Vonnegut's *Cat's Cradle*, would transfigure everyone who heard it, touching off a chain reaction that would spread around the world: a total revolution. At the time, I was engrossed in the struggle to write such a song; my own life had been utterly transformed by a handful of songs, and outdoing them—making songs which might utterly transform the cosmos itself—was my consuming obsession. A year or so after composing that introduction, I read a piece in an issue of Al Burian's *Burn Collector* in which he confessed that there had been a time when he had believed the same thing was possible. Punk rock songs had so affected him that he figured all it would take for everyone to be changed as he had been

(a world of Al Burians... a terrifying thought, really) would be for these songs to be played everywhere—that was why good music was banned from the radio, why the media only broadcast pap and drivel (it was, after all, the 1980's). Accordingly, he set out to play punk rock, to spread it around the world.

Later, after years of band practice, tours, incandescent instants punctuating grueling, disappointing months, Al was sitting in a car, stuck a in traffic jam, listening to corporate radio out of sheer boredom—when one of those old songs came on. He'd long since lost the brash illusions of his youth, but it had been a slow, imperceptible process—now, suddenly, his one-time dream was coming true, but as the most horrible of disappointments. He looked around at the fed up, glassy-eyed people in neighboring cars—it was entirely possible that they were listening to the same station he was, and nothing was happening, nothing at all.

What does that mean, then? Is punk rock powerless to change the world? Have we wasted all those guitar strings and cracked cymbals and eardrums on a pipe dream? Obviously not. What Al and I missed at first was the question of context—we first heard those songs in the drama of gritty basements, as secret weapons we shared with our friends against a world upon which we declared war: small wonder, in such a setting, that those simple, artless songs had the power to forge destinies. Severed from the d.i.y. ecosystem that makes them vital, removed from their natural environment, placed in the zoos of corporation commerce and spectacle, of course they lose their wild beauty, of course they refuse to reproduce. That doesn't mean they weren't ever powerful to begin with—on the contrary, it suggests that that context, d.i.y., dirty basements, and drama, has the potential to make almost *anything* powerful.

So yes, I'm still engrossed in the struggle to write those songs, world revolution through punk rock is still one of my consuming passions. But more than ever I'm aware that we have to fight on two fronts: we have to arrange words and notes and hone structure, sure; at the same time we have to create situations in which "three chords and the truth" can actually matter, can be the beautiful, powerful things they should be. Rocking music and rocking the boat have to go hand in hand, or neither can have the teeth or heart both need.

Where does this leave music journalism, then? If Korn can be life-saving in Yugoslavia and CRASS can be mere kitsch on I-95, if the value of the music depends completely on the context it occurs in, how

[1] *See? Umlaut lyrics can have a positive influence.*

is a 'zinester or scenester to offer any useful perspective at all? Shouldn't we just make 'zines about creating context, then? That is what most of Inside Front has become, anyway—so why have reviews at all? Well, I don't know. Some of the records reviewed here, especially some of the ones I think are fucking great, you may not have heard of before. So here you go, a few reviews, just in case—maybe we won't lead you astray.

And as for you, Music Listener, how should you pick a good record? This is what I've been building up to—it's not just up to the records. If you want to be moved by music, if you want it to matter, then you have to create the context for that in your own life. Live like fire, risk everything for what you love, and records that others dismiss as trite or tired will bring tears to your eyes. Give those world-transforming songs burning worlds within you to resonate with, make liberated spaces in which both people and songs can have power and meaning. Not that you have to move to a war-torn nation or suffer a life of hardship and fear to accomplish this—it should be enough to pursue your dreams and support others in pursuing theirs, and run into the inevitable few nightmares along the way—but the guy who hosted us in Sarajevo who listened to Korn, or for that matter the fourteen-year-old watching his friends play in their first Dis-band and thinking it the best noise the world has ever heard, they are the ones who really know good music, not the critics.

REVIEWER CODE:

-@   Gloria Cubana, queen of the world
-b   Your humble editor
-b-side   Bruce Burnside
-xb   Straight Edge as Fuck Ben!
-s   Stef
-JUG   Juggler Greg Bennick

song with stuff like, "This here's a sawng about settin' in the woods with y'alls buddies round a campfire and watchin' th' ashes go up in the a-yer." After they were done, all of their girlfriends sat down on the floor in front of where Burmese set up, in front of the stage. Burmese played for about 10 seconds before Mike (the little one) stomped all over the women like he hadn't seen them.

He ended up tangled up among them and their suddenly very angry boyfriends. Mike then started doing his usual raging against the audience, getting closer and closer with his bass each time. Finally, one of the Virginians grabbed him and punched his face so hard that his glasses came off and he went sprawling and all his pedals came unplugged.

He plugged them back in and charged the audience, and this time he was thrown into the drum set so hard that the drums fell over. A long buzzing sound followed, and Burmese lurched into another song, hampered by the fact that the hippie metal guys were trying to fight them as they played their show. The set ended 15 minutes after it started, with the lights on and scrawny Mike standing there, his fist raised, challenging someone else to punch him in the face, surrounded by pedals, strings, drum equipment, and the sound of the amplifiers turned up too loud.

ZEGOTA, WASHINGTON DC (farewell show during the National Conference on Organized Resistance, 2002)

I stood outside the show space while Ashley napped in the car, nursing a hangover; but the moment Jon arrived, we promptly took off for a walk around the nearby Mall. We walked in the night shadows of the Capital lights and spoke of the things to come. He was excited and nervous to be at the end of an era; though the band would continue, everything was about to change as they forged off to destinies not yet known. Being present for Zegota's last North American

show for several years to come, preceding their move to Sweden, was a meaningful experience for many of us, as the band had become mingled with our lives over the past four years. In that January of last year after a day at the National Conference on Organized Resistance in Washington D.C. the basement of a church hall downtown was packed with conference goers and people who had come from all over to attend the show. There were many bands that played that night, Kill the Man Who Questions and Redención 9-11 stand out in my mind, but it was Zegota's night, and it was a pleasure to see how far the band had come on the eve of their departure. The lads showed off everything they had learned together, especially since Ard's addition a year and a half previous, holding nothing back. Will opened the set quietly on kora, an African harp, and slowly Jon and Birch, the sometimes brass player for Zegota, followed in on saxophones, intertwining slow and easy, and soon Ard found his way in on the bass. In the midst of all this Jon and Will switched to guitar and drum kit, building and finally bringing the improvisation to a crescendo, a wall of sound and music—the tension built up in the room connecting each person to the next—a brief moment of silence and then total release, launching into the driving "Lesser of Man." Zegota at its best is articulate passionate release and they maintained that electricity and sincerity through the entire set. After "Lesser of Man" they played their two newest compositions, "Thrones for the Worthy, Graves for the Rest" and "15." Ard spoke on the importance of chasing your passions. And before "15" Moe delivered a eulogy to a friend who had taken her life and the importance of being surrounded by friends and allies, as we were then, all brought together by this music and this time. As the finale to the set Jon began by speaking about life during wartime and resistance on all levels. The band played Crosby, Stills, Nash, and Young's "Ohio," still so pertinent to our times, which they had slowly made their own over the years. During a quiet part of

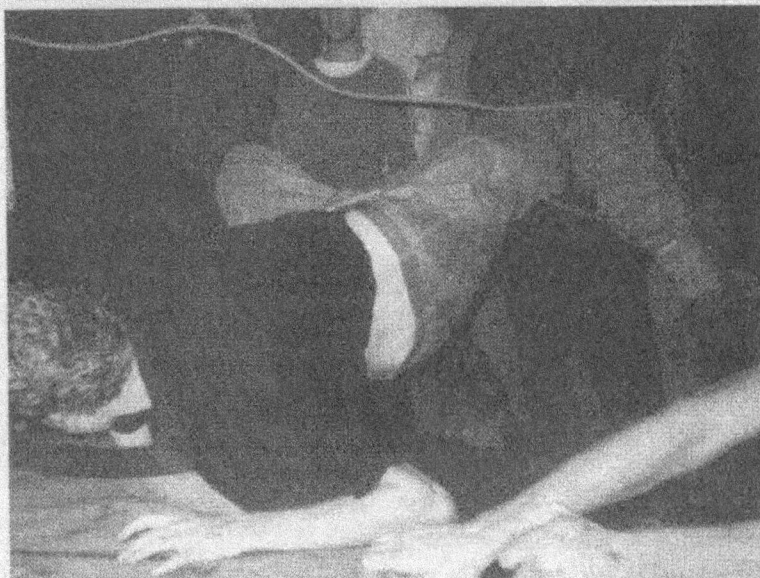

show reviews
FACE DOWN IN SHIT, SAN

FRANCISCO: Copied right out of an email from my friend Jason, their guitarist.

Hey Brian, this is a show 'review' from San Francisco! The offending 'Virginia tree-metaller' is me. And the 'girlfriends' are actually Iman and some other girl who met us up in Portland (from the tour that was two years ago with the LP). I found it really funny, it's from the SF Guardian.

"Burmese with Face Down In Shit"

Face Down in Shit played some kind of Virginian pro-tree metal, prefacing each

reviews

the song before the chorus comes back in Moe and Jon started whispering away from the mikes in unison: "I'm soldiers and Bush is coming," almost inaudibly, and slowly the whole room joined in the chant until our whispers had become a shout and the song came crashing to a finish, everyone and everything in a state of movement. In that last moment of feedback, Jon, on the ground, plucked carefully, the first few forlorn unfinished notes of the composition of a dead composer, and everyone followed him back in, Birch included, to build and break again over the room... The hall was left in an echoing silence comforting everyone in a state of smiling and tears. The band had meant to run "Eternal Flame" over the PA as the outro music, but in the chaos and emotion, it didn't happen; the subtle tribute to Sweden played unheard. It was poignant to be gathered there that night, in that transitioning moment, as if we had all gone down to the train station to wave off our friends who were going on a journey that would change everything. And on the platform we had kissed and laughed and wept and had known that no matter where any one of us went we would all carry this goodbye close, as it pushed us forward.

APPENDIX: A TALK WITH ZEGOTA IN THREE PARTS

ON DUTCH BASS PLAYERS

Bruce: The spring of 2000 you found yourselves without a bass player again, and I think it's quite revealing how you went about finding a new one. It's not every day that people move continents for the sake of joining a DIY punk band. You basically just put on Ard on a plane over here without so much an audition. The previous winter Jon was playing guitar for Catharsis in Europe and had a few days to get to know Ard beforehand—

Johnny G: I think at that time I had got a pretty good feel for Ard over there.

Moe: You didn't seem that way that spring when we deciding whether or not to do this.

B: It was a big decision. But what I see is an ordering of priorities for your band.

IG: That's true, what was important about it was not technical skill, but that we felt that Ard was coming from the same place in terms of what is

important about music: music as emotional expression. But also that Ard shared our idea of music as a tool and a revolutionary means of communication. I knew that he would be down with our lifestyle activism, which is a pretty big deal if you're going to be in a band. To be down with dumpster diving, and going extra lengths. And so being sure of those few things, overpowered our uncertainty about is technical skill or the fact that he wasn't really a bass player or that he had no experience touring. His political and emotional wavelength was the highest priority. We had good bass players before, but they turned out to be on different wavelengths, and it was ultimately destructive. We were all shaped by that. This time so far it's turned out well although sometimes I want to murder Ard and he wants to murder me.

B: Ard, what did Zegota offer you before you came, when you were still sitting at home on your farm in Holland? You're looking at the "Movement" record in your hands... What did this chance offer you in your life?

Ard: At that time I felt as if I needed something new, something refreshing, something that could absorb me totally, not a small change for a few hours a day, or on the weekend. I wanted something to take me to a place I had never been too. Take me to worlds I would not have access to by myself. It wasn't so much that I couldn't change myself, but my longing for others who were trying to do the same things, whose input was total, rigorous. The willingness to go all the way, that was something I totally

lacked where I was. Maybe it isn't necessary to have done things the way I did. But at the time it was the absolute best decision I could have ever made. Partly it was simply the excitement of not knowing what was coming. I knew the change would provide the qualities of which I was seeking, but not what form. I knew Jon a little, and the record and the writings, they meant a lot to me. I decided that they would be the people that would have the impact I was seeking.

ON THE MAKING OF THE "NAMASTÉ" LP

B: Where did Zegota take this project with the "Namasté" LP? What new directions have you all forged out, where did you go that the first full length ["Movement in the Music"] didn't?

IG: We had a different approach to it with "Namasté"—whereas, at least for me, when we recorded before I was way too focused on getting everything exactly right: chord changes, playing all the strings, making sure that every rhythm was right, everything on time. This time our emphasis is much more emotional—just trying to create a space, open ourselves up and bash out what ever comes to our heads. And trying to work on that level where we boil down all this technical considerations into what is important, which is the emotion of the music—and trying to capture that instead of being the best that we technically can.

A: I feel, even though I wasn't part of the first LP ["Movement in the Music"] recording, that this one is not so constrained. It seems that we allow ourselves to take some more risks, to take a more uncommon approach. Really when we came into the studio to record this we really didn't know how the puzzle would work—but by the end it pieced together automatically without being forced. I felt that this is a documentation of what really is going on instead of robotizing what we did before and making it into a clinical recording.

IG: Yeah, that was an important element in recording this: documentation. We wanted to reflect the ways we have grown and progressed since we recorded "Movement In The Music." We have a new band member since then – we don't have a whole lot of new songs. It takes us a long time to write songs and we had to spend a lot of time getting Ard up to speed on a lot of things—we were touring and we just didn't have a lot of time for songwriting. A lot of it is just documenting what was happening while we

STEF'S "DISCLAIMER":

Perhaps I'm not totally qualified to do reviews. In fact, these are the first reviews that I've written. I don't make much of an effort to keep up with punk "trends" and I generally don't buy records or read reviews (unless they're about my friends' bands). The only time I hear new music is when a touring band comes through my town (which is actually frequently), my own band goes on tour, or when stuff arrives for Inside Front. Don't get me wrong—I love music, it's one of the most important parts of my life. There's usually just a small handful of releases that I'm excited about and everything else I don't pay much mind to. I'd rather see a live band any day. So pardon my lack of references for comparison, especially when it comes to the more metallic stuff. I've tried really hard here and I don't feel like I've done that bad of a job.

My five favorite bands when I was 16:
Naked Aggression, Nirvana, the Pist, Crass, Bikini Kill

My five favorite current bands:
Tragedy, Breed/Extinction., Kylesa, Diallo, Gehenna

My five favorite bands of all time at age 23:
His Hero Is Gone, PJ Harvey, Nirvana, Catharsis, Youth of Today

Bands that have been frequenting my stereo in the past few weeks:
Del Cielo, Tragedy, the Pixies, HHIG, Kylesa, Axegrinder, Breed/Extinction, Amebix, the Breeders, Dystopia, Diallo, the Awakening, Fugazi, Bold, Diamanda Galas

were on the road, the ways we changed, the ways we found to keep things fresh and new.

B: What I like about it is that way it reflects the organic process of touring—especially being on tour for five months. Ideas develop, songs, especially when you're allowing space for improvisations like you did.

JG: To keep it vital you have to, otherwise it just becomes an opaque routine without emotion and without feeling. I don't think any of us are about to become robots.

ON THE PUNK BAND AS COLLECTIVE

M: I think first we try to give each other personal space to move around in and also to trust one another's judgments and intentions, even when they might not seem the most rational thing at the time. To have trust and faith with one another. Whereas so-called authority figures like bosses and politicians—these people who make all the decisions I don't know and surely don't trust. They make irrational decisions, and fuck, I don't trust them at all. I don't have faith in these people who have created this image based society that we live in—look what they've done to the world. Whereas Jon can be making a decision that seems irrational to me, but if his heart is in it I support it, because I trust him enough. I give him the benefit of the doubt, to make the decisions that need to be made and run with them.

JG: It basically boils down to a respect we have for each other. I think that's what Moe is getting at too. I respect these people to, number one, trust them with my emotional safety and emotional health and that feeds my ability to be able to express myself with them. This is essential in a musical group where the goal is to express. People who don't live hard and with fire and passion might not understand and be able to work in this manner. The fact that we all know what it's like to have to fight with the whole world just to give your desires a bit of honor and respect means we can be there for each other when the world comes crashing in and deal with it.

B: This is why I consider Zegota not only a valuable but a dangerous band. The common societal consensus is that living with fire and passion is going to ultimately be self-defeating—the example made of rock stars constantly reinforces this "truth,"

that you can only burn so long before you devour everything around you. While Zegota is saying, Let's make it sustainable for the four of us, for all of us—creating a space where that can be a reality.

A: I think that living with passion is easily maligned by society because anger (towards others or oneself) is so often portrayed as the flaw of intense feeling. We don't deny anger's truth but try and incorporate it into the greater spectrum of passion and give it a healthy space to live it and not totally self destructive. To admit to it and not cast it in some dark corner.

JG: But also we reserve the right to self-destruct and to be unafraid to hate if that's what you need to go through.

B: So it's okay to scrape the floor and be in the muck, if you need to be there—and hopefully when you look up someone will be there for you—

JG: When you're ready to come back.

ZEGOTA PRODUCTION UPDATE: as of May 2003 gathering storms in Sweden (shows? recordings? soon?). To get in touch with the band, write: Zegota/ 1104 Buckingham Rd./ Greensboro, NC/ 27408/ USA

multimedia reviews

CREATION IS CRUCIFIXION "CHILD AS AUDIENCE" CD AND BOOK:
Here we have an intersection of technical math-metal, digital-technology hacking, and cultural warfare—fascinating, and definitely not something you encounter regularly in any one of those three contexts. The foundation for this opus is a hacking project, in which the programmers hacked into a Nintendo Gameboy and taught it a subversive, home-made game in place of the one it was designed for; the CD includes "development software" so the user can carry out this hacking herself, which—practicing Luddite that I am—I have not yet been able to open. The basic idea here is to infiltrate the daily environment constructed by adults which children take for granted, and crack the facade to show that other worlds are possible.

The audio portion of the CD includes a spoken word piece over a noise track, laying out the case for their child-liberation program(ming), alternating with, as I said, technical math-metal—growling vocals, unbelievable technical proficiency in the playing, excessively complex compositions. When I saw them, singer Nathan was screaming his vocals while programming the noise track on his laptop, creating a strange spectacle that didn't exactly create an emotional connection between the band and the audience but certainly left an impression. Afterwards, I told him their songs sounded to me like the music I imagined martians would make if they decided to form a hardcore band with only a copy of HeartattaCk, 2600 magazine, and a few death metal mix tapes to work from; I'm not sure if he took that as a compliment, but I intended it as one! The book, which includes complete text in German, French, and Dutch as well as English, gives the necessary schematics and instructions for the Gameboy hacking, as well as a lengthy discussion of the colonization of childhood by Capital and how to undermine it—oh, and lyrics and that stuff. At the bottom of it all, it's unclear to me whether the Carbon Defense League (another of the groups involved in this release, and essentially an alternate incarnation of Creation Is Crucifixion) is actually opposed to silicon technology, or just seeks to contest the monopoly over its social application held by the powers that be; but I like that ambiguity. I think it gives them strength to accomplish things on various fronts at once, rather than limiting themselves to a single platform and method. I believe we need subversive groups who can't be pinned down, who can be recognized not for their rigid ideological stances but for the fact that wherever they go, they stir up shit and leave everyone confronting new questions. This project gets full marks for that—and also for providing the resources to enable anyone else who is interested to join in.

Before this review is concluded, let me point out something very wise that these folks are doing here, which others involved in the d.i.y. "record industry" should take note of: they are mass-producing resources for committing crime, and distributing them as entertainment products. This is brilliant, because it expands and dilutes the pool of potential suspects should the powers that be try to crack down on this particular hack. If thousands of music fans have this CD, and there is evidence that some people have been applying the technology on it, the State will have no idea where to start to track them down. If this same technology were available in a more limited context, it would be easier for those fuckers to keep up with who has access to it. Next time you mass-produce a CD

ALL BRUTE & NO FORCE

reviews

yourself, put a generic bomb threat on it, or a program to be broadcast over pirate radio, or something else along those lines! –b www.hacktivist.com is your best bet to track this down, or other projects by these folks.

forgotten classics

CONCRETE "NUNC SCIO TENEBRIS LUX" CD: I'm not sure how old this one

was. He told me it was Concrete, a band from Rome, and then adhered to what seems to be an Italian custom by insisting that I keep the tape. I listened to it the next six months until it would barely play any longer. Luckily, Gavin at Stickfigure had the CD in his distro so I got him to send me one. I know absolutely nothing about this band beyond these songs—I have no idea what their politics are, what other music they have made or if they're even still together. The CD starts strong with

complex, clocking in at just under forty minutes. Some of the songs move from total chaos to nearly inaudible ambiance to tribal-sounding drums built around the toms in a matter of minutes without ever sounding abrupt or unnatural. There's even a section in the middle of the CD that is structured much like a Godspeed, You Black Emperor! song although, chronologically, I doubt it was influenced much by them. The part comes out of chaos and starts with a simple, slow bass progression that slowly adds guitar, piano, violin, cello and contrabass. It is devastating and triumphant. I like this band very much. If anyone out there has anything else they have recorded and wants to dub me a copy in trade for something, get in touch through I.F. please. –s

SOA Records, via Oderisi da Gubbio 67/69, 00146 Rome, Italy

EDITOR'S TOP TEN LITTLE-KNOWN HARDCORE MASTERPIECES

1. Systral "Fever" 10"—I still stand by this as a record that makes the overused words "brutal" and "devastating" meaningful again.

2. Kriticka Situace 12"—This Czech band, at their peak, had all the soul and spirit of 7 Seconds and all the energy and adrenaline of Metallica at their best; their LP is, in my opinion, one of the best punk records of all time.

3. Headsman "The Morning" 12"—I may well be one of the only people outside of Northern Italy that noticed this record, but it's been really important to me: the broken English lyrics are deeply poetic, the singing vocals behind the screaming are sad and beautiful, the musical experimentation opens new possibilities for the attentive listener. The bass sound is still one of the worst ever produced, though!

4. Mayday "The Underdark" 7"—Perhaps no one remembers the dark, crazy, strange seven inch first recorded by this hardcore band from the early '90's. It still sounds as unique, and as scary.

5. Stalingrad and Hard to Swallow split 7's with Underclass (not the Underclass stuff, though, I'm sad to say)—The Stalingrad songs are totally primitive, yet unforgettably vicious and desperate and catchy. In my opinion, their only song after this that lived up to these was the last one on their picture disc 7." The Hard to Swallow stuff is packed with adrenaline, brilliant transitions, and unusual musical ideas, too.

6. G.I.S.M. (everything they did)—One of the weirdest bands of all time, punk or not. Listen to this to cleanse your system when you've heard too many punk rock clichés. Their occasional Iron Maiden moments are powerfully moving, too, believe it or not.

7. Libertinagem CD and 'zine: This is the top of the heap when it comes to youthful, intellectual, hyper-radical anti/art punk rock. No one ever heard of this outside Brazil.

8. Antidote 7"—This is the record Youth of Today spent their career trying to live up to; listening to it helps one understand better what they were going for. Watch out for the nationalist/quasi-racist song about "protecting American jobs," though—you can just leave that one off the mix tape!

9. Axegrinder "Rise of the Serpent Men" 12"—Very few bands ever really captured the Amebix style or ambience. This LP, though, sounds like the extra tracks cut from the "Monolith" record.

10. demos: Bloodlet (they swiftly became jaded rock stars, but this was their best work—spooky, tense hardcore in the vein Mayday had just opened up), Headway (they were one of the most creative, soulful French hardcore bands of the 1990's, but they never recorded anything during their best phase... their demo, recorded shortly before that time, is the closest one can get), Earth Crisis (not that I actually liked their demo, but it was the best thing they ever did, by far, and few of their fans ever got to hear it)

is since I can't read Italian, but I thought it'd be important to let y'all know about it because this CD has been really important to me over the past eighteen months or so. If "registrato, missato, masterizzato" translates to "recorded, mixed, mastered" then this was made in 1998, but like I said, I don't know Italian. We played at a squat somewhere in Italy one night and as we were winding down and getting ready for sleep, this album was playing on the stereo. It immediately caught my ear, so I asked our host who it

a double-kick fill that brings in a chunky metal hardcore riff. The vocals are insane—I think they're great, someone else might find them highly annoying. I think the singing sounds like a punk version of Perry Farrell (from Jane's Addiction) on crack. It's pretty monotone—the one note being out of key most of the time, throaty and obnoxious. The lyrics which are in Italian, fit the vocal style well, or perhaps vice versa, as there are a lot of rolled "r"s and held out vowels mid-scream. These five songs are long and

KRITICKA SITUACE "" CD: If I did a top ten list of bands you never heard of but should have, Kriticka Situace would be at #3 for sure. They would follow Pistols At Dusk (from Seattle) at #2, and Negate (from Belgium) at #1. Kriticka Situace was around in the late 80's and the very early 90's in the Czech Republic. No wonder you haven't heard of them. You were probably five when they put out this CD. Just kidding there, champ. So, to help enlighten you to the brooding rock and roll that was Kriticka Situace, I will start by telling you that they play this energized fast punk which doesn't fall into convention, and in fact rises constantly above it through poetic lyrics. Any band who uses the following words all on the same CD is a keeper: "subterranean", "insects", "myrmidons", "searchlights", and "graves". (By the way, I had no clue either: www.dictionary.com defines "myrmidons" as "a faithful follower who carries out orders without question"... thus proving once again, that aside from being endowed with a sense of history unparalleled in the US, and aside from all being bi and tri lingual, Europeans could mentally out-box Americans any day of the week with only a third of their brain cells intact. Americans are just a bunch of goddamn myrmidons). So, this CD: lots of bass breaks leading into fast guitar driven punk rock with lyrics about violence and oppression. But don't get me wrong, these aren't armchair warriors singing about how bad violence is and how we must all end oppression, or some similar empty garbage. What separates this CD from so many others is the perspective brought to the issues. When Kriticka Situace sings "You're proud of your truth / that sweet sensation of the victor, you want to live through it again and again / with flames in your eyes and your clenched fist / you throw yourself blindly into the night hunt" they are striking at the core of what makes myrmidons myrmidonic: the need to feel greater through following a leader into conflagration, even and especially through the loss of the individual's sense of self. Given the insanity going on now in Iraq, this song takes on new meaning. The band takes another angle on war and violence with their song Majority, in which they sing "We admire movies with military themes /

We listen to music with brutal lyrics / Our eyes widen, thrilled with violent fights / and we don't care who they dig the graves for". The sense throughout is of an awareness not only of violence, but more importantly, of the power dynamics and hierarchies that keep violence in place, and which in fact, use violence and unrest and dis-ease as tool to maintain status quos. Make sense? One thing you should know about this band is that they sing entirely in Czech with the lyrics translated into English. This is always a preferred method in my opinion because the art inherent in the delivery of the words can be more intense when presented in the original language. I am sure the Czech word for "myrmidons" is much easier to say in Czech when sung at 150 beats a minute. Then again, Czech is one of the most difficult to pronounce languages in the world as far as I can tell. I am pretty sure that sometime in history, the world decided to strip Czechoslovakia of all their vowels, but you might want to check my facts just to make sure. Modern

day cities like Brno and Plzen used to have a much higher vowel proportion, or V.P., before this ruling went into effect. So, the point is, that "myrmidons" might in fact not be simpler to say in Czech, which would just make me more impressed with this band. These guys get bonus points for using the words of Czech poet Frana Sramek as the lyrics to a full song. The words were written in 1914, and I am not sure how well the poem translates, but I like the bringing together of the two worlds of words and passions. Overall: fast punk without stereotypical sound or style meeting head to head with passionate spoken style screaming combined with basic production (but a good mix) and lyrics of which sincerity is not a question. You might have to look really hard to find this disc... and I wish you a successful quest. -JUG

Day After, c/o Mira Paty, Horska 20, 352 01 As, Czech Republic

music reviews

1905 "VOICE": The intro had me on totally the wrong track for this: feedback, discord, and a snare drum roll overloaded to sound somewhere between a bomb explosion and one of those great shitty live recordings of early '80's punk bands. But it ends suddenly, and we're suddenly in a sort of pop punk territory with soft singing vocals. As the record progresses, a rougher edge comes in and out again, with some hoarse-throated screaming and more punk intensity (on the eleventh track, they even

hazard pairing a blast beat with melodic vocals, an interesting experiment that I'm afraid doesn't work out well). At that point I'm already a little confused, but there are some strange moments yet to come: at one point, both vocalists scream "I don't want to look at the stars with you until you can look at strangers with me!!!" and the band goes into a crazy noise part (think Refused at the high point of their song "Shape of Punk to Come")—huh? The lyrics range from that kind of impenetrable venting on personal issues to more explicit, dare I say political, material, all suffused with an earnest longing. I think the drums are too high in the mix, and the guitars too quiet. I'll give them credit for this, though: they don't really sound like anyone else. I imagine they'll develop what they're doing a little more by the next record, and it could turn out to be something interesting and original. I don't want to give the wrong impression, either—there are definitely high-energy moments, and haunting ones. My favorite part is the piano interlude near the end. -b
Exotic Fever Records, P.O. Box 297, College Park, MD 20741-0297

ALCATRAZ "NI DIEU NI MAITRE, A BAS LA CALOTTE ET VIVE LA SOCIALE" CD (WHEW!): Wow, reviewing this is a pretty overwhelming prospect: twenty five songs from three different recording sessions totaling about 70 minutes of music, previously split up between about eight earlier releases, collected here with a 60 page booklet featuring lyrics, in-depth discussions of every song, and other texts in both their native French and also English, not to mention Spanish and Italian. Musically, this is raw, abrasive emo/hardcore, in the tradition that still shows signs of the influence of Acme as well as Rites of Spring. The tempo keeps pretty close to the middle of the spectrum, but blast beats break that trend from time to time, and there's plenty of variety in the compositions, and plenty of spirit and anger in the music—and hope, too. Most of the time someone's shrieking, but one of the vocalists sings sometimes, and she has a beautifully clear voice. A horn and violin make a brief appearance mid-way through—good for them, more of that! That song, a sprawling improvisation, turns out to be my favorite one. The recordings are clear and crisp and powerful, even the older ones. Ideologically, they're coming from an anti-authoritarian left-wing perspective (I think they identify as communists of some kind, but they don't really set off the bullshit alarms for me), with thorough discussions of the evils of corporate globalization, the difficulties in confronting

reviews

entrenched patriarchy, the class war, and even one of those silly little traditional rants about how hardcore sucks now. Let's forgive them for that, and sum up: this is an exemplary example of a great punk record, and miles ahead of almost everything else out there in terms of content and packaging. Even the layout is artistic and yet clear! If only every band would go to the trouble of building this much content into each release. –b
Stonehenge c/o Christophe Mora, 21 Rue des Brosses, 78200 Magnanville, France

ANTI OTPAD "RDNICKI SAN" CD:
This is punk rock at its best with charmingly bad sound quality and a whole lot of energy. This style reminds me of spiking my bi-hawk, getting a ride from Dad and circle pitting at the local teen center where we would book shows. I hear a bit of the Pist, Crudos, Naked Aggression and even a touch of Pennywise and Bouncing Souls. This is all in Croatian but the English translations, included on a separate photocopy—which perhaps was slipped only into the copies going to stupid self-centered Americans

like myself—indicate that the songs are about consumerism, authority, parents, killing your boss and drug addicts to name just a few topics. The vocals range from screaming to melodic singing to group shouts. The playing is not all too impressive but the sincerity and Black Flag guitar solos make up for anything that may have been lacking. This band has a youthful energy and urgency that is missing in a lot of modern punk. All in all this is a keeper. I'll be listening to this one at least a few more times. –s
Darko Hocevar Koparska 54, Pula Croatia

ANTIMANIAX "AS LONG AS PEOPLE THINK" CD:
"As long as people think that animals don't feel, they have to feel that people don't think," reads the slogan in its entirety inside their packaging—it's also the chorus of their first song. That song

actually has some stuff in it that sounds like ska, and a lot of stuff in it that's essentially pop punk, with major key rock riffs, nasal melodic singing in harmony, the whole bit. Almost anything in that whole genre just makes my stomach turn, and most of this is no different, so I'll focus on their content: there's a Noam Chomsky sample about U.S. hypocrisy regarding the treatment of the Kurdish people by Iraq and Turkey, and all the song lyrics address important stuff (con: religion, the entertainment and animal exploitation industries, war, globalization... pro: freedom, non-consumer values, burning down banks!). I appreciate that, and really, as a pop punk band, they're not bad—I'm thrilled they're out there in a different milieu than my favorite bands work in, having a good influence on pop punk fans. Right on. –b
Household Name, P.O. Box 12886, London, SW9 6FE, England

BREED/EXTINCTION "ALASKA" CD:
Since I know all of the people involved in the production of this CD, from the guy who released it, to the kid who did the artwork for the layout, to the dude who recorded it, it's probably impossible for me to give any sort of unbiased review, but, fuck it—this band rocks my world.

Breed/Extinction has gone through many line-up changes in the past few years and I'm not even sure who is in the band at this very moment, but I've at least known Rob, the guitarist and vocalist, for nearly a decade now. We probably first met when his Oi band and my street punk band played together at some Connecticut teen center. I think it was B/E's second show that I saw somewhere in Brookfield, CT several years later, and I was completely blown away. Over the next twelve or eighteen months I made sure I made it out to every B/E show. I probably saw them play over fifty times and I even followed them on their first tour (a week or so) as to not miss any action. There have been few bands that have meant that much to me.

I eventually moved to North Carolina and only saw those kids when I went home to visit or one of them ended up traveling through the south... until the band I was in all-of-a-sudden lost it's bass player within weeks of a five month tour. Rob came to the rescue, the ready-to-go motherfucker that he is, and did the entire tour with us.

So what do they sound like? Well, their other releases are somewhat easier to pinpoint: somewhere between HHIG and Catharsis, but at times a bit more metallic. This record, however, is much different. I was caught off guard on the first listen. They definitely seem to have moved in their own direction. The songs are very intricate and well-written, giving each instrument (including vocals) a chance to shine and take the "lead" during different parts. There are a lot of well thought out harmonies and odd time patterns that fortunately avoid coming off sounding "math-y." a lot of this record is instrumental but it never gets boring. They cover a lot of ground from long, crazy build-ups to beautiful quiet parts that sound quite similar to some Godspeed, You Black Emperor! material, to full-blown chaos.

I only have two small criticisms of this record. There is a three second intro to one of the songs that sounds like a bad version of Botch—I could have done without that. And I do miss their old dual vocals that they no longer have because I thought the brutal low growls (that are no longer there due to their main singer parting ways) and the high-pitched howls complimented each other well.

If you have half of a brain in your head, check this record out. –s
Losing Face Records, P.O. Box 14641, Albany, NY 12212

APES OF THE UNION "" CD:
I think I've got their name right, though I'm not certain... the kind of packaging the bands (is that even the right term?) in this genre (the wave of noise/dada/experimental stuff coming from the likes of Lightning Bolt, USA IS A MONSTER, Monster Attacks King Noise Machine, Herds and Words, etc.) opt for is usually deliberately confusing. Besides, I have a suspicion that this is actually a recording of a band I saw perform under the name "Ground Monkeys": like their performance, the basic fair here is guitar noise, ranging from psychotic to totally abstract, over chaotic drum improvisations. What I really liked about seeing them was the way they reinterpreted the use of the instruments, the drums especially: the drums weren't there to keep a rigid beat so much as to experiment with different speeds and intensities, increasing and decreasing them at will—while the guitarist, left to fend for himself, made parallel, if often artistically disparate, noise. There are also some quieter pieces on here, more spooky perhaps, but not exactly evocative. There are forty one

BURN HOLLYWOOD BURN "IT SHOUTS AND SINGS WITH LIFE... EXPLODES WITH LOVE!" CD: It took me a few listens to figure out what kind of music they're playing for the first minute of this CD: surf music? It arrives through the filter of their cutting edge soulful hardcore aesthetic (think Zegota, perhaps?), so it wasn't easy to pin it down, but that's what's going on. After that part, the Zegota comparison becomes more appropriate in the actual parts and composition for the remainder of that song, but there are definitely some surf rock parts elsewhere on the record. Really, the seamless transitions between parts drawing on entirely disparate segments of music history demonstrate what skilled musicians and songsmiths they are. Things get really interesting around the middle of the third song: there's a quieter break, with intensifying guitar noise, and the singer's declamation is suddenly the center of all attention, in a moment distantly descended from Jim Morrison. That song ends, to name a more recent reference, with the same spent acidity as the end of that older Breed/Extinction song that closed with Greg spitting "boxes... inside boxes..." The fourth song is an instrumental from the lineage of Godspeed, You Black Emperor!, named after an ancient Latin palindrome that probably comes to this band through Guy Debord's use of it—if that doesn't identify for you the recent punk tradition they hail from, I don't know what will! The recording itself is a little dry, reminiscent (as are their title and cover art, snatches of their lyrics—"where do we go from here?", and perhaps some of their politics) of Refused's "Shape of Punk to Come," and I think a less clinical, warmer, more ragged recording might have flattered this more—it could have made them sound more like a band showing off their heart and soul than flaunting their technical precision. My favorite moment on the record is probably the opening riff of the fifth song, which sounds like a cover of some lost segment of Orff's epic *Carmina Burana*. Politically, this band doesn't stray too far from their forebears here—the liner notes emphasize that this is a commodity, and as such cannot compare to the immediacy and preciousness of a life lived for desire's sake—but their personality is apparent in the elements they choose to emphasize: their variation on Zegota's "Wreck Your Life" motto is "fuck it all," or, elsewhere, "we fuck your world," and elsewhere, "we fuck ourselves." It's ambiguous whether this is a sex-negative avowal of nihilism or an invitation to the world to make endless (and potentially sado-masochistic?) love, and in that playing with terms and fire there is an unfettered, volatile, dangerous power—one that rarely is engaged except by young punks too wild-eyed to know better! In that context, of course, when the vocalist, whose pronouncements throughout would be hard to interpret as anything other than individualist/adventurist, declares (in the Dennis/Refused tradition) "we'll get organized," it's clear he's just borrowing the anarcho-syndicalist lingo to refer to something much more disruptive than recruiting factory workers to the union. And—fuck, oh no!!!—finishing this review, I realize to my horror that we have put my *least favorite* Burn Hollywood Burn song on the CD that comes with this Inside Front, and it's far too late to rectify the situation. God, what a disaster. -b

Bisect Bleep, P.O. Box 80249, 35102 Rennes Cedex 3, France

---

fucking tracks in all here—that's pretty overwhelming, not to say self-indulgent. See these guys play (assuming I've pegged their band right) and try to glean your own interesting perspectives from what they're doing, rather than starting with this CD— that's my suggestion. -b
www.massivedistribution.com

ASIDE FROM A DAY "MAIEUTICS" CD: This is metallic hardcore from France that is certainly more metal than hardcore. They sound like a combination of the Black Hand and Isis with shrieking vocals,

layered guitar harmonies and impressive instrumentation from every angle. This CD sounds pretty good too. There are full-on double kick assaults, vulnerable pretty pieces, noise samples here and there and tense build-ups. It has metal harmonies in strange keys, starts and stops, blast beats, bass slides, mosh parts, d-beats—you name it. They're not necessarily doing anything original but there's enough variety to keep it interesting throughout the twenty five minutes that these songs fill. If you're into metallic hardcore certainly check this out. -s
Art-Scenic Production 13 rue de Vignier 25000 Besancon France

---

THE AWAKENING CD: This is a burned CD with hand-made packaging (beautifully crafted, may I add) with songs from three different 7"s, so I'm not sure if this is an "official" release or something they made only a few of. The music is fucking great and the recording is not bad at all. I've never heard a band quite like this. They seem to have taken the best parts of From Ashes Rise and Kill the Man Who Questions and tainted it with a bit of thrash and a whole lot of old school hardcore. The songs are loaded with d-beats, snare rolls, stops, breakdowns and metal harmonies. The vocals are youthful and urgent and remind me a bit of Ruination or some old youth crew band maybe like Bold except without the machismo. The lyrics are pretty good—apocalyptic and poetic with a hint of hope inspiring us to keep struggling: "toxins choke out the sun, your machines continue to seek us out, but our moment of clarity will come, rhythms of the earth cradle our children, the caress of the soil feeds our power within, in our darkest visions we have seen the end, in our darkest visions we are the burning wind, in all of our confusion we know our place in this world, we are the hungry and you have the food, crawling and kicking, fingertips bleeding, you cannot tear us from the sun." The song containing the lyrics I scrawled down [editor's note: she's not joking, Stef wrote all these reviews by hand] just came on and it's fucking great. I'm a fan of all sorts of hardcore with His Hero is Gone and Youth of Today being among my favorites, so this is right up my alley. This band is quite good. -s
The Awakening 1579 Indianola Ave. Columbus, OH 43201

THE BARNHOUSE EFFECT "..." CASSETTE: Clean-channel guitars build an atmosphere, before distortion and shrieking kick in, the band still playing the same chord progressions. They're coming from the same scene as Cathode, although they lack that band's dedication to and mastery of the Gehenna aesthetic, leaning instead towards a less distinctive take on the noisy, screaming hardcore genre. The best moments for me in this recording are the ones when they push the intensity of the guitars, cymbals, and shrieking vocals almost to the point of white noise; the tempo rarely really accelerates, but the moments when it does are also among the best. Maybe they could do with more speed, or maybe that's just my own tastes. For the last song, there's a sample of a Kafka story (the guy who waits his whole life at the gate for access to the Law); a sort of light-hearted, clean improvisation (and—is that a cowbell?) begins over it, switches suddenly over to distortion and screaming and chaos, and back and forth a

ALL BRUTE
AND NO FORCE

BREWT
GOES TO
WAR

BEING ALL THAT
WE CAN BE IN
2003

WATCH OUT FOR
THAT LANDMINE!

-BOOM!-

couple times more. The demo comes with a little pamphlet version of the excellent Kurt Vonnegut story that is their namesake, in which "dynamopsychicism," the force of the mind, and its ethical applications, are

you!" before the vocals come in on the fifth track, which also begins with that sample from Romper Stomper (the Australian movie about racist skinheads), "We came to wreck everything, and ruin your life." The

downtuning, totally overloaded production, and unearthly atmosphere, Carahter manages to capture the same atmosphere Systral did on their amazing "Fever" 10". In fact, I'll be damned if they haven't been listening to that record—the occasional metal leads and harmonies, deep rumbling and high shrieking dual vocals, and discordant chords are all here... let's cover the differences, then: Carahter lack the punchy bass drum Systral used, they don't work with samples (there's a noise track in the middle of the CD that I believe is from Kubrick's 2001, but that's not the same), and they tend to employ a pretty arbitrary song structure—the transitions make sense enough, but parts never come back around. That last quality might make the actual songs a little less memorable, but if you're listening to the record for its terrifying, dark ambiance, it won't bother you. The packaging includes extensive liner notes in both Portuguese and English about third world resistance to neo-liberalism, consumer culture, and imperialist capitalism in general, which is awesome. -b
Liberation, Caixa Postal 4193, Sao Paulo, SP 01061-970

CATHODE "A MACHINE THAT NEVER FALTERS" CD: Some of you may know that one of my favorite bands of all time was Gehenna. Gehenna, in their early years, made the most stomach-twisting, rage-filled, disgust-spitting hardcore punk the world has ever heard, in my opinion. After they recorded their 7", I was holding my breath for their full length, but a long time passed before they finally got around to recording it. By then, the band had changed a bit, and that record wasn't quite what I'd been hoping it would be: it was fast, furious, destructive, but lacked the complexity their earlier recordings had hinted they were capable of. This CD here, by Cathode, is the full length I'd been hoping Gehenna would record: it's fucking amazing. It's good enough that I can say that without meaning that it's simply derivative. It's not Gehenna, it lacks their bitter soul, but musically, everything is here—even the things that Gehenna should have gotten around to doing, and didn't: wide-ranging dynamics, unique drum patterns complementing equally unusual guitarwork, relentless rhythms and vocal attack, and a general atmosphere of ominous darkness and desperate agony broken up by flashes of the kind of rare beauty that can only be experienced under such conditions. Above all, as I've mentioned in a few other reviews—having original, timeless *songs* as well as good musical abilities is the dividing line between a good band and a great band, and Cathode has a whole record of songs here, all their own. Indeed it's one of the best records of the past few years, hands down, and I hope everyone who reads this 'zine gets the chance to hear it—or at least those of you with the same psychotic/maniacal emotional problems I have that make me relate to this so deeply. The d.i.y. packaging (yes, they released this themselves, as if I wasn't impressed with them already!) is starkly beautiful, black-on-grey images of our modern wasteland so abstract that they really capture a feeling of existential loss and lostness. The lyrics are the only place they could stand to improve; some songs are excellent in their simplicity (the first one, for example), but elsewhere they take too much from other bands in the genre (I hate to say it, but I think there are some actual lifts from lines off the "Passion" album)—though even then, as the guttural growls and throat-tearing screams are hardly intelligible, this doesn't hold the music back at all. If these guys can write lyrics that reflect their own unique experience of the world a bit more clearly, their next record will be a classic for all times. Assuming, that is, they're still together. -b
Mark van de Maat, Nijlandstraat 55, 7462 rz Rijssen, The Netherlands (markvdmaat@hotmail.com)

discussed—presumably this is a metaphor for the power we all have to control our own destinies, and thus the world, if we only take responsibility for ourselves. I'm really sympathetic to this band, their lyrics are earnest and passionate and they're going about everything the way I love to see d.i.y. bands go. I've got my fingers crossed that their next recording will really cross the line to be something unbelievable. -b
Thale, Schonauvensingel 8, 3523 JG Utrecht, The Netherlands

BURNING BRIDGES "THE BEST REVENGE" CD: This is precisely-recorded tough hardcore a little bit further into the tough-guy spectrum than Walls of Jericho was. There are fast parts, which helps to keep the music interesting outside the kickboxing pit, and the playing is tight. Hardcore kids familiar with the history of Albany hardcore will know exactly what tradition this band hails from, and it's clear in the gruff vocals and mosh-parts with double bass blasts that they're set on carrying that torch forward. The singer counts off "one-two-fuck

lyrics are starkly individualistic, covering the various letdowns and frustrations of friendships gone awry. The burly, bearded singer has x's on his hands in the live photos, and kids are singing along—maybe straight edge is not dead yet after all! -b
Losing Face Records, P.O. Box 14641, Albany, NY 12212

CARAHTER ""CD: North American and European metal/hardcore listeners take note, especially if you have political convictions, for you will probably not read about this great record in other hardcore publications from the global North. With their dramatic

CEMENTARIO SHOW "" CD: I love this band on their split with Sin Dios (reviewed below), and while I think this recording might be a little older, I'm thrilled about it too. At their best (say, tracks 7 and 10) they mix up their frantic, top-speed hardcore punk with a sort of surf/devil rock thing, and it's fucking great. The drummer's love affair with the snare drum is also in evidence here, everything from the raging vocals to the hyper-kinetic riffs evidences attitude with a capital 'A', and no part goes on any longer than it should. The recording is fine, but somehow I feel like it would be possible to make a more flattering mix of this, one with a scarier atmosphere perhaps. The lyrics appear in translation on the last page: attacks on child-worker exploitation, religious dogmatism, the mass media, soul-killing routine, even controlling parents—yes, this is punk rock. -b
W.C. records, Juan I. Herrero, Apdo. 41019, 28080 Madrid, Spain

CWILL "NATIONS" 10": Here it is, the real thing—a fucking hardcore punk record, in the classic sense! Breakneck speed, a dirty, fierce recording, a photo of a filthy latrine on a cover which reads "nations" in case their politics were unclear, epic drama in the climax of every song, band photo of punks playing in ski masks, deranged maniac screaming "we will never get out of this world alive because we are poisoned and enslaved by the horror we commit every day—hell is here" through torn vocal cords into a dented, rusted microphone. And the beautiful, mournful violin that distinguished this band before still soars above on some songs, adding a sadness that deepens the rage. The lyrics are gritty and yet soulful enough that the two songs which take their words from earlier poets—Pablo Neruda and Erich Fried—don't even stand apart from the others at first glance. These are both adeptly adapted, and make excellent punk songs, as it turns out. In my mind's eye, this band is playing a benefit at a squat the night before a political demonstration; the squatters watching out the windows lest the pigs close in ahead of time, the room steamy in mid-winter from all the bodies dancing and shouting along to the words of a dead South American poet; fists pump the air, guitarists leap and strike chords, promises are made internally to never back down, and everyone sleeps just a couple hours before shaking off the chill to hit the streets. Yes, we need records like this. -b
Cwill and Prawda, Scholastikastr. 24, CH-9400 Rorschach, Switzerland

CHESTERFIELD SYMPHONY ORCHESTRA "" CD: Yes, an anarchist symphony orchestra! In a time when the evolution of punk and hardcore forms and conventions seems to have stagnated, this is exactly what we need! This could be something in the genre Neutral Milk Hotel plays in, if you know them: strings, strummed acoustic guitar, classical horns, theatrical narration. The third song works with those same elements, but adds another narrator; the variety of voices and the layers they form intensifies the effect. It would be easy to be annoyed with the vocalist in this format, but he sounds so earnest that it's hard not to find him endearing: I imagine him a young Walt Whitman, waving his script emphatically, starry eyes swimming in youth and dreams, delivering these spoken word pieces with all he's got—"the walls will spill, encouraging the waves—and the waves will triumph, when we are the making of freedom!" Trust me, it's not bad. He's still there on the fifth track, but in place of the orchestral background, there's an a capella piece sung smooth as silk by a group of women—at least for the first minute, before the ensemble kicks in again. The mood throughout is subdued but complex, melancholy and reflective; the playing itself is spectacular, symphony orchestra-quality to my untrained ears. And speaking of Whitman, and Allen Ginsberg for that matter—these five songs are followed by a fucking hilarious, eloquent take-off on those poets' compositions, composed and narrated on the evening of September 11, 2001: "America, why don't we enjoy the real explosions as much as the video games? America, why are the dumpsters locked?" Three more spoken word pieces by two other speakers follow: depression, confessions of troubled dreams, responding to rape. I don't think this band is still together in this format (that is, if these folks ever thought of themselves as a band), but hopefully this CD can still be tracked down. -b
Try this address (good luck!): Kalie, 3415 Juno Street, Pittsburgh, PA 15213

CONFUSIONE "[?]" 7": Fast, anxious, distraught punk rock. Lots of starts and stops—and nine songs on a 7," no less. The tense melodies only add to the desperation conveyed by the shrieking, broken-voiced vocalist, whose lyrics express a self-destructive nihilism that seems to be overstated—I think this is the sign of an idealism that still lies beneath the surface, wounded but unwilling to die, revealing itself through its opposite. -b
Heroine records c/o Boris Battistini, Via Galilei n. 6, 47020 Montiano (FC), Italy

DAWNCORE "WE ARE YOUNG... SO WE SCREAM... JUST TO FEEL ALIVE" 7": I'm sure these kids have something new out now, maybe a couple records—but this is the latest one in my box, and part of what I do with my part of this 'zine is catalog my passage through the hardcore world, so here this is. The Budapest scene sure did figure out the whole metal hardcore thing to a t—this is top notch hyper-complex, hyper-speed, hyper-intense, hyper-moshable hardcore, coming in at the top of its class: tight machine-gun bursts of double bass, intricate guitar-work, the whole thing. If I have any reservations, they would be (first) that it seems to be difficult to compose memorable songs in this genre—the parts hold together well and are memorable individually, but I think the world has yet to hear a classic in this genre that will have the staying power of some of those old blues songs that still get played today—and (second) that the lyrics put me in a sort of personal quandary: there is a song entitled "Let's Set The World On Fire," and another, better yet, called "Killing of the Spectators," and that kind of rhetoric gets me really excited, but I think they just mean it metaphorically, whereas I actually want to see the world in flames and spectators bleeding to death outside the bullfighting rings. So should I be frustrated with them for posing, or just enjoy this as "brutal metal, dude," or urge them to become actual arsonists? -b
Burning Season, Auf der Scheibe 20, 3130 Herzogenburg, Austria

DEAD THINGS "BECAUSE SOMETIMES YOU JUST WANT TO RIDE YOUR BIKE TO THE SHOW" CD: It's hard for me to think of what to say about this band. Musically, they're not really my thing, but I love them anyhow. They must truly be a great band if their actions, personalities and sincerity win me over as a fan when I generally steer clear of anything that sounds like this. I'll first make a lame attempt to describe their music and then I'll get down to why I'm really into this band. Pardon my comparison if it's a little off due to lack of knowledge: I guess to me they sound like back-woods, more DIY version of Against Me! They definitely have that catchy pop/punk/folk feel to them with melodic guitars, harmonized male/

DEARBORN S.S. "" 7": This record exemplifies anarcho-punk at its best—confrontational, historically as well as politically conscious, with a local focus (in this case, on the secret history of the midwest from which they hail) to make it all that much more urgent. Songs fast enough to fit seven on a 7" (just barely!), busy drumming (even a few blastbeats), punk rock riffs, plenty of transitions in the songwriting, dual vocals (and yes, one male and one female vocalist... if I had to come up with comparisons, I would say a more vicious, pissed off Amy from Nausea, and then that guy from Rorschach), all these make for great listening, and the liner notes go into great detail about the connections between industrialist Henry Ford, anti-Semitic proselytizing, and the Nazis (Hitler said of his friend Ford "I wish I could send some of my shock troops to Chicago and other big American cities to help in the elections.. we look to Heinrich Ford as the leader of the growing fascist movement in America," according to the Chicago Tribune). The lyrics even come translated into Spanish, French, and German! Of course these assholes broke up years ago now, but seek out this record at the least—and when you form a great band, stick together through a few tours. -b
Dearborn S.S., P.O. Box 220691, Chicago, IL 60622

DAVID SANDSTROM "OM DET INTE HANDER NAT INNAN IMORGON SA KOMMER JAG" CD: This is David's (yes, the drummer in Refused, and a member of Text) epic record dedicated to and telling the story of his grandfather, who lived and died struggling in northern Sweden. It's at once austere and eclectic: each part takes its sweet time to develop, leaving some space in which the listener finds himself alone with his thoughts, as the lines continue (not a bad thing, in this case); but if you consider the record as a whole and look at all the different instruments and arrangements going on, you find everything from post-classical compositions for strings and piano (think A Silver Mount Zion), to rock parts a la Bruce Springsteen, early Dire Straits, and Neil Young, to more atmospheric jazz-influenced stretches such as Cerberus Shoal might have played, theatrical a capella sections, and even Portishead moments with turntables and all. The closer you listen, the more treasures are revealed to you, as every last detail has been painstakingly fashioned, gauged, and slipped into place: this is a record to listen to on headphones as you take a long walk through snowy fields—perhaps every day for a month. It's clearly the work of one author, working alone, and I imagine if there had been others involved in the creative process, some stretches would have been a little denser in terms of—not diversity or ideas, exactly, as both are present in abundance here, but perhaps—perspective; at the same time, this particular record could probably only have entered the world as the work of a lone individual, and it's good enough that we've got it. To answer your question, hardcore boy, there are indeed a couple moments that are reminiscent of that punk band David played in and wrote for, and it's fascinating how he's translated that energy into a different aesthetic—a reminder that punk rock and, say, gospel music are not all that far apart, where it really matters. All the lyrics are in Swedish, but the music really is eloquent enough to convey the story alone; on the other hand, if you pestered Dave through the post for the English, he would probably oblige you.
Demon Box, Box 1043, SE-172 21 Sundbyberg, Sweden

female vocals and a generally upbeat, happy
energy. The instrumentation on this record
is skillful and tight although the sound
quality itself is somewhat thin and distant.

DEL CIELO "WISH AND WAIT" CD: I
grew up listening to Kill Rock Stars stuff so
this one wins my
approval almost
immediately.
These three ladies
definitely have
their own style,
but I'll compare
them to Sleater
Kinney for
lack of a better
reference. This is
mid-tempo rock
with dual female
vocals and a lot
of emotion. The
songs are catchy
and I totally find
myself singing
along. The lyrics
seem to be mostly
personal about
relationships and
self-reflection,
which is
refreshing for me
since I generally
listen to bands
with straight-up
political lyrics.
These ladies might
not be singing
about what I
feel are vital and
urgent issues, but

FACE DOWN IN SHIT "SHIT BLOODY SHIT" CD: This band has
really matured into something amazing, as the first (and most recently
recorded) track shows. It begins with a beautiful, sad buildup, violins
and piano over guitars, such as Neurosis might have done at their best.
Once the engines get running, though, it takes off like a Motorhead
song, and when the screaming vocals come in the gears shift again to
something that sounds a little more like the mid-'90's Bremen hardcore
characterized by Acme, Systral, and Morser. You can tell from some
of the fast-and-chunky riffs that these kids listened to metal bands in
the '80's; but none of this is derivative. FDIS have a very distinctive
style of their own—and, most importantly, *soul*. You can recognize it
in the stoner rock bass lines, the dramatic, dragged-out hanging open
notes a la early His Hero Is Gone—when they're slow, they're painfully
slow with a grit you can almost taste, and when they get going, it's
like a monstrous machine tearing through the underbrush, kicking
up dirt and rocks. The layout and design are remarkably well done for
Greensboro slackers like these folks, and I love that they never shy away
from going over the top: song titles include "Born in Fucking Chains"
and "Bleeding in the Street," and the lyric booklet actually has a photo
of someone hugging a tree (in keeping with their pro-nature bent) on
the back. This CD collects the song from their elusive split 10" with
Cold Electric Fire, their "Concrete World" LP (which they released
themselves—right on), and their demo. The demo is almost unlistenable
compared to the other recordings, which are much more vital and
dynamic—despite having each been done, against all common sense,
in only one day. I just find myself listening to the first track over and
over—it's a fucking *song*, a unique song that stands apart in an era when
thousands of bands are playing music but few are actually writing songs
that will be remembered years from now. Yes, this is the real thing. -b
Crimes Against Humanity, P.O. Box 1421, Eau Claire, WI 54702-1421

**DIVINITY OF TRUTH "UNTITLED"
CD:** This CD has some of the craziest
packaging I've ever seen. Sometimes
packaging like this just gets in the way when
you just want to listen to the music, but
this is so well-done that it's worth the extra
effort. And that says a lot, because I'm pretty
lazy. The whole shebang is wrapped in a
piece of black cardstock, with no less than
3 screen prints on it, including lyrics. The
CD is wrapped in black tissue paper (with
handwritten words on it) and mounted
on a brad. The entirety is wrapped in a
piece of black ribbon, and also includes a
small insert with thank-you's and credits.
Someone really loves their band. The music
doesn't let me down, even after they raised
my expectations with their fancy packaging.
Divinity Of Truth play really competent
metallic hardcore, with seamless transitions
into slower, more vulnerable-sounding
parts. The vocals are heartfelt, with well-
written lyrics about greed, remorse, pain,
and finding your own path through it all.
I wholeheartedly recommend this, but it's
limited to 450 hand-numbered copies (with
this packaging, at least), so you might be out
of luck. -xb
DOT, P.O. Box 208, Kapowsin, WA 98344

**E150 [PARTIAL DISCOGRAPHY]
CD:** Through all forty five minutes here,
E150 are always incredibly energetic, often
catchy, and sometimes unforgettable. It's
not one of those classic records that will
never fade from relevance (there's just
not quite enough to set these songs apart
from songs by the other great bands in
this genre), but it's pretty close to the top
of the heap of runners-up, and makes for
great fucking listening if you love punk
rock. This is a collection of eight different
releases, from 7"s to split 7"s to compilation
tracks, ranging from '96 to '00 and totaling
28 tracks (covers: Poison Idea, Beyond
Description, Toreros after ole, and a twenty
second Lärm song). Lots of fucking d-beats
of all kinds, occasional blastbeats and plenty
of snare drum rolls, grainy distorted bass,
two vocalists: one shrieking, one yelling.

The artwork and layout are great and there
are fifteen songs. Alright, let's get down to
business. Dead Things are rad because they
did a tour (playing shows) of the entire state
of North Carolina—one of the larger states
on the East coast—on their bikes. Also, they
have lyrics such as "stop building your big
houses on out mountain sides ya yuppies,
we've got garden tools!" and "more than two
wheels is too many for me, gonna run your
car into a fucking tree." I want to hear more
songs in the world about beating up yuppies
with shovels! -s
Slave PO Box 10093 Greensboro, NC 27404

they certainly are active. They're involved
with a lot of projects in their community,
the D.C. area. Plus, they're just really nice,
charming people. They stayed at my house
on their way to a show in Georgia and
immediately made friends with my foster
brother, Justin. Several days later, a mix tape
arrived in the mail for him from the band.
Anyone that makes Justin happy gets a
"thumbs up" in my book. -s
*Eyeball Records PO Box 1653 Peter
Stuyvesant Station NY, NY 10009*

DIALLO "DIAGRAM OF A SCAM" 7": This is another band that I have some background with. We came from the same scene and
sort of grew up together—we weren't from the same town or anything and never really hung out much, but our various bands played many
shows together. This is by far the best band that any of these kids have done. They are fucking relentless, brutal, passionate and full of energy
and sincerity. Living far away from them now, I had heard a good deal about them before I actually got to listen and boy was I stoked when
I finally heard them. This band is totally the new His Hero Is Gone and possesses all the skill and heart needed to fill those big old-school
skate shoes. Yes, indeed they sound very much like HHIG, which is great for me and I don't mind at all that it's not that original because I'm
at a place in my life where that particular style is still what drives me, makes me shake my fists and want to destroy everything and reminds
me that I'm alive. They have it all—slower crushing heavy parts, gnarly pick slides, thundering bass, powerful fast d-beats, ear-piercing guitar
leads, eerie clean parts and strange vocal layouts that accent the songs perfectly. The vocals themselves are a bit more their own style with
three singers that are giving it their all for every syllable as if it might be their last breath. They also have brutal double-kick, which gives
certain parts the bite they need to set them apart from their predecessors. The first song starts with a three second clean guitar intro that
almost leads you to believe that you have a while to relax, but then the song slams in, much earlier than one might expect, and knocks you on
your ass. And it's non-stop brutality from then on. This is great! The first song goes directly into the second song and for the remainder of the
record there is never more than a second gap between songs. I like my hardcore like this, with no time to breath—there's no time to waste and
every second counts. FUCK, I want to live my life like this!... and I'm able to, due to the inspiration I get from bands like this. This is one of
my top three of the year and it's only a 7". I can't wait to hear a full-length from these guys. Fuck, I want to put it out. I'm stoked on this band
(obviously). Oh, I think they could benefit from a slightly better recording, although this one is not bad by any means. Fans of HHIG—get
this now! -s
(this is on a German label, so I'll give that address for the Europeans and the band's address for the yanks:) *Yellow Dog Box 550208, 10372 Berlin
Germany / Diallo PO Box 1004 Windsor CT 06095*

Some of my favorite stuff happens in the fourth song, where they complement the all-out craziness with some more haunting breaks. Political lyrics (in Spanish, with explanations in English too) covering

personalities, catchy choruses, and streamlined structure! They're a little like the Ramones, in that there's one thing they do really well, and they're hell-bent on exploring every corner of that little space, but you can't blame them, since they are good at it and there can never be enough good songs in the world. Anyway, despite the major key, which is basically my musical nemesis, the raw energy, screaming vocals, and occasional melodic leads keep me connected to this. And, for all ye of little faith, the mighty Umlaut is on their thanks list—of course! –b
Combat Rock Industry, P.O. Box 139, 00131 Helsinki, Finland

FILTH OF MANKIND "THE FINAL CHAPTER" CASSETTE:
This is a modern band that plays old style crust. Judging by the packaging and band photo I assumed that this band would sound like the Amebix and I wasn't too far off. I'd have to say that they tend to lean towards sounding metal a bit more than the Amebix though. This band hails from Poland and their lyrics are in their own language instead of English, which is refreshing. There are English translations of the songs and they are some of the better apocalyptic crust lyrics that I have read: "no one cares to admit that the helm is broken, blinded they count on salvation in the lifeboats, meanwhile like rats they fight...," "I'm suffocating in a concrete jungle without sun or rain, locked inside walls, I'm suffocating, breathing in lead, in an endless traffic jam on the road to nowhere." The vocals sound somewhat similar to those of Zygote, although a bit rougher, with lots of reverb and echo. The songs are generally pretty long and hypnotic with driving bass and drums, chunking guitars with melodic parts in between, synthesizer here and there, and atmospheric noise samples at some points. If you're into bands like the Amebix, Axegrinder, Zygote, etc., I would suggest checking this out. –s
Scream Tapes/ Pawel Rzoska / PO Box 118/ 80 470 Gdansk 45/ Poland

FROM ASHES RISE—1ST LP AT THE WRONG SPEED:
I'd definitely have to say that I'm a fan of these guys. I've seen them play several times and they were always great, even the time when they were sick. I heard their second LP when I was traveling in Europe over a year ago and I remember it being pretty impressive. When I returned home a few months later I wrote to the band and requested a review copy—of course, I was also trying to get a free record out of the deal. In any case, they never got back to me so I've decided to review their first record at the wrong speed—a much slower version of it at 33 revolutions per minute instead of 45.

This must be the His Hero Is Gone LP that was never released. From Ashes Rise normally play pretty fast, have high pitched vocals and aren't tuned ridiculously low (I believe they're playing in D when the record is playing at the correct speed) so when it's all slowed down, it doesn't sound totally unnatural. It's actually quite good. In fact, some of the parts even sound better at the wrong speed. So, if you own this record try it yourself. –s
From Ashes Rise 7038 Bonnavent Dr. Nashville, TN 37076

THE GOONIES "" CD:
In high school I attended a show by a band made up mostly of close friends, who despite their short life recorded two or three amazing thrashing punk songs. That show, which happened in our friend's Lindze's apartment with people flying off the couches, friends hugging, everyone screaming along, the police showing up with video camera, then *leaving* so we could finish, was a mark for our community and a great band we didn't even have to share with the world. The Goonies seem to serve a similar function in their scene in Massachusetts. The documentation of the time and space of those moments with their self titled release must mean a great deal to the community around them.. The CD comes with a seven-inch sized booklet made up of written contributions from the band and their friends, the lyrics interspersed throughout. It is reminiscent of Reversal of Man's efforts with their *Revolution Summer* CD in which they attempted something similar. The writers address, living outside the constraining expectations of a conventional life, rape (including male same-sex rape), critical analysis of world economic policy, personal antedates of wandering city streets, some sound poetry (!?!), growing older in punk, straight edge and more. All the contributions are thoughtful and come across as sincere. We can do nothing but applaud a band that goes that very critical extra length in attempting to communicate beyond the music and lyrics, and the Goonies efforts are quite successful and well considered. There is even a great Nietzsche quote in the inside of the cover. Now for the music: The intro to the first song sounds almost like the beginning of a guitar-heavy 80's pop anthem, but once the song kicks in there is an early thrash punk sound that the Goonies are trying for, something like the first Suicidal Tendencies record; but they also mix in some horns and

multinationals, nationalism, violent dancing, other sources of injustice... I first saw this band play one of the last His Hero Is Gone shows, and they later turned up in my life to rescue me from the sterile atmosphere of an oversized hardcore fest in Belgium, transforming everything for the few minutes of their set—suddenly the squatters, anarchists, and feminists appeared out of the crowd, to have a wonderful time moshing together. –b
Don't Belong, Apdo. 8035, 33200 Xixon, Spain

EMPLOYER, EMPLOYEE "SIC [SIC]" CD:
This is total A.D.D. chaos. I initially thought As the Sun Sets meets Converge with vocals via Cradle of Filth but then realized that they're doing stuff that is mostly their own. The recording isn't as clear as it could be so it quickly turns into a big mess. The lyrics are poetic and vague—in fact, they're so vague that I can't figure out what the fuck they're trying to get at with any of these songs. The packaging is equally strange—totally computer-generated with weird geometric shapes and other imagery that I'm just not comprehending. The music and the packaging work great together, I'll give them that much. If you're into that spastic, A.D.D., part-part-part-part-part-part kind of sound you have a new favorite band. –s
Robodog Records 12001 Aintree Lane Reston, VA 20191

ENDSTAND "FIRE INSIDE" 10":
It's the irrepressible, ever-active Endstand, with another eight major key punk rock hits brimming with sincerity and enthusiasm. I say "hits" not because they're getting up there in the pop charts, but because these guys know how to write songs—yes, that's right, real songs with individual

something like ska-punk (I promise that is not intended as an epithet!) The Voodoo Glow Skulls tried a similar sound, but the Goonies pull it off with a lot more energy and heart. You know, the singer sounds like Sam from Born Against on the first song! The next song sounds a bit like the Dead Kennedys. The third song is more ska based, and turns in something of a punk anthem. The lyrics are mostly straight forward: dealing with the rape of a loved one, frustrated youth, straight edge and consumerism and fit well with the music. The next song sounds like one of those short and to the point Descendents songs. Their straight-edge song (which they are retiring) again starts with ska, transitions to punk—Inside Front favorites Otis Reem come to mind, their song "The Sophomore" maybe. The band thrashes through "No More" and comes to the last studio song of the album (of which there are seven) "Consumed"—which is the best written, the horns are really well integrated here, the transitions make a lot of sense, everyone seems a bit more comfortable with their instruments; and it has great lyrics about rethinking the values were given by our society and finding better ways to communicate, love, and live. Most of the tracks were recorded in a single evening, the energy really comes across from that. But the recording and mix suffered some, it's quite muddled in places. The Goonies have set themselves up for a great follow up. "Consumed" shows that they can grow as songwriters while maintaining that energy of the ska/punk sound that gave them their start. The last track is 18 minutes of a live show recorded in a basement. The recording—well, the recording sounds like it was recorded live in a basement! But I think it was worth including for a couple of reasons. One, you can get an idea of the energy of a Goonies show (I saw one about 2 and half years ago, and loved it), it's probably a great document for anyone who was at the show. Two, it's great to hear what the band has to say between songs—bands trying to communicate, hell yeah! And three, they play some new songs (for which they included an additional lyric sheet) and confirm for me that the Goonies are moving in some awesome directions! - B-Side
High Score Records - no address! Try writing the band at: The Goonies c/o Kevin Driscoll, Box 368, 500 Salisbury St., Worcester, MA, 01615

HEADWAY "" CD: Oh, Headway—the terrible tragedy of it all. In 1998 or so, they were probably the most creative and challenging band working in French punk rock/hardcore. They were gifted with deep-seated soul, fearless artistic curiosity, undeniable creativity; I even saw them play an Acme cover and pull it off perfectly. Yet no one succeeded in getting them into a studio, and the moment passed. This is the feeble trace of the final incarnation of Headway, somewhat later, as an experimental instrumental jazz band, pure and simple. The music is still soulful and the creative risk-taking ambitious—it's just not recognizable as anything that ever proceeded from the hardcore community. The material here varies from soft-lit, sometimes-haunting evening music to more frenetic, chaotic departures. The recording is

GLORIA CUBANA'S TOP TEN PATHS TO THE 4ᵀᴴ DIMENSION

1. Gogol Bordello live in Carrboro, NC, March, 2003
2. Interpol, Turn On the Bright Lights and live in Carrboro, December 2002
3. Art by Yasmina Reza, performed in Chapel Hill, NC, February 2002
4. Voyage Around My Room by Xavier de Maistre
5. Drums & Tuba live, Carrboro, August, 2002
6. The Death and Life of Great American Cities by Jane Jacobs
7. A History of Reading by Alberto Manguel
8. Second Nature by Michael Pollan
9. The Wau-Wau Sisters live a couple of times in 2002
10. The best salad dressing in the world: Blend together 1 cup canola oil, 1/3 cup cider vinegar, 1/4 cup soy sauce, 1 tablespoon toasted sesame oil, 1 tablespoon minced dried shitake mushrooms, and 1 1/2 tablespoons toasted sesame seeds.

excellent and complements everything they do nicely. My only complaint, besides my above-mentioned regret that so much of what they did at their peak has been lost to us, is the same complaint I have with almost all jazz recording: since there is no vocalist, it's somehow hard for me (you may not have this problem) to connect intimately with the music. It sounds great, it's soaked in mood and feeling, but I feel like I'm listening to something outside me, rather than within me. -b
Stonehenge c/o Christophe Mora, 21 Rue des Brosses, 78200 Magnanville, France

HEAVEN SHALL BURN "WHATEVER IT MAY TAKE" CD:

Pretty straightforward metal, with lyrics about various political movements, defending nature, and personal strength and conviction. Like many bands in this genre, it's pretty heavy on the personal conviction part ("they will never extinguish my flame"), evoking the tired image of the lone vegan warrior struggling in a world of impurity. If you liked Arkangel or Undying, you will probably like this band. At The Gates immediately comes to mind, but I don't mind that. The intro sounds like a sample from Star Wars, with creepy music and laser sounds. In case you didn't know, Star Wars is totally crucial. The last track has clean, sung vocals, which don't really grab me, but the rest of the album is good. My, um, associate says these dudes look like ads for sportswear, so I guess civilization will be toppled by guys in Adidas running suits. I thought black Carhartts were the uniform for the revolution. Someone better tell Heaven Shall Burn. Hell, I'll settle for anything at this point, but, for some reason, the idea of kids humming metal riffs as they set a McDonald's on fire appeals to me more than the idea of those same kids humming David Roviks or Against Me songs. One question: where are the d-beats? Mother Culture, look out... you're about to get windmilled. –xb
Life Force Records, P.O. Box 938, Chemnitz, Germany

HERDS AND WORDS

CASSETTE: This represents a much earlier stage in this band's development from the one covered elsewhere in this issue. This is basically a selection of neo-jazz songs with drums, guitar, bass clarinet, and a few other instruments (is that an accordion, or a harmonica, or what?), with occasional whimsical vocals. Most of the musical themes they later applied in their less music-centered performances appear here, and there's a little clapping and yipping and craziness, but it's nothing like the atmosphere of what they

KYLESA "" CD: Kylesa is one of the best sounding bands that played in my basement. The members of Kylesa have been playing in great bands for years and years and it shows. Live, they're tight and loud and totally succeed in creating a dark and urgent mood in the room. Recorded, they're fucking amazing—layers upon layers of down-tuned guitars (A-flat, believe it or not), one of the best bass tones I've yet to hear—super low end but really clear at the same time—pulsing single-kick drums that are always doing something unexpected but steady, layers of high pitched male vocals and super-guttural female vocals and even a bit of singing, and crazy samples, effects petals and studio magic throughout the entire record. The musicianship and songwriting are expert—they seem to have spent much time trying different possibilities to perfectly craft each part and each song (and album) as a whole. I normally wouldn't like a band like this—there is not a single d-beat to be found on this record, in fact it's all pretty mid-tempo—I think maybe it's even metal, but I'm not sure. But there is something mesmerizing, passionate and hypnotic about this record that keeps me listening to it again and again. Kylesa is doing something unique and vital and I'd suggest giving them a listen. –s
Prank PO Box 410892 San Francisco, CA 94141-0892

did with this stuff a few months later. The recording isn't exactly murky, but everything does sound like it's happening far away, which is the opposite of everything I've seen them do. You'll be hard-pressed to find one of these in any distro, I bet.

try writing them at their address printed in the interview section

HOPELESS DREGS OF HUMANITY "REVOLUTIONARY ROCK APOCALYPSE" CD:

This CD starts off with an on-site sound clip of people yelling those protest chants that I never participate in cuz I'd feel like a fucking sheep: "What do we want? Revolution! When do we want it? Now!" and "Whose streets? Our streets!" The music comes in with a sleazy rock riff and snotty vocals. This is definitely not my thing, but at least they are good at it. It's tight and the bass lines are impressive. The recording quality is decent with the exception of the vocals sitting too loud in the mix which is rather unfortunate as they're somewhat annoying. The name of this record is quite appropriate—this is anarchist party music. The rest of the CD sounds somewhere between pop punk and street punk with a touch of rock and roll. The lyrics are super political but light-hearted at times with lines like "What muthafuckin' time is it? It's time for revolution!" and "There's nothing more macho then filling bunnies full of lead." Like I said, this isn't my thing, but I think they're doing a great service for the punk community. Much like Propaghandi, I can totally see some high school kid, who is into bullshit bands like NOFX, getting really into this and then flipping to the back of the booklet to find a list of about twenty different anarchist and activist organizations and/or web-sites to check out. These seem to be good kids. Oh, there is a fabulous collage on the back of the CD worth checking out. -s

Ever Reviled Records PO Box 1904 New Brunswick, NJ 08903-1904

HUMAN RACIST "" DEMO

CD: This starts out with two out-of-tune guitars feeding back and continues to be out of tune for the remainder of the CD. This rocks pretty hard at times with fast parts, crusty vocals and decent breakdowns. It's nothing really out of the ordinary, just typical modern crust. The only distinguishing quality it possesses is this strange drum beat that comes in every time it sounds like there would be a d-beat otherwise—the snare and kick

are opposite of where they typically would be placed. The drummer is not bad at all so it's hard to tell if it's intentional or if he/she hasn't been exposed too much of the d-beat hardcore that they are trying to sound like. This, however, is a plus, since everything else this band does is pretty ordinary. Human Racist sound like they could be a pretty good band down the road if they find a bit of their own flavor, tune up and maybe change their name. This has good energy. –s
humanracist_wv@yahoo.com

IN RUINS OF "" 7":

The whole downtuning thing has totally fucked up my life as a record reviewer. I this is the third record in the row I've listened to all the way through on one speed before concluding I probably had it set wrong. Anyway—leave it to the Swedes to get a great, mean recording, thanks to their socialized arts establishment and so on. This sounds thick, mean, and clear all at once; it flatters the music well. They're playing the hardcore that falls on the fast side of the slower spectrum, if that

LACK "BLUES MODERNE: DANOIS EXPLOSIFS" CD[2] : There is a beautiful part in the first song where the guitars are working furiously, the drums driving everything along and everyone comes to a full stop; only the vocalist comes back in for a moment, his screams torn but controlled—the rest of the band comes back in, but with a surprising shift in tone, almost a moment of reflection drawn out a bit before tearing into the rest of the song. The band's first LP does an excellent job of creating a tone of despair and hope, musically and lyrically throughout the record. I really can't convey enough how powerful it is lyrically! The band has an amazing grasp of the English language and engages in some very philosophical ideas made ready and pertinent to our times. I can't fault them for not singing in their native language, considering their command of English. Part of one song is in Danish, that works really well; and Lack goes where so many hardcore bands never dare to go and sings about sex. It's refreshing to feel a real humanness present amongst the very serious political and social critiques they develop throughout the record. "Achilles and the Tortoise" is a harangue on the danger of just singing these songs without any consequence. ("And if this is not the world for me than I will set it on fire and watch it burn 'til there is nothing but ashes left/ I can't believe my eyes/ I thought we were changing the times/ Are we changing the times?/ And are these flames of discontent really firestorms to purify?/ Have we lost our will to tear down the wall, burn the flags, and start again?/ History shall judge us/ We're history.") This song begins with a quick build, rolling snare, tight guitar and as they come they characteristically take you to a slightly different place than you awaited, in this case a clean guitar riff climbing step by step up the neck over an almost mechanical drumming. It has an intense effect, which they come back later to in the song to push its extreme; Thomas' voice dripping with anger and question and final proclamation as he sings over a deep open bass string the last words of the song, "we're history." "Solipsist Letter to the World" is probably my favorite song on the record. The opening guitar sound feels just like a touch, something like the beginning of a Godspeed lullaby (and which appears again unexpectedly several songs later), but the drumbeat that comes in is bouncy, almost new wave-ish, the band waiting to thrash you around the first corner. The bass guitar I think is mixed best in this song, (sometimes the other guitar is mixed too high throughout the record—but generally they sound great; they are quick and scratchy, but quite distinct in the mix, which seems characteristic of many Scandinavian Hardcore-Punk bands, like Separation or Intensity). But the bass has a couple great moments in this one. There is a nice little break down, smooth, but keeping the song moving, where Thomas sings in Danish—hell except for the man screaming in Danish on this part, this sounds a whole lot like Joy Division! The last part of the song is the only time that shows off on the record the fact that Thomas can do something like actually sing, as in notes, and does so over an energetic hardcore-swinging-guitar part, sounding like his heart is breaking. Musically I would say this record feels in a lot of ways like a logical follow up to Refused's "*Songs to Fan the Flames of Discontent*" LP. There is no wacky electronica, but there is a fair amount of playing with the hardcore formula and experimentation, while maintaining the energy and focus. The great thing about that Refused record was how rooted it was in Hardcore and yet so unique to the band, and Lack has managed something similar here. There is a great part at the end of "Even the Most Honest of Emotions turns in to a Commodity" where Thomas is pacing his growl over the bass rumbling like thunder, while in the back ground an atmosphere, not quite noise, not quite a recognizable tone, builds slowly, eventually a drumbeat joins the thundering bass, the tone is brought to the fore, and they march all of this off, the haunting echoes left. Lack goes on to tackle body image, consumerism, marred heroes, and our attempts to assemble something meaningful in this shattered world. But right through to the end with "Great Russian Nihilists (the Truth Hurts...)" the themes of hope and despair are the focus of the record. ("So I'm caught in between hating a world that I do not want and another world I cannot have/ But I demand the impossible/ because its possible... Defy this deathculture and crawl out of this grave/ I will be a demon to you/ My wings come of the soil/ Fierce eyes shall smile as I lead you to your scaffold/ Come now, insignificant mortal/ Don't give up/ Don't give in"). There is so much to discover from this record (including a beautiful, thoughtful insert/ manifesto), and though its now two years ago since its release, it is still one of the most important hardcore records out there for our time. I'm very excited to witness what Lack will bring us in the future. And like the last song broken off, unfinished on the Trial "Our These are Lives?" record, Lack's final notes break up, incomplete, part of a song of which the last has not yet been heard. - B-Side

Nova Recordings/ Gladbache Str. 44/ 50672 Koeln/ Germany and in the USA thru Stickfigure Distro/ Po Box 55462/ Atlanta, GA/ 30308/ USA

[2] *Graphic Designer's Apology: Honestly—who writes reviews this long without line breaks?! Argh!*

reviews

makes sense: the drums do that At the Gates one-two beat or beats I can imagine Botch (?) doing, not the speedy d-beats of the punk world, and the songs are spiced up with various breaks and transitions while maintaining essentially the same tone and tempo throughout. I wish the lyrics were a little easier to read (they've been artistically rendered in one great block of brushstrokes, without spaces between words), but as far as I can tell they're pretty right on, arguing angrily in favor of d.i.y. hands-on politics and just being angry in general. –b
Black Star Foundation, Suite 757, 21165 Malmo, Sweden

KENJI "DEMONSTRATIONS '02"
CDR: This is packaged in a DVD case, which makes it pretty durable for a demo—it also means it takes up a lot of space. The recording on the first four songs somehow makes everything sound far away—but, now that I realize it's a live recording, I'm really impressed by how clear and well-balanced it is. This is competently played, energetic melodic punk rock, with an attitude that comes across in the gravelly singing (um, Hot Water Music or Planes Mistaken For Stars, maybe, for genre comparisons more so than individual similarities—though this is more rugged) and brash guitars. The lyrics are kind of vague, in that way that lyrics featuring poetic statements around pronouns ("I" and "you" a lot, with some "we" too, and one song filled with "her") often are in this genre. There's a part in the second song that surprised me, with drum rolls and double picking, that could almost have been played by the Amebix—that really helped spice this up for me. And then, hey, there's a feedback wasteland in the third song, and I'm starting to take this seriously! I'd really like to see this band play, they sound like they could really rock together in a tightly packed basement show. Yes, by the end of the fourth song, I'm a believer, and there are still five more tracks, older recordings, on here. Not only that—I'm starting to wish more bands would get good live recordings for their demos, instead of those studio recordings which can often be so clinical and dry. –b
P.O. Box 3441, Ventura, CA 93006

KEVES "NEM EVTETEK, HANEM MIALTATOK" CD: God, this is just bad. They've been listening to way too much Shelter and Limp Biscuit. They do a lot of annoying guitar rhythms that sound almost like funk or something and there's time that the bass sounds like it's from Seinfeld or the Red Hot Chili Peppers. I'm not digging this at all. On some positive notes—the artwork is good, the words are in Hungarian, the recording is good, the musicianship is tight and impressive and they do a variety of different stuff (I just think it's all bad). Man, I feel bad writing shitty reviews, especially

since their thank-you list includes some of my friends in Hungary. My apologies. –s [Editor's note: I remember being interested in these guys when I saw them play—they were doing some unusual stuff, and had distinctive personality. I don't remember Shelter or Limp Biscuit influences, but we'll have to trust Stef on this CD, as I haven't heard it. Out of all of us reviewers, she's the one who listens to Shelter, anyway!]
Nagy Laszlo, 9024 Gyor, Babits M. 71—Hungary

THE LOUISVILLE ANARCHESTRA "TRIBUTE TO J20 BLACK BLOC"
CD: This is totally what I'm talking about! It's a d.i.y. experiment, at once self-indulgent and artistically liberating, connected explicitly to anticapitalist street

NOS SOMOS NADA "" 7": These are some of my friends who were in By All Means, and as far as I'm concerned they can do no wrong. They maintain the dark atmosphere their music had then, take on a singer with quite a fierce high shriek, and keep the heartfelt anarchist politics. If I had to find another comparison for the music, I'd have to say Concrete, Stef's favorite Italian band, only with more nervous energy and perhaps shorter songs. Phenomenal drumming, freight train double bass included, that complements the discordant guitars with perfectly-timed transitions. The packaging is lovely, exemplifying all the best qualities of a certain hands-on d.i.y. aesthetic with printing in red, yellow, and black, and rough-textured illustrations with a style all their own framing the text. The lyrics and explanations (Italian, with English translations) cover conflicts with the State and fascists in the ongoing struggle for freedom—the first one, "reduction of charge," about a court case that is dragged on by the "justice" system to terrorize an activist that they must eventually admit is innocent rings particularly true with me, as one of my friends is in the same situation right now (at least, I hope they'll fucking have to admit his innocence...). Oh yeah, like Dearborn S.S. and many of the other great punk bands of the last couple years, they've broken up, too, but this record is still worth finding on its own virtues. –b
Santa Sangre Discos, c/o Luca Mamone, Piazza P. Togliatti 9, 00030 Vallemartella, Roma, Italy... or write guitarist Matteo, who is lazy at letter-writing but a great person, at Matteo Verri, C.P. 6, Succ 7, 41100 Modena, Italy

resistance (the "J20 Black Bloc" was the masked bloc of anarchist militants that fucked things up at the inauguration of George Bush back in 2001). The concept (and the liner notes that expound on it) here is at least as important as the commodity itself: this is an experiment in process-centered, participatory music, intended to deconstruct the idea that art and activism are the domain of specialists. (One wonders, perhaps, why it would be necessary to release such a thing on CD; if

I had to answer for the creators, I would say 1. to drive those points home to everyone who encounters it, and 2. this isn't exactly mass-produced.) Musically, it's something of a cacophony: against a mumble of background instruments, clicks, taps, piano and woodwind notes, and occasional bangs follow one another in arbitrary flourishes that have some personality, if no pattern. A friend of mine speculated that the author(s?) of this project had just copied some obscure Sun Ra free jazz experiment (it is just a burned CDR, after all—and the recording sounds suspiciously high-quality, not to mention the playing somber, if not actually skilled) and sent it out into the world as their own work, so as to save the trouble of actually having to record an improvisation with others; if that is the case, and this is just an elaborate prank pulled on us all, all the better—I'm all for those, too! I don't think this was ever seriously distributed, but I'll bet the address still works; you could write and demand one of your own. Why not? -b
P.O. Box 4964, Louisville, KY 40204-0964

MALEFACTION "CRUSH THE DREAM" CD: This band is like Doom. No, they don't sound anything like the British crust band, but like Doom, you only need to hear one song. If you've heard one, you've heard them all. And that one song is pretty fucking good, but Christ—the same song twenty three times?! This band plays super fast thrash-metal-punk much like Phobia. Each song, with very few exceptions, starts with a blast beat, does something else for one to three seconds and then returns to the blast beat for the remainder of the song. The recording is pretty clear, the musicianship is not lacking by any means, but where's the creativity? I really can't believe that they do this for twenty-three songs. I'd imagine that this band is fucking incredible live, but for me at least, does not translate on to record very well... which actually is exactly what I think about Phobia. Fans of relentless blast beat brutality check this out. –s
G7 Welcoming Committee (see Swallowing Shit review for address)

MANIFESTO JUKEBOX "DESIRE" CD: As strange as it sounds, my first reaction to this is that it sounds somewhere between Rites of Spring and the first Foo Fighters album. This is good. It's mid-tempo dirty rock with a ton of emotion, good short guitar solos and vocals that are very similar to those of Guy, from the aforementioned Rites of Spring (and Fugazi) except a bit more melodic at times. The recording is great for them—any clearer and they might sound marketable, or something, like the aforementioned Foo Fighters. The guitars play a lot of open chords and then harmonize over the bass, which is usually

holding down the song structure along with the drums. That's a great formula for rock music that has been tested time and time again and works very well. These songs do allow for the bass to take the lead at times though, which is good because otherwise I might forget it is there. Wow... As I continue to listen I notice more and more cool guitar harmonies happening. The cover is a picture of some city with fire superimposed in back of it, which is amusing since it is very similar to the Umlaut record that is on the same label that I believe came out some time later. I wonder if Umlaut ripped off their cover image just as they rip off everything else. Hmmm. [Editor's note: Combat Rock Industries just bit the bullet after that and made their logo a city in flames—good for them!] This CD is just under a half an hour long, perhaps the perfect length as to keep up the momentum and not start to get boring. It's good all the way through. This band is great—I wish I hadn't missed seeing them play when they toured the states last year. [Editor, again: P.S., Stef, not only did you miss them on tour in the USA, our band played with them in Finland and you missed them that night too! Oops!] –s
Combat Rock Industry, PL 139, 00131 HKI, Finland

for me to connect myself to this music as a human being—the only signs of organic life throughout are brief, distorted samples of people screaming, and even those evoke horror movies and techno music rather than actual human beings. I harbor no great love for that fucker Baudrillard, but in cases like these he was right—there is no reality here, just references to references, reconstructions of constructions: it's like the sound of machines talking to each other, using human beings as an interface at best. My favorite parts are when the double bass and stranger computer sounds are dominating, but Ministry still did it better for me. –b
Hai Nguyen Dinh, Tandstadveien 10, 3140 Borgheim, Norway—though he encourages us to use email instead: assbasher@altavista.com

NOTHING TO PROVE "ERASE THE METRONOME" CD:
There's a late '90's chaos-hardcore thing going on here, maybe drawing a little on Botch or Converge, without any of the unpleasant masculine energy that often characterized bands in that genre. There's some interesting sample collagework done here and there, the song construction and the parts themselves are complex, the playing and recording are competent, the vocals even cover plenty of ground between speaking, singing, and

them." The layout is fascinating and original: photos drawing out the terrifying absurdity of death row, and connecting it to the emptiness of modern/techno-slave life in every context, the capital punishment that begins at birth. –b
Nothing to Prove, Pion Lucien, 9 rue de Monthouton, 25230 Dasle, France

PANOPTIKON [?] "[?]" 7":
Fucking crazy! I've had this beat up 7" sitting in or around the review box since—I'm afraid—some time in 1999 or 2000; I think I brought it back from New Jersey on some long-ago tour. I wasn't planning on reviewing it, I just threw it on out of curiosity—and here's the deal, it's fucking soundalike Bad Brains! Seriously! Reggae that merges into Rock-for-Light-era noisy punk, H.R.-sounding vocalist, lyrics that appear to show heavy Rasta influence, the whole thing—and it's not even bad, not at all! Now, this will probably be a challenge to track down, but I think it's worth mentioning here, since there are so few records in this style. I could use another whole genre of bands following the leads Bad Brains set out on that Rock for Light record, myself. –b
10 Garvey Drive, Monroe Twp., NJ 08831

PARAGRAF 119 "MUSIC TIL ULEMPE" 7":
This may not even be this band's latest release, and it's not especially current (I can't tell how long ago it was recorded, because the band opted to include a page on legal rights in confrontations with the pigs in their home nation of Denmark in place of more conventional liner notes), but this is such a classic example of great pro-direct-action punk rock that it has to get coverage here. The cover alone says it all: masked people chiseling up the concrete (yes, to make stones to throw at the pigs!), something I've only been lucky enough to be present for once in my life so far—what a good time that was! The centerfold, too, is classy—a picture split down the middle: what we must do—on the left, burning franchises, trashed cop cars, molotov cocktails, masks and riot gear—and what we want—on the right, gardens, squatted buildings open to the public, communal campfires and friendship. I saw a 12" by this band that had band photos of them in it—each of them was of a different member getting aggressively arrested! No rehashed youth-crew crowd shots for these kids! Six songs, in Danish with English translations, cover subjects such as not forgetting the injustices we've suffered at the hands of the State, breaking their monopoly on violence, and outrageous police brutality and lies—that last one insults the Danish police press secretary by name, reminiscent of the

PLEDGE ALLIANCE "TRUMMER EINER ZERBORSTENEN WELT" CD:
Out of the wave of passionate, adventuresome, anticapitalist bands that appeared in Europe a couple years ago inspired by a mixture of Refused and more metal d.i.y. hardcore, Pledge Alliance have probably recorded the best record yet—this one. It's hard to get complex metal to convey emotion—usually the polish and technicalities take the place where the soul would otherwise be—but this has all the urgency and immediacy that the rare great metal album has. Imagine, if you can, double bass, guitar leads, blastbeats once again expressing human desperation, desire, fear, fury! It helps a lot that they utilize the full range of octaves and dynamics, from heavy driving parts to high melodies and harmonies to heartbreakingly beautiful feedback, like a mourner's wail. And their vocalist is going all out, holding nothing back—he's got a powerful deep scream and a range of expression inside it, and there are frequent breaks in which he is basically reciting poetry. These speaking parts would sound melodramatic if they weren't so earnestly delivered—you have to believe in him, he obviously means it. The lyrics come across the same as his delivery: they are indeed poetry, and they could come across as overwrought if it wasn't so clear that he really feels them, really means every word. This kind of sincere idealism and fire makes me feel like we can fucking make it—it's such a gift to hear someone sing like it matters, dream like it's possible, sing and scream and dream until everything that matters *is* possible. Anyway, the recording and mix are fierce and hard-hitting, complementing the music perfectly. If I was going to suggest any possible route for improvement for here, I would encourage them to compose less conceptually, more traditionally: their songs are good, but the structures might actually complement their soul more if they were less complex, more organic (think old blues songs, rather than "Justice for All"-era Metallica)—a sudden transition from one part to another that has nothing to do with it is something that should happen about once a record, if you ask me.

To those with better Deutsch than me, I apologize if I got the name of the record wrong—handwriting isn't easy to read in a foreign language. Not that the layout is inaccessible in any other way. –b
Erdkampf Style, Brücknerstr. 24, A-8010 Graz, Austria

NEXT LIFE "RED END" 7":
"Songs are made using Amiga and distorted guitar," the back cover of this gatefold reads, and clearly Amiga is some kind of computer program for making music that sounds like it could be used for an '80's video game soundtrack. The electric guitar, for its part, sounds a little tinny. There aren't many points of contact

screaming; all they really lack are unique, unforgettable song compositions, but if you listen to this a few times and get to know everything by heart that doesn't really matter. The lyrics are in English and cover general anti-commodification, anti-hierarchy, and gay-positive subjects; one of my favorite lines: "the toys prepare themselves for the cruel world awaiting

Rambo song that addresses the police commissioner who beat up one of my closest friends and then charged him with assault. The music is pretty standard up-tempo punk rock, with dual scratchy vocals, not especially outstanding; but if these kids keep it up on the action front, I'll get their records just to have them around as conversation starters. Oh—and what does "Paragraf 119" refer to you, you ask? It's the section of Danish penal code forbidding assault upon employees of the State, such as police officers. –b
Paragraf 119, Box 578, 2200 Copenhagen, Denmark—assuming they're not in prison by the time you read this

PISTOLS AT DUSK "DEMO 2003" MP3:

Please do the following things in order. 1. Get access to a computer that has both internet access, and a comfortable and ergonomically correct chair. 2. Sit in the chair and turn on the computer. 3. Open an internet browser window. 4. Go to www.lonelybullet.com/pistolsatdusk/ 5. Download all four demo songs by clicking on the song titles individually. 6. Listen to the songs. 7. Check www.wordsasweapons.com/punkpistols.htm and read the interview I did with Bill from Pistols at Dusk and also check out the lyrics to the first song. 8. Repeat step 6 until head falls off and rolls under the kitchen table. 9. Turn off computer. 10. Stand up and walk into kitchen. 11. Kneel and attempt to find head. 12. Reattach head using any necessary means. -----If you do all of the above, I promise you both an adventure and a great time, even before you bust out the duct tape to reconnect your severed head to your body. This demo will have that effect though, I promise you. Every once in a while a band comes along that just kills me... leaves me wanting to pound nails with my fists, scream until my voice bleeds, and makes it impossible to sit still. Pistols At Dusk is that band right now, and I see them poised to leave the world in flames. The four songs deal with personal heartache, hardcore values, and despair, and I have no doubt that Bill At Dusk could scream about anything and make me feel like I was ready to jump out of my skin. The music is guitar driven, but not in terms of predictable riffs... it is more an assemblage of emotions transferred through musicianship into constant motion. That is the one thing which just keeps hitting so hard throughout this CD: it is constantly changing direction and tempo without ever losing for a second the focus and intensity which makes the

each song and the entire disc so powerful. The screams are from the guts... from deep in the guts... and when on track two Bill lets out "I have only one last wish / I hope you fucking burn" all I know is that I am ready to light the goddamn flames, regardless of who he is talking about. You can't help but get swept up in this thing. I have added this demo to my top ten list of records to own in order to laugh uncaringly in the face of the apocalypse. I recommend you do the same. After all, you can't beat the price. And while you are on the web, sitting there next to the kitchen headless and stoked, contact bill_baker@attbi.com for more information on the band and their future plans. -JUG
Greg provides only internet addresses, so we can imagine this is an entirely virtual band.

PLANES MISTAKEN FOR STARS "FUCK WITH FIRE" CD:

I had only heard one of their songs before on a mix tape and I remember it being good. And they have such a great name, so I was excited to pick this one out of the review box. This Denver band sounds like they should be from D.C. The closest things I can compare them too are Rites of Spring, "In on the Killtaker" era Fugazi and a little bit of Nation of Ulysses, but they definitely have something modern sounding about them too. This is heavy punk rock and

RETORICA "1ST COMMUNIQUÉ" CD:

This is another brilliant, courageous experiment destined to be forgotten by the punk community because it wasn't released by some popular North American group—but if you can get your hands on it, the potential still exists that you could have a new secret favorite record of your own to steal strange inspirations from with which to confound your fellow bandmates. The language almost doesn't exist yet for me to review this—it's that unprecedented, that out there. Musically, this is a collage of live home-recordings and electronic noise, wound together and layered to form sprawling, spare soundscapes; there are guitars, drums, feedback, obscure media samples, the whine and distorted crunch of electronic signals, and occasional yelling riot-grrl vocals in the background—but combined, it takes on a new form with a strange beauty and alien aesthetic of its own: it sounds like a time capsule sent back from some alternative future. The packaging is a very important part of what's going on here: it's all hand-cut, -printed, and -assembled screenprints and stolen x-rays and all, and once again the medium is the message here: you-can-d.i.y, process not product, liberation through contestation of cultural forms as well as political and social structures. The liner notes are clever and conversational, while drawing on the heritage of hyper-radical writing from the Situationists to *Fight Club* to present the whole project in a light that is at once personal and uncompromisingly insurrectionist. The same people are involved in making this who were in Libertinagem; I wish I knew what they are up to now.

If I had to think about other records that could possibly be along the same lines, the only two I'd hazard would be the audio Hunter/Gatherer CDR, and the first Countdown to Putsch release. But now that I think about it, what I really love about this record is not the music itself, but the spirit of fearless experimentation in which it was obviously undertaken. Maybe you don't need a copy of this record—maybe you just need to get together with some friends for a one-month thinktank in which you undertake to create an alien music of your own. But hearing this and looking through these inserts, or at least hearing *about* it, that it exists and can be done, might help a lot. –b
Collectivo Retorica, R. Paulo Simoni, 54, B. Horizonte, M6

roll type stuff with sleazy, nasally vocals that I find just fine, although I know that vocal style can annoy the shit out of some of my friends. The guitars are pretty heavy sounding with a lot of distortion and on the more laid back parts, it sounds like any other band would have backed off of it a bit, but they haven't, and it gives them their own sound. I think most other bands that play this style of music would have chosen a much weaker guitar sound and I give Planes props for trying this out and in my opinion, succeeding. Come to think of it, the bass has a bit of distortion on it too, I think. Hmm. Think of that sort of His Hero Is Gone wall-of-guitar sound that a lot of heavy hardcore bands are going for (including my own) but being applied to mid-tempo, up-beat, almost poppy rock songs. And the songs have a lot of obvious emotion and energy. This is pretty good. –s
No Idea Records P.O. Box 14636 Gainesville, FL 32604

PLANES MISTAKEN FOR STARS "KNIFE IN THE MARATHON" CD:

Stef says this band has one of the best names ever, and I'm inclined to agree. I've been hearing about them forever, it seems, but I'm honestly pretty out of touch. This is pretty good emotional hardcore, somewhere between Hot Water Music and the Exploder. The more I listen to this, the more I like it, especially the 4th track, which is more ambient and brooding than the others. All 5 songs are well-written, and the lyrics aren't too abstract for my tastes (sorry, Jerome's Dream), just songs about love and trying to keep it. I give this one a thumbs-up. –xb
Deep Elm Records, P.O. Box 36939, Charlotte, NC 28236

POINT OF NO RETURN "IMPOSED FREEDOM, CONQUERED FREEDOM" CD:

This needs saying first: the layout of this record sets a new standard for great punk/hardcore layouts that I can only hope other bands will rise to themselves. In masterfully constructed juxtapositions of photos from the last two decades of international conflict, the tension between the fake freedom that the neo-liberal "first world" would enforce at the end of a gun and the freedom won by those courageous men and women who oppose it is dramatized—it's more eloquent than any words could be, and serves to perfectly

frame the lyrics; these draw on the conflict in occupied Palestine, the struggle for agrarian reform, the injustice done political prisoners and all prisoners, and the twin faces of military and cultural imperialism to present a picture of a world in struggle between the dreams and solidarity of ordinary people and the heartlessness of their oppressors. A lengthy booklet (in Portuguese, translation on the internet somewhere) discussing the necessity of redefining such social constructs as straight edge (yes, PONR are a vegan straightedge band!) for oneself is also included—that text almost made it's way into the "straight edge" feature of this very magazine, in fact, but it was too long. And—no, I didn't forget—the music: PONR represent the (soy) cream of the crop of the dance-floor oriented, metallic hardcore bands that came out in the late '90's. Typically they alternate between slow, open chords and really sinister metal riffs, the rhythms switching up beneath them to bring out different aspects of each part. There are fast parts, too, which break things up nicely. The three singers sound like thunder over the cataclysm evoked by the music. The recording is thick and powerful, complementing everything perfectly; yes, everything is in place here. -b
Liberation, Caixa Postal 4193, Sao Paulo, SP 01061-970

REDENCION 9.11 "97-01" CD: At first, I couldn't put my finger on it, but then I figured out what's going on in the first couple tracks: it's like an emo/screamo band playing streetpunk/oi music! The third track is a little electronica experiment, and the fourth track could have been written by Fugazi, perhaps: rocking guitar and drums figure repeating, bass adding different colors to it, distorted speaking over it. As the record progresses, there are also places where they seem to be working from a more metallic hardcore tradition, or even old school hardcore; all this, through the aesthetic of their grainy, aggro-emo sound—and it all holds together better than you'd expect it to, thanks to that. Whoa, the eighth track is a free jazz break, although I'm not convinced they're serious about it. The lyrics, in Spanish with English translations, are a good mix of personal reflection and political incitement. This is well-played music, but somehow I'm not finding a point of personal connection to it—maybe I've just reviewed too many records today. -b
Amor y Lucha, 6107 43rd Street, Riverdale, MD 20737 (www.amorylucha.org)

POESTENKILL "[(?)]" DOUBLE CD: This comes from the same label and aesthetic as the "Apes of the Union" (?) CD I just reviewed above. The music, packaging, and entire aesthetic gives one the impression that these kids are doing everything they can to sabotage the functioning of the artists-who-play-music-and-release-it-on-CD system, without leaving it entirely. Everything about their presentation and music itself screams "inaccessible"—not in a tone of defiance, but of self-preoccupation, or perhaps simply distraction. This kind of spirit is healthy, and can open the way for much freer creative ventures than those that usually take place in our culturally conservative music scene, but it certainly makes my job as reviewer (let alone listener) hard, if not unrewarding. There was another CD in the review box, a long string of poorly recorded basement experiments, that at the time I took out because I couldn't even figure out from the packaging who the label or band were, but now I'm pretty sure it was these folks. Anyway, after that frustrated and not-so-promising introduction, here's the news: there's some great stuff in the music on these CDs! The first one begins with a very slow buildup, so by the middle of the song (many minutes into it) when the pace picks up it's actually really exciting. This is the first out of all the CDs in this vein that I'm really responding to—that's a relief! The rugged, improvised quality of the music—it sounds, in general, like a bunch of fucking maniacs at their first jam on instruments they haven't played for long, but without all the hesitance that usually characterizes such sessions—actually gives it an "anything can happen" quality that makes the songs come alive: it's like listening to punk bands from the first couple years of the genre. Also, there are vocals (yelling, singing, rough stuff) present, which really helps me connect with this as a human being. By the sixth track of the first CD, I'm in the groove with them enough that the jarring collage of backwards music is pulse-quickening, not annoying. Fuck, when the dark-atmosphered, post-metal/goth experiment comes in at the end, I'm a fucking believer—this is raw, real, over-the-top stuff! I'm just putting on the second disc right now, it begins with semi-human wailing unlike anything you'll hear from any genre-specific punk band... oh no, these fucking assholes! Just to make sure they weren't being too predictable, I guess, almost all 64 minutes of this second CD are composed of five minute-bursts of inarticulate wailing and moaning, a capella, broken up by minute after minute, track after track, of total silence. At the very end there's another fucking great, spooky, His-Hero-Is-Gone-meets-Godspeed-You-Black-Emperor! track, for those with patience—that lasts for a minute, before reverting to high-school-band-covering-Led-Zeppelin chaos, and then back again for the stirring conclusion. I can get pretty pretentious myself in my role as "music/art critic," but I'm definitely not in on what's going on here, if there is any method to the madness at all. But anyway, taken as one CD, there's some great stuff going on here—if you're considering getting a strange CD in a badly screenprinted piece of cardboard, for the sake of hearing some unearthly, non-traditional stuff, this is the one to try, for sure. -b
www.massivedistribution.com

REVERSAL OF MAN "DISCOGRAPHY" CD: Not a complete discography, this CD is comprised of 27 songs that were never released on CD, including their demo. Reversal of man were one of the screamy, energetic, socially conscious SXE bands of the mid—to late 90's and, in my opinion, one of the best bands from that era. This disc came out a while ago, and if you were going to get it, you probably already have. For anyone who still likes Prevail, Inkwell, Hourglass, Frail, etc., and didn't manage to get all the Reversal of Man records, go get this. -xb
Schematic Records, dist. by No Idea, P.O. Box 14636, Gainesville, FL 32604

SELFISH "BURNING SENSATION" 12": Yeeeeaah! This starts with a bang with an intro that packs all the punch and drama of the best Iron Maiden, finger-tapping leads and all. Once things get going, this is more Oi/street punk than Maiden, with guitar solos here and there to maintain the '80's metal presence. This is really urgent, intense stuff, though—it doesn't sound sentimental at all. The power and dirt in the mix are balanced at just the right proportions—and even the lyrics, where I can make them out, are positive, about seizing the day and so on. Where I can't make them out, they're more along the lines I was expecting: "Fight the fight dead people vomiting, right, no cry no tear from my dead eye—kill murder a sickly smile, just now as the fist bites!!!" Christ, every once in a while the vocalist sounds a bit like Roger Miret on old Agnostic Front albums... that's not too overwhelming, though, thankfully. What else remains to be said? Well, there are shouted backing vocals on the choruses, and the artwork harkens back to those halcyon days of early metal: full color, amateur illustrations of skulls, mysterious women with spiders, a naked winged bodybuilder angel with a flaming loincloth that makes the title appear a reference to venereal disease. And yes, these guys are Finnish, they're Finnish as fuck. -b
my friend who released this is so humble about his label that he just listed it as "available through Ebullition (P.O. Box 680, Goleta, CA 93116, USA)" on the cover

SHACKLES AWAIT "" 7": Dark atmosphere, primitive overloaded recording, fuzzy guitars and roaring, guttural vocals. There are parts that start out sludgy and crunchy and slowly pick up speed (think "Cave In" on the Gehenna 7"), there are parts where the guitarists will hit one note on two strings at once and then bend one up, there's even a part where echo pedals are used by the guitarists during a spare, atmospheric part.

roxie

I don't know if they've been raised on Gehenna and His Hero Is Gone and, god forbid, Botch, or just on other bands that were, but that lineage is definitely present here. The recording, which seems to have been done in a cave with a boom box in front of the guitar amplifiers, doesn't interfere with the soul here—you know, "bad" recordings can sometimes preserve soul where cleaner ones would lose it. The last song in particular comes in with such a burst of noise and screams mangled by distortion and overload that I feel like I'm listening to some old Negative Approach bootleg or something—and it's great! The composers in this band know their minor keys, and there are dynamics enough to keep it interesting. The first line of lyrics is "force fed lies," so you can sketch out the rest of the content on those lines (although, and this may surprise some, the first place I remember hearing those words as lyrics was the last Agnostic Front record before their 1992 breakup, not some pre-Born Against band). The chorus they take their name from is in a song called "For Those About to Revolt... We Salute You!" Need I say more? –b

[Now another reviewer checks in on the same record:] This band played at my house a year or so ago and they were a lot of fun. They kept talking about their show the night before in which people kept trying to trade them drugs for merch. But not just any drugs—homemade science project drugs made with Robitussin that the locals had named "Voodoo." Apparently some local addict explained, "We drank straight 'tussin for about twelve years before we figured out how to extract the DSM. Now, we have Voodoo." This band is a ton of fun. We received their demo in the mail a few months before the show and it's fucking great. It made us super-stoked for their arrival. And live, they lived up to our expectations. This 7," however, despite its lovely hand-made packaging with silk-screened cover and free patches (with grenades on them!) does not excite me nearly as much as the demo tape. They play crusty hardcore, as many do, in the vein of His Hero with a variety of different tempos and cool guitar work, high and low screaming vocals and a lot of heavy parts. I'd write to them and ask for their demo! –s

These goddamn fucking assholes have no street address in here, just an email address, which, Luddite that I am, I am loath to list, but the slackers leave me no choice: shacklesawait666@yahoo.com

THE SPECTACLE" 10": Here's the old story, once more: Somewhere in some small town, far from anything hip or happening, a few bored teenagers find a record by some old punk band that has long since declared punk rock to be dead and meaningless. Maybe the town is San Diego, maybe it's Umea, Sweden, whatever, but no punk bands ever come through, so, inspired by the record and whatever others like it they can find, the kids make their own crazy punk rock, basing it on the stories they have made up to go with the impressions those first records gave them—and it's amazing, what they make, it becomes the most important thing in the world for them and then for everyone who encounters it. Suddenly the whole world is looking at their little dead-end corner, seeing it as the center of the cosmos; people start moving there in droves, whole battalions of copycat bands form, new generations found their own passionate life projects on the foundation of the music made by these former teenage nobodies. Eventually, under all this pressure, things cave in. "Punk is dead, dude," they all swear, and everyone moves away or tries to get on MTV or "grows up" and dies. But far away, far from all this action, in fact north of the arctic circle, at the northernmost tip of Norway, in Bodo, some kids have found a record left from this brief explosion... and punk rock is born to triumph again.

But let's talk about this record, specifically. This is a good fucking record! It's exactly what I want to see in a band's first release: the music is soulful, the packaging is extensive and original and includes lengthy essays about their intentions and politics (which I'd say are pretty damn close to the politics and intentions of, say, the people who do the magazine you're reading) as well as discussions of each song—and yes, they've released the whole thing themselves. The lyrics are stunning in some places: "let others scurry for cover—we rush to bear witness." For their sound, let me give the reference points you and I probably share: when I saw them play I thought of early Zegota, in that they were so unaffectedly passionate and earnest, pushing themselves like young maniacs, giving it their all; the guitarist, and possibly the vocalist, seem to listen to Undying—it comes out in some double-picked leads, especially, which all the same don't alter the much grittier, punker aesthetic of their sound (possibly influenced by His Hero Is Gone's recordings); the vocalist's painful, guttural delivery makes me think of Gehenna; I imagine, from their politics, that the interest Refused showed in Situationist thinking may have rubbed off some, too. But like any great record, this isn't just a mishmash of things other bands did better; indeed, no comparison to any of those great bands would be warranted if The Spectacle were just a second rate imitation of one or a few of them. No, they have that soul that makes bands matter. Now, there's a lot of fucking music out there in the world, and a lot of it sounds the same, while being generally uninspired, lacking that requisite soul—so you may have to listen to this a few times to recognize that it's of a different caliber than all that other stuff. But if you do, you'll be rewarded: you'll find these songs sticking with you as copycat hardcore doesn't, you'll find yourself reaching for it in times of intense emotion. Yes, this is a good record of real songs.

Or perhaps I'm telling this all wrong, as if I'm a voice from the sky, not involved in the tale at all. Here's what this record means to me personally. In 1999, horribly ill on tour in Scandinavia, I totally lost my voice; for a week I actually thought I'd destroyed it forever and I'd never be able to speak or sing again—it was really scary. Maybe some of you have heard this story before... now, in the last two days before I became completely mute, I was still able to sing, though I was really sick. We were on tour in Norway, and the first of those two days we played a fucking great show at the Blitz squat in Oslo. At least one of these kids was there; I think a few of them were. I was a wreck, but, sustained by the spirit of the crowd, we still reached that beautiful place a room full of screaming, sweating people can reach; I remember when we finished the set, I made a break for the gap at the edge of the stage, through which I hoped to escape to the toilets to crash out in utter exhaustion—but the huge, wild, woolly squatter-punk descendents of the Vikings beat me to it and blocked my way, pushing me back and shrieking "YOU PLAY MORE NOW!" as they brandished their vodka bottles. "We can't play more now." Matt informed the crowd—"our singer is going to die." Later that evening a somewhat-inebriated squatter punk without very good English approached and, solemnly, addressed me: "I am very sorry to hear that you are going to die." I was mute, of course, and couldn't correct the misunderstanding... but I'm getting off the subject. The next night we played a hardcore festival a few hours away, and the kids from Bodo were there again, having come over a thousand kilometers south for the two shows. That night I was on my last legs, barely able to move; I'm sure it was painful for everyone there to have to watch me struggling to make something beautiful when it was all I could do to stand up. If we made any real music that night, it was the inaudible music, the music we couldn't make but wanted to so desperately that it must have been wrenching for folks there, like the Bodonites, to see. We had to cancel our show in Trondheim the next day, and that was the first of the days I woke up without any voice in my throat at all. Anyway, two years later, we returned to play in Oslo at the Blitz again. The Spectacle played, too, and they were great—and we were in good health, so we were able to return the favor; I recognized them from the earlier tour, and probably bragged about how healthy I was this time around. A few nights later, we were to play with them in Trondheim—but, of course, I had suddenly become so sick again that I couldn't even stand up. I slumped in the room behind the club, doing my best to talk with the Bodo kids; I imagine we talked about how important it is to make music despite the costs and challenges, that sort of thing. That night I couldn't do it—my friends took me back to a house and laid me on the floor, where I lay in fever-delirium—but the rest of our band played, and I heard later that the kids from Bodo had taken the microphone and passed it around the crowd, everyone singing and having a wonderful time. That made me feel good, to know that even when I can do nothing others are still out there making it happen; and getting this record was a wonderful reminder of that. To all of you who will keep punk and passion and music alive, even when I'm too fucked up or ill or defeated to participate, here's a salute. Maybe I'll never make most of that inaudible music audible, though I'm sworn to try; but I know if I don't, you will. Thank you. –b

Smart Patrol, Kirkeveien 5, N-8009 Bodo, Norway, www.smartpatrolrecords.com, ihatethespectacle@yahoo.com

SICK OF SILENCE "CRUSADER OF INDIVIDUALITY" CD:

When passionate young people are getting started making music of their own, they often start out trying out the words and songs of others on their own tongues, as a way to develop their own voices. This record definitely shows the influences of Refused's last record: the first song actually has that breakdown from Refused's "Protest Song '68" about how much more our music could be, impassioned manifesto and jazz buildup included. It has a catchy chorus, and I'm happy every time it comes around, so that's good! The second song kicks in with a part that could be a more rocking Tragedy, for my favorite part on the record; it has a break that sounds like something out of Botch, and then the clean channel parts with narration that could be the result of listening to various modern emo bands, or parts of the "Shape of Punk to Come" record. The third song has another breakdown with a string section, and the vocalist exhorting "let's set the world on fire, let's start tonight." The fourth song starts with some more rock'n'roll stuff that I like least out of everything here—when they get to the chorus, I wonder if they've been listening to Propagandhi, too. Anyway, derivative or not, I feel like these kids mean what they're saying, and that's the really important thing. If they take what they're doing seriously, and develop their own sound, their own style, their own voice (just

TRAGEDY (FIRST 12", 7", AND "VENGEANCE" 12"):

I'm at the end of my career as a music critic, writing the final review in the reunion issue of the 'zine I started as a teenager, so for once I can afford to be speechless before a record, to decline to attempt to describe it. In fact, I'm not going to attempt to describe any of these three records; all I can say is, since the last issue of this magazine, as fewer and fewer records came out that I could get really excited about, this band has maintained my faith that punk rock can still surprise and transform me as much as an adult as it did when I was a kid. Even when I couldn't listen to the records, these songs were definitely playing in my head in every ridiculous, miserable, or triumphant situation I've survived or celebrated over that time, keeping my spirits up and my resolve firm. Thank heaven for punk rock, that's all I can say. If you haven't heard these recordings, hunt them down—not to put anyone on a pedestal, but for me, in my world, this is the Amebix of our generation. -b

Try the address in the interviews section

TIMEBOMB "THE BEAT IS HERE FELLAS" CD:

This is the CD on which Timebomb surprised all of us by totally changing their style. I think after this they changed it all again in some other direction, and quite possibly have since disappeared into the bottomless pit of history, or else perhaps they're out there right now putting the finishing touches on a record of Gregorian chants. Anyway, this record shows the influence of some Fugazi (the third song can be traced back, in places, to "Suggestion"), but it has a brighter, more joyous tone to it. The songs sound like they are crafted to some pop aesthetic from a parallel world, one unrecognizable to my ears at least but still strangely familiar. I usually can't stand anything upbeat or poppish, but for some reason I just think this is great. Unlike just about everything else in the world in a major key (with the obvious exception of Beethoven's Ninth), listening to this actually makes me happy, rather than annoyed. The photo collage in the layout, not to mention the '60's sentimentality and "live your dreams" politics, all point to Refused as the culprit in making these kids think they could get away with doing whatever they wanted, not trying to follow up one record with another in the same genre. That's great, though—I think this is the best thing they ever did, even at the peak of their straight edge metal phase. -b
Cane records, Paolo Gaiarsa, via s. Cristoforo 12, 36061 Basano del Grappa, Vicenza, Italy

repeating another band's departures from the genre will not set you free!)—well, that's the next step they have to take. For now, I'm thrilled they're singing about something, not just rocking out. -b
Freedumb Recordz, 101 Place Charles Lemoyne Longueul, Quebec, J4K 2T3, Canada

SPEAK UP! "THIS DAY IS THE PERFECT DAY" CD:

Western imperialism rears its ugly head again, as the lyrics for this old-school Hungarian hardcore band are in poorly-translated English. I just wish to hell bands could feel safe singing in their native tongues. Though the points the band are making(condemnations of war, the class system, and animal exploitation) are right on, I don't really like this album. The music isn't catchy or powerful enough to make up for the old youth crew formula, and the singer doesn't have very good delivery. A lot of the energy is probably lost by the words being in English, and this just doesn't sound desperate enough for me. Altogether, not a bad release, but not outstanding enough to stay in my stereo. -xb
Bertalan Andras, Gazdag 13, Szombathely 9700, Hungary

STRIKE ANYWHERE "UNDERGROUND EUROPE 2001 GENOA BENEFIT EP" 7":

This is this band's 1999 demos, but the fact that they're released here as a benefit for arrestees at the Genoa protests makes this record worth mentioning even at this late date. I get the impression that Strike Anywhere, at least here, is the band some of us wished Avail would have been—they're out of the closet about their antiauthoritarian politics, keep a high energy level throughout and a youthful idealism in the foreground, their music is fast and gritty but they're not afraid of melody in the vocals or, for that matter, major key guitar parts—which still often have an undertone of sadness. Listening to this, I can sort of tell that Against Me was

just around the corner in punk history at that point. If you like Strike Anywhere, or, fuck it, Against Me, I'm sure you'd really enjoy this: as they sing in the last song, "1999, but it could be anywhere, any year"—that's almost too perfect a note to end this review on. What is this, Rolling Stone magazine? So instead, I'll conclude by complaining that they actually sing "Oi Oi Oi!" in that song, too, at one point—what is this, 1979? Anyway, pay no attention to the grumpy editor. -b
Scene Police, D.P.M., Humboldtstrasse15, 53115 Bonn, Germany

SWALLOWING SHIT "PROMO COPY—NOT FOR RESALE" CD:

Okay, so that's not the name, but I thought it was funny that our review copy was stamped with that. It's actually self-titled. This is an anthology of this Canadian band that was together from around 1995 to 1997 whose members have since moved on to play in bands that you've probably heard of. These songs are over before you possibly could get bored. They're fast, intense, to the point with non-stop energy and great recordings (with the exception of the last few songs). They sound like Crudos, then Drop Dead, then Slayer, then Umlaut and then Tear it Up. These guys are all over the place. But even with such short songs they manage to break into parts that sound totally original. This band is really tight as well. The lyrics are political, serious and straight to the point. On the contrary, the song titles themselves are fucking hilarious: "Lyrics That May Offend the Honkys," "Burn Winnipeg to the Fucking Ground," "Christian Metal=Nazi Reggae," "You're Not Old School, You're Just Old," "If Assholes Could Fly, This Place Would Be an Airport," etc. This is great! If you're a fan of fast, relentless hardcore definitely check this out. And check out the record label's name... -s
The G7 Welcoming Committee PO Box 27006, 360 Main Street Concourse Winnipeg, MB R3C 4T3 Canada

UNCONFORM "THE PURSUIT OF HAPPINESS" CD:

This is some of the first punk music I've heard from Moscow, and I'm not disappointed. It's basically old school hardcore, but it's top notch, and there's plenty of variety and personality to set it apart: the two guitar parts complement each other well, the rhythms often switch up in interesting ways, the recording and playing are both excellent, and there are many flourishes and experiments that are above and beyond anything any old school band from this hemisphere has tried in a decade and a half: the intro features some

reviews

beautiful cello playing that really sets it apart (think Cwill), another song includes sweet-voiced singing as a counterpoint to the usual gruff yelling and occasional youth crew vocals. Those unexpected moments are my favorite parts—the intro is so good, Unconform should ask the cellist to sign on for the long haul—but even in the moments when they're doing what many bands have done before, choruses, breakdowns, and all, they don't sound like anyone else; their transitions are still original, and their riffs are really good. The lyrics are sung and printed in Cyrillic, but the explanations also appear in English; they are about the individual struggle for dignity, as straight edge band lyrics often have been, but they come across as sincere. I'd recommend this highly to anyone who liked any of the various waves of self-consciously "old school" hardcore, and to anyone who enjoys punk bands who reinterpret old traditions to make them interesting again. -b
Unconform, P.O. Box 64, 109147, Moscow, Russia (unconform@mail.ru)

UPSILON ACRUX "LAST TRAIN OUT" CD:
I'm going back and forth between being annoyed and intrigued with this one. It's a quiet, spare sound, clean-channel guitars and bass and jazz drums in front exploring math-rock rhythms—presumably with a calculator in hand, as these time signatures are confusing the fuck out of me! At my favorite moments, the music is alien but softly beautiful, capturing the natural, almost non-musical beauty of distant rain; the second track is definitely an example of this. In those cases, their strange aesthetics work to throw the listener off in a way that forces her to open herself up to what's going on more. In the more annoying moments, the actual sounds the instruments are making are unpleasant and jarring enough (think—the alarm on a digital wristwatch) that, combined with the foreign time signatures, one can't help but wish it would just stop. As a musician, I'm fascinated by some of what they're doing, and would like to listen to this over and over until it makes sense to me intuitively; as a music lover, there are a couple tracks I'd like to hear often, and then some I'd like to skip from now on. Not bad, though, for something so out there compared to what I usually listen to. They get full credit for exploring, anyway; without bands out there doing that, it would be hard for other bands to keep composing new heart-rending, timeless anthems out of the same old materials. No vocals, so no lyrics; presumably no political pretensions, so no liner notes or essays. -b
www.hactivist.com

UWHARRIA "FURY IN THE FOOTHILLS" CD:
I think this band used to be a side-project for the people involved, but they recently converged in North Carolina and have been more active. I saw them play the other night and Rick, the

singer, proclaimed, "We play three kinds of music: thrash, metal and mosh." And he's right. This CD is nearly impossible to sit still to. It's a concept record for sure (or perhaps a concept band) with each song written about a different plant or animal that resides (or used to reside, prior to their extinction) in Uwharria, the bio-region that we live in here in NC. This recording is raw and fast with some of the most snotty, unintelligible vocals I've heard. I'm really glad that this band exists because I think that a great deal of thrash bands are apolitical bullshit. This band does a great job of letting people know what their songs are about when they play live. Their explanations are concise, accessible and even humorous and have gone over surprisingly well in Greensboro, of all places, where it is often difficult to speak about any sort of politics at a show because someone is always too drunk to let band members speak. Up the Uwharria punx—these guys are right on. ~s
Slave, PO Box 10093, Greensboro, NC 27404

VANILLA "FANTASTIQUE" DOUBLE 12":
Wow, this really is a double LP of melodic, moody, sad and pretty emo rock songs. This music proceeds from the tradition of punk that proceeded from Fugazi, rather than Minor Threat, so I'm not especially qualified to write about it. There's a pop aesthetic, but more in sweet, smooth texture than in the song structures: they're expansive, exploratory, patient. The tone and intensity doesn't vary too much, so you'd better like what they do a lot if the whole record is going to hold your attention. Don't get me wrong, though, they're good at it—it's just near the opposite end of the punk spectrum from Tragedy, in a terrain I don't venture into much. The lyrics paint a world of disintegrating relationships, alienating cityscapes, and uncaring gods. -b
Plastik Culture c/o Broussard Dorian, 17 rue Rifle-Rafle, 13100 Aix-en-Provence, France

WHEN WE DIE "DIGITAL ANGEL E.P." CD:
I'm not sure exactly what these cats are going for. This is screamy, repetitive hardcore. The songs never seem to go anywhere. There is an awkward tension throughout nearly the entire album. The vocals are choppy, and the whole thing is lacking any real energy or sense of direction. This just isn't driving enough for my tastes, musically or lyrically. ~xb
www13@prodigy.net

ANALENA/UNISON SPLIT 7":
Analena is such an incredible band. Their vocalist, Ana (it's a coincidence—"analena" is Sanskrit for fire) has such emotive power, she's able to evoke a series of widely divergent emotions in just a few syllables.

CHARLIE DON'T SURF/UNISON/ INTENSITY "LIVE FROM THE DOM OMLADINE, BEOGRAD" THREE WAY SPLIT CD:
Check this out—fuck you and your bourgeois limited edition colored vinyl records by spoiled North American hipster "hardcore" bands, records like this one are what I love about punk rock! This is a live recording (and over 77 minutes!) of the first real d.i.y. punk show in Belgrade (May 5, 2001), following a five year vacuum caused by the war in Yugoslavia. The drama of that setting alone distinguishes this from all the uninspired records pouring out of uninspiring suburbs (not that you can't make great music in the suburbs, but you have to contest those suburbs to be able to do anything good there). The recording quality is great—and for my part, I often really prefer the unmediated, raw quality of a live recording to any studio fanciness. The first two bands are from Belgrade—Charlie Don't Surf starts out with a Charles Manson sample ("who put your voice up over my voice? who says your god's bigger than my god?", in part), chilling, which repeats as they begin playing a powerful, energetic, yet deeply sad introduction—the whole effect is really moving, it layers a number of different emotional responses over each other. Their music, once they get going, is fast and crazy, punk and fuck, really powerful yelling vocals cutting through—they're fucking great! Unison are a little less direct—they work more with dynamics, moving back and forth between restrained tension with melodic vocals and buildups and moments when everything busts out into intensity and screaming. They do manage to build to some great climaxes near the end, though. Intensity are in their natural environment here, playing the straightforward high energy hardcore that they do (did?) so well. This is as good as any of their studio stuff, in my opinion—all the intensity is here!—and has extra personality, thanks to their songs explanations and banter. They play twenty songs, including a Citizen's Arrest cover, compared to Charlie Don't Surf's fifteen and Unison's seven. The packaging, also very classy as a d.i.y. three-panel cardstock design, includes liner notes describing the context of this record and emphasizing the importance of keeping punk/hardcore "a permanent struggle against nationalism, racism, homophobia, sexism, and all forms of exploitation." Right on. Contact these folks and demand a copy of this, if you want some more nutrients in your punk rock diet. -b
Dreamstate, Milesevska 61, 11000 Beograd, Yugoslavia (dreamstate99@yahoo.co.uk)

She can sing so sweetly, sounding almost childlike, then shriek with such hurt and anger and strength that it cuts right to my marrow, then sing sweetly again, this time lower, like one who has lived and suffered and is not guarded, exactly, on account of it, so much as deepened. And the band is behind her, ready to carry her everywhere with their music, just as she carries us. At the time I saw them play in Yugoslavia and Bosnia, I somehow had the idea that they were the Baltic Fugazi, but now I'm not sure exactly where that was coming from; they're tight and expressive, like Fugazi, but I think they play their fast parts a little faster, and generally use more emo musical

conventions ('emo' in the very best sense, I promise!)—lots of melodies intertwined, sudden dynamic changes. To sum up: this is great, such poetic, touching, expressive music, and I only wish for a full record of their music. Now, Unison: the first beat is distinctly a d-beat, but their aesthetic is far from the standard dis-band—the recording is a little thin and small, not dirty and overloaded, and some stuff sounds more youth crew than hardcore punk. They experiment with a huge reverb effect on the vocals in parts of the first song, a build-up with guitar noise in the background in the second one, and make their third song by far my favorite with some eastern European guitar lines and a related percussion part in the middle. All around, I can't say I'm as excited about them as about Analena, but that was a tall order. –b
LibberTea records, c/o Davor Bolant, Ivana Mazuranica 32, 10362 Kasina, Croatia

Bob Barker Youth/And I Can't Wait split 12":
When I was in my mid-teens, a punk kid I knew was in a band called Bob Barker and the Abortions, so my life has pretty much come full circle. The latest tribute to Bob features those crazy, barking vocals that come across in a vehement, screaming, indecipherable monotone, fast punk with a recording that may be a little overloaded in the bass register, and that general atmosphere of excitement and recklessness that kids making this music for the first time can create. There's a section of static noise at the end that had me really concerned about the condition of the record player needle for a minute. And I Can't Wait, who have the audacity to put xs around their name at this late date (wow!) have a better recording that makes their impassioned, inexperienced punk rock come across a little more clearly. They play a little slower, but their vocalist is also screaming one anguished note over and over throughout most of the songs—and wait, those are breakdowns with youth crew vocals! And, oh shit, their side ends with a screaming call and response that gets me really excited: "Where's your heart/It's right here!" Fuck yes! B.B.Y. puts information about Food Not Bombs and vegetarianism on the back of their lyric sheet, while A.I.C.W. has a song called "Outnumbered 70 to 1" about "straightedge sisterhood! With my heart on my sleeve and an x on my hand I'm breaking into your boys' club." That's fucking awesome! I hope there is a small army of teenagers listening to this record in their parents' basements, their hearts pounding at the notion that their peers make records they like more than anything in the malls, slowly hatching commitments to d.i.y. that will last the rest of their lives. –b
Damn it, FUCK everybody who can't be bothered to provide a street address! There's just one email address in here, and if I know email, it won't do you any good: kingcobra recording@hotmail.com... and oh, here's a webpage: www.andicantwait.com

Cementario Show/Sin Dios "El Hombre Contra Si Mismo" 7":
Sin Dios has been around forever, working hard at spreading their old-fashioned Spanish anarchism with CDs that come packaged in books of history and political theory, and I'd seen them a couple times already in Poland (once in a squat, no less), but all the same this listening is the most excited I've been about their music yet. Fast punk rock with all the traditional drum beats, earnest, angry singing, occasional guitar leads; the lyrics are in Spanish, but "la etica no existe para el capital—la vida no es mercancia" is clear enough, at least to me—especially accompanied by a photo of an armored pig hitting an old man in the head with a baton. I saw Cementario Show in their native western Spain, after over four fucking months of straight touring, and I was still thrilled about their d-beats—I danced their whole performance, waving my fist in the air and guessing right every time a new transition was about to hit! A band with good d-beats is a thing of beauty, not to be taken lightly. And they don't sound like every other excellent d-beat band, either—the drummer does some original stuff on the snare drum, keeping a roll going throughout one whole part as a beat rather than a rhythm, and the hoarse vocalist has his own personality, as do the songs. Memorable songs—that's the dividing line between a good band and a great band. The riffs have something of a blues sensibility to them, under all the distortion, I think. Anyway, in my book, there's something to be said for any band that plays d-beats with those high guitar leads at the end of verses and doesn't sound like a total dis-clone. I was a little worried about some of the lyrics, until I recognized that was a G.G. Allin cover—now I'm more concerned about their musical taste. Regardless, I'd love to see them again just wave my fist in the air in time to the bass drum. –b
La Idea, Difusion Libertaria, Apdo. 18.251, 28080 Madrid —c, Santa Barbara, 9, Spain

Infect/Discarga split CD:
Infect is a high energy, fast, intense straightforward hardcore band quite possibly influenced by Infest and reminding me of Sweden's Intensity at their best. My comrade here in the kitchen I've occupied to compose reviews is thinking more along the lines of Melt Banana and Super Junky Monkey, but I think their blastbeats and catchy choruses are more directly connected to the U.S. forerunners of those bands. They're rocking here, full power, and their singer's clear voice cuts through over everything with great personality and fury. Yeah! And then Discarga comes in, even faster—yes! faster!—with over-the-top blastbeats, yelling vocals, and plenty of energy of their own. I wish they'd offered more originals, though—after that great first song they offer a good Circle Jerks cover, a painful-to-listen-to Kiss cover, a good Nations on Fire cover, and a half-decent Motorhead medley (sorry,

Northern Ireland's Bleeding Rectum did it better) before finally playing one more song of their own and ending with a big drum finale. Both bands print their lyrics only in the original Portuguese—but from what I know of them, they're all right on people, so don't worry about that. –b
78 Life records, Caixa Postal 2505, cep 09190, Sto Andre, SP, Brazil

Makhnovshchina & Guardia Negra Demo CD:
This is two Boston bands sharing a CDR with a color-copied cover/insert for each band. Both covers are impressive for a demo, especially the Guardia Negra one, and both bands have pretty rough sound quality. Makhnovshchina (that's a mouthful!) play mostly crusty hardcore sometimes leaning towards street punk and sometimes towards metal, strangely enough. There are a lot of d-beats, blast beats and fast rock beats. Their lyrics are straightforward and deal with topics ranging from destroying the World Bank to killing cops to stopping gentrification. I like this. I'd love to see this band live and I look forward to hearing a better recording from them in the future. Guardia Negra are a bit sloppier musically but they sing in Spanish, which is exciting. They play simple four-chord street punk rock with melodic vocals that sometimes almost come to a scream... but not quite. I wish this band had a bit more energy. The songs sound sort of laid back and I don't think that is intentional. The singer could help improve this if he sang a bit harder and sounded like he was giving it his all. There are English translations of the songs and they seem to generally be well-researched words about class struggle and revolution. I'm not digging this one too much, but it is sure nice to hear North American bands singing in Spanish. –s
Barricada PO Box 73 Boston, MA 02133

Overmars/Donefor "In the Arms of Octopus" split CD:
This is two French bands splitting a CD. One song is in French and the rest are in English with all the song explanations in French. Overmars starts off the CD with a long minor key clean guitar intro that I suspect is intended to slowly build tension before the heavy part of the song kicks in—but doesn't quite succeed, as it gets pretty boring about half way through. The song finally comes in as heavy sludge similar to some of the stuff that Face Down in Shit or Neurosis play. There's some effects and impressive guitar work now and then, but for the most part, the ten minutes and twenty-six seconds that comprise this first song are pretty uneventful. The second song, however, comes in really rocking. It starts with a down-tuned, shitty sounding bass guitar and then the rest of the band comes in with upbeat drums and high droning guitar notes. This song is much better—they should have put it first. Unfortunately, much like the first song, the parts go on for much

too long without any exciting changes and I'm bored again. Same with the third song though they do suddenly break into a quiet part in the middle of the chaos. I'm only into six, eight or ten minute songs if they're interesting enough to captivate my attention for that long. Donefor is a whole lot more interesting with their first song ranging from parts that sound like Converge to Sonic Youth to Earth Crisis. The band continues to encompass a great deal of variety throughout their other three songs with different tempos and guitar tones and an indication that they are working from many different influences. All of the parts flow together really smoothly too. This is good song composition although I'd have to say there are a few too many "mosh" parts for my liking. –s

Overmars 21 Grande Rue La Guillotiere 69007 Lyon, France; Donefor 27 Rue Des Combes 69250 Curtis Au Mont D'or, France

UNSANE CRISIS/EKKAIA SPLIT

CD: As I listened to the first few songs from Unsane Crisis I thought I was in for seventeen songs of non-stop blast beat that was going to be difficult for me to get through since songs like that usually make me want to rip my hair out and poke out my eyes. But I was in for a surprise as I got a little further into the CD. They do a good variety of stuff that keeps it interesting. Don't get me wrong—the majority of this is blast beat chaos, but now and again they break into good d-beat parts, fast street punk sounding stuff, powerful "floor-punching" parts and even some slower heavy parts that sound like Korn, but surprisingly not in a bad way—perhaps it only sounds like that cuz they're tuned so low. The vocals are ear piercing shrieks for the most part but there's some cookie monster grunts and growls here and there. If you like fast thrash metal sounding stuff and can deal with a bad recording that really buries the guitars than this might be for you. Oh, the lyrics are great—English sung by a Spanish band: "Just another more song. Why would have any sense. I only want to fun". Ekkaia, who have four songs on here, sing in Spanish and fall somewhere in between screamo, metal and thrash. This band has a lot of skill and a decent recording, but even though they are doing some really interesting stuff, it's not really moving me. They sort of remind me of Converge at times—really good technically, but I can't find much emotion. Maybe I take some of that back. It may be that I'm just worn out by the first band's seventeen songs. I think I'd enjoy seeing both of these bands live, but this CD is just mediocre. –s

Difusion Liberataria La Idea Apdo 18251, 28080 Madrid, Spain

VUUR/SEEIN' RED "ANOTHER FINE

PUNK PRODUCT" SPLIT 7": Vuur is rocking, taking everything that was good about Systral's "Fever" record and going with it: grainy bass, chord progressions that

occasionally sound like they were composed by Martians, blastbeats to keep the listener awake, over-the-top screaming vocals backed by low-bass-rumbling vocals, great stuff. Their first song is about working on improving yourself rather than criticizing others who stick their necks out—I wish that attitude was more prevalent in certain activist corners of the punk world. This is truly fist-pounding, head-banging, glass-smashing stuff, top notch. And, speaking of Systral, whose indecision and uncertainty was so touching on that record (though it later panned out into apolitical apathy), the lyrics to their last song are similarly ambiguous and conflicted: "RAGE!! I am gonna set your world on fire! I don't want to set your world on fire. Rage... rage!!! I apologize for my rage!" Seein' Red are fucking maniacs to have been hammering out hyper-energetic, short-attention-span punk rock songs for the last two decades and still be at it in it top form, but here they are doing exactly that. Four songs, covering homophobia, conformity, ignorance of world suffering, and capitalism—ending with a wild-eyed call not only to smash the state and capitalism, but also to kill the oppressor. Punk rock indeed. –b

Day One, Nico, Olenseweg 151, 2260 Westerlo, Belgium

"VARNA HARDCORE POINT OF

VIEW" COMPILATION CD: This is a compilation of eight bands from Varna, Bulgaria: Never Again, Crowfish, Indignity, Outrage, Not Broken in Spirit, BFH, No Values and Another Day. I was hoping that because this is from half way across the world, I would be exposed to something new and different when I put this in my stereo. But apparently American imperialism has infected every corner of the planet—nearly all of these bands sound like bad NY hardcore from one year or another and when they stray from that, it sounds like Pantera or Korn. Each band has a slightly different sound, I guess, but share a common ground of being all boys and having purposefully-macho vocals. I don't like any of this—sorry guys. –s

unitedandstrong@gbg.bg

949 MARKET: This is fucking great, a stellar example of the heroic endeavors and creative documentations that come out of our community. In spring of 2001, a vast building in downtown San Francisco was squatted; it hosted a punk show attended by 600 people, enormous servings of free food, and the dreams and ambitions of a wide circle of people from all walks of life who cleaned and rewired it, and decorated it floor to ceiling with graffiti murals. This is their story, told through various accounts and interviews and photographs, from the moment the space was discovered to the eviction and its aftermath. This account does exactly what it should do—it captures those events in a way that makes the reader feel like similar adventures might be possible in other contexts, rather than glorifying some past achievement. I'd recommend this highly to anyone interested in squatting or messing with the fabric of reality in general in this repressive country. –b

Zara, 3288 21rst St., P.M.B. #79, San Francisco, CA 94110

A KIND OF EPIC: Everyone sit up and take note, though I can't promise it will do you any good! This little 'zine, probably produced in a print run of only a few dozen, is one of the finest collections of poetry I've read in some time. I'm very rarely excited about poetry—when I find a great poem, or even a great line, I dwell or soar on it for weeks, but that's extremely rare. Rita Mae Brown's "The Hand that Cradles the Rock" is my latest favorite discovery in the world of poetry, and it was 1997 when I came across it. This 'zine is up there with that book, for me—all the more impressive, since the author is from mainland Europe. His English is effortless like only a true poet's can be, though, shot through with those occasional moments of revelation when the language and the world you thought you'd known all your life suddenly, simultaneously open up new horizons before you. Yes! But good luck getting your hands on this. Some of my favorite poems in here are not actually part of the 'zine—they're written on scraps of paper, tucked into it (when I was in Europe, I was lucky enough to bump into the author and get him to give me copies of some unpublished ones)—so your best bet is just to try to track this guy (Maarten Das is his name) down and get him to share something with you. He's since released another 'zine of poetry, which I don't like as much (he works more with straightforward rhymes in it, which gives a singsong quality to the work), but I'll print the email address from that one, since the contact on this 'zine doesn't work anymore. –b

whydaredevilspray@hotmail.com

COMMUNICATING VESSELS VOLUME

1, #7 AND WILLFUL DISOBEDIENCE VOLUME 3, #5: These 'zines are two of a kind: both feature consistently intelligent anarchist theory from an insurrectionist/ultraist perspective, balance historical

and even statistical precision with a taste for surrealist fantasy, are illustrated with borrowed woodcuts and cartoons that xerox nicely, and appear at remarkably regular intervals. C.V. is more prone to artiness, with significant parts given over to poetry and somewhat overwrought narratives one might expect to see from the Chicago Surrealist Group; it also focuses more on a politics of daily life resistance, as opposed to the hyper-theoretical critiques, abstract glorifications of revolt, and dry news blurbs of W.D. The highlights of this issue of C.V. are two reprints—an excellent analysis of the differences between "antiwar" movies that subtly glorify war and works which succeed in undermining its grip on the psyche, and an anti-work manifesto translated from German—and a contribution from a food service worker who interprets his (?) experiences engaging in on-the-job resistance in terms from class struggle theory. If the similarities in format and subject matter were not enough, this issue of Willful Disobedience quotes the same British 'zine in the same discussion of how anti-war agitation cannot convincingly be pro-peace, either. Of the two, W.D. has the deeper analyses, and this issue is one of the better ones—the arguments about anarchism being about means as well as ends, the role of festival as pressure valve in oppressive society, and the centrality of desire in anarchist economics are convincing, and might even usefully inform one's practice. Still, I have to admit, I want to like both these 'zines more than I succeed in liking them—if only the poetry in C.V. could actually move me, I would be deeply faithful to it, but it has yet to; and W.D., on the other hand, is demoralizing in that it tends to include a lot of abstract ranting about stuff I deeply believe myself (immediate struggle against alienation and oppression in all their forms, etc. etc.) that still fails to leave me with any particularly new ideas of how to realize those abstractions, coupled with news reports about real life exciting things happening very far away—which offer no practical information on how I could be involved. Mere thinking about revolt won't help us—we have to think and act, and my favorite papers are the ones that offer equal proportions of philosophical and practical armaments. All the same, between these two I'd recommend Willful Disobedience, especially, as a stellar example in the tradition of verbosely theoretical revolutionary anarchism. Just make sure you leave the armchair after reading. -b
Communicating Vessels: Mutual Aid Portland, P.O. Box 7328, Portland, ME 04112 Willful Disobedience: Venomous Butterfly Publications, P.O. Box 31098, Los Angeles, CA 90031

CREACTIV@ [#4?]: El ateneo ha publicado una colección de pequeños ensayos políticos en un 'zine de 32 páginas. Queda énfasis en la cuestión de los presos en España, y también hay escritos sobre el espacio libre imaginativo, físico, y psicológico que debemos ofrecerles a nuestros hijos para ayudarlos a crecer mejor; algunos contra los efectos aniquilizantes y estandardizantes de la escuela y del trabajo; una biografía de Louise Michel, educadora libertaria francesa del Siglo XIV, y una descripción corta de la utopía protoanarquista Sinapia. No profundizan mucho en estos temas, pero la mayoría tienen una energía sincera e idealista. Aparece también una lista de las publicaciones que tiene el ateneo en su biblioteca.-@

Ateneo Libertario Eliseo Reclús, Apdo. 586, 11480 Jerez Fra., Cádiz. España

DISORDERLY CONDUCT #6 AND GREEN ANARCHY #12: Like Disorderly Conduct and Communicating Vessels, this 'zine and paper are so closely tied to one another in terms of content, tone, and even personnel that it makes the most sense to review them together. Both of these, taken together, constitute the best-known voices of anarcho-primitivism in North America, or at least the really confrontational strains of it (I'm not counting Derrick Jenson here, nor Daniel Quinn, for good or for ill). Do I like them? I go back and forth—when the contents just seem too outlandish to do anyone any practical good in the actual struggles for freedom and authentic living that are going on, or, worse, when too much space is given over to vitriolic attacks on other radicals, I can get really fed up (especially with Green Anarchy, which seems to be edited by people with scant social skills in the important field of conflict resolution!); on the other hand, on good days, I enjoy the fact that there is a wing of the anarchist community at least as far out as I am, and take interest in their perspectives for the sake of diversity at least (this is more the case for Disorderly Conflict). So what are the differences between the two? The obvious distinction is depth: Green Anarchy is a tabloid, with coverage of environmental direct action, radical struggles from around the world (seen through a primitivist lens, of course), infighting between various anarcho-splinter groups, and intermittent essays (that, when they don't just boil down to another repetition of the obvious "Destroy Civilization, Already!", can be interesting: the fall of Rome, how to prepare and eat roadkill); Disorderly Conduct, on the other hand, has the space to add some subtleties and diversity. In addition to direct action news and exhortations, this issue includes, to its credit, a story by Italo Calvino, an account of a trip through the anarchist squat circuit in southern Europe, a piece on the Aborigine concept of Dreamtime, and even my now all-time favorite poem on the subject of spelling and grammar elitism (no, it wasn't a competitive running, but anyway): "its or it's"; "it's or its, I really don't care—it's its 'it's' and 'its,' it's its shit, not mine." Of the two, then, I'd recommend

BEATING HEARTS OF THE WORLD UNITE: This is such a beautiful project, the kind that takes a deep generosity to undertake, since it's easy to feel like this world just doesn't deserve anything beautiful like this, and that it won't shelter anything like this that is brought into it. This is a 130 page handcrafted book, one of quite a few they must have put together, hand-binding them, hand-gluing in photographs of haunting landscapes, hand-stamping the covers, hand-writing in words. Rather than selling them, they offer them in trade for other gifts or works of art or imagination from others, a grand gesture in itself. And the content is absolutely top-notch—it's essentially everything I would want to read in the d.i.y. press, gathered together. There's fiction, personal narratives, essays and manifestos, art and poetry, even a little news, all covering the spaces where anarchist and activist politics, sex and love and sexual/amorous liberation, and passionate living in general intersect and intertwine. Some of it is plagiarized, some reprinted, much of it original, all of it high quality and yet very personal, even intimate, as if everything here was done by someone you knew, with you in mind. By the time you're reading this, it may well be a couple years since they put these together, but you should write them all the same, sending something beautiful you've dared to make yourself, so this quixotic gift won't be entirely wasted on this world after all. -b

Beating Hearts Press, P.O. Box 444, Wollongong, NSW 2520 Australia

Disorderly Conduct more, in view of it offering more variety (and balancing out the vindictiveness with humor and even verse), though it might be easier for the indigent reader to get her hands on Green Anarchy free. -b
both available from P.O. Box 11331, Eugene, OR 97440

ILEGAL #2: Este 'zine español es bien escrito e interesante. [También está un poco viejo (del enero de 2002)—pero eso es por la culpa del programa de publicación de Inside Front, no por otra cosa.] Se trata de ka escena punk con un enfoque en la política (específicamente en el anarquismo y movimientos asociados con ello). Hay columnas sobre el rol de la música en cuanto a la difusión de las ideas; sobre cómo podamos vivir unas vidas DIY, no sólo comprar discos y leer 'zines DIY; sobre la prostitución, los okupas en Holanda y en España (los dos un poco pesimistas), y el vegetarianismo. "EL PUNK ES ODIO" nos anima a reclamar el punk por afirmar nuestro asco a la gente, pero su tema más grande es cómo hacer que el punk como movimieno pueda escaparse de su asimilación enervante a la corriente principal cultural. Hay entrevistas con Submission Hold (muy larga e interesante: tratan temas como la crianza de niños, el

separatismo en Quebec, Canadá, las drogas y los ordenadores), Tragedy, un hombre de la escena punk de Groningen, Holanda, Ruidoactivo (de un pueblo pequeño español), y, por dios, otro con Catharsis. Las preguntas por lo general son originales y las respuestas no aburren. Hay dos artículos sobre ateneos colectivos, uno de ellos en Brasil. Las reseñas tienen personalidad propia.-@
Don't Belong, Apdo. 8035, 33200 Gijón, España

PROFANE EXISTENCE #40:

I've always been perplexed when little magazines like Inside Front reviewed much more widely-circulated ones like Profane Existence—what good could that possibly do? But in this case, it offers me a chance to think through some things I've been preoccupied with anyway—so damn the torpedoes, I'm gonna do it, and hopefully you'll get something out of it too. Now, as a younger punk rocker, I was all about innovation—everything had to be new, an unheard-of idea, a challenge to everything taken for granted, a break with the past even if that past had just been a break with the past before it. Getting a little older, though, I discovered within myself a profound love for longstanding punk conventions—d-beats, patches, dreadlocks, badly xeroxed 'zines and basement shows, sullen teenagers, the works. Every time I saw, heard, met, or went to one of these, it felt like less of a ritual and more of an affirmation of persistence: twenty-some years into this counterculture, literally tens of thousands of sell-outs, age-outs, arrests, prison terms, and catastrophes later, and we're still at it—the punk community is still somehow spawning new generations of anarchists, activists, squatters, radical

feminists, local communities, and even, occasionally, good bands! So at this point, sometimes I'm more thrilled just to see a new issue of an old, old (I mean old in punk years) paper like Slug and Lettuce than I am to see a brand new band demonstrate some strange new hybrid of punk and cutting-

> **HALF WILD:** I lack the poetry to extol this 'zine as it deserves to be extolled. Suffice to say, it is an eloquent, intensely personal testimony written very much from inside the world of emotionally conflicted, mentally unstable, nature-loving social dropouts—and yet possessing the power to communicate far outside that context. It is the equal, and yet the opposite, of a 'zine like Burn Collector: where Burn Collector is astute but cynical, this author achieves wisdom through her insistent, impractical artlessness, flaunting her raw idealism and the unhealed wounds it occasions. It is as moving as, and yet utterly different from, any literature in the vein of Harbinger: it is not a manifesto, nor an exhortation—it has far more in common with the personal 'zines of old—but yet communicates and inspires with that power, a power deriving here from the intimacy and openness of the author. I have to say—I've gotten a lot of really important insights out of reading and rereading this, as I have out of few 'zines in a long time, and I know others who have too; at her best moments, the author looks at the world through a sort of permaculture perspective, piecing together different ecosystems and the ways they function (or, tragically, break down). In case all this praise still leaves it unclear what this is actually "about," let me offer some selections from the contents: "crazy," "glory tramps," "nonmonogamy," "disaster," "creatures out of their element." Got it? -b
> *Rika Kat at the Grubumkin House, 726 Frederick, Olympia, WA 98501*

edge jungle techno. That would make you think I'd be overjoyed to see this new issue of the mainstay publication of the U.S. anarcho-punk community, and I am, but... I've got to air some misgivings, too. The problem for me is that P.E. has changed so little over the years that I'm afraid it can't possibly be as useful to the new generations of punks as it was almost fifteen years ago. I mean, "making punk a threat some more" is critical, but the original punk scene they formed to radicalize no longer exists—their readership and "target audience" is now made up of kids raised on the bands that were reading this magazine in the early '90's, while kids in other parts of the punk scene seem to languish on without any connection to radical possibilities. It would be ridiculous for me to think these folks would move on to radicalizing the emo scene or the metalcore scene, so I guess what I'm saying is that they (and all of us anarcho-punks) need to focus on how to keep developing our scene, and our role in it. Is it

> ## JACK FROST'S TOP TEN SOURCES OF MOTIVATION WHILST LAYING OUT THIS ZINE:
> 1. Fear of Editor's swift reprisal[1]
> 2. Envy - *Any recording I can get my mits on*
> 3. Memento Mori: *s/t*
> 4. Lightning Bolt: *Wonderful Rainbow*
> 5. Mirah - *Advisory Committee*
> 6. Spring landscape in bloom right outside the library window *(damnit!)*
> 7. Pizza dumpster awaiting me after every night's work
> 8. Panda Cam: *http://www.sandiegozoo.org/special/pandas/pandacam/*
> 9. Explosions in the Sky - *Peel Sessions*
> 10. Asschapel - *Total Worship (don't let the band name fool you—they're fucking amazing!)*

enough to keep doing exactly the same stuff, printing interviews with young anarchist bands and ranting simply against the government and religion over and over year in and year out? I wonder if there are any elements missing in the anarcho-punk scene (more tactical information, new insights into the advantages of a marginal lifestyle, new connections to others communities, new anticapitalist strategies to try) that Profane Existence and others like them could come up with and spread, elements which could really make punk twice as dangerous as it already is, just as this magazine succeeded in doing in the '90's. Anyway—in this issue, you'll find middle-finger anti-government/war political rants, a little activist news (including an exchange about squat legalization reprinted from the fucking internet—are we living in the last days of print culture, or what?), angry demands that punx "live up to their patches" based on the age-old notion that punk rock isn't as right on as it once was, Felix von Havoc's history of Crust punk in the U.K. (which is fascinating for us old folks, and probably also for young folks who were in diapers at the time—but it's troubling to me, too, since for our scene to be powerful and healthy we have to focus primarily on the present, not on the old days), and, on the back cover, even a good old-fashioned attack on Christianity. The most troubling parts are the interviews, which are so superficial as to read like interviews from Maximum Rock'n'Roll, and the reviews, which are similarly superficial for the most part (and, though I'm sure reviewer Nate didn't mean for this to come off as badly as it does, I really cringed when he wrote "most bands can't pull off the female vocals" in the Tem Eyos Ki review). If my fears that this is all too rooted in the past were not great enough already, the magazine cover is taken from one of the first Metallica records. Here's my dilemma: just existing, even without any evolution in content, approach, or quality, is an achievement for Profane Existence and everyone associated with it—so maybe it's OK that their contents don't challenge me today the way they did a decade ago, maybe they challenge some modern-day teenager instead. But, on the other hand, maybe today's average teenager needs to be challenged in some other way, too, since the world is evolving—and I really hope anarcho-punk will be able to remain a challenging, empowering force for the next generation, somehow... so how could P.E. evolve to address the needs of these new kids, assuming they are different? It certainly can't help that many of us older

[1] *Just kidding!*

punks are now twice the age of the kids getting involved now, when it comes to the question of what we should be doing to be useful. Maybe it's Profane Existence's job just to hold down the fort doing what they've always done well, and Inside Front's job to try out the complementary stuff—but Inside Front doesn't exist anymore, so who's ready to take that on? –b
Profane Existence, P.O. Box 8722, Minneapolis, MN 55408

SOFAKARTOFFEL #4: This 'zine reminds me a lot of Lieve's *Ugly Duckling* 'zine, one of my favorites from Belgium: like that 'zine, Sofakartoffel (that's literal German for "couch potato," but the 'zine is largely in English, with little flourishes of Spanish) is mostly written in handwriting, with all the intimacy that can create between the writer and reader, and ranges from personal confessions and reflections to explicit considerations of such issues as "pro-life" bullshit (represented here by a debate between editor Sandra and some Italian holdover from the ghost of hardline past) and whether it is anti-Semitic to criticize Israel for their genocidal oppression of Palestinians. The hardcore scene is present throughout, not so much as a subject of coverage as a backdrop. There's a massive account of her travels last summer, including a trip through Argentina that I believe is the counterpart of Cyril's Argentinean scene report in this issue. The reader will probably come away from *Sofakartoffel* with an invigorating dose of optimism and idealism, and a finer sensitivity to the precious things in life. –b
Sandra c/o A. Fleischer, Bachbohlweg 47, 78467 Konstanz, Germany

WASTELAND AND PROLEFUTTER: These are two excellently produced graphic works by the same artist. Wasteland is a dystopian story in pictures (think Lynd Ward, only grittier, bleaker, more terrifying), about an individual lost in a literally heart-rending world; there is some text in Deutsch, but it's not central to understanding or appreciating the work. The line drawings are simultaneously raw and precise, and convey alienation and disconnection without distancing the viewer from the sadness they portray. Prolefutter is more provocative, even political, art/manifesto than narrative; the graphics are largely collage-based (think early CRASS layouts, plus twenty years of

INTERNATIONALE PSYCHOGEOGRAPHIC: "THE AMSTERDAM EPISODE": This is one of those near-unintelligible yet precious gifts to an unresponsive world that can come out of moments when individuals trust their own whims and subjective responses enough to act on them instead of limiting themselves to established forms. In this case, that approach has produced a subjective map of two (?) observers' wanderings through the foreign city of Amsterdam: it's a patchwork of witty intellectual commentary, scrawled personal accounts and notations, and jarring collages assembled from on-the-spot photo documentation, sketches, and xeroxes of tickets/schedules/other souvenir-artifacts. It reads like a letter from your most deranged and creative friend's winter hitchhiking trip (which, in my case, it actually is—not that this colors my opinion!). The maps of Amsterdam would not help even the most accomplished C.I.A. agents retrace the steps of our erstwhile authors, let alone enable a newcomer to Amsterdam to navigate its streets, but that's not the point here; if anything, they might encourage other travelers to feel like their own private journeys are as worth mapping as any "objective" space is. The commentaries, covering anti-expert iconoclasm ("of course they write long and fancy books, but if you were stuck in a small cubicle for forty years, you would write books as well!"), squatter ethnography ("living at a place without paying rent?! That's like an object with mass not being affected by gravity"), and tourist pathology ("tourists need help. 'Help' would be kind—tourists need electro-shock treatment") and its cure ("once you are predictable, you can be stopped—but unleashed upon the world, operating by sheer fancy, taking note of the most mundane scenes, nothing will be safe... we don't need the camera, the camera needs us"), are hilarious and insightful, and the already-irregular margins of my copy are now filled with my own additional notations, from inspirations that hit me in the course of reading ("'For an Imaginarian Antinational!'"..."on the side of the angels,' i.e., against all of us""...a lost glove senses the moment of its former master's death..."). Who knows if these authors can be tracked down to mail out copies of this to folks like you, but if you write us at the Greensboro or Atlanta CrimethInc. addresses, we have a few copies, and I'd be willing to send you one myself. It's worth the read for nonsense like this alone: "...the bargain basement is also the torture chamber, the concentration camp, the charnel house with Christmas tree decorations..." –b
email addresses to try: blackandgreen@ziplip.com, kaviat@graffiti.net, everyangelisterrible@doityourself.com

development), with really intricate work throughout. Rape, patriarchy, capitalism are portrayed with the kind of graphic genius and mental acuity that lays everything frighteningly bare. There is more text— English for the bold statements, Deutsch for the fine print—but again, an English speaker would still get a lot out of this. Not every picture is worth a thousand words, but these two compositions are worth their weight in Cometbus 'zines and George Orwell books. If you take d.i.y. visual arts seriously, try to track these down, or other work by this artist. –b
Flatline-Imperium c/o M99, Manteuffelstr. 99, 10997 Berlin, Germany

TOOLBOX OF WEAPONS FOR LIBERATION/
CATALOG OF MERCHANDISE FOR CONSUMPTION
(it's up to you!)

CrimethInc. Far East is, by far, the most efficient distributor of CrimethInc. materials. Those motherfuckers are horribly overworked, though, so only send them simple, paid orders. Send generic requests for free stuff, special requests, and personal letters to the Urban Pirates address instead. The Urban Pirates also mail out vast quantities of free literature—'zines, posters, etc.—whenever they have the money to afford the postage. For that matter, they're the ones who could get you shirts or patches (various anarchist, Catharsis, Zegota, Blacken the Skies, etc. designs). Send impersonal orders for CDs and copies of Inside Front to Stickfigure, along with all inquiries about buying those items wholesale. Stickfigure is the best place for retailers and distributors to order items from the record label division of CrimethInc.

Payment to CrimethInc. Far East can be made in cash or money order made out to CrimethInc., or order online with credit card (yes, that's disgusting, but let's not be coy: this is the getting-our-hands dirty-in-commerce part, that hopefully somehow finances and enables the creating-community-and-killing-heads-of-state part). Payment to the Urban Pirates should be in the form of well-concealed cash or blank checks. Payment to Stickfigure can be made in cash, check or money order made out to Stickfigure, or you can order online or over the phone with credit card; customers that order only one record have to pay an additional $.50 for shipping, customers that order one record or CD and want it sent by priority mail need to pay an additional $3, and all Georgia orders add 7% sales tax—isn't that fucked!

PAPER:

Inside Front postscript issue: This is what you're holding, silly.
1 copy/$5 postpaid in the USA ($7 world), 5+/$3.50 each postpaid in the USA ($5 world)

Inside Front #13: The supposed final issue of the magazine you're reading! This issue focuses on how to create communities that both foster freedom in the lives of those involved and fight for positive change on a larger scale; it also includes extensive reports from many of the activist demonstrations and similar undertakings of 1999-2001, discussions on alternatives to monogamous relationships and gender roles, and the usual pages and pages of fine-print columns, how-to guides, reviews, etc. 164 pages, and comes with a cd compilation featuring an international cast of punk/hardcore bands: Milemarker, Newborn, Endstand, Point of No Return, Newspeak, Constrito, Shank, Abuso Sonoro, Ruination, Cwill, many more.
1 copy/$5, 5+/$3.50 each

Inside Front #12: Features a lengthy retrospective/interview with Refused, an interview discussing hardcore imperialism and the third world with Brazilian band Point of No Return, a new take on the old tradition of scene reports (including the Appalachian Trail and Lewisburg, North Carolina), an analysis of Reclaim the Streets protests, and a whole lot more. 136 pages, and including the already-classic eleven song 6" by Finland's most notorious roadsters, Umlaut.
1 copy/$3, 5+/$1.50 each

Stone Hotel: This book of poetry is a no frills ride through one man's experience in the United States prison system, and all of the lunacy, horror, and meditation that entails.
1 copy/$10, 2/$17, 3/$22, 4/$26, 5-9/$6 each, 10 or more/$5 each (this is a fund-raiser for the upcoming Fighting For Our Lives reprint)

Days of War, Nights of Love: Crimethink "for beginners"—your ticket to a world free of charge.
1 copy/$8, 2/$14, 3/$19, 4/$23, 5-9/$5 each, 10 or more/$4.50 each

Evasion: The controversial account of one boy who left his destined place in society behind to steal, scam, and hitchhike to personal freedom.
1 copy/$6, 2/$11, 3/$15, 4/$23, 5-9/$4 each, 10 or more/$3.50 each

Fighting For Our Lives: This free paper discusses, in simple language, what is anarchist in everyday life, and how those spheres of cooperation can be expanded. It addresses common questions that often deter people from exploring anarchist ideas and approaches, and endeavors to help introduce new terms and possibilities into the public consciousness.
Individual copies free to all. Bulk orders will be possible again one day, hopefully by the time you see this—we have to raise the money to reprint them.

Hunter/Gatherer—CrimethInc. Journal of Folklore and Folkwar, #1: A manifesto of confusion to make war on nonsense! A journal celebrating the decentralized, radically participatory do-it-yourself underground, mass-produced and distributed by a vanguard elite? A broadside emphasizing your capabilities by glorifying the adventures and achievements of a privileged few? A fable chronicling traditions of revolt, a pioneer expedition into the past, a retelling of time to rescue the future? History or story, legend or legerdemain, anthropology or propaganda?
Individual copies free to all.

[Note: the Urban Pirates distribute many of the various follow-up issues of Hunter/Gatherer, most recently including the audio Hunter/Gatherer on CDR, which can be obtained from them for $2 and 2 postage stamps.]

D.I.Y. Guide #2: This rugged little urban pirate handbook includes practical information on participating in demonstrations, direct action, shoplifting, software piracy, d.i.y. spelling and grammar, traveling on trains, backpacking, urban camping and evasion, herbal gynecology, d.i.y. abortion, sewing, d.i.y. oil change, making your own quarter pipe for skating, forearm guards, pressing records, CD's, and zines, book publishing, beating the postal system, food not bombs, plaster casting, black and white photography, and safety pin tattoos.
Individual copies free to all, bundle of 40/$15 donation

CrimethInc. Far East
P. O. Box 1963
Olympia, WA 98507
www.crimethinc.com
house@crimethinc.com

CrimethInc. Urban Pirates
P.O. Box 2133
Greensboro, NC 27402
stef@crimethinc.com

Stickfigure Distribution and Mailorder
P.O. Box 55462
Atlanta, GA 30308
(404) 752-7399
www.stickfiguredistro.com

The Walls Are Alive: A how-to graffiti guide, including wheatpasting.
Individual copies are free. 30 copies/$8, 100 copies/$15

Off the Map: Personal travel 'zine by two young women dead set upon making their lives what they dream of and vice versa. 94 delightful pages across Europe squatting, hitching, and creating new worlds in which to frolic. Amazingly well-written and much more than just another mindless recounting of traveling stories. Highly recommended.
Free to all, donations appreciated

Dropping Out: Rather than a comprehensive foray into the subject of dropping out, this zine aims to provide some practical tips along with some personal writing on the experience of dropping out of high school. Strongly recommended for those in the heart of high school hell, and them alone.
Free to all, donations appreciated

ROCK:

Blacken the Skies CD: Punks/activists push the anarcho-punk musical tradition to a new level of creativity, intensity, and emotional expression. Imagine Zegota as a d-beat band like Diallo or From Ashes Rise: the heart and soul, the long improvisations, but with fist-waving, dreadlock-swinging crust parts! Ten soulful, dark, wide-ranging songs in 50 minutes.
1 copy/$9, 5+/$5.50 each

Countdown to Putsch "" double CD: Pioneering political hardcore drawing on the radical traditions of free jazz improvisation, spoken word performance, and experimental noise—absolutely unique, and breaking important new ground to keep the genre vital.
1 copy/$10, 5+/$6 each

Catharsis "Arsonist's Prayer"/Newborn "Ready to Leave, Ready to Live" CD/LP: The last recording from Catharsis (one ten-minute song) and Newborn (three songs on the CD—the LP has four: hectic, intricate, soulful compositions from this incredible Hungarian band), packaged with the usual creative (i.e. ripped off) CrimethInc. finesse.
CD-1 copy/$8, 5+/$5 each; LP-1 copy/$10, 5+/$6 each

Catharsis "Passion" CD: To sew seeds in barren fields where there is no more fertile ground. To bear the fragile worlds within through the ruined one that surrounds. To lift us up, to bring empires down.
1 copy/$10, 5+/$6 each

Catharsis "Samsara" CD: A Pandora's box of suffering and tragedy, with hope trapped at the bottom... includes four tracks from now-unavailable 7" record (once on the now-unavailable eponymous first cd).
1 copy/$10, 5+/$6 each

Zegota "Namaste" CD: The much anticipated sophomore record from this North Carolina punk band. For those of you who've seen them live, this record truly captures the spirit, energy and artistry of a live Zegota show, from beginning to end, creating a record that captivates the body, soul and mind. 71 minutes of musical improvisations, new songs, medleys, and their cover of Neil Young's "Ohio." When I first got this record it was the only thing I listened to for an entire week (and I listen to music almost non-stop). Comes with hand-screened packaging and elaborate booklet, etc.
1 copy/$8, 5+/$5 each

Zegota Movement in the Music CD/LP: Their soulful, youthful, idealistic debut record.
CD-1 copy/$8, 5+/$5 each; LP (import)-1 copy/$10, 5+/$6 each

Umlaut "Havoc Wreakers" LP: Ready to wreak whatever havoc must be wrought... Holy Shit! Song titles like "Thrill of the Open Road" and "Duct Tape and Distortion" with matching lyrics: *Come on! Let's blow this town, raze the streets to rubble—set a land speed record for causing trouble—I want to ride a sonic boom across a land with no borders. I'll be the crash test dummy of the No World Order! Yeah!* 28 songs of wild abandon and an utter refusal to give in, this record will break your fuckin' record player. Comes with an elaborate 28 page half-size booklet. Released by Finland's Combat Rock Industry Records. *So don't rock the vote—vote with the rock, mothers and fuckers! The hand that cradles the rock rules the world! Rock around the clock!*
(import) 1 copy/$10, 5+/$6 each

Aluminum Noise "Totally Fucking Lost" CD: A d.i.y. experimental noise project undertaken by kids who set out to broaden the spectrum of the audio arts, challenging everyone's conceptions of what music itself is. This recording has a haunting beauty, made sharper by a tension that steadily increases over the seventy minutes of music, rather than discharging itself. We think it's fucking amazing, like feeling new chambers of the heart being carved out—but the average pop punk listener will probably find himself alienated and confused.
1 copy/$6, 5+/$4 each

Ire "What Seed, What Root?" CD: Their last recording. Five songs of their great political sludgy French Canadian hardcore.
$10, 5+/$6.60

Timebomb Full Wrath of the Slave CD: Italian, vegan straight edge, anarcho-communist black metal.
1 copy/$7, 5+/$4

"In Our Time" LP: compilation with Damad, Systral, Gehenna, Timebomb, Jesuit, Final Exit, Congress and an elaborate insert discussing standardization of our world under capitalism... and what to do about it. Beautiful packaging and vinyl.
1 copy/$8, 5+/$4 each

SCISSORS

Wheatpasting Posters: A variety of 11"x17" posters celebrating resistance and lampooning the war on terrorism, the psychiatric-industrial complex, etc.—perfect for public redecorating.
Free with orders

Stickering Kits: For adjusting public spaces to broadcast messages that line up with reality. Currently, two designs are available: "this phone is tapped" (as per the Patriot Act) for telephones, and "fortified with 100% pure Iraqi blood" for gas pumps/SUVs.
$5 for 100—sorry about the high price, we're selling these at exactly what it costs to make and mail them

PickAxe/Breaking the Spell video: The second edition/reprinting of this 158 minute tape featuring these two excellent documentary films. *PickAxe* revolves around an anarchist struggle to save a forest (Warner Creek) in Oregon from logging; *B.T.S.* covers the events at the infamous W.T.O. meeting in Seattle, and the ensuing media focus on "Eugene Anarchists." Arrange a public showing at your school, house, or community center.
1 copy is $12, 2-4/$12 each, 5-10/$8 each

Coming next: A new issue of our free tabloid Harbinger, a new Face Down in Shit CD/LP, discography CD sets from Umlaut and Catharsis, a new anarchist cookbook... then we'll get down to fucking business.

Anarchy Triumphs Again

In autumn of 2001 I sat with my band in the Kopi squat in Berlin, eating a delicious meal prepared for us by a local friend. The many residential floors above us hummed with activity, squatters and artists and dissidents of literally dozens of nations and cultures chatting and cooking and repairing together; around us, hundreds of punk rockers were gathering for the show. The room with the stage was huge, and featured the most sophisticated sound equipment I had ever seen in a d.i.y. space; in fact, Rage Against the Machine had asked to play here on their last European tour, but the squatters had turned them down on account of all the compromises the band had made with the capitalist culture industry. The neighborhood around the squat was alive with infoshops and gathering places and radical culture, so much so that the yearly Mayday festivals inevitably turned into violent clashes with the repressive police.

As I sat and looked around at all these beautiful, crazy people and all the structures they'd created and defended against the demands of the market and its enforcers, it hit me: sixty years ago there were no anarchists or queers or rebels in Germany—they were all dead, imprisoned, or overseas. Just two generations back, there was nothing like this in Berlin or within a thousand miles of it. I was looking upon solid proof that the burning passion of human beings for freedom and creation cannot be extinguished: the bureaucrats and fascists can threaten us, bully us, even slaughter entire generations (Latin America, the Soviet Union, Palestine), but their very children will grow up to defy them, as if raised by the ghosts of their parents' foes. A mere three decades after the Nazis reigned supreme here, squats like Kopi were appearing all around this city, thousands were filling the streets to contest the status quo, white children of the middle class were even taking up arms and risking their lives to fight in solidarity with those in the third world whose exploitation benefited their rich parents.

Maybe we haven't beaten fascism and oppression once and for all yet, but they've had their chance to finish us off, and failed.

So before the war—any war, every war—even begins, we know who the winners will be: us, the anarchists. Call us by that name or any other—we who treasure freedom-to above power-over, who stake our lives on mutual aid rather than cannibalism, we shall prevail as we have always prevailed. We've been defeated in every revolution, crushed by every regime, persecuted with every torture known to humanity, and still we come out on top.

Wait—isn't that pure arrogance, the ultimate in over-privileged disregard for the suffering of those who die under the bombs of the empire-builders? And—historically speaking—isn't it just plain inaccurate? Haven't we in fact lost everything over and over, failed whenever we had a chance, been conquered in every struggle?

No, my friends, we haven't, and it's not arrogant to celebrate the miracle of our survival. Let's look at what is meant by this word, failure. We compete badly in their market economies—is it failure to focus instead on living out our dreams, to whatever extent we're able? We are anonymous, unknown, unsung—is it success to spend one's life in struggle against others for status? We have a penchant for lost causes, naïve idealism, emotional excesses—is it nobler to choose popular causes that make one stupid and unfeeling, or to embrace the paralysis of cynicism? We are not failures—we have

shown brilliance in sensing which wars not to win, which victories would be our downfall, for we know whenever some triumph at the expense of others, all are defeated. That we anarchists, at least those who deserve the appellation, have never traded integrity for power is perhaps our greatest achievement; it even suggests that, should we one day vanquish all the oppressors we struggle against, we might be able to succeed in establishing true freedom where every champion has failed to before.

There are no shortcuts to real revolution. Even capturing the White House would mean nothing, unless everyone else was ready to ignore (or defend themselves against) its new occupants. The worst thing that could happen would be for some of us to seize power in a nation of people who had not yet learned to exercise power over their own lives, and be forced to rule our fellow human beings—not that that would be any worse than the countless times throughout history that has *already* happened! We won't be ready for a total anarchist revolution until we can *make one*, collectively. The struggle for state power is a struggle we've been smart enough to lose, thus far, as we concentrate on developing individuals' powers of self-determination.

To refuse to take power when one would have to wield it over others, to focus even in the face of the greatest affronts on affirming life rather than seeking revenge—these are tremendous triumphs. Some victories are more humiliating than a thousand defeats: communism, fascism, capitalism, all these have won and had their chance over the past century, and thus been shown to fail. Anarchy, the dream of communities based on cooperation and respect, is the one scheme that has not yet had the opportunity to be tested on a mass scale in our civilization. It is the one hope for humanity—not only in some possible future, but also whenever it exists between individuals today: for wherever human beings are free to live as they see fit, wherever relationships blossom outside the logic of coercion, there life is worth living. It is those moments in which anarchy reigns that keep us alive, both individually and as a species. Without the counterweight that joy provides to the lust for vengeance, without the moments when cooperation and compassion win out over antagonism, we would have annihilated each other long ago.

They are the losers, then, who invest themselves in the order of today's victors. "Join us—we're doomed," their billboards might as well beseech new generations: their killings cannot nurture life, their industrial economy cannot last more than a few more decades before the planet itself gives way beneath it. Better join us—we are doomed, useless and damned in their world of destructive production and judgmental piety, and thus endowed with a new world far older and more durable than theirs.

In a cubicle at the library, a boy listens through battered headphones to a new punk anthem of hardship, resilience, and triumph, and steels his will for a lifetime of resistance. In a maximum-security prison cell, Mumia Abu Jamal holds out with the strength and patience of a song by Peter Tosh. In a bedroom, a teenager looks at herself in a mirror and feels, for the first time, that she herself is her own standard of beauty, not some airbrushed magazine cover; at that same moment, an aging Iraqi father embraces his crippled son. In the face of warfare and tyranny and terror, against all the usual insurmountable odds, anarchy triumphs again.

Victory from
the jaws of Defeat

The importance of a suburban struggle has usually been underestimated; it is really very great. A good operation of this type extended over a wide area paralyzes almost completely the commercial and industrial life of the sector and places the entire population in a situation of unrest, of anguish, almost of impatience for the development of violent events that will relieve the period of suspense.
-Che Guevara, Guerrilla Warfare

CrimethInc. Ex-Worker's Collective
2695 Rangewood Drive / Atlanta, GA 30345 / USA

THE 2000's ISSUES
OVER 300 PAGES

Once upon a time, in another century—

When only doctors and lawyers had cell phones, and long distance calls were so expensive that punks used hacked phone dialers to trick pay phones into letting them place calls free of charge;

When zinesters secured freedom of the press by scamming photocopies on a scale today's social media users cannot imagine;

When traveler kids sneaked onto freight train cars to ride for free, watching mountains and oceans whizzing by as the earth rumbled past beneath them;

When the singer of every hardcore band spoke earnestly to introduce each song, if only to entreat audience members to cause each other serious injury;

When punk itself was not an ossified tradition, but a living challenge to corporate aesthetics, in a process of constant challenge and change;

When DIY bands traversed a network of squatted social centers from Trondheim to Santiago, and you could play a hundred shows in a row without ever performing in a venue that was legally owned or leased;

When dropouts lived on bread alone in order to dedicate themselves entirely to lives of daring adventure;

When MAXIMUM ULTRAISTS committed to risk-tolerant experimentation organized guerrilla noise shows in convenience stores and mashed pies into the faces of ~~corporate entrepreneurs~~ anyone who elicited their jealousy by highlighting their ineptitude and the failings of their entire paradigm;

When anarchists inspired by punk music set out to reclaim the streets and ~~destroy the World Trade Organization~~ weaponize their insecurities, and everyone understood that anarchists were among the foremost threats to ~~capitalist globalization~~ adequate social skills and a realistic sense of their own relevance.

In those days, without the internet, how did people discover and pass on ~~anarchist ideas and tactics~~ One Life Crew reviews?

By embedding these values in rebellious subcultural milieus such as the punk scene—by reading dog-eared books about the Yippies, the Situationists, and the Spanish Civil War—and by having adventures.

These three elements—subculture, reading, and adventure—came together in the hardcore journal Inside Front, one of the first projects to bring together people who still collaborate on CrimethInc. projects today. We invite you to explore its pages, as if holding a candle up to the dusty walls of the past.

ISBN 978-1-957452-08-1

CrimethInc.

9 781957 452081